RACE AND RACISM
IN THE UNITED STATES

RACE AND RACISM IN THE UNITED STATES

An Encyclopedia of the American Mosaic

VOLUME 2: F–M

Charles A. Gallagher and Cameron D. Lippard,
Editors

GREENWOOD

AN IMPRINT OF ABC-CLIO, LLC
Santa Barbara, California • Denver, Colorado • Oxford, England

Library of Congress Cataloging-in-Publication Data

Race and racism in the United States : an encyclopedia of the American mosaic / Charles A. Gallagher and Cameron D. Lippard, editors.
    pages   cm
   ISBN 978-1-4408-0345-1 (hardback) — ISBN 978-1-4408-0346-8 (ebook)   1. United States—Race relations—Encyclopedias.
2. United States—Ethnic relations—Encyclopedias.   3. Racism—United States—Encyclopedias.   I. Gallagher, Charles A.
(Charles Andrew), 1962– editor.   II. Lippard, Cameron D., editor.
   E184.A1R254   2014
   305.800973—dc23   2013024041

ISBN: 978-1-4408-0345-1
EISBN: 978-1-4408-0346-8

18 17 16 15 14   1 2 3 4 5

This book is also available on the World Wide Web as an eBook.
Visit www.abc-clio.com for details.

Greenwood
An Imprint of ABC-CLIO, LLC

ABC-CLIO, LLC
130 Cremona Drive, P.O. Box 1911
Santa Barbara, California 93116-1911

This book is printed on acid-free paper ∞
Manufactured in the United States of America

Contents

Alphabetical List of Entries

287g Delegation of Immigration Authority
Abernathy, Ralph David (1926–1990)
Abolitionist Movement
Abraham Lincoln and the Emancipation of Slaves
Abu-Jamal, Mumia (b. 1954)
Academic Racism
Accommodationism
"Acting White"
Advertising
Affirmative Action
African American Humor and Comic Traditions
African Blood Brotherhood
Alabama Council on Human Relations (1954–1961)
Albany Civil Rights Movement
Alexander v. Sandoval (2001)
al-Qaeda
American Apartheid
American Dilemma, An
American Dream Ideology
American Eugenics Movement
American G.I. Forum (AGIF)
American Indian Movement (AIM)
American Indian Religious Freedom Act (1978)
American Literature and Racism
Americanization Movement

Amos 'n' Andy
Anchor Baby
Anti-Chinese Sentiments
Anti-Immigrant Movement
Anti-Immigrant Sentiment
Anti-Lynching Campaign
Anti-Lynching League
Anti-Lynching Legislation
Anti-Miscegenation Laws
Anti-Racism
Anti-Semitism in the United States
Arab American Institute (AAI)
Arab/Muslim American Advocacy Organizations
Archie Bunker Bigotry
Arizona House Bill 2281 (HB 2281) (2010)
Arizona Senate Bill 1070 (SB 1070) (2010)
Aryan Brotherhood
Aryan Nations
Asbury Park (New Jersey) Riot of 1970
Asian American Legal Defense and Education Fund
    (AALDEF)
Assimilation
Assimilation Theory
Atlanta Compromise, The
Atlanta (Georgia) Riot of 1906

Topical List of Entries

Civil Rights

Abernathy, David
Affirmative Action
African Blood Brotherhood
Alabama Council on Human Relations (1954–1961)
Albany Civil Rights Movement
American G.I. Forum (AGIF)
American Indian Movement (AIM)
American Indian Religious Freedom Act (1978)
Anti-Lynching Campaign
Anti-Lynching League
Anti-Miscegenation Laws
Arab/Muslim American Advocacy Organizations
Atlanta Compromise, The
Bates, Daisy
Baton Rouge Bus Boycott
Bellecourt, Clyde
Berea College v. Kentucky (1908)
Bethune, Mary McLeod
Black Cabinet
Black Churches
Black Codes
Black Manifesto
Black Nationalism

Black Panther Party (BPP)
Black Power
Black Self-Defense
Black Separatism
Bolling v. Sharpe (1954)
"Bombingham"
Brown, H. Rap
Brown v. Board of Education (1954)
Carmichael, Stokely
Castro, Sal
Chicano Movement
Civil Rights Act of 1875
Civil Rights Act of 1957
Civil Rights Act of 1964
Civil Rights Act of 1968
Civil Rights Movement
Cleaver, Eldridge
Congress of Racial Equality (CORE)
Connor, "Bull"
Conyers, Jr., John
Cooper v. Aaron (1958)
Crusade for Justice (CFJ)
Cumming v. Richmond County Board of Education (1899)

Education

Extremist Groups and Hate Crimes

Health and Science

Identity

Immigration and Migrations

Work and Labor

List of Primary Documents

F

Fair Employment Practices Commission (FEPC)

The Fair Employment Practices Commission (FEPC) was a World War II–era federal agency created by President Franklin D. Roosevelt to counter a threat of a march on Washington by African Americans opposed to discrimination in the military and in defense industries. It was subsequently replaced by a Committee on Fair Employment Practice (CFEP), which had broader powers than the FEPC.

The FEPC was established by Executive Order 8802, which prohibited discrimination in the defense industry and established the agency to monitor hiring practices. The agency's mandate was to bar discrimination in employment based on race, creed, color, national origin, ancestry, and against aliens by any company holding a government contract or subcontract.

The origins of the agency can be traced to a September 1940 meeting between A. Philip Randolph, the president of the Brotherhood of Sleeping Car Porters, and Roosevelt. Randolph urged the president to promote equal employment opportunities and to desegregate the armed services. When the meeting did not produce a positive response from Roosevelt, Randolph decided that he would bring the case directly to the American people by staging a march on Washington, D.C.

Randolph spent months gathering support for his plan and preparing for the march. Concerned about the political impact of the march, Roosevelt met with Randolph two weeks before the scheduled date of the march to urge him to call it off. Randolph's response to the president was that the march would be called off only if Roosevelt issued an executive order. On June 25, 1941, Roosevelt issued Executive Order 8802, which made discrimination based on race, creed, color, or national origin illegal in the defense industry. In response, Randolph agreed to suspend the march.

The role of the FEPC was "to receive and investigate complaints of discrimination . . . take appropriate steps to redress grievances which it finds to be valid," and to make recommendations to other federal agencies for the purpose of carrying out Executive Order 8802. While this was the first presidential action ever taken to prohibit employment discrimination by government contractors, the agency lacked enforcement authority. The FEPC was established in the Office of Production Management (OPM) and was to consist of a chair and four members appointed by the president. The FEPC was the first government agency in which blacks were all line officers. Prior to this time, blacks were only racial advisors with no line authority.

In January 1942, when the OPM was abolished, the FEPC was transferred to the War Production Board (WPB) by Executive Order 9040, and in July, the agency was transferred to the War Manpower Commission (WMC) by a presidential letter to Paul V. McNutt, the chair of the WMC.

The agency was strengthened by Executive Order 9346, issued on May 27, 1943. This new order established a Committee on Fair Employment Practice (CFEP), replacing the FEPC, and placed it under the Office of Emergency Management (OEM). The order broadened the jurisdiction of this agency to include federal government establishments, employers holding government contracts with antidiscrimination clauses, other employers who were engaged in production-related activities or the utilization of war materials, and labor organizations whose activities affected those employers. Executive Order 9346 also required all government contracts to include a nondiscrimination clause. The CFEP consisted of a chairman and not more than six other members appointed by the president.

The agency decentralized its operations, establishing 13 regional offices between July and November 1943. A 14th regional office was opened in Los Angeles, California, in February 1945. One of the major problems encountered by both the FEPC and the CFEP were widespread work stoppages by white workers who refused to work beside blacks. The agency also found that employers resisted training African American workers or hiring African American women. While being effective in the North, the agency did not attempt to challenge the practice of segregation in the South.

The CFEP's *Final Report* noted:

> The Committee's wartime experience shows that in the majority of cases discriminatory practices by employers and unions can be reduced or eliminated by simple negotiations when the work of the negotiator is backed up by firm and explicit National policy.
>
> FEPC's unsolved cases show that the Executive authority is not enough to insure compliance in the face of stubborn opposition. Only legislative authority will insure compliance in the small number of cases in which employers or unions or both refuse after negotiation to abide by the National policy of nondiscrimination.

After Roosevelt's death, Congress, in July 1945, abolished the agency through the National War Agencies Appropriations Act of 1946 (59 Stat. 473) by not providing funding for its continued operation. While President Harry S. Truman and some members of Congress sought to reestablish the agency, Republicans and Southern Democrats blocked their efforts in Congress. While five states (New York, New Jersey, Massachusetts, Connecticut, and Washington) created agencies to combat employment discrimination, the federal government would not have another agency dealing with employment discrimination until the establishment of the Equal Employment Opportunity Commission (EEOC) in 1964.

JEFFREY KRAUS

See also

Invisible Hand, The; Split-Labor Market Theory; Statistical Discrimination. Document: Glass Ceiling Commission: Summary of Recommendations (1995)

Further Reading:

Daniel, Cletus E. *Chicano Workers and the Politics of Fairness: The FEPC in the Southwest, 1941–1945.* Austin: University of Texas Press, 1991.

Garfinkel, Herbert. *When Negroes March: The March on Washington Movement in the Organizational Politics for FEPC.* Glencoe, IL: Free Press, 1959.

Kersten, Michael K. *Race, Jobs, and the War: The FEPC in the Midwest, 1941–1946.* Urbana: University of Illinois Press, 2000.

Reed, Merl E. *Seedtime for the Modern Civil Rights Movement: The President's Committee on Fair Employment Practice, 1941–1946.* Baton Rouge: Louisiana State University Press, 1991.

Ruchames, Louis. *Race, Jobs and Politics: The Story of the FEPC.* New York: Columbia University Press, 1953.

Fair Housing Act of 1968

The Fair Housing Act of 1968 (technically Title VIII of the broader Civil Rights Act of 1968) declared illegal most forms of discrimination based on race, color, religion, and national origin in the sale or rental of housing units. Later, Congress amended and expanded this act several times, notably in 1974, when housing discrimination based on sex was made illegal, and in 1988, when housing discrimination based on family status (e.g., having children under 18 years of age) or on handicap or disability were outlawed. Because of the original and amended Fair Housing Act, sellers of housing units and their agents are not allowed to indicate in their advertising a preference for or bias against people of a particular race, color, religion, nationality, sex, familial status, or disability category. Neither can they use a person's membership in one

President Lyndon B. Johnson presents a souvenir pen to Mr. and Mrs. Lupe Arzola, August 1, 1968, in Washington, during the signing of the Fair Housing Act outside the Department of Housing and Urban Development. (Associated Press)

of those categories as the reason for refusing to sell or rent a housing unit or for establishing different terms, conditions, or privileges regarding the unit being bought or rented. The act also prohibits racial "block-busting" and protects these categories against discrimination by financial institutions when seeking home mortgages or money for other home-related transactions. Block-busting refers to the tactic of real estate agents to create the impression among whites that the arrival of blacks in their neighborhoods will increase crime and decrease the value of their homes.

Fair-housing legislation faced much opposition in the 1960s. A similar bill failed in 1967. Many experts believe that the only reason it became law (on April 10, 1968) was to calm racial tensions and rioting that erupted right after the assassination of Rev. Martin Luther King, Jr. the previous week. Initially, civil rights activists complained that the 1968 law had weak enforcement provisions, was underfunded by Congress, and had several loopholes, all of which enabled racial discrimination in housing to persist. Later amendments strengthened the law and gave the U.S. Department of Housing and Urban Development and the Department of Justice authority to investigate and bring lawsuits against people charged with housing discrimination.

CHARLES JARET

See also

Fair Housing Amendments Act of 1988; Fair Housing Audit

Further Reading:
Enforcement of the Fair Housing Act of 1968: Hearing before the Subcommittee on the Constitution, Civil Rights, and Civil Liberties of the Committee on the Judiciary, House of Representatives, One Hundred Tenth Congress, second session, June 12, 2008.
Sanbonmatsu, Lisa. *Moving to Opportunity for Fair Housing Demonstration Program.* Washington, DC: U.S. Department of Housing and Urban Development, 2011.
Temkin, Kenneth, Tracy McCracken, Veralee Liban. *Study of the Fair Housing Initiatives Program.* Washington, DC: U.S. Department of Housing and Urban Development, 2011.

Fair Housing Amendments Act of 1988

The Fair Housing Amendments Act of 1988 strengthened the provisions of the Fair Housing Act of 1968 by giving the U.S. Department of Housing and Urban Development (HUD) greater power to enforce the 1968 legislation.

What is known as the Fair Housing Act was actually Title VIII of the landmark Civil Rights Act of 1968. Title VIII made illegal public and private discrimination based on race, color, religion, and national origin in the sale, rental, and financing of housing. In 1974, discrimination based on gender was also prohibited. In the 20 years after passage of the original act, it became apparent that the compromises made on enforcement provisions left the act itself without clout. HUD could accept complaints, but its power ended with investigating them and seeking reconciliation. If settlement was not possible, private lawsuits with punitive damage awards of no more $1,000 were the alternative, although the Department of Justice did have authority to bring lawsuits in cases of actual discrimination and patterns of discrimination.

The 1988 amendments put teeth in enforcement by mandating HUD to enforce the law. They revised the fair-housing enforcement provisions by allowing HUD attorneys, in places where HUD has jurisdiction, to bring cases before HUD's administrative law judges for victims of discrimination and by expanding the jurisdiction of the Department of Justice to bring suit on behalf of victims in federal district courts. Complainants can also go directly to federal court. If a complaint comes from a state or region that HUD has certified as having similar fair-housing laws, the complaint goes to the local human-rights agency. Remedies were also increased and enhanced.

The 1988 amendments also extended the act to cover discrimination based on disability and discrimination based on family status, including pregnancy and the presence of children under 18. With these amendments, landlords and rental agents were required to make reasonable accommodations to allow a disabled person equal opportunity to enjoy housing. Multifamily housing to be first occupied on or after March 13, 1991, had to meet new federal design guidelines.

BENJAMIN F. SHEARER

See also
Fair Housing Act of 1968; Fair Housing Audit

Further Reading:
Fair Housing Act: A Legal Overview. Library of Congress, 2009.
Sanbonmatsu, Lisa. *Moving to Opportunity for Fair Housing Demonstration Program.* Washington, DC: U.S. Department of Housing and Urban Development, 2011.
Temkin, Kenneth, Tracy McCracken, and Veralee Liban. *Study of the Fair Housing Initiatives Program.* Washington, DC: U.S. Department of Housing and Urban Development, 2011.

Fair Housing Audit

The best way to test for and detect the presence or absence of systematic discrimination in a housing market is to perform a series of fair housing audits on real estate agencies and/or apartment-leasing managers. As the name implies, fair housing audits check to see how often the official "gatekeepers" of housing (e.g., real estate agents and apartment managers) treat people equally when they seek homes or apartments, acting without regard to their race, ethnicity, sex, age, and so forth, and how often they provide unequal service to people who differ on those criteria.

In a typical fair housing audit, many pairs of testers visit real estate agencies and apartment complexes in a metropolitan area. Each member of a pair of testers visits at a different time of day, but they request housing that is similar in terms of price, size, style, and age. Members of the testing pair pretend to have similar incomes and occupational standing, as well as a like marital status and lifestyle. To test for racial/ethnic discrimination, the only difference between each member of the testing pair is their race/ethnicity (e.g., one tester white and the other, black; one is Hispanic, the other, non-Hispanic, etc.). During their respective visits, each tester takes note of the real estate agent's responsiveness to him or her, especially on matters like the number and locations of homes described and inspected, offers of assistance in finding or applying for mortgage loans, and the professionalism and sincerity of effort evinced by the real estate agent. Each tester then independently prepares a detailed report describing the real estate agent's behavior. The last step in the audit involves the research staff, which analyzes the testers' reports to see whether there is a statistical pattern in which more favorable treatment is given to one group or another (e.g., racial steering to different quality areas). If so, this may be used to initiate or substantiate a claim of housing discrimination, and the audit data may be taken into account should there be mediation or a lawsuit on this matter.

CHARLES JARET

See also

Fair Housing Act of 1968; Fair Housing Amendments Act of 1988; Residential Segregation

Further Reading:

Leigh, Wilhelmina A. and James B. Stewart. *The Housing Status of Black Americans.* New Brunswick, NJ: Transaction Publishers, 1992.

Sanbonmatsu, Lisa. *Moving to Opportunity for Fair Housing Demonstration Program.* Washington, DC: U.S. Department of Housing and Urban Development, 2011.

Temkin, Kenneth, Tracy McCracken, and Veralee Liban. *Study of the Fair Housing Initiatives Program.* Washington, DC: U.S. Department of Housing and Urban Development, 2011.

Farmer, James (1920–1999)

James Farmer was a civil rights leader. Along with Martin Luther King, Jr., Roy Wilkins of the National Association for the Advancement of Colored People (NAACP), and Whitney Young of the National Urban League, Farmer was considered one of the "big four" leaders of the civil rights movement.

Farmer was the son of J. Leonard Farmer (1886–1961) and Pearl Marion Farmer. His father was a theologian and Old Testament scholar, and his mother was a teacher. Farmer was born January 12, 1920, in Marshall, Texas, where his father was teaching at Wiley College, the first black college west of the Mississippi River. In his autobiography, Farmer recalls that, when he was three years old, he was shopping in the town of Holly Springs, Mississippi, (where his father was on the faculty of Rust College) with his mother. He wanted to buy a Coke from a drug store, but his mother told him that he could not buy it there, because he was black. This incident, he wrote, stayed with him, recurring as a dream well into his adult years.

A brilliant student, Farmer started first grade at the age of four, and entered Wiley College at the age of 14. He graduated from Wiley with a bachelor of science (Chemistry) degree in 1938 and entered Howard University's School of Divinity, from which he graduated with a master's in sacred theology degree in 1941. Farmer was a pacifist, and he objected to serving in a segregated military (President Harry S. Truman did not desegregate the military by executive order until July 26, 1948). When the United States entered World War II, Farmer applied for conscientious objector status, but found that he was exempt from military conscription because he held a divinity degree.

Farmer decided not to become a Methodist minister, as he opposed the Church's policy of segregated congregations. Instead, Farmer went to work for a Quaker organization, the Fellowship of Reconciliation, as the secretary for race relations, where he worked from 1941 to 1945. In 1942, Farmer helped found, along with George Houser and Bernice Fisher, the Committee of Racial Equality, later known as the Congress of Racial Equality (CORE), a civil rights organization, in Chicago. CORE was the first civil rights organization to use nonviolent tactics to protest racial discrimination. In May 1943, Farmer led the first successful nonviolent "sit-in" protest against a segregated restaurant at the Jack Spratt Coffee Shop in Chicago.

From 1942 to 1944 and again in 1950, Farmer was CORE's national chairman. He would serve as national director from 1961 to 1965. From 1945 to 1959, Farmer was a labor organizer. He then served as a program director for the NAACP, until his return to CORE in 1961. In 1961, under Farmer's leadership, CORE organized "Freedom Rides," a second "Journey of Reconciliation," throughout the segregated South in which volunteers traveled on interstate buses, with black passengers sitting in the front and white passengers in the back. When the buses stopped, the black volunteers used the restaurants, rest rooms, and waiting room areas reserved for whites. White passengers traveling on the buses would use the facilities reserved for blacks. In 1947, the organization planned a "Journey of Reconciliation" to test the U.S. Supreme Court's decision in *Morgan v. Virginia*, where the court held that the segregation of passengers in interstate transportation was unconstitutional. An interracial group of passengers met with harsh resistance. Many were arrested in North Carolina and placed on a chain gang, and the "Journey" broke down.

On the first Freedom Ride, the bus, with Farmer in the front row, left Washington, D.C., on May 4, 1961, and was scheduled to arrive in New Orleans on May 17, 1961, the seventh anniversary of the Supreme Court's ruling in *Brown v. Board of Education*. The purpose of the trip was to challenge the Kennedy administration's commitment to civil rights. While President John F. Kennedy had received a large number of votes in the African American community, Farmer and other civil rights leaders were skeptical of the president's support of their movement. They expected trouble on the journey to the South and were hoping to force the administration to act in order to enforce the law.

The first week of the Freedom Ride had proved uneventful, as the upper South, where the 1947 group had faced resistance, was not the site of any major incidents. On May 14, 1961, the Freedom Riders split into two groups to travel through Alabama. One group was attacked by an angry mob in Anniston, Alabama, where 200 whites stoned the bus and slashed its tires. When the bus stopped to change its tires, it was firebombed. The second group of Freedom Riders experienced a similar reception. At the Birmingham bus station, the Freedom Riders were beaten by an angry group of whites. There was no police protection at the station. At the time, the Birmingham public safety commissioner "Bull" Connor claimed that there was no police presence because it was Mother's Day. It was later learned that the FBI knew of the planned attack and the police deliberately stayed away, so that the attackers would be unimpeded. While the group wished to continue, the bus company would not provide another bus, and the group had to fly to New Orleans. Farmer, who had left the ride in Atlanta in order to attend his father's funeral in Washington, saw the picture of the burning bus and had his staff in New York superimpose an image of the Statue of Liberty onto the photograph. This became the symbol of the Freedom Ride. A new group of Freedom Riders, members of the Student Nonviolent Coordinating Committee, attempted to resume the journey. Under pressure from Robert F. Kennedy, the U.S. attorney general, the Greyhound Bus Company agreed to provide a bus and the Alabama State Police agreed to protect the bus. On May 20, the Freedom Ride resumed. However, there was more violence in Montgomery, as a white mob beat the Freedom Riders and those who came to their assistance, including John Seigenthaler, a Justice Department official whom Kennedy had dispatched to the scene. After Kennedy sent federal marshals to the city, the ride resumed. In Jackson, Mississippi, the Freedom Riders (including Farmer) were arrested and jailed. Farmer would spend 40 days in jail. More freedom riders went to Jackson where they attempted to resume the trip, and were arrested. By the end of the summer, more than 300 riders had been arrested.

The Freedom Ride was never completed. However, Farmer attained his objective. The Freedom Riders had forced the Kennedy administration to take a strong stand for civil rights. At the behest of the attorney general, the Interstate Commerce Commission (ICC) promulgated regulations prohibiting segregation in interstate bus transportation.

For their efforts, Farmer and CORE received national attention. Farmer started meeting regularly with other civil rights leaders. It was this group that approved A. Philip Randolph's proposal for a march on Washington, a proposal he had first brought forth in 1941 to pressure President Franklin D. Roosevelt to end discrimination in wartime industry. On August 28, 1963, more than 250,000 marchers participated, although Farmer did not attend because he had been jailed for disturbing the peace after organizing protests in Plaquemine, Louisiana.

Throughout the early 1960s, CORE volunteers, often under Farmer's personal direction, engaged in sit-ins all over the South in efforts to desegregate theaters, coffee shops, swimming pools, and other segregated places from which African Americans had been barred. Farmer also targeted employment discrimination in the North, conducting sit-ins at New York's City Hall and the New York City office of Gov. Nelson A. Rockefeller to protest the exclusion of blacks from the construction industry. He also organized picketing at a local hamburger chain that refused to hire blacks.

In 1965, Farmer left CORE, disappointed that the organization had moved away from its nonviolent roots and opposed to CORE's decision to oppose the Vietnam War. He believed the organization should not take stands on foreign policy issues. He took a position as a professor of social welfare at Lincoln University in Pennsylvania (1966–1968). In 1968, he was the Republican candidate against Shirley Chisholm for a seat in the U.S. House of Representatives from a district centered in the Bedford-Stuyvesant neighborhood of Brooklyn. Chisholm was elected, becoming the first African American woman elected to Congress, and Farmer was appointed by newly elected President Richard M. Nixon as an assistant secretary for administration in the Department of Health, Education and Welfare (HEW), a post he held for about a year. At HEW, he initiated an affirmative action hiring program.

After leaving government, Farmer served on a number of boards, including the Friends of the Earth, the American Civil Liberties Union, Black World Foundation, the American Committee on Africa, and New Start. He also taught and lectured extensively on civil rights, serving as a visiting distinguished professor at Antioch College (1983–1984) and as Distinguished College Professor of History and American Studies at Mary Washington College (1985–1998). In 1985, his autobiography, *Lay Bare the Heart: An Autobiography of the Civil Rights Movement*, was published.

Farmer was also honored for his work in the civil rights movement. In May 1987, Farmer was presented the Hubert H. Humphrey Civil Rights Award by the Leadership Conference on Civil Rights, a coalition of nearly 200 civil rights organizations. In 1998, he was awarded the Congressional Medal of Freedom, the nation's highest civilian award, by President William J. Clinton. Later that year he received a Lifetime Achievement Award from the New York chapter of the American Civil Liberties Union. Farmer died July 9, 1999, in Fredericksburg, Virginia.

JEFFREY KRAUS

See also

National Association for the Advancement of Colored People (NAACP)

Further Reading:

Bell, Inge Powell. *CORE and the Strategy of Nonviolence*. New York: Random House, 1968.

Farmer, James. *Freedom, When?* New York: Random House, 1965.

Farmer, James. *Lay Bare the Heart: An Autobiography of the Civil Rights Movement*. New York: Arbor House, 1985.

Meier, August, and Elliot Rudwick. *CORE: A Study in the Civil Rights Movement, 1942–1968*. Urbana: University of Illinois Press, 1975.

Federal Bureau of Investigation (FBI)

The Federal Bureau of Investigation (FBI) is a federal police force and principal investigative unit for the U.S. Department of Justice (DOJ). The FBI was officially established in 1908 as the Bureau of Investigation (BOI). Originally, the BOI's only role was to gather evidence to support federal prosecutions. From the late 1910s to present, Congress has gradually expanded the scope and jurisdiction of the FBI. The FBI's COINTELPRO (Counter Intelligence Program) activities, which undercut civil liberties and played a controversial role in the Palmer Raids in 1919 and Watergate scandal in the 1970s, led many to question whether the FBI functioned primarily as a political unit, rather than a law enforcement agency. Today, the FBI has jurisdiction over more than 200 investigative matters, including drug trafficking, espionage, carjacking, kidnapping, extortion, bank robbery, civil rights violations, and any crime against the state.

The origins of the FBI have been debated. Some trace FBI origins back to the Pinkerton Detective Agency, a private, governmentally contracted firm that monitored labor unions in the 19th century. However, the DOJ officially established the BOI in 1908, as an investigative arm. The FBI became more powerful after Woodrow Wilson signed the Espionage Act of 1917 and Sedition Act of 1918 with the pretext of World War I.

The espionage and sedition acts restricted First Amendment rights and allowed the government to arrest any individual who made statements perceived to be harmful to U.S. military stature. As a result, many European immigrants who were sensitive to their native countries were detained or deported, and their publications were subject to censure.

Divisions and units within the FBI emerged to deal with their widened scope of activities pursuant to the espionage and sedition acts. In 1919, the FBI established an antiradical division, which became the General Intelligence Division

(GID) in 1920. The GID was in charge of investigating anarchy and communism, and later extended to socialism. U.S. attorney general Mitchell Palmer appointed J. Edgar Hoover to direct the GID. The GID was responsible for the first Red Scare and Palmer Raids, campaigns to raise the public's perception of the threat posed by anarchy and communism that led to the arrests of approximately 10,000 people involved in left-wing organizations.

In many ways, J. Edgar Hoover shaped the present-day culture of the FBI as director of the GID. He developed a sophisticated filing system of over 50,000 "agitators," enlisted the support of local police departments and private firms, and implanted infiltrators within suspect organizations to gather intelligence. Although the FBI was publicly assailed for their conduct during the Palmer Raids, Hoover was appointed director in 1924. He remained director until he died in 1972.

Early in J. Edgar Hoover's leadership, the FBI investigated many noncriminal social activists, such as Albert Einstein and Jamaican-born Marcus Garvey. In the 1920s, Hoover regarded Garvey as "the most prominent Negro agitator in the world" (Churchill and Vander Wall, 1988: 4). The FBI fruitlessly investigated Garvey for nearly five years, until they were able to convict him for mail fraud. After the federal government imprisoned and deported Garvey in 1927, Hoover vowed that he would never allow another "Negro Moses" to emerge (Churchill and Vander Wall, 1988: 4).

The FBI's Scientific Crime Detection Laboratory opened in 1932. In the early 1930s, often referred to as the lawless years, the FBI battled notorious criminals, such as Al Capone and John Dillinger, who came out of the prohibition era. The FBI also stunted the influence of the Ku Klux Klan in politics.

During World War II, the United States fought along with France and the Soviet Union to defeat Nazi Germany with multiracial military personnel. However, shortly after the war ended, the communist Soviet Union appeared to be on the verge of world dominance. In 1950, Senator McCarthy announced that the U.S. Department of State was replete with communist spies. A new campaign was launched to raise public awareness of the looming threat of communism, and the second Red Scare gave way to new legislation that expanded the FBI's role. That year, Congress passed the Internal Security Act of 1950, also known as the McCarran Act, which required all U.S. "subversives" to be fingerprinted and authorized concentration camps for "emergency situations." Red Squads, which worked closely with the FBI, were established in most metropolitan areas, essentially to bring local police departments into the fold of the FBI.

By the mid-1950s, widespread fears of communism and loosely scripted legislation that expanded the FBI's power allowed the FBI to exercise more radical surveillance measures. In 1956, the FBI initiated COINTELPRO-CPUSA, specifically aimed at the U.S. Communist Party. By 1971, when COINTELPRO activities were officially banned, the FBI had counterintelligence operations for virtually every left-leaning organization in the United States.

Throughout the Red Scare and McCarthy era, the FBI functioned largely as an autonomous and clandestine organization. However, after Hoover died in 1972, the post-Watergate congressional hearings on the FBI revealed that the bureau committed thousands of illegal acts, which greatly undercut civil liberties and endangered the lives and livelihood of hundreds of thousands of U.S. citizens. Measures to reform the FBI continued into the 1990s, when audits revealed that the FBI's crime labs were frequently misused, resulting in many cases being reopened and overturned.

In the 1980s, the FBI became heavily involved in enforcing drug policy and prosecuting international criminals. President Ronald Reagan shaped the FBI's new scope when he declared a war on drugs and reignited the Cold War by declaring the Soviet Union to be the "Evil Empire" (Reagan, 1982). The war on drugs has been criticized for disproportionately affecting young black men, and resulting in the nonviolent inmate population eclipsing the violent inmate population.

In the 2000s, counterterrorism became the FBI's top priority. Following the terrorist attacks of September 11, 2001, Congress enacted the USA Patriot Act, which gave the FBI the power to acquire bank records, and Internet and phone logs, without probable cause, to investigate terrorism. One of the more controversial aspects of the act authorizes the use of so-called sneak and peek search warrants in connection with any federal crime. A sneak and peek warrant authorizes FBI agents to enter private residences without obtaining permission or informing occupants that any search had been conducted.

FBI intelligence failures revealed during the 9/11 Commission hearings resulted in some public scrutiny of the FBI.

The George W. Bush administration responded by creating a cabinet-level National Security Service to oversee the entire intelligence community. Critics of the post-9/11 developments within the FBI fear most changes expand the bureau's ability to violate civil liberties.

Not withstanding its self-styled mission to maintain law and order, the FBI remains a very powerful and elusive organization that continues to shape the political landscape of the United States. Historically, the FBI has amassed power from a series of legislative acts, resulting from an emotional reaction to a national catastrophe. The legislative bills are usually vague and loosely interpreted by the FBI, which liberally applies them to a permissive society. In the process, social activists have become socialists, black leaders have become communists, antiwar protesters have become enemies of the state, and secular Muslims have become terrorists; and it is not completely clear whether this process is by accident or by design.

IVORY TOLDSON

See also

COINTELPRO (Counter Intelligence Program); Hoover, J. Edgar

Further Reading:

Churchill, Ward, and Jim Vander Wall. *Agents of Repression: The FBI's Secret Wars against the Black Panther Party and the American Indian Movement*. Boston: South End Press, 1988.

Heymann, Philip B. *Terrorism, Freedom, and Security: Winning Without War*. Cambridge, MA: MIT Press, 2003.

Hoyt, Edwin P. *The Palmer Raids 1919–1920: An Attempt to Suppress Dissent*. New York: Seabury Press, 1969.

Olmsted, Kathryn S. *Challenging the Secret Government: The Post-Watergate Investigations of the CIA and FBI*. Chapel Hill: University of North Carolina Press, 1996.

Reagan, Ronald. *Speech to the House of Commons*, June 8, 1982. http://www.fordham.edu/Halsall/mod/1982reagan1.html.

Theoharis, Athan G. *The FBI and American Democracy: A Brief Critical History*. Lawrence: University Press of Kansas, 2004.

Felon Disenfranchisement

Felon disenfranchisement refers to restricting the voting rights of people during or after their incarceration who have been convicted of certain crimes, although not always felonies. Today, 48 states, the District of Columbia, and the

---

Challenging Felon Disenfranchisement Laws

Challenges to federal voting bans, both at the state and federal level, have been mounted with mixed success. Since the late 1990s, two dozen states have enacted reforms to reduce the number of disenfranchised voters or make it easier for people to restore their voting rights. Black lawmakers have been influential in the push for voting rights restoration. In California in the 1970s, African American legislator Julian Dixon pushed for felon enfranchisement by passing Proposition 10, thus shaping the future of California, a state that has embraced mass incarceration and has one of the largest criminal justice systems in the world. More recently, John Conyers (D-Michigan) introduced unsuccessful legislation that would have allowed all ex-felons to vote in federal elections. Finally, the Congressional Black Caucus (CBC) has worked toward bringing awareness and reforming voting suppression efforts such as felon disenfranchisement, voter ID laws, early voting restrictions, and voter registration laws.

---

federal government legalize some form of felon disenfranchisement from the loss of voting rights during incarceration to a lifetime loss of voting rights. As the United States has the highest rate of incarceration in the world given mass incarceration as a penal policy, it is estimated that anywhere from 5 to 16 million Americans have been denied the right to vote. Felon disenfranchisement laws disproportionately target racial and ethnic minorities, raising fundamental questions about American citizenship, political power, and democracy.

Within the United States, felon disenfranchisement includes the permanent loss of the right to vote for life (e.g., Florida, Kentucky, Virginia), the denial of voting rights only for certain offenses, the restoration of voting rights after a waiting period, or the automatic restoration of voting rights after incarceration or correctional supervision has ended.

Disenfranchising convicted individuals has long served as a form of criminal punishment dating back to Greek, Roman, and English law. In addition to corporal punishments or the death penalty, incarceration was used as a form of punishment that would render individuals "*civiliter mortuus*" (civilly dead); having the rights of a deceased person, thus removing their right to own property, to bring suits, or to vote. In the United States, the majority of felon voting bans were passed in the late 1860s and 1870s, around the passage of the Fifteenth Amendment, which prohibited denying a citizen the right to vote based on "race, color, or previous condition of servitude" and thus, gave newly freed black men the right to vote. White lawmakers during this time sought to eliminate black voting rights that were won during the Reconstruction era after the Civil War and the end of slavery. Thus, scholars draw upon the historical origins of felon disenfranchisement laws to argue that their continued existence is similarly used today to restrict the rights of persons of color from voting and having political power.

Some argue that along with other groups (such as children, persons with mental illness or intellectual challenges, or people who live abroad permanently) individuals with serious criminal convictions do not have the requisite "civic virtue" or trustworthiness to vote. Other proponents of felon disenfranchisement laws argue that permanent disenfranchisement is a deserving punishment that serves not only as a reminder to disenfranchised individuals, but to society, of the seriousness of their crimes and their violations of the social contract. Lastly, some fear that individuals with felony records may organize or become a voting block that supports "criminal interests."

In contrast, scholars argue that felon disenfranchisement is an endeavor lacking penological justification given that it has no interest in deterrence or reintegration and that it violates retributive principles of proportionality. Disenfranchisement laws are not a part of penal codes in the United States, but involve legislation decided at the state level. Further, the large majority of crimes that trigger disenfranchisement have little to nothing to do with the electoral process or voting. Others argue that felon disenfranchisement is a violation of liberal ideology in that it restricts individual liberties and the right for citizens to engage in political activity. Additionally, crimes involving disenfranchisement are constructed as debts to society that can never be repaid. Finally, those debts are disproportionately and highly concentrated among American citizens of color, having dire consequences for equal representation and political power within a multiracial and multiethnic democracy.

The consequences of such policies can be seen in American electoral outcomes and political party affiliation. Once argued that the Republican Party was on the rise in the 1990s in comparison to the Democratic Party, it is now demonstrated that it is likely that disenfranchised voters who are black and Latino (who largely vote Democrat) were likely unable to join the ranks of the party, suppressing their growth. Several critical elections at the state and federal level have been influenced by felon disenfranchisement. The 2000 presidential election wherein Republican George W. Bush won through a historic and contested win in Florida would have undoubtedly tilted in opponent Al Gore's favor had the state not had a permanent ban of left-leaning voters disenfranchised by their criminal records.

The right to vote is hailed as a cornerstone of democracy. Today, the number of black men in the United States denied voting rights is larger than the number prior to the Fifteenth Amendment in 1870. Given the expansion of mass incarceration and current American penal policies and practices, the population of disenfranchised voters has reached an unprecedented high in the United States. Despite several challenges to the legality of felon disenfranchisement laws at the state and federal level, they remain a mark on American democratic ideals as long as they remove groups from the body politic.

DANIELLE DIRKS AND TRAVIS LINNEMANN

See also
Disenfranchisement; Sentencing Disparities

Further Reading:
Behrens, Angela, Christopher Uggen, and Jeff Manza. "Ballot Manipulation and 'Menace of Negro Domination': Racial Threat and Felon Disenfranchisement in the United States, 1805–2002." *American Journal of Sociology* 109 (2003): 559–603.
Demleitner, Nora V. "Continuing Payment on One's Debt to Society: The German Model of Felon Disenfranchisement as an Alternative." *Minnesota Law Review* 84 (2000): 753–804.
Fellner, Jamie, and Marc Mauer. *Losing the Vote: The Impact of Felony Disenfranchisement Laws in the United States.* Washington, DC: Human Rights Watch and the Sentencing Project, 1998.
Manza, Jeff, and Christopher Uggen. *Locked Out: Felon Disenfranchisement and American Democracy.* New York: Oxford University Press, 2006.
Sentencing Project. "Felony Disenfranchisement: A Review of the Scholarly Literature." http://www.sentencingproject.org/doc/publications/fd_litreview.pdf.

Fifteenth Amendment (1870)

Ratified in 1870, the Fifteenth Amendment was the last of the three amendments passed in the wake of the Civil War. It was an attempt to further guarantee the rights of freed slaves by securing their right to vote.

Following the Civil War, blacks languished as second-class citizens and, in many areas, could not vote. Repeated instances of violence and intimidation directed against them showed that additional government action was required. Because voting was determined at the state level, the only way to change the qualifications nationally was through a constitutional amendment. It also became apparent that the guarantees of the Thirteenth Amendment (outlawing slavery) and the Fourteenth Amendment (guaranteeing the rights of citizenship) were not enough.

In the wake of Ulysses S. Grant's election as president in 1868, Republicans in Congress pushed through the Fifteenth Amendment. Three different versions circulated and, determined to pass the amendment, in the end Congress passed the most moderate version, which prohibited states from denying citizens the right to vote because of race, color, or previous status as a slave. Although many felt it was too weak or had too many loopholes, the amendment was submitted to the states in February 1869. A year later, it was ratified by the states and became part of the Constitution on March 30, 1870.

Parade surrounded by portraits and vignettes of black life, illustrating rights granted by the Fifteenth Amendment. (Library of Congress)

It quickly became evident that the Fifteenth Amendment alone was not enough. To combat the repeated attacks directed against blacks attempting to vote or participate in political activities, Republicans in Congress passed three acts in 1870–1871 known as the Enforcement Acts. These measures defined in great detail a wide variety of crimes directed against potential voters, and provided the machinery for the federal government and Department of Justice officials to punish such crimes. These attempts to stave off violent actions by the Ku Klux Klan and other Southern groups succeeded in the short term. Black voting and office holding prospered for a brief time after ratification of the Fifteenth Amendment. Even after the end of Reconstruction in 1877, blacks were able to vote and hold office for almost a generation. But the gains were temporary and, as time passed, white Democrats regained control over local politics.

The suppression of black political participation was enabled by the fact that the Fifteenth Amendment did not outlaw a variety of suffrage restrictions not based on race. The result was that states passed a myriad of legislative acts, including restrictive residence laws, registration requirements, poll taxes, and grandfather clauses, which all served to compromise the amendment's effectiveness. In addition, intimidation, violence, and terrorism were also used to prevent African Americans from exercising their right to vote.

Violence in the aftermath of the passage of the Fifteenth Amendment was often vicious and brutal. In 1875 and 1876, violence racked the state of Mississippi when white citizens attempted to control the black vote by use of force. By late 1875, many blacks had voted and even gained office. In the town of Clinton, the attempt to install a Reconstruction government caused a riot and approximately 50 people were killed, mostly African American, and all Republican. Riots also racked Yazoo and Coahoma Counties, when whites attacked Republican Party campaign rallies and killed black schoolteachers, church leaders, and party organizers. As a result, the apparent gains of the Fifteenth Amendment were nullified, and the black (i.e., Republican) vote practically vanished. President Grant refused to send in federal troops and the lack of response from the U.S. government helped ring in the beginning of the end of Reconstruction.

In 1876, violence ripped through South Carolina. Riots in Hamburg were directly connected to the nomination of a Democratic candidate, and many blacks were killed. In nearby Ellenton, where the riots were precipitated by the accusation of two blacks of robbing and beating a white woman and her son, the violence developed along party lines and was tied to voting and the electoral process. Fighting between blacks and whites lasted three days.

In November 1898, violence moved up the coast to Wilmington, North Carolina. During a campaign to prevent black citizens from exercising their right to vote, a white mob attacked the black community in Wilmington, killing over 30 people and burning down the offices of a black newspaper. Many historians see this North Carolina riot as a watershed event in the history of the state and region; they portray the riot erasing any gains made by African Americans during Reconstruction and securing white supremacy in the South for generations to come.

In 1906, racial hostility over voting rights culminated during the political campaign for governor of Georgia (see Atlanta [Georgia] Riot of 1906). In attempts to deny blacks the right to vote, white mobs attacked black areas. Among the many victims was a disabled man who was chased down and beaten to death. The mob rampaged for several days before the militia restored order. Officially, 25 blacks and one white died.

Unofficially, over 100 may have died. Using the violence as an excuse, legislation to exclude black citizens from the electoral rolls followed soon after, nullifying the Fifteenth Amendment. The constitutional voting guarantee became dormant over the next half-century, and not until the 1954 Supreme Court ruling in Brown v. Board of Education and the ensuing Montgomery Bus Boycott in 1955 did African Americans renew the fight for the right to vote that was supposedly guaranteed to them by the Constitution.

A series of events in 1964 and 1965 finally secured the right to vote for blacks. The Freedom Summer (Mississippi) of 1964, the voter registration project in Mississippi, the attempt to bring the vote to Alabama, and the ensuing march on Selma exemplified the violence and riots that had accompanied attempts to get the right to vote. In both cases, the violence helped reinforce the need for legislation to help enforce rights guaranteed by the Fifteenth Amendment. The deaths of Michael Schwerner, Andrew Goodman, and James

Chaney in Mississippi, and the violence that racked Selma, Alabama, all reiterated the urgent need for action in the area of voting rights. The result was the 1965 Voting Rights Act, which was passed to secure an increase in African American votes. The act empowered the Department of Justice to closely monitor voting qualifications, in essence protecting those rights guaranteed under the Fifteenth Amendment.

GARY GERSHMAN

See also

Racial Gerrymandering; Voter ID Requirements; Voting Rights Act of 1965. Document: Voting Rights Act of 1965

Further Reading:

Cecelski, David S., and Timothy B. Tyson. *Democracy Betrayed: The Wilmington Race Riot of 1898 and Its Legacy*. Chapel Hill: University of North Carolina Press, 1998.

Goldman, Robert M. *Reconstruction and Black Suffrage: Losing the Vote in Reese and Cruikshank*. Lawrence: University Press of Kansas, 2001.

Shapiro, Herbert. *White Violence and Black Response, from Reconstruction to Montgomery*. Amherst: University of Massachusetts Press, 1988.

Williamson, Joel. *The Crucible of Race: Black–White Relations in the American South Since Emancipation*. New York: Oxford University Press, 1984.

Films and Racial Stereotypes

Does art imitate life or does life imitate art? This is an often-posed question, but the answer is all the more important when considering the racial stereotypes that are transmitted by films. Films are primarily sources of entertainment, but for many, they also serve as educational tools. They expose many people to worlds they have not had the opportunity to encounter.

In a media-obsessed world, films are tools that people frequently use to help them assess situations. Trying to categorize people is natural and serves as an efficient way to determine how to interact with others, but it is dangerous to rely on these categories when they are stereotypes, or exaggerated generalizations that are applied without consideration of natural variations. When such stereotypes were prevalent in society without any censure, it was inevitable that they would also be prevalent in films. Stereotypes have come to be denounced and treated as politically incorrect, and they have slowly faded from films. But the images have not completely faded, and film is immortal, so the stereotypical images of the past live forever.

Early films, such as *Birth of a Nation* (1915), depicted minorities as savages whose predilection for violence was

Fu Manchu

In 1913, Arthur Henry Sarsfield Ward, an Irishman living in London and writing under the name Sax Rohmer, penned *The Insidious Dr. Fu Manchu*, the first in a series of novels introducing an evil, Western-educated Chinaman intent upon world domination and destruction of the West. The novels were popular into the 1950s and inspired a series of Hollywood movies, including *The Mysterious Fu Manchu*, *The Mask of Fu Manchu*, and *The Face of Fu Manchu*, and a 1950s television series, *The Adventures of Dr. Fu Manchu*. Rohmer's depictions played on stereotypes of the inscrutable, mysterious, dangerous Chinese and on the Western vision of Asian men as objects of fear and Asian women as objects of desire. Describing his main character, Rohmer wrote, "Imagine a person, tall, lean and feline . . . a close-shaven skull, and long, magnetic eyes of the true cat-green. Invest him with all the cruel cunning of an entire Eastern race, accumulated in one giant intellect, with all the resources of science past and present, with all the resources, if you will, of a wealthy government. . . . Imagine that awful being, and you have a mental picture of Dr. Fu-Manchu, the yellow peril incarnate in one man" (*The Insidious Dr. Fu Manchu*: 25–26).

The Fu Manchu movies, in which the title role was played by white actors in "yellowface," including Warner Oland, Boris Karloff, and Christopher Lee, continued to market these Asian stereotypes. The evil and dangerous Fu Manchu was eventually replaced in the entertainment media by the more benign and lovable Charlie Chan, a second-generation Chinese detective who displayed his insights in short Confucian-style proverbs. The success of the Fu Manchu series built upon anti-Asian sentiment of the time, and critics have suggested that Rohmer's writings revealed Western xenophobia and Orientalist ideas of Asian race, class, and sexuality, more than they portrayed truths about Asia and Asians.

KENNETH J. GUEST

Vivien Leigh and Hattie McDaniel in a scene from *Gone with the Wind* (1939). (MGM/Photofest)

a constant threat to civilized white people. By the 1930s, minorities were no longer primarily depicted as savages. Instead, they were most often cast as servants for white families, e.g., *Gone With the Wind* (1939). Despite society's penchant for political correctness, examples of stereotypical images still abound. African Americans are frequently depicted as being sexually promiscuous, loud, uneducated, poor, and criminal. Few mainstream films depict African American males in intimate relationships. Most images of the African American family in film continue to promote the notion that all African American families are dysfunctional.

Images of Hispanic Americans in films have been every bit as stereotypical as images of African Americans. Silent films such as *Tony the Greaser* (1911), *Bronco Billy and the Greaser* (1914), and *The Greaser's Revenge* (1914) depicted Mexican Americans as violent, dishonest, and criminal. By the 1950s, Hispanic actors continued to receive few leading roles. Instead, white actors were frequently asked to portray Hispanic characters, as in films such as *Touch of Evil* (1958) and *Viva Zapata!* (1952). In the 1960s, the greaser image dominated films about Hispanics once again and led to the emergence of the image of the urban greaser in films such as *The Warriors* (1979), *Boulevard Nights* (1979), and *Walk Proud* (1979). By the end of the 20th century, independent filmmakers began to provide more diverse images of Hispanic Americans. Still, many mainstream films continue to present Latinos as uneducated, unable to speak English, poor, and primarily employed in menial occupations. Latino men in particular are treated as hypermasculine, cartoonlike characters.

Four dominant images of Asian Americans have emerged in mainstream films. The stock image treats Asian characters as expendable or interchangeable. The mysterious villain image plays into anti-immigrant attitudes. The Banzai war crime image became popular during World War II when the loyalty of Japanese Americans was called into question. The image that has been most difficult to shake is the China Doll or Geisha character. Asian American women were portrayed as submissive, exotic sex objects in films such as *The Thief of Bagdad* (1924), *Old San Francisco* (1927), and *The World of Susie Wong* (1959). In modern films, Asian Americans are portrayed as docile, industrious, conservative, and cliquish. They are identified as America's "model minority." This term seems positive, but it also trivializes challenges that are faced by members of the Asian American community by suggesting that they have no problems that need to be addressed by the larger society. Although Asian Americans continue to be treated as foreigners in films, their role as the instantly recognizable villain has been passed onto Arab Americans in films such as *The Siege* (1998).

Perhaps the most influential stereotype is the most subtle one. Minority actors are frequently relegated to second-class status in films. Even at the start of the 21st century, minority actors are not equal to white actors in their roles. In most instances, African American actors are used to support or prop up the lead actors, who typically are white. Even in films in which equal billing is given to the lead white and nonwhite actors (e.g., *Lethal Weapon* movies), the white character usually takes on the high-profile, take-charge, heroic role. These limited images are transmitted time and time again, with very few alternative images to balance them. Certainly, white Americans are stereotyped in films as well. The difference, however, is that many alternative images of whiteness are offered.

ROMNEY S. NORWOOD

See also

Beauty Standards; Cosby, Bill; Hollywood and Minority Actors; White Savior Films

Further Reading:

Bernardi, Daniel, ed. *Classic Hollywood, Classic Whiteness.* Minneapolis: University of Minnesota Press, 2001.

Miller, Randall, ed. *Ethnic Images in American Film and Television.* Philadelphia: Balch Institute, 1978.

Toplin, Robert B., ed. *Hollywood as Mirror: Changing Views of "Outsiders" and "Enemies" in American Movies.* Westport, CT: Greenwood Press, 1993.

Financial Institutions and Racial Discrimination

In spite of federal laws that prohibit discrimination in lending, studies continue to demonstrate that racial discrimination persists in the lending of funds for homes, cars, businesses, and farms. A landmark study by the Federal Reserve Bank of Boston in 1990 documented disparities in mortgage-lending patterns between nonwhites and whites in the Boston area. It also found that African Americans were three times more likely than whites to have a loan application rejected. A supplemental report that controlled for important economic factors, like credit histories, still left whites with higher approval rates than blacks. The Geographic Information System Action for Economic and Social Justice project conducted a larger study of 16 metropolitan areas in 1993 and found absolute evidence of redlining— lenders drawing theoretical red lines around minority neighborhoods—and not making mortgages available within those lines. This practice can account for higher loan costs to the borrowers and thus lower home ownership ratios for those affected. If African Americans were no longer to bear the brunt of illegal lending policies, the federal government had to begin enforcing its laws. The government had indeed begun enforcing the law when the Justice Department brought suit against the Decatur Federal Savings and Loan Association of Atlanta in 1992. In a consent decree, Decatur paid damages of $1 million to loan applicants and agreed to adopt a marketing plan that did not exclude black neighborhoods or discriminate against potential loan applicants.

Still, discrimination continued. A 1998 study by the California branch of the Association of Community Organizations for Reform Now (ACORN) looked at 9,000 lenders in 35 cities around the country. It found that nationwide, of all those applying for conventional mortgages, African Americans were 2.1 times more likely, and Latinos, 1.76 times more likely, to be rejected than whites. Furthermore, as the number of conventional loans made to whites increased 24 percent between 1995 and 1997, loans to African Americans increased only 5 percent, and loans to Latinos, 1 percent. The Urban Institute reported in 1999 that mortgage-lending discrimination existed from the beginning of the process to its end. Another ACORN report found that, in 2001, the likelihood of loan rejections for African Americans and Latinos had not changed much. Even as the Department of Justice continued to prosecute discriminatory lending cases, like the 2002 redlining case against MidAmerica Bank in Chicago, many studies showed that the pattern of discrimination goes on in mortgage lending. A National Community Reinvestment Coalitions report issued in 2003 found that African Americans were more likely than whites to have high-cost subprime loans rather than conventional loans, even when their credit risk was factored out. That 74 percent of whites and only 47 percent of blacks nationwide are homeowners reveals the reality of mortgage-lending discrimination.

Lending discrimination in car loans is also a problem. It is legal for car dealers to increase the interest rates fixed by lenders, which are determined by credit history and income. When dealers mark up the rate charged to the customer, they split the profit with the lenders. However, if black car buyers' loans are marked up more than white car buyers' loan, there is discrimination. Studies showed that nationally, blacks were charged over $600 more than whites through these markups. General Motors settled a class-action suit against it alleging discriminatory markups by its General Motors Acceptance Corporation early in 2004. Class-action suits are pending against WFS Financial, Inc. (a lender that works with thousands of dealers), American Honda Finance Company, and Toyota Motor Credit Corporation.

It is estimated that minorities own nearly 15 percent of small businesses nationwide—Hispanics about 6 percent, and blacks and Asians each around 4 percent. However, numerous studies have consistently found that minorities do not have equal access to capital, or put another way, are discriminated against when applying for business loans. One study even found a loan denial rate for whites of 27 percent and for blacks, 66 percent. The National Community Reinvestment Coalition found disparities in small-business loans by income and percentage of minorities in Washington, D.C., neighborhoods. Most controlled studies confirm a loan denial rate for black-owned small businesses twice that of white-owned businesses. Financial institutions make less than 1 percent of their small-business loans to black-, Latino-, and Asian American-owned businesses.

Black farmers have also experienced lending discrimination, most notably by the federal government itself. It came to light in 1997 that employees in the U.S. Department of Agriculture had for decades been systematically denying black farmers crop loans and other federal support to which they were entitled. In several Southeastern states, the county committees that granted the loans processed loans of whites three times faster than those of blacks. Most of these local committees had no minority representation. As a result, many lost their land. Only 18,000 black farmers of the 925,000 who were counted in 1920 remained by 1992. In the class-action suit that followed this revelation, black farmers and former farmers who documented loan denials were compensated with over $630 million.

Benjamin F. Shearer

See also

Housing Discrimination; Laissez-Faire Racism

Further Reading:

Myers, Samuel, and Tsze Chan. "Racial Discrimination in Housing Markets: Accounting for Credit Risk." *Social Science Quarterly* 76 (1995): 543–61.

Shlay, Anne B. "Not in That Neighborhood: The Effects of Population and Housing on the Distribution of Mortgage Finance within the Chicago SMSA." *Social Science Research* 17 (1988): 152–63.

Fire Next Time, The

The Fire Next Time consists of two 1962 essays by James Baldwin, "My Dungeon Shook: Letter to My Nephew on the One Hundredth Anniversary of the Emancipation," published in the *Progressive*, and "Down at the Cross: Letter from a Region in My Mind," published in the *New Yorker*. The two essays were released together as a book in 1963. The title, drawn from the second essay's final resonant phrase, is both a vague threat and a call to arms in the service of peace, which has become shorthand for the specter of violence promised by persistent racial injustice: "If we do not now dare everything, the fulfillment of that prophecy, recreated from the Bible in song by a slave, is upon us: God gave Noah the rainbow sign, No more water, the fire next time!" (347).

In the brief first essay, "My Dungeon Shook," Baldwin sets out for his nephew the challenges facing him as a black man in late-20th-century America. The second essay, "Down at the Cross," integrates Baldwin's observations about race and religion from several directions—Baldwin's childhood church experiences and his adult encounter with Elijah Muhammad and the Nation of Islam—with a meditation on how black and white Americans might move peacefully, with a full and candid knowledge of violent history, into the future together.

Across the two essays, Baldwin focuses on the rightful grudge but ultimate responsibility African Americans bear toward white people who have been responsible for, or at best ignorant of, black oppression. "It is the innocence which constitutes the crime," Baldwin writes (292). "This innocent country," he explains to his nephew, "set you down in a ghetto in which, in fact, it intended that you should perish" (293). The tension between reprisal and reconciliation is at the heart of Baldwin's formulation on how to integrate the desire for revolution with the responsibility of participating as citizens in building the United States: "Do I really *want* to be integrated into a burning house?" (340).

Narrating his meeting with Elijah Muhammad, Baldwin expresses skepticism of Muhammad's gratitude that black men are increasingly feared, and resists the idea that black and white must be opposed in America, that, in Muhammad's words, "The white man's heaven . . . is the black man's hell" (312). Rather, Baldwin articulates a vision of two communities stuck together, that must overcome past wounds and strive for something larger: "Relatively conscious whites and . . . blacks . . . must like lovers, insist on, or create, the consciousness of others . . . end the racial nightmare, and achieve our country, and change the history of the world" (346–47). Baldwin's closing plea for unified struggle recalls his quotation from St. Paul at the start of "Down by the Cross," that it is "better to marry than to burn," and transfigures Paul's affirmation of God-fearing monogamy into an interracial embrace of spiritual reconciliation (297).

ALEX FEERST

See also
American Literature and Racism; Baldwin, James

Further Reading:
Baldwin, James. *Collected Essays*. New York: Library of America, 1998.
Balfour, Katharine Lawrence. *The Evidence of Things Not Said: James Baldwin and the Promise of American Democracy*. Ithaca, NY: Cornell University Press, 2001.
Campbell, James. *Talking at the Gates: A Life of James Baldwin*. New York: Viking, 1991.
Porter, Horace A. *Stealing the Fire: The Art and Protest of James Baldwin*. Middletown, CT: Wesleyan University Press, 1988.

Florida Effect

During the 2000 presidential elections, Florida became the center of a nationwide spotlight. The Florida controversy involved a month-long legal battle after the election was completed, along with numerous recounts before a winner was declared. The battles began when, after voting was completed, many reports began to emerge from Florida of instances of minorities being disfranchised during the voting process. The combination of these seemingly isolated instances of voter suppression had a huge impact on the outcome of the election, with many claiming that Florida was ultimately the deciding factor. Examples of events or policies that prevented minorities from being able to vote in the 2000 election included poor ballot designs, use of outdated machinery, purging voter lists, labeling eligible voters as felons thereby making them ineligible to vote, shortening early vote periods, making access difficult to voters with special needs, and passing unfair election laws. The combination of these incidents and others created a huge impact on the election's outcome, as Republican George W. Bush won the election against Democrat Albert Gore with a laser thin margin of 537 popular votes in Florida. Ever since, the "Florida Effect," as it has been nicknamed, became a symbol of state-sponsored efforts of voter suppression.

The Florida Effect is viewed as the work of Republicans because up until 2000, no Republican since Calvin Coolidge had been able to win the presidency without winning Florida. Republicans have since come to see Florida as a "gateway" to the White House. However, Democrats have won the presidency without winning Florida, as President Obama did in 2008 and again in 2012. Historically, Florida voted

---

The U.S. Commission on Civil Rights Investigation

The U.S. Commission on Civil Rights conducted extensive investigation of irregularities that allegedly took place in the November 2000 presidential election in Florida. The commission utilized its subpoena power in the investigation that involved three days of hearings, over 30 hours of testimony from over 100 witnesses, and a systematic review of more than 118,000 sheets of paper. Among several of its findings, the report confirmed:

- Approximately 3.9 million Americans are disenfranchised or separated from their right to vote in public elections due to their status as former offenders.
- Over 36 percent of the total disenfranchised population of these offenders consists of African American men.
- Thirteen percent of African American men are disenfranchised.
- Thirty-one percent of the Florida disenfranchised population consists of African American men.
- Florida's recently enacted electoral reform law failed to change the state's policy of permanently disenfranchising former felons, which produces a stark disparity in disenfranchisement rates of African American men compared with their white counterparts. The state also failed to reform the laborious and protracted executive clemency application procedures.

A complete report is available online at: http://www.usccr.gov/pubs/vote2000/report/main.htm

---

consistently for Democratic candidates from Reconstruction until 1952. Because of its rapid population growth over the last 60 years, Florida's electoral importance has grown from a mere 8 electoral votes at the end of World War II to its current count of 29 electoral votes. The state of Florida currently has the fourth highest number of electoral votes. The Cuban exodus during the1980s along with the influxes of retirees and service workers to the theme park economy helped the state become much more diversified economically and politically than other Southern states. This has made the Florida of today a swing state, though it has tended to lean slightly Republican. Florida's swing state reputation reached new heights in the 2000 election with the mountain of legal battles and voting recounts that accompanied that election.

The largely contested election in 2000—especially as it played out in Florida—exhibited common tactics of voter suppression, especially when it came to the technology used to score citizens' votes. The Votomatic-style punch card technology system used in the 2000 election has been criticized by many as contributing to residual votes—that is, the votes that cannot be counted in a given election—which has in turn affected the minority vote. Specifically, there are allegations that many minority votes in Florida were not counted because of this residual effect, which may have altered the election outcome by propelling Republican

George W. Bush into the White House. Indeed, during the controversy surrounding the 2000 election, a public suspicion emerged that Bush stole the election. As Florida worked to correct the issues surrounding the Votomatic-style punch card in 2000, the system was deemed flawed, prejudiced, and discriminatory. A careful review of the Votomatic scoring system in Florida showed that a majority citizen's vote counted with 1.026 more times the weight of a minority person. In other words, minority votes are invalidated more frequently than nonminority votes with Votomatic-style punch card systems, showing that this particular technology is less reliable and objective than newer voting systems such as optical scan. Along with the outdated technology, many attributed the racial gap in the Florida election to confusing ballot designs. One such design was the "butterfly ballot" used in Palm Beach County, where the Votomatic systems required voters to fully line up the correct holes on a nameless ballot with the correct names on the device into which the ballot is inserted.

After the 2000 election, debates continued in Florida around the suppression of minority votes. In 2004, George W. Bush comfortably won the presidential election in Florida, especially in counties closest to military bases. In 2008, Florida swung the other direction when Democrat Barack Obama won the state. Obama did exceptionally well in 2008 compared to his Democratic predecessors, perhaps largely due to the rapid increase in diverse populations in the Sunshine State. This led many Florida Republican politicians to believe that the move to expand early voting that year by then-governor Charlie Crist had favored Obama. To remedy the situation, in 2012 Florida legislature cut the number of days for early voting from 14 to 8 and prohibited it on the last Sunday before the election. This caused incredibly long lines on Saturday of the final weekend, forcing voters to wait in lines for sometimes more than eight hours and forcing polls to stay open past midnight in some cases. Despite these problems with voter access, current Republican governor Rick Scott emphatically refused to open polls on Sunday during the 2012 election. To circumvent the situation, some local election officials handed out absentee ballots on both the Sunday and Monday before Election Day. Nevertheless, all of the obstacles and inconveniences in Florida's current voting policies kept many Florida voters from casting their ballots in the 2012 presidential election until 1:30 A.M., well past Obama's victory speech. Many voters complained that longer early voting lines dissuaded them from voting in person and the frustration grew higher because of longer lines on Election Day. Data shows that the voter turnout rate (71 percent) in 2012 was smaller than in 2008 (75 percent) or 2004 (74 percent). Looking at the issue from a different angle, only 80,351 more eligible voters in Florida participated in 2012 than in 2008, even though voter registrations went up by 686,812 during this time period. Because of the long lines and other obstacles to voting, Florida was not called until the Saturday following the election, although in this election the delay did not have a big impact on the outcome since Romney conceded and Obama gave his victory speech on the election night itself.

The 2000 Florida elections stand as an example of state-sponsored efforts to suppress minority votes, as the state has had a long history of implementing policies that seem designed to impede minorities from voting and in some cases, exclude their ballots altogether. In 2000, these policies had a profound impact on the outcome of the presidential election, as Florida was in the spotlight that year for being the swing state in that election. This election shows that seemingly trivial events or policies surrounding voting, such as ballot design and poll hours, can actually have a pronounced effect on an election's outcome. Twelve years later, election problems continue to plague Florida. Ballot design continues to be a hotly contested issue in the state, along with other such issues as technology, reducing early voting periods, eliminating Sundays before elections as voting days, purging voter lists, and labeling eligible voters as criminals, among others.

KOMANDURI MURTY

Further Reading:

Edwards III, George C. "The 2000 U.S. Presidential Election." *Taiwan Journal of Democracy* 2 (2006): 37–50.

Hines, Revathi. "The Silent Voices: 2000 Presidential Election and the Minority Vote in Florida." *Western Journal of Black Studies* 26 (2002): 71–74.

Wattenberg, Martin P. "Was the 2000 Presidential Election Fair? An Analysis of Comparative and Retrospective Survey Data." *Presidential Studies Quarterly* 33 (2003): 889–97.

Wolter, Kirk; Diana Jergovic, Whitney Moore, Joe Murphy, and Colm O'Muircheartaigh. "Reliability of the Uncertified Ballots in the 2000 Presidential Election in Florida." *American Statistician* 57 (2003): 1–14.

Folsom, James (1908–1987)

James Elisha Folsom was a two-time Alabama governor who took a moderate stand on civil rights issues and segregation during the middle portion of the 20th century. Folsom was born October 9, 1908, in rural Coffee County, Alabama. He is known as a populist governor who sought to improve the standing of black and white Alabamians. During his campaign for governor in 1946, Folsom earned his nickname, "Big Jim." Standing six feet seven inches, he towered over most men. A hallmark of Folsom's campaign was "Y'all Come"; the intention was to show an openness of government with citizens. Many disenfranchised black Alabamians interpreted this openness as a sign of taking down barriers of segregation. After his election to the governorship, Folsom pursued policies perceived by many at the time to be liberal regarding issues of race. In particular, his populist agenda involved eliminating poll taxes that discouraged many poor whites and blacks from voting and implementing a comprehensive public defender program. He also publicly spoke against the formation of a White Citizens Council in Alabama.

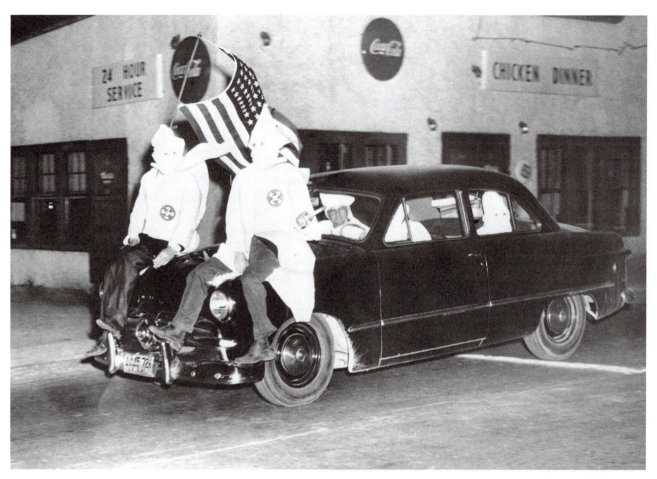

An 18-car parade staged by the Ku Klux Klan in Gadsden, Alabama, March 5, 1949. Observers said all license tags were uncovered in accordance with Gov. James E. Folsom's order. One of the cars chased the car of the photographer who took the photograph, but gave up the chase upon reaching a downtown intersection. (Associated Press)

Elected governor of Alabama twice, he served from 1947 to 1951 and from 1955 to 1959. As the civil rights movement gained steam, Alabama voters signaled a desire for elected officials to take a hard line against complying with federal mandates concerning integration. Despite this growing opposition to the civil rights movement, Folsom promised to work within the legal realms in making the adjustment to integration. During the first year of Folsom's second administration, many of his programs to expand state services were passed by the state's legislature. While enjoying great success with the legislature for his reforms of state government and moderate stand on civil rights issues, subsequent federal court rulings and the civil rights movement began to erode public support for compromise on issues of civil rights.

Folsom's moderate stand on issues concerning race, and his refusal to exploit race relations to achieve his agenda or gain political capital, eroded his support base among white voters. In 1962, Folsom was defeated in his third bid for governor by George Wallace. Wallace's more aggressive stand against integration propelled him past other candidates and into the governor's office. Although Folsom continually ran for governor, he was never again elected to public office, being relegated to an also-ran in elections during the later years of his life. Folsom spent his golden years managing his insurance business in Cullman, Alabama.

Folsom and his second wife, Jamelle Moore, had seven children. The oldest, James Elisha Jr., followed in his father's political path, having served as Alabama's governor and lieutenant governor. Folsom died of heart failure on November 21, 1987, in Cullman.

JAMES NEWMAN

See also
Civil Rights Act of 1964; Civil Rights Movement; Segregation

Further Reading:
Grafton, Carl, and Anne Permaloff. *Big Mules and Branchheads: James E. Folsom and Political Power in Alabama.* Athens: University of Georgia Press. 1985.

Football

Many organized sports in the United States have a history of excluding African Americans. Football is no exception. From its origins in a professional league and as a intercollegiate sport, football was almost an exclusively white sport.

Integration in the professional leagues also came slowly. In the premier professional football league, the National Football League (NFL), integration came slowly. The first signs of integrated teams seemed closer to tokenism than an outright recruitment of talented black athletes. There were several subtle and not-so-subtle slights against black players. For example, many NFL teams did not allow the integration of athletes at dining facilities and boarding during training camp.

The arrival of the American Football League (AFL) hastened the process of integration. In an effort for the upstart league to develop a fan base, the AFL chose to locate many of its franchises in cities that were not home to NFL franchises. In the 1960s, many of the NFL teams were located in states with few or no Jim Crow laws and customs. While this did not prevent slights and other forms of racial discrimination from occurring, it did not open the black players to the societal and legal system of segregation that existed in the South.

While the AFL resisted placing franchises in the South, it did place teams in Dallas, whose team shortly moved to Kansas City, and Houston. This move into the South was considered risky because the AFL planned to openly recruit African Americans. To provide funding for the new league, the AFL was able to use a new medium, television, and its contract with the National Broadcasting Company (NBC)

to pay players wages comparable with the NFL. Nonetheless, team owners, and many fans, believed the talent level of the AFL would not be up to par with the more established NFL. In an effort to look for competitive talent, the AFL was aggressive in recruiting players from historically black colleges and universities. Almost immediately, AFL teams consistently employed more African Americans than NFL teams. Upon merger of the two leagues in 1970, the NFL began to follow suit in employing more African Americans as players.

By 1970, the Jim Crow restrictions that prevented professional football from expanding in the South were erased. The removal of these laws allowed for rapid expansion into an underserved market. In 1965, the only NFL franchise south of Washington, D.C., was in Dallas, Texas. By 1993, there were NFL teams in Dallas, Houston, New Orleans, Atlanta, Charlotte, Jacksonville, Tampa Bay, and Miami.

In the college ranks, many large state universities throughout the South did not accept nonwhites and therefore did not have any nonwhite student athletes. This segregation spilled over into football throughout the South. In the segregated system of higher education, African American student athletes had two options; play at a historically black college or leave the South. Many black football players chose to play for historically black universities. Some universities, such as Grambling, in Louisiana, experienced enormous success with talented African American football players. Grambling's head football coach for 57 years, Eddie Robinson, retired with 408 wins, the most of any head football coach in National Collegiate Athletic Association (NCAA) history at the time.

As segregation ended, many of the most talented African American student athletes chose to accept athletic scholarships at traditionally white universities. By the 1990s, African American student athletes outnumbered white student athletes on many team rosters of large, traditionally white universities playing in NCAA Division I-A.

Opportunities for African Americans in college and professional football have improved greatly. Many major NCAA Division I-A football teams award a majority of its athletic scholarships to African American players. An overwhelming majority of the players on NFL rosters are black. Despite these gains, the coaching ranks continue to be dominated by whites. While most major college teams have at least one black assistant coach, the overwhelming majority of NCAA Division I-A schools do not have a black head coach. In the NFL, the situation is similar but not as bleak. Currently, the percentage of NFL franchises with an African American as head coach is greater than the percent of African American coaches in the college ranks, but still considerably lower than the percentage of African Americans who are currently playing in the NFL. The NFL has taken several steps to improve opportunities for African Americans to become a head coach. Anecdotal evidence of this exists in that in 2007, the head coaches of both teams playing in the NFL's Super Bowl were black. This was the first time any team playing for the NFL championship had a black head coach.

JAMES NEWMAN

See also
Basketball; Sports and Racism

Further Reading:
Barnhart, Tony. *Southern Fried Football: The History, Passion and Glory of the Great Southern Game.* Chicago: Triumph Books, 2000.

Dunnavant, Keith. *The Missing Ring.* New York: St. Martin's Press, 2006.

Levy, Alan H. *Tackling Jim Crow: Racial Segregation in Professional Football.* Jefferson, NC: McFarland, 2000.

Ross, Charles K. *African Americans and the Integration of the National Football League.* New York: New York University Press, 1999.

Forman, James (1928–2005)

Born in Chicago, Illinois, on October 4, 1928, James Forman believed himself to be the oldest of the two children of Octavia and James "Pop" Rufus. However, at the age of 14, he discovered that his biological father was Jackson Forman, a Chicago cab driver. Forman spent most of his first six years on his grandmother's farm in Marshall County, Mississippi, where he received a harsh education in the rules of segregation. He was once threatened with lynching for not saying "Yes, ma'am" to a local white storekeeper, and was told that black boys could not eat ice cream at the parlor counter or drink Coca-Colas from the deposit bottles.

Returning to Chicago, Forman attended a predominantly African American Catholic school until a spiritual crisis in the sixth grade sent him to public school. Forman grew up reading the *Chicago Defender* and the work of prominent African Americans, such as Richard Wright and W.E.B. Du Bois. His academic career took a brief detour when he enrolled in, and was expelled from, a vocational high school and joined a gang of juvenile delinquents. Re-enrolling in Englewood High School's general studies program, he earned the *Chicago Tribune*'s student honors award in 1947, graduating with honors and enrolling in Wilson Junior College.

Seeking to avoid the draft, Foreman joined the U.S. Air Force, serving from 1947 to 1951. He then enrolled for a semester at the University of Southern California before a false arrest and abuse by the Los Angeles Police Department sent him into a long physical and mental convalescence and led to his return home to complete his bachelor's degree at Roosevelt University in 1957. While pursuing a master's degree in African Studies at Boston University, Forman secured press credentials as a reporter for the *Chicago Defender* and went to Little Rock, Arkansas, to cover the 1957 school desegregation struggle.

In 1960, Forman joined the Emergency Relief Committee, an initiative sponsored by the Congress of Racial Equality (CORE) to assist Fayette and Haywood County, Tennessee, farmers displaced from their land by white landlords and by the local White Citizens' Council for attempting to register to vote. In the summer of 1961, Forman and several others from the committee participated in CORE's Freedom Rides and joined the direct-action wing of the Student Nonviolent Coordinating Committee (SNCC), with Forman intending to write and engage in direct-action protest. He was later asked by SNCC members to consider assuming the position of SNCC executive director, a position that primarily involved organizing and providing direct logistical support to the famously decentralized multistate network of SNCC field workers.

Forman eventually agreed and, in 1964, blended his administrative talents with a more mature and seasoned approach to the essential direct-action training, protest, voter registration, logistical support (food, clothing, shelter) and other fieldwork of the SNCC. Forman assumed responsibility for preparing the biracial group of students who participated in the Freedom Summer (Mississippi) of 1964 (see entry).

His attitude toward the work reflected that of his SNCC colleagues. They were highly suspicious of what they termed the "messiah complex" that looked to top-down leadership; they echoed the call for group-centered, grassroots work made by their advisor, Ella Jo Baker.

SNCC debates over tactics, direction, and strategies in the wake of the 1964 successes and the subsequent passage of the Civil Rights Act of 1964 and the Voting Rights Act of 1965 led the organization and Forman into an alliance with the rapidly emerging Black Panther Party for Self-Defense (BPP), even as Forman advocated that the SNCC remain open to white members. Faced with the BPP's lack of effective administrative structure, internal conflicts, and other issues, Forman left both the BPP and the SNCC in 1969 to pursue the agenda of economic development for black communities. Forman, who had also traveled to southern, eastern, and central Africa in 1964 and 1967 to promote the internationalization of the SNCC and BPP agendas, had accelerated his advocacy of an internationalist framework for analyzing the conditions of blacks in the United States.

On April 26, 1969, a National Black Economic Development Conference (NBEDC) called in Detroit, Michigan, by the Interreligious Foundation for Community Organization adopted the Black Manifesto, a call for white churches and synagogues to pay $500 million in reparations for the enslavement of Africans and the effects of ongoing systematic racism and oppression. The document, prepared by Forman and the League of Black Revolutionary Workers, stated that the money was to be used to fund a Southern land bank for the use of poor people, four major publishing and printing enterprises for black people, four TV networks, a communications training center, a black labor strike and defense fund, and a black university.

On May 4, 1969, Forman interrupted the morning service at New York City's Riverside Church to read the Black Manifesto from the pulpit. Of the approximately $500,000 eventually collected from the demand, 40 percent came from Riverside alone, which was selected because of its ties to the family of John D. Rockefeller, who had built the church. Some white religious institutions responded by increasing contributions to new or existing programs they had initiated. The Federal Bureau of Investigation investigated the NBEDC, and only a fraction of the funds collected went to the organization, most of the money going to various reform projects,

which had ironically been criticized by the Black Manifesto. The NBEDC formed Detroit's Black Star Publications from its part of the proceeds; Black Star published Forman's *The Political Thought of James Forman* in 1970.

Forman remained active politically throughout the remaining three decades of his life, accepting the leadership of the Unemployment and Poverty Action Committee in Washington, D.C., in 1974. His work with this organization included, among other things, voter registration and political education, lobbying for D.C. statehood, and working against the appointment of Robert Bork to the U.S. Supreme Court. In later years, Forman participated in symbolic commemorations of his earlier struggles, such as the 40th anniversary of the Freedom Rides in 2004.

In 1969, Forman published his first book, titled *Sammy Younge, Jr.: The First Black College Student to Die in the Black Liberation Movement*. Younge was a Tuskegee Institute student and friend of Forman's who was murdered in 1966 for his participation in the civil rights movement. Three years later, Forman published his memoir, *The Making of Black Revolutionaries*, which has undergone several editions (1985, 1997). He earned his MA in Africana Studies at Cornell University (1980), and a PhD from the Union of Experimental Colleges and Universities (1982). The research he conducted for these degrees was partially published in his 1984 book *Self-Liberation: An Examination of the Question and Its Application to the African American People*. In 1994, Forman also published *The High Tide of Black Resistance (and Other Political and Literary Writings)*, a mixture of essays, speeches, oral history, and short fiction that revealed dimensions of the civil rights movement in which he had participated. Forman died of colon cancer in January 2005. He was married to, and divorced from, Constancia Romily, with whom he had two sons. James Jr. worked as a public defender and educator, helping to found the Maya Angelou Charter School (named for his godmother) in Washington, D.C. Chaka is a member of the Screen Actors' Guild.

GREGORY E. CARR

See also

Congress of Racial Equality (CORE); Freedom Summer (Mississippi) of 1964; Lynching

Further Reading:

Forman, James. *The Making of Black Revolutionaries*. Seattle: Open Hand Publishing, 1985.

Smith, Jessie Carney, ed. *Notable Black American Men*. Detroit: Gale, 1999.

Valentine, Victoria. "In the Fore of the Movement." *Emerge Magazine* (April 1996): 24.

Fortune, T. Thomas (1856–1928)

Timothy Thomas Fortune was born into slavery in Marianna, Florida, on October 3, 1856. Shortly after the Civil War, Fortune began to attend school at the Freedmen's Bureau in Marianna, where he became an exceptional student. Fortune lived a rather privileged life in comparison to other former slaves because his family purchased some land and became farmers. For a short time, he worked at the *Marianna Courier* where he learned the printer's trade and became actively interested in journalism. His father became involved in politics during the Reconstruction period; however, Fortune's family was forced to move from Marianna to Jacksonville because his father had received death threats in regard to his political beliefs and actions. Fortune stayed in Tallahassee, where he was serving as a page in the state senate after his family's move. Upon returning to Jacksonville, Fortune attended school at the Stanton Institute. In 1874, he traveled to Washington, D.C., and attended Howard University.

During his collegiate years, Fortune worked for several African American newspapers such as the *People's Advocate*. After graduation, Fortune and his wife, Carrie, returned to Florida where he worked for the *Jacksonville Daily Union*, but their stay there was short as the opportunity arose to work at the *Weekly Witness* in New York City. While working for the *Witness*, Fortune became the managing editor for the *Rumor*, a weekly tabloid run by George Parker, an African American who shared the same beliefs and interests as Fortune. Fortune insisted the paper's name be changed to the *New York Globe*, which subsequently became the *Freeman* and the *New York Age*, and survived until 1960, making it one of the longest-running African American newspapers.

Fortune's professional career was not limited to journalism; he became actively involved in politics as well. In 1890, Fortune cofounded the Afro-American League, which was a precursor of the Niagara movement and the National Association for the Advancement of Colored People. Fortune also became acquainted with African American activist Ida B. Wells-Barnett, who had been born after the Civil War, taught school in rural Mississippi, and worked at the *Memphis Free Speech*. It was during her time at the *Free Speech* that Wells-Barnett began to speak out against lynching. After learning of threats against her life in Memphis, Wells-Barnett went to work for Fortune at the *Age* where they combined their efforts in an anti-lynching campaign. It was in 1892 that they printed a seven-column article stating the names and dates of victims who had been lynched because of their supposed involvement in various crimes. Wells-Barnett became involved in speaking engagements leading the charge against lynching. In 1895, Fortune spoke at the National Federation of Afro-American Women, a group in which Wells-Barnett had played an integral part.

Fortune continued his political interests in 1896 when the reviving of the Afro-American League occurred in response to deteriorating conditions for African Americans in the South. In 1898, Fortune and other prominent African American leaders met in Rochester, New York, for a conference regarding race relations. During this conference, Fortune's fellow activist and friend Ida B. Wells-Barnett was named secretary of the newly renamed National Afro-American Council, whose purpose was to incorporate religious, political, and benevolent organizations for the good of all races.

Throughout his career, Fortune continued to use his newspaper, the *Age*, to speak out against lynchings in both the North and South. His 1884 *Black and White: Land, Labor, and Politics in the South* was a reply to the poor treatment of Southern freedmen. His other book, *The Negro in Politics*, published in 1885, was a result of Fortune's belief that the Republican Party was exploiting African American voters. His career as a journalist and writer allowed him the opportunity to speak out against racial injustices and, along with other prominent African Americans such as Booker T. Washington and Marcus Garvey, to create opportunities for the financial, social, and civil furtherance of African Americans. Fortune was editor of Marcus Garvey's *Negro World* and the *Colored American Review*. He died in 1928, but not before his career, politics, and activism gave voice to the cause and place of his race.

MARY J. SLOAT

See also
Garvey, Marcus; Washington, Booker T.

Further Reading:
Andrews, William L., Francis Smith Foster, and Trudier Harris,
    eds. *Oxford Companion to African American Literature.* New
    York: Oxford University Press, 1997.
Page, James A. *Selected Black American Authors.* Boston: Page,
    1977.
Thornbrough, Emma Lou. *T. Thomas Fortune: Militant
    Journalist.* Chicago: University of Chicago Press, 1972.

Fourteenth Amendment (1868)

Although the Fourteenth Amendment pertains to all U.S. citizens, it was originally created to grant former slaves in the South protection against violence and discriminatory laws and to safeguard their voting rights. Congress passed the Fourteenth Amendment in 1866, but it was not ratified by all 10 Southern states until 1868 as one of the requirements of readmission to the Union during Reconstruction. Nevertheless, whites consistently violated the Fourteenth Amendment (often without repercussions) while blacks remained the target of a long and turbulent period of violence, riots, and social, economic, and political oppression. Significant intervention to enforce the Fourteenth Amendment did not occur until after the achievements of multiple individuals and grassroots organizations during the 1950s and 1960s.

The Fourteenth Amendment comprises five sections. The first section grants state as well as federal citizenship to all individuals born or naturalized in the United States. It outlaws the states from constructing laws denying any individual their rights and freedoms. The states are also obligated to protect the rights and freedoms of every individual and forbidden to victimize any person in any way without a formal process of law. The second section punishes any state obstructing suffrage by reducing the number of its political representatives. The third section thwarts rebels by withholding any federal or state position from any individual not conforming to the Constitution. The fourth section indicates that the United States will not pay for any debts incurred during acts of rebellion and will not compensate slave owners for any slaves that were lost or emancipated. The last section gives Congress powers to enforce this amendment.

A scene outside the galleries of the U.S. House of Representatives during the passage of the Fourteenth Amendment. This amendment was intended to enforce the end of slavery and protect the rights of free blacks. Although typically considered in the context of its meaning for African Americans, the Fourteenth Amendment, which established the basis of American citizenship, is also considered to be a significant piece of legislation in the fight for women's rights. (North Wind Picture Archives)

Notwithstanding Congress's progressive maneuver, vicious attacks against blacks continued unabated even after the South had consented to the terms of the Fourteenth Amendment. In an effort to regain political power, white conservatives, or Democrats, engaged in bribery and hostile acts against blacks to prevent them from voting and to maintain white supremacy.

Some whites made efforts to protect blacks and their supporters. These efforts were ephemeral. Governors in Tennessee, Texas, and Arkansas declared martial law. They ordered droves of armed men to subdue the violence that engulfed the South. As a result of the Enforcement Acts of 1870 and 1871, hundreds of members of the Ku Klux Klan were arrested. Nevertheless, many of them served short sentences, paid mild fines, or eluded prosecution altogether. Also problematic was the fact that the federal government had limited finances and resources to handle the overwhelming number of aggressors. Nevertheless, white Democrats regained political power in the South by 1877, using the very methods the Fourteenth Amendment ruled against. They disenfranchised blacks and assaulted them and their property with no regard to due process. Shortly thereafter, the federal government withdrew the Union troops, and Northern interest in helping to protect blacks waned.

Unfettered by external interference and restraints, the Democrats established Jim Crow laws and permitted—and in some cases instigated—the onslaught of violence and oppression that permeated the South. Jim Crow laws limited the freedoms and rights of blacks, defying the decrees of the Fourteenth Amendment. The laws designated colored-only and white-only sections of towns, drinking fountains, restaurants, schools, and seating on public transportation. These laws were backed by a series of Supreme Court decisions made between 1875 and 1900 that further limited the rights the Fourteenth Amendment guaranteed blacks. For example, the Supreme Court sanctioned separate but equal accommodations on railroads in the *Plessy v. Ferguson* case (1896). The Court believed the Fourteenth Amendment concerned racial equality before the law and not social matters.

However, blacks did not receive equal protection in the court system, either. Police brutality was common and unchecked. Juries remained all white. Judges and juries almost always sided with whites, whether innocent or guilty. Blacks, when convicted, received harsher sentences. Whites were rarely charged in crimes against blacks. In the late 1800s and early 1900s, white mobs regularly lynched blacks they accused of crimes, and destroyed black communities without due process of law. In response, some blacks fled the South, or turned to leaders who extolled Black Nationalism. Others supported racially mixed (though predominantly black) organizations such as the National Association for the Advancement of Colored People and, later, the civil rights movement of the 1950s and 1960s.

The Fourteenth Amendment was a powerful instrument used to combat injustices in the courts and to defeat discriminatory laws during the 1950s and 1960s. One of the most celebrated cases to end segregated schools was *Brown v. Board of Education of Topeka* (1954). The National Guard protected black students from white mobs. Many protested, marched, participated in sit-ins, and boycotted for the rights guaranteed by the Fourteenth Amendment. They were often met with mob violence and police brutality. Members of the Congress of Racial Equality and the Student Nonviolent Coordinating Committee traveled to Mississippi during the Freedom Summer (Mississippi) of 1964 (see entry) to galvanize black suffrage. These protests resulted in legislation, such as the Civil Rights Act of 1964, which authorized action against segregation in public accommodations, public facilities, and employment and was pivotal to the enforcement of the Fourteenth Amendment. Nearly 100 years later, blacks finally reaped the benefits of the Fourteenth Amendment. They voted with greater ease and enjoyed more freedoms and opportunities. Nevertheless, violence against blacks, racism, and discrimination were not completely eradicated as evident in impoverished black ghettos where frustrations gave way to racial consciousness, militancy, and riots.

GLADYS L. KNIGHT

See also
Birthers; Naturalization and Citizenship Process; Reconstruction Era

Further Reading:
Meyer, Howard N. *The Amendment That Refused to Die: Equality and Justice Deferred, the History of the Fourteenth Amendment.* Lanham, MD: Madison Books, 2000.

Frazier, E. Franklin (1894–1962)

E. Franklin Frazier, who became a renowned sociologist and preeminent scholar, was born Edward Franklin Frazier in Baltimore, Maryland, the son of James Edward Frazier, a bank messenger, and Mary E. Clark. Because his father had taught himself to read and write as an adult, young Frazier quickly learned to use formal education to escape poverty. He also articulated a strong interest in sociology and race relations during this time. This awareness seemingly started as a result of Frazier's daily discussions with his father about the harsh and explosive atmosphere among the African American and white residents of Baltimore and of Atlanta,

Georgia, expressed in numerous newspaper articles and editorials.

After graduating from Baltimore Colored High School in 1912, Frazier entered Howard University, in Washington, D.C., on an academic scholarship. Upon the completion of his studies at this institution in 1916, Frazier quickly illustrated his mastery of several languages, literature, and mathematics. Specifically, he taught mathematics at Tuskegee Institute (1916–1917) and English, French, and history at St. Paul Normal and Industrial School in Lawrenceville, Indiana (1917–1918).

In 1919, Frazier enrolled into the graduate program in sociology at Clark University in Worcester, Massachusetts. There, under the direction of Professor Frank Hankins, he became a skilled sociologist by immersing himself in the various methods and theories of the discipline. In 1922, Frazier married Marie Brown. However, no children came from this union. This same year he became the director of the summer school program at Livingstone College in Salisbury, North Carolina. Five years later, he became the director of the Atlanta University School of Social Work as well as an instructor in the Department of Sociology at Morehouse College in Atlanta. Once he received his MA in 1929, Frazier spent a year as a researcher at the New York School of Social Work and the following year at the University of Copenhagen in Denmark on a university fellowship.

During these years, Frazier also published more than 30 articles on topics such as the African American family, the emergence of African American business leaders, and the development of the black American middle class. Soon he began to be read widely by both black and white Southerners. However, Frazier's readership greatly declined when his research focus changed. His article titled *The Pathology of Race Prejudice* appeared in June 1927 in an academic journal, where he claimed that racial prejudice and racism were pathological societal norms in the South. Eventually these same views were published in the *Atlanta Constitution* and the *Atlanta Independent* newspapers. As a result, he began to receive many harassing phone calls and death threats. These actions, along with some heated discussions with several close friends, caused Frazier to leave the South.

Upon leaving the region, Frazier entered the University of Chicago as a graduate student and research fellow. In 1929, he accepted a position as a lecturer in the Department of Sociology at Fisk University in Nashville, Tennessee. Once he completed his PhD in 1931, Frazier became a research professor of sociology in the Department of Social Science. Three years later, he became chairperson of the Department of Sociology at Howard University. He retired as professor emeritus of sociology in 1959 but continued to teach courses in the African Studies Program at Howard University and the School of Advanced International Studies at John Hopkins University until his death in 1962.

Two of Frazier's prestigious publications were *The Negro Family in Chicago* (1932) and *The Negro Family in the United States* (1939), which won him the Anisfield Award for publishing the most important book in field of race relations. However, his most controversial book was *Black Bourgeoisie* (1957), an analysis of the development of the African American middle class from its origin during the time of enslavement to the 1940s, which was shaped by various racial prejudice and discriminatory forces. In general, Frazier concluded in this study that the "black bourgeoisie," or black American middle class, lacking any real economic power and being socially marginalized, had created a moral foundation and value system that was identical to the white upper class rather than the white middle class.

Throughout the rest of his illustrious academic and scholarly career, Frazier received numerous honors, such as serving as the president of the District of Columbia Sociological Society, being appointed as vice president of the African Studies Association, and becoming the first African American president of the American Sociological Society in 1948. All in all, there is no question that E. Franklin Frazier was a pioneer and trailblazer within the field of sociology.

Eric R. Jackson

See also

Black Bourgeoisie; Du Bois, W.E.B.

Further Reading:

Blackwell, James E., and Morris Janowitz. *Black Sociologists: Historical and Contemporary Perspectives*. Chicago: University of Chicago Press, 1974.

Edward, G. Franklin. "E. Franklin Frazier: Race, Education, and Community." In *Sociological Traditions from Generation to Generation*, edited by Robert K. Merton and Matilda W. Riley. Norwood, NJ: Ablex Publications Corporation, 1980.

Odum, Howard. *American Sociology*. New York: Longmans, 1951.

Platt, Anthony, M. *E. Franklin Frazier Reconsidered*. New Brunswick, NJ: Rutgers University Press, 1991.

Vlasek, Dale R. "E. Franklin Frazier and the Problem of Assimilation." In *Ideas in America's Cultures from Republic to Mass Society*, edited by Hamilton Cravens. Ames: Iowa State University Press, 1982.

Freedom Rides

The Freedom Rides were a form of nonviolent protest conducted on buses by an interracial group of civil rights activists in the early 1960s. Freedom Rides, which occurred during the broadly defined civil rights movement of the 1950s and 1960s, constituted a challenge to legalized racial segregation. Southern whites reacted violently to the rides, while the riders refrained from fighting back. Ironically, the violence that was committed by whites against the peaceful

---

Boycotts

Boycotts are a tactic that social movements and other groups use to put pressure on their opponents so that they will change laws, policies, or behaviors. This tactic involves refusing to support an organization or corporation financially by not purchasing its products, going to its stores, or spending money that it will benefit from. One reason for the popularity of boycotts is that the risk of physical or economic harm to those who participate is slight. As a result, groups engaged in boycotts can often induce individuals who are not part of their group but are sympathetic to their cause to participate, thus increasing the incentive for the target to change its ways. Martin Luther King, Jr. and his followers, who were greatly influenced by Mahatma Gandhi, used boycotts and other forms of nonviolent action in the civil rights movement; the Montgomery Bus Boycott is one of the most famous examples. Other well-known instances of groups sponsoring boycotts are the boycott of grapes in sympathy with migrant agricultural workers in California in 1965 and boycotts of Korean grocery stores in New York and Los Angeles by African American and Latino groups who perceived the grocery store owners as racist.

MIKAILA MARIEL LEMONIK ARTHUR

---

protesters generated nationwide attention and sympathy for the riders, eventually prompting a major win in the struggle for civil rights.

The precursor to the Freedom Rides was the Journey of Reconciliation, which took place in 1947 when the Congress of Racial Equality (CORE) and the Fellowship of Reconciliation joined forces to test a Supreme Court decision that declared segregation on interstate buses to be unconstitutional. Activists limited their rides to the upper South, which posed a lesser threat than the Deep South. Their trip was cut short when they were arrested in Chapel Hill, North Carolina.

More than a decade later, following the unprecedented desegregation at lunch counters across the nation as a result of staged sit-ins, CORE organized the Freedom Rides. In 1960, the Supreme Court had forbidden segregation on interstate transport in *Boynton v. Virginia*. This ruling had expanded the 1947 decision by including bus terminals, waiting rooms, restaurants, restrooms, and other interstate travel facilities. The freedom riders planned to test the ruling in the Deep South. They hoped for an explosive reaction from white Southerners, which would help them gain significant support and success. Although no deaths occurred during the Freedom Rides, many victims sustained permanent injuries.

The first Freedom Ride took place on May 4, 1961. Seven blacks and six whites mounted two buses in Washington, D.C. Among the first freedom riders were James Farmer, a CORE leader; John Lewis, a member of the Student Nonviolent Coordinating Committee (SNCC); and James Peck, who had also participated in the 1947 ride. The objective was to arrive in New Orleans, Louisiana, on May 17, the anniversary of the *Brown v. Board of Education* ruling of 1954, which had declared separate but equal facilities in the schools to be unconstitutional.

The first major violence occurred in Rock Hill, South Carolina, where riders who attempted to use the restrooms and lunch counters were beaten and arrested. None of the white assailants was arrested. On May 14, one of the buses encountered 200 members of the Ku Klux Klan in Anniston, Alabama. The mob stoned the bus and slashed the tires. The bus escaped, only to be firebombed a few miles down the road. The mob then attacked the riders as they ran off the bus. Rev. Fred Shuttlesworth and several local blacks rescued the freedom riders and transported them to Birmingham, Alabama.

Police officers watch from a sidewalk as a Trailways bus carrying freedom riders arrives in Jackson, Mississippi, in the summer of 1961. The Freedom Rides, organized by the Congress of Racial Equality, ended when the Interstate Commerce Commission mandated an end to segregated facilities in interstate travel. (Library of Congress)

A white mob attacked the other bus when it arrived in Birmingham. The police were absent that day, as Public Safety Commissioner T. Eugene "Bull" Connor had auspiciously given the cops the day off for Mother's Day. Although the Federal Bureau of Investigation was aware of the threats against the freedom riders, they also withheld their protection. Overwhelmed by the violence suffered en route to Birmingham, James Farmer called a halt to the first Freedom Ride. Although they had failed to reach New Orleans by bus, the freedom riders did gain significant media exposure.

Determined to keep the Freedom Rides going, the SNCC sponsored a second trip on May 17, 1961. Before setting off from Nashville, Tennessee, for Birmingham, Alabama,

they requested protection from the Department of Justice, but to no avail. In Birmingham, the riders were arrested. Unable to procure a bus driver to resume the trip to New Orleans, Attorney General Robert Kennedy intervened and contacted the Greyhound Bus Company. In addition, John Seigenthaler, a Kennedy aide, accompanied the riders to help ensure safe travel. Nevertheless, more than 1,000 whites attacked the riders in Montgomery, Alabama. A white rider, James Zwerg, and Seigenthaler were seriously injured and sent to the hospital. The police ordered them all to discontinue the Freedom Ride. Finally, President John F. Kennedy sent several hundred federal marshals to aid the riders.

Martin Luther King, Jr. also responded to the situation. Leaving a speaking tour in Chicago, Illinois, he flew to

Montgomery, where he conducted a rally at Rev. Ralph Abernathy's church. As a white mob seethed outside, he spoke out against the violence imposed upon the riders and the lack of federal and state protection. The mob fought with the federal marshals. King called Attorney General Kennedy, who impelled Gov. John Patterson to send in the state police and the National Guard. The National Guard subdued the mob with tear gas, and the freedom riders and other supporters inside the church evaded a deadly attack.

Robert Kennedy repeatedly urged the freedom riders to bring the perilous rides to a stop. Even so, more than 300 riders attempted to finish the journey to New Orleans. Through the violence inflicted upon them, the freedom riders captured the interest of the world, thereby prodding the Kennedy administration to act. On December 1, 1961, the Interstate Commerce Commission banned racial segregation in interstate transport and facilities.

GLADYS L. KNIGHT

See also

Congress of Racial Equality (CORE); Connor, "Bull"; Greensboro Four; Jim Crow Laws; Parks, Rosa; Sit-Ins

Further Reading:

Barnes, Catherine. *A Journey from Jim Crow: The Desegregation of Southern Transit*. New York: Columbia University Press, 1983.
Halberstam, David. *The Children*. New York: Fawcett Books, 1998.
Peck, James. *Freedom Ride*. New York: Grove Press, 1962.

Freedom Summer (Mississippi) of 1964

From June to August 1964, the state of Mississippi witnessed an influx of volunteers, mostly white, affluent college students from around the nation, who were recruited by the Student Nonviolent Coordinating Committee (SNCC) to help African Americans register to vote, to establish freedom schools, and to support grassroots leadership. This movement became known as the Freedom Summer.

The efforts by the SNCC and the volunteers produced important gains for civil rights, and their efforts also produced a reaction of violence by racist whites, which was later depicted in the film *Mississippi Burning* (1988). Three young men disappeared within 24 hours of their arrival in

Philadelphia, Mississippi, on June 21, 1964. The men were James Earl Chaney, age 21, a native of Meridian and active in the Congress of Racial Equality (CORE) since 1963; Andrew Goodman, age 20, an anthropology student from New York; and Michael Schwerner, age 24, a married social worker from New York, who had previously been active in the civil rights movement in Mississippi and was thus particularly hated by the Ku Klux Klan (KKK). The bodies of the three men were not found for 44 days. The disappearance and murders of these three volunteers, which were later depicted in William Bradford Huie's *Three Lives for Mississippi* (1964), became a rallying point for Freedom Summer participants, whether locals or out-of-state people. All the civil rights workers lived in mortal danger. The Freedom Summer resulted in 6 deaths, 80 beatings, 1,000 arrests, 37 burnings of African American churches, and the burning or bombing of 31 homes.

The voter registration process for African Americans in Mississippi was the worst in the nation. To register, an African American was required to interpret two sections of the U.S. Constitution to the satisfaction of the registrar, a local white, and pay a poll tax. Intimidation also played a role in keeping people away from registering. Nightriders, usually members of the KKK, practiced drive-by shootings, arson of homes and churches, beatings, and lynchings. In Greenwood, the county seat of Le Flore, only 9 percent of the eligible black population was registered to vote, yet blacks comprised 64 percent of the total population. This issue, the denial of American citizens' right to vote, united different groups. The SNCC, created in April 1960, conducted sit-ins in an effort to end segregation of public facilities and helped people register to vote. Bob Parris Moses, a graduate of Hamilton College, who also studied philosophy at Harvard and received a teaching certificate, barely escaped injury in 1963 when 13 bullets were pumped into his car. Moses, who became the SNCC's field secretary in 1960, helped CORE organize the Freedom Rides, which brought civil rights workers to the South to challenge Jim Crow laws. He then became the project director for the SNCC's Freedom Summer in Mississippi. By 1964, he was co-director of the Council of Federation Organization (COFO), composed of various organizations committed to improving the lot of people of color in Mississippi. This organization directed logistics for Freedom Summer and distributed funds for voter registration.

COFO comprised the Southern Christian Leadership Conference, CORE, the National Association for the Advancement of Colored People, and the SNCC.

In the spring of 1964, the SNCC held a major campaign to register voters. They hoped to attract national attention, including the attention of and protection by the U.S. Department of Justice. Sixty-two of the 67 SNCC members were arrested and jailed, 45 of whom were sentenced to hard labor. Two years earlier Bob Moses had conceived of a way to gain national attention and to pressure the Department of Justice to intervene—get whites to participate—and his plan was implemented. In 1964, the SNCC recruited volunteers from universities across America, and many Northern, idealistic college students responded to the invitation. More than 50 percent of the students who signed on for training at the Western College for Women in Oxford, Ohio, were students at elite universities. COFO moved its staff headquarters to Jackson, Mississippi, and opened 44 sites in Mississippi in preparation for Freedom Summer. The SNCC's headquarters moved from Atlanta to Greenwood, Mississippi. COFO promoted grassroots support, refused to glorify its leaders, desired a loosely structured hierarchy, and, of course, had the major goal to end racial oppression. Not all COFO members favored the inclusion of Northern, white, rich students because they believed they would undermine the project, but Moses and Allard Lowenstein, a white law professor at the University of North Carolina and an activist, believed the students would bring national attention to the area. National attention was garnered when 700–1,000 volunteers entered Mississippi after they completed a screening process and trained at the Western College for Women. There were two training sessions in June; both instructed the volunteers on the goals of the project and provided intensive training on nonviolent self-defense.

Like all the volunteers, Chaney, Goodman, and Schwerner, were to be housed, fed, and protected by local participants in Mississippi. After arriving in Oxford, they drove into rural Neshoba County to investigate a church burning. When they did not return by 4:00 P.M. on June 21, which was the designated check-in time for all workers, the alarm was sounded. The COFO offices at Meridian and Jackson were notified, a search was activated, and jails were called. Since there were no Federal Bureau of Investigation (FBI) offices in Mississippi, the Atlanta office was notified of the disappearances, as were the *New York Times* and the families of the three volunteers. Sheriff Lawrence Rainey and Deputy Sheriff Cecil Price admitted to arresting the three for speeding, but they stated they had released them. Not until later was it discovered that the officers had turned them over to the KKK. On June 22, 1964, reporters came to the small community and were threatened by a mob. COFO requested assistance from President Lyndon B. Johnson. The burned-out car was found and the media circus began, which, in fact, did bring the plight of African Americans and those trying to help to national attention. Still, federal help to find the missing men was slow in coming. Attorney General Robert Kennedy ordered a full investigation, and FBI agents from New Orleans were dispatched to Mississippi. Agent Joseph Sullivan was appointed the major case inspector. President Johnson ordered U.S. sailors into Mississippi to assist with the search. White racists used the disappearance of Chaney, Goodman, and Schwerner as a threat to other workers. Communities such as Hollandale, Mississippi, passed ordinances forbidding any white volunteer to live with Negroes. Only local citizens could appeal the ordinance. The disappearance of the three young men did not stop the second wave of volunteers from entering the state as soon as they finished their training in Oxford, Ohio.

Eleven days after the murders of Chaney, Goodman, and Schwerner, President Johnson signed into law the Civil Rights Act of 1964, which prohibited segregation in public places, created the Equal Employment Opportunity Commission, and established the right of the federal government to withhold funds from segregated public schools and to deny federal contracts to any business that practiced segregation. The legislation increased the violence in the South. Bob Moses held firm that the Freedom Summer workers would not test the new law. He reiterated the goals of the project: grassroots leadership development, voter registration, freedom schools, community centers, food and clothing drives. It must be remembered that in addition to having the lowest African American voter registration in the country, Mississippi also had one of the highest percentages of poverty. The average number of years of school for an African American child was 4.3; the median annual family income was $595. Freedom schools were an effort to combat these statistics. Workers were not quite prepared for the response. In Hattiesburg alone, 600 people, ages 8 to 82, signed up for the freedom schools. During the summer, over 3,000 children participated. The schools' goals were reading, writing, arithmetic, instilling pride, and the need for activism necessary for the creation of present and future leaders. One of the most notable occurrences took place near the end of the summer when freedom school teacher Sandra Adickes of the Priest Creek Freedom School in Hattiesburg took six students, on their urging, to the public library. When they applied for library cards, the librarian called authorities, and the mayor sent the police chief to close the library. The teacher and her students then went to an S. H. Kress Co. lunchroom, where the children's orders were taken, but not the teacher's. They all left; Adickes was arrested a short time later for vagrancy. This case eventually made it all the way to the Supreme Court.

Sniper fire at voter registration rallies, beatings, burnings, and bombings continued during the long, hot summer. Arrests skyrocketed. For example, at a registration rally in Greenwood, 112 people were arrested, including activist Stokely Carmichael. Violence and the lack of punishment for the perpetrators became all too familiar. While the search for the missing civil rights workers continued, searchers found other bodies, or partial bodies, of African American males. In one instance, Klansmen were arrested; they confessed to the murders of two black men, yet state officials refused to prosecute. J. Edgar Hoover, director of the FBI, finally opened an FBI office in Mississippi, under pressure from President Johnson, who himself was under great pressure from the public to do something about the situation in the state. In July, Martin Luther King, Jr. visited Greenwood; the state refused a police escort even though threats had been made against his life. Tensions increased as allegations of communist backing for the Freedom Summer project were made, as were rumors that the disappearance of Chaney, Goodman, and Schwerner was a hoax to get national attention.

Neither was true. King's visit precipitated more violence. Two churches were burned; two African American activists, brothers, were trapped in a movie theater with a mob waiting for them outside, but the police did not act. The SNCC sent cars and volunteers to rescue them. Later in the summer, one of the brothers, Silas McGhee, was murdered.

On August 2, 1964, a search warrant was executed after FBI investigator Sullivan received information that the bodies of Chaney, Goodman, and Schwerner were buried in an earthen dam on the Olen Burrage farm, located only five miles from Philadelphia, Mississippi. The bodies, with bullet wounds and broken bones, were unearthed, which resulted in a mass meeting in Greenwood at which workers wanted to arm themselves for self-defense. Since the bodies were found in Neshoba County, the FBI had to share jurisdiction with the very men, Rainey and Price, who were under suspicion for involvement in the murders. The Imperial Wizard of the KKK, Sam Bowers, had ordered Schwerner's death; Chaney and Goodman had been in the wrong place at the wrong time with the wrong person. Although 19 members of the White Knights of the KKK were indicted three years later, they were not charged with murder but with conspiracy to injure, oppress, threaten, and intimidate. Not until 2005, over 40 years after the murders, was Edgar Ray Killen arrested and charged with three counts of murder. In June 2005, the jury convicted Killen of three counts of manslaughter.

In August 1964, Harry Belafonte and Sidney Poitier went to Greenwood; they were pursued by the Klan from the airport. Belafonte brought $60,000 in cash to help the project extend beyond summer. They spent the night barricaded inside the freedom house. Also in August, a three-day summit was held at Tougaloo College. The group decided to extend or replace 200 volunteers after summer's end. The summit precipitated a riot that resulted in 250 arrests and 52 beatings. Efforts were also being made to send the Mississippi Freedom Democratic Party (MFDP) to the 1964 Democratic National Convention in Atlantic City, New Jersey, with the goal of unseating the regular party, which was segregationist. Over 80,000 Mississippians voted in the MFDP elections. Led by Fannie Lou Hamer, the MFDP attended the convention. Although the MFDP did not unseat the regular party, they did have a partial victory, being allotted two at-large delegate seats and winning a promise that delegates who promoted discrimination would no longer be seated.

As the summer drew to a close, a new attitude surfaced. The SNCC veered from nonviolence to armed self-defense and a more militaristic approach. After the discovery of the bodies, the continuing intimidation by violence, the summit at Tougaloo College, and the Democratic National Convention, the split in the SNCC's direction became obvious. Bob Moses wanted to continue to focus on freedom schools and voter registration; James Forman leaned in the direction of promoting Black Power. Moses resigned as the leader of

COFO; he never resumed his leadership in Mississippi after the convention. By 1965, the SNCC decided to no longer include whites in their activities.

The Freedom Summer brought progress. Freedom schools, libraries, community centers, and food and clothing drives all continued to operate after the summer. The nation entered Mississippi via radio, television, and the newspaper; hence, as Bob Moses had hoped, pressure was put on the government to tend to the injustices and to stop the violence. The Civil Rights Act of 1965, which can be viewed as a direct result of the efforts of those involved in the Freedom Summer, outlawed literacy tests for voter registration and poll taxes, and stipulated that only authorized federal examiners could register voters; and the MFDP made inroads into the Democratic Party.

CLAUDIA M. STOLZ

See also
Civil Rights Movement; Ku Klux Klan; Student Nonviolent Coordinating Committee (SNCC); Voter ID Requirement

Further Reading:
Burner, Eric. *And Gently He Shall Lead Them.* New York: New York University Press, 1994.

Chaney, Ben. "Schwerner, Chaney, and Goodman: The Struggle for Justice." *Human Rights Magazine* 27, no. 2 (Spring 2000). See American Bar Association: Section of Individual Rights and Responsibility.

Randall, Herbert. *Faces of Freedom Summer.* Photographs by Herbert Randall. Text by Bob M. Tusa. Foreword by Victoria Jackson Gray Adams and Cecil Gray. Tuscaloosa: University of Alabama Press, 2001.

Steigerwald, David. *The Sixties and the End of Modern America.* New York: St. Martin's Press, 1995.

Fugitive Slave Act (1793)

The Fugitive Slave Act of 1793 was a piece of legislation signed by Congress and President George Washington in 1793 that monitored and relegated fugitive slaves. Southern states believed that this law was necessary because although the U.S. Constitution made it unlawful for a slave to escape to another state to be free, many slaves continued to flee to Northern states in search of a new life. Because abolitionists—both white and black—created a support network for fugitives, opponents felt that there was a need for clearer legislation regarding runaway slaves, especially the issue of returning slaves to their owners. One incident in particular indirectly led to the Fugitive Slave Law of 1793: the kidnapping of John Davis, a suspected runaway slave. Three white men kidnapped Davis from Pennsylvania and took him to Virginia, where they claimed he had been a slave. Pennsylvania authorities wanted Virginians to arrest the men and send them to Pennsylvania to face kidnapping charges. U.S. attorney general Edmund Randolph refused to arrest the three white men because he said that Virginia did not have sufficient legal jurisdiction.

This incident highlighted the constitutional problems regarding capturing and returning runaway slaves. Randolph claimed that both governors were at fault and that the governor of Philadelphia should have provided the governor of Virginia with a copy of the law that had been broken. Randolph submitted his report regarding the incident and policy to President Washington, who forwarded the report to the Congress. The result was the Fugitive Slave Act of 1793.

The Fugitive Slave Act of 1793 outlined the process for returning runaway slaves to their owners. After significant debate and revision, the Senate passed a bill on January 17, 1793, and a similar version was passed by the U.S. House of Representatives on January 30. The final bill was signed into law by President Washington on February 12, 1793. The final Fugitive Slave Act of 1793 includes four sections. Sections 1 and 2 of the law addressed the role of the states in returning criminals. This part of the law claimed that it was the governor's responsibility to act. Once the harboring state had received an indictment from the governor seeking the fugitive, it was the responsibility of the state to arrest the fugitive and notify the state from which the fugitive had committed the crime. These sections of the law also placed a fine of $500 and imprisonment up to one year on anyone who aided in rescuing a fugitive.

Sections 3 and 4 of the law addressed fugitive slaves. These sections did not put the responsibility of enforcing this law on any one person. Section 3 outlined a three-stage process for taking a runaway slave into custody: (1) the slave owner must first seize the runaway; (2) the runaway was to be brought before a federal judge, state judge, or magistrate; and (3) the claimant must offer proof that the suspected fugitive was a fugitive owned by the claimant. A certificate of removal would then be issued to the claimant. The last section, section 4, said that any person interfering could be sued by the owner for $500 and for any injuries caused.

The Fugitive Slave Law of 1793 was important for several reasons. This legislation allowed Congress to direct states on how they must deal with runaway slaves, a matter that eventually led to significant debate and court battles because many critics argued that Congress should not have been given such extreme power. The law was also important because it ignored the rights of any free black person. Free blacks could be kidnapped and sent into slavery although they had been citizens of their communities. Many free blacks in the North feared that they would be captured and taken into custody, regardless of whether they had actually escaped from slavery. This problem was highlighted by the fact that alleged slave owners were not required to provide tangible proof that a person was a runaway slave. The magistrate could accept an affidavit or oral proof that the person was a runaway. This lack of precise evidence allows for the possibility of tainted evidence to force free blacks into slavery. Runaway slaves now were forced to escape to Canada rather than be subjected to this treatment in the free states.

The Supreme Court upheld the constitutionality of the Fugitive Slave Act of 1793 in *Prigg v. Pennsylvania* (1842). In this case, Edward Prigg had assaulted a black woman, Margaret Morgan. He kidnapped her from Pennsylvania and took her to Maryland to serve as a slave. Pennsylvania had passed a law that did not allow the state to help in returning runaway slaves and made it a crime for anyone to try to capture a black person for the purpose of enslaving him or her. The Supreme Court ruled that Pennsylvania's law was unconstitutional but also argued that states did not have to enforce the Fugitive Slave Act of 1793. This remained a point of conflict between the Northern and Southern states until 1850, when the Fugitive Slave Law of 1793 was revised as part of the Compromise of 1850. This new law, the Fugitive Slave Act of 1850, called for federal assistance in the recapturing of fugitive slaves and mandated that federal marshals be used to capture and return slaves to their owners.

CLARISSA PETERSON

See also

Runaway Slave Advertisements; Slave Codes; Slave Families; Slave Revolts and White Attacks on Black Slaves; Slave Women and Sexual Violence; Slavery

Further Reading:
David, C. W. A. "The Fugitive Slave Law of 1793 and Its Antecedents." *Journal of Negro History* 9, no. 1 (1924): 18–25.
Finkelman, Paul. "The Kidnapping of John Davis and the Adoption of the Fugitive Slave Law of 1793." *Journal of Southern History* 56, no. 3 (1990): 397–422.
Riddell, William Renwick. "The Fugitive Slave in Upper Canada." *Journal of Negro History* 5, no. 3 (1920): 340–58.

Furtive Movement

Furtive movement is a notoriously vague law enforcement term encompassing suspicious, shifty, or stealthy behavior. Police officers are legally allowed to stop and search suspects they believe to be dangerous if suspects are displaying furtive movement and attempting to avoid notice or attention. In these cases, furtive movement is assumed to be indicative of guilt and symptomatic of the suspect trying to conceal evidence. However, research shows that minorities are disproportionately targeted for displaying furtive behavior, suggesting that the policy is highly discriminatory.

The Fourth Amendment protects citizens against unreasonable searches and seizures and requires search warrants to be judicially sanctioned and supported by probable cause. However, under *Terry v. Ohio* (1968), law enforcement officers are permitted to conduct limited warrantless searches if they have a level of suspicion of probable cause. This suspicion is permissible only under certain circumstances, such as if an officer witnesses unusual conduct leading him or her to believe the suspect has a weapon and is dangerous. In these cases, the officer can search and frisk the individual to determine if he or she is carrying a weapon. In August 2009, the Wisconsin Court of Appeals upheld that a suspect's furtive-type movement can be the basis for a protective search.

However, it has been noted that in such police searches, there is generally a high correlation between furtive behavior and skin color. Law enforcement training encourages officers to become aware of the preconscious feelings they may develop when thinking about whether suspects are acting suspiciously, but often these preconceived notions—especially around race—are responsible for officers identifying a suspect as suspicious. Because officers cannot testify in court that the reasonable suspicion they used to stop or search a suspect was intuition, they will often state that the person displayed furtive movement. The intuitions informing officers' decisions are subjective and often based on preconceived notions of suspects, such as race-based stereotypes. Frequently, these preconceived notions are not probable cause indicators that the officers themselves can even articulate. Furtive behavior can also be generated by the very presence of police officers themselves, as it is reasonable to assume that people may be fearful of the police and therefore exhibit strange behavior that could be interpreted as suspicious.

Several studies have shown that police officers are racially biased when it comes to what they deem suspicious behavior and who they choose to stop and search. Scholars often discuss furtive movement as a catch-all category used by police to stop whomever they please. Often, these stops include a disproportionate number of racial minorities. One example of furtive movement being used to discriminate against racial minorities is in the New York City housing project of Brownsville, Brooklyn, where data suggests that police use the excuse of furtive movement to determine who may come and go. At Brownsville, police spend an unreasonable amount of time stopping, questioning, asking for identification, and running warrant checks on people who are merely entering or near the building. According to a *New York Times* study in 2010, in the 52,000 stops conducted in the previous four years, furtive movement was listed as the reason for half of those stops. The arrest rate in these instances in Brownsville was less than 1 percent compared to the 6 percent arrest rate in the rest of the city. In addition, only 25 guns were recovered during these stops. The Brownsville example shows that furtive movement is by no means an indicator of criminal activity and that it is instead often used to harass and demean racial minorities.

Several reports emerging since 2010 have suggested that police target blacks and Latinos when making decisions about whether to stop individuals or frisk them for weapons. In one 2011 report from the New York Civil Liberties Union (NYCLU), blacks and Latinos composed the majority of police stops, even in areas where blacks and Latinos represented 14 percent or less of the population. According to this study, blacks and Latinos were stopped in over 70 percent of all cases and were more likely to be frisked than whites who

Racial Profiling

Controversy surrounding the issue of furtive movement is intertwined with the concept of racial profiling. Racial profiling can be defined as law enforcement's use of an individual's race, ethnicity, or national origin as a deciding factor in taking some kind of action or no action against that individual. Recent Arizona (2010) and Alabama (2011) legislation requires law enforcement officers to verify the citizenship status of anyone who they deem suspicious of being an illegal immigrant. Critics of these laws argue that this is a form of racial profiling where individuals are targeted as suspicious because of their race. The impact of these controversial laws in both Arizona and Alabama has resulted in significant drops in school attendance, medical treatment, and reports of domestic abuse among those who fear deportation.

were stopped. The NYCLU report also suggested that youth of color are exceedingly overrepresented in these types of stop and search procedures. This is especially troubling considering that New York Police Department (NYPD) reports confirm that 90 percent of the young black men and Latinos they stopped were innocent. No research has ever proven the effectiveness of the stop-and-frisk regime, and reports such as this one from the NYCLU show that blacks and Latinos are unfairly targeted by police. This has led many to call for reform of police stop-and-frisk practices and the furtive movement policies upholding them.

ADRIENNE N. MILNER

See also

Arizona Senate Bill 1070 (SB 1070) (2010)

Further Reading:

New York Civil Liberties Union. *Stop and Frisk Facts.* http://www.nyclu.org/node/1598.

Pinizzotto, Anthony J., Davis, Edward F., and Charles E. Miller. "Intuitive Policing." *FBI Law Enforcement Bulletin* 73 (2004): 1–11.

State Bar of Wisconsin. *Suspect's 'Persistence' in Furtive-Type Movement Can Be Part for Search, Court of Appeals Says.* http://www.wisbar.org/AM/Template.cfm?Section=News&Template=/CM/ContentDisplay.cfm&ContentId=847362012.

G

Galton, Francis (1822–1911)

Born into a successful English family that included men of industry, finance, science, and medicine, Sir Francis Galton was well known in his day as a public spokesman for the sciences and a pioneer in applied statistics. His talents, privilege, and hard work made him very popular in scientific societies, and he made a number of remarkable contributions to numerous fields including geography, meteorology, statistics, psychology, and anthropology. This made his advocacy for eugenics, the cause that consumed all his energy late in life, all the more authoritative and influential.

As a young man Galton spent a considerable amount of time traveling through Egypt and Sudan before embarking on an expedition into far southwest Africa, an area almost completely unknown to Europeans at the time. While on his expedition Galton encountered "savage races," by which he meant African tribal peoples, and the experience was profoundly important for how he would come to write about race. He believed Africans to be far inferior to Europeans and documented this in his ethnographic notes, although his major African publications focused on geography and natural history.

As a statistician Galton made many important contributions to psychology, particularly in differential psychology or the measuring of differences between individuals. He was the first to use correlation and regression in quantitative methods, techniques he would also apply to the study of kinship. In his groundbreaking twin studies, Galton laid the foundations for what was to become behavioral genetics. He sought to measure general intelligence by devising the first tests of mental ability to be administered at a specialized testing center, another of his innovations. With his statistical work Galton was the first to apply normal distribution patterns to human intelligence. All of this exemplifies his research agenda, which was to identify and measure human variation.

Galton was profoundly influenced by his cousin, Charles Darwin, and his *On the Origin of the Species* (1859). Upon returning to England after sailing around the world on the HMS *Beagle*, Darwin went to study animal husbandry where he learned that farmers selectively bred their animals so as to conserve desirable traits like fecundity and eliminate undesirable ones such as aggression. In his theory of evolution by natural selection Darwin was essentially arguing for a similar process in which nature, rather than human agents, was the selective force. Galton was especially keen to extend this research to human populations, and the two enjoyed a lively correspondence. Darwin, out of concern that he would antagonize the religious community, intentionally avoided detailed discussion of evolution and humanity, saving this topic for his later work, *The Descent of Man and Selection in Relation to Sex* (1871). Though Galton was also shy around controversy, he felt passionately that racial degeneration threatened everything that was great about England and his nation's place in the world. This passion motivated him to push back on the topic of human evolution in a way that Darwin refused.

What vexed biologists of the 19th century most was the absence of any understanding of the mechanism of heredity. Genetics as we know it today was completely nonexistent, and Gregor Mendel, who inferred the existence of genes at about the same time, still labored in obscurity. Although hampered by an inaccurate theory of heredity, Galton wanted to learn if the inheritance of physical characteristics extended to personality, intelligence, and talent. To test this possibility, Galton conducted several studies on upper-class Brits such as himself. In one of his best known eugenic studies, Galton demonstrated that successful men were more likely to have other successful people in their family. He was able to document that this was the case by using a methodology wholly new to the social sciences, the questionnaire. Galton concluded that the clustering of successful men in select families such as his own proved that talent and ability must be heritable. Their privileged standing in society was therefore due to superior genetic make-up.

The social situation Galton and his contemporaries witnessed in late-19th-century England concerned them greatly. As England industrialized and the cities boomed, so too did the lower classes grow as peasants dispossessed of their land streamed into the urban ghettos. How could it be that the manifestly inferior poor were reproducing a greater rate than the upper class? Combined with the threat of inferior races outside of Europe, this was indeed alarming. In order to preserve and protect English society, which Galton referred to as "civilization," it would be necessary to carry out an "improvement of the race." *Eugenics* was the term he gave to this task. For Galton an ideal society would be one in which individuals were allowed to succeed according to their own abilities with the most talented and successful being helped on their way up with monetary incentives to encourage the most beneficial marriage pairings. The weak and unfit of society were to be humanely cared for, but kept celibate. Through selective parenthood Galton hoped to improve the very biological make-up of the human species itself. Galton spent many years campaigning for the cause of eugenics, and his efforts paid off as its popularity continued to rise well after his death.

Matthew D. Thompson

See also
American Eugenics Movement

Further Reading:

Galton, Sir Francis. "The Possible Improvement of the Human Breed under the Existing Conditions of Law and Sentiment." *Nature* 64 (1901): 659–65.

Galton, Sir Francis. *Hereditary Genius: An Inquiry into Its Laws and Consequences.* London: Macmillan, 1925 [1869].

Gillham, Nicholas Wright. *A Life of Sir Francis Galton: From African Exploration to the Birth of Eugenics.* Oxford: Oxford University Press, 2001.

Garment Workers

Garment workers are involved in the production of clothing. Most workers are trained on the job and require no special training prior to employment. However, the work is extremely labor intensive. Garment manufacturing serves as a common source of employment for immigrants in the United States. Today, garment workers find themselves at the intersection of globalization, mechanization of garment manufacturing (especially in the United States), and the utilization of sweatshops as a cost-cutting measure in uncertain economic times.

Garment manufacturing is a fairly simple, mechanized industry. There are only a handful of unique jobs in garment manufacturing, and nearly all are now machine oriented. Each machine has operators who run the equipment, setters who adjust the machine settings for the operators, and tenders who supply the raw resources needed. Production follows an orderly pattern. First, textile machinists create the fabric used in the garment. Textiles are manufactured using machine looms and weavers run by workers in mill settings. Synthetics (like rayon) are spun from liquids pressed out of machines as filaments. Next, the textiles are cut into specified shapes using the patterns provided by designers. Cutters typically utilize machinery rather than scissors. Third, sewing machine operators assemble the patterns into the final

Former Seo employees Faviola Munoz Aguirre, 20, left, and her sister Maria Aguirre, 23, jot down addresses of midtown Manhattan garment factories, June 12, 1996, before searching for work in New York's garment district. The sisters lost their jobs when the Seo factory where they were employed closed after it was found to be producing garments for Kathie Lee Gifford's clothing line while violating state and federal labor laws. (AP Photo/Kathy Willens)

product. This can be done at a factory or done by individuals in their homes. Finally, a contingent of testers, sorters, and inspectors prepare the clothing for distribution along a factory line.

The U.S. garment industry is amid a period of dramatic economic change. Currently, U.S. garment manufacturing is severely threatened by production abroad. Overseas manufacturing (including mills in Hong Kong, Thailand, and Vietnam) now produces much of the world's textiles and clothes at lower costs due to reduced labor costs. U.S. companies face wage requirements, unionization, and employee costs such as insurance that overseas companies simply do not have. Another major issue has been China's entry into the

World Trade Organization and the subsequent removal of WTO quotas in 2005 on apparel exports, especially those from China. Low-cost imports quickly overcame the much higher production costs of U.S. sites.

U.S. companies still enjoy the benefits of laws requiring armed services and Transportation Security Administration clothing to be made domestically. U.S. companies also have lowered costs of operations by being close to distributors and buyers and are subject to fewer export restrictions, meaning less capital must be budgeted for distribution to retail and wholesale markets in this country. Despite this, the U.S. garment industry is in a state of restructuring. The labor process has been simplified through machinery, allowing

Ethnic Niches

Ethnic niches occur when an ethnic group is *overrepresented* in a particular job compared to other workers employed in the same job. Common examples of ethnic niches include Vietnamese nail salons, Latino construction workers, Latino *jardineros* (lawn workers), Latino maids and housekeepers, and Asian Indian engineers. Garment manufacturing is also an ethnic niche. Chinese workers and entrepreneurs are frequently found in the garment manufacturing niche in San Francisco and New York City. This niche acts as an important source of work for undocumented workers and often includes sweatshop operations. However, the worker-employer relationship found in the Chinese ethnic niche does not necessarily match the classical view of sweatshops. For example, owners often work alongside workers, and co-workers may often include family members. Workers may also receive more flexibility in bringing their young children to work, receive entrepreneurial training in the niche, or, in the case of family members, benefit from the profits of the business.

extraneous workers to be laid off. Advanced equipment also improves productivity per worker. However, mechanization usually requires additional training, thus adding to expenses in the short run. Machines require fewer workers but create higher investments and overhead that must be addressed in the cost of the items produced. Other companies have elected to close U.S. operations and move to international sites. This allows U.S. manufacturers the benefits of U.S. ties while employing (and enjoying) the benefits of low-wage laborers abroad. In other cases, competitors have merged into larger companies, creating mass layoffs between 2005 and 2008 and increased overhead via the merger. This has essentially ended most U.S. manufacturers' capacity for making small-quantity production runs, focusing on large-quantity runs for profits.

Over the next 10 years, the Bureau of Labor Statistics predicts that U.S. garment industry jobs will be cut in half across the board. The number of employees is expected to decline by 55 percent. Unskilled positions such as sewers will be hit the hardest, and these are positions frequently held by immigrant laborers. U.S. companies are now closing inefficient old mills and opening large, highly mechanized sites requiring only skilled machinists capable of using the modern equipment. These changes seemingly doom the pools of laborers (including immigrant workers) currently employed in the garment manufacturing industry.

Today, sweatshops represent a prominent productive force in the garment industry that has helped revolutionize production levels without much thought about human rights. Sweatshops are an exploitative labor process in which garment manufacturers employ workers at illegally low wages, often paying based on piece-work, and often under appalling conditions. Sweatshop labor marks by far the most significant approach to cutting domestic labor costs, but does so at the expense of garment workers. Sweatshops create profits through low labor costs, minimizing investment in machinery, and remaining flexible in terms of what they can produce. While most U.S. companies focus on completing large production runs, sweatshops are designed for flexibility in smaller production runs. Instead of using machines that produce a single product, sweatshops utilize human labor and multiuse machinery to create products as demand dictates. Companies selling garments benefit directly from the cost-cutting nature of sweatshops, while garment workers experience reduced access to unionization and compensation for job-related injuries. Sweatshops do provide certain benefits to workers, such as plentiful unskilled labor employment opportunities (including work for unauthorized workers), flexible work arrangements, child care options, and family employment, but accompany this with extremely low wages, long hours, and often unethical working conditions.

JAMES MAPLES

See also
Migrant Workers

Further Reading:
Bender, Daniel E., and Richard A. Greenwald. *Sweatshop USA: The American Sweatshop in Historical and Global Perspective.* New York: Routledge, 2003.
Bonacich, Edna, and Richard P. Appelbaum. *Behind the Label: Inequality in the Los Angeles Apparel Industry.* Berkeley and Los Angeles: University of California Press, 2000.
Esbenshade, Jill. *Monitoring Sweatshops: Workers, Consumers and the Global Apparel Industry.* Philadelphia, PA: Temple University Press, 2004.

Garvey, Marcus (1887–1940)

Marcus Garvey was a publisher, journalist, businessman, and one of the most famous proponents of Black Nationalism. Garvey was also founder of the Universal Negro Improvement Association (UNIA) and a champion of the back-to-Africa movement, which encouraged African Americans and other people of African ancestry to return to their ancestral homelands.

Marcus Garvey was born in St. Ann's Bay, Jamaica, on August 17, 1887. During his formative years he was not aware of racism. In adolescence, however, he experienced his first act of racism when called *nigger*. It was then that he realized he had been surrounded by racism all his life. That early experience stimulated the desire to process the effect of racism and inequality by whites on blacks. From 1910 to 1912, this process led to writing, publishing, entering politics, and traveling throughout Central America and other continents to see if blacks there experienced the same injustices as blacks in Jamaica. Garvey concluded that with the exception of England, blacks experienced racism and inequality in other countries. Therefore, he elected to attend Birbeck College in England and was inspired to ignite the Pan-Africa movement to unify black people.

Garvey's experiences in England convinced him it was time to do something about the condition of poor blacks. In 1914, he established the UNIA. The objectives of the UNIA were: improving black life in Jamaica and in the world, promoting the spirit of race pride and love, reclaiming the fallen

---

Marcus Garvey Calls for a Bill of Rights for African American Men, 1920

Marcus Garvey and his Universal Negro Improvement Association directly challenged the legal aspects of Jim Crow in their revision of the Bill of Rights. The *Baltimore Afro-American* claimed that Garvey and the movement should adopt a bill of rights "calling on whites to leave America":

Whereas all men are created equal and are entitled to the rights of life, liberty, and the pursuits of happiness, and because of this, we, the duly elected representatives of the Negro people of the world, invoking the aid of the just and almighty God, do declare all men, women, and children of our blood throughout the world free denizens, and do claim them as free citizens of Africa, the motherland of all Negroes.

We declare that no Negro shall engage himself in battle for an alien race without first obtaining the consent of the leader of the Negro peoples of the world, except in a matter of national defense.

We believe in the freedom of Africa for the Negro peoples of the world, and by the principle of Europe for the Europeans, and Asia for the Asiatics, we also demand Africa for the Africans at home and abroad. We believe in the inherent right of the Negro to possess himself of Africa, and that his possession of same shall not be regarded as infringement on any claim or purchase made by any race or nation.

We assert that the Negro is entitled to even-handed justice before all courts of law and equity, in whatever country he may be found, and when this is denied him on account of his race or color, such denial is an insult to the race as a whole, and should be resented by the entire body of Negroes.

We deprecate the use of the term "nigger" as applied to Negroes, and demand that the word Negro be written with a capital "N."

We demand a free and unfettered commercial intercourse with all the Negro peoples of the world. We demand that the governments of the world recognize our leader and his representatives chosen by the race to look after the welfare of our people under such governments. We call upon the various governments of the world to accept and acknowledge Negro representatives who shall be sent to the said governments to represent the general welfare of the Negro peoples of the world.

We demand that our duly accredited representatives be given proper recognition in all leagues, conferences, conventions, or courts of international arbitration wherever human rights are discussed. We proclaim the 31st day of August of each year to be an international holiday observed by all Negroes.

Source: "Adopt Bill of Rights Calling on Whites to Leave America," *Baltimore Afro-American*, August 19, 1920.

race, and promoting the spirit of conscientious Christian worship among the native tribes of Africa. Another goal of the UNIA was to establish universities, colleges, and secondary schools for further education of children and conducting a worldwide commercial and industrial relationship.

Garvey's next project was the Black Star Shipping Company, developed in 1919 to further the back-to-Africa concept. The concept was to create a strong central African power base structure that would protect blacks around the world from imperialism. Garvey believed the Black Star Shipping Company would not only improve blacks as a commercial and industrious people, it would also re-create the drive needed to overcome poverty. The company was to bring business industry to black communities along with conducting international trade between America and Africa. The ships were to be manned by all-black crews. The success of the Black Star Shipping Company transformed Marcus Garvey into a hero to black communities, a threat to white communities, and—finally—a national politician. With the Black Star Shipping Company, blacks were inspired to move from economic dependence to independence.

The impetus for Garvey's ideals was the three stages he believed had affected the blacks' contact with the white man. The stages were: 1) being shackled in Africa and kept in bondage for 250 years; 2) emancipation, enjoyment of which for the previous 50 years was equated to partial freedom and limited ability to earn a wage; and, finally, 3) after the first two stages, to try 50 years of African American self-direction. The third stage was the rationale for the Black Star Shipping Company, the call for manhood within the race and for economic, industrial, and political involvement. A major concern of Garvey's was blacks' inability to follow orders within the organization, and a lack of discipline or a check-and-balance system, which in the end limited progress. Marcus Garvey died in London, England, in 1940.

DENISE D. McADORY

See also

Black Nationalism; Universal Negro Improvement Association (UNIA)

Further Reading:

Cronon, David. *Black Moses: The Story of Marcus Garvey*. Madison: University of Wisconsin Press, 1955.
Dumenil, Lynn. *The Modern Temper*. New York: Hill & Wang, 1995.
Jacques-Garvey, Amy, ed. *The Philosophy & Opinions of Marcus Garvey: Or Africa for the Africans*. New York: Universal Publishing House, 1923.
Stein, Judith. *The World of Marcus Garvey: Race & Class in Modern Society*. Baton Rouge: Louisiana State University Press, 1986.
Universal Negro Improvement Association and African Communities League, http://www.unia-acl.org.

Gatekeeping

Gatekeeeping refers to the ability of real estate brokers and agents to determine which potential homebuyers are able to live where. Real estate agencies and organizations constantly make decisions about what information to share with homebuyers, which ultimately allows these real estate associates to determine the geographic areas where potential homebuyers can reside. Gatekeeping can often result in racial steering, where real estate brokers guide prospective homebuyers towards or away from neighborhoods based on their race. Real estate agents are described as gatekeepers because their expertise and responsibilities make them involved in all aspects of home buying. More significantly, realtors often see their role as being responsible for developing and shaping the social structure of a neighborhood, leading them to feel justified in screening potential residents. Gatekeeping often revolves around race, as realtors have been known to guide customers towards homes in certain neighborhoods and away from others on the basis of race. The practice of gatekeeping has often been cited as a contributing factor to the perpetuation of racial segregation in the United States.

One way gatekeeping is accomplished is through racial restrictive covenants. Developing in the 19th century, racial restrictive covenants were written agreements between buyers and sellers of property to avoid selling, renting, or leasing to minority groups. These minority groups were usually blacks but could also refer to other nonwhites. Up until 1948, racial restrictive covenants were considered private contracts legally enforceable in court. Local and national real estate boards, in addition to neighborhood and homeowners associations, developed racial restrictive covenants. Real estate boards strictly enforced these covenants and advocated for homeowners associations to use them as well.

Restrictive Racial Covenants

The typical wording of a restrictive housing covenant appeared as follows:

> In consideration of the premises and the sum of five dollars ($5.00) each to the other in hand paid, the parties hereto do hereby mutually covenant, promise, and agree each to the other, and for their respective heirs and assigns, that no part of the land now owned by the parties hereto, a more detailed description of said property, being given after the respective signatures hereto, shall ever be used or occupied by, or sold, conveyed, leased, rented, or given to, Negroes, or any person or persons of the Negro race or blood. This covenant shall run with the land and bind the respective heirs and assigns of the parties hereto for the period of twenty-one (21) years from and after the date of these presents.

Such covenants assisted in the rise of racially segregated neighborhoods and the continued practice of racial steering. Even though racial restrictive covenants are no longer legally permissible, gatekeeping practices that exclude racial minorities still continue to this day.

Gatekeepers in the form of real estate agents and organizations possess expertise in all areas of home buying; therefore, they are able to influence both formally and informally the shaping of the social structure of a community. Although they are no longer in formal practice among realtors, restrictive covenants in the form of personal and selective value systems are still known to be used by gatekeepers to structure neighborhoods. These value systems often include preconceived racial stereotypes, and gatekeeping is frequently used to exclude black homebuyers from entering predominantly white neighborhoods.

Real estate agencies and organizations continue to practice gatekeeping in the form of racial steering, as statistics reveal that prospective black homebuyers are seldom shown available homes in suburban and exclusive neighborhoods. This form of discrimination is technically illegal under federal legislation, but it persists often covertly, making it difficult for prospective black homebuyers and other minorities to purchase homes in certain neighborhoods. Research indicates that when black couples are shown homes, they are likely to be an average of $3,300 less expensive than the homes shown to their white counterparts. This is mainly due to the location of the houses shown to blacks in areas with overall lower housing values. Gatekeeping is difficult to prove and to prosecute legally, unlike other forms of discrimination such as employment discrimination and discrimination in educational settings. There are many agencies and organizations that deal with real estate, from realtors to homeowners associations to mortgage agencies, and many have institutionalized practices that perpetuate racial steering and racial segregation. Although the discriminatory practices associated with gatekeeping are difficult to prove, they nevertheless continue to be a powerful determining factor in the racial geographic distribution of the United States.

SONJA V. HARRY

Further Reading:

Jones-Correa, Michael. "The Origins and Diffusion of Racial Restrictive Covenants." *Political Science Quarterly* 115, no. 4 (2000): 541.

Pager, Devah, and Hana Shepherd. "The Sociology of Discrimination: Racial Discrimination in Employment, Housing, Credit, and Consumer Markets." *Annual Review of Sociology* 34 (2008): 181–209. DOI: 10.1146/annurev.soc.33.040406.131740.

Pearce, Diana M. "Gatekeepers and Homeseekers: Institutional Patterns in Racial Steering." *Social Problems* 26, no. 3 (1979): 325–42. http://www.jstor.org/stable/800457.

Gates/Crowley Incident, The

On July 16, 2009, Professor Henry Louis Gates Jr., an African American faculty member at Harvard University, was arrested outside of his Cambridge, Massachusetts, home for disorderly conduct. Shortly before this, a 911 caller reported that two African American men were breaking into his residence; the alleged "burglars" turned out to be Gates and his driver. Police Sergeant James Crowley, a white officer, initially responded to the call and was the one who eventually became embroiled in a national controversy over the state of race relations and police-citizen encounters in the United States.

Cambridge police Sergeant James Crowley, left, stands with Sergeant Leon Lashley, right, as police from various unions hold a news conference in Cambridge, Massachusetts, on July 24, 2009, to express support for Crowley in connection to the incident in which he arrested Harvard professor Louis Gates at his home. (Associated Press)

Postracial America

Following the election of Barack Obama, an election in which he easily beat out opponent John McCain, many citizens of the United States believed that we had moved beyond skin color, into a state of postraciality. Although voting patterns revealed a significant racial divide, they also provided evidence of a measure of equality, with white votes around the nation helping to elect the first African American president. Theoretically, a postracial America would mean the elimination of racial bias, discrimination, and stereotypes based on skin color. However, the Gates incident cast doubt on whether American has truly moved beyond race as a factor in decision making, and brought race, once again, to the forefront of discussions of social justice within political spheres.

Independent statements on what ensued between Gates and Officer Crowley differ, but Gates had been attempting to open the door to his home after returning from China, where he was working on a PBS documentary series. According to the account given by Gates, the front door was jammed, so after he and his driver placed his luggage on the front porch, he went around the back of the house to let himself in. After entering through the kitchen and attempting to open the front door from inside, the door remained jammed, so the driver used his shoulder to force the door open. Gates was in the process of placing a call to the maintenance service at Harvard University, the owner of the home in which Gates resided, when police appeared at his door. Gates reported that the police officer asked him to step out onto the porch, a request that he initially refused.

Officer Crowley asked Gates for his identification. Gates complied and gave the officer his university identification card and his state-issued identification, which listed the address of the home. As the interaction unfolded, Gates reported repeatedly asking the officer, "What is your name, and what is your badge number?" According to Gates, he followed the officer onto the porch to get his information, in the midst of a sea of officers that had arrived on the scene. Once stepping onto the porch, he was arrested.

Officer Crowley, in the official incident report filed with the Cambridge Police Department, indicated that Gates was exhibiting "loud and tumultuous behavior" during their interaction. Responding to the call about two black males with backpacks attempting to enter a residence, Officer Crowley spoke with the 911 caller and then proceeded to the porch of the home occupied by Gates. Crowley asked Gates to step onto the porch, at which time Gates allegedly asked him if it was because he was black. The officer also reported that Gates called him racist and was generally uncooperative. After verifying his identification, Crowley began to descend the stairs, while Gates continued yelling at him and threatening that he "had not heard the last of him." With a small crowd assembling, and members of the Cambridge and Harvard University Police Forces present, Gates finally exited his residence. Sergeant Crowley reported that he warned Gates that he was becoming disorderly. After two ignored warnings, Crowley handcuffed Gates and placed him under arrest.

Less than a week after the incident, after the charges against Gates had been officially withdrawn and he was released from police custody, President Barack Obama spoke about the incident. During a press conference, the president declared publicly that the officer involved had "acted stupidly" in arresting someone who had already shown identification that proved that he was a lawful resident of the home where they were investigating a possible break in. He also insinuated that Gates's anger was understandable given the circumstances. The remaining presidential comments regarding the incident focused on the larger issue of race relations, highlighting the incredible progress that has been made, but pointing to the need to continue working with police forces to improve policing practices. Days later, President Obama expressed regret over his choice of words and indicated a desire to make the incident a teachable moment.

DANIELLE LAVIN-LOUCKS

The Gates/Crowley Beer Summit

The "Beer Summit," as it has been named in popular media, the culmination of the media storm that brought race relations into the political spotlight, was President Obama's attempt at uniting Gates and Crowley, and opening up a national conversation about race. In an effort to have the two parties discuss the event at a neutral location, President Obama invited Gates and Crowley to the White House Garden to enjoy a beer. In attendance at the July 30 meeting were President Obama, Vice President Joe Biden, Henry Louis Gates Jr., and Sergeant James Crowley. While the Beer Summit lasted only 40 minutes, Gates and Crowley agreed that their perceptions of the incident would likely never coincide. However, the meeting was amicable. Details on the specific points of discussion remain largely hidden from the media, but Gates has publicly deemed Crowley a "nice guy, when he's not arresting you," and Crowley has made positive comments about Gates's character. As a gesture of reconciliation, Crowley presented Gates with the handcuffs he used during the arrest at the meeting. At the conclusion of the meeting, both Gates and Crowley contend they would meet up again without President Obama as the moderator, but no official reports of such a meeting exist.

See also

Disproportionality Index Scores; Racial Profiling

Further Reading:

CQ Transcription. "Transcript of Obama Prime-Time News Conference." *Washington Post.* http://voices.washingtonpost.com/44/2009/07/22/transcript_of_obama_prime-time.html.

Crowley, James. "Incident Report #9005127." *Cambridge Police Department.* http://i.cdn.turner.com/cnn/2009/images/07/23/0498.001.pdf.

Ogletree, Charles J. *The Presumption of Guilt: The Arrest of Henry Louis Gates, Jr. and Race, Class, and Crime in America.* New York: Palgrave Macmillan, 2010.

Olopade, Dayo. "Skip Gates Speaks." *The Root.* http://www.theroot.com/views/skip-gates-speaks.

Reed, Wornie L. "Social Justice in the Age of Obama." *Research in Race and Ethnic Relations* 16, no. 16 (2010): 193–213.

Wilkes, Jr., Donald E. "The Professor with the Limp and the Cane and the Cop with the Gun and the Badge." *Flagpole Magazine.* http://www.law.uga.edu/dwilkes_more/69gatesgate.pdf.

Genocide

Genocide may be defined two ways. It can be a crime as defined under international law, or it can serve as a politicized label to affix to certain historical events in which a population or group, whether they are identified in terms of race, nation, or religion, is subjected to a highly organized form of violence that systematically seeks to destroy the group itself. This contrasts sharply to other acts of war, which are typically fought over the control of natural resources or to wrest some political concession, and as such genocide is a highly symbolic form of violence. Genocide may be carried out through the large-scale murder of group members, inducing famine or otherwise destroying the conditions necessary to life, preventing births within the group, and forcibly transferring children out of the group to nongroup members.

In sum genocide refers to coordinated efforts to destroy an entire human population by erasing its very existence. This usually requires considerable bureaucratic organization and is usually codified in various governmental policies. The systematic implementation of very specific kinds of attacks is what makes genocide unique. Targets might include political or social institutions, outlawing language and cultural practices, undermining economic and subsistence activities, and bringing about the widespread ruin of the group's health and well-being. In addition to the killing of a group of people, genocide often coincides with the deliberate destruction of culturally significant objects, landmarks, sacred sites, or neighborhoods.

The various perpetrators of historical genocides show very different motivations for carrying out their plans. For example, the Nazis undertook to exterminate the Jews in the Holocaust in 1933–1945 because they perceived the Jews as the central problem of world history. From the Nazi point of view the future of humanity itself depended on carrying out this objective, which they termed the Final Solution. By contrast the Armenian people became the victims of genocide at the hands of the Ottoman Empire in a fit of nationalist fervor between the years 1915–1923. The Ottomans undertook to exterminate the Armenians within Turkey, but they were not concerned about the lives of Armenians outside their borders. In Indonesia from 1965–1966 a mass extermination of Communist Party members was carried out by the ruling political party in order to consolidate power. The Indonesian Communist Party was destroyed as a result. The Rwandan genocide of 1994 was more like an elaborate revenge scheme and arose from long-standing animosity between the minority Tutsi who ruled over the majority Hutu people, exasperated by decades of Belgian colonialism.

Genocide is a crime under international law and sometimes results in accused parties being prosecuted in national or international courts. This legal definition was formulated in part through one of the best known of these trails, the Nuremberg Trials of 1945–1946, during which members of the German Nazi leadership were prosecuted for war crimes and crimes against humanity. The United States signed the Convention on the Prevention and Punishment of the Crime of Genocide in 1948; however, it is immune from prosecution before the International Court of Justice.

Genocide may be covered up or denied. In Turkey, for example, it is illegal to speak of the Armenian genocide as such or to imply that the Turkish government is culpable for it. There still exist people who believe that the Holocaust is an elaborate hoax perpetrated by Jews to illicit sympathy for Israel. Few people in the United States today perceive the colonization of North America as a genocide of native peoples even though from the point of first contact until the close of the Western Indian Wars at the end of the 19th century, the native population of the continent declined about 90–95 percent. The primary difference between early American policy towards natives and the genocides of the 20th century is industrialization. Innovations in science and technology as well as the growth of complex state bureaucracies and industrial economies expedited the rapid mass murder of populations. This is why genocide is principally associated with the modern world. Industrialization and the nation-state allowed for death and destruction to be carried out on a greater scale and with greater efficiency than was previously possible.

Related to genocide is so-called ethnic cleansing, which can include mass deportation, mass arrest, or the forced displacement and confinement of a people. The Roma people, also known as the Gypsies, are often subject to this in France, for example.

Matthew D. Thompson

See also
American Eugenics Movement; Cultural Genocide

Further Reading:

Balakian, Peter. *The Burning Tigris: The Armenian Genocide and America's Response*. New York: Harper Perennial, 2004.

Gourevitch, Philip. *We Wish to Inform You That Tomorrow We Will Be Killed with Our Families: Stories from Rwanda*. New York: Picador, 1999.

Hoxie, Frederick E. *A Final Promise: The Campaign to Assimilate the Indians, 1880–1920*. Lincoln: University of Nebraska Press, 2001.

Totten, Samuel, and William S. Parsons, eds. *Century of Genocide: Critical Essays and Eyewitness Accounts*. New York: Routledge, 2008.

Genotype versus Phenotype

A genotype is the internally coded, inheritable genetic information that is stored by all living organisms. A phenotype is any outward, observable structure, function, or behavior of an organism. Phenotype—how a person appears, acts, or functions—is the consequence of both a person's genotype and his or her environment. People with the same genotypes may have the same phenotype, or they may have different phenotypes. For instance, siblings may have different eye and hair color. Likewise, people with different genotypes may have the same phenotype. Thus, inferring genetic characteristics or qualities (i.e., what genes a person has inherited from his or her parents) from phenotype can be very difficult. This is strikingly true in the classification of race, because race has no genetic component and is based solely on the subjective classification of phenotypical features, that is, the outward appearance of skin color, hair texture, eye color, and so on.

TRACY CHU

See also

Biological Determinism; Biological Racism

G.I. Bill of Rights (1944)

The Serviceman's Readjustment Act of 1944, labeled the G.I. Bill, was passed by Congress after an intensive lobbying campaign by the American Legion. The legislation, signed by President Franklin D. Roosevelt, was a comprehensive set of benefits for soldiers returning from service in World War II. The G.I. Bill provided funding for higher education, business and farm loans, money for unemployment, and home loans. The law served the dual purposes of rewarding the sacrifices of a generation of soldiers and providing a significant amount of stimulus to the economy. These public investments paid dividends throughout the postwar boom in terms of economic growth, technological innovation, and increased levels of civic participation.

The impact of the legislation on the United States was dramatic, especially in the area of access to higher education. Although many prominent university presidents (both privately and publicly) expressed reservations about the admission of so many new students whom they would not have previously thought qualified, the students who entered colleges and universities across America on the G.I. Bill graduated faster and with higher grades than many traditional-aged students. In addition to the sociocultural change in the economic makeup of college and university students, this aspect of the G.I. Bill was important in the sheer number of students who entered higher education. In 1946, half of all new college students were veterans, with a total number of over 1 million students. Over 10 million veterans had used the G.I. Bill's education payments by the mid-1950s. Many flagship and land grant state universities saw their student bodies double and even triple in size in less than a decade.

However, the benefits of the G.I. Bill did not benefit equally all of the men and women who served. Some areas of military service were not covered at all, such as the Merchant Marine, even though they sustained high casualty rates. Women, African Americans, and other minority groups were not able to receive the full benefits of the G.I. Bill because of existing laws and traditions outside the scope of the legislation. Women often had to defer entry into college because of the postwar baby boom, and other women, who would have been able to attend college before the influx of new students, were turned away. African Americans faced social, economic, and political barriers to the use of their benefits on numerous fronts.

For African Americans, usage of the educational benefits was particularly problematic across the nation, but especially in the segregated South, where African Americans were

Young men attending college on the G.I. Bill acquire school supplies on January 28, 1945. Books and notebooks, as well as tuition and other fees, up to a total of $500 for an ordinary school year, were furnished to World War II veterans under the Servicemen's Readjustment Act of 1944, also known as the G.I. Bill. (UPI/Bettmann/Corbis)

legally prohibited from attending most colleges and universities. Not until *Brown v. Board of Education* (1954), and even longer before James Meredith's successful integration of the University of Mississippi, were educational opportunities open to all citizens.

In the area of housing, the G.I. Bill benefits for African Americans were also difficult. Many white veterans took advantage of the home loan part of the law and moved to the suburbs. Technically, these loans were available to African American veterans as well, but they faced de facto housing segregation, even in the wake of the elimination of de jure segregation in *Shelley v. Kraemer* (1948).

The G.I. Bill has continued beyond the postwar era of World War II in various forms for the veterans of the Korean conflict, Vietnam veterans, and other service members when the military became an all-volunteer service in 1973. However, the impact of these succeeding eras of benefits did not have the same, substantial impact of the original legislation.

Aaron Cooley

See also
World War II

Further Reading:
Bennet, Michael. *When Dreams Came True: The G.I. Bill and the Making of Modern America.* Dulles, VA: Potomac Books, 1999;
Mettler, Suzanne. *Soldiers to Citizens: The G.I. Bill and the Making of the Greatest Generation.* New York: Oxford University Press, 2005.

Gibson, Althea (1927–2003)

The first African American to win one of tennis's Grand Slam events with her victory in Paris at the French Open in 1956, Althea Gibson eventually won 11 major tennis championships in singles and doubles, shattering the sport's color barrier along the way. Born on April 25, 1927, to sharecropping parents in Silver, South Carolina, Gibson moved with her family to New York City as a young girl. A school dropout at age 14, Gibson found her focus when she picked up the sport of paddleball, competing in city tournaments of the New York Police Athletic League. Her success at paddleball eventually led to free tennis lessons at Harlem's Cosmopolitan Tennis Club, and in 1942, Gibson won the New York State Negro Girls' Open.

At this time, most tennis tournaments were held at private clubs, which excluded blacks from all nonservice positions. In keeping with the all-white policies of most clubs, the United States Lawn Tennis Association (USLTA; now the United States Tennis Association) excluded blacks from all of its events, including the national championships. In response to this exclusion, as they did in numerous other instances during the Jim Crow era, African Americans created a parallel institution, the American Tennis Association (ATA) in 1916, which held its own tournaments and national championships. Gibson competed in the ATA's national championship for the first time in 1942, and won the girls' singles title in 1944 and 1945. In 1947, Gibson won the first of her 10 consecutive ATA women's singles crowns.

Gibson's performance at the 1946 ATA championships (which, ironically, she did not win), caught the eye of the physician and former ATA national champion Hubert Eaton of Wilmington, North Carolina. Eaton and fellow physician Robert Johnson of Lynchburg, Virginia, offered to mentor Gibson. She moved into Eaton's home, which had its own tennis court, and reentered high school in Wilmington. She flourished under the tutelage of the two doctors, who served as her coaches and traveled with her to ATA tournaments. While living with Eaton, she also graduated from high school and went on to college at Florida A&M University, where she majored in physical education and played both tennis and basketball.

Despite her success in both ATA and intercollegiate events (where she sometimes competed against white athletes), the USLTA refused to bend its "whites only" policy and extend Gibson an invitation to participate in its national championship at Forest Hills, New York. Only after an outcry from some prominent white players about Gibson's exclusion from the event, most notably from four-time U.S. champion Alice Marble, did the organization finally relent and offer her an invitation to participate in the 1950 national championship, becoming the first African American to participate in the event. Gibson won her opening match of the tournament before falling to former U.S. and Wimbledon champion Louise Brough, 9–7 in the third set.

Gibson's appearance at the 1950 U.S. championships opened doors to other events previously closed to her, but she initially struggled to duplicate the success she had enjoyed on the ATA circuit. In 1953, she graduated from college and accepted a teaching position at Missouri's Lincoln University. While teaching at Lincoln, she contemplated retiring from competitive tennis, but in 1956, she broke through with victories in both the women's singles and doubles at the French Open, becoming the first black person to win a Grand Slam tennis event. She followed up her success in Paris with a victory in the women's doubles at Wimbledon and a runner-up finish in the women's singles at Forest Hills later that summer.

Her Grand Slam breakthrough in 1956 propelled Gibson to one of the great stretches in women's tennis. She won both the U.S. and Wimbledon singles titles in 1957, becoming the first black person to win either event, and was the runner-up in Australia. She repeated as champion in both New York and London the next year, and established herself as the dominant player in the women's game. Then, in 1958, Gibson stunned the tennis world by announcing her retirement from competitive tennis, having won a total of 11 Grand Slam events in both singles and doubles. At that time, the major tennis events were reserved for amateurs, so Gibson turned professional and played a series of exhibition matches, often held before Harlem Globetrotters games.

Following her retirement from tennis, Gibson pursued careers in both music and professional golf, with middling success. In 1968, she married W. A. Darben and settled in New Jersey, where she taught tennis. In 1971, she became the first African American inducted into the International Tennis Hall of Fame in Newport, Rhode Island. Althea Gibson died in 2003.

Thomas J. Ward, Jr.

See also
Sports and Racism

Further Reading:
Biracree, Tom. *Althea Gibson: Tennis Champion*. Los Angeles: Holloway House, 1990.
Gibson, Althea. *I Always Wanted to Be Somebody*. New York: Harper, 1968;
International Tennis Hall of Fame. http://www.tennisfame.com (accessed June 10, 2008).

Goddard, Henry H. (1866–1957)

Henry Herbert Goddard was a major proponent of the idea that Southern and Eastern European immigrants entering the country in the first decade of the 20th century were intellectually inferior. In 1912, Goddard was asked by U.S. government officials to use the newly developed intelligence test on immigrants entering the United States at Ellis Island in New York. The newly arriving immigrants were given a test in English that covered information about American life that was unfamiliar to most of them. Naturally, Goddard found that Italian, Jewish, Hungarian, and Russian immigrants did poorly on the IQ test compared with native-born Protestants. He labeled those immigrants with low IQ scores as "feebleminded." The results of his intelligence test were used by policymakers and other white supremacists to legislate restrictive immigration laws in the early 1920s, including the National Origins Act of 1924.

PYONG GAP MIN

See also
Biological Racism

Further Reading:
Kamin, L. J. *The Science and Politics of I.Q.* Hillside, NJ: Earlbaum Associates, 1974.

Gonzales, Corky (1928–2005)

Chicano activist Corky Gonzales helped to catalyze the Chicano Movement by organizing the National Youth Liberation Conference in Denver, Colorado, in 1969. In addition, Gonzales wrote the iconic poem *Yo Soy Joaquin/I Am Joaquin*, which became a touchstone in Chicano literature.

Rodolfo "Corky" Gonzales was born in Keenesburg, Colorado, on June 18, 1928. He was the youngest of seven siblings, and he and his family worked as farm laborers on the outskirts of Denver. His mother, Indalesia, died when he was two years old; his father, Federico, who had immigrated to the United States from Chihuahua, Mexico, never remarried. At the age of 10, Gonzales began assisting his family in the fields. His family moved frequently; nevertheless, Gonzales graduated from Manual High School in 1944 and briefly attended the University of Denver. In the mid-1940s, Gonzales began a successful career as a boxer in the bantam and featherweight classes. He won the National Amateur Athletic Union bantamweight title in 1946 and turned professional a year later. Gonzales forged a successful boxing career, tallying a 47–3 record overall in his six-year professional career (1947–1953).

Gonzales was involved in Denver political organizations in the mid-1950s. Although he eventually embraced separatist politics, his first exposure to politics was through the traditional Democratic Party. After becoming active in the Democratic Party in 1957, he became a district party captain for the city—the first Latino ever appointed to that position in Colorado. Following John F. Kennedy's successful nomination as the Democratic presidential candidate, his campaign team realized that winning the Latino voting bloc could have enormous consequences in the election. To that end, Viva Kennedy clubs arose throughout the Southwest. In 1960, Gonzales was tapped to chair Colorado's Viva Kennedy campaign.

One of President Lyndon B. Johnson's core programs instituted after John F. Kennedy's assassination was the War on Poverty. In Denver, poverty was conspicuously present, especially among Latinos. With prior experience in Denver politics, Gonzales was tapped to chair one of the War on Poverty programs for the city: the Neighborhood Youth Corps. In 1965, he was appointed to oversee the citywide War on Poverty program. Gonzales devoted much of his attention to the city's poor, who, in many cases, were Latinos; however, the Denver mayor fired him for giving preferential treatment to Latinos. As a result, in April 1966, shortly after Gonzales's dismissal, the local Latino community organized a rally to protest the city's actions. The gathering provided

Jose A. Gutierrez, left, of Texas, and Rodolfo "Corky" Gonzalez of Colorado, stand before the Raza Unida Party national convention in El Paso, September 4, 1972. (AP Photo/Fred Kaufman)

the impetus for the Crusade for Justice, a grassroots organization aimed at improving the conditions of Latinos, or as Gonzales quipped, "This meeting is only the spark of a crusade for justice which we are going to carry into every city in Colorado."

The Crusade for Justice was based on the twin pillars of the Chicano Movement—self-determination and cultural nationalism. Gonzales believed that economic and political autonomy was possible by projecting a unified positive self-image of *la raza* (the community). To that end, Gonzales penned the iconic poem, *Yo Soy Joaquin /I Am Joaquin* in 1967. Divided into three parts, the poem used powerful metaphors to convey a history of oppression, a transformation

into a proud Mexican people, and finally, an affirmation of the Chicano experience. The poem circulated widely among Mexican American political organizations before being published in 1972.

Initially, the Crusade for Justice focused on the widespread problem of police brutality. However, as an integral participant in Denver politics for a decade, Gonzales had witnessed the virtual absence of Latinos and believed that the Crusade for Justice could provide Latinos with a springboard for political activism. The Crusade also highlighted the disproportionate numbers of Latino Americans fighting in Vietnam, although it would be the Los Angeles–organized Chicano Moratorium that took up the mantle of antiwar protest. The Crusade also advocated better education, jobs, and housing. It printed its own newspaper *El Gallo* (The Rooster) to publicize its political agenda. In 1968, the Crusade purchased and renovated an old church to serve as its main headquarters.

In April 1968, the Crusade for Justice participated in the Poor People's Campaign in Washington, D.C. Gonzales and Reies Tijerina, a prominent Chicano leader from New Mexico, organized the "western caravan" composed of Latinos from the Southwest. Gonzales articulated the need for improved education, jobs, and housing, as well as the message of cultural nationalism. In the end, many perceived the Poor People's Campaign as a failure because of the splintered agendas that often extended beyond class concerns.

By early 1969, the Crusade for Justice had begun to plan a national conference for Chicano youth known as the National Youth Liberation Conference (NYLC) in Denver. Attended by 1,500 Chicanos, the conference brought together individuals from diverse backgrounds, including a large contingent of Chicano high school and college students, gang members, and ex-convicts. The Chicano Movement's core ideas of cultural nationalism and self-determination crystallized at the conference through the foundational document penned by Chicano poet Alurista. "El Plan Espiritual de Aztlan" conveyed the organizational goals of the movement, including cultural unity, economic autonomy, bilingual education, self-defense, and political liberation. As a result of the NYLC, the La Raza Unida Party formed, and several independent schools opened, including Escuela Tlatelolco, to better address the needs of Chicano youth. By the late 1970s, however, the Crusade for Justice—like the Chicano Movement—began to fall apart due to internal conflicts and competing agendas.

Gonzales continued his political activism until 1987 when he suffered a heart attack while driving, causing a serious accident. A year later, he was inducted into Colorado's Sports Hall of Fame.

Gonzales died of congestive heart failure on April 12, 2005, at his home in Denver, surrounded by his family, including his wife, Geraldine, and his eight children.

ABC-CLIO

See also

Chicano Movement

Further Reading:

De Baca, Vincent, ed. *La Gente: Hispano History and Life in Colorado.* Denver: Colorado Historical Society, 1998.

Fresquez, Cristina. "Corky's Dance with Life." *El Semanario,* June 15, 2006.

Sahagun, Louis. "Rodolfo Gonzales, 76; Prizefighter, Poet, and Fervent Chicano Activist." *Los Angeles Times,* April 14, 2005.

Vigil, Ernesto. *The Crusade for Justice: Chicano Militancy and the Government's War on Dissent.* Madison: University of Wisconsin, 1999.

Gonzales v. Abercrombie & Fitch Stores (2003)

During the first decade of the 21st century, Abercrombie & Fitch Company (A&F), a prominent retailer of contemporary casual clothing for teenagers and young adults, encountered several controversies and lawsuits accusing A&F of committing racial and gender discrimination in their hiring and promotion practices, promoting sexual promiscuity and pornography in their marketing materials, and selling racially offensive clothing. Of the myriad controversies that embroiled A&F, the accusations of racial and gender discrimination detailed in *Gonzalez v. Abercrombie & Fitch Stores, Inc.* (No. 03-2817 SI [N.D. Cal. April 11, 2005]), a class action lawsuit filed in 2003 in the Northern District of California, received the most notoriety. The crux of the charges was based on Abercrombie & Fitch's aggressive deployment and stringent maintenance of its putative "A&F Look" policy, a policy that imposed onerous grooming and style restrictions on its sales associates, called "Brand Representatives," to ensure that they represented the brand's narrow conceptualization of American style. After its original filing, the *Gonzalez* case was amended and consolidated to include two additional lawsuits: *West v. Abercrombie & Fitch Stores, Inc.* (No. 04-4730), a case that advanced substantially the same facts and legal claims as *Gonzalez* but added complaints of gender discrimination; and *Equal Employment Opportunity Commission v. Abercrombie & Fitch, Inc.* (No. 04-4731), a case that affirmed the same facts and legal claims as *Gonzalez* and *West* but added additional charges that resulted from the Equal Employment Opportunity

Jennifer Lu, 22, left, addresses reporters as several of her fellow plaintiffs in an employment discrimination lawsuit against Abercrombie & Fitch, Brandy Hawk, 20, second from left; Patrice Douglass, 20, center; Carla Grubb, 21, second from right; and Eric Fight, 23, listen during a news conference, November 16, 2004, in downtown Los Angeles. Abercrombie & Fitch agreed to pay $40 million to black, Hispanic, and Asian employees and job applicants to settle the class-action federal discrimination lawsuit that accused the clothing retailer of promoting whites at the expense of minorities. (Associated Press)

Commission's (EEOC) exhaustive investigation of five years of complaints of discrimination against A&F.

Court documents detail the scope and seriousness of the complaints: the plaintiffs in the *Gonzalez* case accused Abercrombie & Fitch of violating Title VII of the Civil Rights Act of 1964 and the California Fair Employment and Housing Act by discriminating against female, African American, Latino, and Asian American job applicants and employees in A&F's hiring, firing, promotion, job assignment, and compensation practices.

Plaintiffs in the *Gonzalez* case alleged that the "A&F Look" represented a corporate policy of discrimination since A&F conceived and defined the "A&F Look" as "exclusively white." The plaintiffs also accused A&F of aggressively enforcing this exclusively white image by excluding persons of color from employment, relegating them—when they were hired at all—to stock or night positions, zeroing out their hours, denying them advancement in the company, and/or firing them for their inability to conform to the "A&F Look" because of their race, gender, national origin, and color. According to court documents, A&F considered the plaintiffs not white enough to serve as Brand Representatives, visually displaying A&F's ostensibly unique look, or to work in one of its stores at all. A&F allegedly painstakingly maintained this all-white image across all of its stores by exercising employment practices that ensured an all-white workforce.

Abercrombie and Fitch Parodied on *MADtv*

Abercrombie & Fitch's commodification of white identity was famously parodied by *MADtv*, a sketch comedy series that aired on FOX for over a decade, during the show's ninth and 10th seasons. These seasons aired concurrently with the adjudication of the *Gonzalez* racial and gender discrimination case. As a result, several of the skits made reference to or provided commentary on A&F's packaging of white identity. These skits can be viewed on YouTube by typing "Mad TV-Abercrombie Skits" into the search bar.

For instance, A&F recruited students from predominantly white sororities and fraternities, required that managers hire only persons who conformed to the "A&F Look" (i.e., young, white, preppy males), regulated this policy by having regional and district managers scrutinize stores and review pictures of employees to ensure compliance, and reinforced the policy by displaying almost exclusively white models in its publications, store displays, and marketing campaigns.

In 2005, EEOC, the private plaintiffs in *Gonzalez* and A&F amicably resolved the case by entering into a consent decree enjoining A&F from discriminating against applicants and employees due to race, color, gender, and national origin for a six-year period. While disavowing any guilt, A&F avoided the negative consequences of protracted litigation by agreeing to the consent decree and its provisions. The consent decree stipulated a $50 million settlement: $40 million was paid out to potentially thousands of female and minority claimants who may have been victims of discrimination because of their race, color, gender, and national origin; and an additional $10 million was appropriated for attorneys' fees and the costs associated with monitoring A&F's compliance during the six years that the agreement was in force. The consent decree also established several additional conditions. For instance, A&F was required to establish benchmarks for the hiring and promotion of women and minorities and hire a vice president of diversity, as well as 25 diversity recruiters. The consent decree specifically prohibited A&F from targeting fraternities, sororities, and colleges for recruitment purposes, a recruiting practice that virtually guaranteed an all-white work force, and mandated that A&F populate its publications and marketing materials with racially and ethnically diverse models.

Although lauded by civil rights groups as an agreement that promised to dramatically alter A&F's all-white image, that promise may not have materialized. Since the resolution of the *Gonzalez* case, A&F has faced complaints of religious discrimination relating to employment practices that allegedly discriminated against Muslim women for wearing the hijab, a religious head covering, prompting the EEOC to sue A&F again for violating Title VII of the Civil Rights Act of 1964. This suit, like *Gonzalez*, centers on A&F's aggressive application of the all-white image that the "A&F Look" embodies, indicating that A&F must continue to modify its policies to integrate diversity.

Nicholas N. Behm

See also

Criminal Justice System and Racial Discrimination; Discrimination; White Privilege; Whiteness Studies

Further Reading:

Consent Decree. *Gonzalez v. Abercrombie & Fitch Stores, Inc.,* No. 03-2817 SI (N.D. Cal. April 11, 2005) (accessed October 4, 2012).

Gonzalez v. Abercrombie & Fitch Stores, Inc., No. 03-2817 SI (N.D. Cal. June 10, 2004) (accessed October 2, 2012).

Greenhouse, Steven. "Clothing Chain Accused of Discrimination." *New York Times,* June 17, 2003.

Greenhouse, Steven. "Abercrombie & Fitch Bias Case Is Settled." *New York Times,* November 17, 2004.

Joint Notice of Motion. *Gonzalez v. Abercrombie & Fitch Stores, Inc.,* No. 03-2817 SI, *West v. Abercrombie & Fitch,* No. 04-4730, *Equal Employment Opportunity Commission v. Abercrombie & Fitch,* No. 04-4731, (N.D. Cal. November 15, 2004) (accessed October 4, 2012).

Lepore, Meredith. "Abercrombie: How a Hunting and Fishing Store Became a Sex-Infused Teenybop Legend." *Business Insider,* April 6, 2011.

Mexican American Legal Defense and Educational Fund, NAACP Legal Defense and Educational Fund, Asian Pacific American Legal Center, and Lieff, Cabraser, Heimann, & Bernstein, LLP. "$40 Million Payment, Detailed Plan for Diversity in Employment Discrimination Suit Against Retail Giant Abercrombie & Fitch," press release, November 16, 2004.

Rozhon, Tracie. "Abercrombie & Fitch May Be Cool. But Cool Only Goes So Far." *New York Times,* July 13, 2004.

U.S. Equal Employment Opportunity Commission. "Court Finds for EEOC in Religious Discrimination Suit Against Abercrombie & Fitch," press release, July 15, 2011.

Good Hair

Hair is a biological attribute of the human body that is imbued with social meaning. It is a medium that, when groomed in a particular manner, informs us about the individual, society, and the relationship between the two. The symbolic importance of hair is visible in social institutions and categories like religion and gender, but the notions of "good hair" and "bad hair" are closely tied to race. Within the context of race, "good hair" is long and straight while "bad hair" has a texture of tightly coiled curls. Aside from skin color, hair texture has been one of the most stigmatized physical features of black people in general and black women specifically.

Hair has played an important role in the lives of black women dating back to antebellum slavery. The texture of one's hair played an important role in determining the type of work a slave would perform. Darker-skinned slaves with kinky hair were relegated to the fields. Women who worked outdoors covered their hair with scarves while the men wore hats or cut their hair short. Lighter-skinned slaves with straighter hair, on the other hand, worked indoors as housekeepers or craftsmen. Many scholars believe that light-skinned, straight-haired slaves were given domestic work because they were the offspring of the master (or his son). Other scholars argue that they may have been favored because of owners' association of physical attributes with personality characteristics.

During the 17th and 18th centuries, naturalists, philosophers, and early social scientists began to categorize racial groups based on features such as skin color, lip size and shape, hair texture, and skull angle and attributed certain personalities to each race. Swedish botanist Carolus Linnaeus (1707–1778), for example, proposed four subcategories and behaviors of humans: *Europæus albus* (ruled by law and custom), *Americanus rubescens* (ruled by habit), *Asiaticus fuscus* (ruled by belief), and *Africanus niger* (ruled by impulse). Because light-skinned, straight-haired slaves more closely approximated whiteness, slave owners believed that they were more intelligent and were more comfortable having them work in their homes. In addition to having less physically demanding jobs, slaves who worked inside the home were more likely to be educated and had a higher chance of being released from slavery than slaves working outdoors. The differential treatment of slaves produced a plantation hierarchy that created and maintained notions of "good" and "bad" hair that, some propose, were internalized by many black people.

Following the end of slavery, hair was thought to be a critical indicator of black people's desire to become a part of mainstream American society. To express their commitment, many adopted white standards of appearance and behavior. Women, and men to a slightly lesser degree, straightened their hair using products from a growing black hair-care industry. While many felt hair straightening was necessary in the fight for social acceptance and economic opportunity, there were others who argued that hair straightening was a form of black self-hate. This rhetoric reached its apex in the late 1960s during the Black Power movement. During this time many blacks stopped straightening their hair in an effort to challenge Eurocentric standards and promote the idea the "Black Is Beautiful" campaign. Despite the progressive ideas supported during this time period, the fervor was short-lived as many blacks believed that achieving economic success was more likely if they adhered to mainstream styles of hair and dress.

SHEENA KAORI GARDNER AND MATTHEW W. HUGHEY

See also

Cosmetics; Cosmetic Surgery

Further Reading:

Banks, Ingrid. *Hair Matters: Beauty, Power, and Black Women's Consciousness.* New York: New York University Press, 2000.

Byrd, Ayana D., and Lori L. Tharps. *Hair Story: Untangling the Roots of Black Hair in America.* New York: St. Martin's Press, 2001.

Mercer, Kobena. "Black Hair/Style Politics." *New Formations* 3 (1987): 33–54.

Patton, Tracey O. "Hey Girl, Am I More than My Hair?: African American Women and Their Struggles with Beauty, Body Image, and Hair." *NSWA Journal* 18 (2006): 24–51.

Gospel Music

Gospel music emerged out of African American Protestant churches in the early 20th century, with its development and instrumentation reflecting the impact of migration, urbanization, commercialization, and secularization on gospel musicians and their genres.

African American Pentecostals made the earliest contributions to gospel music at the turn of the 20th century. Charles Harrison Mason, founder of the Church of God in Christ (COGIC), encouraged early black Pentecostals to celebrate the African expression of their faith, and he made a direct effort to maintain the exuberant worship style of plantation praise houses, where body percussion, the shout, and personal testimony were common. Many mainline worshippers viewed gospel music as undignified and worldly. But those who appreciated it continued to use upbeat rhythms and creative instrumentation, including vocals, guitar, drums, piano, and a preference for the Hammond organ. The chord structures used often approached blues and jazz.

Many early black gospel musicians figured among the millions of black Southerners who migrated to Northern and Midwestern cities, where commercial opportunities were more prevalent, new instrumentation and styles developed, and secularization was imminent. Pentecostal solo evangelists used gospel music as missionary work in the 1920s and 1930s and created their unique brand of musical evangelism, as Rosetta Tharpe demonstrated. Reared in COGIC, Tharpe spent her early years traveling and singing with her mother in churches and on city streets to spread the gospel. Tharpe's commitment to musical evangelism and that of other Pentecostal solo evangelists and musicians, including pianist Arizona Dranes and guitarists Ann Bailey and Nancy Gamble, helped to set the stage for the commercialization of gospel music. Thomas Dorsey (Baptist) and Sally Martin (Sanctified) are credited with initiating this process by establishing the National Convention of Gospel Choirs and Choruses (NCGCC), an organization that made musicians less dependent on local churches for support.

The commercial interest of large for-profit corporations soon competed with grassroots entrepreneurial efforts of Dorsey and Martin as the appreciation for gospel and race music grew in the postwar years. From 1938 to 1945, the subsequent tension between the sacred and secular was crystallized in the experiences of Rosetta Tharpe. Tharpe sang gospel music, but she privatized her faith, a move that allowed her to perform sacred music in secular arenas like the Cotton Club despite her religious beliefs. Her blend of the sacred and secular was censured from morally conservative black Christians and was the basis for her excommunication from COGIC. Her success was nonetheless a prelude to the popularity of gospel music and ignited debates over the still controversial union of religion and commerce.

Solo evangelists like Tharpe shared the gospel music stage with an increasing number of gospel soloists and groups from the 1940s onwards, including Clara Ward and the Ward Singers, the Staple Singers, and Mahalia Jackson. Of these performers, Mahalia Jackson gained international recognition and performed at a number of historic events, including the inauguration of President John F. Kennedy in 1961, the March on Washington in 1963, and the funeral of Martin Luther King, Jr. in 1968.

By the 1960s, James Cleveland was crowned the prince of gospel music when he introduced choirs to the gospel music performance with *Peace Be Still* in 1962. Cleveland also established the Gospel Music Workshop of America, which, similar to Dorsey and Martin's NCGCC, became an important training ground and launch pad for gospel musicians throughout the country from the 1960s onwards. He shared the gospel arena with a number of award-winning gospel quartets, including the Dixie Humming Birds, Five Blind Boys from Mississippi, and Mighty Clouds of Joy.

As American society of the post–civil rights era diversified, so too did gospel music. By the 1970s, some artists remained faithful to the "down home" gospel styles of previous generations and others to semiclassical art forms, as did Houston's Sara Jordan Powell, then a member of COGIC. Some secular music artists created a secular gospel known as soul music, which carried sociopolitical messages. Marvin Gaye's *What's Going On* (1971) represents this genre. Some who continued to sing traditional gospel eventually gravitated to the fresh new sound of the contemporary gospel music largely produced on the West Coast.

Andrae Crouch was among the first to experiment with new sounds in the 1970s, though his conservative lyrics bore a clear gospel message. Crouch's choices concerned some black Christians, who feared that his contemporary integrationist format did not respect the traditional black gospel sound. While playing for his father's church, Crouch continued to engage the entire gamut of black gospel music expressed through the music styles of holiness churches. Crouch moved away from traditional gospel, creatively fusing country, rhythm and blues, jazz, and Latin rock. His songs *Through It All* and *I Don't Know Why Jesus Loved Me* repackaged the traditional gospel message in the new Tin

Pan Alley of Hollywood. Crouch further distinguished himself by employing a "hip" approach to his vocal delivery.

As Crouch's music was diverse, it was performed and recorded by a variety of artists, including Elvis Presley, the Imperials, and the Jesse Dixon Singers. Crouch also appeared with Billy Preston, Santana, Johnny Cash, Pat Boone, and Billy Graham. Crouch attracted black and white followers and surpassed the boundaries of his COGIC upbringing. Accordingly, many of his songs have become gospel music classics and are frequently anthologized. The Hawkins Family Singers, of COGIC roots, experienced similar success. Edwin Hawkins earned the distinction of being the first gospel singer to have a single, *Oh Happy Day*, secure the number-one spot on both pop and gospel music charts in *Ebony*'s Black Music Poll, the first of which was initiated in 1973.

Sarah Jordan Powell joined the extensive lineup of COGIC-born artists who gained national attention for their contributions to gospel music. She was listed among the nominees of *Ebony*'s 1975 annual gospel music awards voting sheet. Previous nominees and their childhood religious affiliations are as follows: Shirley Caesar (Baptist, now COGIC); Rev. James Cleveland (Baptist); Sam Cooke (Baptist); the Dixie Hummingbirds (Baptist); the Mighty Clouds of Joy (Baptist); the Staple Singers (Baptist); and Clara Ward (Pentecostal).

Jordan's earlier nomination for best female gospel music performer along with the successes of the Edwin Hawkins Singers and Andrae Crouch and the Disciples signified a shift in the vanguard of gospel music. The reigning prince of gospel music, James Cleveland, and long-favored quartet groups now shared the spotlight with a new wave of singers who introduced a fresh gospel sound with innovative instrumentation and embellished traditional Baptist harmonic structures with neo-Pentecostal modalities.

In the post–civil rights era, gospel choirs multiplied on white college campuses throughout the country, and reflected the enduring importance of communal worship for many young black college students. Gospel choirs were largely established to help affirm the racial identity of black students as they adjusted to the demands of white society, although tensions existed on some campuses between students embracing Pentecostal-style gospel music and those preferring quieter sacred music expressions.

Gospel music also found expression in the advent of extrachurch community choirs. Among the community choirs whose performances placed them at the top of radio music charts in the 1970s and 1980s were the Brooklyn Tabernacle Choir of New York, Milton Brunson and the Thompson Community Singers of Chicago, the Mississippi Mass Choir, and the Southeast Inspirational Choir of Houston, Texas, where Yolanda Adams initiated her award-winning career as a gospel music artist. Their continued success brought additional opportunities to perform with Sara Jordan Powell, the legendary Ray Charles, and Twinkie Clark of the Clark Sisters, daughters of Mattie Moss Clark, then head of the International COGIC Music Department.

From the 1980s onwards, gospel music artists embraced a variety of music expressions, including funk, hip-hop, jazz, rap, reggae, and broader categories such as contemporary Christian, inspirational, and praise and worship music, where the music of such artists as Nicole C. Mullen, Larnell Harris, and Israel Houghton are respectively featured. Regardless of the genre or category, discussions continue about the impact of secularization and commercialization on the gospel music expression. Kirk Franklin became a national icon of funky contemporary gospel music in 1993 with the group Kirk Franklin and the Family, and its self-titled album. Franklin's highly-acclaimed *Whatcha Lookin' 4* sold 1 million copies, and his *Kirk Franklin and the Family Christmas* album became a holiday favorite. Kirk Franklin career was launched into enduring fame by his hit tune "Stomp," which he recorded with the group God's Property. Drawing on Pentecostal-Charismatic traditions, Franklin invited his fans to have a "Holy Ghost party" with him to the rhythm of the aforementioned tune. Although Franklin was criticized for the sound and delivery of his music, which some believed was too secular or dance oriented, Franklin insisted on artistic freedom, as did his predecessors and many of his contemporaries, such as Kim Burrell, Fred Hampton, Mary Mary, Donnie McClurkin, John P. Key, Take 6, BeBe Winans, CeCe Winans, the Winans, and other gospel music artists of the latter 20th and early 21st centuries.

KAREN KOSSIE-CHERNYSHEV

See also
Jazz; Rhythm and Blues; Rock and Roll

Further Reading:
Jackson, Jerma A. *Singing in My Soul: Black Gospel Music in a Secular Age*. Chapel Hill: University of North Carolina Press, 2004.

Lornell, Kip. *"Happy in the Service of the Lord": African-American Sacred Vocal Harmony Quartets in Memphis*. Knoxville: University of Tennessee Press, 1995.

Reed, Teresa. *The Holy Profane: Religion in Black Popular Music*. Lexington: University Press of Kentucky, 2003.

Sanders, Cheryl. *Saints in Exile*. New York: Oxford University Press, 1996.

Southern, Eileen. *The Music of Black Americans: A History*, 3rd ed. New York: W. W. Norton, 1997.

Spencer, John Michael. *Black Hymnody: A Hymnological History of the African American Church*. Knoxville: University of Knoxville Press, 1992.

Government Initiatives after the September 11, 2001, Attack on the United States

Immediately after the September 11 attack on the United States, the U.S. government initiated a series of directives aimed at combating terrorists who might have infiltrated the country. These initiatives will be discussed in chronological order to get a sense of the pace, sequence, and scope of the directives as they happened. It should be noted, however, that the long-term repercussions of these initiatives—how they have affected the lives of the immigrant men who were "caught" in the fray, the effects on their families, and the impact on targeted communities, namely, Arab and/or Muslim Americans—remains to be seen. A list of the major initiatives, announcements, and actions is provided.

- On September 17, 2001, the Immigration and Naturalization Service (INS) changed the regulation regarding detentions. A nonresident alien could be detained without charge for 48 hours or more if there were attenuating circumstances.
- On September 21, 2001, chief immigration judge Michael Creppy issues a memorandum regarding "secure" hearings, meaning that in certain cases, proceedings are closed to the public.
- On October 25, 2001, the attorney general, John Ashcroft, announced that the government had arrested or detained nearly 1,000 individuals as part of its antiterrorism offensive.

- On October 26, 2001, President George W. Bush signed the USA Patriot Act into law.
- On November 7, 2001, President Bush announced the creation of the Foreign Terrorist Tracking Task Force during the first formal meeting of the Homeland Security Council. The goal of the task force was to deny entry to, locate, detain, prosecute, and/or deport anyone suspected of terrorist activity.
- On November 9, 2001, the attorney general sent a memo to the FBI to conduct voluntary interviews with some 5,000 men, ages 18 to 33, who entered the United States after January 2000 and who came from countries where Al Qaeda is suspected of having operations. If found in violation of immigration laws, these men were to be arrested and kept without bail.
- On November 19, 2001, President Bush signed into law the Aviation and Transportation Security Act, which established the Transportation Security Administration (TSA). The law empowered the new agency to use information from government agencies to identify individuals on passenger lists who may be a threat to civil or national security, and to prevent them from flying.
- On January 8, 2002, the Department of Justice added to the FBI's National Crime Information Center database the names of approximately 6,000 men who had ignored deportation or removal orders. This is known as the "absconder" initiative. The list profiles men of working age from a number of countries believed to be harboring Al Qaeda cells.
- On February 26, 2002, the Final Report on Interview Project stated that out of 5,000 Arab and/or Muslim men on the list, 2,261 were interviewed and fewer than 20 were taken into custody, three on criminal violations and the rest on immigration charges.
- In March 2002, the State Department updated its list of terrorists and terrorist organizations whose property interests were frozen in September 2001 by presidential order.
- On April 12, 2002, the INS established a new limitation on visitors to the United States of 30 days, depending on the reason. Visitors could not change their status to student or attend a school if their status was pending.

U.S. Attorney General Alberto Gonzales speaks about the renewal of the Patriot Act on Capitol Hill during a news conference with House Judiciary Chairman James Sensenbrenner, left, and House Homeland Security Committee Chairman Peter King, right, December 13, 2005, on the eve of a House vote. The Bush administration and loyal Republican lawmakers demanded that Congress renew the Patriot Act before adjourning for the holidays, saying the nation's security depended on it. (AP Photo/Lauren Victoria Burke)

- On May 9, 2002, the attorney general ordered noncitizens who are subject to deportation to surrender to INS within 30 days of the final order or be barred forever from any discretionary relief from deportation.
- On May 14, 2002, President Bush signed into law the Enhanced Border Security and Visa Entry Reform Act. Like most of the government initiatives, this law was most consequential to individuals of Middle Eastern and South Asian birth, even if they were naturalized Canadian citizens.
- On May 16, 2002, the attorney general introduced the Student and Exchange Visitor System (SEVIS), which

became law on January 30, 2003. SEVIS tracks student enrollment, start date of each semester, failure to enroll, dropping below nine credits per term (i.e., full-time status), disciplinary action by the institution, and early graduation, among other information.
- On June 5, 2002, the attorney general announced a new entry-exit system. Aliens from 25 predominantly Muslim countries (Afghanistan, Algeria, Bahrain, Djibouti, Egypt, Eritrea, Indonesia, Iran, Iraq, Jordan, Kuwait, Lebanon, Libya, Malaysia, Morocco, Oman, Pakistan, Qatar, Saudi Arabia, Somalia, Sudan, Syria, Tunisia, United Arab Emirates, Yemen) were required to register, submit to fingerprints and photographs

upon their arrival in the United States, report to INS field offices within 30 days, re-report annually, and notify the INS agent of their departure, with possible criminal prosecution for those who fail to comply. The National Security Entry-Exit Registration System (NSEERS) was implemented on September 11, 2002, for men from Iran, Iraq, Syria, and Sudan.

- On June 26, 2002, the Department of Justice deported 131 Pakistani nationals who were detained for months at various INS facilities. Most were arrested for ignoring previous deportation orders. Another 100 men were deported on August 21, 2002.

- On July 11, 2002, the Department of Justice declared that most of the September 11 detainees were released and many of them deported.

- On July 24, 2002, the Department of Justice announced that the attorney general can deputize any state or local law-enforcement officer to exercise and enforce immigration laws, under certain provisions.

- On July 24, 2002, the U.S. Commission on Civil Rights reaffirmed its commitment to protect the rights of Arab and Muslim Americans.

- On November 6, 2002, the INS required males older than age 16 who are citizens of Iran, Iraq, Libya, Sudan, or Syria, and who had entered the United States before September 10, 2002, and who were remaining at least until December 16, 2002, to register with the INS before that date. Failure to comply was cause for deportation. On December 16, 2002, other countries were added to this list, which then totaled 20, mostly from the Middle East. Armenia was initially part of that list, but it was removed immediately. Some argue that the government put Armenia on the list to suggest it was not targeting only Muslim countries.

- On November 25, 2002, President Bush signed into law the Department of Homeland Security. This new cabinet-level department merges 22 federal agencies and thus employs about 170,000 individuals. President Bush also signed the Justice Department's operation Terrorism Information and Prevention System (TIPS), which would enlist thousands of truck drivers, mail carriers, bus drivers as "citizen observers," but was defeated through media exposure and the resulting outrage by the American public.

- On January 16, 2003, the INS extended the date of deadlines for registration. Statistics are released stating that almost 1,200 were detained during the NSEERS "special registration." Five countries—Bangladesh, Egypt, Indonesia, Jordan, and Kuwait—were added to the existing list of 20 that requested males older than 16 years of age to register with the INS and be fingerprinted.

- On March 24, 2003, the FBI declared that more than 5,000 Iraqis who live in the United States were "voluntarily" interviewed and, of these, 30 were detained on immigration violations.

- On April 29, 2003, Tom Ridge, Secretary of Homeland Security, launched U.S. Visitor and Immigrant Status Indication Technology (U.S. VISIT). The new system replaces NSEERS and integrates SEVIS. A minimum of two biometric identifiers (e.g., photographs, fingerprints, iris scans) will be used in the future to track all visitors to the country.

- On May 9, 2003, the General Accounting Office (GAO) issued its report on the "voluntary interviews." The report noted that 3,216 Muslim and Arab immigrants were interviewed by the Justice Department out of a possible 7,602 identified individuals. GAO doubted that the interviews were voluntary.

- On June 2, 2003, the Office of the Inspector General of the U.S. Department of Justice issued its highly critical report on the detention initiative that followed the September 11 attacks.

- In November 2003, two facets of what had been NSEERS were suspended: the annual re-registration requirement and the 30- and 40-day follow-up interviews.

Though the government initiatives do not appear to have ended, a preliminary analysis of their impact thus far is warranted. Civil rights organizations, legal experts, immigrants' rights groups, and critical observers of the government's policies claim that these policies in the process of defending the security of the nation, are chiseling away at immigrants' rights and potentially even citizens' civil liberties. They also victimize innocent people. Even the U.S. Department of Justice's own Office of the Inspector General issued a scathing report accusing the attorney general of breaking many laws he was meant to protect.

Arab and Muslim immigrant men suffered the most from these policies, and their ethnic/religious communities were left feeling extremely vulnerable. It is not yet known how many of those detained, interviewed, and registered have been deported, because the government has not published these statistics. However, from available information, one can gather that about 6,000 Arab/Muslim absconders were sought; 42 percent of those invited for supposedly voluntary interviews were questioned and about 20 arrested on immigration and criminal charges; at least 231 individuals were deported, more than half of them Pakistanis; and less than 1 percent of the 5,000 Iraqis were detained after being interviewed. Estimates of the detainees vary between the Inspector General's number of 762 illegal immigrants from the Middle East and South Asia to more than 1,200 from other sources. Almost 1,200 men were detained as a result of NSEERS, or "special registration," whereas by May 2003, it was estimated that more than 80,000 had obeyed orders to register. Although these numbers are not staggering, the dragnet nature of the government initiatives has created a perception that the backlash was far more encompassing.

As men usually contribute the primary income for the household, especially those originating from patriarchal societies, wives, children, and other family members were obviously drawn into the backlash unwittingly. The repercussions on the Arab and Muslim immigrant communities have yet to be assessed. The Pakistani immigrant community in Coney Island, New York, for example, has witnessed the closure of several businesses and rapid sales of vehicles and real estate. More seriously, constitutional scholars and observers of the nation's civil liberties have sounded the alarm. For example, law professor David Cole argues that the United States has adopted a double standard of "their liberty, our security," accepting abuse of foreigners that citizens would not tolerate. He warns that these civil-liberty abuses, if unchecked, may come to haunt citizens in the future.

MEHDI BOZORGMEHR AND ANNY BAKALIAN

See also

Immigration and Customs Enforcement (ICE); Islamofascism; September 11, 2001, Terrorism, Discriminatory Reactions to; Terrorism

Further Reading:

Cole, David. *Enemy Aliens: Double Standards and Constitutional Freedoms in the War on Terrorism.* New York: New Press, 2003.

Gray, Garland (1901–1977)

Garland Gray, nicknamed "Peck," served in the Virginia General Assembly for 29 years as a Democrat from Waverly, in Sussex County, where he founded the successful company Gray Land & Timber. He was a key figure in U.S. Senator Harry F. Byrd's political machine. He is most well known for serving as the staunch segregationist chairman of the Commission on Public Education, also called the Gray Commission. Established by Gov. Thomas Stanley in 1954, the 32-member legislative commission proposed a state response to public school integration. The plan included (1) an amendment of the Compulsory Attendance Law so that no white parents would be required by law to send their child to an integrated school; (2) a local option plan to allow individual school boards to assign students to their various public schools; and (3) a tuition grant program to aid parents in sending their children to private academies. Though the local option aspect of the Gray plan would technically permit integration in more moderate counties, the remaining tenets were attempts by the all-white commission to avoid the U.S. Supreme Court's 1954 *Brown v. Board of Education* decision.

Submitted to the governor in November 1955, the Gray plan soon came under heavy fire from both white supremacists and liberal moderates. Gray almost immediately turned against the local option aspect of the plan because his fellow segregationists feared the snowball effect of allowing integration anywhere in the state. Gray quickly joined with other Byrd loyalists to support the Doctrine of Interposition, an idea set forth by conservative journalist James J. Kilpatrick in a series of editorials for the *Richmond News Leader*. The Doctrine of Interposition, reminiscent of similar constitutional arguments made on the eve of the Civil War, insisted that the Tenth Amendment protected state autonomy from the federal government on issues not clearly enumerated as federal powers in the Constitution. Thus, if those limitations were violated, the state could impose itself between federal mandates, including Supreme Court decisions, and the citizens of Virginia.

The resurrection of this modern version of the Doctrine of Nullification further radicalized Senator Byrd as well as his loyal supporters at home, including Gray. They embarked upon the new Massive Resistance campaign, passing legislation to strengthen the governor's powers over school decisions. Gray was rumored to be Byrd's choice to replace Governor Stanley in the 1957 election, but Lindsey Almond, who had argued the Prince Edward County, Virginia, integration case before the Supreme Court, secured the nomination. Nevertheless, Gray remained an active member of the Byrd organization, and continued to promote programs that would halt integration in his state. Even as late as 1959, when even Governor Almond began to see the futility of Massive Resistance, Gray proposed a budget revision that would reallocate all public school funding to the tuition-grant program that had originated in the commission's 1955 report. Gray's integral role in the relentless efforts to maintain segregation though legal maneuverings in the years following the *Brown* decision represents the depth and intensity of Southern, white attachment to the Jim Crow system. He retired from the Virginia General Assembly in 1971 and died in 1977.

ANGIE MAXWELL

See also

Gray Commission

Further Reading:

Ely, James W. *The Crisis of Conservative Virginia: The Byrd Organization and the Politics of Massive Resistance.* Knoxville: University of Tennessee Press, 1976.

Wilkinson, J. Harvie, III. *Harry Byrd and the Changing Face of Virginia Politics, 1945–1966.* Charlottesville: University Press of Virginia, 1968.

Gray Commission

On August 20, 1954, in the wake of the aftermath of the landmark *Brown v. Board of Education* decision, Governor Thomas Stanley of Virginia appointed a 32-member commission to study the economic and social impact of the ruling on the state and to craft a state response to integration. On September 13, 1954, at the first meeting of the Gray Commission, also known as the Commission on Public Education, Senator Garland Gray was elected chairman and delegate Harry B. Davis from Princess Anne County was elected as vice-chairman.

Governor Stanley had originally promised to appoint a diverse committee of public leaders in education and community affairs. However, in the wake of public and political pressure, Stanley dictated that the commission would be legislative. Thus, of the 32 members, 13 served as Virginia state senators and 19 served as Virginia house delegates. The legislative makeup of the committee ensured the exclusion of African American representatives, since the legislative body of the Commonwealth included no African American members. Garland Gray's reputation as a staunch segregationist preceded his election as chairman; he had, in fact, directed a meeting of southern Virginia political leaders earlier that June that resulted in the original call (sounded by the city council of Hopewell, Virginia) for Governor Stanley to define the Commission on Public Education as a legislative initiative. Two other significant events occurred at this initial meeting, both of which would reveal the budding anxiety of the pro-segregation delegates charged with directing the course of the Virginia school system. First, Chairman Gray established a subcommittee, called his executive council, that was heavily stacked with delegates from Virginia counties with large African American populations—counties that would experience the greatest change if school integration was enforced. And second, the entire commission adopted a privacy rule that insisted that the meetings would be wholly confidential. The only exception was granted to public hearings, which would be expressly defined by the commission; such a hearing was held once in November 15, 1954 in a mosque in Richmond and was attended by over 2,000 people.

For almost a year after that public hearing, the commission remained fairly inactive. Though the issue of public school integration was rarely absent from the news, most Southern political leaders chose to wait for the Supreme Court addendum to be decided in what would be called *Brown* II. Reargued in April 1955, *Brown* II hinged on the efficacy of integration and the uncertainty of the enforcement power and execution timeline of the original opinion. At the heart of the second hearing stood one major question: What means should be employed to realize fully the Warren Court's ruling in *Brown v. Board*? The implementation decision, announced on May 31, 1955, dictated that integration should occur "with all deliberate speed." The Commission on Public Education met again in August 1955, charged with laying out in detail a proposed solution to the integration debate in the state of Virginia. Their deliberations resulted in a three-point plan, submitted to Governor Stanley on November 11, 1955, that would emphasize local control while providing legal means for white students and their parents to avoid attending school with African Americans.

First, the commission recommended that the state law of compulsory attendance be amended to no longer force white students to enroll in integrated schools. In other words, students would not be compelled to attend school at all if their only option was attending an integrated school; such an act was primarily relevant in rural communities. Second, the report to the governor recommended that a pupil assignment organization be established so that each county could determine how many African American students would be integrated into the white public schools. Thus, the local control option could potentially open the door to integration in some of Virginia's more moderate counties. Finally, Chairman Gray reported that a system of tuition grants, made available by public funds, could be used at private schools, which remained outside of the reach of *Brown v. Board of Education*. The tuition grant aspect of the plan proved the most controversial because it required a change to the Virginia state constitution to allow government funds to be spent on private education. Liberals and some moderates in Virginia were concerned that these grants would result in the abandonment of the public school system. And the local control option provoked staunch segregationists who insisted that any integration in any part of Virginia was unacceptable. Support for the plan quickly collapsed as the political leaders of the state, such as U.S. Senator Harry F. Byrd, implemented the more radical, defiant Massive Resistance plan that eventually resulted in the closing of public schools in several Virginia counties.

ANGIE MAXWELL

See also

Bolling v. Sharpe (1954); *Brown v. Board of Education* (1954); *Brown v. Board of Education* Legal Groundwork; *Cooper v. Aaron* (1958); *Cumming v. Richmond County Board of Education* (1899); Gray, Garland; School Segregation. Document: *Brown v. Board of Education* (May 1954)

Further Reading:

Gates, Robbins L. *The Making of Massive Resistance: Virginia's Politics of Public School Desegregation, 1954–56.* Chapel Hill: University of North Carolina Press, 1962.

Muse, Benjamin. *Virginia's Massive Resistance.* Bloomington: Indiana University Press, 1961.

Wilhoit, Francis M. *The Politics of Massive Resistance.* New York: G. Braziller, 1973.

Great Depression

The Great Depression was a severe economic downturn impacting the United States and other industrialized countries. Lasting from 1929 through the early 1940s, the period was characterized by bank failures, massive unemployment, and a dramatic decrease in the production and sale of manufactured goods. In the United States, the economic collapse led to a dramatic transformation in the role that the federal government plays in regulating the economy. President Franklin D. Roosevelt's New Deal programs sought to alleviate suffering through unprecedented government intervention. Roosevelt's economic policies proved to be a turning point in the agricultural South, as federal funds led to the mechanization of agriculture and to the eventual displacement of many of the region's agricultural workers.

The Great Depression startled many, coming as it did on the heels of the 1920s, a time of reputed national prosperity characterized by an ebullient national mood and unprecedented consumer spending. Although many people did see an upswing in their standard of living during this decade, many of these changes were only surface deep. Wealth remained unequally distributed, and many Americans, particularly in the South, continued to live in poverty. In order to maintain the lifestyle promoted by the advertisements of the era, many bought luxury items on credit and were ultimately unable to support their lifestyle. Some investors also borrowed money to buy stocks on margin, initially paying as little as 10 percent of the face value in the hopes of paying off these debts as the stock's value increased. Speculation of this kind led to inflated stock prices, whose values could not be maintained, and on October 29, 1929, the bubble burst. The stock market fell in value by $14 billion in a single day. Industrial production quickly fell by half, and the unemployment rate reached a devastating 25 percent by 1932.

The events on Wall Street and the pain felt by the nation's industrial sector initially meant very little to the inhabitants of the largely rural Southern United States. In 1929, Southerners were already suffering from the decline in agricultural prices that followed the end of World War I as international production outpaced the demand for agricultural goods. Natural disasters in the form of an infestation of boll weevils, which plagued the cotton-producing South, and the

African American farmer plowing, Alabama, June 1936. Photo by Dorothea Lange for U.S. Farm Security Administration. (Library of Congress)

devastating Mississippi River flood of 1927 brought severe damage to the Southern economy well before the onslaught of the nationwide depression.

The federal government dramatically increased its role in regulating the economy and in providing for the needs of its citizens during this era. After his election in 1932, Roosevelt set out to provide needy Americans with the "New Deal" he had promised in his campaign. These government programs were designed to regulate businesses and agriculture, shore up the nation's banking system, provide relief to the needy, and reduce unemployment. In theory, many of these programs prohibited discrimination on the basis of race, but in reality, such discrimination continued to occur.

Throughout the country, African Americans were disproportionately impacted by the Great Depression. They were typically the last hired and the first fired. During the height of the Depression, half of black workers were unemployed. Like other workers, African Americans became increasingly radicalized in response to dire economic need and joined labor unions, such as the biracial Southern Tenant Farmers'

Union founded in Arkansas in 1934, in an attempt to protect their economic interests.

Blacks also suffered disproportionately as they were less likely than needy whites to receive aid—in the form either of payments or of food subsidies. Particularly in the South, blacks who did receive relief typically received less money and food than whites. This was due to the prevailing belief that African Americans were prone to laziness and would not work if given too much assistance. To compound matters, prominent Southern whites generally controlled relief funds and supplies, even those donated by the Red Cross, and were able to use their control over these resources to influence black behavior.

One of the federal programs that most dramatically impacted the South was the Agricultural Adjustment Act. Passed in 1933, this bill was designed to increase agricultural prices by limiting production by means of government subsidies to farmers. Southern plantation owners enthusiastically participated in the program, but for the most part, they refused to share New Deal monies with the sharecroppers and tenant farmers who worked on their land. Furthermore, as large landowners began to decrease production, they began to evict unneeded farm workers from the land. The displacement of the agricultural workforce accelerated in the following decades as landowners used federal funds to mechanize agricultural production, further reducing their dependence on individual laborers.

Both black and white farm laborers began to migrate to cities in search of other kinds of work, and many African Americans in particular set their sights on the North. Blacks had begun migrating northward in large numbers to take advantage of opportunities in manufacturing as the stream of European immigrants dried up during World War I. Although many waited out the lean years of the Great Depression in the South, African Americans began migrating again in great numbers as the country mobilized in preparation for World War II. In the process, African Americans went from residing primarily in rural areas of the South to becoming a predominantly urban population that resided in increasing numbers in the North.

As the 1930s progressed, the South continued to lag behind other parts of the nation on the road to economic recovery. The South failed to measure up in terms of per capita income. The region's inhabitants also suffered from a lack of access to adequate health care and a lackluster commitment to providing quality public education for all Southerners. In 1938, Roosevelt soberly labeled the region "the nation's No. 1 economic problem."

Recovery did come to the nation after the United States entered World War II and the effort to prepare for war jump-started the economy. The South began increasingly to industrialize, and machinery such as tractors and mechanical cotton pickers continued to displace laborers as the dramatic transformation in the Southern economy that began in earnest during the lean years of the Great Depression continued.

JENNIFER JENSEN WALLACH

See also
Works Progress Administration (WPA)

Further Reading:
McElvaine, Robert S. *The Great Depression: America, 1929–1941.* New York: Crown, 1984.
Shlaes, Amity. *The Forgotten Man: A New History of the Great Depression.* New York: HarperCollins, 2007.

Great Migration, The

After the broken promises of Reconstruction, African Americans looked to the North as a place where their dreams could be fulfilled. From towns and farms they poured into Northern cities in search of the American Dream. The apex of this Diaspora lasted from 1915–1920, and is referred to as the Great Migration.

In a matter of 10 years, 1910–1920, 1 million blacks migrated out of the South and into Northern, industrialized cities. Most notably, Detroit witnessed an astounding 611 percent increase in its black population. The cities of Cleveland, Ohio (307 percent increase); Chicago, Illinois (148 percent increase); New York (66 percent increase); Indianapolis, Indiana (59 percent increase); and Pittsburgh, Pennsylvania (47 percent increase) also experienced significant growth resulting from this mass exodus out of the South. In raw numbers, however, Chicago experienced the greatest growth, as over 65,000 new Southern black migrants moved to the city; New York expanded by 61,000, and Detroit grew by 36,000.

Although the Great Migration stands as the most significant black exodus out of the South, it was not the first.

From 1862–1900, for instance, groups of disgruntled and downtrodden blacks started moving into the northern and western regions of America. This initial exodus began as a result of the Civil War (1861–1865), the Emancipation Proclamation (1863), and the dismal failure of Reconstruction (1865–1877). As the outlook of a better future quickly faded, thousands of blacks headed toward states such as Kansas, Pennsylvania, Ohio, and New York.

From 1890–1910, a second, smaller migration had begun. This time, however, Southern blacks remained south of the Mason-Dixon Line, moving into Southern industrial towns and cites, west to Texas and Oklahoma where wages were rumored to be higher, and to the burgeoning iron and coal mines of Alabama, Tennessee, and Georgia.

Although both of these early migrations were relatively small in scope and significance, white Southerners, who had grown accustomed to cheap labor, incredulously viewed these black efforts toward social, political, and economic betterment. Interestingly, many black leaders were also unsupportive. In 1879, Frederick Douglass, the nation's foremost black leader, urged Southern blacks to remain home and work through their problems.

Two decades later, Booker T. Washington similarly exhorted Southern blacks to "Cast down their buckets where they are" (Washington, 1901). Even Robert S. Abbott, staunch supporter of the Great Migration and owner and editor of the *Chicago Defender*, was telling Southern blacks as late as 1915 "to stick to the farm" (January 16 and 23, 1915).

By 1915, however, many Southern blacks had enough of the farm and of the South. With their continued oppression at home and the growing need for industrial labor in the North, African Americans, in unprecedented numbers, set out in search of the Northern Promised Land.

The most obvious factors that contributed to the migration were the racist and economic conditions of the South. Although Reconstruction idealistically should have ameliorated the devastation left in the wake of the Civil War, its impact on blacks was barely detectable. With the Compromise of 1877 that repealed most of the postwar recovery programs, Southern whites soon regained their old political and economic power, leaving many blacks penniless and homeless.

Perhaps the most immediate obstacle that many blacks faced during this period was the physical destruction caused by the Civil War. Throughout the South, entire towns and cities were looted and burned to the ground, and with them, the farms, factories, stores, warehouses, machine shops, and mills that once employed their inhabitants.

For the few blacks who owned farm land, other troubles awaited. From 1913 to 1915, black and white farmers suffered from a severe agricultural depression. On the heels of this disaster, farmers faced the devastation of the boll weevil on their cotton crops. Hit hard by both, many black farmers were forced to give up their land and become tenant farmers or sharecroppers for white landowners. Blacks found themselves, once again, financially dependent on Southern whites, and, in many cases, more impoverished than before.

Along with such economic obstacles, many Southern blacks were also confronted with an equally corrupt criminal justice and peonage system. Once arrested, African Americans were rented out to white landowners in need of cheap labor. When white landowners needed more labor, compensated local law enforcement simply found more bogus reasons to arrest more blacks. As many historians have observed, there was little difference between the postwar peonage system and prewar slavery. Blacks were still being sold and whites were still profiting from their sweat and labor.

There were also Jim Crow laws passed throughout the South and designed to impede black advancement. These laws were specifically structured to restrict the rights of blacks and to relegate them to a subordinate status in virtually all aspects of life. In the realms of education, legal justice, religion, democracy, and the inalienable right to pursue happiness, Southern blacks had no rights that whites were obligated to respect.

Serving to augment this postwar legal system, violence and lynching increased throughout the South as membership in the Ku Klux Klan (KKK) rose to over 5 million. White-on-black violent crimes reached an all-time national high, with the Southern states of Alabama (248 fatalities), Mississippi (323 fatalities), and Georgia (374 fatalities) leading the list of vigilante lynching. It should come as no surprise that blacks in these three states also comprised a disproportionate share of Southern migrants.

In contrast to the racially oppressive life in the South, the industrial North during the second decade of the 20th century promised downtrodden blacks a far brighter social, legal, and financial future. In 1914, World War I erupted in Europe. By 1915, the United States began preparing for combat through a substantial military buildup. With the new and growing need for factory workers, an exigency intensified by the decline of foreign immigration because of the war in Europe, blacks had their first real opportunity to enter industry in sizable numbers.

In April 1917, Congress, acting on President Woodrow Wilson's call, declared war against Germany. While hundreds of thousands of white American men prepared for combat, black Americans were told that they did not have the right to fight in the armed services. Consequently, white men left Northern cities and went to Europe to fight. At the same time, black Americans were recruited to Northern cities to help fill the manufacturing voids left vacant by their white counterparts.

As important as these push-and-pull forces were to the Great Migration, they would not have been enough in and of themselves to create a mass exodus if there were not persuasive voices both detailing the striking contrasts between the two regions and overtly encouraging migration. There were, for instance, labor agents from every major industrial city sent to the South in search of hardworking manual laborers. These agents would often pay for a migrant's passage north, procure their living quarters, and promise countless opportunities for financial and social betterment.

Confirming such promises, many neighbors and family members who had previously left the South wrote home to extol the many wonders of the North. Entire Southern communities would hear the letters from contented migrants about the opportunities that awaited blacks in the North, the ease of obtaining employment, unprecedented social justice, and the magic of big-city life.

These first-person narratives and testimonies, as effective as they were in stimulating migration, reached a relatively small and localized populace. It was the black press, however, that had the power to spread the word about the advantages of the North to millions of black Southerners every week. And no newspaper was more dedicated to the migration cause than the *Chicago Defender*. Along with being the most popular black newspaper in the United States, it also published more stories more often on the oppressive South, the promises of the North, and the immediate need for migration. Unflinching, it refused to succumb to calls from both blacks and whites for moderation.

Although life in the North may not have been everything that it was promised to be, it was still a significantly better place to live for most blacks than Dixie. According to 1919 U.S. Department of Labor findings, for example, blacks in Chicago were being paid four to six times more than blacks in the South for comparable work. Many migrants also found themselves joyfully overwhelmed by the social nightlife of the big city. For the first time, many of these newly arriving rural migrants encountered a vibrant black community with black-owned nightclubs, movie theaters, restaurants, dance halls, saloons, and retail shops selling a myriad of imaginable, and many unimaginable, luxury items.

Life in the North, unfortunately, was not solely composed of high wages, materialistic consumption, and exciting nightlife. Although the North generally provided a better standard of living than the South, it was still scarred with inequalities. Many blacks left the South believing that the stench of racism would be left behind. It would not be long, however, before they realized that bigotry knows no boundaries. Many Northern whites, who grew accustomed to their racially homogenized life, fiercely resisted black migrants using public beaches, swimming pools, playgrounds, libraries, restaurants, hotels, and movie theaters in the white sections of Northern cities.

The workplace was also marked with racial inequalities. Although it is true that blacks received higher wages than they had in the South, it is also true that blacks made less than their Northern white counterparts. In fact, blacks, many of whom were from families that had been part of the American experience for generations, made less than newly arriving, non-English-speaking immigrants from Germany, Poland, Italy, and Russia. This general attitude of white workers was illustrated by the policies of most industrial labor unions that refused membership and its subsequent benefits to all blacks.

As a result of poor wages and Northern racism, blacks were forced to locate in what are now commonly referred to as the ghettos of the Northeast and Midwest (e.g., Harlem; the Southside of Chicago; Gary, Indiana; East St. Louis, Illinois; and a myriad of other segregated enclaves in the cities of Philadelphia, Pennsylvania; Baltimore, Maryland; Camden, New Jersey; Washington, D.C.; and Boston, Massachusetts). At first, this de facto segregation helped migrants obtain a sense of community, security, and culture. It was not long,

however, before the problems of overcrowding, poor conditions, crime, disease, and high rent began to outweigh the positive aspects of these black communities. Consequently, blacks were forced to spread into outlying areas designed for Whites Only. With the threat of decreasing property values and the fear of race mixing, whites passed restrictive covenants that legally segregated the races and stopped black expansion.

When legal means of housing segregation failed, Northern racists reverted to the use of violence, bombing being the technique of choice. Unfortunately, bombings motivated by housing disputes were not the only violence blacks encountered in the North. As more African Americans migrated into Northern cities, homicides and assaults, although not as prevalent as in the South, became a growing reality. Along with the threat of isolated violence, blacks in most cities also had to tolerate the Northern equivalent of the KKK—the athletic clubs. The members of these white supremacy clubs were mainly comprised of white teenage boys, whose primary athletic outlet was bullying and assaulting newly arriving migrants. Clubs such as Ragen's Colts, the Hamburgers, Our Flag, and the Sparklers made it their mission to affirm white power in a rapidly changing and diverse North.

This ever-growing violence culminated in the Red Summer Race Riots of 1919, when a series of race riots spread throughout the United States. Fueled by returning soldiers anxious to reaffirm the prewar/premigration caste system, blacks were painfully reminded that although the Civil War had been won by the North, the struggle for equality and justice was far from over.

ALAN D. DeSANTIS

See also
Great Retreat; Jim Crow Laws; Labor Movement, Racism in; Labor Unions

Further Reading:
DeSantis, Alan D. "Selling the American Dream Myth to Black Southerners: The *Chicago Defender* and the Great Migration of 1915–1919." *Western Journal of Communication* 62, no. 4 (1998): 474–511.

Drake, St. Clair, and Horace R. Cayton. *Black Metropolis: A Study of Negro Life in a Northern City*. New York: Harcourt, Brace & World, 1970, 1962, 1945.

Ginzburg, Ralph. *100 Years of Lynchings*. New York: Lancer Books, 1969.

Goodwin, Marvin E. *Black Migration in America From 1915– 1960*. Lewistown, NY: Edwin Mellen Press, 1990.

Griffin, Farah Jasmine. *"Who Set You Flowin'?" The African American Migration Narrative*. New York: Oxford University Press, 1995.

Grossman, James R. *Land of Hope: Chicago, Black Southerners, and the Great Migration*. Chicago: University of Chicago Press, 1989.

Henri, Florette. *Black Migration: Movement North 1900–1920*. New York: Doubleday Anchor Books, 1975.

Lemann, Nicholas. *The Promised Land: The Great Migration and How It Changed America*. New York: Vintage Books, 1991.

Trotter, Joe William, Jr., ed. *The Great Migration in Historical Perspective: New Dimensions of Race, Class, & Gender*. Bloomington: Indiana University Press, 1991.

Washington, Booker T. *Up from Slavery*. New York: Doubleday, Page & Co., 1901.

Great Retreat

In the antiracist euphoria of Reconstruction, African Americans moved almost everywhere across America. By 1890, blacks were living and working in northeast Pennsylvania river valleys, in every Indiana county save one, deep in the north woods of Wisconsin, and in every county of Montana and California. In that year, the proportion of black Illinoisans living in Cook County, which included the city of Chicago, 26 percent, was less than that for whites, 31 percent.

Then, from 1890 to the 1930s, the nadir of the Negro set in, triggered by three developments: the massacre of Wounded Knee, ending American Indian independence; the new Mississippi constitution, which removed African Americans from citizenship yet drew no protest from the federal government; and the failure of the U.S. Senate to pass the Federal Elections Bill. At that point, the Republican Party largely abandoned its commitment to civil rights.

Throughout the traditional South, whites copied Mississippi by passing laws that took away the voting and citizenship rights of African Americans. Elsewhere, whites took a different tack. White opposition in town after town, county after county—even whole regions—drove out African Americans. Whites in Liberty, Oregon (now part of Salem), for example, ordered their blacks to leave in 1893. Caucasians used various methods, including social and economic boycotts, making schooling difficult or impossible for black children, and acts by local government such as seizure of black homes by eminent domain. Violence and threat of violence played a key role. Residents in many communities indulged in little race riots that until now have been lost to history. In Anna, Illinois, after a nearby lynching of an African American in 1909, whites rioted and forced out Anna's African Americans. Nearby Pinckneyville followed suit probably in 1928. Harrison, Arkansas, required two riots before the job was done—in 1905 and 1909. White workers in Austin, Minnesota, repeatedly drove out African Americans in the 1920s and 1930s. Other towns that drove out their black populations violently include Myakka City, Florida; Spruce Pine, North Carolina; Wehrum, Pennsylvania; Ravenna, Kentucky; Greensburg, Indiana; St. Genevieve, Missouri; North Platte, Nebraska; Murray, Utah; and many others. Some of these mini-riots in turn spurred whites in nearby smaller towns to have their own, thus provoking little waves of expulsions. White residents of Vienna, Illinois, set fire to the homes in its black neighborhood as late as 1954.

Many African Americans wound up in black neighborhoods in larger Northern cities. This Great Retreat went on from 1890 at least to 1940, with isolated retreats occurring as recently as 1954. In its wake, the Great Retreat left a new geography of race in the United States. From southern Florida to northwestern Washington state, the nation is dotted with thousands of all-white sundown towns that are, or were until recently, all white on purpose.

The Great Retreat of African Americans was preceded by a dress rehearsal in the West, from the mid-1870s to about 1920, as whites forced Chinese Americans from many towns and entire counties. Chinese fled from almost every county in Wyoming and from at least 40 towns in California. Their retreat from Idaho was especially striking: in 1870, Chinese made up 24 percent of that territory's population, but by 1920, fewer than 600 remained, only 1 percent. Most communities that expelled Chinese Americans also banned African Americans. This "Chinese Retreat" resulted in the concentration of that minority in Chinatowns in Seattle, San Francisco, Los Angeles, and a few other cities.

The Great Retreat was even more striking. Many counties drove out their black populations, usually following the lead of their county seats. In 1902, for example, Decatur, county seat of Adams County in northeastern Indiana, drove out its small black population. By 1920, all of Adams County had not a single African American. By 1930, even though many more African Americans now lived in the state, six Indiana counties had no blacks, while another 14 counties had fewer than 10. Sometimes the countywide "cleansing" process took decades. In 1906, a white mob in Greensburg, seat of Decatur County, 50 miles southeast of Indianapolis, rioted, tried to lynch a black prisoner, failed, and beat other African Americans. Black residents fled the town, but whites did not force them from the county; as late as 1920, the census counted 51 African Americans in Decatur County, but whites continued to intimidate them. At some point around World War II, Greensburg residents put up a typical sundown town sign that read, "Nigger, don't let the sun set on your back in Greensburg," only instead of "Greensburg," it read "Decatur County," according to a long-time resident. By 1960, not one African American remained in the county.

County and town statistics paint a dismal picture across the United States. Eleven counties in Montana had no blacks by 1930, and the proportion African Americans were of that state's population fell from 1.1 percent in 1890 to 0.2 percent. In the Upper Peninsula of Michigan (UP), there were more than 400 African Americans in 1890. By 1930, although its white population had increased by 75 percent, the UP was home to only 331 African Americans, 180 of whom were inmates of the Marquette State Prison. Ironwood, the largest town in the western part of the peninsula, grew so racist that as recently as the 1960s, porters on passenger trains "experienced enough harassment . . . that they wouldn't step onto the depot platform while the train was in the station," in the words of the daughter of a track inspector for the Chicago & Northwestern Rail Road. While Oregon's white population tripled in the four decades between 1890 and 1930, its black population remained constant, and 70 percent of them wound up in Portland, having been banned from Ashland, Grants Pass, Medford, Eugene, Tillamook, and other Oregon towns and cities.

The Great Retreat left large areas of the United States virtually barren of African Americans. Among these are the Ozarks, the Cumberlands, a thick band of sundown counties and towns on both sides of the Iowa-Missouri border, almost every town and city along the Illinois River except Peoria, most of western Oregon, a 4,000-square-mile area southwest of Fort Worth, Texas, and a V-shaped area encompassing more than six counties from Forsyth County, Georgia, north to the Tennessee line. None of these subregions became so white by accident. Consider the Ozarks. In 1890, Arkansas had no county without African Americans, and only one with fewer than 10. By 1930, three counties had none, and another eight had fewer than 10, all in the Ozarks. All 11 were probably sundown counties; six are confirmed. Polk County drove out its African Americans in 1901, for example; Boone (Harrison) in 1905 and 1909. By 1923, William Pickens saw sundown signs across the Ozarks.

The Great Retreat antedated and channeled the flows of the Great Migration. Like the concentration of Chinese Americans in big-city Chinatowns, the Great Retreat resulted in such huge black ghettoes as Harlem, Cleveland's Hough, the South Side of Chicago, and Watts in Los Angeles. The proportion of black Illinoisans living in Cook County, 26 percent in 1890, had risen to 76 percent by 1940, while among nonblacks, just 50 percent did so. Moreover, African Americans did not live across Chicago, but were concentrated in just two areas. At the same time that independent towns and counties were closing themselves to African Americans, so were many suburbs and city neighborhoods. The Index of Dissimilarity, "D," used by social scientists to measure how segregated a city or metropolitan area is, ranges from 0 to 100. When D = 0, integration is perfect: every census tract has the same racial composition. A D of 100 represents complete apartheid: not one black in any white area, not one white in any black area. In 1860, the average Northern city had a D of 45.7—only moderately segregated. Southern cities were even less segregated spatially, with an average D of 29.0. After 1890, hostility ranging from shunning to violence forced the involuntary retrenchment of African Americans from across many parts of the city to concentration in inner-city ghettoes—an intracity manifestation of the Great Retreat. Already by 1910, Northern cities averaged 59.2 and Southern cities 38.3. By 1940, at the end of the Great Retreat, Northern cities averaged 89.2, Southern cities 81.0. These are astonishing levels of segregation.

The retreat can also be seen in suburban areas. Most suburbs formed between 1900 and 1970. In many places—across the South, of course, but also as far north as Edina, Minnesota, and Dearborn, Michigan—developers had to get rid of African Americans, who already lived where the suburbs were going in, to create the white communities.

Americans until recently took this for granted. In Minnesota, a Quaker village already existed where Edina was to be built. Quakers had welcomed African Americans after the Civil War, and many black families lived among them. "Over the ensuing decades," according to Edina historian Deborah Morse-Kahn, African Americans "became very involved in community life—very often as leaders." But after World War I, developers attached to all deeds for new homes racial covenants like this one:

> No lot shall ever be sold, conveyed, leased, or rented to any person other than one of the white or Caucasian race, nor shall any lot ever be used or occupied by any person other than one of the white or Caucasian race, except such as may be serving as domestics for the owner or tenant of said lot.

Before Dearborn incorporated, among the 2,300 people living in Dearborn township in 1870 were 30 African Americans. Incorporated Dearborn's 2,470 residents in 1920 included just one African American. And so it went, from Long Island to the suburbs of Los Angeles.

As with the Chinese retreat, knowledge of the Great Retreat was lost. Somehow, Americans came to think it "only natural" that mostly rural black Southerners would wind up concentrated in the inner cities of America's largest metropolitan areas. Conversely, it seemed "only natural" that affluent stock brokers would subject themselves to a 70-minute commute from all-white enclaves in Connecticut and New Jersey to Wall Street.

African Americans never passively accepted the Great Retreat. Better records of racial incidents exist for Wyandotte, Michigan, than for any other community, owing to local historian Edwina M. DeWindt. She collected accounts of attempt after attempt by black workers and families to enter Wyandotte, then an independent city, now a suburb of Detroit. Again and again, whites drove them out. After 1968, when Congress passed what is commonly called the "Fair Housing Act," African Americans met more success. Wyandotte's black population rose from 0.04 percent in 1970 to 0.52 percent in 2000. Wyandotte's experience is fairly general. Since 1970, African Americans have often encountered civility and sometimes even goodwill as they work to reverse the Great Retreat.

JAMES W. LOEWEN

See also
Great Migration; Jim Crow Laws

Further Reading:
Blocker, Jack S. *A Little More Freedom: African Americans Enter the Urban Midwest, 1860–1930*. Columbus: Ohio State University Press, 2008.
Jaspin, Elliot. *Buried in the Bitter Waters*. New York: Basic Books, 2007.
Loewen, James W. *Sundown Towns*. New York: New Press, 2005.
Newman, Dorothy K., et al. *Protest, Politics, and Prosperity*. New York: Pantheon, 1978, 144.
Pfaelzer, Jean. *Driven Out*. New York: Random House, 2007.
Pickens, William. "Arkansas—A Study in Suppression." Reprinted in *These "Colored" United States: African American Essays from the 1920s*, edited by Tom Lutz and Susanna Ashton, 34–35. New Brunswick, NJ: Rutgers University Press, 1996.

Greensboro Four

In the mid-1950s, many people described Greensboro, North Carolina, as a unique place because it was seen as a symbol of racial reforms in the New South. However, the city was not different from other places in America where Jim Crow laws were enforced by adherents of racial segregation in public locations such as restaurants, dance halls, shops, cinema halls, schools, hospitals, and other public facilities. From the 1940s through the 1960s, as enforcement of Jim Crow laws intensified, black people were constantly kept from having the same access to public facilities as whites.

Jim Crow laws were enforced directly and indirectly all over America, but these race-based practices had a potent presence in the South. In Greensboro, black and white residents did not see Jim Crow laws the same way. For instance, many whites who were privileged by the institution of the racist laws wanted segregation to continue without any legal or social interruption. White merchants enforced the laws by enforcing segregated lunch counters, posting "White Only" and "Black Only" signs in public locations, while white city officials took a neutral position. Black people, on the other hand, wanted an immediate end to the racist tradition.

Four teenagers from North Carolina, David Richmond, Ezell Blair, Joseph McNeil, and Franklin McCain, lived most of their life in Greensboro, where they were members of the National Association for the Advancement of Colored People (NAACP) Youth Wing in North Carolina during their high school days. The Greensboro Four, as they became known, witnessed most of these discriminatory practices in their community, especially when they traveled in public buses and visited public places within and outside Greensboro. Through their participation in the NAACP Youth Wing, they became well informed about the effects of Jim Crow laws on their lives, their family, and the black community. Therefore, they decided to take action when they were freshmen at North Carolina Agricultural College (now North Carolina Agricultural University and Technical State University).

Although some African Americans made efforts to desegregate lunch counters elsewhere in the country prior to this time, they were not successful. On February 1, 1960, the four college students started their journey to change how blacks and whites related to each other in public places. There were several places to challenge Jim Crow laws, but they chose Woolworth's, a national chain. The idea was that the success of their approach could create similar demonstrations, desegregating Woolworth's stores across the country. According to Franklin McCain, Jim Crow laws in Woolworth's stores in Greensboro allowed black customers to purchase merchandise, but they could not eat with white customers sitting by the counters. Also, blacks could eat while standing, and work as cooks, but they could not be employed as waitresses.

The Greensboro Four were successful in the sit-in movements partly because they employed nonviolent strategies. They were influenced largely by Mahatma Gandhi's nonviolent approach and by the examples that were laid down by Martin Luther King, Jr. and his followers. Also, the Greensboro Four were mindful of other freedom struggles in Africa, Asia, and other parts of the world that fought against different forms of white oppression. For Joseph McNeil, the public protest was racially uplifting and a payment for manhood. To confront Jim Crow laws in a way that would generate white support and sympathy, the Greensboro Four demanded that other students who supported their movement for change adhered to a dress code—dress in suits and ties. The February 1, 1960, Greensboro movement continued for several months and drew more people from the community and nearby colleges such as Bennett College, Greensboro

Women's College (now the University of North Carolina at Greensboro), and several others. As these and many more students from Duke University, Wake Forest University, and several other colleges in the country targeted other desegregated facilities, Jim Crow laws started crumbling.

The Greensboro Four also gained support from the media as news of the sit-ins rippled across various towns and cities in America. Although the white media criticized the Greensboro Four for creating chaos in public facilities, black newspapers and liberal journalists gave their support to the students' movement. During this tumultuous period, other issues such as World War II and the Cold War between the 1940s and the 1960s created more problems for the U.S. government as it attempted to spread democracy in Europe and other parts of the world. These international events offered an opportunity for enemies of the United States to criticize the government for its double standards by attacking Jim Crow laws. The Greensboro Four continued their campaigns for desegregating lunch counters until July 26, 1960, when the Woolworth's store in Greensboro finally pulled down the White Only and Black Only signs. Although other merchants resisted desegregation for a fairly long time, Jim Crow laws collapsed around downtown Greensboro and other business centers in the area.

The grassroots student mobilizations triggered by Richmond, Blair, McNeil, and McCain did more than facilitate the demise of Jim Crow laws in Greensboro. Locally, in 1961 and 1962, Greensboro was chosen as the site for the Congress of Racial Equality and for further attempts to open other desegregated public facilities to blacks all over America. Nationally, the most far-reaching results of the confrontational tactics inspired by the Greensboro Four during the sit-ins contributed to the 1963 March in Washington, the Civil Rights Act of 1964, and the passage of the Voting Rights Act in 1965.

KWAME ESSIEN

See also

Civil Rights Movement; *Plessy v. Ferguson* (1896). Document: *Plessy v. Ferguson* (1896)

Further Reading:

Carson, Clayborne. *In Struggle: SNCC and Black Awakenings of 1960.* Cambridge, MA: Harvard University Press, 1981.
Chafe, William. *Greensboro Sit-Ins.* New York: Oxford University Press, 1979.

Chafe, William. *Civilities and Civil Rights*. New York: Oxford University Press, 1980.

Wolff, Miles. *Lunch at the 5 & 10*. Chicago: Ivan R. Dee, 1990.

Greensburg (Indiana) Riot of 1906

The Greensburg, Indiana, riot of April 1906 was a precursor to the more deadly and destructive race riots that would occur in Northern industrial cities during the period from 1907 to 1919 as whites reacted to the influx of blacks from the South and to the increased economic, social, and civic competition that they represented.

Indiana was one of the five states carved out of the Northwest Territory, where the 1787 Northwest Ordinance prohibited slavery. The institution was also outlawed in Indiana by the 1816 state constitution. However, because the state bordered on slave-holding Kentucky to the south, Indiana was attractive to escaping slaves. Thus, antiblack feeling in the state was extremely strong and African Americans in Indiana faced deep-seated hatred and discrimination. They could not serve in the militia, vote, enter public schools, or testify in court. Like neighboring Ohio, Indiana required blacks to post a $500 bond to secure their good behavior. Those who could not post the bond could be sold to the highest bidder for a period of six months. Yet blacks continued to move into the state, often settling near Quaker communities that were more tolerant of blacks and active in the abolitionist movement, until 1851 when the Indiana legislature encouraged blacks to emigrate and began fining whites who hired blacks. During the Civil War, conditions for free blacks in Indiana worsened, and many of them left the state for Canada.

Blacks who stayed in the state developed their own communities, building schools, businesses, and churches; however, strict segregation remained in force into the early 20th century. By 1900, only 57,000 blacks lived in Indiana, where they comprised just 2.28 percent of the state's population. Black residents were periodically run out of towns in which they had been long settled, and were prohibited from stopping in many towns for even a short period of time. Blacks who dared to flout the rules were often visited by the men in the community, who used intimidation to encourage them to leave. One such community was Greensburg.

Located about 45 miles southeast of Indianapolis, Greensburg in 1906 was a small, prosperous town with a rural flavor, the quaint values of an earlier age, and a population of less than 8,000. A small number of blacks had lived in the city for years. They were known as the better kind of blacks, who were hardworking, self-respecting, and good citizens. They maintained their own separate society, lived in nice homes, and supported a church and a full calendar of social activities. Some of them worked in the local mill. The first black graduate of the local school became an instructor at Hampton Institute. In spite of this, blacks generally were not welcome in Greensburg; indeed, in 1902, blacks living in the city had been forced to flee for their lives.

As the city modernized, a railroad was built to serve it. The efforts required hundreds of workers, so unskilled black laborers from the South were imported. After the railroad and depot were completed, a number of them remained in Greensburg. They lived in substandard, segregated housing and found it difficult to find steady work. Moreover, the mayor of the city owed his office to businessmen who were in the tavern and liquor trades; he recognized it was to his advantage to ignore the enforcement of various vice and liquor laws. Thus, a saloon was allowed to exist in the black section of Greensburg, and it attracted the idle, the unemployed, and a fair amount of trouble and criminal activity, including a murder in 1905, the year before the riot. Citizens in the city protested, but to no avail. Thus, an atmosphere of lawlessness, introduced by white citizens, was not only permitted, but encouraged in the black portion of Greensburg.

In early April 1906, a black laborer named Green, who had been brought up from the South to work on the railroad and who was known to be mentally impaired, allegedly raped a well-liked and highly respected white widow for whom he had been performing odd jobs. After the rape, he was quickly apprehended, tried, and convicted. Several weeks later, whites in the town were still seething over the incident. On April 30, a crowd of white men and boys tried to take Green from the jail, but were held off by law enforcement officials. They then went on a rampage in the black section of Greensburg, shooting and torching homes, destroying businesses, and beating blacks at random.

Many blacks were driven out of town, never to return. The riot was quickly contained, and although no one was killed, there were thousands of dollars in damages and a number of injuries. No one was ever arrested or tried for participating in the riots.

MARILYN K. HOWARD

See also

Great Migration; Jim Crow Laws; National Association for the Advancement of Colored People (NAACP); Rape As Provocation for Lynching; Race Riots in America. Documents: The Report on the Memphis Riots of May 1866 (July 25, 1866); Account of the Riots in East St. Louis, Illinois (July 1917); The Cook County Coroner's Report Regarding the 1919 Chicago Race Riots (1919); A Southern Black Woman's Letter Regarding the Recent Riots in Chicago and Washington (November 1919); The Final Report of the Grand Jury on the Tulsa Race Riot (June 25, 1921); Testimony from *Laney v. United States* Describing Events during the Washington, D.C., Riot of July 1919 (December 3, 1923); The Governor's Commission Report on the Watts Riots (December 1965); Cyrus R. Vance's Report on the Riots in Detroit (July-August 1967); The Reports of the Oklahoma Commission to Study the Tulsa Race Riot of 1921 (2000-2001); The Draft Report of the 1898 Wilmington Race Riot Commission (December 2005)

Further Reading:

Baker, Ray Stannard. *Following the Color Line: An Account of Negro Citizenship in the American Democracy*. Williamstown, MA: Corner House, 1973.

Du Bois, W.E.B. *The Souls of Black Folk*. New York: Library of America, 1903.

Loewen, James W. *Sundown Towns: A Hidden Dimension of Segregation in America*. New York: New Press, 2005.

Marks, Carole. *Farewell—We're Good and Gone: The Great Black Migration*. Bloomington: Indiana University Press, 1989.

Greenwood Community (Tulsa, Oklahoma)

Situated in the northeastern part of Tulsa, Oklahoma, the Greenwood community developed into a thriving black business and residential district during the first two decades of the 20th century. As Tulsa grew during the oil boom of the early 1900s, Greenwood prospered as well. Prevented from patronizing stores in the white section of town, black Tulsans developed their own enterprises in Greenwood instead. Its main street, Greenwood Avenue, became known popularly as the black Wall Street. In June 1921, fueled by resentment of black gains and aspirations, a white mob of Tulsans leveled 35 blocks of the black community in a race riot precipitated by false allegations of an attack on a white woman in downtown Tulsa by a black man. Although some of the area recovered after the destruction, Greenwood never regained the prominence it enjoyed during its heyday.

Greenwood began attracting black residents when a group of African Americans purchased land there around 1905. As the area lured more people, black Tulsans soon enjoyed their own newspaper, a barber, two doctors, and three grocers. By 1910, blacks comprised 10 percent of Tulsa's inhabitants, and in the next few years, the city had a black police officer and several new black-owned businesses along Greenwood Avenue. At the time of the riot, Tulsa's black population had expanded to 11,000, with around 8,000 living in Greenwood itself. Greenwood's vibrant streets at this time also held two schools, 13 churches, three fraternal organizations, a hospital, two newspapers, two theaters, and a public library. On Greenwood's side streets, Tulsans could find other types of successful businesses—prostitution houses and speakeasies, where jazz blared and alcohol flowed freely.

On the morning of May 30, 1921, Dick Rowland, a black shoe shiner, stepped into an elevator in downtown Tulsa operated by a young white woman named Sarah Page. While the police attempted to piece together the story of what happened next, Tulsans took the matters into their own hands. An angry white crowd—fed by newspapers that typically used words such as *Little Africa* and *Niggertown* to depict Greenwood, and manned by a flourishing local chapter of the Ku Klux Klan—began to congregate in front of the courthouse, where authorities had detained Rowland. When a group of men from Greenwood converged on the building to protect the young man, a scuffle ensued, a shot was fired, and chaos ensued. The white mob charged into the center of Greenwood, looting, burning, and attacking residents with abandon. Several hours later, the once bustling community lay in ruins. Death estimates ranged from 27 to more than 250. Property loss amounted to millions of dollars.

An initial investigation blamed the residents of Greenwood for inciting the crowd at the courthouse and for stressing equal rights. Like many of their counterparts, a number of black Tulsans had served in the military during World War I. Upon their return home, they asserted a new sense of purpose and a demand for equality. White Tulsans, like whites across the country, felt threatened by these measures. But no white Tulsans ever served prison time for the murders, destruction, and looting that took place in Greenwood. Not until some 75 years later would an official reckoning of the annihilation take place, when the Oklahoma state legislature established the 1921 Tulsa Race Riot Commission in 1997 to clarify what transpired and rectify some of the injustices that prevailed.

ANN V. COLLINS

See also

Race Riots in America; Tulsa (Oklahoma) Riot of 1921. Documents: The Report on the Memphis Riots of May 1866 (July 25, 1866); Account of the Riots in East St. Louis, Illinois (July 1917); The Cook County Coroner's Report Regarding the 1919 Chicago Race Riots (1919); A Southern Black Woman's Letter Regarding the Recent Riots in Chicago and Washington (November 1919); The Final Report of the Grand Jury on the Tulsa Race Riot (June 25, 1921); Testimony from *Laney v. United States* Describing Events during the Washington, D.C., Riot of July 1919 (December 3, 1923); The Governor's Commission Report on the Watts Riots (December 1965); Cyrus R. Vance's Report on the Riots in Detroit (July-August 1967); The Reports of the Oklahoma Commission to Study the Tulsa Race Riot of 1921 (2000-2001); The Draft Report of the 1898 Wilmington Race Riot Commission (December 2005)

Further Reading:

Brophy, Alfred L. *Reconstructing the Dreamland: The Tulsa Riot of 1921: Race Reparations, and Reconstruction.* Oxford: Oxford University Press, 2002.

Ellsworth, Scott. *Death in a Promised Land: The Tulsa Race Riot of 1921.* Baton Rouge: Louisiana State University Press, 1982.

Griffith, D. W. (1875–1948)

David Wark Griffith was the director of the controversial film *The Birth of a Nation*, a racist view of the Reconstruction period that is believed to have sparked a revival of the Ku Klux Klan in the 1920s.

Griffith was born in LaGrange, Kentucky, in 1875. His father was a Confederate Civil War veteran and Kentucky legislator, who died when Griffith was 10 years old, leaving the family in difficult financial circumstances. Eventually, Griffith dropped out of school to earn money to help support his family. He originally wanted to be a great playwright but turned to writing and acting in the film industry to pay the bills. In 1908, he began his film career with the Biograph Company as an actor and scenario writer. He is credited with introducing film techniques like the fade in, fade out, long shot, full shot, close-up, moving camera shot, and flashback. He also started United Artists in 1919 with Douglas Fairbanks, Mary Pickford, and Charles Chaplin.

In 1915, he created Hollywood's first feature-length film, *The Birth of a Nation*, which ran for over three hours on 12 reels. Because of its overt racism, *The Birth of a Nation* is also seen by many as the most controversial film in the history of cinema. It is also Hollywood's longest-running film and played in movie theaters well into the mid-20th century. The film arrived in theaters during a time of racial unrest in the South, where Jim Crow laws created an environment conducive to lynchings of African Americans and their unequal protection under the law.

The movie is also credited with promoting the resurgence of the Ku Klux Klan, which used the film to recruit members and promote their ideology of white supremacy. The Klan especially used the film in cities of the North and West where there was an increase of African Americans who had fled the terror of Jim Crow but who were met with resentment from whites when they began taking jobs in industry that were vacant due to a shortage of cheap Eastern European labor during World War I.

The National Association for the Advancement of Colored People, formed in 1910, publicly condemned the movie, which Griffith defended with the argument that it was not his intention to make a racist film. Many found it hard to buy his argument since the movie was based on Thomas Dixon's *The Clansman*, which espoused racist propaganda and called for the day the Klan would rise again and solve the race problem.

Griffith also incorporated scenes from an earlier Dixon novel called *The Leopard Spots: A Romance of the White Man's Burden, 1865–1900.* Griffith also used ideology about Reconstruction that he interpreted from Woodrow Wilson's

A film about the American Civil War and white domination by the Ku Klux Klan, *The Birth of a Nation* sparked major controversy across the United States when it was released in 1915. (Hulton Archive/Getty Images)

The History of the American People. Others in the black community condemned the movie. Entrepreneurs like Oscar Micheaux began to open small, black-owned movie companies to make movies that answered *The Birth of a Nation* and to address the racist imagery of African Americans in Hollywood films. Black intellectuals such as W.E.B. Du Bois and Booker T. Washington involved themselves in making the film *The Birth of the Race*, a response to Griffith's movie. They felt it was important for more African Americans to get into media production to combat racist imagery of African Americans in film.

On Thanksgiving night, 1915, in Atlanta, Georgia, approximately 25,000 Klansmen marched down Peachtree Avenue to celebrate the film's opening. The film, the first shown in the White House, was endorsed by President Woodrow Wilson. During the period from 1915 to 1919, there were at least 22 race riots. The summer of 1919 is called Red Summer because of all the people who were killed in race riots at that time. Militant black activity was hampered mainly due to the fact that blacks were not permitted in most movie theaters.

The Birth of a Nation was Griffith's most famous film. His subsequent films never made as much of a splash as this one did. The film set the framework for the image of blacks in films for many years to come and aided in maintaining the racist stereotypes that still exist in the United States today. Although demonstrations and protests were unsuccessful in getting the film completely banned, it was banned in eight states. In 1999, the National Board of the Director's Guild of America voted to rename the D. W. Griffith Award it had given since 1953 because they believed his film helped racial stereotypes flourish in the United States. After a 16-year absence from filmmaking, Griffith died in 1948 of a brain aneurysm.

CATHERINE ANYASO

See also

Birth of a Nation, The

Further Reading:

Barry, Iris, and D. W. Griffith. *D. W. Griffith, American Film Master.* New York: Museum of Modern Art, 1940.

Gurrero, Ed. *Framing Blackness: The African American Image in Film.* Philadelphia: Temple University Press, 1993.

Leab, Daniel J. *From Sambo to Superspade: The Black Experience in Motion Picture.* Boston: Houghton Mifflin, 1975.

Griggs, Sutton (1872–1933)

Sutton Elbert Griggs was one of the most prolific and militant writers of his generation. He wrote both fiction and nonfiction that described the plight of African Americans during the post-Reconstruction era. Jane Campbell, in her book *Mythic Black Fiction*, states that Griggs's fiction emerges out of a sense of "post-Reconstruction despair" (Campbell 1986: 42) and he strives to give voice to a black heroism in the face of devastating odds.

Griggs was born on June 19, 1872, in Chatfield, Texas. He was the oldest child of Alan Ralph and Emma Hodge Griggs. Alan Griggs was a Baptist minister and editor of the *Western Star*, a local African American newspaper. Sutton attended high school in Dallas, Texas; graduated from Bishop College in Marshall, Texas; and studied theology at the Richmond Theological Seminary (now the Virginia Union University) in Richmond, Virginia. Ordained in 1893, Griggs served as pastor of the First Baptist Church in Berkeley, Virginia, and was later minister of the First Baptist Church in East Nashville,

Tennessee; corresponding secretary of the National Baptist Convention; and pastor of the Tabernacle Baptist Church in Memphis, Tennessee. Griggs founded Orion Publishing Company (1901) and the Public Welfare League (1914) to assist African American businesses and other enterprises.

Griggs wrote an autobiography titled *The Story of My Struggles* (1914) and numerous religious and political pamphlets and tracts. But his five novels—*Imperium in Imperio* (1899), *Overshadowed* (1901), *Unfettered* (1902), *The Hindered Hand* (1905), and *Pointing the Way* (1908)—stirred the most controversy. These novels depicted the dilemma African Americans faced during the post-Reconstruction era of disenfranchisement, when Southern states enacted black codes and Jim Crow laws designed to enforce segregation and deprive, or disenfranchise, African Americans of the political, social, and economic gains they had won during Reconstruction (1866–1877). When laws and codes failed to fully restrict the constitutional rights of African Americans, white supremacist groups like the Ku Klux Klan terrorized black people with lynching and other forms of mob violence. The Wilmington (North Carolina) Riot of 1898 is but one example of violence by white mobs.

Although the repression of African Americans was a major theme in Griggs's writings, he also felt compelled to challenge the racial stereotypes of black people perpetrated in the writings of white Southern writers like Thomas Nelson Page and Thomas Dixon Jr. Page favored the plantation motif, which characterized the antebellum South as one the most beautiful civilizations the nation had ever known. He painted portraits of benevolent slave masters and contented, doting slaves. Similarly, in his books *Leopard's Spots* (1902) and *The Clansman* (1905), Dixon portrayed African Americans as degenerate, inferior, and bestial. *The Clansman*, a romantic history of the Ku Klux Klan, was made into a movie by D. W. Griffith called *The Birth of a Nation* (1915). Griggs used his literature to counteract these negative stereotypes and to paint a more positive, realistic portrait of black people.

He also used his novels and nonfiction to explore themes and solutions that would lead to a better way of life for black people in the United States. For example, *Imperium in Imperio* (Nation within a Nation) tells the story of African American militants who create a separate nation within the United States with a functioning government and a disciplined army whose sole purpose is to end the injustices black people have suffered in the United States. The leaders of this separate nation also intend to publicize to the world crimes committed against their race. Although Griggs would later reevaluate the militant stance he took at the beginning of his career, he continued to devote his life to the struggle for civil rights for African Americans.

JOHN G. HALL

See also

American Literature and Racism; Black Nationalism; Du Bois, W.E.B.; White Supremacy

Further Reading:

Bone, Robert A. *The Negro Novel in America*. New Haven, CT: Yale University Press, 1958.

Campbell, Jane. *Mythic Black Fiction: The Transformation of History*. Knoxville: University of Tennessee Press, 1986.

Fleming, Robert E. "Sutton E. Griggs: Militant Novelist." *Phylon: The Atlanta University Review of Race and Culture* 34, no. 1 (March 1973): 73–77. Reprinted in *Twentieth-Century Literary Criticism* 77.

Gloster, Hugh M. "The Negro in American Fiction." *Phylon: The Atlanta University of Race and Culture* 4, no. 4 (Winter 1943): 333–45. Reprinted in *Twentieth-Century Literary Criticism* 77.

Griggs, Sutton E. *Imperium in Imperio*. Cincinnati: The Editor Publishing Co., 1899.

Griggs, Sutton E. *Overshadowed*. Nashville: Orion Publishing Co., 1901.

Griggs, Sutton E. *Unfettered*. Nashville: Orion Publishing Co., 1902.

Griggs, Sutton E. *The Hindered Hand; or The Reign of the Repressionist*. Nashville: Orion Publishing Co., 1905.

Griggs, Sutton E. *Pointing the Way*. Nashville: Orion Publishing Co., 1908.

Griggs, Sutton E. *The Story of My Struggles*. Memphis: National Public Welfare League, 1914.

Logan, Rayford W., and Michael R. Winston, eds. "Sutton Elbert Griggs." In *Dictionary of American Negro Biography*, 680. New York: W. W. Norton, 1982.

Guadalupe Hidalgo, Treaty of

Named for the city in which it was signed on February 2, 1848, the Treaty of Guadalupe Hidalgo concluded the Mexican-American War. The treaty called for Mexico to

---

Creation Generation

The term *creation generation* refers to the generation of Mexicans who became U.S. citizens as a result of the 1848 Treaty of Guadalupe Hidalgo, which ended the war between Mexico and the United States. The treaty is now considered to have unduly benefited the United States. Under this treaty, in an exchange for a payment of $15 million, Mexico surrendered 55 percent of its territories: areas that currently include New Mexico, Arizona, Texas, and parts of California, Colorado, Nevada, and Utah. In addition, Mexican citizens residing in these areas were granted U.S. citizenship.

The notion of involuntary immigrants (i.e., individuals who belong to social groups that were forced into becoming Americans) has primarily been applied to the experiences of African Americans, but other minority groups in the United States fit the same criterion. The creation generation of Mexicans is among them. Although the treaty provided an opportunity for these individuals to remain Mexican citizens, most did not opt to do so. Rather, they became Americans not through due democratic process, but simply by virtue of remaining at their own residences, which now fell on the American side of the new border. As an involuntary minority group, they encountered Anglo-centered ethnocentrism, economic exploitation, and political disfranchisement.

DAISUKE AKIBA

---

cede 55 percent of its territory, including the land area that later became the states of Arizona, California, and New Mexico, and parts of what are now Colorado, Nevada, and Utah. In exchange, the United States agreed to pay $15 million in compensation for war-related damage to Mexican property. In addition, the treaty established the border between Texas and Mexico at the Rio Grande River, 150 miles south of the traditional border on the Nueces River (Article V). Articles VIII and IX called for the United States to protect the property and civil rights of Mexican nationals living within the new U.S. border. The treaty also stipulated that the United States would police its side of the border (Article XI) and provided for compulsory arbitration of future disputes

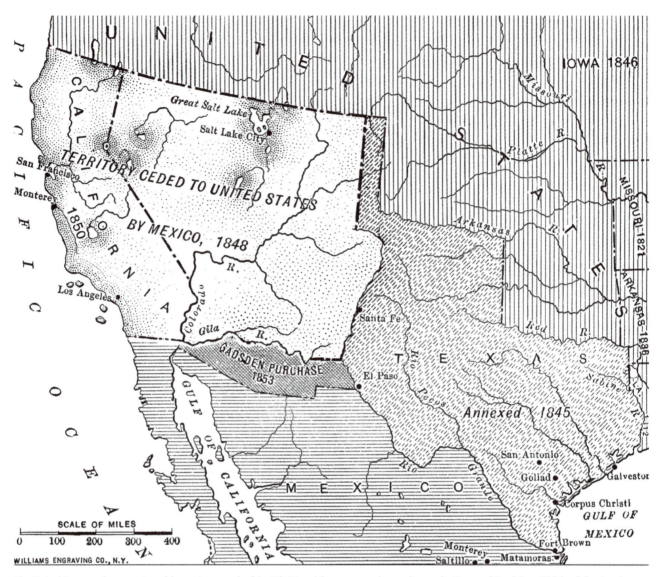

The United States took possession of the territory north of the Gila River (shown on map) according to the Treaty of Guadalupe Hidalgo following the Mexican-American War in 1848. In 1853, the Gadsden Purchase (Treaty of La Mesilla) added the territory south of the Gila River. (North Wind Picture Archives)

between the two countries (Article XXI). Article X originally guaranteed the protection of Mexican land grants, but the U.S. Senate deleted this clause when it ratified the treaty in March 1848. The treaty made Mexican Americans the only minority group in the United States, besides Native Americans, who were annexed by conquest and whose property rights were legally usurped.

The legitimacy of the war and the U.S. territorial ambition have been disputed from the beginning. In 1846, with the war barely begun, pacifist and naturalist Henry David

Thoreau refused to pay taxes, denouncing the Mexican-American War. Newspaperman Horace Greeley doubted that the predictable military victories and annexation of half of Mexican territory would enhance liberty, morality, and industry. General Ulysses S. Grant declared the Mexican-American War to be "the most unjust war ever undertaken by a stronger nation against a weaker one." But in a widely circulated article written in 1911, David Saville Muzzey, a historian at Barnard College, Columbia University, justified the war, arguing that the United States had a right to annex Texas, which had been independent for nine years, and that the admitted military weakness of a country should not give immunity to continued and open insolence. With the Treaty of Guadalupe Hidalgo, he concluded, "The work of westward extension was done. Expansion, the watchword of the decade 1840–1850, was dropped from our vocabulary for fifty years."

Notwithstanding the promises of the treaty to protect property rights and civil rights of the former Mexican nationals (now Mexican Americans), the U.S. government and judiciary have denied their claims to the ancestral land formerly granted under Spanish and Mexican rule. Recently, an increasing number of Mexican American families have begun to fight for the return of the land taken from them for decades by the injustice of predominantly Anglo-Saxon courts. Now those bringing land-related claims, disillusioned by the treaty's unenforceability under the current judiciary procedure, have started focusing their attention on the federal legislature. Consequently, a small number of bills were introduced in Congress: House Resolution 2538 sought to create a presidential commission to determine the validity of the land-related claims; a Senate bill proposed to acknowledge the property claims outright and to develop a method of compensation; and in 2000, Senate Bill 2022 recognized that the loss of property subsequent to the war with Mexico has had serious repercussions in the Mexican American community in the southwestern United States, and specifically questioned whether the United States fulfilled its obligations under the treaty. These bills are significant in that Congress admits the accountability of the federal government and the Territory of New Mexico in the mid-to-late 19th century for the massive dispossession of Mexican American landholders. But the proposed legislation does not directly address the key issue, the Unites States' blatant failure to adhere the provisions of the treaty, but merely mentions the issue of fairness and equity in administrative process, thus blurring the necessity of an official apology on the part of the federal government to those illegally dispossessed.

DONG-HO CHO

See also

Mexican-American War; Mexican Repatriation

Further Reading:

Muzzey, David Saville. *An American History*. Boston: Ginn Company, 1911.

St. Mary's Law Review on Minority Issues (Spring 2001): 231–67, 232–36. http://www.loc.gov/exhibits/ghtreaty.

Zinn, Howard. *A People's History of the United States*. New York: Perennial Classics, 2003.

Gutiérrez, José Angel (b. 1944)

Writer and civil rights activist José Angel Gutiérrez earned degrees from Texas A&M University at Kingsville (BA, 1966), St. Mary's University in San Antonio, Texas (MA, 1968), the University of Texas at Austin (PhD, 1976), and the University of Houston, Bates College of Law (JD, 1989). He has done other postdoctoral work at Stanford University, Colegio de México, the University of Washington, and the Centro de Estudios Económicos y Sociales del Tercer Mundo (Center for Economic and Social Studies of the Third World) in México City, México.

A key figure in the Chicano Movement, José Angel Gutiérrez began his career in 1963 by helping to elect five Mexican Americans to the city council of Crystal City, Texas. As a student at St. Mary's University in San Antonio in 1967, Gutiérrez and four other young Chicanos—Mario Compeán, Nacho Pérez, Willy Velásquez, and Juan Patlán—founded the Mexican American Youth Organization (MAYO), the forerunner of the La Raza Unida Party (LRUP). MAYO sought to effect social change for the Mexican American community and to train young Chicanos for leadership positions. Under the guidance of political science professor at St. Mary's, Charles Cotrell, Gutiérrez produced a master's thesis entitled "La Raza and Revolution: The Empirical Conditions of Revolution in Four South Texas Counties" that became the basis for the Winter Garden Project, an initiative that led to the founding of the LRUP in later years.

MAYO members led by Gutiérrez held to the belief that confrontational tactics could convince cowed Texas Mexicans that the *gringo* was vulnerable. For example, by engaging in public confrontations with the feared Texas Rangers, they demonstrated that at least some Mexicans were willing to stand up to those often-despised law enforcement officials. But MAYO's highly publicized tactics also provoked the ire of established Anglo liberals and Mexican American *políticos.* San Antonio's Congressman Henry B. González, for example, almost single-handedly eradicated most of the funding sources for the young militants.

After being stymied in their community development efforts, in 1968 the young activists turned to gaining electoral power. Naming their effort the Winter Garden Project (WGP), they chose to start in Crystal City, Gutiérrez's hometown. Although the population of this agricultural town in South Texas was more than 80 percent Mexican, the power structure in both local government and private business was Anglo American. Gutiérrez and his MAYO cohorts returned to Crystal City to reestablish a Mexican American majority on the city council. But unfolding local dissatisfaction with the school system prompted the organizers to put gaining electoral goals on hold temporarily.

When Mexican American students at Crystal City High School led a walkout in 1969, the WGP, led by Gutiérrez, joined high school students and their parents to form the Ciudadanos Unidos (United Citizens). In December, when the school board did not accede to their demands, practically all of the Chicano students walked out of their classes. The strike ended on January 6, 1970, when the school board acceded to the reforms demanded by strikers. The next move for Gutiérrez and the group was to gain political power in Crystal City. After the successful school boycotts, Gutiérrez and other MAYO members formed an LRUP chapter and won five positions on the city council and school board in 1970.

The LRUP spread to other regions in the United States, exerting particular strength in Colorado, where the popular Chicano leader Rodolfo "Corky" Gonzales headed the effort and also called for a national political party. Although Gutiérrez was reluctant to begin a national effort at this point, arguing that it could jeopardize his regional strategy, he decided to accede to the national focus and was elected chairman of the LRUP at its 1972 convention in El Paso, Texas. The most important issue at the meeting became whether the pragmatic Gutiérrez or the ideological Gonzales would be elected party chairman. Colorado LRUP leaders encouraged rumors that accused Gutiérrez of making deals with the Republicans to obtain funding for LRUP programs in Texas. Nonetheless, Gutiérrez won, provoking a bitter split that could not be bridged by any number of overtures for unity; the national Chicano party initiative was still-born. Later, disaffected LRUP members in Zavala County formed a breakaway faction; José Angel Gutiérrez resigned in 1981. In 1986, Gutiérrez earned a PhD in government at the University of Texas at Austin and later graduated from law school at the University of Houston. Gutiérrez has served as executive director of the Greater Texas Legal Foundation, a nonprofit organization seeking justice for poor people, and is currently a lawyer in Dallas and a professor of Chicano studies at the University of Texas at Arlington. He continues to research and publish on the Chicano Movement and heads the Greater Dallas Foundation, a civil rights litigation unit.

Like Corky Gonzales, José Angel Gutiérrez often expressed his militant experiences and his aspirations for his people in poems that were often published in movement and community periodicals. Gutiérrez also furthered the movement by issuing *El Político: The Mexican American Elected Official* (1972) and a self-published handbook detailing how Chicanos could attain power in society: *A Gringo Manual on How to Handle Mexicans* (1974). It was not formally published until well after the Chicano Movement was over, in 2001. He followed this up with *Chicano Manual on How to Handle Gringos* (2003). In 1999, Gutiérrez published an autobiography, *The Making of a Chicano Militant: Lessons from Cristal.* In 2005, he adapted the book for young adults as *The Making of a Civil Rights Leader* and he also penned a biography of Severita Lara, a civil rights leader who got her start during the Crystal City school walkouts: *We Won't Back Down: Severita Lara's Rise from Student Leader to Mayor.* His other books include *A War of Words* (coauthored in 1985) and *Chicanas in Charge: Texas Women in the Public Arena* (coauthored in 2005). In addition, Gutiérrez translated *My Struggle for the Land: Autobiography of Reies Lopez Tijerina* (2000). He has also has written several articles and book chapters over the years.

Gutiérrez has been the subject of many articles and film documentaries, the most recent being the PBS four-part video series, *CHICANO! The Mexican American Struggle for Civil Rights*, and his life and work are studied in many Chicano history and political science books. His many honors include being named one of the "100 Outstanding Latino Texans of the 20th Century" by *Latino*

Monthly (January 2000) and "Distinguished Texas Hispanic" by *Texas Hispanic Magazine* (October 1996), as well as being awarded the Distinguished Faculty Award from the Texas Association of Chicanos in Higher Education (June 1995) and the National Council of La Raza's Chicano Hero Award in 1994.

F. Arturo Rosales

See also

Chicano Movement

Further Reading:

Gutiérrez, José Angel. *The Making of a Chicano Militant: Lessons from Cristal.* Madison: University of Wisconsin Press, 1999.

Rosales, F. Arturo. *Chicano! History of the Mexican American Civil Rights Movement.* Houston: Arte Público Press, 2000.

H

H-2A Visa

The H-2A nonimmigrant status visa allows non-U.S. residents from specific nations to work in temporary agricultural jobs in the United States. H-2A workers may receive the visa for up to a one-year period and renew the visa up to three years, at which point the worker must return to their country of origin for at least three months before applying again. As of January 18, 2012, workers from 58 nations are eligible for H-2A visas, with most going to Mexican agriculture workers. Under extenuating circumstances, workers can also be recruited from other nations not on the list of approved countries. H-2A visas are intended to address overwhelming shortages in the U.S. labor market for unskilled seasonal agriculture workers. H-2A visas allow U.S. employers to recruit non-U.S. workers to fill seasonal jobs generally regarded as undesirable to most unskilled workers in the United States. H-2A workers and their U.S. employers work under contracts intended to protect workers from potential exploitation by enforcing U.S. labor laws. Additionally, employers must provide employees housing, transportation, and meals while employed. The H-2A visa first appeared as part of the 1986 Immigration Reform and Control Act (IRCA), outlining procedures for acquiring agriculture laborers long after the end of the Bracero Program in 1964.

H-2A workers enter into a contract with their employer stating the start and end of the work contract, the conditions of employment (such as housing), all holidays, the definition of the work day, the location of the work site, and the pay rate. Every worker must receive a copy of the contract by the first day of work. The contract must be in the language spoken by the worker. This contract, along with legal requirements of employers utilizing H-2A workers, is intended to limit worker exploitation. As part of the contract, workers are partially monitored while in the United States. Employers must notify Citizenship and Immigration Services (USCIS) if a worker is terminated. Employers must also report workers that do not report to work for five days, and must notify USCIS if the scheduled work period ends early. Employers must pay workers at least 75 percent of the work days in the contract if work ends early. H-2A visa workers are protected under U.S. wage laws. This includes the application of minimum hourly and piecemeal wages, worker's compensation if injured, and the creation of a safe work space.

Employers requesting H-2A workers must offer jobs that are temporary or seasonal agricultural jobs. Additionally, employers must demonstrate a lack of qualified U.S. workers who are willing and available to do the work. Employers must attempt to recruit U.S. workers before applying, including coordinating recruitment efforts with the State

Workforce Agency (SWA) where the work is located. Additionally, employers may be required to recruit outside the state using other SWAs to ensure that U.S. workers have received access to the jobs. Employers must also show that H-2A workers will not depress U.S. worker wages in similar jobs. Employers must also meet a surety bond demonstrating their ability to meet payroll and obligations for workers such as housing, transportation, and meals.

As a condition of receiving H-2A workers, employers must provide free housing to workers unable to return to their homes at the end of the work day. Housing is subject to Occupational Safety and Health Administration (OSHA) or Employment and Training Administration (ETA) standards depending on when the housing was built. Housing built after April 3, 1980, is subject to OSHA requirements, including one washbasin per six workers, 50 square feet of sleeping space per worker, and one shower per 10 workers. Additionally, housing must be at least 500 feet from livestock. Older housing (built or under construction before April 3, 1980) falls under more lenient ETA standards: one wash bin and shower per 15 workers and only 40 square feet of sleeping space. Additionally, there is no language limiting housing location from livestock or other hazards. However, in both OSHA and ETA standards, state laws that are stricter will prevail. Employers may instead elect to have workers live in rental properties (such as motels). In this case, the employer must visit the site to ensure the rental location is in compliance with local and state laws, and must pay all expenses to the owner.

Further, employers must supply transportation to and from work each day, as well as access to meals and the tools needed to complete the job. This also applies for non–H-2A workers that are employed at the same job site. Prior to employment, employers must help transport workers from their home nations to the site and back home once the contract is completed. Employers can charge workers for the costs of transportation from their home nation to the work site, but must refund it once the employee has worked for half the contract. Additionally, the employer must provide free transportation back to their home nation once the contract has been completed. Employers must also ensure that their workers are fed and have the necessary tools to complete the job. Employers must provide three meals a day (including off days) to each worker or provide kitchens where workers may prepare their own meals as a group or individually. If the employer provides the three meals, they are entitled to charge workers a disclosed fee. Employers must also offer the tools needed for the job. Generally, workers are not expected to provide or pay for the tools needed to complete the work.

The use of H-2A visas is not without controversy. Few visas are requested and certified in comparison to the number of migrant workers used in previous agriculture worker programs such as the Bracero Program. H-2A visas are not attached to statutory limits, yet less than 90,000 visas were requested in 2010 (with 88 percent being later certified). This means that employers are likely seeking out unauthorized workers instead of seeking visas while fueling the debate about the importance of this program to the agriculture industry. Further, unauthorized workers are not subject to the same protections as those under H-2A visas, exposing workers to situations such as wage theft, unsafe work environments, and even debt bondage.

JAMES MAPLES

See also

Bracero Program; Day Laborers; Migrant Workers

Further Reading:

Massey, Douglas S., Jorge Durand, and Nolan J. Malone. *Beyond Smoke and Mirrors: Mexican Immigration in an Era of Economic Integration.* New York: Russell Sage Foundation, 2002.

Massey, Douglas S., and Magaly R. Sanchez. *Brokered Boundaries: Creating Immigrant Identity in Anti-Immigrant Times.* New York: Russell Sage Foundation, 2010.

Waldinger, Roger. *Strangers at the Gates: New Immigrants in Urban America.* Berkeley and Los Angeles: University of California Press, 2001.

Hamer, Fannie Lou (1917–1956)

The granddaughter of slaves, civil rights pioneer Fannie Lou Townsend was born into a sharecropping family in Montgomery County, Mississippi, on October 6, 1917. She was the youngest of Jim and Ella Townsend's 20 children, and grew up facing the worst ravages of the Jim Crow South's discrimination. As an adult, she faced violence and economic ruin when she challenged Mississippi's policies of segregation and disfranchisement, but eventually emerged as one of the most forceful voices for freedom and equity during the civil rights movement.

Fannie Lou Townsend began picking cotton at age six on a plantation in Sunflower County, where her family had moved when she was two, deep in the heart of the Mississippi Delta. While the county was predominately black, it was run politically and economically by a small number of powerful whites, most notably Senator James Eastland, who owned large tracts of land in the county and lived in the town of Doddsville. Sunflower County was so identified with the segregationist senator that it was often referred to as "Eastland's Plantation." On Eastland's Plantation, the segregated schools for black children were open only about five months of the year, in order to not conflict with cotton chopping and picking seasons. Townsend received only six years of formal education in her life, dropping out to help her family survive financially, and seemed to be relegated to the lot of most blacks in the Mississippi Delta, working for shares on white plantations.

In 1944, Townsend married Perry "Pap" Hamer, five years her senior, and the two moved to Ruleville, about three miles from the plantation where she had grown up. The two became tenants on the Marlow Plantation and began working for shares. The couple had no children of their own (she was sterilized by a physician in 1961 without her consent), but raised four adopted daughters. The Hamers lived and worked on the Marlow Plantation until 1962, when the burgeoning civil rights movement made its way into the Mississippi Delta and changed Fannie Lou Hamer's life.

"I had never heard, until 1962, that black people could register and vote," recalled Hamer in a 1971 interview. But in the summer of 1962, she attained a mass meeting conduced by the Council of Federated Organizations (COFO) which included members of the SNCC, CORE, the SCLC, and the NAACP, designed to encourage black citizens of Mississippi to register and vote. The civil rights workers had found little success enlisting volunteers up to that point, as the combination of economic dependence on whites and threats of violence kept most local blacks from trying to register. Hamer, now 44, was inspired to challenge the system and volunteered along with 17 others to go to Indianola to try to register. Upon attempting to register, she had to list her place of employment and pass Mississippi's notorious literacy test.

Fannie Lou Hamer, a Mississippi field hand for most of her life, became a prominent advocate of civil rights. As Mississippi's Democratic Party refused African American members, Hamer helped form the Mississippi Freedom Democratic Party (MFDP), whose members attempted to unseat the regular party delegation at the Democratic National Convention in 1964. (Library of Congress)

When she was unable to give the registrar an acceptable explanation of the facto laws in Mississippi's constitution, she was told she had failed the test and could not register.

Fannie Lou Hamer's failed attempt to register to vote cost her both her job and her home, as her family was thrown off the plantation where they had lived and worked for 18 years for her challenge to white supremacy. Blackballed along with her husband from other plantations because of her actions, Hamer became a field secretary for SNCC, earning $10 a week, while often having to live with friends or relatives. Her dedication and sacrifice inspired the young SNCC volunteers, most of whom were less than half her age. She became famous among them for both her bravery and her magnificent singing voice. In 1963, she was beaten mercilessly by police while returning from a voter education seminar, sustaining permanent kidney damage, but refused to yield. The following year, she was part of the founding of the Mississippi Freedom Democratic Party (MFDP), an interracial group that sought to inspire black Mississippians to register and vote, and to pressure President Lyndon B. Johnson and the national Democratic Party, which voiced support for civil rights, to deal with the contradiction of Southern Democrats who openly resisted civil rights legislation and barred black members from the party. Hamer even challenged Jamie Whitten in the Democratic primary for his congressional seat, allowing her to remark that in 1964, "I cast my first vote for myself, because I was running for Congress. The first vote, I voted for myself."

It was as a delegate for the MFDP that Fannie Lou Hamer emerged on the national stage at the 1964 Democratic National Convention in Atlantic City, New Jersey. The MFDP sent a delegation of 68 delegates (four of whom were white) to Atlantic City in an attempt to unseat the all-white regular Mississippi delegation, which opposed not only civil rights, but virtually all aspects of the Democratic Party's platform that year. Conversely, the MFDP argued that not only was it the only delegation from Mississippi open to all of its citizens, but that it heartily endorsed all the major planks of the national party. A number of other state delegations supported the MFDP, and the decision was made to allow the members of the MFDP to testify before the credentials committee to plead their case. It was in front of this committee that Hamer gave an emotional appeal to the committee and the nation, describing her beating by police in 1963, and closing by stating, "If the Freedom Democratic Party is not seated now, I question America. Is this America, the land of the free and the home of the brave where we have to sleep with our telephones off the hooks because our lives be threatened daily because we want to live as decent human beings, in America?"

A national television audience saw the beginnings of Hamer's testimony, but not its conclusion, because President Johnson called an impromptu press conference in an attempt to get her off the air. Johnson, while a supporter of civil rights, did not want any division at the national convention, which was poised to nominate him for election in his own right. He dispatched one of his lieutenants, U.S. Senator

Hubert Humphrey of Minnesota, to broker a deal with the MFDP. A compromise was proposed where two delegates of the MFDP would be seated as at-large delegates, while the other 66 members of the MFDP would be treated as guests of the convention. The regular Democrats would still be the official delegation from Mississippi, but a promise was made that in 1968, no delegation that discriminated upon race would be seated. A number of black leaders, including Martin Luther King, Jr., Andrew Young, and Roy Wilkins, urged the MFDP to accept the settlement, but the delegation rejected it as an insult. As Hamer summed it up, "We didn't come here for no two seats."

Despite not getting what it wanted, the MFDP's challenge did have wide-ranging effects. It forced the issue of voting discrimination into the national consciousness, helping to set the stage for the Voting Rights Act of 1965. It also changed the Democratic Party. As promised, all-white delegations were not allowed at the 1968 convention, but this was in part due to the defections of many Southern whites to the Republican Party as a result of the support for civil rights by Johnson. Finally, Atlantic City had made Hamer a major face of the civil rights movement. In the wake of her performance at the 1964 convention, the uneducated former sharecropper toured Africa and spoke at colleges across the country. In 1968, she served as a delegate at the Democratic National Convention in Chicago, and was elected to the Democratic National Committee.

Hamer spent the bulk of the rest of her life working to improve the conditions for poor blacks in the Mississippi Delta. In 1969, she founded the Freedom Farm Cooperative back in Sunflower County to provide food for low-income people in the Delta, and she worked to have Head Start programs administered in the black communities of Mississippi. She again ran unsuccessfully for public office in 1971, losing a bid for the Mississippi state senate. She was diagnosed with breast cancer in 1976 and died the following year at age 59.

THOMAS J. WARD, JR.

See also
Civil Rights Movement

Further Reading:
Lee, Chana Kai. *For Freedom's Sake: The Life of Fannie Lou Hamer.* Urbana: University of Illinois Press, 1999.
Mills, Kay. *This Little Light of Mine: The Life of Fannie Lou Hamer.* New York: Dutton, 1993.

An Oral History with Fannie Lou Hamer. Center for Oral History and Cultural Heritage, University of Southern Mississippi.

Sewell, George A. "Fannie Lou Hamer." In *Mississippi Black History Makers.* Jackson: University Press of Mississippi, 1977.

Hammerskin Nation

The Hammerskin Nation is a conglomeration of groups that ascribes to the white power ideology and skinhead lifestyle and is heavily involved in the production of white supremacist music. According to the group's Web site, they live by 14 words: "We must secure the existence of our people and a future for white children." They are considered to be the most organized, respected, and feared racist skinhead group in operation today.

The group was originally formed in Dallas, Texas, in 1987 under the name of Confederate Hammerskins. The original group was inspired by symbolism in the Pink Floyd movie *The Wall* and adopted the Confederate flag and two crossed hammers as their logo. After the original group was founded, various factions with different identifying names developed across all regions of the United States as well as in various foreign countries. It is estimated that there are 19 chapters in the United States and 10 chapters abroad. Currently they are all subsumed under the umbrella term *Hammerskin Nation.*

The Hammerskin Nation actively uses the Internet to recruit disillusioned, young, white males through the use of their webpage, e-mail lists and bulletin boards. Unlike other racist, skinhead groups, the Hammerskins are very selective in who joins and require that potential members prove their loyalty to the cause by demonstrating knowledge of their history, ideology, and goals. As a result of the application process and probationary period that prospective members must go through, the overall numbers of Hammerskins around the world are relatively low compared to membership numbers in other racist, skinhead groups.

The main focus of the Hammerskin Nation is the production and promotion of white supremacist music, which they use not only as a main source of funding for their organization but also as another source of recruitment. They have attempted and successfully organized several large concerts to promote not only their hate rock music but also their group's ideology. The most recent "Hammerfest" was held in 2000 on private land outside Bremen, Georgia. There were an estimated 300 people in attendance and 14 bands. The music produced by white supremacist groups as Bound for Glory, Blue Eyed Devils, Extreme Hatred, and Hatecrime includes violent and racist lyrics that have inspired some members to engage in hate crimes.

The Hammerskin Nation is well known for their involvement in acts of harassment, assault, and murder. For example, members have been involved in vandalizing Jewish synagogues, cemeteries, and community centers; shouting racist slurs at various minority groups; firebombing minority-owned night clubs and homes of minorities; assaulting minorities to keep them out of various places they believe should be reserved for whites only; and committing race-related homicides. Most recently Wade Michael Page, a member of the Hammerskin Nation, killed six people and then himself in a Sikh temple in Oak Creek, Wisconsin.

VIRGINIA R. BEARD

See also

Hate Groups in America; Nazism

Further Reading:

Gerstenfeld, Phyllis B. *Hate Crimes: Causes, Controls and Controversies.* Los Angeles: SAGE, 2011.

Perry, Barbara. *In the Name of Hate: Understanding Hate Crimes.* New York: Routledge, 2001.

Ryan, Matt E., and Peter T. Leeson. "Hate Groups and Hate Crime." *International Review of Law and Economics* (2011).

Harlan, John Marshall (1833–1911)

U.S. Supreme Court Justice John Marshall Harlan was born in Boyle County, Kentucky, on June 1, 1833. His family was wealthy, politically connected, and owned slaves. Harlan's father was a distinguished lawyer who served as a congressman. Harlan's family standing allowed him to attend Centre College. Thereafter, he studied law at Transylvania University, graduating in 1853. He became active in politics as a Whig and, then, in other parties after the Whig Party splintered. Harlan became a county judge for a time before joining the Union army in the Civil War.

Although Harlan was an ardent Unionist, he believed in the legality of slavery so fervently that he threatened to leave the army if President Abraham Lincoln carried out the Emancipation Proclamation. However, he did not leave the service and, after the war, his views on slavery and rights for African American changed dramatically. Harlan twice campaigned for the governorship of Kentucky; both attempts were unsuccessful. In 1877, President Rutherford B. Hayes nominated Harlan to the Supreme Court.

John Marshall Harlan served as a Supreme Court justice from 1877 to 1911. His 34-year career on the bench made him one of the longest serving justices in the history of the Court. Harlan became known for his dissents from the majority opinions of the Court, which totaled 361 in all. He was an independent jurist who interpreted the Fourteenth Amendment broadly, leading to impassioned pleas for justice in some of the most famous Supreme Court cases of the day, including the *Civil Rights Cases* (1883) and *Plessy v. Ferguson* (1896).

In the *Civil Rights Cases*, Harlan was disappointed with the majority of the Court that found the Civil Rights Act of 1875 to be unconstitutional because the law went beyond the inherent legislative power of Congress. Vociferously voicing his sole dissent, Harlan decried the Court's holding as undercutting the intent of the post–Civil War amendments to the Constitution that sought to equalize the rights of all persons in the United States.

Another landmark case in which Harlan dissented was *Plessy v. Ferguson*. In this instance, Harlan again was the only justice to depart from the majority. He clearly believed that the Court's "separate, but equal" standard as a matter of policy and practice would be at odds with the Fourteenth Amendment right to equal protection. His argument in his dissent for a "constitution [that] is color-blind" marked him as a legal light of hope in a decision that history looks upon with disdain. Presciently, Harlan thought that the *Plessy v. Ferguson* ruling would eventually be overturned, which it was, 58 long years later in *Brown v. Board of Education* (1954).

Harlan is usually thought of a progressive figure on issues of civil rights and equal protections, but in many other cases, less well known than his famous dissents, Harlan registered no objection to the curtailing of rights for African Americans or other minority groups. A prime example of a step back was in *Cumming v. Richmond County Board of Education* (1899), where, writing for the Court, Harlan did not find any "clear and unmistakable" violations of equal protection and deferred to the state and local boards of education to make decisions about access to education. Yet, even with the above caveat, Harlan's erudite and impassioned opinions inspired civil rights pioneers, and his clear and unpopular judgments on controversial cases still have significance into the present day.

AARON COOLEY

See also

Brown v. Board of Education ((1954); Civil Rights Movement; *Cumming v. Richmond County Board of Education* (1899); *Plessy v. Ferguson* (1896)

Further Reading:

Beth, Loren. *John Marshall Harlan: The Last Whig Justice.* Lexington: University of Kentucky Press, 1992.

Przybyszewski, Linda. *The Republic According to John Marshall Harlan.* Chapel Hill: University of North Carolina Press, 1999.

Harlem (New York) Riot of 1935

Often considered the end of the Harlem Renaissance because it shattered the image of Harlem as a neighborhood of nightclubs and cabarets open and welcoming to white patrons, the riot of March 1935 revealed the anger and frustration that racism, police brutality, and economic hardship had bred among Harlem residents. Unlike most previous 20th-century race riots, the violence in Harlem in 1935 was not characterized by white mobs attacking black victims, but by black rioters destroying white property.

During the Depression, there were two main causes of discontent in Harlem, a New York City neighborhood that, since the turn of the century, had been increasingly populated by African Americans. One cause was tension between the residents and the police, who were frequently accused of brutality in their interactions with blacks. For instance, in March 1934, at a Harlem rally held in support of the black men accused in the Scottsboro case, eyewitnesses claimed that police officers drew their weapons on the crowd and beat several demonstrators, including a young girl. The anger and distrust born of such incidents grew among Harlemites when the police commissioner, ignoring a finding of excessive force made by his own chief inspector, exonerated the officers under investigation.

A more powerful cause of discontent, especially in view of the high unemployment of the time, was the refusal of local white merchants, who made their living largely off the Harlem community, to employ African Americans as clerical and sales staff. Since 1933, various citizen groups in Harlem had organized boycotts against the merchants but, by 1935, these actions had achieved only limited success, with only a few jobs being offered to African Americans and then only to lighter-skinned individuals. Not surprisingly, it was an incident involving the police and occurring in one of the white-owned stores on West 125th Street that ignited the riot.

On March 19, 1935, rumors spread that the police had beaten and killed a 16-year-old boy, Lino Rivera, who had been accused of stealing a knife from a Kress Store. Although Rivera was not beaten, he later testified that store employees had threatened to take him to the basement and do so. To avoid causing any further agitation among the store's customers, the police hustled Rivera out the back door and released him. The boy's sudden disappearance led to excited speculation that he had indeed been taken to the basement to be beaten. The unfortunate and entirely coincidental appearance in the area of an ambulance and a hearse only fueled this notion, which, given the state of community and police relations, was quickly and completely believed.

By late afternoon, a large and angry crowd had gathered outside the store, forcing its closure. Violent confrontations erupted between blacks and whites and between the police and the rioters. Over 600 windows were smashed and many stores were looted and vandalized. Although they did not cause the rioting, communist groups, which had been active in the community attempting to create solidarity between black and white workers, attempted to seize control of the crowd to focus its anger on the white merchants and the city's political leaders. The Young Communist League and other leftist groups encouraged the rumor of Rivera's death and called for the arrest of the Kress Store managers. The league also distributed leaflets calling for blacks and whites to unite against their capitalist bosses. This communist involvement in the disorders led to later claims by the police and the city administration that the riot had been caused by leftist agitators.

With over 500 police officers on the streets, the rioting eventually subsided, only to break out again on the evening of March 20. After a second night of violence, the disorders ended. In his initial comments on the rioting, made before it had ceased, New York mayor Fiorello La Guardia blamed the violence on criminals and other riffraff. However, the 13-member commission later appointed by the mayor to investigate the causes of the riot rejected both the riffraff and communist agitator theories and, in an unprecedented set of conclusions, placed blame for the disorders on economic depression, racial discrimination, and indifference or racism within the city administration. Because the report was so critical of the city government, Mayor La Guardia delayed its official release, and it was first made public by the *Amsterdam News*, which printed a leaked copy in July 1936.

The commission's unusual composition—it had a black majority that included Howard University sociologist E. Franklin Frazier as director of research—may have accounted for its unorthodox conclusions—most previous riot commissions accepted criminal activity or political agitation as the chief cause of disorder. Although the mayor became somewhat more responsive to the needs of Harlem, appointing more blacks to city office and speaking more frequently before black audiences, his administration did little to improve economic conditions in the neighborhood. Because economics had been such a large factor in the violence, some commentators, such as writer Claude McKay, refused to even call the 1935 disorders a riot, preferring instead to see the episode as an economic revolt.

JOHN A. WAGNER

See also

Locke, Alain LeRoy; Race Riots in America. Documents: The Report on the Memphis Riots of May 1866 (July 25, 1866); Account of the Riots in East St. Louis, Illinois (July 1917); The Cook County Coroner's Report Regarding the 1919 Chicago Race Riots (1919); A Southern Black Woman's Letter Regarding the Recent Riots in Chicago and Washington (November 1919); The Final Report of the Grand Jury on the Tulsa Race Riot (June 25, 1921); Testimony from *Laney v. United States* Describing Events during the Washington, D.C., Riot of July 1919 (December 3, 1923); The Governor's Commission Report on the Watts Riots (December 1965); Cyrus R. Vance's Report on the Riots in Detroit (July-August 1967); The Reports of the Oklahoma Commission to Study the Tulsa Race Riot of 1921

(2000-2001); The Draft Report of the 1898 Wilmington Race Riot Commission (December 2005)

Further Reading:

Fogelson, Robert M., and Richard E. Rubenstein. *The Complete Report of Mayor La Guardia's Commission on the Harlem Riot of March 19, 1935.* New York: Arno Press and the *New York Times,* 1969.

Greenberg, Cheryl Lynn. *Or Does It Explode: Black Harlem in the Great Depression.* New York: Oxford University Press, 1991.

Greene, Larry. "Harlem: The Depression Years—Leadership and Social Conditions." *Afro-Americans in New York History* 17 (July 1993).

Locke, Alain. "Harlem: Dark Weather-Vane." *Survey Graphic* 25, no. 8 (August 1936): 457.

Naison, Mark. *Communists in Harlem during the Depression.* Urbana: University of Illinois Press, 1983.

Harlem Youth Opportunities Unlimited (HARYOU)

Harlem Youth Opportunities Unlimited (HARYOU), founded in 1962 by members of the Harlem community and led by Kenneth B. Clark (1914–2005), was a program dedicated to alleviating the distressed conditions of black youth in Harlem, New York. HARYOU was a heroic effort and was well supported by the federal and state government. Nevertheless, it did not achieve the success that Clark and others had hoped. In fact, conditions in Harlem went from bad to worse following a riot there in 1964.

Clark, best known for his compelling and extensive studies on the effects of racism on black youth, was an ambitious HARYOU leader. He himself knew intimately the obstacles facing blacks. As a youth, he lived in New York City, near Harlem, where he and his mother were once forced out of a white-only restaurant. His guidance counselor tried to persuade Clark to attend a vocational high school rather than an academic one. This reflected an attitude that has existed in the United States since Reconstruction, that blacks should be navigated toward servile and unchallenging positions in life.

During his undergraduate years at Howard, a historically black university, Clark protested racial segregation inside the U.S. Capitol. He was later denied admission to Cornell because of his color, but went on to Columbia University to receive a PhD in psychology. He then got a job as a research assistant working for Gunnar Myrdal's book *An American Dilemma* (1944). He worked closely with his wife, Dr. Mamie Phipps Clark, on pioneering research that used dolls to analyze the damage done to blacks' self-image due to racism and segregation. These studies, and Clark's direct involvement, were pivotal to the 1954 U.S. Supreme Court decision in *Brown v. Board of Education* to outlaw segregation in public schools.

In 1961, the concept of a social program to help Harlem youth was first reported in the *New York Times.* The New York City Youth Board and the Community Mental Health Board planned to work together with the Jewish Board of Guardians to establish programs to assist three communities in New York City. Members from the community, particularly the Harlem Neighborhoods Association (HANA), jumped at the chance to participate. HANA members put together a grant proposal and generated the ideas and objectives for HARYOU. The President's Committee on Juvenile Delinquency contributed $230,000, to be used to cover the costs for the 18-month planning period. The City of New York granted the group $100,000. Individuals on all levels genuinely supported and encouraged programs to assuage the mounting problems in Harlem.

The issues that beset Harlem youth were not that different from those in ghettos across the nation: poverty, broken families, crime, drugs, unemployment, and poor housing conditions. Racism and racial segregation also took their toll. Police brutality and racist white gangs, which caused many young blacks to form their own gangs, were rampant. Racial profiling and racism in the judicial system put a disproportionate number of blacks in jails. Immured by the squalor of their racially segregated physical environment and by social and economic oppression, blacks were overwhelmed with feelings of hopelessness and frustration.

The HARYOU planning committee produced a comprehensive plan of action. It detailed their objectives, the issues concerning black youth to be addressed, the structure of the organization, the programs to be implemented, and the analysis to be used to evaluate the effectiveness of these programs. The plan formed a template for many similar programs used across the nation.

The HARYOU programs were categorized as follows: community action, community services, arts and culture,

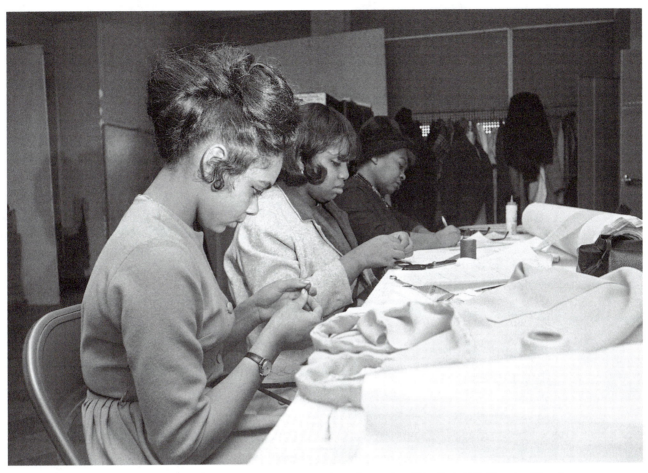

Young girls learn sewing and dress designing at the HARYOU-ACT center in the Harlem section of New York, 1964. (Associated Press)

and business enterprises. The group planned to train and employ Harlem youth to be leaders in each of these areas. Participants in the community action programs were responsible for organizing activities alongside such organizations as the National Association for the Advancement of Colored People, Community Council on Housing, Student Nonviolent Coordinating Committee, Congress of Racial Equality, and local neighborhood boards.

Participants in the community service programs were employed as assistants with organizations such as the Junior Academy, the Senior Academy, the After-School Center, and the Neighborhood Board (Health Services). Participants in the arts and culture program performed at venues within HARYOU, the Harlem community, and beyond. Participants in the business enterprises programs worked to establish coffee shops, cultural centers, and a film and sound laboratory. They also helped to develop renovation projects within

the community. In 1963, the HARYOU committee implemented its plan of action and published its findings in *Youth in the Ghetto* (1964).

In 1964, Harlem erupted in an urban rebellion after a white police officer fatally shot a 15-year-old black youth. Demonstrators, largely black youths, attacked their own community. Although HARYOU continued to promote its programs, it never did recover, nor did it achieve the results the organizers had intended. Shortly after, black youths instigated race riots in the urban ghettos in the North across the nation.

GLADYS L. KNIGHT

See also
Long Hot Summer Riots (1965–1967)

Further Reading:
"An Architect of Social Change: Kenneth B. Clark." In *Against the Odds*, edited by Benjamin P. Bowser and Louis Kushnick, with

Paul Grant, 147–57. Amherst: University of Massachusetts Press, 2002.

Clark, Kenneth B. *Dark Ghetto: Dilemmas of Social Power*. New York: Harper & Row, 1965.

HARYOU. *Youth in the Ghetto: A Study of the Consequences of Powerlessness and a Blueprint for Change*. New York: Harlem Youth Opportunities Unlimited, 1964.

Tyson, Cyril deGrasse. *Power and Politics in Central Harlem, 1862–1964: The HARYOU Experience*. New York: Jay Street Publishers, 2004.

Harlins, Latasha (1976–1991)

The violent shooting death of 15-year-old Latasha Harlins exacerbated racial tensions in Los Angeles, California, and has often been cited as a mitigating factor in the civil unrest that fueled the riots that occurred in Los Angeles between April 29 and May 2, 1992. The Los Angeles (California) Riots of 1992 have been characterized as the worst race riots in U.S. history. The frustration of L.A. residents seemed to be connected to the videotaped beating of Rodney King during an arrest made by L.A. police officers.

Although the Rodney King beating was a travesty, many L.A. residents recognized that the pent-up rage that exploded after the acquittal of the police officers who beat King was deeply rooted in another tragic incident that occurred the same month as the King beating and was also on videotape.

On March 6, 1991, 15-year-old Latasha Harlins walked into the Empire Liquor Market located at 9172 South Figueroa Street in Compton, California. She entered the store, walked over to the refrigerated cases, and pulled out a bottle of orange juice costing $1.79. According to other children who witnessed the events and later testified in court, Harlins placed the orange juice in her open backpack and walked to the counter with $2 in her hand prepared to pay for the juice. Soon Ja Du, the 49-year-old Korean woman who owned the store, immediately began to accuse the girl of attempting to steal the orange juice when she approached the counter. The African American girl and the Korean American woman argued over the orange juice. The videotape showed Soon Ja Du grabbing and pulling Latasha Harlins's backpack. Harlins hit Du in the face a few times as the fight escalated.

Soon Ja Du threw Harlins's backpack behind the counter and tossed a stool at the girl. Du grabbed a .38-caliber gun that she had behind the counter. During the melee, the orange juice bottle had dropped to the floor near Harlins. Harlins turned to pick up the orange juice from the floor and placed it on the counter and Du swatted the bottle off of the counter and pointed the gun at Harlins. Harlins turned around and started to walk out of the store. Soon Ja Du pointed the gun at Harlins and the gun went off with a bullet hitting Latasha Harlins in the back of the head.

The videotaped shooting was shown repeatedly on local news channels in Los Angeles for days after the shooting. In November 1991, a jury convicted Soon Ja Du of voluntary manslaughter. Judge Joyce Karlin presided over the case and ultimately sentenced Du to 400 hours of community service, a $500 fine, reimbursement of funeral costs to the Harlins family and five years' probation.

The incident and the court ruling instigated further hostility between African American residents and Korean American merchants who owned stores in predominantly African American communities throughout South Central Los Angeles. During the L.A. riots, there were over 2,300 documented injuries, 55 deaths, and $1 billion in damage. Many of the Korean-owned businesses were targeted due to deep-seated resentment against their existence in the areas. The memory of Latasha Harlins still haunts many residents of Los Angeles who believe that justice and peace were thwarted by her death.

KIJUA SANDERS-MCMURTRY

See also

Hate Crimes in America; Los Angeles (California) Riots of 1992

Further Reading:

Coleman, Wanda. "Remembering Latasha: Blacks, Immigrants and America." *Nation* 256 (March 1993): 187–91.

Ford, Andrea, and John H. Lee. "Slain Girl Was Not Stealing Juice, Police Say." *Los Angeles Times* (March 1991): 19.

Hu, Arthur. "Us and Them." *New Republic* 206 (June 12, 1992): 12–14.

Stevenson, Brenda E. "Latasha Harlins, Soon Ja Du, and Joyce Karlin: A Case Study of Multicultural Females and Justice on the Urban Frontier." *Journal of African American Life and History* 89 (Spring 2004): 152–76.

Wood, Daniel. "L.A's Darkest Days: 10 Years Later." *Christian Science Monitor* (April 29, 2002).

Hate Crimes in America

Hate crime, also called "bias crime," is a criminal offense motivated by prejudice based on, but not limited to, race, religion, ethnicity, national origin, sexual orientation, or disability. The definition and reporting of hate crimes began in 1985, when Representatives John Conyers (D-Michigan), Barbara Kennelly (D-Connecticut), and Mario Biaggi (D-New York) cosponsored a bill to require the Department of Justice to collect and publish statistics on the nature and number of crimes motivated by racial, religious, and ethnic prejudice. In 1990, President Bush signed the Hate Crime Statistics Act (HCST) into law, which gave national recognition to hate crimes as a bona fide category of crime that manifests evidence of prejudice.

Hate crime involves actions that have already been defined as illegal in state or federal statutes such as assault, battery, rape, vandalism, and arson and does not criminalize new behaviors, but rather recriminalizes and increases punishment for behaviors that are already against the law.

The classification of an offense as a hate crime requires that a designated legislative prejudice such as racism or homophobia had some role in inspiring the criminal act. However, because no federal statute prohibits hate crime where defining hate crime is left up to the states, there are no specific sets of individuals protected by federal law, thus creating controversy on whether certain groups such as women should be shielded under hate crime legislation. The discrepancies between states in how they define hate crime and differences in law enforcement procedures across geographic areas also makes it difficult to record, measure, and analyze hate crime. In addition, the stigma attached to being a victim of hate crime and belonging to a marginalized population contribute to the underreported and underestimated nature of bias crime in the United States. For example, a transgendered person who is violently attacked may not disclose to police that they are transgendered for fear of even further victimization or humiliation.

Council on American Islamic Relations (CAIR)

The Council on American Islamic Relations (CAIR) was established in 1994, but in the wake of the backlash against Muslims that followed the events of September 11, 2001, it has come to national prominence as the leading civil rights advocate for the growing number of Muslim Americans. This is probably because of its ability to fill an important void in addressing issues that are pressing for Muslim Americans in a period of crisis and to respond quickly to events through the use of electronic communication, and to the strength of its programs.

Through political and social activism, CAIR works to debunk negative stereotypes of Islam and empower its constituents. Its slogan, "Faith in Action," explains CAIR's programs, which include (1) media relations: monitoring the media for stereotypes and projecting a positive image of Islam, as in the "Islam in America" advertisement campaign in major newspapers; (2) publications: for example, the "Know Your Rights Pocket Guide," "An Employer's Guide to Islamic Religious Practices," and "Teaching About Islam and Muslims in the Public School Classroom"; and (3) action alerts: encouraging grassroots activism.

CAIR has been tallying cases of hate crimes and bias incidents that individuals report over the phone or via e-mail, as well as stories from the press. Periodically, a report is published summarizing this work, such as the May 2002 report entitled "The Status of Muslim Civil Rights in the United States: Stereotypes and Civil Liberties." Among CAIR's most popular programs is the daily electronic news it sends to its Listserv group summarizing mentions of Islam, Muslims, and Arabs in the local, national, and international press. These daily e-mails also disseminate information on community events and fundraisers and encourage readers to write protest or encouragement letters to officials and the press. In its work, CAIR educates its membership on how to function effectively in the United States. CAIR's primary goals, however, remain the education of the larger American public about Islam.

MEHDI BOZORGMEHR AND ANNY BAKALIAN

Hate Speech and the International Community

The United States has yet to follow the lead of other nations such as Canada, France, Great Britain, Germany, and Ireland, which have all passed laws prohibiting at least some forms of hate speech. Long tradition of free speech protection has resulted in the United States' refusal to address the issue of hate speech where even on colleges campuses, which are often designated to be progressive spaces, speech codes have been met with resistance (Levin and McDevitt, 1999). In March 2012, 21-year-old English college student Liam Stacey was sentenced to 56 days in prison for posting racially offensive remarks on Twitter about Fabrice Muamba, a black soccer player who had a heart attack on the field and almost died. Whereas this incident would be protected under the guise of freedom and civil liberties in the United States, it was classified as racial abuse in Britain and the offender was punished accordingly.

It is important to remember that hate crimes do not necessarily involve hate and are more about bias and prejudice, while crimes that perhaps do involve hate, such as crimes of passion, are not necessarily hate crimes. Hate speech is also different than hate crime, where prohibiting hate speech has often been ruled unconstitutional in the United States. In addition, there is a difference between hate crime and hate groups, where hate groups are infrequently involved in hate crimes because they are often secluded. That is not to say, however, that hate groups do not provide the ideological framework from which perpetrators of hate crime may legitimize their behavior.

Hate crimes are more than isolated, bigoted acts; they are embedded in structural and cultural context in which groups use violence as an instrument of intimidation to control and reaffirm both perpetrators' and victims' place within the social hierarchy. This is evident in the way in which dominant groups such as whites, males, heterosexuals, and American-born citizens have utilized violence and the threat of violence to reinforce their privilege and simultaneously reinforce the stigmatized and marginalized position of racialized, sexualized, and religious others. Throughout history, Native Americans, freed black slaves, and immigrants, and in recent times, blacks, women, and homosexuals who have fought for equal rights and thus challenged the social structure have been targeted for victimization. Aside from the way in which current legislation downplays the oppressive nature of the racialized and gendered social order in the intent of hate motivated crime, scholars have criticized the way in which hate crime is legally defined in that it does not account for violations that may be legal, such as the Holocaust. Because there is currently no federal law that prohibits discrimination against homosexuals or non-gender-conforming individuals, denying employment or housing to gay or transgendered people is not considered a hate crime even though

Hate Crimes Statistics Act of 1990

Sponsored by Rep. John Conyers Jr. of Michigan, and having over 100 co-sponsors, the Hate Crimes Statistics Act was passed in 1990. Hate crimes are defined in the legislation as "manifest prejudice based on race, religion, sexual orientation, or ethnicity." The act requires the U.S. Department of Justice to compile national data annually on the incidence of hate crimes and to publish an annual summary of findings. The act was intended to help create a hate-crime index and to allow for the tracking of the incidence of hate crimes. The act arose out of a growing concern in the late 20th century over an increase in hate crime.

The FBI collects this information through the Uniform Crime Reporting System, which compiles aggregate data based on crime statistics reported by state and local policing agencies. The Higher Education and Reauthorization Act of 1998 mandated that hate crimes on college campuses be included in these data. Since the passage of the act, the federal definition of hate crimes has been expanded. In 1994, the Violent Crime Control and Law Enforcement Act amended the Hate Crimes Statistics Act to include manifest prejudice based on disability. The Hate Crimes Statistics Improvement Act of 2003, introduced in the House by Rep. Carolyn Maloney of New York, would also add manifest prejudice based on gender.

VICTORIA PITTS

the behavior is motivated by prejudice, since a hate crime is predicated only when another violation of an existing criminal code occurs.

Throughout the 1990s, nearly two-thirds of the motivations for hate crime were race-based, and hate crimes tended to be more severe than criminal actions alone. For instance, those injured in nonbiased assaults were not nearly as likely to need medical treatment as victims of hate crimes. This trend still continues today where more than 80 percent of hate crimes reported in 2009 were associated with violent crime such as rape, assault, and robbery. In 2006, the FBI reported 7,722 incidents of hate crimes, 52 percent of which were directed at individuals because of their race. Of the bias hate crimes in 2009, 48.8 percent were racially motivated and of racially motivated incidents, 71.5 percent were inspired by an offender's antiblack bias (U.S. Department of Justice 2009). The percentage of race-based bias crime has declined in recent years due to a dramatic spike in crimes targeting Muslims and sexual minorities. However, the Southern Poverty Law Center (2011) predicts that the 2011 data will show a rise in anti-Latino hate crimes due to the anti-immigrant rhetoric surrounding the passage of Arizona's S.B. 1070.

Though the defining and recording of hate crime is seen as a positive step toward equality, the ever-changing landscape of diversity in the United States continues to result in bias crimes similarly to the way in which violence has been used against minorities throughout American history.

ADRIENNE N. MILNER

See also

Arizona Senate Bill 1070 (SB 1070) (2010); Hate Groups in America; Southern Poverty Law Center (SPLC)

Further Reading:

Jacobs, James B., and Kimberly Potter. *Hate Crimes: Criminal Law and Identity Politics*. Oxford: Oxford University Press, 1998.

Levin, Jack, and Jack McDevitt. "Hate Crimes," in *Encyclopedia of Violence, Peace, And Conflict, Volume 2, F-Pe*, edited by Lester R. Kurtz and Jennifer E. Turpin, 89–102. New York: Academic Press, 1999.

Morris, Steven. "Student Jailed for Racist Fabrice Muamba Tweets." *Guardian*. 2012. http://www.guardian.co.uk/uk/2012/mar/27/student-jailed-fabrice-muamba-tweets.

Perry, Barbara. *In the Name of Hate: Understanding Hate Crimes*. New York: Routledge, 2001.

Southern Poverty Law Center. *Hate and Extremism*. 2013. http://www.splcenter.org/what-we-do/hate-and-extremism.

U.S. Department of Justice. *Hate Crime Statistics*. 2009. http://www2.fbi.gov/ucr/hc2009/victims.html.

Hate Groups in America

A hate group is defined as individuals or groups that have beliefs or practices that attack an entire class of people, typically for such immutable characteristics as race, religion, disability, sexual orientation, or ethnicity/national origin. Hate groups have been on the rise in the United States since 2000. One organization estimates that in 2012, the total number of active, known hate groups in America was 1,018, a figure that represents a 60 percent increase since 2000. Researchers have put the total number of active members in these hate groups at anywhere from 20,000 to 30,000. The most prevalent and visible types of hate groups included in these statistics include neo-Nazis, Klansmen, white nationalists, neo-Confederates, racist skinheads, black separatists, border vigilantes, and others. Among these groups, white supremacists are the most prevalent hate group in America, evidencing that racial prejudice and discrimination remains a pressing issue in the United States even to this day.

While hate groups vary widely in their individual member characteristics, they generally share two common characteristics. First, hate groups are defined by being bigoted against some other group. In the United States, the vast majority of hate groups are white supremacist in nature, meaning they define the term *white* very narrowly and consider anyone who does not fit into this definition of whiteness to be inferior. While these white supremacist groups are the dominant form of hate group in America, there are many other bigoted groups, such as the Nation of Islam and Black Separatists. The second characteristic shared by all hate groups in America is that they are organized. This means that hate groups have an identifiable leader, as well as symbols to represent their solidarity, and traditions in which they engage.

Many hate groups also share a common set of ideologies. Included among these is the ideology of power. An ideology is a system of ideas that forms the basis for an operating

---

Revolutionary Action Movement (RAM)

The Revolutionary Action Movement (RAM) was a militant organization founded in the 1960s by Max Stanford (also known as Muhammad Ahmad). RAM was notorious for its reputed role in the conspiracies to assassinate civil rights leaders and in the ghetto riots of the 1960s.

Stanford fashioned RAM from an amalgam of the philosophies endorsed by Malcolm X (Black Nationalism), Robert F. Williams (black self-defense), and Queen Mother Audley Moore (Marxism). RAM recruited youth from within black ghettos, prisoners, and ex-convicts as members. It influenced blacks who had rejected the nonviolent methodology and integrationism of the original Student Nonviolent Coordinating Committee (SNCC) and the Congress of Racial Equality (CORE), and supported the rise of like-minded militant organizations such as the Black Panther Party (BPP), the Black Liberation Army, and the League of Revolutionary Black Workers. Stanford himself cofounded the African Liberation Support Committee and was instrumental in the struggle for reparations.

The violent orientation of RAM made it a target of the Federal Bureau of Investigation (FBI), which infiltrated the organization with its agents. In 1967, Stanford and several other members were arrested for allegedly plotting to assassinate several civil rights leaders. RAM claimed that the charges were never substantiated. RAM was also accused of plotting the violent rebellions within the nation's ghettos. Despite the fact that Roy Wilkins was one of the reputed targets of RAM's assassination plot, he stated in its defense that the riots were the independent responses of poor blacks who felt "abandoned by his government and his country" and "isolated, of no importance in the United States" (Wilkins 1982: 324–26).

Gladys L. Knight

---

theory, and among hate groups, power is the driving ideology, as these groups are often concerned either with gaining power or with their perceived loss of power in a society. As the vast majority of hate groups are white supremacist, a common belief among these groups is that the white race is supreme to all other races and should therefore maintain positions of power in the United States. These groups believe that whites are losing power and privilege through the actions of various minority groups such as racial and ethnic minorities, women, and homosexuals. In attempts to maintain power for their race, white supremacist groups are known to vilify minorities and characterize them in derogatory ways. Other hate groups, such as Black Nationalists and the Nation of Islam, are concerned with their lack of power in the United States and are striving to obtain more power. A second common ideology among hate groups is the ideology of racial separatism, meaning that these groups aspire, at the extreme, to have separate societies reserved only for their members. To a lesser extreme, this ideology allows for only a few "outsiders" as long as these outsiders adhere to a strict attitudinal and behavioral code that recognizes the supremacy of the main group. In the United States, the ideology of racial separatism is most often espoused by white supremacist groups and the Nation of Islam.

Most hate group "meetings" are rather informal, as members simply spend time together reinforcing their ideologies of hate. In some cases, group members will engage in hate speech, which is defined as derogatory words or symbols that vilify a person or group on the basis of a minority group's status. While it is a commonly held belief that the majority of hate crimes are carried out by hate groups, research has indicated that most of these crimes are instead committed by individuals who are not formally affiliated with a hate group.

Hate groups build membership in a variety of ways. For the most part, individuals who eventually become members of organized hate groups already hold the ideologies that are consistent with the group, often joining the group because they have personal contact with someone in the group and are looking for common understanding. However, hate groups are known to engage in some methods of recruitment, including distributing propaganda such as fliers and pamphlets and hosting radio talk shows. Technological developments have also helped hate groups to disseminate information more easily and recruit new members more efficiently. The unregulated World Wide Web is now being widely used by hate groups for purposes of recruitment and unification, which has allowed hate groups to expand their audiences worldwide.

In fact, the Internet can be considered a major contributing factor to the growth of hate groups in the United States in recent years. In the past, hate groups have relied on low-tech propaganda such as fliers, newsletters, mailings, small rallies, and interpersonal contact to spread their ideas and recruit members. However, today, hate groups are increasingly using the Internet for these purposes in a phenomenon that is referred to as "cyber-hate." In 1995, there was only one recorded hate group–related Web site. By 2000, there were an estimated 3,000 Web sites containing messages of hate, racism, terrorist agendas, and bomb making instructions. Studies estimate that anywhere from 5,000 to 10,000 people visit these sites on a regular basis. This number has remained relatively constant since that counting. These Web sites are largely targeting young, white males as statistics show they are the most likely groups to use the Internet to view hate material. Perhaps one reason for the expansion of "cyber-hate" is that the Internet provides hate groups an anonymous link to people around the world wherein they can share their racist ideologies.

The first known hate group Web site was developed by U.S. citizen Don Black on March 27, 1995. Black was a former Klansman who learned computer skills while in a federal prison, later using those skills to launch his white pride worldwide online campaign through a site he named Stormfront. Stormfront is a launch pad site providing links to other white supremacist Web sites. Black argued that the mainstream media in the United States was dominated by liberal whites and Jews and that his Web site would provide an alternative media outlet for like-minded, white supremacist individuals to interact and exchange ideas. Since the launching of Stormfront in 1995, many other hate groups have developed online platforms, most of them white supremacist in nature.

As hate groups have increasingly used the Internet to spread their racist ideologies, there has been a parallel increase in the number of hate crimes being committed by individuals who have accessed hate propaganda on the Internet. For example, David Copeland, the mastermind behind the 1999 London bombings, is cited as an individual whose primary contact with racist politics was by way of the Internet. Copeland is also known to have found his recipe for the nail bombs used in the attack online. Despite the increasing number of hate crimes inspired by online material, online hate speech is almost impossible to regulate because of the First Amendment right to free speech. Nevertheless, several organizations, including the Anti-Defamation League, are now spending considerable resources in an attempt to combat online hate speech.

Despite great strides made in civil rights in American society over the last several decades, hate groups are still active and are even on the rise, as they have recently experienced an upsurge in membership, perhaps due to the Internet emerging as a new platform. There is a great variety of hate groups within the United States, but they all share certain common characteristics and ideologies, the most common of which being white supremacy. Since these groups have begun to utilize the Internet as a platform to disseminate their ideologies, both within the United States and abroad, hate groups today are even more difficult to monitor and suppress.

Virginia R. Beard

See also

Black Panther Party (BPP); Black Separatism; Christian Identity Hate Groups; Ku Klux Klan (KKK); Student Nonviolent Coordinating Committee

Further Reading:

Ahmad, Muhammad, Ernie Allen, John H. Bracey, and Randolph Boehm, eds. *The Black Power Movement (Black Studies Research Sources)*. Bethesda, MD: Lexis Nexis, 2002.

Gerstenfeld, Phyllis B. *Hate Crimes: Causes, Controls and Controversies*. Los Angeles: SAGE, 2011.

Perry, Barbara. *In the Name of Hate: Understanding Hate Crimes*. New York: Routledge, 2001.

Ryan, Matt E., and Peter T. Leeson. "Hate Groups and Hate Crime." *International Review of Law and Economics* (2011).

Southern Poverty Law Center. "Active U.S. Hate Groups." http://www.splcenter.org/get-informed/hate-map (accessed December 20, 2012).

Southern Poverty Law Center. "Hate Map." http://www.splcenter.org/get-informed/hate-map (accessed December 20, 2012).

Wilkins, Roy, with Tom Matthews. *The Autobiography of Roy Wilkins: Standing Fast*. New York: Penguin Books, 1982.

Hawkins, Yusef (1973–1989)

Yusef Hawkins was an African American student whose 1989 murder by Italian American youths in Bensonhurst, New York, created severe racial tensions between the African American and Italian American communities.

During the evening of August 23, 1989, Yusef Hawkins traveled from the mostly African American Bedford-Stuyvesant area in Brooklyn to the predominantly Italian American working-class community of Bensonhurst. The 16-year-old Hawkins went there with three friends to look at a used Pontiac car for sale. While in Bensonhurst, a group of about 30 local young men accosted Hawkins and his friends because they believed that Hawkins had been invited to a party hosted by a girlfriend of one of the youths. Armed with bats, the young men chased Hawkins and his friends. While running after them, one of the youths fired four shots at Hawkins and his friends. Two of the bullets struck Hawkins, and he later died.

The incident sparked outrage and an increase of racial tension between African Americans and Italian Americans. Demonstrations also soon followed, and one of the largest rallies was held on August 31, 1989. Proclaimed as the Day of Outrage, approximately 8,000 people gathered on Flatbush Avenue in Bensonhurst to protest the death of Hawkins. Their massive cry of "No justice, no peace," called for equality and freedom from oppression. Two weeks later, on September 19, African American activist Jesse Jackson led a group of high school students in Bensonhurst to protest the racially motivated killing. The shooter, Joseph Fama, received a sentence of 32 years; several other defendants received lesser sentences in 1991. Outraged by what he considered lenient sentencing, the Rev. Al Sharpton organized a protest in Bensonhurst that same year. He was met by angry demonstrators and one, Michael Riccardi, stabbed him in the stomach. Sharpton also became the spokesperson for Diane Hawkins and Moses Stewart, the parents of Yusef Hawkins.

DORSÍA SMITH SILVA

See also

Hate Crimes in America

Further Reading:

Thernstrom, Stephan, and Abigail Thernstrom. *America in Black and White: One Nation, Indivisible.* New York: Simon & Schuster, 1997.

Hayes-Tilden Compromise of 1877

The controversial results of the 1876 presidential election between Samuel J. Tilden, a Democrat from New York, and Rutherford B. Hayes, a Republican from Ohio, led to a political deal that dramatically affected Southern history and race relations throughout the United States. This election was so tainted by allegations of voting fraud and other irregularities that it was unclear who won the popular vote in four states. Supporters of each candidate claimed the electoral votes of the states in question, and the decision as to who would be declared the winner was given over to the House of Representatives. In February 1877, after intense political negotiation, a deal was struck whereby Democrats conceded the election to Hayes (the Republican), and in return Hayes promised to remove all remaining federal troops from the South and to recognize the white-dominated state governments that remained committed to undermining political and social gains that blacks had made during the Reconstruction era.

Although some saw this arrangement as a gesture toward regional reconciliation and a first step toward ending Northern dominance over the South, many others saw it as sign that Northern whites had lost interest in protecting African Americans' civil and social rights, as established by the Thirteenth, Fourteenth, and Fifteenth Amendments to the Constitution. In more partisan terms, it was seen as evidence that the Republicans—the party of Abraham Lincoln, "The Great Emancipator," and congressional leaders such as Thaddeus Stevens and Charles Sumner, who supported equal rights for freed slaves—had "sold out" the cause of black equality in exchange for taking over the office of the presidency. Indeed, in the decades after this compromise, black oppression deepened in cruel and brutal ways as whites disenfranchised African Americans, exploited their labor, institutionalized "Jim Crow" segregation laws in many facets of life, and without fear of punishment lynched thousands of blacks.

Given the ineffectiveness and corruption of the previous Republican administration led by President Ulysses S. Grant, the Democrats had appeared likely to win the 1876 election, and Tilden actually won the total popular vote. But disputes over ballots cast in South Carolina, Louisiana, Florida, and Oregon prevented either candidate from obtaining the needed number of electoral votes to become president. The House of Representatives then created a

The controversial way in which Rutherford B. Hayes was elected has tended to overshadow his presidency. (Library of Congress)

bipartisan commission to investigate the election and resolve the matter. Its deliberations were contentious, and a bargain was worked out to give each side something. In return for Republican candidate Hayes receiving all the electoral votes of the states in question (which would allow him to become president), Hayes promised several things that Southern Democrats wanted. The most important of these was to withdraw federal troops that were still stationed in the South and have the federal government refrain from interfering in white Southerners' efforts to subordinate blacks. Other elements of the compromise involved Hayes promising to include at least one Southern white in his cabinet, to appoint some Democrats to patronage offices in the South, and to support federal legislation that would assist in industrializing the South. Soon after he was inaugurated in March 1877, Hayes ordered federal troops out of the South. This set the stage for many years of social and political control by supporters of white supremacy. Among other things, they established whites-only primary elections, created racially

segregated schools, and tolerated Ku Klux Klan violence. Until Franklin D. Roosevelt was elected president in 1932, the federal government remained mute as blacks were ensnared in racist systems that denied them their rights and excluded them from a host of educational, economic, political, and social opportunities.

CHARLES JARET

See also
Voting and Race

Further Reading:
Blauner, B. *Still the Big News: Racial Oppression in America.* Philadelphia: Temple University Press, 2001.
Bonilla-Silva, E. *White Supremacy and Racism in the Post-Civil Rights Era.* Boulder, CO: Lynne Rienner Publishers, 2001.
Feagin, J.R. *Racist America: Roots, Current Realities, and Future Reparations.* New York: Routledge, 2010.

Health Care Access

Racial and ethnic minorities tend to receive a lower quality of health care access. Even when factors such as access to health insurance status and income are controlled, minorities still witness a significant gap in health care access. Some of the factors that determine the gap in health care access are related to socioeconomic status, poverty, and access to health insurance. When racial and ethnic minorities receive health services, there is evidence of receiving lower-quality health care. Racial attitudes of health care providers are also an important factor. Finally, the influence of racial bias in white opposition to the new more universal health care law shows that health access continues to be racialized.

There is a much higher probability that minorities will be uninsured. In 2011 for individuals under 65, 11.1 percent of whites were uninsured. In contrast, 19.5 percent of African Americans and 30.1 percent of Hispanics were not covered by any insurance. Native Americans have the highest rates of uninsured individuals at 44.2 percent. Uninsured Asians were between whites and African Americans at 16.8 percent. When racial and ethnic minorities are insured they are much more likely to be covered by Medicaid than whites. The only exception is Asians, who are more likely to have private insurance.

The economic recession at the beginning of the 21st century impacted African Americans and Hispanics to a much greater degree than their white counterparts. High unemployment rates in conjunction with differences in savings and wealth resulted in lapses in health coverage and difficulties in paying for adequate health care. Hispanics are overrepresented in occupations with the highest unemployment rates such as construction and maintenance.

Hispanics and African Americans report more difficulty affording and accessing health coverage and care than whites. In 2009 38 percent of Hispanics reported having trouble paying for health care in contrast with 25 percent of African Americans and 22 percent of whites because of the economic downturn. Loss of health coverage has directly affected 25 percent of African Americans, 21 percent of Hispanics, and 13 percent of whites. A higher percentage of Hispanics and African Americans than whites also report either postponing or skipping needed health care due to cost.

This was related to the decline in median household income. In 2011 there was a significant disparity in median income between racial and ethnic groups. Blacks had the lowest median income at $32,229, a negative 2.7 percent change from 2010. Hispanics median income remained approximately the same between 2010 and 2011 at $38,624. Asians had the highest median income at $65,129. Non-Hispanic whites also experienced a decline in income from 2010 to 2011. Their income declined 1.4 percent to $55,412. Income has a significant influence on the ability to afford health insurance.

For racial and ethnic minorities particularly, poverty status and lack of health insurance make it difficult to get necessary health and medical care. Once they do visit health providers, poor, uninsured minorities often report racial discrimination when communicating with health care professionals. Especially for uninsured blacks and Hispanics, lack of insurance is related to increased perceptions of racial and ethnic bias in health care. This is a significant problem because individuals who experience discrimination are more likely to put off medical tests and procedures.

Physicians tended to perceive African Americans and low socioeconomic groups more negatively than whites and higher socioeconomic patients. The patient's race was associated with the physician's assessment of the patient's intelligence, and the beliefs about the patient's likelihood of risk behavior and likelihood of following medical advice. The socioeconomic status of the patient and race and ethnicity were also associated with the physician's perceptions of the patient's personality, abilities, and behavioral tendencies.

Taken together, lack of health insurance, higher poverty rates, discrimination, and skepticism of health care providers means that racial and ethnic minorities receive inferior health care. Another important variable is the attitude of physicians' perceptions of patients, which is more negative generally toward African Americans and members of low socioeconomic minorities.

The Affordable Care Act of 2010 (ACA) would close some of the significant racial and ethnic gaps in health access. The public perception and antagonism against the new law is significantly correlated with race, according to the Kaiser Family Foundation. In November 2012 African Americans held a 68 percent favorable attitude toward the ACA. In contrast whites' perception was more negative than positive with only 35 percent favorable to the law. Hispanics were between the two groups; 52 percent viewed the law favorably. It appears that some opposition to President Obama's health care reform law is linked to racial bias.

CAROL SCHMID

See also
Health Gap

Further Reading:
Berndt, Julia, and Cara James. "The Effects of the Economic Recession on Communities of Color." Race, Ethnicity and Health Care Issue Brief. Henry Kaiser Family Foundation. July, 2009. http://www.kff.org/minorityhealth/upload/7953 .pdf (accessed November 8, 2012).
Kaiser Family Foundation. "Health Tracking Poll: Exploring the Public's View on the Affordable Care Act (ACA)." http://www .kff.org/dataviz/index.html (accessed December 3, 2012).
Medical News Today. "Poor, Uninsured Perceive More Discrimination during Health Care Visits." December 13, 2007. http://www.medicalnewstoday.com/printer friendlynews.php?newsid=91625 (cited November 24, 2012).
U.S Census. "Income, Poverty and Health Insurance Coverage in the United States: 2011." September 12, 2012. http://www .census.gov/newsroom/releases/archives/income_wealth/ cb12-172.html (cited November 8, 2012).
Van Ryn, M., and J. Burke. "The Effect of Patient Race and Socioeconomic Status on Physicians' Perception of Patients." *Social Science & Medicine* 50, no. 6 (March 2000): 13–28.

Health Gap

In the first decade of the 21st century there continue to be pervasive and significant health care gaps between African Americans, Hispanics, Native Americans, and non-Hispanic whites as documented by the Office of Minority Health. These health disparities are recorded in the areas of asthma, cancer, chronic liver disease, diabetes, heart disease, hepatitis, HIV/AIDS, infant health, mental health, obesity, oral health, organ and tissue donation, and stroke (Office of Minority Health). The major sources of these disparities are related to health care access, lack of adequate health insurance, higher unemployment among minorities, and lower social class than non-Hispanic whites and Asian Americans.

Asthma has increased in the general population in the last two decades. Minorities, however, have been particularly affected, particularly children. African American children have an 80 percent higher incidence of asthma than white children. They were also seven times more likely to die from asthma between 2003 and 2005. Native Americans were 20 percent more likely to be diagnosed with asthma in 2008 than their white counterparts.

Cancer in its many forms is overrepresented among minorities. African American men are twice as likely to die of prostate cancer as whites. African American women are less likely to be diagnosed with breast cancer, but 40 percent more likely to die of the disease than white women. Hispanic women are 1.9 times more likely to be diagnosed with cervical cancer than non-Hispanic white women.

Chronic liver disease is much more common among African American men than non-Hispanic whites—they are 70 percent more likely to have the disease. Both Hispanic men and women have a chronic liver disease rate that is twice that for their white counterparts.

Diabetes is another disease that is more common among minorities. In 2012, over 13 percent of Hispanics 18 years and older had diabetes. African American and Native American adults were twice as likely to be diagnosed with diabetes as whites. African American women are particularly affected with the disease.

Heart disease strikes minorities more than their white counterparts. African American men and women are 30 percent more likely to die from heart disease than white, non-Hispanic males. Premature death among Mexican Americans is more likely than among non-Hispanic whites (23.5 percent versus 16.5 percent).

Despite the decline of hepatitis A and B with new vaccines (there are currently no vaccines for hepatitis C), minorities still die more from the disease than whites. In 2009, African Americans were 50 percent more likely to die from viral hepatitis as compared to non-Hispanic whites. In 2010, American Indians were almost three times as likely to develop hepatitis C compared to the white population. Hispanics are twice as likely to be diagnosed with hepatitis A as non-Hispanic whites.

HIV/AIDS has a devastating impact on American minorities. African American males have 7.6 times the AIDS rate as white males, and African American women have almost 20 times the HIV rate of non-Hispanic white women. For Hispanic females, the AIDS rate is four times as great as non-Hispanic white females.

The United States has made substantial improvement on reducing infant deaths, but disparity still exists between racial and ethnic groups. In 2008, the infant death rate among African Americans was more than twice that for comparable whites. Among Native Americans the infant death rate is 1.6 times higher than their white counterparts.

Mental health treatment is underutilized with patients reluctant to seek services and insurers reluctant to pay for services. Individuals living under the poverty level are particularly susceptible to psychological distress. In 2010 adults living below the poverty level were three times more likely to have serious psychological distress as compared to adults over twice the poverty level. Both African Americans and Hispanics are disproportionately in poverty (in 2010, the poverty rate for non-Hispanic whites was 9.9 percent, for blacks 27.4 percent, and for Hispanics 26.6 percent). In general, minorities have less access to mental health services.

Obesity is a national problem in the United States in that it is associated with increased mortality rates and higher rates of heart disease, diabetes, and some types of cancer. Unfortunately obesity is concentrated in the minority population. In 2012, African American women had a 40 percent higher obesity rate than non-Hispanic white women. Mexican American children (between ages 6 and 17) in 2009–2010 were 60 percent more likely to be overweight than their non-Hispanic counterparts. Obesity is also much greater among

American Indians and Alaskan natives, approximately 70 percent higher than non-Hispanic whites.

Dental and oral care is also worse for the minority population. In 2004, only 30 percent of African Americans had annual dental visits in comparison to half of the white non-Hispanic population. Hispanics were twice as likely to have untreated tooth decay as whites. These trends start with children and continue to adulthood.

Minorities are disproportionately candidates for organ transplants. They make up 55 percent of individuals on waiting lists but they comprise only 34 percent of organ transplants performed. On the other hand, white patients make up 45 percent of those on the waiting lists but comprise 66 percent of transplants performed.

Strokes are much more common among African Americans and American Indians/Alaska natives. African Americans are 1.6 times more likely to suffer from a stroke than whites. For American Indians/Alaska natives the rate is even higher—they are 2.4 times as likely to have a stroke as their white adult counterparts.

Taken together these medical trends show pervasive and worse outcomes for African Americans, Hispanics, and American Indians/Alaskan natives. Even at higher incomes whites and Asians have better health status than African Americans and Hispanics (Staveteig and Wigton 2000). Multiple factors contribute to racial/ethnic health disparities including socioeconomic factors associated with income, education, and employment; racial discrimination; lack of preventative health care services; and lower rates of health insurance. Health disparities lead to earlier deaths, decreased quality of life, and higher health care costs (Center for Disease Control 2005).

CAROL SCHMID

See also
Health Care Access

Further Reading:
Centers for Disease Control. *Health Disparities Experienced by Black or African Americans—United States.* January 14, 2005. http://www.cdc.gov/mmwr/preview/mmwrhtml/mm5401a1 .htm (cited November 5, 2012).
Office of Minority Health. U.S Department of Health and Human Services. *Data by Health Topic.* http://minorityhealth.hhs.gov/ templates/browse.aspx?lvl=2&lvlid=9 (cited November 10, 2012).
Staveteig, S., and Wigton, A. "Racial and Ethnic Disparities: Key Findings from the National Survey of American's Families." Urban Institute. Series B, no. B-5, February 2000. http://www .urban.org/UploadedPDF/anf_b5.pdf (cited November 5, 2012).

Hereditarians versus Environmentalists

The age-old debate over which shapes human behavior, nature or nurture, is at the root of the debate between hereditarians and environmentalists. Hereditarians tend to emphasize the importance of inherited traits. Hereditarians have often argued that some racial groups are inherently superior to others and that inherent racial differences explain why some racial groups are generally more advantaged than others. Environmentalists tend to stress the importance of the environment and opportunity structures in which a person is embedded. Today, this debate might be seen as being between genetics and environment, but the differences between hereditarians and environmentalists have historically been more complex. For example, social Darwinists of the Progressive era were strongly hereditarian, but they tended to see inherited traits as being shaped by the behavior of the parents. In other words, in their view, a child born to parents who had been criminals could inherit a criminal tendency that they would not have inherited if those same parents had not engaged in criminal behavior.

This is a much more flexible view of inherited traits than we have today. It is as if DNA, which had not yet been discovered in the Progressive era, could be changed by the actions of individuals. Although this might seem to be a less-restrictive view of human potential than the contemporary genetics-based view, it had within it frightening implications: for instance, that the downward spiral of a family could continue with each generation, becoming progressively more criminal, stupid, or otherwise undesirable. Hereditarians of this era viewed this process as being similar to the process of breeding animals for particular traits: with generations of breeding, it would be difficult to reverse the traits. Today, hereditarians tend to focus more on genetic predisposition. There is relatively little talk of people being genetically programmed to be criminals. Instead, hereditarians tend to focus on inherited traits as setting the parameters for behavior. In other words, they may view aggression as an inherited trait, but whether that aggression is expressed as criminal violence or corporate advancement depends on personal choices and social opportunities. Similarly, few contemporary environmentalists deny any role to biology or genetics in shaping behavior. The idea that children are blank slates and can be turned into anything at all has fallen out of fashion. Today, the main difference between hereditarians and environmentalists is in which is seen as the dominant factor in people's lives: inherited traits or social and environmental factors. Hereditarians and environmentalists also tend to differ in their assessment of social inequality.

Hereditarians as a group view social inequality as reflecting innate differences between groups. For example, in the early 1990s, prominent hereditarians such as Arthur Jensen have argued that there are real and measurable differences in the intelligence levels of different racial groups. These real—in other words, biological—differences, they argue, account in part for social inequality. In contrast, environmentalists tend to view social inequality as primarily the result of social structures that perpetuate the power of some groups over others.

Hereditarians are often accused of being racists. In response, they argue that scientists must study the world as it is and not as they wish it to be. Critics of hereditarianism, such as Stephen Jay Gould, argue that hereditarians misuse science to justify social inequality. Debates between hereditarians and environmentalists often focus on both concrete issues of research methodology and more abstract philosophical questions, such as how much science can be detached from its social context.

ROBIN ROGER-DILLON

See also
Biological Racism

Further Reading:
Gould, Stephen Jay. *Mismeasure of Man*. New York: Norton, 1981.
Herrnstein, Richard J., and Charles Murray. *The Bell Curve: Intelligence and Class Structure in American Life*. New York: Free Press, 1994.

Hidden Curriculum

The hidden curriculum refers to everything the formal curriculum does not explicitly cover but that students learn through the organizational arrangement, unwritten rules, routines, rituals, and cultural milieu of their schools. Through the hidden curriculum, students are taught dominant values and attitudes, such as obedience to authority and conformity to cultural norms, hard work, punctuality, "proper English," and acceptable manners, that employers would require of their workers. The hidden curriculum embodies and reproduces at the same time the structural inequality of a society by class, gender, race, national origin, religion, and sexual orientation. The hidden curriculum works against the optimistic hope of educator John Dewey that universal education would eventually lead to democracy and equality.

Even well-intended educators, when they are not fully aware of the hidden curriculum, may contribute unwittingly to the perpetuation of racial stratification. The hidden curriculum is present in the formal curriculum, the teaching process, and the culture of the school. In the formal curriculum, what counts as knowledge reflects the cultural biases of the white middle class. Even the IQ test, which appears neutral and objective, is culturally tilted in a way that disadvantages ethnic minorities as well as lower-class and female students. Assessment procedures in general that are culturally and racially biased can lead to misevaluation and reinforce racial stereotypes. Teaching materials often contain linguistic expressions and graphic illustrations that reproduce racial and ethnic stereotypes.

In the teaching process, teachers' preconceptions and expectations of their students based on their race play a significant role in students' development. Generally, black students get less attention and encouragement from teachers and thus tend to have lower self-esteem. Even though African American girls start out with positive behaviors, teachers give them less academic feedback. Even worse off are African American males, who are more likely to be negatively labeled as "a problem" and referred to special-education programs. In contrast, Asian American students tend to be viewed as the best. Often, teachers encourage ethnic minority children to participate fully only in stereotypical areas. For example, African American boys are often thought to be naturally good at sports.

The culture milieu of the school is also an important part of the hidden curriculum. The rules of conduct, ceremonies, and rituals in the U.S. school system represent the dominant white Anglo-Saxon Protestant culture. They are not updated yet to represent the cultural diversity of ethnic groups that make up U.S. society. The specific religious reference in the Pledge of Allegiance and the insistence on school prayer can alienate students who are from non-Western religious backgrounds. The historic symbols that are inherited from the bygone years of ethnic extirpation, slavery, Jim Crow, and colonialism still survive in ceremonies and rituals to damage the self-esteem of the nonwhite students. For example, the use of the Confederate flag or war whoops, tomahawks, and "savage" mascots at sports events creates a hostile environment for African American and Native American students.

Although the hidden curriculum has a significant influence on students, students are by no means passive containers. The process of socialization always involves struggle and conflict. For example, as Paul Willis's 1970s ethnographic study shows, working-class kids may develop a rebellious counterculture, a possibly embryonic form of working-class culture, against the dominant culture the school system embodies. In this sense, the hidden curriculum may be said to be a cultural battlefield, in which the dynamics of social, political, and economic conflicts unfold around the assumptions, stereotypes, and social structure taken for granted in everyday routines.

DONG-HO CHO

See also

Clark Doll Study; Ideological Racism; Meritocracy; *Savage Inequalities*

Further Reading:

Gillborn, David. "Citizenship, 'Race,' and the Hidden Curriculum." *International Studies in the Sociology of Education* 2, no. 1 (1992): 57–73.

Irvine, Jacqueline Jordan. "Teacher-Student Interactions: Effects of Students' Race, Sex, and Grade Level." *Journal of Educational Psychology* 78, no. 1 (1986): 14–21.

Willis, Paul. *Learning to Labor*. New York: Columbia University Press, 1977.

Wren, David J. "School Culture: Exploring the Hidden Curriculum." *Adolescence* 43 (1999): 593–94.

Hip-Hop

Hip-hop is a musical style that is often characterized by stylized rhythmic music that is commonly accompanied by rapping. Some have labeled this art form as racist, while others argue it is simply a reflection of a unique culture. Scholars argue it developed in New York in the 1970s, during block parties where artists would mix portions of different songs and combine them with shouts and yells from the audience. The art progressively developed as part of a larger hip-hop subculture, defined by MCing/rapping, DJing/scratching, break dancing, graffiti writing, and sampling and beat boxing.

The term *hip-hop music* is sometimes used synonymously with the term *rap*, though rapping is not a required component of hip-hop music. Hip-hop is often seen as a mirror reflecting American society, in particular, and is composed of the society's positive and negative traits. The art form can also be thought of as uniquely American and is largely the combination of old and new forms of music based upon the process of sampling, which seeks to update and incorporate classic records. It follows in the footsteps of earlier American musical genres, such as blues, and has become a worldwide phenomenon.

The art form has, for some time, been largely criticized for espousing racism, especially when performed by African Americans. This criticism has been framed in a way that rebukes critiques of larger society and suggests that the lyrics reflect a "self-fulfilling prophecy" of pathological inferiority of African Americans. Critics claim the art is promoting racism and should be subsequently ostracized as the lyrics provide "proof" that black behavior creates the conditions of ghetto life. For example, Tricia Rose (2008: 5) suggests that some critics argue the art is composed of five racist ideologies:

1. Causes Violence
2. Reflects Black Dysfunctional Ghetto Culture
3. Hurts Black People
4. Destroys American Values
5. Demeans Women

The accusation that hip-hop promotes racism is largely unfounded as the arguments espoused ignore the culpability of larger social and political contexts. These critics often

Portrait of members of the hip-hop group, NWA, including DJ Yella, MC Ren, Eazy-E, and Dr. Dre. (Getty Images)

ignore the economic, political, and structural factors that may lead to some of these themes appearing in the music.

Hip-hop also has its defenders who argue that the art is not racist; rather, it is a form of artistic expression that allows for critiquing racism seen in larger society. These defenders suggest that the anger and dissatisfaction espoused in the lyrics is reflective of the individual experiences of racism the artists encounter (Taylor and Austen 2012). In addition, the lyrics are often seen as a way to express dissatisfaction regarding race-based biases related to employment, politics, and larger society. In this view, hip-hop is an art form that, like many other art forms, is counterhegemonic—it attempts to challenge the social status quo.

When the art is observed from the perspective of the artists one can observe that, at least in part, the music provides an avenue for rebellion. Hip-hop provides artists one of a few available venues to communicate ideas, values, and norms that are not in line with the larger American society. This is essential because "appropriate" modes of communication or dissent often restrict the content communicated and promote the dominant viewpoint of society.

Despite the mainstream success of hip-hop, racism in the art continues to be a primary criticism, which is often compounded by issues of race-based exploitation. Many have characterized the business of hip-hop as a modern-day minstrel show or a contemporary sharecropping arrangement,

---

Hip-Hop Worldwide

Many argue that hip-hop is an art form that originated as a response to oppression and racism, particularity in the United States. However, with the advent of mass communication and other global technologies, hip-hop has spread and is often used to challenge the social status quo in different societies throughout the world. The most recent evidence of this phenomenon was during the Arab Spring as many throughout the Middle East used hip-hip to rebel against repressive regimes.

The "Arab Rappers Spring" started with a hip-hop song titled "O Leader!" performed by El General, a Tunisian musician. The song gained popularity on the Internet and aided in starting an uprising that overthrew the Tunisian regime. Subsequently, two songs from the popular Egyptian rap group Arabian Knightz—"Not Your Prisoner" and "Rebel"—also hit the airwaves. These songs became the soundtrack of a revolutionary wave that swept throughout most of the Middle East and brought down several oppressive regimes.

Source: *USA Today*, "Rappers Provide Anthem For Arab Spring." http://usatoday30.usatoday.com/news/world/story/2012-05-21/ arab-spring-hip-hop/55120262/1 (accessed December 15, 2012).

---

and use this art for profit making or artistic challenges to the racial and social status quo.

JAMES W. LOVE

See also
Rap Music; Rhythm and Blues; Rock and Roll

Further Reading:
Chang, Jeff. *Can't Stop Won't Stop: A History of the Hip Hop Generation*. New York: Macmillan, 2005.
Collins, Patricia Hill. *From Black Power to Hip Hop: Racism, Nationalism, and Feminism*. Philadelphia, PA: Temple University Press, 2006.
Lhamon, W. T. *Raising Cain: Blackface Performance from Jim Crow to Hip Hop*. Cambridge, MA: Harvard University Press, 1998.
Mitchell, Tony. *Global Noise: Rap and Hip Hop Outside the USA*. Middletown, CT: Wesleyan University Press, 2002.
Morgan, Marcyliena. *The Real Hip Hop: Battling for Knowledge, Power, and Respect in the LA Underground*. Chapel Hill, NC: Duke University Press, 2009.
Patterson, Orlando. "Ecumenical America: Global Culture and the American Cosmos." *World Policy Journal* 11(1994): 103–17.
Rose, Tricia. *The Hip Hop Wars: What We Talk about When We Talk about Hip Hop and What It Matters*. New York: Basic Books, 2008.
Taylor, Yuval, and Jake Austen. *Darkest America: Black Minstrelsy from Slavery to Hip Hop*. New York: W. W. Norton, 2012.

---

which, in both cases, allows whites to economically prosper while promoting negative and demeaning stereotypes of African Americans (Lhamon 1998). Often this arrangement is fostered in the name of profit as hip-hop artists sign record deals without much control over the content of the music they produce; therefore, they are often underpaid, mistreated by management and record companies, and exploited for profit. This, unfortunately, leads some artists to replicate and buttress stereotypes attached to racial minorities in the modern age.

Whether one sees hip-hop as advocating racism or espousing the values of a unique American subculture, the art form has had a considerable impact on American society and the world. The art remains a prime moneymaker for the recording industry while also being a powerful influence on culture throughout the world. Mass communication has created a global hip-hop scene, which allows individuals throughout the world to absorb the American hip-hop scene

Hiring Practices

Researchers Philip Moss and Chris Tilly set out to find what skills American employers seek in their employees. Through phone surveys and face-to-face interviews with employers in Atlanta, Boston, Detroit, and Los Angeles, they discovered that not only do minorities lack the skill set needed for jobs, but employers' attitudes also bias the hiring process.

Many Americans think that in today's digital age using technology, such as computers, makes it more difficult to hire minorities. The assumption is minorities do not have the required skill set to compete in the high-tech service sector. However, in their examination of entry-level jobs, Moss and Tilly found out that most people can handle the computer skills needed in those jobs. Employers said the use of computers was not "rocket science," and most could learn how to use the computer very quickly.

Employers and Race Discrimination

In Australia, two sociologists, Farida Tilbury and Val Colic-Peisker, discovered that employers use discursive methods to deflect from themselves the responsibility of race discrimination. There are a number of honest responses employers could use to explain the unequal treatment of minorities, who are mostly immigrants from the ex-Yugoslavia, Middle East, and African countries. Those explanations could include using methodological shortcomings, discussing how there are legitimate differences in productivity, education, and trauma. They could say that past discriminatory effects have spilled into the present. They could note how immigrants or migrant workers do not have the social network connections to find a job. They can also point to institutional discrimination, such as requiring employees to speak English. They can also candidly say those who make the hiring decisions have bias.

However, most of the employers did not give those explanations. Instead, the explanations they gave fell in two spheres: (1) Discrimination is in the past, and (2) the market does not look at ethnicity. These two spheres enforce the notice that racism does not exist. If racial discrimination does rear its ugly head, employers shift the blame to others, including: (1) clients, who might not want to interact with minorities; (2) the market, because it arbitrarily enforces the idea that productivity must be immediate which puts minorities at a disadvantage; and (3) placing the blame on the employee, saying past experiences they have had with minorities and immigrants did not work. Thus, they did not want those negative experiences to happen again, so they will not hire those minorities. Placing the blame on others allows the employers to portray themselves in a positive manner.

While technology was not the biggest obstacle, Moss and Tilly discovered other skills employers said minorities lacked. They learned that employers exclude applicants from the pool, before meeting them, if they thought the employees lacked certain desirable skills. These skills can be divided into two categories—hard skills that include reading, writing, arithmetic, type of degree, and computer skills, and soft skills which include interaction with customers and the motivation to work. According to the authors, fewer than 6 percent of the employers required no reading, writing, arithmetic, customer interaction, or knowledge on how to use a computer. Fewer than 6 percent of the employers would hire an applicant who had no high school degree. This puts blacks and Latinos at a disadvantage, because they do not have the same opportunities for an education. In addition, the jobs that require no reading, writing, arithmetic, customer interaction, or basic computer skills pay a much lower rate—$6.88 and $5.87 on average compared to the $8.72 of the higher jobs.

Location also exacerbates the problem. The highest skilled job openings are found in central cities, which typically has the highest rate of unemployment for local residents. However, most job openings go to suburbanites. This makes it more difficult for minorities to find a job. It also does not help that more inner-city industries move out of the downtown and into the suburbs than suburban firms that move into the inner city.

Besides these hiring practices, employers' biases seep into the hiring decision. One of the survey questions asked in Moss and Tilly's research questioned whether employers preferred to work with individuals of their own race. About one-fourth of the employers answered by saying customers, employees, and other employers would rather deal with someone of their own race. In addition, survey results showed employers hired a greater number of white applicants compared to black males and females and Latinos. In every case, suburban industries hired a considerably larger proportion of whites than urban industries.

Results show discrimination is still evident in the hiring procedure. However, Moss and Tilly say this problem can be fixed. Moss and Tilly suggest training programs should incorporate classes on soft learning skills, such as how to behave during an interview. They also suggested that more school programs can be tied to the job market. Thus, it will be easier for minorities to get their foot in the door. The two also encourage moving toward what they call an evangelistic approach to affirmative action. They say affirmative action should be geared toward small- and medium-sized businesses that are the least likely to enforce affirmative action.

ALAN VINCENT GRIGSBY AND RASHA ALY

See also

Labor Movement, Racism in; Labor Unions. Document: Glass Ceiling Commission: Summary of Recommendations (1995)

Further Reading:

Feagin, J. R. "Book Review—Stories Employers Tell: Race, Skill, and Hiring in America by P. Moss and C. Tilly." *Work and Occupations* (2001): 506–8.

Moss, P., and C. Tilly. "Big City Labor Markets, Inner-City Workers: An Employer's Eye View." *Regional Review— Federal Reserve Bank of Boston* 9, no. 2 (1999): 16–22.

Moss, P., and C. Tilly. *Stories Employers Tell: Race, Skill, and Hiring in America*. New York City: Russell Sage Foundation, 2001.

Shao, Maria. "Diversity Training: What Is IT? Who Does It?: *Boston Globe*. Special section, Working Together: Exploring Diversity in the Workplace, 1994.

Tilbury, F., and V. Colic-Peisker. "Deflecting Responsibility in Employer Talk about Race Discrimination." *Discourse & Society* 17, no. 4 (2006): 651–76.

Historically Black Colleges and Universities

The term *historically black colleges and universities*, or HBCUs, became a descriptor for what had previously been termed "Negro" or "black" colleges. Colleges thus designated were institutions that existed prior to 1964, and were established specifically to educate African American students. Prior to the 1954 *Brown v. Board of Education* ruling, most states with a substantial black population and Jim Crow laws maintained at least one "Negro college" or other institution for educating black residents beyond the high school level. The existence of such schools fulfilled, at least in theory, the "separate, but equal" doctrine. The first Negro colleges were established for generally benevolent reasons in the decades after the end of slavery, but many became bulwarks of Jim Crow, both through their existence as separate institutions and through their curricula, which tended to prepare black graduates for the occupations deemed suitable for blacks by white-dominated society.

At the same time, Negro colleges became centers of black middle-class respectability and intellectual identity in the South. Students at black colleges often established lifetime networks of mutual support.

Most of the first black colleges were founded without a specific categorization of higher education, and many continued to maintain secondary educational programs as well as collegiate programs throughout their existence. Modern HBCUs offer a wide assortment of programs, from junior colleges to full universities with medical and business schools. The federal government recognizes 110 HBCUs. Other modern colleges with predominantly black student bodies exist, but they either were founded after 1964 or were formally white colleges that have experienced a demographic shift in their student bodies. Most black colleges existed in the South, where Jim Crow laws prevented black students from attending college with whites at either public or private schools. However, a few black colleges existed outside of the South, such as Wilberforce University in Ohio and Lincoln University in Pennsylvania. In general, private black colleges were usually founded or largely supported by Northern-based church groups during Reconstruction, whereas public black colleges were usually founded after the establishment of Jim Crow, specifically to thwart legal challenges to all-white public colleges. Some colleges were established from genuine grassroots efforts, such as what became Grambling State University, where black farmers in northern Louisiana created a college for their children. However, Grambling, like some other private black colleges, was eventually absorbed into the state system.

While the establishment of black colleges by states fulfilled the "separate" clause of the "separate but equal" doctrine, black public colleges were funded far below the level of white public colleges and so failed to maintain the "equal" clause of the doctrine. Black colleges were additionally handicapped by the poor primary and secondary education provided for black students at most segregated public schools. But as the ratio for seats for black students at black colleges was far lower than that for white students at white colleges, many black colleges were able to be somewhat selective in their admissions and to maintain a high quality of graduates.

Most black colleges followed Booker T. Washington's model and focused on subjects that were immediately practical for blacks, such as agriculture and home economics, rather than liberal arts or the sciences. Educating primary and secondary teachers soon became a major role for many of the schools. With the declining acceptance of Washington's ideas in the 1950s, as well as the rapidly declining percentage of African Americans involved in agriculture, black colleges began shifting toward liberal arts, social work, and business. Black public colleges usually had mostly black administrations and faculty, but many private colleges had white faculties and administrations. Increasingly, private colleges came under pressure from students and alumni to employ greater percentages of blacks in faculty and administrative roles. Howard University in Washington, D.C., generally considered to be the most prestigious of the black colleges, received its first black president in the 1920s, but other colleges would take much longer.

The *Brown* decision forced public and private colleges to end racial segregation. Negro colleges were increasingly called historically black colleges and universities. The new term reflected the post-*Brown* reality, as the formerly black colleges accepted students from any ethnic group, while not forgetting their origins as schools for blacks. While the efforts to desegregate previously all-white colleges such as the University of Alabama and the University of Mississippi received wide publicity, the integration of formerly black colleges passed with little notice. More significant were the efforts of black colleges to be integrated into state university systems. The case of *Geier v. Tennessee* dragged on from its initial filing in 1968 until its conclusion in 2001, when a federal district court ordered the state to dismantle its de facto two-race system. The desegregation of mainstream universities had the ironic effect of weakening many HBCUs. Top black academic achievers and student athletes were increasingly recruited by formerly all-white colleges. Some HBCUs have been successful in recruiting significant numbers of non–African American students, while others find competing for students more problematic, as a century of financial neglect and the legacy of Jim Crow left a stigma of inferiority for HBCUs. However, most have built on their legacy and have adapted to the competition from mainstream universities, carving out new niches in higher education.

BARRY M. STENTIFORD

See also

Affirmative Action; College Admissions, Discrimination in; UC Berkeley Bake Sale

Further Reading:

Betsey, Charles L. *Historically Black Colleges and Universities.* Edison, NJ: Transaction Publishers, 2008.

Gasman, Marybeth. *Envisioning Colleges: A History of the United Negro College Fund.* Baltimore: Johns Hopkins University Press, 2007.

Willie, Charles V., Richard J. Reddick, and Ronald Brown. *The Black College Mystique.* Lanham, MD: Rowman and Littlefield, 2005.

History of U.S. Census Racial Categorizations

Beginning with the first census of 1790, race had important political implications. This census included three possible racial categories indicating the legal status of the person in order to determine eligibility for political representation in Congress: (1) free whites, (2) nontaxed Indians, and (3) slaves. Free whites were eligible for full political representation, nontaxed Indians were not eligible for representation, and slaves were counted as three-fifths of a person. The 1820 census began collecting information about the foreign-born population, and census enumerators were, for the first time, to specifically record a person's color based on physical appearance as to whether they were white, black, or American Indian. By 1870, the census was using a six race system including white, black, mulatto, quadroon, octoroon, and Indian. Quadroons were classified as one-quarter black and three-quarters white while octoroons were thought to be one-eighth white and seven-eighths black. The 1890 census kept these six categories but added two additional categories of Japanese and Chinese, reflecting the anti-Asian sentiment at the time. The 1900 census dropped the categories of mulatto, quadroon, and octoroon, leaving respondents with five racial choices of black, white, Japanese, Chinese, and Indian. An Other category appeared in 1910 for respondents that did not fit into these racial categories and remained an option until the census of 2000. The 1920 census represents the only period where the census did not alter any racial categories. The 1930 census added the categories of Hindu, Korean, and Mexican in addition to negro, white, Chinese, Japanese, and Indian, resulting in half of the racial categories reflecting people of Asian origin. The 1930 census is also noteworthy in that enumerators were instructed to follow a one drop rule where any mixed ancestry

1990 Census

The 1990 census resulted in a grassroots social movement led by multiracial individuals and the families of multiracial children. Dissatisfied with being forced into a single race category, multiracial individuals organized to have their race recognized and not be forced into a mutually exclusive racial category. The 1990 census had over 500,000 people mark multiple race boxes despite instructions to choose one. Among these organizations protesting census racial classification was a prominent group known as RACE or Reclassify All Children Equally. This movement is credited with instigating changes to racial choices in the 2000 census.

with Negro blood was to be recorded as Negro, removing the mulatto option. The 1940 census removed Mexican, which was to be considered white. Mulatto reappeared in the 1950 census thus acknowledging black/white and black/American Indian sexual unions, creating some distance from the one drop rule of racial classification. The 1960 census choices grew to 11 categories including new categories of Hawaiian, part Hawaiian, and Aleut and Eskimo. These three categories were removed by 1970, and Korean was reintroduced (which previously appeared from 1930 until 1950). Respondents of the 1970 census were able to self-report their race although census enumerators were allowed to alter answers based on skin color. By 1980, race was completely self-reported and consisted of the largest selection yet of choices, including the new categories of Asian Indian, Samoan, Guamanian, and Vietnamese in addition to the return of Eskimo and Aleut. The 1980 census also included five official racial categories that were chosen by the Office of Management and Budget (OMB) in 1977. Referred to as Directive no. 15, the OMB mandated that all federal agencies collecting data on race must include the categories of American Indians and Alaska Natives, Asians and Pacific Islanders, non-Hispanic black, non-Hispanic white, and Hispanic. The census of 1990 was comparable to that in 1980 and consisted of 16 racial choices.

The 2000 census was a significant departure for racial classification and is notable for allowing respondents to check multiple racial boxes, allowing them to identify as multiracial. Previously, respondents who identified as multiracial were listed as other or were assigned a single racial category. Black-white, for example, was reclassified as black while white-black was reclassified as white. Respondents who identified as multiracial were reclassified as Other. The 2000 census also introduced the some other race category (SOR) which was included in the 2010 census. Fourteen racial categories appeared on the 2010 census, including the option to check some other race and to check multiple racial boxes. The multiracial category (respondents who check more than one race) is among the fastest growing racial groups in the United States with an increasing number of respondents choosing to identify as more than one race.

The history of the racial classification system of the U.S. Census underscores the social construction of race and political concerns over racial groups in the United States. Many racial categories emerged due to perceived concerns regarding economic, cultural, and political threats by a foreign category of people. At present, the Census reflects a diverse racial landscape and an increased acceptance racial diversity and of the social origins of race.

MICHELLE PETRIE

See also
Some Other Race (SOR)

Further Reading:
Anderson, Margo. 1988. *The American Census: A Social History.* New Haven: Yale University Press.
Lee, Sharon M. "Racial Classification in the US Census: 1890–1990." *Ethnic and Racial Studies* 16 (1993): 75–94.
Omi, Michael, and Howard Winant. *Racial Formation in the United States: From the 1960s to the 1990s.* New York: Routledge, 1994.
Snipp, C. Matthew. "Racial Measurement in the American Census: Past Practices and Implications for the Future." *Annual Review of Sociology* 29 (2003): 563–88.
Thompson, Daniel. "Making (Mixed) Race: Census Politics and the Emergence of Multiracial Multiculturalism in the United States, Great Britain, and Canada." *Ethnic and Racial Studies* 35 (2012): 1409–26.

Holiday, Billie (1915–1959)

Billie Holiday is considered one of the greatest jazz vocalists of all time and a major influence on many later performers, such as Janis Joplin and Nina Simone. Holiday's major

Billie Holiday performs in 1947 in New York. (William P. Gottlieb/Library of Congress)

contribution to the fight against racially motivated violence was her brave decision to publicly perform Abel Meeropol's powerful anti-lynching song, "Strange Fruit."

Billie Holiday was born Eleanora Fagan on April 7, 1915, in Baltimore, Maryland. Her father, Clarence Holiday, was a jazz guitarist, and her mother, Sadie Fagan, was just 13 years old when Holiday was born. Due to her mother's age, she was raised by a host of relatives. To escape the hardship and poverty of her early years, she listened to the music of Louis Armstrong and Bessie Smith. Their music inspired her dreams of one day becoming a singer. In 1933, jazz enthusiast John Hammond discovered her, and it was then that she took the name Billie Holiday by combining the first name of an admired film star, Billie Dove, with her father's last name.

Racism was a serious problem for artists of that time, and this was no exception for Billie Holiday. "Colored performers" had to enter through back doors in Harlem establishments and sleep on buses. In spite of those conditions, Billie Holiday performed as if singing to the stars in heaven while masking her inner pains and addictions. In later years,

Holiday's battles with alcohol and drugs—she served eight months in prison for heroin possession in 1947—changed the tone and limited the range of her voice, though her phrasing and emotional power remained exceptional.

Holiday first performed "Strange Fruit" at the club Café Society in Harlem in 1939. She later wrote that upon finishing the song she was greeted by stunned silence, until one patron's nervous applause elicited a thunderous clapping from the rest of the audience. The song's impact was so great and its popularity so immediate that the club owner insisted that Holiday close all her shows with it. As she was about to begin "Strange Fruit," the waiters would stop serving, the house lights would dim, and a single spotlight would illuminate Holiday, who would close her eyes, as if in prayer, before launching into the song. Although many other performers have since recorded "Strange Fruit," that song is most closely identified with Holiday.

Holiday was given the nickname "Lady Day" by musician Lester Young and was renowned for wearing a white gardenia bobby-pinned over an ear during performances. She launched a highly successful European tour in 1954 and appeared on British television in 1959, when she again sang "Strange Fruit." Holiday's story was told in a successful 1972 film starring Diana Ross, *Lady Sings the Blues*. Billie Holiday died on July 17, 1959.

DENISE D. MCADORY

See also
Jazz; Rhythm and Blues; "Strange Fruit"

Further Reading:

Holiday, Billie, with William Dufty. *Lady Sings the Blues*. Garden City, NY: Doubleday & Company, 1956.

Jazz—A Film by Ken Burns. Directed by Ken Burns. A General Motors Mark of Excellence Presentation. Presented by WETA, 2001.

Margolick, David. *Strange Fruit: Billie Holiday, Café Society, and the Early Cry for Civil Rights*. Philadelphia: Running Press, 2000.

Hollywood and Minority Actors

The Hollywood community has long been accused of limiting the talent and the stories that emerge from the minority community. From television shows to films, Hollywood has a history of perpetuating racial stereotypes and presenting content from a predominantly white perspective. Even today, while there are more minority actors, directors, and writers in Hollywood than ever before, many still hold that Hollywood is an industry that privileges white narratives and white actors.

In years past, watchdog organizations such as the National Association for the Advancement of Colored People (NAACP) have called attention to the dearth of roles for minority actors and the lack of programming introducing elements of minority culture. The NAACP even threatened to sue the broadcast networks for violating the Communications Act of 1934, which mandates that broadcasters must act in the public's interest. This resulted in the addition of many supporting roles for minority actors at the end of 1999. In the early 2000s, there were relatively few shows featuring minority characters in leading roles, with those that did frequently ghettoizing those roles. Programs with predominantly minority casts are typically shown in blocks on such newer networks as the CW. Many charge that minority characters on network television are caricatures of racial stereotypes, rather than fully developed, complex characters. For example, the 2009 ABC sitcom *Modern Family* features only one person of color of the six main characters. Played by Sofia Vergara, the character Gloria Pritchard is a Colombian woman whom many popular culture scholars charge perpetuates the stereotype of the oversexed Latina, as an ex-beauty queen who frequently wears tight clothing and is the subject of many jokes on the show revolving around her sensual beauty.

The film industry has not fared much better in providing opportunities for minority actors. The 2002 Academy Awards made headlines when African Americans won Oscars for Male Actor in a Leading Role and Female Actor in a Leading Role. Denzel Washington won the Oscar that year for his role in *Training Day* and Halle Berry won for *Monster's Ball*. This was the first time in history that the Lead Actor Oscar was awarded to an African American woman, and the first time in more than 40 years that an African American man had received the award. In 2003, only two minorities were nominated for acting awards, and neither was considered a front-runner. In 2004, five of the 20 acting U.S. nominees were black. However, in early 2011, when the Academy announced the nominees for the 83rd Oscars, many in Hollywood were shocked when there were no black artists on the list.

When the racial composition of the U.S. population is considered, the proportion of minority nominees in the acting categories at the Academy Awards is not representative. At most, nonwhites have earned only three out of 20 acting nominations in the history of the Academy Awards in any given year. This represents only 15 percent of the nominations, while the nonwhite population in the United States is currently at 37 percent and growing. Statistics show that things seem to be getting worse for minority actors in Hollywood. For example, in the early 2000s, blacks played 15 percent of roles in film and TV, while as of 2013, that number has fallen to 13 percent. This is all despite the recent rise in major Hollywood films being produced that are based on black characters and/or black narratives. Films such as *Django Unchained* (2012) and *12 Years A Slave* (2013) that have received considerable box office success show that there is an increased interest today in films featuring black narratives. However, many have also charged Hollywood with focusing too narrowly on slave narratives over other types of minority experiences.

Not only are there few roles for minority actors, many of the roles written for minority actors offer stereotypical and in some instances degrading images of minorities. Black actors receive an inordinate number of scripts featuring gang members and poor, single mothers. Hispanics receive a great number of scripts about drug dealers and menial workers, and Asian Americans are regularly depicted as foreigners and small-business owners who have poor social skills. Many minority actors feel they must take these limited roles to maintain their visibility and to make a living.

Some insiders believe the entertainment industry is not capable of producing films and shows that address the experiences of minorities, because most of the writers, producers, and directors are white. Moreover, minority actors are being penalized by a system that devalues them. Not only are stories that examine the minority experience less often explored, but minority actors are also marginalized and excluded from films that explore mainstream culture as if they have no relationship to it.

This less-than-diverse view in Hollywood does not reflect the diversity of the viewing audience. Black households watch 50 percent more television than other Americans and account for a quarter of movie ticket sales, although they make up only 12 percent of the U.S. population. Since the target audience for film and television tends to skew young, one might expect to see more roles for minority actors, given the fact that the white population is older than the minority population. Some believe the solution to this problem is to increase the percentage of minority-owned media outlets. Some minority actors have developed their own production companies, talent agencies, and film festivals to showcase their work, in an effort to increase the presence of racial minorities in Hollywood.

ROMNEY S. NORWOOD

See also

Beauty Standards; Cosby, Bill; Cosmetics; Films and Racial Stereotypes; White Savior Films

Further Reading:

Lester, Paul M., ed. *Images That Injure: Pictorial Stereotypes in the Media*. Westport, CT: Praeger Publishers, 1996.

Ryan, Joel. "Fall TV an 'Outrage,' NAACP Charges." July 12, 1999. E!Online. http://www. eonline.com/News/Items/ Pf/0,1527,5033,00.html.

Xing, Jun, and Lane Ryo Hirabayashi. *Reversing the Lens: Ethnicity, Race, Gender, and Sexuality through Film*. Boulder: University Press of Colorado, 2003.

Homelessness and Minority Groups

There is remarkably little solid research on who is homeless in the United States. Part of the problem is that it is difficult to define who is homeless. Most people would agree, for example, that individuals who live exclusively on the street are homeless. Similarly, people who live in homeless shelters are also widely considered to be homeless. But there are other groups for whom it is not so clear. For example, consider a family who loses their home or are evicted from their apartment. If they stay in the living room of friends and family, are they homeless? Many researchers and advocates say yes, because this family has no stable housing. Others say no, because the family, however unstably, is currently housed by friends and family. In addition, this definition of homelessness can include people whom most of us would not consider homeless, such as college students who are temporarily without a place to stay. However, if this group is omitted, there is a risk of missing a large number of people who do not have steady or reliable shelter.

The face of homelessness changes depending on who is counted as being homeless. The homeless who live on the streets are overwhelmingly men. Women and children make up a greater proportion of the homeless who temporarily stay in other people's homes. There are also considerable regional differences in who is homeless. The homeless are a diverse group. Even if one agrees on a definition of homelessness, it is hard to create a reliable demographic portrait of this group, because they are often a hidden population. Simply counting the number of people who appear to be living on the street can be misleading. Some of the so-called street homeless may be in areas that are not easily accessible or visible. In addition, some of the people who may appear homeless to the researcher may, in fact, have a home. Trying to learn who is homeless solely by looking at information from homeless shelters creates similar problems. Not everyone who is homeless will be willing to go to a shelter. More importantly from a demographics perspective, those who go to a shelter may be different from those who do not. It is even more difficult to get an accurate count of the homeless who are temporarily staying with friends or family.

In the early 1990s, Anne Shlay and Peter Rossi conducted an extensive review of the literature on the homeless. This comprehensive review is arguably one of the most reliable sources on homelessness. They found that more than 40 percent of homeless persons were blacks, although the black population accounted for only about 12 percent of the U.S. population in 1990 (1992, 135). Therefore African Americans are disproportionately represented among the homeless. Latinos composed 9 percent of the U.S. population in 1990 but represented 12 percent of the homeless population. There has been considerable growth in the Latino population in the United States since 1990. Therefore, the percentage of Latinos in the homeless population is likely to have grown. The proportion of Asian homeless was too small to note in the early 1990s.

Why are some people homeless? There are two types of explanations, individual and structural. Individual explanations focus on the characteristic of the homeless themselves, such as their prevalence of mental illness and substance abuse. Structural explanations focus on external factors, such as expensive housing and high unemployment. In fact, it is hard to completely separate individual and structural factors. For example, external factors such as a weak economy can create unemployment and homelessness. Housing instability and homelessness can exacerbate substance use and abuse problems, which can make locating stable employment and housing even more difficult. Similarly, more and more people are being incarcerated, and there may be an increase in homelessness as people leave prison and have no stable housing. This would be a result of both individual factors, the decision to commit a criminal act, and structural factors that contribute to criminality and the social response, such as increased criminalization of drug offences in the United States and limited assistance available to former inmates in reentering society.

Although research on the homeless is limited, there are a few clear patterns. First, men and women have different patterns of homelessness. Men are more likely to be single and on the street than are women, and women are more likely to be doubled up and to have children with them. Minorities, particularly blacks and Latinos, are also far more likely to be homeless than are whites. These differences suggest that there are strong structural influences on who is homeless, although these external influences may be mitigated by individual factors such as addiction and mental illness.

ROBIN ROGER-DILLON

See also
American Apartheid; Underclass, The (Ghetto Poor)

Further Reading:
Ringheim, Karin. "Investigating the Structural Determinants of Homelessness." *Urban Affairs Quarterly* 28, no. 4 (June 1993): 617–40.

Shlay, Anne B. "Social Science Research and Contemporary Studies of Homelessness." *Annual Review of Sociology* 18, 129–60.

Hoover, J. Edgar (1895–1972)

John Edgar Hoover was the director of the Federal Bureau of Investigation (FBI) from 1924 to 1972. He had the longest tenure of any FBI director, serving eight U.S. presidents from Calvin Coolidge to Richard Nixon. Over his tenure, he attained unprecedented power and used far-reaching tactics to influence U.S. policy, politics, and culture. Hoover has a long-standing controversial history and has been accused or suspected of being a racist, of having Mafia ties, and of being a closet homosexual, although he publicly assailed alternative lifestyles. Many historians and critics suggest that Hoover was responsible for severely crippling black empowerment organizations and socialist reform, antiwar, and labor movements.

Hoover was born January 1, 1895, in Washington, D.C. He was the youngest of three children born to Dickerson Naylor Hoover and Annie Marie Scheitlin Hoover. From birth until his mother died when he was 43 years old, Hoover lived in his birth home, located three blocks behind the Capitol. In 1916, Hoover completed a bachelor of law degree from George Washington University, where he pledged the Kappa Alpha fraternity and worked as an assistant at the Library of Congress. After graduation, Hoover's uncle helped him get a draft-exempt position with the U.S. Department of Justice, making $900 a year. Within a year, he was promoted to an attorney position that doubled his salary.

Hoover's professional life advanced in 1919 after Attorney General A. Mitchell Palmer's house was firebombed by a suspected subversive. At the time, communism was spreading throughout Eastern Europe, and U.S. labor unions were organizing a series of strikes. Palmer launched a campaign against radicals, and tapped Hoover to head his project under the newly established General Intelligence Division (GID). Within months, Hoover used skills he acquired through library work to compile dossiers on approximately 150,000 people. By mid-1921, the number reached an estimated 450,000. Two benign American communist political parties were Hoover's main targets. By the end of 1919, the Palmer Raids officially commenced and, under Hoover's leadership, deportation orders were given to thousands of so-called radicals. When most of the deportation orders were cancelled by Assistant Secretary of Labor Louis F. Post, Hoover responded by opening a file on Secretary Post. The Palmer Raids came to an embarrassing end when Hoover's prediction of a May 1, 1920, communist revolution failed to materialize.

Attorney General Palmer lost his position after Warren G. Harding became president in 1920. However, during the Palmer Raids, Hoover effectively postured himself as a

J. Edgar Hoover was director of the Federal Bureau of Investigation and created a powerful federal government crime-fighting agency. He served in that post from 1924 until his death in 1972. Hoover has a controversial history that includes accusations of being a racist, and of having ties to the Mafia. (Yoichi R. Okamoto/Lyndon B. Johnson Presidential Library)

nonpartisan, who worked with extraordinary detail and was fanatical about protecting the establishment. In 1921, he became the assistant chief of the FBI. In 1924, he became the FBI director under the Coolidge administration.

In the 1930s, prohibition, the Great Depression, and the gangster era brought new challenges and opportunities for Hoover. Gangsters such as John Dillinger, "Machine Gun" Kelly and "Pretty Boy" Floyd became protagonists in the media, as the public became more disenchanted with the government and law enforcement. Many of the gangsters bolstered an antiestablishment, Robin Hood position, and captured the imagination of the public. Hoover quickly

positioned himself publicly to be the gangsters' antagonist and the foremost defender of the establishment. Hoover adored the media attention afforded by the government's war on crime. He began to recruit special agents who were more physically fit and set more rigorous training standards. However, one of his special agents, Melvin Purvis, became a victim of his own success. Purvis orchestrated the seizure and murders of John Dillinger and Pretty Boy Floyd. In the fallout, Purvis dominated media headlines, while Hoover became vehemently resentful of Purvis for hogging the spotlight. Purvis was later forced to resign and was discredited to all other potential employers. He eventually committed suicide.

In the interim, the Lindbergh kidnapping case of 1933 gave Hoover an opportunity to make public headlines. Although the FBI was not directly responsible for apprehending Lindbergh's kidnappers, Hoover went to New York for the photo opportunity when Bruno Hauptmann was arrested by New York Police. Hauptmann's capture, along with other high-profile arrests, such as Louis "Lepke" Buchalter, paid personal dividends to Hoover. In 1935, the "G-man" movies were produced in Hollywood, which portrayed Hoover as a master crime fighter.

When Franklin D. Roosevelt became president in 1933, Hoover approached the new president about his concern over subversive activity in the United States. Hoover was personally interested in reviving the GID, which he shaped during the Palmer Raids. Roosevelt allowed Hoover to expand the GID. In exchange, Hoover monitored the activities of Roosevelt's political opponents, such as Huey Long. During Roosevelt's administration, Hoover's FBI grew in size and scope. In addition, Hoover learned how to use his powers to become a political tool for any sitting president. When Harry Truman succeeded Roosevelt, he sought to distance himself from Hoover, while limiting FBI appropriations. Hoover responded by raising suspicions of communists working in Truman's administration.

At the time, Hoover developed a working relationship with the House Un-American Activities Committee (HUAC). With Hoover's help, the HUAC had recently spearheaded an initiative to expose communists in the entertainment industry. The FBI drafted an anonymous list of Hollywood communists, which contained many black activist entertainers such as Paul Robeson and Harry Belafonte. When Truman was elected in his own right in 1948, Hoover worked with HUAC member Richard Nixon to indict Soviet spy suspects working within Truman's administration. In 1952, Richard Nixon became vice president under Dwight Eisenhower. Both Eisenhower and Nixon admired Hoover and expanded his power and influence in government.

A relationship between Sen. Joseph McCarthy and Hoover also emerged. Hoover helped spawn the McCarthy era when he provided Senator McCarthy with a list of mostly invalidated communists working for the government. McCarthy used the list to make an inflamed six-hour speech on the dangers of communism and effectively sparked a communist witch hunt throughout the nation. By 1956, the McCarthy–Hoover relationship grew sour after McCarthy's alcoholism and questionable sexual practices became public. Hoover helped the Eisenhower administration neutralize McCarthy, while increasing his own efforts to fight communism with a new initiative called COINTELPRO (Counter Intelligence Program).

By the time John F. Kennedy took office in 1960, COINTELPRO had expanded well beyond investigating communism. Robert Kennedy, who became attorney general and Hoover's boss, was interested in pursuing the Mafia. However, Hoover had not been actively involved with organized crime since the Prohibition era. Rumors suggested that Hoover either had a special relationship with the Mafia or was being blackmailed. The Kennedys' relationship with African Americans was another source of conflict for Hoover. Through his crusade against Marcus Garvey and Martin Luther King, Jr., Hoover clearly acknowledged his bigotry. Although King had a close relationship with Robert Kennedy, Hoover was vehemently dedicated to discrediting King. In the years to follow, John F. Kennedy, Robert Kennedy, and Martin Luther King, Jr., were assassinated. Hoover's FBI remained at the center of controversy surrounding their murder cases. In 1979, years after Hoover's death, the House Select Committee determined that the FBI's investigations into conspiracies leading up to the Kennedy murders were deficient.

Lyndon Johnson and Richard Nixon were the last two presidents Hoover served. For different reasons, Hoover had a close relationship with both presidents, and enjoyed unprecedented autonomy. During this period, opposition to the Vietnam War and the Black Power movement sparked an upsurge in antiestablishment ideas, and civil unrest threatened the status quo. Hoover expanded the scope of COINTELPRO beyond its original purpose and expanded the tactics beyond the boundaries of the law.

In 1971, a series of events occurred that brought public embarrassment to Hoover. First, COINTELPRO was exposed by the Citizens Commission to Investigate the FBI. Next, the media began to assail Hoover and the FBI for the agency's spending and biased hiring practices. One of Hoover's top aids, William Sullivan, openly criticized Hoover's policies, leading to a highly publicized rift within the FBI. Finally, an internal memo surfaced that partially exposed the Watergate conspiracy.

Hoover died on May 2, 1972, before Watergate was completely exposed. His longtime friend and confidant, Clyde Tolson, was the first to be notified. Tolson managed the disposal of thousands of files, of which more than 17,000 pages survived. The secret files were primarily composed of morally and sexually derogatory information that Hoover used to blackmail civic leaders and political opponents. Tolson inherited Hoover's estate. For more than 40 years, the two lifelong bachelors regularly vacationed and dined together, and accompanied one another to social events.

Hoover was posthumously criticized during the post-Watergate congressional hearings. However, elite celebrations of his legacy overshadowed the millions of individuals who denounced him. In 1972, the FBI Building in Washington, D.C., was named in Hoover's honor, although organizations have routinely petitioned to rename the building because of Hoover's contentious legacy.

IVORY TOLDSON

See also

Federal Bureau of Investigation (FBI)

Further Reading:

Bardsley, Marilyn. *J. Edgar Hoover. CourtTV* Crime Library, Criminal Minds and Methods. http://www.Crimelibrary.com/gangsters%5Foutlaws/cops%5Fothers/hoover/.

Gentry, Curt. *J. Edgar Hoover: The Man and the Secrets.* New York: W.W. Norton, 1991.

Powers, Richard G. *G-Men: Hoover's FBI in Popular Culture.* Carbondale: Southern Illinois University Press, 1983.

Powers, Richard G. *Secrecy and Power: The Life of J. Edgar Hoover.* New York: Free Press, 1987.

Housing Covenants

Housing covenants, also known as restrictive covenants, are legal documents designed to ensure that blacks do not move into white neighborhoods. Rather than deed restrictions, which are enforced by individuals, housing covenants must be agreed upon by some majority of neighborhood residents (usually about 75 percent), after which most others are pressured to comply. These covenants forbid the property owners, as well as their heirs, from selling their property to blacks as well as other racial and ethnic minorities. Because of these covenants, if they sold to a minority person, neighbors had the right to go to court to ensure that property and homes did not change hands and became the property of minorities. Therefore, courts in these cases, for generations, were complicit in ensuring and maintaining residential segregation of suburban and urban neighborhoods.

After World War II, a number of historical events and practices of the government, realtors, and private citizens resulted in the suburbanization of former white ethnic city dwellers, particularly white ethnics, and the ghettoization of urban blacks. First, heavy industry and low-skill but high-paying jobs moved to the South and West, while high-paying service-sector jobs located in the suburbs. Second, the government offered housing loans to veterans, while the growth of interstate highways ushered in a new age of suburbs surrounding central cities. Third, as whites left the cities, they sought to ensure that blacks did not follow. Blacks were unable to gain access to low-income loans to buy new homes or improve existing homes through redlining by realtors, resulting in increasing isolation in rapidly deteriorating urban centers. Housing covenants, in conjunction with loan restrictions and urban renewal projects, increasingly locked blacks into public housing as their former homes, which had been in redlined areas, were bulldozed. By locking blacks into urban centers, they were also locked into poor-quality social services, education, housing, and job opportunities, thereby perpetuating social and economic inequality and replicating their place in the Jim Crow racism of America. To ensure residential segregation between blacks and whites in urban and newly suburban areas, many realtors and residents used housing covenants forbidding the owners to sell the home or its land to blacks (as well as Jews, Asians, and other racial groups). These covenants appeared throughout the country in cities as disparate as Seattle, Los Angeles, and Chicago as well as nearly all Southern states. While most were directed at blacks, other cities used housing covenants to ensure that Jews, Asians, or Hispanics did not purchase property in white neighborhoods. For example, in Los Angeles, covenants were used almost exclusively to bar Mexicans from entering white neighborhoods.

Housing covenants were developed primarily by members of "neighborhood improvement associations." Many of these organizations existed to "improve" the neighborhoods by ensuring that blacks and other minorities did not buy homes within them. These covenants were then institutionalized by realtor organizations that encouraged and often required residents to sign to ensure high profits for themselves because of increased house values due to residentially segregated neighborhoods. Conversely, an increase in blacks would lower the values of the homes. Local real estate boards collaborated nationally on the development of model covenants to provide to white homeowners throughout the country as well as conducted citywide drives to ensure all "desirable" neighborhoods were ensured against black encroachment and the maintenance of high property values. Finally, the Federal Housing Administration (FHA) advised, encouraged, and then required residents to use covenants if they wanted to gain access to home loans and mortgages.

These covenants, though not written into law, often appeared in conjunction with state laws prohibiting residential proximity between blacks and whites and, therefore, were similar to the Black Codes enacted during and after Reconstruction that restricted blacks' rights and liberties. These restrictive covenants coincided with a wide variety of laws, statutes, and municipal codes prohibiting blacks from building or buying homes in white neighborhoods or in the same building that were found in Delaware, Illinois, Louisiana, Kentucky, New York, Virginia, and Washington. Chicago was a leader in using restrictive covenants to ensure that blacks remained on the South Side of the city in what was, and continues to be known as, the "Black Belt." These legally binding affirmations of black and white difference served to entrench racial attitudes outside of the South, where black and white residential segregation was deeply ingrained in culture and custom, as well as ensure that blacks did not gain access to higher-quality schools, jobs, and public services often found in and around white neighborhoods. They also allowed for the perpetuation of Jim Crow laws and attitudes in otherwise "liberal" places. Therefore, these covenants reveal whites' real fear of black encroachment on their neighborhoods, in the schools, and in their daily lives.

Blacks recognized the insidious nature of these covenants in limiting their access to educational, social, economic, and political opportunity and challenged their constitutionality in a number of cases. The first of these was *Shelley v. Kraemer*, initially brought by a black family who purchased a home in St. Louis, Missouri. White neighbors seeking to halt their move into their new home argued that the Shelleys' purchase of the home was illegal due to the restrictive covenant barring blacks from purchasing the home. The court argued that the covenants were state-sponsored discrimination, but there were no penalties for those who engaged in this practice, and the ruling was effective only when suits were brought to court and the courts enforced the law. As such, they did not forbid their existence, only with using the courts to ensure their enforcement. The rights and racial attitudes of property owners ensured that this practice persisted well into the 21st century, as many deeds continue to have these clauses written into them.

The 1948 *Hurd v. Hodge* case reaffirmed *Shelley v. Kraemer*, finding it illegal to fail to sell to blacks in Washington, D.C. Congress officially outlawed the practice in the 1968 Fair Housing Act, which also addressed redlining and other discriminatory practices by realtors. The U.S. Supreme Court reaffirmed these previous rulings in the 1968 *Jones v. Alfred H. Mayer* case based in St. Louis, emphasizing the 1866 and 1968 Civil Rights Acts that barred racial discrimination in all housing, both public and private. In doing so, the Court declared restrictive covenants "a relic of slavery" that perpetuated the badge of slavery suffered by all blacks.

Although ruled unenforceable in the *Shelley v. Kraemer* decision, and reaffirmed numerous times since then by both rulings and constitutional amendments, housing covenants continue to exist. Restrictive covenants, though repeatedly ruled to be illegal, continue to preclude blacks' access to suburbs. In 2007, the House of Representatives sponsored a resolution condemning the use of restrictive covenants and urging states to follow California's lead in complying with existing legislature and rulings (including the Fair Housing Act of 1968, *Shelly v. Kraemer*, and *Hurd v. Hodge*) addressing the issue in proactively removing these clauses from housing documents and urging the Department of Housing and Urban Development to educate the public about these issues and collect data on any continued use of covenants.

One of America's most well-known and its first preplanned neighborhood, Levittown on Long Island, New York, offered working-class Americans the opportunity to own homes, but employed housing covenants to ensure that the development would remain white. Built almost entirely during the five years between 1946 and 1951, Levittown comprised nearly 18,000 almost identical homes, which began as an initial 2,000 in Hempstead, then spilled into neighboring Wantagh, Hicksville, and Westbury. Many credit Levittown with the beginning of suburban sprawl and the movement away from cities as it fulfilled the American dream of many families in the 1950s by providing them with affordable homes, plenty of space for children to play, access to good schools, and all the latest appliances.

But Levittown had a dark side for minorities longing to live there. The Levitts, particularly William, enforced racial segregation by restricting the purchase of homes to only whites using restrictive covenants forbidding "any person other than members of the Caucasian race" from living in Levittown homes. After restrictive covenants were outlawed in 1948 and the FHA announced that they would not back mortgages linked to such covenants, Levitt continued to practice discrimination in renting and selling Levittown homes. Levittown was not integrated until the late 1970s.

MELISSA F. WEINER

See also

Fair Housing Audit; Gatekeeping; Housing Discrimination; Residential Segregation

Further Reading:

Lipsitz, George. *The Possessive Investment in Whiteness: How White People Profit from Identity Politics.* Philadelphia: Temple University Press, 1998.

Massey, Douglas S., and Nancy A. Denton. *American Apartheid: Segregation and the Making of the Underclass.* Cambridge, MA: Harvard University Press, 1993.

Vose, Clement E. *Caucasians Only: Supreme Court, the NAACP, and the Restrictive Covenant Cases.* Berkeley: University of California Press, 1973.

Housing Discrimination

Racial/ethnic housing discrimination refers to adverse or inferior treatment of an individual or group based solely on their race or ethnic identity, resulting in a negative impact on their ability to find housing. This type of discrimination can take the form of direct actions or institutional arrangements. In general, housing discrimination hinders minorities' abilities to find, purchase, rent, or live in residential property. Although it was once legally sanctioned, the most significant forms of housing discrimination have since been outlawed. Historically, housing discrimination has had a negative impact on the social mobility of racial minorities and has been responsible for perpetuating racial segregation in the United States.

Racial/ethnic housing discrimination can take many different forms including the use of real or threatened violence to intimidate minorities; refusing to rent or sell particular housing units to members of specified minority groups; property sellers setting more onerous conditions on minority buyers or renters than on white tenants; banks and mortgage companies basing loan awards on race rather than financial stability; or marketers who selectively advertise housing only in majority-group geographic areas. Local residents may use intimidation tactics to prevent minorities from looking for housing in white areas or to frighten them into moving out of the area.

Other forms of housing discrimination revolve around such financial aspects as sellers putting more onerous conditions on minority buyers or renters than white tenants. For example, landlords might require a higher security deposit from minorities than from their white counterparts. Similarly, real estate agents or apartment managers may provide false or misleading information and give poorer-quality assistance to minority-group home-seekers than to white home-seekers. Banks and mortgage companies can also participate in housing discrimination, basing loan awards on race rather than financial stability. Governments have also perpetuated housing discrimination by employing racial zoning, essentially dictating which areas may be occupied by whites versus racial minorities. Finally, marketers can also practice racial discrimination by selectively advertising housing only in majority-group geographic areas. While all of these forms of housing discrimination are now illegal, these practices have nevertheless continued to occur in the United States over the last several decades.

Since the 1970s, the Federal Department of Housing and Urban Development (HUD) has sponsored national surveys to gauge the extent of these forms of housing discrimination. One such survey from 1989 found that real estate agents showed blacks and Hispanics about 25 percent fewer housing units than they did to equally qualified whites, and that in about 10 percent of the cases, blacks and Hispanics were told that no house or apartment was available when in fact there were units available. In 2000, HUD completed another survey, which found a slightly lower amount of housing discrimination against blacks, but a small increase in housing

Federal Housing Administration (FHA)

The Federal Housing Administration (FHA) was created in 1934 as one of the many "alphabet" agencies of Franklin Roosevelt's administration. Its purpose was to stimulate home ownership in the depths of the Depression at a time when millions of construction workers were unemployed, maximum mortgage loans were 50 percent of the property's value, and only 40 percent of Americans owned a home. By 2001, 68 percent of Americans owned their own homes, thanks in large part to FHA programs.

The FHA has increased home ownership by insuring mortgages made by approved lenders, to lessen their risk on unconventional loans. Unlike conforming conventional loans, FHA-insured loans require a smaller down payment and allow for more latitude in determining household income and payout ratios. But the FHA also discriminated against African Americans by using racially restrictive covenants as a means of ensuring the security of neighborhoods. In evaluating the stability of a neighborhood, the agency focused on whether properties there will continue to be "occupied by the same social and racial classes." As a result of this policy, the vast majority of FHA mortgages went to white, middle-class suburbs; few were awarded to black neighborhoods in central cities. The FHA's bias for granting mortgages for suburban white middle-class neighborhoods and pattern of disinvestment in black neighborhoods were most evident in the 1940s, but its racist practices continued in the 1950s. They contributed not only to the huge racial gap in home ownership, but also to racial segregation.

BENJAMIN F. SHEARER

discrimination against Hispanics. Federal legislation initiated by HUD in the 1970s along with private negotiation in the 1990s have attempted to reduce racial housing discrimination, but it still continues to be a problem in some areas of the United States.

Housing discrimination persists because it brings real or perceived benefits to those who practice it. Because laws against housing discrimination are often not well enforced, many individuals or groups who want those benefits ignore the law or seek loopholes in it. One major reason housing discrimination continues to occur is likely because of the psychological sense of elevated status it brings to those who practice it. Some people derive feelings of security, superiority, and prestige from residential exclusiveness, which establishes social and physical distance between them and those who they look down upon. Furthermore, there are important financial and material rewards associated with housing discrimination. Sellers of housing often find that buyers are willing to pay more to live in racially/ethnically exclusive areas, and purchasers in those areas may find their property appreciating in value more than houses in other more diverse areas. Another benefit of housing discrimination for members of a dominant group is that it enables them to claim for themselves many geographically

based advantages, such as better access to the finest schools, the best shopping areas, the least pollution, the best drainage, and the most scenic spots. Real estate agents and banks typically engage in housing discrimination for financial reasons. Although realtors and bankers often cite financial reasoning to justify such discriminatory practices, they are often grounded purely in preconceived racial stereotypes and judgments.

Racial housing discrimination is but one example of larger practices of institutionalized racism that predominated in the United States throughout the early 20th century. Although the 1866 Civil Rights Act stated that blacks have the same property and contract rights as whites, organizations and institutions across the United States devised a variety of ways to deny blacks and other racial minorities freedom of choice in selecting a place to live. However, in the past century, fair-housing advocates have challenged each form of housing discrimination in court and public forums. The first such struggle was over racial zoning. In the 1910s, soon after many U.S. cities started to use zoning to regulate and separate urban land use, some municipalities also passed zoning ordinances specifying that certain streets or districts could only be occupied by whites. Typically, the corresponding areas reserved for blacks had lower-quality housing and received inferior public services. Although courts in 15 states initially upheld laws establishing such residential segregation, in 1917 the U.S. Supreme Court struck down those laws in the *Buchanan v. Warley* case, asserting that government did not have the authority to dictate where people of different races could live.

Following the 1917 ruling against racial zoning, white individuals and associations turned to racially restrictive covenants as their new primary mechanism of housing discrimination. These practices were dominant from the 1920s through the 1940s, and typically they took the form of private agreements made by white homeowners associations stipulating that white residents would only sell their homes to a purchaser who was also white. Racially restrictive covenants covered a significant percentage of the U.S. housing stock in the first half of the 20th century but were actively opposed by civil rights groups such as the NAACP. In 1948, racially restrictive covenants were officially outlawed by the Supreme Court, but many of these covenants continued as "mutual understandings" among whites about excluding minorities in deals to rent or sell housing.

It is not just individual realtors and property owners who have engaged in racial housing discrimination. Throughout the 20th century, federal and local governments often engaged in racial discrimination when designing public housing projects. Despite providing most of the money for public housing projects, the federal government did not require that this housing be racially integrated. As a result, Southern and many Northern public housing authorities used race when deciding where to assign public housing residents. Moreover, in places where public housing became predominantly black, local government officials and public-housing authorities often abided by white residents' demands that these public-housing projects not be built in their neighborhoods. This meant that most federally funded public-housing projects built in the 1950s and 1960s were put in predominantly black neighborhoods or in less-desirable, peripheral areas of cities.

Post–World War II, black resentment over housing discrimination was strong, especially in the North. Major civil rights organizations and coalitions such as the National Committee Against Discrimination in Housing lobbied local, state, and federal government to outlaw housing discrimination. By 1962, they had succeeded in urging President John F. Kennedy to sign Executive Order 11063, which prohibited discrimination in federally funded housing. By this time, more than a dozen states and 56 cities had passed laws against racial discrimination in housing. However, black-white residential segregation was nevertheless increasing, evidencing that these legal actions were doing little to prevent it. The difficulties blacks had in finding housing outside the less-desirable ghetto areas were an important underlying factor in many of the large urban race riots of the 1960s. Indeed, it was the violent turbulence following the assassination of Martin Luther King, Jr. that pushed the federal government to take a more proactive stance against housing discrimination by passing the 1968 Fair Housing Act, which outlawed many forms of housing discrimination. This law has been amended several times to extend protection against housing discrimination to several other categories of people, now covering gender, religion, and national origin beyond just racial/ethnic identity.

Housing discrimination by private individuals rather than by government authorities can take many forms. Although it is illegal and against real estate ethics, some agents nevertheless still practice racial steering, which is defined as behavior that directs a customer toward or away from certain neighborhoods based on their race. Fair-housing audits show that in some areas, racial steering is still very commonly practiced among real estate agents. Apartment managers and rental agents also have been found to discriminate by telling minorities there are no vacancies when in fact there are, by charging higher deposits to racial minorities, and by assigning minority residents to different buildings or parts of the apartment complex.

Other housing "gatekeepers" beyond real estate and rental agents are also still involved in housing discrimination. In some higher-status residential settings such as condominiums and country club communities, a residents committee reviews applicants' financial and personal characteristics and can screen out unwanted racial/ethnic minorities by finding some "defect" on their application. In less-affluent, tight-knit areas, housing vacancies sometimes are made known only through word-of-mouth social networks that are racially or ethnically homogeneous. In these cases, unwanted racial/ethnic minorities are excluded because they

Property Holding and Racial Differences

There are large differences in the wealth and property holding between white and black families in America. These differences go far beyond differences in earned income and account for some of the differences in social and economic outcomes for black and white children from families with comparable household incomes and parental educational levels. For example, low-income black families, those with incomes less than $15,000 per year, often hold no assets, while low-income white families typically have assets of around $10,000. Information about high-income families, those with incomes above $75,000, reveals a similar pattern, with white families having assets around $300,000 and equivalent black families having assets of around $100,000.

Melvin Oliver and Thomas Shapiro's *Black Wealth, White Wealth* (1995) first brought attention to the vast differences in wealth between white and black Americans, even among those with comparable incomes, and the systemic barriers that foster that gap. In the late 1990s, sociologist Dalton Conley further analyzed these differences in his book *Being Black, Living in the Red* (1999). These books documented the pervasiveness and importance of racial differences in property holding. Persistent differences in wealth are largely due to intergenerational transference of assets. Typically, each generation must earn its own income independently of the last generation. Social advantages such as education can be transferred between generations, but there is very little direct transfer of income: children do not inherit their mother or father's paycheck. In contrast, wealth is often directly transferred from one generation to the next in the form of inheritance, such as a house or lump sum of money, or gifts, such as the down payment for a house or money for college tuition. Racial differences in property holding are one mechanism that perpetuates racial disadvantage across generations.

Robin Roger-Dillon

are not granted access to knowledge about available houses or apartments in these neighborhoods.

In the 1970s, fair-housing activists and researchers became concerned about discrimination by banks and businesses that provide mortgage or other home-related loans. Research in Atlanta, Milwaukee, and Boston found that banks did not offer mortgage loans in many black neighborhoods or had much higher rejection rates for blacks than whites, even when applicants were of similar economic status. Racial/ethnic housing discrimination by lending institutions has several negative consequences, such as contributing to lower rates of home ownership among minorities, preventing upgrading and revitalization in minority neighborhoods, and making minority borrowers more likely to rely on companies that make home loans on adverse terms (e.g., higher interest rates and fees). As the extent and seriousness of home-loan discrimination became clearer, civil rights groups pressured and sued banks and sought legislative remedies.

Three important federal laws sought to address home-mortgage discrimination. The 1974 Equal Credit Opportunity Act made it illegal for banks to discriminate against minority groups and made it illegal for them to "redline" local areas, that is, use the racial composition of a neighborhood as a basis for not making loans in that area. The 1975 Home Mortgage Disclosure Act, which was amended and strengthened in 1989, requires each lender to provide census data on its mortgage loans and give additional information about its loan applications, making it more difficult to conceal housing discrimination. The Community Reinvestment Act (CRA) of 1977 reinforced the principle that banks have a responsibility to serve the credit needs of the entire community in its service area, regardless of race or income level. It also required federal financial regulatory agencies to monitor banks' CRA performance and take this into consideration when making decisions on banks' requests for mergers, relocations, and expansions. Some banks have found it expedient to increase mortgage loans to minorities to avoid jeopardizing their merger and acquisition plans. These laws have reduced housing discrimination by lending institutions, but there is debate about how powerful they actually have been in cutting out housing discrimination. Housing discrimination continues to be an ongoing issue in the United States, as the banking industry continues to fight to weaken the CRA, while fair-housing advocates continue to try and strengthen it.

CHARLES JARET

See also

American Apartheid; Blockbusting; Reverse Redlining; Segregation

Further Reading:

DeSena, Judith N. "Local Gatekeeping Practices and Residential Segregation." *Sociological Inquiry* 64 (1994): 307–21.

Ladd, Helen F. "Evidence on Discrimination in Mortgage Lending." *Journal of Economic Perspectives* 12 (1998): 41–62.

Ross, Stephen, and John Yinger. *The Color of Credit: Mortgage Discrimination, Research Methodology, and Fair-Lending Enforcement.* Cambridge, MA: MIT Press, 2002.

Squires, Gregory D., and Sally O'Connor. *Color and Money.* Albany: State University of New York Press, 2001.

Yinger, John. *Closed Doors, Opportunities Lost.* New York: Russell Sage Foundation, 1995.

Houston (Texas) Mutiny of 1917

The Houston Mutiny of 1917 (also referred to as the Houston Riot or Camp Logan Riot) was a violent rebellion of black troops against racist conditions in Houston. The black soldiers, part of the Army's 24th Infantry, mutinied on the night of August 23, 1917, after suffering verbal and physical abuse from members of the Houston Police Department (HPD). One of several pre–World War I riots, the Houston Mutiny was the bloodiest race riot in Houston's history and resulted in the deaths of 16 whites and four black soldiers. It was also one of the only American riots where more whites were killed than blacks. The riot led to one of the largest court-martials in military history, with 18 soldiers condemned to death by hanging.

The origins of the 24th Infantry, and of the use of black troops by the U.S. military, began in the Civil War. After the war, Congress established several new regiments of black troops, and in 1869 two of these regiments were joined to create the 24th Infantry. Like all colored units, white officers commanded the 24th because the Army, and many white Americans, believed that African Americans lacked the necessary courage and intelligence required to command troops and fight. In 1916, the U.S. War Department ordered the 24th Infantry to New Mexico to secure the border and protect American property after Pancho Villa began raiding the area.

The 24th Infantry, which in 1917 consisted of three battalions each with four companies, was split up and each battalion went to a different base. The Army ordered the 3rd Battalion to Houston to perform guard duty at Camp Logan, a training facility and staging area for white soldiers en route to Europe. On July 28, the 3rd Battalion set up camp near present-day Memorial Park, approximately three miles from downtown Houston.

In 1917, Houston was a city of 130,000 at the brink of a period of impressive economic growth. In the early 1910s, the Houston City Council began a reform program that improved city services, streamlined the local government, and attracted bigger businesses to the city. In 1917, Joseph Pastoriza was elected mayor, and he continued these reforms by overhauling the Houston Police Department. Mayor Pastoriza replaced the then chief of police, Ben Davison, with the superintendent of parks, Clarence Brock. Brock's inexperience with the police force, coupled with Mayor Pastoriza's short time in office, led to disorganization in the city government. This disorganization formed the backdrop to the Houston Mutiny of 1917.

One of the major factors that led to the mutiny concerned how HPD officers treated black Houstonians in general, and the black soldiers in particular. Houstonians generally did not respect the police department. There was much corruption among officers, and the host of poorly trained officers frequently abused their authority, especially when dealing with the city's black residents. Police officers treated black Houstonians with the utmost disdain, made frequent use of the n-word and beat jailed suspects. These problems were exacerbated when Mayor Pastoriza died unexpectedly only four months into his term. The local government fell into disarray. When the black troops began to return police violence with their own violence, this disorganization ensured that city officials were incapable of handling the situation.

The initial situation in Houston when the 3rd Battalion arrived, however, was relatively peaceful. The arrival of the black troops in Houston, which local papers had publicized for several weeks, caused little initial reaction. Indeed, many white-owned businesses hoped to benefit economically from the presence of the troops. For black Houstonians, the presence of the troops meant something different. At a time when there were few African American role models, local blacks viewed the soldiers as heroes. But the 3rd Battalion suffered from its own internal disorder, and like the Houston government, the troops were somewhat disorganized.

The base that 3rd Battalion established in Houston was basically a tent camp. The soldiers' main duty involved guarding Camp Logan. While the soldiers' time at the tent camp was hardly problematic, their service at Camp Logan required them to leave the camp. When they did, they often experienced the city's racism. Despite the façade of calm in the city, many Houstonians had a hard time accepting the presence of the black troops, especially after what had happened during the Brownsville Riot of 1906, a conflict involving black soldiers and white townspeople in Brownsville, Texas. The East St. Louis (Illinois) Riot of 1917 also exacerbated racial tensions in Houston. The Illinois riot did not involve black soldiers, but rather local whites and white soldiers from the Illinois National Guard. It was clear that racial tensions were brewing at this time, in Texas and beyond.

Houstonians were not prepared to treat the members of 3rd Battalion as equals. The soldiers came to resent the city's Jim Crow customs and the treatment they received from local whites. On the night of July 28, the day the 3rd Battalion arrived in Houston, overcrowding on streetcars prompted the men to simply rip the "Colored" signs out of the streetcars. These violations of Southern custom infuriated local whites, particularly the white streetcar conductors. Instances of soldiers reacting with violence to white racism on streetcars continued throughout 3rd Battalion's stay. The lieutenant colonel of the battalion took special care to work with Police Chief Brock to ease tensions between the black soldiers and white police officers. This was an important step in smoothing community relations, but one that ultimately failed. HPD officers frequently harassed the black soldiers, and when members of 3rd Battalion reacted angrily to racial affronts, the police responded with violence. There were many instances of HPD officers beating and harassing the black soldiers in Houston during this time.

The disorganization within the city government and in the 3rd Battalion, the incidents of police harassment, and the racism of local whites all led up to the Houston Mutiny. There were several sparks that ignited the riot.

The first involved a confrontation between two HPD officers and two black youths who were spotted shooting craps. A chase ensued, and one of the young black men escaped by fleeing through the home of a private citizen named Sara Travers. After the officers searched Travers' home, a scuffle broke out between her and one of the officers, Lee Sparks. At this time, one of the black soldiers, Pvt. Alonzo Edwards, intervened on Mrs. Travers' behalf. Angered by what he viewed as a challenge to his authority, Sparks withdrew his revolver and beat Edwards unmercifully. At this point, Cpl. Charles Baltimore, a black policeman, intervened on Edwards' behalf. He approached Sparks and Daniels in order to ascertain what had happened to Private Edwards. Dismayed at what he perceived to be another challenge to his authority, Sparks pistol-whipped Baltimore before placing him under arrest.

The soldiers of 3rd Battalion learned of these events almost immediately. Tensions grew when the soldiers heard an erroneous report that the police had killed Baltimore, and they quickly began to plan an attack on the city. After Baltimore was released and returned to the tent camp, he and several other soldiers began planning their revenge.

City officials began hearing rumors that the soldiers were planning a violent retaliation, but the disorganization in the local government ensured that officials ignored these rumors. As night fell, the soldiers began gathering ammunition and guns from supply tents. When one of the black soldiers erroneously reported that he had spotted a white lynch mob near the camp, the men panicked, grabbed weapons and ammunition excitedly, and commenced firing at random. The shooting continued for nearly 15 minutes. Amazingly, only one soldier was shot.

After the shooting, the 3rd Battalion's officers tried to calm the men, but they were too late. Sgt. Vida Henry, one of the few black soldiers entrusted with a leadership position and the rank to match it, ordered the men to form lines and prepare to march on the city. Henry and some of the other mutineers browbeat reluctant men into line, and told those who refused to participate that they would be killed. At approximately 9:00 P.M., around 150 soldiers began marching toward downtown. They specifically headed to the San Felipe district hoping to encounter Officer Lee Sparks. After shooting indiscriminately at a group of teenagers, the soldiers encountered and subsequently shot at three police officers.

The soldiers finally made it to San Felipe district at about 10:00 P.M.

Meanwhile, another mutiny was taking place at Camp Logan. The members of 3rd Battalion who guarded the camp were outraged that Baltimore had supposedly died and they had heard the shooting at the nearby tent camp. These men assumed that local whites had attacked the camp. As a group of soldiers left Camp Logan for 3rd Battalion's camp, they encountered an automobile, commanded the car to halt, and then opened fire. The driver was killed instantly and the passenger badly wounded. The 15 soldiers then broke up into two groups, one returning to the guard post at Camp Logan with the other proceeding to the tent camp. At the same time, a third group of soldiers left the 3rd Battalion camp and indiscriminately terrorized local whites who lived near the camp.

By this time, news of the mutiny had spread around the city. The Illinois National Guard mobilized a riot control squad, while the local police chief organized a civilian posse. Around 1,000 local whites volunteered to serve on the posse and then broke into downtown hardware stores to acquire guns and ammunition. Amazingly, this posse and the riot control squad cordoned off downtown Houston instead of attacking the black soldiers.

Meanwhile, the 3rd Battalion mutineers initiated several more violent confrontations with Houston policemen. After a few such confrontations resulted in the death of several police officers, a few dissenters emerged within the group of mutineers. The men quickly broke into disagreement about whether they should continue the march or return to camp, eventually deciding to return to camp. When the soldiers returned to camp, they attempted to blend in with the men who had not participated in the rioting. The mutiny had ended.

The riot lasted only a few hours, but left 15 whites dead and 12 seriously wounded. Four black soldiers died as a result of the riot. The death rate could have been much worse. The disorganization within Houston's government actually aided the mutineers. Instead of suppressing the riot in a violent counterattack, Houston's leaders were dumbfounded into inaction. By the time the police force swore in the posse and the Illinois National Guard riot control squad swung into action, the principal violence had already occurred. The Houston Mutiny was nevertheless the worst episode of racial violence in the city's history, and it spawned one of the largest courts-martial trials in American military history.

After local authorities restored order, the military began a lengthy investigation to try to determine exactly what had happened. The disorganization at 3rd Battalion's camp hindered this process. Eventually, 151 men were arrested for their participation in the mutiny and ferried out of Houston. The court-martials began on November 1, 1917, and continued throughout 1918. The mutineers engaged in a conspiracy of silence and refused to speak to investigators. However, at trial, several mutiny participants testified against the others in return for lighter sentences. The men were charged with disobeying orders of their commanding officer, mutiny, assault on civilians, and murder. Sentences ranged from death by hanging in the worst cases, to life in prison, to two-year prison sentences.

In the years following, African Americans did not soon forget these cases, many of them deemed unjust. James Weldon Johnson and members of the National Association for the Advancement of Colored People (NAACP) fought for the freedom of many imprisoned soldiers. They met with President Wilson, who commuted the death sentences of 10 soldiers. This meant that Wilson approved the execution of six mutineers, and these men were executed on September 16, 1918, outside of San Antonio. As for the men sentenced to jail terms, most were released early after appeals from the NAACP throughout the 1920s. The last prisoner was paroled in 1938.

The Houston Mutiny stands as one of the worst race riots in American history. It was also one of the worst mutinies in American military history. Unlike any other American riot, the Houston disturbance resulted in the deaths of more white people than blacks. Although 16 white people died, four blacks died as a result of injuries sustained in the mutiny. The riot also spawned one of the largest court-martials in American history and resulted in the execution of 19 soldiers. The people of Houston did not soon forget this event. Decades later, when college students began sit-ins to desegregate Houston's lunch counters in 1960, Houston's leaders remembered the violence of August 23, 1917. They chose to desegregate downtown facilities rather than face another riot. The city's leaders did not do quite enough because another riot occurred in 1967. The Texas Southern University Riot, however, was far less bloody than the Houston mutiny.

Only one person, a white police officer, died. The Houston Mutiny of 1917 marked the start of a long struggle for racial equality in Texas.

BRIAN D. BEHNKEN

See also

Brownsville (Texas) Incident of 1906; Race Riots in America. Documents: Report on the Memphis Riots of May 1866 (1866); Account of the Riots in East St. Louis, Illinois (1917); A Southern Black Woman's Letter Regarding the Recent Riots in Chicago and Washington (1919); The Cook County Coroner's Report Regarding the 1919 Chicago Race Riots (1920); The Final Report of the Grand Jury on the Tulsa Race Riot (June 25, 1921); Testimony from *Laney v. United States* (1923); The Governor's Commission Report on the Watts Riots (1965); Cyrus R. Vance's Report on the Riots in Detroit (1967); The Reports of the Oklahoma Commission to Study the Tulsa Race Riot of 1921 (2000–2001); Draft Report: 1898 Wilmington Race Riot Commission (2005)

Further Reading:

Adams, Thomas Richard. "The Houston Riot of 1917." Masters thesis, Texas A&M University, 1972.

Christian, Garna L. *Black Soldiers in Jim Crow Texas, 1899–1917.* College Station: Texas A&M University Press, 1995.

Haynes, Robert V. "The Houston Mutiny and Riot of 1917." *Southwestern Historical Quarterly* 76 (1973): 418–39.

Haynes, Robert V. *A Night of Violence: The Houston Riot of 1917.* Baton Rouge: Louisiana State University Press, 1976.

Schuler, Edgar A. "The Houston Race Riot, 1917." *Journal of Negro History* 29 (July 1944): 300–338.

Howard Beach (New York) Incident (1986)

On December 20, 1986, three African American men, 23-year-old Michael Griffith, 20-year-old Timothy Grimes, and 36-year-old Cedric Sandiford, were beaten and chased by a gang of local white teenagers. Griffith was killed while attempting to run across the Belt Parkway to escape from his attackers. The incident drew national attention and sparked a wave of demonstrations in one of New York City's least integrated neighborhoods.

According to court testimony, Griffith, Grimes, and Sandiford were traveling through Queens when their car broke down in the almost all-white Howard Beach community.

Hungry and tired, they walked into New Park Pizza to use the telephone but were refused. They later sat down to eat pizza when two police officers responded to the call that "three suspicious black males" were on the premises. When the officers realized the call was unwarranted, they left the scene. John Lester, Scott Kern, and Jason Ladone, all 17, approached the men yelling various epithets.

Some accounts state that the teenagers yelled, "There's niggers at the pizza parlor. Let's get them!" while others said, "There's niggers on the boulevard, let's go fuckin' kill them!" (Hynes and Drury 1990: 19). Nonetheless, as Griffith, Grimes, and Sandiford left the pizza parlor to walk up the street, a gang of white men with baseball bats and tree branches was waiting for them. Grimes managed to escape relatively unharmed while Griffith and Sandiford were severely beaten. Sandiford was knocked unconscious and lay bleeding at the scene. Griffith dove through a hole in an adjacent fence. In an attempt to escape, he ran onto the parkway, was struck and instantly killed by an automobile. The driver of the vehicle left the scene of the crime.

Almost overnight, crowds of black leaders and protesters, including Rev. Al Sharpton, descended on Howard Beach holding signs that compared the small, homogenous community to apartheid South Africa. Demonstrators were met by angry residents who screamed, "Nigger, go home!" Black leaders then called for boycotts of the white-owned Howard Beach businesses. Over the course of the next few months, Howard Beach came to exemplify the tumultuous history of race relations in the United States.

The incident also captured media, national, and international attention drawing comparisons to the segregated South and motivating journalists to comment on contemporary race relations. For example, one editorial in the *Queens Tribune* stated, "We cannot accept a climate that has not changed a lick since the days of 'Bull' Connor in Selma, Alabama. We cannot accept the narrow we–they mentality that gave rise to Hitler and Joseph McCarthy" (Albergotti et al. 2003: 1).

The trial for Michael Griffith's murder began almost a year after his death. The defendants were three 17-year-olds—Scott Kern, Jon Lester, and Jason Ladone—and 16-year-old Michael Pirone. They were each charged with manslaughter, first-degree assault, and second-degree murder. C. Vernon Mason and Alton Maddox, the lawyers

Al Sharpton, center, wearing fur collared jacket, organizer of a rally held in Howard Beach, Queens, New York, and James Bell, third from right, president of the Coalition of Black Trade Unionists, pose with unidentified rallyists, December 22, 1986, in front of the New Park Pizzeria. Four white youths were charged and seven others questioned that day in what New York's mayor termed a "racial lynching"—an attack on three blacks. One of them was killed by a car as he tried to flee. (AP Photo/Ed Bailey)

representing the Griffith family, believed that there was a conspiracy between the police and the mob. For instance, the driver of the car that killed Michael Griffith, Dominick Blum, was a court reporter and the son of a police officer. Although Blum claimed he thought he hit a tire or an animal, the lawyers argued that he was questioned little and was not even held accountable for leaving the scene of an accident. Likewise, there were accounts that mob boss John Gotti and friends, who grew up in Howard Beach, influenced potential witnesses and provided financial support for the defense team. A father of one neighborhood child was reputed to say that he would not let his son testify because he didn't want "to come home from work one day and find a slab of cement where my house used to be" (Hynes and Drury 1990: 87).

Attorneys representing the teens countered Mason and Maddox's conspiracy theory by portraying Griffiths, Sandiford, and Grimes as criminals. In an interview in the *Washington Post*, Ladone's attorney, Ronald Rubinstein, stated,

"We now have evidence of the fangs of the true villains" (Albergotti et al. 2003: 1). Rubinstein revealed that Grimes had once been charged with assault and criminal possession of a gun, had been investigated for burglary as well as trespassing, and for stabbing his then-girlfriend. Grimes also admitted to pulling out a knife when he was confronted by the gang of teens. Sandiford was a former convict who had several gun charges, and the coroner's report showed that Griffith had cocaine in his system at the time of his death.

The dramatic and emotional trial culminated with the conviction of Ladone, Kern, and Lester. The three teens were convicted of second-degree manslaughter and first-degree assault. They were acquitted of the second-degree murder charge. Michael Pirone, however, was acquitted of all charges. Reactions to the convictions were just as mixed as reactions to the incident. The *Queens Tribune* reported that Howard Beach residents were angry about the convictions because they felt the punishment was far too severe for what was just a simple dispute that ended in an accidental death.

Many of those who supported the victims, who saw this as a racially motivated crime, were pleased with the outcome of the trial.

State Supreme Court Justice Thomas Demakos sentenced Lester to 10 to 30 years in prison. At the sentencing he remarked that Lester "showed no remorse, no sense of guilt, no shame, no fear" (Albergotti et al. 2003: 1). Ladone received a five- to 15-year sentence, and Kern received six to 18 years. Lester was released from prison on May 29, 2001, and returned to his native country, England. Ladone was released in April 2001, and Kern was released in the spring of 2002.

DARA N. BYRNE

See also

Hate Crimes in America; Jena Six; Race Riots in America; Sharpton, Al; Vincent Chin Case (1982). Documents: Report on the Memphis Riots of May 1866 (1866); Account of the Riots in East St. Louis, Illinois (1917); A Southern Black Woman's Letter Regarding the Recent Riots in Chicago and Washington (1919); The Cook County Coroner's Report Regarding the 1919 Chicago Race Riots (1920); The Final Report of the Grand Jury on the Tulsa Race Riot (June 25, 1921); Testimony from *Laney v. United States* (1923); The Governor's Commission Report on the Watts Riots (1965); Cyrus R. Vance's Report on the Riots in Detroit (1967); The Reports of the Oklahoma Commission to Study the Tulsa Race Riot of 1921 (2000–2001); Draft Report: 1898 Wilmington Race Riot Commission (2005)

Further Reading:

Albergotti, Reed, Thomas Zambito, Marsha Schrager, and John Rofe. "Racism Comes Home: The Howard Beach Case." *Queens Tribune*, 2003.

Breindel, Eric. "The Legal Circus." *New Republic* 196 (1987): 20–23.

Hynes, Charles J., and Bob Drury. *Incident at Howard Beach: The Case for Murder*. New York: G. P. Putnam's Sons, 1990.

Hughes, Langston (1902–1967)

Langston Hughes was best known for his work as a poet, playwright, novelist, and columnist during the Harlem Renaissance in the 1920s and 1930s. First published in the *Crisis*, the official magazine of the National Association for the Advancement of Colored People in 1921, Hughes had a rich and unique life of international travel, experiences, and publishing. His first published work, the poem "The Negro Speaks of Rivers," was well received and appeared in his first book of poetry, *The Weary Blues*, published in 1926.

Hughes was born on February 1, 1902, to Carrie Langston Hughes and James Nathaniel Hughes in Joplin, Missouri. Langston's father abandoned his family and fled to Cuba and then Mexico due to increasing racial pressure in the United States. The separation of his parents resulted in his grandmother, Mary Langston, caring for Hughes and giving him the sense of racial pride that would vault his career forward in the coming years. After the death of his grandmother, Hughes moved in again with his mother in Lincoln, Illinois, and then to Cleveland, Ohio, where he attended high school. Hughes graduated high school in June 1920 and convinced his father to pay for his tuition at Columbia University if Hughes promised to earn his degree in engineering. He left Columbia in 1922 after increasing racial pressure forced him to do so. Columbia was followed by a stint on the S.S. *Malone* in 1923, where he traveled to West Africa and Europe. He spent time in Paris before traveling back to live with his mother in 1924 in Washington, D.C. As a busboy, Hughes had a fateful encounter with poet Vachel Lindsay, who helped spread the word of Hughes's talent, which was already being compiled into a book of poetry.

Hughes then attended Lincoln University and earned a BA in 1929. In 1930, he published his first novel, *Not Without Laughter*. The novel is about a boy named Sandy whose family must endure racial inequalities and must deal with their place in society. The Jim Crow laws of the United States, enforced between 1876 and 1965, are the "separate but equal" laws enacted in the Southern and border states. They stated that African Americans were to use separate schools, trains, buses, water fountains, and bathrooms than whites. Hughes countered these laws by confronting racial stereotypes and spoke to other African Americans about their own identity through his works. After 1945, the civil rights movement put increasing pressure on the U.S. judicial system to overturn the racist laws. The U.S. Supreme Court declared the legal segregation of schools unconstitutional in 1954. Then in 1964 President Lyndon B. Johnson pushed Congress to pass the Civil Rights Act of 1964, which overturned the remaining Jim Crow laws. Finally, the Voting Rights Act of 1965 ended all discrimination in local, state, and federal voting.

Hughes was incredibly influential internationally and in the United States. He was a key figure in the Negritude movement in France, which asked the black population to examine themselves in the light of European colonialism. He influenced countless poets, playwrights, novelists, and other black artists in Harlem during the Harlem Renaissance and inspired many blues, jazz, and gospel songs with his poetry. In the 1950s and 1960s, during America's movement toward racial integration, Hughes's work was seen to be racially chauvinistic and ethnocentric. Alternatively, Hughes thought that the Black Power movement was too angry in its methods but agreed generally with its fundamental philosophy.

Hughes died on May 22, 1967, after complications from surgery at the age of 65. Hughes was cremated and his ashes are placed under an African Cosmogram, titled *Rivers*, in the floor of the Langston Hughes Auditorium in the Schomburg Center for Research in Black Culture in Harlem.

ARTHUR HOLST

See also

Baldwin, James; Baraka, Amiri; Black Arts Movement (BAM); Ellison, Ralph

Further Reading:

Berry, Faith. *Langston Hughes: Before and Beyond Harlem.* Westport, CT: Lawrence Hill & Co., 1983. See esp. chap. 10, "On the Cross of the South," 150, and chap. 13, "Zero Hour," 185–86.

Joyce, Joyce A. "Hughes and Twentieth-Century Genderracial Issues." In *A Historical Guide to Langston Hughes,* edited by Steven C. Tracy, 136. New York: Oxford University Press, 2004.

Ostrom, Hans. *A Langston Hughes Encyclopedia.* Westport, CT: Greenwood Press, 2002.

Hurricane Katrina

Hurricane Katrina made landfall on the Gulf Coast of the United States on August 29, 2005. It is considered by many to be the most deadly and costly hurricane in U.S. history, ultimately responsible for more than 2,800 deaths and costing the affected states more than $150 billion. Hurricanes are quite common in that region of the country; however, the severity of the damage Katrina caused was extraordinary. The metropolitan areas of New Orleans; Mobile, Alabama;

Disaster Capitalism

Disaster capitalism has been offered as a framework for understanding recovery and redevelopment efforts in New Orleans. Decent affordable housing was somewhat scarce in New Orleans before the storm. Redevelopment efforts in New Orleans and the surrounding areas have been both celebrated and questioned in terms of fairness. Naomi Klein (2005) introduced the concept of "disaster capitalism" in her analysis of several crises around the world. Her concept includes the replacement of public infrastructures of social welfare with private-sector infrastructures through contracts with for-profit corporations. An example of this phenomenon is the decision to demolish New Orleans' public housing units, many of which were not affected by floodwaters, replacing them with mixed-income projects.

---

and Gulfport, Mississippi, bore the brunt of the destruction, but New Orleans also experienced severe flooding as a result of breached levees that were previously keeping the city, which is partially below sea level, from being inundated with water. Beyond the vast destruction that the storm created, poststorm flooding in New Orleans brought attention to racialized poverty and inequality in New Orleans and in the rest of the country. There are a variety of perspectives on the impact of Hurricane Katrina, most of which can be divided into two general approaches. The first, a colorblind ideology posits the storm as strictly a national disaster that happened to impact a predominantly black neighborhood, while the second approach advances the storm as a metaphor for racial and socioeconomic inequality.

Media coverage of the hurricane and the aftermath was particularly important for understanding differences in the response to survivors of Katrina and survivors of other natural disasters, as well as differences between the response to different survivors of Katrina. Many victims of the storm and aftermath were generally admonished by the public for not evacuating, being viewed in one study as passive, careless, and lacking agency. Images of residents stranded on rooftops and the poor conditions at the Superdome were crucial in influencing the disaster relief. Focus on the element of criminality was clear in media accounts

Devastation at Irish Bayou, Louisiana, in the aftermath of Hurricane Katrina in 2005. (iStockPhoto.com)

of the immediate aftermath. Relief centers were described as being chaotic and lawless with stories of rape and other criminal activity like theft were widely circulated. As some survivors attempted to meet their daily needs by taking food and other essentials from stores, they were often described as being "looters," and were associated with rumors of people stealing consumer goods like televisions from abandoned stores. White and rural victims of the storm were likely to be called "victims" or "survivors" in news coverage, while black New Orleans residents were likely to be referred to as "refugees." Characterizing black storm survivors as refugees, looters, and criminals simply served to reinforce long-held racial stereotypes, reinforce victim blaming, and impact the amount of assistance made available in the short term and in the long term.

The role of racial segregation in producing differential post-Katrina outcomes for residents of various parts of the city is one that cannot be overstated. The legacy of racial segregation is that black neighborhoods, especially poor black neighborhoods, were located in the areas most likely to have experienced flooding because they were in low-lying areas of the city. The neighborhoods with the highest number of storm fatalities and people missing after the storm were 80 percent African American, leading to the conclusion that Katrina's disproportionate impact on African Americans cannot be explained by the fact that the storm struck a city with a large black population. Although poverty was associated with not being able to evacuate before the storm, Sharkey (2007) found that poverty was no more prevalent in neighborhoods with high death counts than in those in which no bodies were found. Despite the obvious issues of segregation and inequality that were evident in New Orleans, many observers did not acknowledge these issues and the ways they shaped inequities in the response and recovery of the city.

The long-term impact of Hurricane Katrina is beginning to take shape and be documented. One year after the hurricane, black survivors reported more problems with personal health, emotional well-being, finances and the loss of

---

Katrina Refugees

The designation of "refugee" is a term generally reserved for citizens fleeing their home country and seeking refuge in another, not for citizens. Black hurricane survivors were more likely to be referred to as refugees than were white survivors, who were more likely to be referred to as victims. The use of this label for black Hurricane Katrina survivors in the news media likely had a strong impact on the relief effort, as studies have shown that the degree to which one perceives minorities as Americans affects the degree of empathy and helping behavior extended toward minority victims.

---

friends, relatives, and personal property than white survivors. Three years after Katrina, black survivors were more likely to be living in trailers than white survivors. Job security was another disparate outcome between black survivors and whites. Elliot and Pais (2006) found that black workers from New Orleans were four times more likely than white workers to lose their jobs after the storm, and when income differences were factored into the equation, average black workers in New Orleans were nearly seven times more likely to their jobs than average white workers. This difference in job security has a strong impact on who returned and will return to the city, as well as the structure of the city's workforce in the future.

Renee S. Alston

See also
Racialized Poverty

Further Reading:

Bauzon, K. "Race, Poverty, and the Neoliberal Agenda in the United States: Lessons from Katrina and Rita." *Monthly Review* February (2008):11–13.

Dyson, Michael Eric. *Come Hell or High Water: Hurricane Katrina and the Color of Disaster.* ReadHowYouWant, 2010.

Elliott, James R., and Jeremy Pais. "Race, Class, and Hurricane Katrina: Social Differences in Human Responses to Disaster." *Social Science Research* 35, no. 2 (2006): 295–321.

Gafford, Farrah D. "Rebuilding the Park: The Impact of Hurricane Katrina on a Black Middle-Class Neighborhood." *Journal of Black Studies* 41 (2010): 385–404.

If God Is Willing and Da Creek Don't Rise, directed by Spike Lee (2010).

Sharkey, Patrick. "Survival and Death in New Orleans: An Empirical Look at the Human Impact of Katrina." *Journal of Black Studies* 37, no. 4 (2007): 482–501.

Stephens, Nicole M., MarYam G. Hamedani, Hazel Rose Markus, Hilary B. Bergsieker, and Liyam Eloul. "Why Did They "Choose" to Stay? Perspectives of Hurricane Katrina Observers and Survivors." *Psychological Science* 20, no. 7 (2009): 878–86.

Toldson, Ivory A., Kilynda Ray, Schnavia Smith Hatcher, and Laura Straughn Louis. "Examining the Long-Term Racial Disparities in Health and Economic Conditions among Hurricane Katrina Survivors: Policy Implications for Gulf Coast Recovery." *Journal of Black Studies* 42, no. 3 (2011): 360–78.

Wailoo, Keith, Karen O'Neill, Jeffrey Dowd, and Roland Anglin, eds. *Katrina's Imprint: Race and Vulnerability in America.* New Brunswick, NJ: Rutgers University Press, 2010.

When the Levees Broke: A Requiem in Four Acts, directed by Spike Lee (2006).

Hypersegregation

Hypersegregation is an extreme form of residential segregation. In the most basic sense, residential segregation is the separation of racial groups based on where they live. Although segregation is illegal, residential segregation has persisted despite reforms in laws and in housing regulations. Demographers measure residential segregation using five different dimensions: evenness, isolation, centralization, clustering, and exposure. A group is considered hypersegregated when they experience high levels of segregation on several of these five dimensions.

In order to understand hypersegregation fully, it is important to review the five dimensions of residential segregation a bit further.

Evenness is the degree to which the percentage of minority members within residential areas equals the citywide minority percentage; as areas depart from the ideal of evenness, segregation increases. Exposure is the degree of potential contact between minority and majority members; it reflects the extent to which groups are exposed to one another by virtue of sharing neighborhoods in common. Clustering is the extent to which minority areas adjoin one another in space; it is maximized when minority neighborhoods form one large, contiguous ghetto and minimized when they are scattered widely in space. Centralization is the degree to which minority members are settled in and around the center of an urban area, usually defined as the central business district. Finally, concentration is the relative amount of physical space occupied by a minority group; as segregation rises, minority members are increasingly concentrated within a small, geographically compact area. (Massey and Denton 1989: 373)

Many studies focus on only one or two of these dimensions, especially the index of dissimilarity. However, Massey and Denton argue in their book *American Apartheid: Segregation and the Making of the Underclass* that this narrow focus can underestimate the impact and effects of residential segregation, especially for African Americans. Using data from the 1980 census, they found that African Americans are "highly segregated on at least four of the five dimensions at once" in several U.S. metropolitan areas. Each of the five dimensions is measured on a scale of zero to 100, where zero would mean complete integration and 100 would mean complete segregation. Scores above 60 in any of the dimensions is considered to be high by Massey and Denton. For example, if a city had a dissimilarity score of 60, that would mean that 60 percent of African Americans (or another racial group) would need to relocate in order for there to be evenness residentially. Perfect evenness means that every neighborhood's composition matches the racial proportions in the city. So if a city is 70 percent white and 30 percent African American, evenness would be achieved if every neighborhood was 70 percent white and 30 percent African American. However, this is rarely the case. In fact, Massey and Denton found that in 16 metropolitan areas, blacks were hypersegregated in 1980. "Thus one-third of all African Americans in the United States live under conditions of intense racial segregation. They are unambiguously among the nation's most spatially isolated and geographically secluded people, suffering extreme segregation across multiple dimensions simultaneously, Black Americans in these metropolitan areas live within large, contiguous settlements of densely inhabited neighborhoods that are packed tightly around the urban cores" (Massey and Denton 1993: 77).

Though Massey and Denton's work was written nearly 20 years ago, hypersegregation for African Americans persists. For example, here is the information for Chicago in 2000. The dissimilarity index was 79, the isolation index was 77, the concentration index was 84, the centralization index was 66, and the spatial proximity index was 1.73. Note that the spatial proximity index reported was developed by White. "Spatial proximity equals 1.0 if there is no differential clustering between minority and majority group members. It is greater than 1.0 when members of each group live nearer to one another than to members of the other group, and is less than 1.0 if minority and majority members live nearer to members of the other group than to members of their own group" (Census). It is important to note that each of these measures decreased slightly from 1980 and 1990, however high levels of residential segregation continue to exist. Chicago was ranked 9, making it one of the top 10 most segregated cities in 2000.

The effects of hypersegregation are important to note. Living in a hypersegregated community fosters a number of disadvantages for African Americans. A racially segregated society cannot be a race-blind society; as long as U.S. cities remain segregated—indeed, hypersegregated—the United States cannot claim to have equalized opportunities for blacks and whites. In a segregated world, the deck is stacked against black socioeconomic progress, political empowerment, and full participation in the mainstream of American life.

KATHRIN A. PARKS

Further Reading:

Frey, William H. "The New Metro Minority Map: Regional Shifts in Hispanics, Asians, and Blacks from Census 2010." Metropolitan Policy Program at Brookings Institute. August 2011.

Massey, D.S., and N.A. Denton. "Hypersegregation in U.S. Metropolitan Areas: Black and Hispanic Segregation along Five Dimensions." *Demography* 26 (1989): 373–92.

Massey, D.S., and N.A. Denton. *American Apartheid: Segregation and the Making of the Underclass*. Cambridge, MA: Harvard University Press, 1993.

United States Census Bureau, "Housing Patterns, Appendix B." http://www.census.gov/hhes/www/housing/housing_patterns/app_b.html

Wilkes, Rima, and John Iceland. "Hypersegregation in the Twenty-first Century." *Demography* 41 (2004): 23–36.

Hypodescent (One Drop Rule)

Colloquially referred to as the "one drop rule," hypodescent refers to the automatic assignment of children of mixed unions or parentage to the less socially privileged group. In the United States, the concept has de facto applied primarily to blacks, meaning that anyone with any amount of black blood is automatically categorized as black. Despite this exclusive application, the concept forms the foundation of race relations in the United States, exposes the power and application of racial binaries, and showcases how race has been understood and determined both historically and in contemporary times.

Historically, mixed black-white offspring were classified as black in order for slave owners to evade their paternal responsibilities. Tracing back to the anti-Roman traditions of Northern Europe and continuing with early Dutch and English Americans, the idea of hypodescent grew to justify taboos against racial mixing, particularly as other differences between communities became less obvious. During slavery in the United States and other colonies, the growing dependence on monoracial responses on government forms ensured that offspring of white slave owners and female black slaves were categorized as black. The underlying purpose of this categorization was to maintain a slave labor force and free slave owners from their paternal responsibilities. Under slavery, white women could give birth to free children, whereas black women's children would always be classified as property. The concept of hypodescent, however, was most strongly entrenched in legal discourse in the early 20th century. For example, the landmark 1896 Supreme Court decision, *Plessy v. Ferguson*, by holding that anyone with any traceable amount of African American descent was deemed African American, set a judicial precedent for future legal definitions of blackness. The *Plessy* ruling led to the creation of Jim Crow laws that enforced racial segregation in railway travel and eventually in schools and other public facilities. The one-drop rule was officially adopted as law in the 20th century, beginning in 1910 in Tennessee and then in 1924 under Virginia's Racial Integrity Act.

The purpose of hypodescent was to delineate boundaries between black and white groups, maintain white superiority, and limit African American equality. Thus, up until the civil rights movement, a person's work and housing options were legally determined by one's racial categorization. This meant that anyone with any amount of black ancestry could be classified as black and thus be subject to segregation laws. Although not its intent, the rule also led to a burgeoning black identity and sense of community, which culminated in the civil rights movement of the 1950s and 1960s. The civil rights movement dismantled Jim Crow segregation laws and eliminated overtly racist legal discrimination. Notable was the 1967 *Loving v. Virginia* decision, which eliminated laws against interracial marriage. The result of the *Loving* decision, many scholars contend, led to a growth in interracial marriage and multiracial offspring who eventually came to challenge rules of hypodescent in an effort to honor their multiracial identities.

Today, the idea of hypodescent continues to be debated. Although the historical reasons behind the enforcement of hypodescent no longer exist, and although more people today are identifying with multiple races and cultures, the practice of identifying black-white Americans as black is still often advanced and adhered to. Some scholars contend that the historical effect of hypodescent has meant that black-white biracial individuals tend to highlight their black identity because this is how they are perceived and expected to identify. Others advocating the "right" to identify as racially mixed see resistance to informal rules of hypodescent as mandatory and claim that the rule is racist, exclusionary and not in tune with today's reality of multiracial diversity. Critical race theorists and whiteness studies scholars maintain that the logic behind the rule of hypodescent also inaccurately suggests that race is fixed at birth and not subject to change. Such scholars further contend that hypodescent sustains a racial hierarchy where whiteness is upheld at the top of a racial hierarchy and defined in relation to blackness. In this view, hypodescent is a biological notion of race that upholds white purity because it "allows for whiteness to participate in blackness, but not for blackness to participate in whiteness owing to the fact that whiteness cannot remain white when mixed with blackness" (Spencer 2010: 6). U.S. critical race scholarship holds that in our goal to challenge racism we must also debunk hypodescent and the binary framework of white purity and black impurity on which it depends and which continues to form the basis of the U.S. racial paradigm.

LEANNE TAYLOR

See also

American Eugenics Movement; Blood Quantum; Multiracial Identity; Race; Racial Profiling

Further Reading:

Daniel, Reginald. *More Than Black: Multiracial Identity and the New Racial Order*. Philadelphia: Temple University Press, 2002.

Ferber, Abby. *White Man Falling: Race, Gender and White Supremacy*. Lanham, MD: Rowman and Littlefield, 1998.

Fernandez, Carlos. A. "Government Classification of Multiracial/Multiethnic People." In *The Multiracial Experience: Racial Borders as the New Frontier*, edited by Maria M. P. Root, 15–36. Philadelphia: Temple University Press, 1996.

Harris, Cheryl. L. "Whiteness as Property." *Harvard Law Review* 106 (1993): 1707–91.

Hollinger, David. "Amalgamation and Hypodescent: The Question of Ethnoracial Mixture in the History of the United States." *American Historical Review* 108 (5) (2003): 1363–90.

Ibrahim, H. *Troubling the Family: The Promise of Personhood and the Rise of Multiracialism*. Minneapolis: University of Minnesota Press, 2012.

Roediger, D. R. *How Race Survived U.S. History: From Settlement and Slavery to the Obama Phenomenon*. New York: Verso, 2008.

Spencer, R. *Reproducing Race: The Paradox of Generation Mix*. Boulder, CO: Lynne Rienner Publishers, 2010.

I

Identity Politics

Not limited to activity in the traditionally conceived political sphere, identity politics refers to activism, politics, theorizing, and other, similar activities based on the shared experiences of members of a specific social group (often relying on similar experiences of oppression). Many of the groups that engage in identity politics are racially, ethnically, or pan-ethnically organized, but people have also organized around identities such as gender, sexuality, and disability. They engage in such activities as state-oriented social movements, movements for change at colleges and universities, consciousness-raising support groups, and education and awareness in the outside world. The most important and revolutionary element of identity politics is the demand that oppressed groups be recognized not in spite of their differences but specifically because of their differences: it was an important precursor to the emphasis on multiculturalism and diversity in certain facets of modern political and educational culture.

Identity politics movements have suggested that those who do not share the identity of and the life experiences that it brings to an individual thus cannot understand what it means to live life as a person with that identity—they cannot understand the specific terms of oppression and thus cannot find adequate solutions to the problems that the members of the group face. Thus, identity politics movements have pushed for self-determinism on the part of oppressed groups. This has meant, for example, that proponents of identity politics believe that ethnic-studies courses should be taught only by those who share the ethnic identity that the course addresses, and that faculty and students of color should have sole responsibility for determining the policies of curriculum and faculty hiring in such departments and the admission of students of color to colleges and universities. In spheres of action beyond academia, identity politics movements have pushed for self-determination in local politics through the institution of community boards controlled by people of color and the establishment of social-service agencies staffed by people of color to deal with the specific problems faced by communities of color.

Conservative politicians and back-to-the-basics academics have criticized identity politics movements as being naïve, fragmenting, essentialist, or reductionist. They have stressed the importance of unified "American" identities in moving away from discriminatory pasts and suggested that focusing attention on the specific histories of identity groups disadvantages these groups by ensuring that they do not possess the cultural capital they will need to get ahead. One important aspect of this debate is that those engaged in identity politics believe that legacies of discrimination can only be overcome by drawing attention to the oppressed difference, while traditional liberal analysis promotes color blindness

Russell Means, American Indian Movement (AIM) leader, speaks to a crowd of followers in South Dakota in 1974. AIM was an American Indian activist group that sought restitution from both state and federal governments. (Bettmann/Corbis)

communities are racist. Black women who turn to support organizations to build their identity have found that "all the blacks are men and all the women are white." Those with multiply oppressed identities have sometimes responded by forming new, more specific identity politics groups (e.g., lesbians of color). This fragmentation counters the original point of identity politics, which is to encourage recognition of the vast numbers of people who share identities that are outside the mainstream. However, these communities can also provide support and consciousness raising to those who become involved in them.

MIKAILA MARIEL LEMONIK ARTHUR

See also
Intersectionality

Further Reading:
Arthur, John, and Amy Shapiro, eds. *Campus Wars: Multiculturalism and the Politics of Difference.* Boulder, CO: Westview Press, 1995.
Giroux, Henry A. *Living Dangerously: Multiculturalism and the Politics of Difference.* New York: P. Lang, 1993.
Heyes, Cressida. "Identity Politics." In *The Stanford Encyclopedia of Philosophy*, Fall 2002 ed., edited by Edward N. Zalta. http://plato.stanford.edu/.
Reed, Ishmael. *MultiAmerica: Essays on Cultural Wars and Cultural Peace.* New York: Viking, 1996.

as a way to overcome discrimination and believes that paying attention to difference merely highlights its salience in interactions. Additionally, critics worry that multiculturalism brings with it a call to moral relativism, a philosophy that prevents judgment of the practices of other groups that might be found reprehensible. Identity politics movements counter with the idea that it is possible to preserve cultures and identities without allowing the practice of certain objectionable elements within it.

Criticism does not stem only from critics who do not share the oppressed identity. There are conflicts within identities as well. Of chief importance is the fact that many people's identities are multifaceted, and thus involvement in one identity politics does not suffice. For instance, Asian American gay men often struggle to find a place when their Asian American communities are homophobic and their gay

Ideological Racism

An ideology is a strongly held set of beliefs of an individual or group and often guides action; for example, a strong ideology in the United States is that of meritocracy, the idea that one's hard work will result in rewards. Ideological racism, then, is the belief that based on biology and/or culture, racially superior and inferior groups exist. Ideological racism is most often analyzed at the individual level as it is seen as a person's beliefs, but it can be applied to understand how groups subscribe to racist ideologies in order to govern their actions.

Race is a social construction (a group defined by socially assigned meaning), not a biological, genetic reality, yet society does have "races" that are easily recognized by most. Thus, ideological racism aids in understanding the transition from "group of people" to "race" such as how the group of enslaved Africans from a range of African tribes came to be known as "black." Ideologies are used to categorize some racial groups as inferior and apply negative characteristics to them. For example, the "ideology of savagery" was applied to Native Americans during colonization and, as could be surmised, subscribers to this ideology believed that Native Americans were barbaric, crude, and uncivilized. White colonists then used this ideology to justify pushing Native Americans off their land and later their systematic genocide. White colonists also applied this ideology of savagery to other people of color. In the 18th century Chinese immigrants were viewed as "mongrels" unsuitable for relations with whites, Mexicans were viewed as lazy and incapable of governing their land, and blacks were considered subhuman. The power of the ideology of savagery is that once understood and utilized, it can easily be transferred to other racial groups in order to justify their racial subordination. This type of ideological work still operates in contemporary United States. Pre-9/11, Arab Americans were generally seen as "white," but post-9/11 the ideological beliefs about Arabs changed so that collectively they were deemed as potential terrorists. This new set of beliefs about Arabs resulted in "racializing" (to make a race) them as "Muslim" and/or "nonwhite."

Classical racial theorists most often define racism as an ideology, a set of prejudiced attitudes and beliefs that then later inform discriminatory actions. Two examples of theorists that rely on this racism as ideology perspective are Marxists who explain racial discrimination as a result of upper-class groups who use racial ideologies to maintain class divisions, and similarly colonial theorists who place colonization at the center of analysis and maintain that racism is the ideological underpinnings of colonial oppressors. In this vein, racism as an ideology comprises a set of strongly held beliefs and is thus largely restricted to the field of psychology, or perhaps to the field of social psychology.

Analyzing racism as an ideology has been criticized as too simplistic and inaccurate as it reduces racism to attitudes and beliefs, rather than structure. Michael Omi and Howard Winant (1991) advanced the theory of ideological racism with their "racial formation thesis," which states that ideology has structural, institutional consequences (racist beliefs result in racist institutions) but also that institutional

---

Ideologies about Racial Groups

Ideologies about racial groups can help sustain racism and are a component of how some groups are racialized, or in other words, how a group becomes a race. For example, pre-9/11 Arab Americans were generally seen as white and were classified on the U.S. Census as white. However, post-9/11 discrimination against Arab Americans has spiked, and incidents against them have persisted. In the weeks following 9/11 there were approximately 700 documented violent crimes against Arab Americans as reported by the American-Arab Anti-Discrimination Committee (ADC). Ideas that Arabs are to blame for 9/11 and that they are terrorists have led not only to hate crimes against them but also distinguishing them from whites and identifying them as "other." Some also argue that there has been the creation of "Arab" or "Muslim" as a racial group recognized by U.S. society.

Read more on the report on hate crimes against Arabs: http://www.civilrights.org/hatecrimes/united-states/050-arab-hate-crimes.html

---

organizations give rise to ideologies (racist institutions lead to racist beliefs). Omi and Winant thus argue there is an intense and bicausal arrow between structure and ideology, which creates and sustains the belief that nonwhites are inferior to whites. Bonilla-Silva (1997), however, suggests that Omi and Winant and other theorists of racism do not go far enough in articulating racism as distinct from just ideology; he, instead, pushes for the concept of "racialized social systems" where economic, political, social, and ideological levels are structured partly by race.

Ideological racism is both a viewpoint and a type of racial analysis. As a viewpoint, it is the set of beliefs that individuals or groups hold against an opposing group; it is most often associated with how whites view racial minorities as biologically and/or culturally "less than." As a theoretical concept, ideological racism explains how many theorists choose to understand what racism is and how it operates. From their perspective, racism largely operates via prejudiced attitudes, which can affect social structures but is not *of* social structures.

Hephzibah Strmic-Pawl

See also

Color-Blind Racism; Cultural Racism; Laissez-Faire Racism; Racism; Symbolic Racism; Systemic Racism

Further Reading:

Bonilla-Silva, Eduardo. "Rethinking Racism: Toward a Structural Interpretation." *American Sociological Review* 62 (1997): 465–80. http://www.jstor.org/stable/2657316. Accessed December 6, 2012.

Jamal, Amaney, and Nadine Naber, eds. *Race and Arab Americans Before and After 9/11: From Invisible Citizens to Visible Subjects*. Syracuse, NY: Syracuse University Press, 2008.

Omi, Michael, and Howard Winant. *Racial Formation in the United States: From the 1960s to the 1990s*. New York: Routledge, 1991.

Takaki, Ronald. *A Different Mirror: A History of Multicultural America*. Boston: Back Bay Books, 1993.

Illegitimacy Rates

In the 1950s, American law and policy centered on the ideal family as the nuclear family: a husband, wife, and their biological children. Children born out of wedlock are referred to as "illegitimate births." Pejorative terms are used to describe the children as "bastards." Since the 1965 report, "The Negro Family: The Case for National Action" by Daniel Patrick Moynihan, researchers have been concerned with the growth of out-of-wedlock births. In 2010, the Centers for Disease Control and Prevention, U.S. Department of Health and Human Services, National Center for Health Statistics, and National Vital Statistics System found that 40.8 percent of all births were to unmarried women. Premarital births are caused by in vitro fertilization or sex before marriage. The context as to what causes premarital birth is due to social, economic, and religious factors.

World War II opened social spaces for interracial contact. During World War I, military directives forbade black soldiers from speaking with white women or visiting public places where they could socialize with them. In military towns in the Asia-Pacific region, hostess bars cropped up where locals entertained servicemen. Oftentimes the women in the bars were expected to offer sex to their customers. During World War II, the U.S. government realized that they could not control interracial relationships between African

American soldiers and white women with soldiers deployed to Europe. Therefore, the military censored the stories in the American press, and segregated bar nights were implemented. In 1945 the War Brides Act was passed, enabling war soldiers to bring military brides home. However, many children, referred to as Amerasians, were abandoned. Amerasian children are any person fathered by a citizen of the United States (American servicemen, American expatriates, and U.S. government employee) whose mother is or was an Asian national. The Amerasian Act of 1982 gave permission to Amerasian individuals to migrate to the United States—people born in Cambodia, Korea, Laos, Thailand, or Vietnam after December 31, 1950, and fathered by a U.S. citizen. Amerasian children were seen as objects of shame and stigmatization, due to the reminders they represented of inequalities between Asia and the United States and the assumption of how their mothers met their fathers.

Immigrants have high rates of illegitimate birth, in spite of the stereotypes that they have a strong commitment to traditional families. Between 1980 and 2003, the percentage of immigrants giving birth to children out of wedlock increased from 13 percent to 32 percent—from 45,000 illegitimate births to 300,000. Forty-five percent of migrants who lack a high school diploma gave birth to children out of wedlock. In 2003, 1 out of 12 unmarried immigrant women gave birth, contrasting the 1 out of every 25 for U.S. citizens. Immigrant groups are more likely to be missed in census counts due to their legal status. College students who are migrants have a triple rate of illegitimacy in comparison to college students who are citizens. The rates differ for racial minorities; Hispanics have higher rates (nearly 42 percent) than Asian migrants (11 percent).

Since the 1980s teen mothering has become a visible social problem. Teen motherhood is represented in popular culture and the media in films such as *Juno* and an MTV show titled *Teen Moms*. Popular attitudes toward teen mothers assume pregnancy is an individual disease, a social illness, and even an epidemic. Children born to unmarried parents are at risk for a variety of social problems that include poverty, incarceration, low academic achievement, and becoming unmarried parents themselves. However, it is essential to centralize race and teen motherhood to offer a nuanced understanding of the stereotypes and realities for young mothers. In 2010 Hispanics between the age of 15 years and

19 years old held the highest rate of illegitimacy rates at 55.7 percent. The second highest rates of teen pregnancy occur among black Americans. Overall, since 1991 teen pregnancies have declined.

U.S. laws continue to address illegitimate births. In 1972, Title IX was passed ensuring that single mothers have access to education and school activities. In 1996, the Clinton administration passed the Welfare Act that replaced Aid to Families with Dependent Children with Temporary Assistance for Needy Families (TANF). TANF offered aid to individuals who were married and required parents to work, reinforcing the assumption of a family. Although the first four years of TANF decreased poverty, it did not do so after four years suggesting the challenges of the program to address poverty and the diverse types of families such as unmarried mothers or fathers. In 2012, the Obama administration loosened the concept of work in the Welfare Act; however, the new legislation continues to maintain the assumption that families are defined by a two-parent household (TANF Waiver Section 1115, July 12, 2012).

ANNIE ISABEL FUKUSHIMA

See also
Ant-Miscegenation Laws; Domestic Violence; Mixed Race Relationships and the Media; Tripping over the Color Line

Further Reading:
Camarota, Steven A. "Illegitimate Nation: An Examination of Out-of-Wedlock Births Among Immigrants and Natives." *Center for Immigration Studies.* 2007. http://www.cis.org/illegitimate_nation.html.

Gage, Sue-Je Lee. "The Amerasian Problem: Blood, Duty, and Race." *International Relations* 21 (2007): 86–102.

Gregson, Jaonna. *The Culture of Teen Mothers.* New York: SUNY Press, 2009.

Institute on Women and Criminal Justice. "Quick Facts: Women & Criminal Justice—2009." *Women's Prison Association.* 2009. http://www.wpaonline.org/pdf/Quick%20Facts%20Women%20and%20CJ%202009.pdf.

Martin, Joyce A., Brady E. Hamilton, Stephanie J. Ventura, Michelle J. K. Osterman, Elizabeth C. Wilson, and T. J. Mathews. "Births: Final Data for 2010." National Vital Statistics Reports 61, no. 1 (August 28, 2012): 1–71.

Romano, Renee C. *Race Mixing: Black-White Marriage in Postwar America.* Cambridge, MA: Harvard University Press, 2003.

Sugarman, Stephen D. "What Is a 'Family'? Conflicting Messages from Our Public Programs." *Family Law Quarterly* 42, no. 2 (Summer 2008): 231–61.

Immigration Acts

Intended or not, the Immigration and Naturalization Act of 1965 brought a momentous change in the country-of-origin composition of immigrants to the United States. In that sense, the act truly represents a historical shift in U.S. immigration policies. To understand its significance, the history of U.S. immigration laws prior to the passage of the act must be reviewed.

With the opening of the western frontier, the U.S. economy demanded a large influx of workers. This pull factor in America that began in the 17th century and remained until the Civil War brought a surge in European immigration. Most of these immigrants came from the British Isles and other Western European countries and were Protestants. These white Protestant immigrants and their descendants emerged as the dominant group in the United States. Their dominance generated the image of America as a white, Protestant society.

As expected, there was a lull in immigration during the Civil War. Immediately afterward, though, the industrialization of the U.S. economy again required large numbers of workers. Once again, America obtained the needed labor force from immigrants. But the immigrants of this period came mostly from Eastern and Southern European countries. A great majority of these new immigrants were not only illiterate but also brought religious traditions—Catholicism, Judaism, and Eastern Orthodoxy—different from those of the dominant group. They suffered prejudice, discrimination, and even physical violence by the dominant white Protestant group. For a long time, these immigrants and their children were treated as second-class citizens at best. World War I eventually halted immigration from Eastern and Southern European countries. Then, as blacks began migrating to the North in significant numbers, these white immigrants and their descendants were gradually assimilated into mainstream America.

Several groups of non-Europeans began arriving in the United States in the middle of the 19th century. For example, as the United States acquired Texas and what would become California, New Mexico, and other western states from Mexico through annexation or war between 1845 and 1848, a large number of Mexicans became members of U.S. society, but they were treated as immigrants. In the early part of the 20th century, many Mexican migrant workers moved to the

United States as well. As a whole, though, Mexican Americans were relatively small in number and concentrated in the former Mexican territory.

Beginning in the mid-19th century, a limited number of Chinese immigrants arrived in Hawaii and California. When the Chinese Exclusion Act of 1882 prohibited the Chinese from immigrating to the United States, the immigration of the Japanese to Hawaii started. A small number of Korean immigrants also arrived to the United States between 1903 and 1905. Then, Japanese labor migration was stopped by the Gentlemen's Agreement in 1908, and Filipino workers immigrated in substantial numbers. But most of these Asian immigrants and their descendants, numbering about a half million, were confined to the Hawaiian Islands and the West Coast. As expected, these non-European immigrants were too small in number to dent the image of the United States as the land of white men.

This short review of American immigration history bespeaks the racial stratification in the United States that existed in the 19th century and in the early part of the 20th century. The native-born whites, the descendants of Western European immigrants, enjoyed a highly respected racial position and were regarded as the dominant group. Although the immigrants from Eastern or Southern European countries and their descendants were eventually accepted as white Americans, they were not socially well respected. Nonwhite and non-European immigrants were in the worst situation, at the bottom. They were brought to meet the need for cheap labor, but the United States did not want to accept them as a part of America. Even their U.S.-born descendants were not allowed U.S. citizenship for a long period of time.

The U.S. government began a sweeping regulation of the immigration flow in the early part of the 20th century. The immigration law that faithfully reflected this regulation was passed in 1924. The 1924 National Origins Act spelled out the national origins of immigrants the United States would accept. As reflected in its name, it stipulated that the number of immigrations allowed from European countries should be based on the race/ethnic composition of the U.S. population. This law heavily favored immigration from the British Isles and other Western European countries, as Western European Americans maintained a numeric dominance among the U.S. population.

The 1924 immigration law did allow for immigration from Eastern and Southern European countries. But their number was limited because of a small proportion of the native-born population of Eastern and Southern European ancestry. The number of immigrants from these parts of Europe was further reduced when the calculation of the ethnic composition of the population was made on the basis of the 1880 census, instead of the 1920 census, as originally conceived. The 1924 immigration law virtually prohibited immigration from non-European countries, with the exception of Mexicans. It also had a special provision that completely banned immigration from Asian countries. With the enforcement of the 1924 National Origins Act, no Asian country, with the exception of the Philippines, a U.S. colony at that time, was able to send immigrants.

The 1924 immigration law was enforced until the end of World War II in 1945. Afterward, the United States was forced to critically review the immigration laws for several reasons. First, the experience of World War II made Americans more tolerant of racial and religious differences. Second, the civil rights movement in the 1950s and 1960s sensitized the issue of racial equality. Viewed with this perspective, U.S. immigration laws clearly violated the principle of racial equality. Third, in the early 1960s, the heart of the Cold War period, the United States had to abolish its racist immigration policy for the diplomatic purpose of gaining more support from Third World countries at the United Nations. Fourth, the escalation of Cold War tensions rendered the racist U.S. immigration policy problematic. Along with the escalation of the Cold War, U.S. military involvement in various parts of the world greatly expanded the numbers of refugees. Fifth, the growing globalization of mass media spread the American way of life throughout the world and increased the number of people in the other parts of the world eager to move to the United States. Sixth, there was a growing need for professional workers, especially medical professionals, in the 1960s, which could not have been met by the native workforce alone.

Even though a couple of small-scale changes had already been made to the 1924 National Origins Act, the McCarran-Walter Act of 1952 was the first attempt to address these issues. Nevertheless, it was a reluctant, transitional response at best. This law reaffirmed the national origins system of the 1924 law but eased some restrictions, such as the ban on non-European immigrants and their descendants acquiring U.S. citizenship. It also legally accepted some non-European immigrants and refugees. Since this law had maintained the main tenet of the 1924 National Origins Act, however, U.S. immigration policies remained racially restrictive until 1965.

President John F. Kennedy sent his immigration reform law to Congress in July 1963; it was intended to eliminate the racially biased national-origins system. This bill called for an abolition of the national-origins system over a five-year period but retained the nonquota system for the Western Hemisphere. It also specified that the total number of immigrants outside the Western Hemisphere be only 165,000 annually, with no one country permitted to have more than 10 percent of the total. Visas were expected to be granted on the basis of preference categories in which one-half of immigrant visas would be granted to persons with special skills, training, or education advantageous to the U.S. economy and the rest to close relatives of U.S. citizens.

The Johnson administration also stressed admitting persons with skills, education, and desirable occupations and wanted to grant half of the visas to such people. Preferences to those with close family ties in the United States came second. Congressman Edward Feighan won his battle with the Johnson administration and reversed these preferences, though. Congressman Feighan's preferences heavily favored immigration based on family reunion. As a result, the final proposal contained only two preference categories—the Third and Sixth Preferences—and allowed 20 percent maximum of total immigrant visas to be granted for those with professions, skills, occupations, and special talents needed in the United States.

The act phased out the national-origin quotas over a three-year period. Effective July 1, 1968, the act provided 170,000 visas for persons from the Eastern Hemisphere and 120,000 from the Western Hemisphere per year. No one country in the Eastern Hemisphere was to have more than 20,000 visas. However, immediate family members, such as spouses, minor children (under age 21), and parents of American citizens, and a few others such as ministers, were exempt from the numerical limits. In 1978, the U.S. Congress passed a law providing for a worldwide immigration cap of 290,000 without differentiating Eastern and Western Hemispheres.

President Lyndon B. Johnson (left) speaks after signing the Immigration and Naturalization Act of 1965 below the Statue of Liberty. The act granted Chinese immigrants equal status to that of European immigrants. (Lyndon B. Johnson Library/Yoichi R. Okamoto)

After World War II, the United States experienced rapid suburbanization and high rates of interethnic marriages among descendants of various white immigrants. Eventually, various white ethnic groups merged into one single group: white Americans, or European Americans. As the U.S. Congress amended immigration laws to abolish discrimination based on national origin and to open the door for immigration to non-European countries, many legislators nonetheless preferred to have more European immigrants. As a way to facilitate European immigration, they supported the legal device that stressed family reunion. Legislators thought that heavy emphasis on family reunion would definitely favor immigration from European countries, because a great majority of Americans were descendants of past European immigrants.

However, contrary to policymakers' expectations, emphasis on family reunification has instead facilitated immigration in large numbers from Asian, Latin American, and Caribbean countries. Right after the passage of the act, Greece, Italy, Portugal, and some other Southern European countries sent more people than before to the United States, while fewer immigrants came from Northern and Western European countries. By the mid-1970s, however, immigration from Southern European countries, except Portugal, also decreased. While European immigration declined, immigration from Asian countries, Mexico, the Caribbean Basin, and Latin American countries increased. These non-European Third World countries accounted for three-quarters of the 4 million immigrants of the 1970s. Since then, the immigration flow in the United States has consisted predominantly of immigrants from two areas of the world: Mexico and other Latin American countries, and Asian countries.

To explain the dominance of non-European immigrants in the post-1965 era, the following factors need to be considered. First, immediately after the full enforcement of the 1965 Immigration Act, many Asian and Middle Eastern professionals, especially medical professionals, immigrated as beneficiaries of occupational immigration preferences. But Western European professionals were not motivated to come here because they were paid well in their native countries. Soon, these occupational immigrants from Asian and Middle Eastern countries became naturalized citizens and brought their parents and married brothers and sisters. Since there were few Latino and Asian naturalized citizens in 1965, policymakers did not realize the "multiplier effects" of family-based immigration.

Second, the U.S. military and political involvement in Asian, Latin American, and Caribbean countries has brought in huge numbers of refugees and women who are married to U.S. soldiers. After the fall of South Vietnam, more than 1 million South East Asian refugees have come to the United States. Large numbers of refugees have also originated from Cuba, El Salvador, Ecuador, Haiti, and even China, and the presence of the U.S. forces in the Philippines, South Korea, and Vietnam has brought many Asians married to U.S. service men and women. These refugees and U.S. soldiers' spouses have brought many more married brothers and sisters and their own family members, using family-union

preferences that grant eligibility for naturalization after only three years. Many Jews from the former Soviet Union and many people from other Eastern European countries have entered the Unites States as refugees since the early 1990s, but no significant number of refugees has originated from the politically stable Northern and Western European countries.

Third, the 1965 Immigration Act has gone through some revisions, and two revisions have affected the dominance of non-European immigrants as significantly as the original law did. The 1986 Immigration Reform and Control Act provided for an amnesty program for illegal residents. As a result, about 3 million illegal residents became permanent residents at the end of the 1980s and the early 1990s. Two-thirds were Mexicans, and the vast majority originated from non-European countries. They have brought their immediate family members and many of them have invited their brothers and sisters and parents through naturalization.

The Immigration Act of 1990 further revised the 1965 Immigration Act, which has had a strong effect on the increase in the number of Asian professional immigrants as well as in the total number of annual immigrants. It increased the total number of immigrants per year by about 40 percent, to 700,000 through 1994 and thereafter to 675,000. It also increased employment-based visas (heavily professionals) by three times, to 140,000, to meet the shortage of professionals, especially in the information technology (IT) field. Many Asian professionals, especially those in the IT industry, have come as beneficiaries of the occupational immigration since the early 1990s. Many of these professional Asian immigrants have become naturalized citizens and brought their family members. Computer specialists and other professionals from India, China, and the Philippines are strongly motivated to immigrate to the United States because of a big gap in their earnings potential, but professionals from Northern and Western European countries have little motivation because they do well in their own countries.

There were several intended and unintended effects of the act. First, the overall numbers of immigration increased dramatically. In fact, the United States would have experienced a population decrease without the increased immigration. According to U.S. censuses, the major population growth in the last several decades was coming from either immigration itself or children of immigrants. In that sense, without

McCarran-Walter Act of 1952

Retaining a large part of the 1924 Immigration Act, the McCarran-Walter Act regulated the quota system for immigration based on national origin. Under this law, 70 percent of all immigrant slots were allotted to natives of the United Kingdom, Ireland, and Germany, most of which remained unfilled, while only a few quotas were granted to Asian nationalities. Moreover, the Act replaced the 1917 Asiatic Barred Zone with a territorial concept called the Asia-Pacific Triangle. Although this particular statute somewhat liberalized the entry of Asian immigrants, it still included highly racialized provisions against Asians in comparison to Northern and Western Europeans. It limited the number of immigrants who were indigenous to the Asian-Pacific Triangle to no more than 2,000 annually and the number of those who were natives or descendants of each Asian country within the Triangle to a mere 100. The McCarran-Walter Act is considered a significant step toward ending the long-standing racial discrimination in the U.S. immigration policy, but it continued to endorse racist practices in immigration law.

Reflecting the shift toward ending racial discrimination, the McCarran-Walter Act repealed all previous exclusion laws against naturalization of Asians. It made Japanese and Korean immigrants eligible for citizenship, whereas special measures taken in the 1940s made Chinese, Filipino, and Indian immigrants eligible for citizenship. The act also provided for family reunification and occupational-skills preferences within the national quotas for immigration. The Immigration and Nationality Act of 1965 finally dismantled the national-origins quota system, but these provisions of the McCarran-Walter Act remained an integral part of the liberalized immigration law of 1965.

ETSUKO MARUOKA-NG

substantial increases in immigration, the U.S. economy could not have maintained its robustness.

Second, the racial/ethnic composition of the U.S. population has altered drastically due to a large influx of non-European immigration. In 1970, Hispanics (4.5 percent) and Asian Americans (.07 percent) composed only tiny fractions of the population. The 2000 census reports a huge increase in both minority groups, with Hispanics accounting for 13 percent of the U.S. population and Asian Americans 3.5 percent. The proportion of white Americans decreased from 87 percent in 1970 to 70 percent in 2000, and it will continue to decline to the extent that white Americans will turn into a numerical minority. Most experts predict that whites will account for a little more than a half of the U.S. population by the mid-21st century. The vast influx of non-European immigrants since the mid-1960s has changed the United States from a black-white, biracial society to a multiracial society.

Third, a large proportion of the post-1965 immigrants from non-European countries, particularly Asian countries, brought human capital in the form of high education and professional skills, as well as vast amounts of money to the United States. Although these middle- and upper-middle-class immigrants

struggle to adjust to life in the United States, a great majority of their children are likely to receive a college education and will work as professionals. They will be highly visible and active in the mainstream American society. This is seen today, and, in the future, their visibility will only increase. One consequence of this is the high out-marriage among children of immigrants. It will only accelerate the race/ethnic multiplicity of the U.S. population.

By contrast, the 1990 Immigration Act has brought a heavy influx of Latino and Caribbean immigrants from lower socioeconomic groups, which is very different than the post-1965 immigrants. Compared with Asian immigrants, immigrants from Mexico, other Latin countries, and the Caribbean Islands include more political refugees, many low-skilled workers, and many undocumented workers. Researchers have indicated that because many of their families are poor and have settled in minority neighborhoods, the children of Caribbean black and many Latino immigrants generally have poor performance in school, and many have failed to complete high school. Given racial discrimination and a lack of blue-collar jobs owing to deindustrialization, these children have bleak prospects for jobs without a high school diploma. Researchers cautiously predict that they may fill the low layers of the racial hierarchy in the United States in the future.

Fourth, the influx of Third World immigrants in the post-1965 era has contributed to cultural and religious diversity. Because of transnational ties, the children of post-1965 immigrants have advantages over European immigrants from the early 20th century and before in preserving their ethnic cultural traditions and language. The children of Latino immigrants have a huge advantage in retaining their mother tongue because many Latinos speak the same common language. According to one analysis of data from the 1989 Current Population Survey that provides monthly labor force data, the majority of second-generation Latinos aged 24 to 44 are perfectly bilingual. The mass migration of Third World immigrants has also contributed to religious pluralism in the United States. The influx of immigrants from Asia and the Middle East has brought several non-Judeo-Christian religions—Islam, Buddhism, Hinduism, and Sikhism—into the mix of American culture. Also, the mass migration of Catholics from Latin America, the Caribbean Islands, and Asia has contributed to the diversification of American Catholics as well as the substantial increase in the Catholic population.

Shin Kim and Kwang Chung Kim

See also

287g Delegation of Immigration Authority; Anchor Baby; Anti-Immigrant Sentiment; Immigration and Customs Enforcement (ICE); National Origins Act of 1924; Operation Wetback; Unauthorized Immigration; United States Border Patrol

Further Reading:

Bryce-Laporte, Roy S. *Sourcebook on the New Immigration*. New Brunswick, NJ: Transaction Books, 1980.

Hing, Bill Ong. *Making and Remaking Asian America through Immigration Policy, 1850–1990*. Stanford, CA: Stanford University Press, 1993.

Keely, Charles B. *The Immigration Act of 1965: A Study of the Relationship of Social Science Theory to Group Interest and Legislation*. New York: Keely Publishers, 1978.

King, Desmond S. *Making Americans: Immigration, Race, and the Origins of the Diverse Democracy*. Cambridge, MA: Harvard University Press, 2000.

Min, Pyong Gap, ed. *Mass Migration to the United States: Classical and Contemporary Periods*. Walnut Creek, CA: AltaMira, 2002.

Reimers, David M. *Still the Golden Door: The Third World Comes to America*. New York: Columbia University Press, 1986.

Immigration and Customs Enforcement (ICE)

Immigration and Customs Enforcement (ICE), a component of the Department of Homeland Security (DHS), is primarily responsible for the criminal and civil enforcement of federal laws that govern border control, trade, customs, and immigration. In 2003, ICE was created and incorporated under the DHS in order to integrate the investigative and enforcement aspects of the U.S. Customs Service and the Immigration and Naturalization Service. Today, ICE has more than 20,000 employees and an annual operating budget of more than $5.7 billion dollars.

ICE is the principal investigative division of the DHS, focusing mainly on interior enforcement (as opposed to border enforcement) of immigration law. Its two major components are Enforcement and Removal Operations (ERO) and Homeland Security Investigations (HSI). ERO is tasked with the implementation and enforcement of federal immigration laws, including the identification and apprehension of unauthorized immigrants. To accomplish this, ERO functions through a number of programs—including the Criminal Alien Program, 287(g) delegation of immigration authority, and Secure Communities—which promote information sharing and cooperation between federal immigration agents and state and local law enforcement agencies. ERO also manages the nation's immigration detention facilities

---

Department of Homeland Security (DHS)

The Department of Homeland Security was created in 2002 in order to increase communication and cooperation across agencies that dealt with matters of national security, border security, immigration enforcement, and citizenship services. Prior to the creation of the DHS, these organizations operated independently and often did not communicate with one another. Following the 2001 attacks on the World Trade Center, reports documented the need for a single, comprehensive organization to coordinate and respond to matters of national security. The creation of the Department of Homeland Security, which was designed to integrate 22 different federal departments, was created to address these needs.

and oversees the detention and removal (deportation) of unauthorized immigrants.

Through the ERO, ICE has overseen a record number of removals in recent years. Since 2008, ICE has removed approximately 400,000 unauthorized immigrants per year, a sharp increase in the annual total removal of unauthorized immigrants. However, removals are heavily skewed by ethnicity and national origin. Data from the Office of Immigration Statistics of the Department of Homeland Security indicate that Mexican nationals account for 75 percent of all removals in 2011, although they compose only 59 percent of all unauthorized immigrants in the United States.

HSI, the second major component of ICE, investigates criminal activities and organizations related to the unlawful movement of people or goods, including suspected terrorist and other criminal organizations that pose a threat to public safety and national security. In particular, HSI investigates those suspected of terrorist activities, war crimes and human rights violations, weapons and drug smuggling, human trafficking, and cybercrime.

In 2010 and again in 2011, ICE director John Morton issued memos identifying agency priorities for the apprehension, detention, prosecution, and removal of noncitizens. Given that ICE has sufficient funds to deport only 400,000 noncitizens per year—approximately less than 4 percent of the total unauthorized population—the guidelines articulated in these memos focused on utilizing ICE's limited resources to prioritize the apprehension and removal of the most serious immigration offenders.

The articulation of ICE priorities for immigration enforcement and prosecutorial discretion has caused a great deal of controversy. Advocacy organizations, such as the American Immigration Lawyers Association and the Immigration Policy Center, argue that ICE has been slow to implement these guidelines and that ICE agents lack sufficient oversight and public accountability to ensure compliance with these priorities. In particular, advocacy groups claim that ICE has not complied with its stated priorities, pointing to empirical and anecdotal evidence demonstrating that ICE continues to deport unauthorized immigrants who have not been convicted of a crime or those who present little risk to public safety. Moreover, such groups argue that the reprioritization of immigration enforcement and removal actions should not substitute for comprehensive immigration reform.

Morton Memo on Prosecutorial Discretion

In 2010, ICE director John Morton issued an agency-wide memo prioritizing the apprehension and removal of unauthorized immigrants who present a risk to national security and public safety, including those suspected of terrorism, gang activity, and those who have been convicted of a crime. Criminal offenders are further prioritized based on the severity of the crime committed, with top priority given to those who are convicted of an aggravated felony and low priority given to those convicted of misdemeanors. This memo also prioritizes those who present a risk to border security (such as recent entrants) and those who obstruct immigration controls (such as those who reenter the United States after a prior removal or who fail to depart after ordered removed). In 2011, Morton issued a second memo reaffirming these priorities and identifying guidelines for the application of prosecutorial discretion in immigration-related matters. Prosecutorial discretion refers to ICE's authority to selectively enforce immigration laws in accordance with the priorities outlined in the first Morton memo. The second memo advocates the use of discretion in cases involving minors or the elderly, those present in the United States since childhood, victims of crime, and those with mental or physical disabilities or serious health conditions.

Advocates of stricter enforcement of immigration law, including the Federation for American Immigration Reform (FAIR), argue that the reprioritization of federal enforcement priorities constitutes an "amnesty" for unauthorized immigrants. In 2012, Kris Kobach, the secretary of state of Kansas and an attorney with the Immigration Reform Law Institute (IRLI)—the legal arm of FAIR—filed suit against the Department of Homeland Security on behalf of several ICE agents who claim that the new enforcement priorities require them to violate federal immigration laws.

MEGHAN CONLEY

See also

287g Delegation of Immigration Authority; Anchor Baby; Anti-Immigrant Sentiment; Immigration Act of 1965; National

Origins Act of 1924; Operation Wetback; Secure Communities; Unauthorized Immigration; United States Border Patrol

Further Reading:

Immigration and Customs Enforcement. *Exercising Prosecutorial Discretion Consistent with the Civil Immigration Enforcement Priorities of the Agency for the Apprehension, Detention, and Removal of Aliens.* http://www.ice.gov/doclib/secure-communities/pdf/prosecutorial-discretion-memo.pdf.

Immigration and Customs Enforcement. *Memorandum on Civil Immigration Enforcement: Priorities for the Apprehension, Detention, and Removal of Aliens.* http://www.ice.gov/doclib/detention-reform/pdf/civil_enforcement_priorities.pdf.

Simanski, Jonathan, and Lesley M. Sapp. "Immigration Enforcement Actions: 2011." Washington, DC: Department of Homeland Security, 2012.

Implicit Bias

There are two types of biases: implicit and explicit. Explicit biases are thoughts, feelings, and beliefs that people can consciously identify with relative ease; in lay conversation, they are often referred to simply as "biases." Conversely, implicit biases are thoughts, feelings, and beliefs a person holds subconsciously, and are innocuous. Implicit and explicit biases are usually similar, but when they differ, research suggests that implicit bias has measurable effects on a person's behavior.

In U.S. culture, implicit bias is most often discussed in terms of prison sentencing, career promotion, and interpersonal interactions. U.S. culture has become more sensitive to overt racism, but since implicit biases are subconscious and socialized by the dominant culture, they are difficult to notice, challenge, and revise. Implicit association tests and microaggression research are two leading areas of implicit bias research.

The implicit association test is a computer-assisted test that measures human reaction to stereotypical stimulus. During the test, the individual is shown pictures or words (e.g., good, bad, smart, ignorant, fast, slow, etc.) and are instructed to tap one of two keys; the keys are associated with two opposite groups (e.g., blacks or whites, males or females, rich or poor, etc.) The software then calculates the responses, response time, and determines the extent to which the participant associates the stimuli with each response category. Stimuli are administered rapidly, so that the participant has little response time; this is done, in theory, to measure subconscious associations.

Proponents of the implicit association test believe that results indicate the extent to which the participant is subconsciously biased in favor of or against certain groups. According to test designers, pairing racially charged stimuli (e.g., a picture of a black male) with negative words (e.g., murder, violent, crime) indicates an implicit bias against members of that racial group. Conversely, pairing racially charged stimuli with positive words (e.g., kind, happy, pleasant) indicates an implicit bias in favor of that racial group.

Opponents of the implicit association test challenge the validity of the test. According to this criticism, test responses (which are recorded in milliseconds) are poor measures of subconscious bias. Microaggressions are another area of subconscious bias research.

Microaggressions are subtle insults or acts that can be interpreted as racist remarks, regardless of the intent of the actor. Often, microaggressions tap into racial stereotypes and operate on the subconscious level. Microaggression literature is centered in counseling psychology literature, although social psychologists and race scholars have begun to conduct microaggression research. Microaggression research is most often credited to the work of D .W. Sue, although its roots go back to research in the 1970s.

According to Sue, there are three types of racial aggressions. The first are microassaults: overt, consciously employed insults or actions against a racial minority that are intended to offend the minority (e.g., calling a black person a "n*gger"). Microassaults are commonly recognized as racist behavior. The second are microinsults: backhanded compliments or statements that may have positive intentions, but negative implications drawn from common stereotypes (e.g., a Japanese woman may be told, "You drive really well, for an Asian," drawing upon the stereotype that Asians are poor drivers). The third are microinvalidations: questions and statements that question the legitimacy of a person in a specific place, occupation, or role (e.g., a college counselor in New York asks a student from Hawaii, "Why would you leave Hawaii for here?" This well-intentioned question invalidates the Hawaiian student's right to belong in New York, at a university, and/or on the continental U.S.).

Although microaggressors may be well intentioned, the implicit biases within their statements may have latent meanings that are offensive, hurtful, and racist. The negative effect of microaggressions is that minorities spend more time on self care, are at greater risk of stereotype threat, and feel persecuted but unable to express their slight due to the good nature of the assault. More maliciously, microinsults and microinvalidations allow closet racists to appear progressive, while communicating racist messages.

Both implicit association tests and microaggressions draw on implicit biases. Implicit biases are difficult to accurately measure, but hold great potential for challenging subtle acts of racism, whether consciously or unconsciously motivated. Implicit Association Tests and microaggression research are promising tools for examining implicit biases, and the extent to which implicit biases harms U.S. culture remains an area of future research.

LEIGHTON VILA

See also

Clark Doll Study; Color-Blind Racism; Institutional Discrimination; Stereotype

Further Reading:

Greenwald, Anthony G., Debbie E. McGhee, and Jordan L. K. Schwartz. "Measuring Individual Differences in Implicit Cognition: The Implicit Association Test." *Journal of Personality and Social Psychology* 74 (1998): 1464–80.

The Microaggressions Project. *Microaggressions: Power, Privlidge, and Everyday Life.* http://microaggressions.tumblr.com/.

Sue, Derald Wing, Christina M. Capodilupo, Gina C. Torino, Jennifer M. Bucceri, Aisha M. B. Holder, Kevin L. Nadal, and Marta Esquilin. "Racial Microaggressions in Everyday Life: Implications for Clinical Practice." *American Psychologist* 62 (2007): 271–86.

Indian Claims Commission

Established in 1946 as an independent, quasi-judicial branch of the U.S. Congress, the Indian Claims Commission operated for 32 years, adjudicating the long-standing land and accounting claims of Native Americans against the federal government. By the end of 1951, the deadline year for filing, some 600 claims had been brought before the commission by almost all of the 176 known tribes or bands in the United States. Approximately $800 million was awarded to these tribes through the Indian Claims Commission. When divided by the number of acres of land that those particular cases involved, the sum represented approximately 50 cents an acre paid to the Indian people.

The history of American Indian land claims begins in the 18th and 19th centuries. During this treaty-making period, separate Indian tribes were considered foreign nations, and the U.S. government negotiated 370 treaties with them, giving the federal government 2 billion acres of land and leaving Native Americans with 140 million acres by 1868. The tribes were placed on some 200 reservations, most of them west of the Mississippi River. The General Allotment Act of 1887 divided these reservations into individually owned parcels and removed another 90 million "surplus" acres from Indian ownership.

Barred by the U.S. Constitution from bringing suit against the United States, Native Americans sought redress in the Court of Claims, which was created in 1855. In 1863, however, they were barred from that court as well. A reversal of that decision allowed claims to proceed after 1881, and these claims increased after 1924, when Native Americans were granted U.S. citizenship. The Indian Claims Commission was created to bring closure to these and other claims. While Congress was partly motivated to provide a fair settlement to the tribes, the act creating the commission was also part of a policy of "termination," whereby the government hoped to eliminate the Indian as an unassimilated minority within the United States.

The majority of claims brought before the commission were for loss of land, and the majority of the remainder were for mismanagement of tribal funds by the U.S. government, which claimed to be the legal guardian of the Indian tribes. The land claims required the tribes to prove exclusive tribal use and occupation of the land from time immemorial, and that definition did not account for the overlapping lands of migratory tribes. After title was proven, the value-liability was calculated, and the decision was made to disallow any interest accrued on the 19th-century value of the land. Finally, any offsets paid by the government to the tribes were factored in. Gratuitous offsets, however, which had reduced previous awards to the Indians by about 60 percent, were not allowed. The consolidated California claims case was concluded in 1968 when President Lyndon B. Johnson signed a

Cherokee Nation v. Georgia (1831)

In December 1828, the Georgia legislature passed a law stipulating that the land in Georgia occupied by the Cherokee be divided into parcels and opened up for white settlement. The next year, it passed law declaring that all laws made by the Cherokee nation were null and void and that no Cherokee could testify in court against a white man. With the two new laws, the state of Georgia tried to evict the Cherokees out of the state. But the Cherokees responded with a lawsuit, claiming that the two Georgia laws were contrary to the U.S. Constitution, congressional legislation, and a treaty between the federal government and the Indians (the Treaty of Hopewell, 1785). The U.S. Supreme Court rejected the claim, arguing that the court did not have the legal jurisdiction to hear the Cherokees' complaint because Indians were "domestic dependent nations" rather than foreign nations and that only the latter had the right to use the Supreme Court in a dispute with a state.

In 1831, Samuel Worcester and other white missionaries were arrested for living with Cherokees in violation of a law designed to prevent whites from encouraging the Cherokees to oppose the new state laws. Challenging his conviction, Worcester took the case to the court, claiming that this and other anti-Indian laws passed by Georgia were invalid. The case went to the Supreme Court, which this time gave a decision favorable to Worcester and the Cherokees. The chief justice, John Marshall, declared that the Cherokee nation was "a distinct community, occupying its own territory, with boundaries accurately described, in which the law of Georgia can have no force" (Jaret 1995: 543). He further declared that only the federal government had control over relations between Native Americans and U.S. citizens.

Pyong Gap Min

bill to provide compensation in the amount of $29 million, approximately 47 cents per acre of land claimed.

After numerous extensions of its tenure, the commission finally expired in 1978 and its remaining 68 cases were transferred to the Court of Claims. In all, the tribes won awards in about 58 percent of the cases and paid approximately $100 million in legal fees. Rather than "terminating" the Indian, the commission's work seems to have had the opposite effect. The Indian claims helped redefine the identity of many tribes and reawakened the cultural pride of all. The essential injustice of the procedure from a Native American point of view, however, was that it only provided payment in money and not in land. Indians continue to seek the return of their tribal lands, but normally if they received compensation for their claims, they cannot get their land back.

ABC-CLIO

See also

Bureau of Indian Affairs; Dawes Act (1887); Indian Removal and the Creation of Indian Territory; Indian Reservations; Native Americans, Forced Relocation of. Documents: Andrew Jackson: Indian Removal Message to Congress (1829); Indian Removal Act (1830); *Cherokee Nation v. Georgia* (1831); The Dawes Act (1887)

Further Reading:

Cothran, Helen, ed. *The Conquest of the New World*. San Diego: Greenhaven Press, 2002.

Forman, Grant. *Indian Removal: The Emigration of the Five Civilized Tribes of Indians*. Norman: University of Oklahoma Press, 1953.

Sokolow, Gary. *Native Americans and the Law: A Dictionary*. Santa Barbara, CA: ABC-CLIO, 2000.

Indian Removal and the Creation of Indian Territory

By the 1820s, plans to relocate tribes to areas far from their homelands were already well under way. The idea of exchanging tribal lands in the East for tracts in the Midwest was not a new idea. As far back as 1804 the Louisiana Purchase had made the scheme plausible, and President Thomas Jefferson began to see removal and assimilation as viable solutions for American Indian survival and American expansion. Jefferson's overall objective was to encourage the tribes to migrate voluntarily to the Midwest, where they could reside in lands protected from white intrusion. Other politicians such as James Madison saw the southern tribes as obstacles to securing the nation's borders and argued in favor of a western land exchange. In 1825, Madison presented a plan for land exchange to Congress, and in 1827, President John Quincy Adams again raised the issue.

In 1829, removal became a key political objective of President Andrew Jackson's administration. Millions of acres of rich agricultural lands in the South were owned by a handful of tribes. The Cherokee, Chickasaw, Creek, Choctaw, and Seminole all held title to lands in Georgia, North Carolina, Tennessee, Alabama, Mississippi, and Florida. In the early 1800s, however, controversy arose between Cherokee and white settlers in Georgia. Despite the tribe's assertion of sovereignty and its written constitution, the state claimed jurisdiction over the tribe and declared its laws null and void. When the discovery of gold in Cherokee lands prompted a land rush, the tribe turned to the U.S. Supreme Court for help. Two pivotal cases resulted.

In *Cherokee Nation v. Georgia* (1831), Chief Justice John Marshall described Indian tribes as "domestic dependent nations" that could not appeal to the Supreme Court. Marshall's opinion greatly encouraged removal efforts by the state. In *Worcester v. Georgia* (1832), Marshall wrote that the United States recognized through its treaty relations with the Cherokee that American Indian nations are "distinct, independent political communities retaining original natural rights." The Cherokee Nation, he argued, was a separate sovereign nation with legal title to its lands. Jackson, angered by Marshall's decision exclaimed, "Let him enforce it."

Through the auspices of the Indian Removal Act (1830), Congress authorized the creation of a new western domain set aside for relocated Indian tribes. In 1834, Congress set the final policy of the Indian Intercourse Acts in place. The policy set aside lands that included the area of present-day Oklahoma north and east of the Red River, Kansas, and Nebraska, to be known as Indian Territory.

Although Chief Pushmataha called for the Choctaw people to resist removal at all costs, in 1831, the Choctaw became the first tribe to move west. Nearly 4,000 died during Choctaw removal. In 1832, the Creek signed a treaty opening a portion of their Alabama lands to white settlement but were guaranteed protected ownership of the remaining portion. By 1836 they were destitute, and the secretary of war

ordered Creek removal. One year later, some 15,000 Creek were pushed west despite the fact that they had never signed a removal treaty. Seeing removal as inevitable, the Chickasaw signed a treaty in 1832 in which the federal government promised suitable western lands and protection. Federal promises went unfulfilled, however, and in 1837, the Chickasaw were compelled to pay the Choctaw for the right to reside on lands in their western allotment.

In 1833, a small faction of Cherokee entered into an unauthorized treaty agreement that effectively signed away the tribe's ownership of its southern lands. As a result, Chief John Ross led the Cherokee in a well-publicized campaign to garner public support to resist removal. Ross and his followers refused to leave, so in 1838, thousands of Georgia militiamen descended on them, throwing them out of their homes at gunpoint and forcing them into stockades. More than 4,000 died on their subsequent march to Indian Territory.

A Seminole faction also signed an unauthorized removal treaty in 1833, but the majority of the tribe refused to leave, and many took up arms. Thousands died in the resulting Second Seminole War (1835–1842) and Third Seminole War (1855–1858), which cost the U.S. government nearly $60 million. The Second Seminole War ended in 1842 with an agreement that a few hundred members of the tribe could remain in Florida. Their descendants remain in Florida today.

More than 3,000 Seminole were removed to Indian Territory. Those who remained continued under the leadership of Olactomico (Billy Bowlegs). In the mid-1850s, encroaching whites and their militiamen constantly harassed and attacked the remaining Seminole. The tribe retaliated, and its guerrilla-style resistance came to be known as the Third Seminole War. The war finally ended with the surrender of Bowlegs and 40 warriors on May 7, 1858.

The Indian Removal Act also led to the eviction of the Potawatomi from their Illinois and Indiana homelands. Tribal leaders signed the Treaty of Yellow River in 1836 exchanging their lands for lands in Kansas, but when the tribe missed the set deadline for westward migration, Gen. John Tipton pushed them out. He first seized their most influential leaders and rounded up the people, marching them at gunpoint some 700 miles to Kansas in 1838, a journey of two months. The tribe had been promised provisions for the trip, but food provided by federal contractors was rancid, shelter was inadequate, and water was in short supply. At journey's end, approximately 40 children had died of typhoid fever, and 110 persons had simply disappeared. In 1867, the tribe signed a new treaty selling its Kansas lands to buy lands in Indian Territory. At that time, the tribe's members accepted U.S. citizenship and became known as the Citizen Potawatomi.

PATTI JO KING

See also

Native Americans, Conquest of; Native Americans, Forced Relocation of; Trail of Broken Treaties (1972). Documents: *Cherokee Nation v. Georgia* (1831)

Further Reading:

Deloria, Vine, Jr. *Behind the Trail of Broken Treaties: An Indian Declaration of Independence*, 3rd ed. Austin: University of Texas Press, 1990.

Foreman, Grant. *Indian Removal: Emigration of the Five Civilized Tribes of Indians*. Norman: University of Oklahoma Press, 1989.

Hall, Ted Byron. *Oklahoma, Indian Territory*. Fort Worth, TX: American Reference Publishers, 1971.

Remini, Robert V. *The Legacy of Andrew Jackson: Essays on Democracy, Indian Removal and Slavery*. Baton Rouge: Louisiana State University Press, 1990.

Sturgis, Amy H. *The Trail of Tears and Indian Removal*. Westport, CT: Greenwood Press, 2007.

Indian Reorganization Act (1934)

The more than 70 years since the passage of the Indian Reorganization Act (IRA) in 1934 have provided many opportunities for examination of the conventional wisdom that it was a signal example of federal administrative reforms favorable to American Indians, reversing decades of land alienation and cultural abuses caused by the 1887 Indian Allotment Act. John Collier was Indian commissioner from 1933 to 1945 during President Franklin D. Roosevelt's Democratic administration, and the IRA was Collier's brainchild and the centerpiece of the reforms. Collier, a radical social worker who became an anthropologist, was both a prolific writer and a skilled propagandist. His books, *Indians of the Americas* (1947) and *From Every Zenith* (1962), have been widely read and put the best possible interpretation on the Indian New Deal. Until recently, conventional wisdom has followed Collier's interpretation. The question remains, however, was the IRA truly an Indian agenda, and was it fairly and intelligently applied? In short, how should one evaluate the IRA legacy?

A 20-year appraisal of the IRA took place in conjunction with the annual meeting of the American Anthropological Association in 1953. It included John Collier himself, along with several prominent Indians and anthropologists. When the 50th anniversary of the IRA occurred in 1984, scholars, Indian leaders, and political activists began another reevaluation. The Institute of the American West, for example, held a conference at Sun Valley entitled "Fifty Years Under the Indian Reorganization Act—Indian Self-Rule," in which many notables participated in a series of panels. Both appraisals during these past reevaluations were uniformly positive.

In the past few decades, however, scholars have taken yet another look at the IRA and Collier's administrative reforms. Kenneth Philp's biographical study, *John Collier's Crusade for Indian Reform, 1920–1954*, came out in 1977, and Lawrence Kelly's *The Assault on Assimilation: John Collier and the Origins of Indian Policy Reform* appeared in 1983. Philp generally follows Collier's favorable view of the IRA. Kelly, on the other hand, emphasizes the failure of the IRA legislation as passed by Congress to attain Collier's idealistic reform goals. He also faults the Collier administration for its failure to extend the act's limited benefits to the majority of Indians. Two other scholars who have written major reevaluations are Graham Taylor and Lawrence Hauptman. They, too, are critical of the Indian New Deal as not being all that it was purported to be. We should also mention Deloria and Lytle who present an insightful analysis of the IRA in *The Nations Within: The Past and Future of American Indian Sovereignty*.

In 1977 the American Indian Policy Review Commission reported its findings to Congress on the economic, social, and political conditions of the Indian tribes and nations. Its findings, as Graham Taylor observes, seem to indicate that the twin goals of the IRA (Indian economic development and the restoration of Indian self-determination through a council system of government) have been notable failures of existing Indian policy. As a result, as the Meriam Report found in 1928, American Indians continued to rank at the bottom of virtually every social indicator 50 years later.

New criticism of the IRA incorporates the views of traditional Indians, many of whom opposed the IRA and the

Secretary of the Interior Harold Ickes presents the Confederated Tribes of the Flathead Indian Reservation with the first constitution and bylaws to be issued under the Indian Reorganization Act (1934). The act advocated tribal organization on reservations as a formula for the improvement of Indian life. (Library of Congress)

Indian New Deal from its very beginnings. The traditional Indian movement has historically struggled to achieve three goals: (1) a viable land base for economic self-sufficiency and nationhood; (2) political self-determination through sovereignty under the treaties; and (3) cultural rights—language, religion, and heritage. John Collier's two aims under the Indian New Deal, on the other hand, were (1) to preserve the Indian people as a "race" and as distinct cultures—which Collier termed "grouphood"; and (2) to preserve and develop resources, including land. The means to achieve these goals for Collier were "tribal" organization and economic incorporation under the IRA. For traditional Indians, however, the means to their goals is for the United States to return to the treaty relationship (treaty federalism), and to recognize the Indian peoples as sovereign with the right to self-determination.

The first two decades of the 20th century were particularly onerous for American Indians within the borders of the United States. Not only had the 1887 Indian Allotment Act resulted in reservation land loss and impoverishment, but the government's policy of Americanization and cultural assimilation ushered in a virulent period of ethnocide. One of the worst manifestations was the federal crackdown on Indian religious ceremonies. The proassimilationist Indian Rights Association led an attack on "indecent" ceremonies among the Indian Pueblos of the Southwest, and the Board of Indian Commissioners deplored the fact that tribal rituals were still being conducted on many Indian reservations. In its 1918 report, the Board described the Indian dances as evil and a reversion to paganism. On April 26, 1921, Indian Commissioner Charles H. Burke issued Circular 1665 that outlawed the Plains Sun Dance and other traditional religious ceremonies, to be punished by fines or imprisonment. The Native American (peyote) Church also came under attack. This period of Indian policy also saw many other instances of religious abuse.

About the same time that the assault on Indian culture and religion was occurring, Secretary of the Interior Albert B. Fall led an attack on Indian rights through his sponsorship of the Bursum and Indian Omnibus bills in Congress. The former bill would have confirmed white encroachment on 60,000 acres of Pueblo Indian land, while the Omnibus bill sought to individualize remaining tribal assets, including timber, coal, and other minerals, thereby ending federal trusteeship responsibility. Fall also attempted to create a national park out of part of the Mescalero Apache Reservation that bordered his Three Rivers ranch that would enhance the value of his own property. When oil was discovered on the Navajo Reservation in 1922, he issued a ruling that opened all executive order reservations to exploration by oil companies under the 1920 General Leasing Act. These were the federal Indian policies that struck at Indian sovereignty, especially in New Mexico, and which led to the protest from the Pueblos and the entry of John Collier as an advocate for Indian rights.

Instead of destroying Native societies and cultures through forced assimilation, John Collier believed in a policy of cultural pluralism and Indian administration through indirect rather than direct U.S. rule. The controversy over the Pueblo land grants (part of a larger struggle against landlessness stemming from allotment) and religious dancing led to the formation of the American Indian Defense Association in May 1923. Facing criticism from Collier and the Pueblo Indians, New Mexico Democrats, and the 2 million–member General Federation of Women's Clubs, Fall was forced to resign from the Harding administration. He was replaced in 1923 by Dr. Hubert Work, who was described as the last of the frontier commissioners. Secretary Work was under the influence of Christian missionaries and opposed Indian dancing, but he had to back off from former Commissioner Burke's order prohibiting the theocratic Taos and Zuni Pueblos from withdrawing selected Indian youth from Bureau of Indian Affairs schools for traditional religious training.

Despite Collier's advocacy work, the bureau continued its policy of suppressing Indian religious ceremonies. The issue came to a head during the summer of 1925 at Taos when the Pueblo's officials disciplined two members of the Native American Church for invading traditional religious ceremonies. The Indian Bureau thereupon arrested virtually the entire governing body of Taos Pueblo. Collier's Defense Association provided bail and lawyers, and the All-Pueblo Council swung into action, denouncing the bureau's effort to destroy Indian self-government. Collier took Pueblo representatives on a tour of Utah and California in the cause of Indian religious freedom and to raise money for its defense. Secretary Work denounced these activities, saying that "propagandists are touring part of the country with a company of dancing and singing Pueblos in full Indian regalia in order to awaken people to the 'crime' in New Mexico. There is no crime in New Mexico." Congressman Scott Leavitt of Montana sponsored a bill drafted by the bureau that would give Indian superintendents the power to throw any reservation Indian in jail for six months and levy a $100 fine without trial. Because of the work by the Defense Committee the Leavitt bill did not get out of committee.

In 1928, on the eve of the Indian New Deal, a government commission issued a landmark report to Congress, "The Problem of Indian Administration." Collier declared that the Meriam Report, as it was popularly called, had "blasted apart the walls of the dungeon called the Indian affairs system" and constituted a major indictment of the Indian Bureau. The report made it clear that allotment policy had not produced assimilation and was, in fact, an unmitigated disaster judging by any social or economic indicator one could apply. The Indian population had actually decreased since the passage of the 1887 Indian Allotment Act. There were more landless Indians than before; Indian trust lands had decreased in value; family income was as low as $48 per year on some reservations; the annual death rate had increased; and the Indian land base had shrunk from 137 million acres to a mere 47 million. Collier saw horrible material and spiritual decline as a result of the allotment policy.

As the Depression deepened, the bureau began a retreat from instituting reform, and Congress was less inclined to vote for Indian appropriations. In March 1932, representatives of 49 Indian tribes petitioned the U.S. Senate, alleging that the Hoover administration had reneged on its promises for Indian reform as recommended in the Meriam Report. After his election in 1932, President Roosevelt received a document signed by more than 600 educators, social workers, and other concerned citizens, drawing attention to the extreme situation of the American Indians. The signers asserted that "your administration represents almost a last chance for the Indians."

Harold Ickes, who became FDR's new secretary of the interior, was a Chicago Progressive reformer and former director of the American Indian Defense Association. Collier became commissioner of Indian affairs on April 2, 1933. A cultural pluralist, Collier sought to reverse the policy of forced assimilation and its detrimental economic exploitation and land dispossession. He still believed in eventual assimilation, but at a slower and more equitable pace and without the loss of community solidarity and Indian values. He proposed that government follow a colonial policy known as indirect administration.

Upon taking office, Collier immediately instituted recovery measures legislated under the "New Deal" FDR administration. He successfully established a separate Civilian Conservation Corps (CCC) for Indians known as Emergency Conservation Work (ECW). The conservation of reservation lands and the training of Indians to utilize their own lands and resources distinguished it from the regular CCC, a jobs program for the unemployed. Before its demise in 1943, the ECW had employed 85,349 enrollees from 71 different reservations with a total of $72 million in appropriations. This Indian CCC was perhaps the most successful of Collier's Indian New Deal reforms, and it was very popular at the grassroots level on the reservations.

Collier initiated many other reform measures as well, all of which became known as the "Indian New Deal." The assimilationist-minded Board of Indian Commissioners was abolished in May 1933, and by the following August Collier persuaded Ickes to declare a temporary cessation of further Indian land allotments, sale of allotted lands, the issuance of certificates of competency, and similar measures. Of equal importance was the cancellation of debts owed by Indian tribes to the federal government. Because of the debt cancellation and the appropriation of more than $100 million in relief programs, American Indians were able to survive the worst years of the Great Depression and even enjoy a higher standard of living than they had a decade earlier. In some respects, the impact of the Depression in the wider society was already reversing the process of assimilation by driving Indians back to their reservation homelands for economic survival.

Other Indian New Deal reforms included the creation of an Indian Arts and Crafts Board, a reservation court system, and a directive ordering the Indian Service to observe "the fullest constitutional liberty in all matters affecting religion, conscience and culture." The ban against religious dances was lifted, and government repression of Indian languages in bureau schools was ended. The major accomplishment of the Collier administration, however, was the passage of the Indian Reorganization Act.

In a meeting held at the Cosmos Club in Washington, D.C., in January 1934, Collier laid out his ideas for a basic piece of legislation to correct the evils of 47 years of allotment policy. To this meeting he had invited representatives from organizations that formed the nucleus of Indian reform: the American Indian Defense Association, Indian Rights Association, National Association on Indian Affairs, American Civil Liberties Union, National Council on American Indians, and the General Federation of Women's Clubs. Later the same month, he tested the waters for his ideas in a circular to reservation superintendents, tribal council members, and individual Indians in a document entitled "Indian Self-Government." Despite the mostly negative replies, Collier nevertheless advanced plans to draft a bill for major Indian reorganization. The primary thrust of Collier's draft legislation was self-government, a policy that ran directly counter to the previous policy of assimilation. The completed Collier Bill contained 48 pages and 4 major titles, each divided into a number of substantive sections. The final Indian Reorganization Act (IRA) as passed by Congress, on the other hand, omitted important parts of two of Collier's original titles and one title altogether, the one dealing with a proposed Court of Indian Offenses. Although the three remaining titles—self-government, education, and Indian lands—were all substantively reduced in content, they at least made it into the new law.

The bill was signed into law June 18, 1934, as the Wheeler-Howard, or Indian Reorganization Act, but it bore little resemblance to Collier's original bill. Opposition to the Collier Bill came from Indians who favored assimilation, western Congressmen (many of whom were reflecting special interests in their home states containing Indian reservations), missionaries, and bureau personnel. The powerful Indian Rights Association still favored the melting-pot concept, but hoped that the legislation with its provision for educational training would promote assimilation. Only the section of Title II in the original bill that dealt with education came through relatively unscathed. The act in its final form eliminated four key features of Collier's draft bill: (1) the tribes were denied the right to take over heirship lands; (2) the section setting up a reservation court system was eliminated; (3) social units smaller than the tribe, e.g., local or community level groups, were not empowered, although Alaska Native villages were later included when the IRA was amended in 1936; and (4) the section on promoting Indian culture and traditions was deleted.

Title I of the IRA gave Indian tribes the right to organize for the purposes of local self-government and economic enterprise. Collier's bill would have conferred limited self-government on reservation Indian groups or communities, treating them as municipalities, but the final version of the IRA limited this provision to tribal units only. The first step in the process was for a tribal committee to draft a constitution. Then an election would be held to ratify the constitution, with a majority vote of reservation members necessary for adoption. Approval by the secretary of the interior was also required. Congress modified this section of Collier's bill by cutting the annual appropriation for the organization of tribal governments from $500,000 to $250,000.

Deloria and Lytle in *The Nations Within* point out that the self-government provision of the IRA helped to define important powers of Native American political entities. With the support of Collier, after the IRA was passed, a ruling by the solicitor of the Interior Department found that the powers conferred under the act's self-government provision were inherent in the tribes' and nations' status as domestic, dependent nations. These powers are a tribe's right to adopt its own form of self-government, to determine tribal membership, to regulate the disposition of tribal property, and to proscribe the rules of inheritance on real and personal property.

An emphasis on economic development was an important feature of the IRA. Upon receiving a petition from at least one-third of the adult reservation Indians, the Secretary of the Interior could issue a charter of incorporation. When ratified by a majority of reservation members, a Native tribe or nation could then engage in business enterprises. The IRA also established a revolving loan fund of $10 million for economic development. This was twice the amount that Collier had suggested in his original bill.

The education provisions of Title II were not controversial, and Congress raised the appropriation from Collier's $50,000 to $250,000. Congress, on the other hand, limited the amount to loans rather than outright grants and training was primarily for vocational education. An important clause in Title I waved a civil service requirement for employment in the Indian Service, thus establishing the principle of "Indian preference" in hiring. Omitted from Title II was Collier's draft section declaring that it would be the policy of Congress "to promote the study of Indian civilization, including Indian arts, crafts, skills and traditions," This entire section was struck out. Congress, it would seem, was not interested in promoting the Indian heritage.

A key part of Title III was the section abolishing the 1887 Indian Allotment (Dawes) Act. Title III also declared it the policy of the United States to undertake a constructive program of Indian land use and economic development, with a pledge to consolidate Indian land holdings into suitable economic units. $2 million was set aside annually for land acquisition.

The new law also extended indefinitely the trust period of allotted lands as a protection against loss of Indian lands to non-Natives. Under the previous system, allotted lands were held in trust for 25 years, after which they were vested into the ownership of the Indian allottee. At the same time, however, they became subject to state taxes. As a result, the Indian landowner almost always lost his land because of nonpayment of taxes, or else was forced to sell to a non-Indian.

The lands provisions of the Collier Bill were so controversial in the Congressional debate that its original 21 sections were reduced to 8, thus negating many of Collier's plans for significant land reform. The Collier Bill had addressed the land alienation and heirship problems with language ensuring that previously allotted lands would be returned to tribal ownership. In the Collier draft, the secretary of the interior was empowered to compel the sale or transfer of trust allotments to tribal governments, and trust allotments not immediately returned would revert to tribal status upon the death of the landowner. Congress modified this section by making it voluntary rather than compulsory. In addition, the land title would now pass to the heirs and not to the tribe upon the death of the Indian landowner. This dealt a deadly blow to Collier's efforts to consolidate fragmented Indian parcels and return them to the tribal estate.

Under the IRA as passed by Congress, the Bureau of Indian Affairs became a real-estate entity for thousands of Indian heirs possessing an interest in ever-smaller pieces of inherited land from an original allotment. Today, the number of heirs to an original 160-acre allotment distributed under the 1887 Allotment Act in many cases exceeds 100. Tens of millions of dollars are lost every year to Indian tribes through the Bureau's practice of renting or leasing these uneconomical interests in allotted or heirship lands to non-Indian farmers and ranchers at low rates, who then combine the parcels into viable economic units. The heirship problem has continued to become more unmanageable with each passing generation. Because of allotment, which the IRA stopped but did not reverse, 25 reservations have greater non-Indian than Indian populations and 38 have lost at least half of their original reservation land base to non-Indians.

Title IV of the Collier Bill that would have created a Court of Indian Affairs was eliminated entirely from the Indian Reorganization Act. It also would have removed IRA tribes from state jurisdiction in Indian cases, heirship cases, and appeals from tribal courts. Title IV also stipulated that law and order must be consonant with Indian customs and traditions. Although the then existing tribal court system needed significant improvement and stability, and the federal attempt to deal with Indian legal problems was woefully inadequate, Collier realized that it was politic to give up Title IV more or less as a sacrificial lamb to a not-too-friendly Congress.

Part of the congressional debate concerned the voting or ratification by the tribes and nations for self-government under the IRA provisions. An early version of the bill merely specified "three-fifths of the Indians on the reservation or territory covered by the charter." The House bill changed this to a simple majority vote. Finally, a supplementary act passed in 1935 resolved the question to "the vote of a majority of those voting."

Collier lost out to Sen. Burton Wheeler, a sponsor of the legislation, with respect to the blood quantum legal definition of an American Indian under the IRA legislation. Collier wanted one-fourth "blood," but Wheeler insisted on one-half "blood."

Within a year from the date of passage of the IRA the secretary of the interior was to call for a referendum election on the reservations. Each tribe was to discuss the provisions of the act and then vote on whether to accept or reject it. Senator Wheeler favored a simple majority vote, but Collier managed to insert language that would make the IRA operative on a reservation *unless a majority of the tribal members voted to exclude themselves from the act.* In other words, those adult Indians not voting could be counted as voting for the IRA. In this way, Collier's stratagem resulted in more tribes and nations coming under the IRA than would otherwise have been the case. No matter how small the number of eligible Indians voting in favor of the IRA, by counting the nonvotes as "yes," IRA acceptance was virtually assured. A case in point is the Santa Ysabel tribe in California that came under the IRA because 62 eligible tribal members who did not vote were counted as being in favor of adoption. Another example is the vote manipulation that took place on the bitterly divided Hopi Reservation. A plurality of Hopi "progressives" voted for the referenda while a larger number of traditional Hopi "voted" by not voting. The Collier administration nonetheless ruled that the Hopi had voted to accept the IRA. As Kenneth Philp points out in his biography of Collier, at least 17 Native American polities that voted to reject the IRA were considered as being in favor of it. Collier knew that on many of the reservations the more traditional, full-blood Indians would refuse to participate in the IRA elections, preferring instead to assert their tribal sovereignty under the treaties.

A related feature of the IRA was the provision that allowed a tribe only one chance to either accept or reject it. Any benefits of the new law would be lost forever if a tribe wanted to take a "wait and see" approach.

When administrative manipulation of the voting was exposed, Collier was forced to agree that Congress should amend the IRA. In June, 1935, an amendment was passed that extended the deadline for referenda for another year. It also clarified the voting requirements by stipulating that a majority of those voting would determine whether a tribe accepted the IRA or not. At the same time, a distressing feature of the majority rule amendment was that it also contained a provision that 30 percent of the eligible adult Indian population had to participate in the referendum in order for a majority of "no" votes to reject the act. If the number of voters did not amount to 30 percent, then even an overwhelming number of "no" votes could not result in the IRA being rejected. On the other hand, the same rule did not apply for a tribe voting to accept the IRA. Theoretically, even a 1 percent voter participation could effect acceptance of the IRA.

Because a number of nations and tribes did not want to participate in certain provisions of the new law, and because of political pressure brought by special-interest groups, a section of the IRA provided for exclusions and modifications.

Congress passed the Alaska Reorganization Act on June 1, 1936, that included Alaska Natives at the village level under the IRA provisions. The original IRA, on the other hand, had limited its provisions to tribes only. Ultimately, 66 Alaskan Native groups adopted constitutions and corporate charters under this law. The Oklahoma Indian Welfare Act was passed in the same month, which included the Indian tribes of that state.

According to the reorganization plan, after a tribe or nation voted to accept the IRA, then it would draw up a constitution and by-laws, submit them to a referendum, have the secretary of the interior certify the results, and then start operating as a corporate tribal council. Of the 181 tribes accepting the Indian Reorganization Act between 1934 and 1945, only 96 adopted a tribal constitution, and only 73 tribes ever received corporate business charters. Seventy-seven tribes with a population of 86,365 members rejected the IRA outright. Several of these were large reservation groups, such as the Klamath Indians of Oregon and the Crow of Montana. An especially bitter blow to Collier was the rejection of the IRA by the Navajo Nation. With 98 percent of the eligible Navajo voting, the tribe rejected the Act by 419 votes. The Navajo had not forgiven the Collier administration for its drastic livestock reduction program on the reservation that had reduced many of the small herding families to destitution.

Graham Taylor stood alone as the only contemporary critic to raise the question of Native political organization and the nature of Indian communities at the time the IRA went into effect. He believed that the Indian responses to the act differed because each Indian group was at a different point on the assimilation-traditional continuum. There were great differences among the reservations in terms of intermarriage, English literacy, Anglo American education, and acceptance of Christianity. These differences provoked factional strife on most reservations at the time. Many of the monolingual, full-blooded, traditional Indians were unfamiliar with parliamentary procedures, their aboriginal political systems having been a council of elders and chiefs acting on the unanimity principle. Consequently, many of the traditionals boycotted the IRA proceedings altogether. For most reservation Indians, the "tribal governments" established under the IRA constitutions were a totally new and unfamiliar form of political organization. For the Hopi it was primarily the more acculturated villages on the First Mesa that strongly supported the IRA and drew up the tribal constitution, while the villages on the other mesas, being more traditional, either vacillated or withheld their support.

The misreading by Congress and Collier on the question of Indian social organization defies explanation because many of Collier's closest advisers were anthropologists. Yet Collier and his Applied Anthropology Unit, in pressuring Native American peoples to accept the IRA, neglected the existing social organization of Indian communities, the nature of which varied tremendously from reservation to reservation. Many of the Six Nations Iroquois were still committed to a confederacy based on the clan system; the Choctaw, Cherokee, Chickasaw, and Creeks had a history of secular Indian republics; the Shoshones and Paiutes of Nevada, Utah, and Wyoming were organized only at the level of the extended family band; the Rio Grande Pueblo societies were settled, agricultural villages run as theocracies; and the full-bloods among the Plains Indians were organized into a complex of band councils under traditional chiefs. If the goals of the

Indian reform were cultural preservation and economic self-sufficiency, then it would have made sense for reorganization to be tailored to each specific situation. Instead, the "tribal" governments established under the IRA constitutions were a totally new and unfamiliar level of socio-political organization for many Indian populations.

John Collier continually defended the IRA and the Indian New Deal programs during his tenure as commissioner of Indian affairs. He was forced to appear before Congress several times to justify the reforms, and there were two attempts by Congress to repeal the Act, although both were ultimately unsuccessful. The House Appropriations Committee underfunded IRA programs, and by 1944, the Senate Committee on Indian Affairs had also come to oppose the commissioner and his program of Indian reform. Among the most active Indian opponents of the IRA was the American Indian Federation, which joined forces with American pro-Nazi groups in labeling Collier a communist.

In hindsight one can conclude that the self-government provisions of the IRA, although important, were problematic in their impact on Indian communities, but Collier's most lasting achievement was economic development. Much of the Indian New Deal involved bringing needed resources to economically depressed reservation communities. Collier's economic policies also helped Indians rebuild their badly depleted land base, if only modestly; Indian land holdings increased from 48 to 52 million acres, and almost 1 million acres of surplus land was returned to Native tribes and nations.

Following Collier's resignation in 1945, federal Indian policy became stridently regressive for the next two decades during the termination and relocation policy periods in which the limitations of Indian "self-government"—the relative powerlessness of the tribes under the IRA—became apparent. Federal policy did not improve until the federal War on Poverty in the early 1960s and the resurgence of American Indian activism.

STEVE TALBOT

See also

Bureau of Indian Affairs; Dawes Act (1887); Indian Claims Commissions; Indian Removal and the Creation of Indian Territory; Indian Reservations. Documents: Andrew Jackson: Indian Removal Message (1829); Indian Removal Act (1830); Cherokee Nation v. Georgia (1831); The Dawes Act (1887)

Further Reading:
Deloria, Jr., Vine, and Clifford Lytle M. *The Nations Within: The Past and Future of American Indian Sovereignty*. New York: Pantheon Books, 1984.

Hauptman, Lawrence M. "The Indian Reorganization Act." In *The Aggressions of Civilization: Federal Indian Policy Since the 1980s*, edited by Sandra L. Cadwalader and Vine Deloria, Jr., 131–48. Philadelphia, PA: Temple University Press, 1984.

Jorgensen, Joseph G, and Richard O. Clemmer. "On Washburn's 'On the Trail of the Activist Anthropologist': A Rejoinder to a Reply." *Journal of Ethnic Studies* 8 (2) (1980): 85–94.

Kelly, Lawrence C. *The Assault on Assimilation: John Collier and the Origins of Indian Policy Reform*. Albuquerque: University of New Mexico Press, 1983.

Philp, Kenneth R. *John Collier's Crusade for Indian Reform, 1920–1954*. Tucson: University of Arizona Press, 1977.

Taylor, Graham D. *The New Deal and American Indian Tribalism: The Administration of the Indian Reorganization Act, 1934–45*. Lincoln: University of Nebraska Press, 1980.

Indian Reservations

Indian reservations are land set aside for the use, possession, and benefit of an Indian tribe and its members by the president and Congress. Ordinarily, such reservations are considered to be Indian land where the exercise of some measure of self-government is allowed. In reality, reservations frequently represent a struggle on the part of Indians for autonomy, self-sufficiency, religious freedom, and cultural identity as being eroded by the path of white settlement.

Continuing the 17th-century English colonizers' reservation tradition, the U.S. government controlled Native Americans by forcing them to live within clearly defined zones based on treaties, executive orders, or congressional decrees. These treaties involved promises to provide food, goods, and money and to protect them from attack from other tribes and white settlers, but these treaties were often broken. The reservation policy also reflected the view that forcing the Indians to live in a confined space with little opportunity for nomadic hunting would make it easier to "civilize" them. Indians on reservations, however, have preserved many of their traditional values, beliefs, and

Alaska Native Claims Settlement Act of 1971

To understand the Alaska Native Claims Settlement Act, one must first know something about the history behind the territory of Alaska. It was the Russians who first showed interest in Alaska, because they perceived there was much profit to make in the fur seal and sea otter skin trade. Once this industry was depleted, the Russians proceeded to negotiate with the United States over the sale of the territory. The United States purchased Alaska from Russia for $7.2 million in 1867. In this transaction, the rights, status, and land ownership of Alaska natives were never considered. The United States declared that the "uncivilized tribes" in Alaska would be subject to U.S. laws and regulations.

The United States took more than 100 million acres of land for its own use from the territory's public domain, which caused a great controversy. The natives demanded that a freeze on federal land transfers be placed into effect on territorial land. This land freeze was imposed until Congress acted on the issue of how much land would be distributed to those who claimed it. There was a big debate over who exactly would receive the land. The natives claimed 40 million acres of land and also wanted part of the profits made by companies that mined resources from other parts of Alaskan land. The discovery of oil became a critical factor in determining the distribution of the territory.

Debate over land ownership came to a resolution in April 1971 when President Richard M. Nixon proposed to Congress that the Alaska natives would receive 44 million acres of land, $500 million in compensation from the federal treasury, and another $500 million in profits from the lands. Twelve regional corporations would be major recipients of the land. The Senate and the House passed separate bills in support of the president's original proposal to Congress. The Alaska Native Claims Settlement Act was passed as a compromise between the two bills.

TIFFANY VÉLEZ

customs rather than being assimilated to American ways of life.

The passage of the General Allotment Act in 1887, which began dividing reservation lands into individual parcels, had a profound impact on reservations. Many Indian nations lost most of their land because reservation residents had to sell their allotments for income or to pay delinquent state taxes or mortgages. In addition, the allotment policy undermined tribal sovereignty on reservations because federal agents began dealing primarily with individual Indians rather than with their tribal governments.

By the time Congress passed the Indian Reorganization Act (IRA) in 1934, Indian tribes began to reassert their authority over reservation lands. The IRA was significant in that it discontinued the allotment policy, allowed reservation residents to form their own governments, protected Indian culture, and promoted traditional arts and crafts.

Today, Indian reservations make up less than 2 percent of their original area. These reservations also vary in size and demographic composition. In 1990, the federal government recognized 278 Indian land areas as reservations. The Navajo (Diné) Reservation consists of some 16 million acres in Arizona, New Mexico, and Utah; others contain fewer than a hundred acres. The 2000 U.S. census reported that 921,322 people lived on reservations and 52 percent of the reservation residents were American Indians. About half of the land on reservations belongs to Indians; significant portions are owned and inhabited by non-Indians. The Indian-owned land is usually held in trust by the federal government, meaning that this property is exempt from state and federal taxes and can be sold only in accordance with federal regulations.

SOOKHEE OH

See also

American Indian Religious Freedom Act (1978); Bureau of Indian Affairs; Dawes Act (1887); Indian Removal and the Creation of Indian Territory; Indian Reservations; Native Americans, Forced Relocation of. Documents: Andrew Jackson: Indian Removal Message to Congress (1829); Indian Removal Act (1830); *Cherokee Nation v. Georgia* (1831); The Dawes Act (1887)

Further Reading:

Banks, Dennis, and Richard Erdoes. *Ojibwa Warrior: Dennis Banks and the Rise of the American Indian Movement.* Norman: University of Oklahoma Press, 2004.

Indian Self-Determination and Education Assistance Act of 1975 (ISDEAA)

In 1975 Congress passed the Indian Self-Determination and Education Assistance Act (ISDEAA) to implement tribal self-determination policy. Before passage of this law, the Bureau of Indian Affairs (BIA) and other federal agencies regulated and maintained federal control over the delivery of educational, health, and other services to American Indians. Congress recognized the obligation of the United States to respond to the strong expression of Indian people for self-determination by assuring maximum Indian participation in the educational services as well as other federal services to Indian communities. This recognition would enable Indian communities to assume their rightful role in control of their own lifeways. Although this Act deals primarily with the delivery of educational services, nearly all other federal support to Native Americans is also within the extent of the act. Such services include agriculture, health care, law enforcement, and other programs in support of tribal government.

The ISDEAA permits the tribes or any group chartered by the tribe's governing body to take the responsibility for delivering federal services to tribal members. Contracting organizations must meet certain requirements before they are eligible to enter into such agreements with the federal government. Elementary and high schools located on a reservation are among the most common organizations. Although tribes and allied organizations now deliver these services using their own employees, buildings, and equipment, the federal government still retains significant oversight over these contracts.

SOOKHEE OH

Institutional Discrimination

Institutional discrimination can be defined as policies of dominant group institutions and the behavior of individuals who implement these policies and control these institutions that are intended to have a differential and/or harmful effect on subordinate groups. In 1966, Stokely Carmichael and Charles Hamilton coined the term *institutional racism* to differentiate the discriminatory actions of governments and large corporations from the behavior of individuals and small groups.

A classic international example of institutional discrimination would be the apartheid (i.e., separate development) system in South Africa prior to 1993, where the laws sharply limited the rights of both black and mixed-raced people in all areas of life even though they were the numerical majority. Blacks were legally barred from white schools, jobs, and neighborhoods and were relegated to the least desirable areas of the country. They also had no power in national politics.

The United States also had a system of legal segregation, sometimes referred to as Jim Crow, from the late 1870s through the 1960s. The separate-but-equal schools were decidedly unequal. Employment discrimination was rampant. Blacks were prevented from voting through coercion and terrorism. Even the U.S. military was segregated during World War II, with black and Japanese soldiers fighting in segregated units with white officers. Both South African apartheid and American Jim Crow go far beyond the actions of individuals.

A series of U.S. Supreme Court decisions (e.g., *Brown v. Board of Education*, 1954) and laws (e.g., the Civil Rights Acts of 1964 and 1965) outlawed and dismantled much of the legal segregation in education, voting, employment, and housing that existed in the South. The civil rights and Black Power movements struggled to get the federal government to pass and enforce these laws.

With the decline of explicit, legal segregation, some observers have argued that institutional discrimination is no longer a problem in the United States. Especially after the election of President Barack Obama in 2008, some have argued that we have entered a postracial society where race no longer matters. Although there has been great progress since the 1870s and the 1970s, the evidence shows that institutional discrimination is still an important problem in both the public and private sectors.

The Great Recession, beginning in late 2007, exposed institutional discrimination in the mortgage industry. Two lawsuits alleged that major banks knowingly participated in racial discrimination in granting home mortgages. Wells Fargo and the Countrywide Financial unit of Bank of America were charged with giving whites more favorable rates

Chicago Fire Department Case (2010)

In 2010, the U.S. Supreme Court ruled against the Chicago Fire Department and a lower federal court ruled against the New York City Fire Department for using racially biased exams to screen applicants. In the Chicago case, the court ruled that the city used an arbitrary cut-off point of 89 even though studies showed that applicants scoring in the 70s and 80s were capable of succeeding as fire fighters. In the New York case, the court ruled that the department continued using a test that they knew was biased.

than comparable blacks and Hispanics and of steering blacks and Hispanics to more expensive subprime loans when they could have qualified for conventional loans. These policies negatively impacted at least 230,000 households around the country. In 2012, Bank of America agreed to a settlement of $335 million and Wells Fargo agreed to pay $175 million.

Institutional discrimination can still be found in government. The federal government agreed to a $1.4 billion settlement in 2009 to resolve a claim that Indian land was illegally sold to non-Indians a century earlier. In 2010, the federal government paid $4.55 billion to settle claims that black farmers had been discriminated against by the departments of agriculture and the interior.

In order to combat institutional discrimination, discriminatory policies must be changed. This goes far beyond changing the attitudes and actions of individual people. Although legislative and judicial bodies actually make the changes, powerful social movements must demand the changes and then demand that they be enforced.

The 1965 Voting Rights Act, for example, outlawed policies like literacy tests and poll taxes that many Southern states used to prevent blacks from voting. The act also sent federal marshals to enforce the new policies. In spite of this, it took years to make voting rights a reality. The conservative policy of requiring voter identification cards in some states during the 2012 presidential election may be part of a new, indirect means of preventing blacks and Hispanics from voting. Although conservatives who support voter ID cards insist that their goal is to prevent voter fraud, it is clear that subordinate groups, who tend to vote for more liberal candidates, are the least likely to have the required documents.

FRED L. PINCUS

See also

Cumulative Discrimination; Discrimination; Reverse Discrimination; Structural Discrimination

Further Reading:

Better, Shirley. *Institutional Racism: A Primer on Theory and Strategies for Social Change.* Lanham, MD: Rowman and Littlefield, 2008.

Feagin, Joe R. *Racist America: Roots, Current Realities and Future Reparations,* 2nd ed. New York: Routledge, 2010.

Pincus, Fred L. *Understanding Diversity: An Introduction to Class, Race, Gender, Sexual Orientation and Disability,* 2nd ed. Boulder, CO: Lynne Rienner, 2011.

Institutional Racism

Social institutions are organized in such a way that they discriminate against minority members. This type of discrimination, or racism, is referred to as institutional racism. In their 1967 book *Black Power*, Stokely Carmichael and Charles Hamilton first used the term *institutional racism* to differentiate individual acts of racism from institutional policies that affect blacks and other minorities in all spheres of life. Institutional racism encompasses discriminatory mechanisms and policies that adversely affect minorities, even though the institution itself may have an official policy against discrimination. Institutional racism can also involve actions where those who work for the institution have no intention to discriminate against minorities but result in doing so because of the policies that are already in place. Sometimes rules and regulations that were established over time to protect the institution may result in discrimination against minorities today because they are outdated and no longer reflect current racial and social attitudes.

Race expert Joe Feagin identified two types of institutional racism. The first is direct institutional discrimination, which includes actions or policies that are consciously devised by an institution to discriminate against people on the basis of their race, color, religion, or national origin. The employees who are aware of its discriminatory policy usually carry out direct institutional racism. The second is indirect institutional racism, which includes practices and policies that have a negative impact on a group of people even though there is no official policy to discriminate against that group. As Carmichael and Hamilton note, "When five hundred black babies die each year because of the lack of proper food, shelter, and medical facilities and thousands more are destroyed and maimed physically, emotionally and intellectually because of conditions of poverty and discrimination in the black community, that is a function of institutional racism" (1967: 4).

Another important difference between direct and indirect forms of institutional racism is that the former has been legally banned in our society so that even private institutions such as clubs, golf courses, and universities that practice direct institutional racism have been under tremendous pressure to end these practices. However, indirect institutional racism still exists today, 50 years after the passage of the Civil Rights Act by Congress in 1964. Indirect institutional racism takes place through mechanisms and policies that have an impact on minorities in the community where they live in the areas of employment, health, housing, education, and other spheres of life.

There are several reasons why indirect institutional racism continues to exist in society today. First, most of the people who write the rules and regulations for these institutions are often whites who have little or no knowledge of the distinct needs of the particular minority communities. Second, it is more difficult to root out indirect institutional racism because it is difficult to pinpoint who is responsible for discrimination. The structure of the organization or the agency that is implementing a set of policies may be guilty of indirect racism without knowing it. Unless certain practices or policies are challenged, the institution may not be aware that it is engaged in indirect institutional racism.

The health-care industry is an example of how institutional racism adversely affects African Americans. According to data from the 2000 census, a white person born today can expect to live to 79 years, while a black person is expected to live only to 69 years. Diseases and conditions such as prostate cancer, high blood pressure, stroke, and diabetes that can be controlled when caught early are often the leading killers of African Americans. The U.S. government supports institutions that do research on health issues through grants and tax exemptions. However, there is no requirement that they include minorities in their research design. These institutions may already have white researchers who were hired at a time when black and other minority scientists were denied employment in these fields because of official discrimination policies. Therefore, when these researchers create their research design, there may not be any black or other minority group present to provide the viewpoint of their community. As a result, the major illnesses that the minority populations suffer from may be omitted from the research design.

According to law, anyone who shows up in an emergency room has to be treated. However, studies have shown that white doctors tend to perform fewer tests on black patients who show up in emergency rooms than on whites. In a study of asthma among racial and ethnic groups that use Medicaid, Lieu et al. (2002) concluded that black and Latino children had a more severe asthma status and less use of preventive asthma medication than white children within the same economic group. Even though white and black children have access to the same insurance group, black children tend to use inhalers less often than whites and are more likely to go to the emergency room whenever they have an asthma attack. The authors note that the disparity between the white and black children in obtaining care for their asthma because of communication barriers between doctors and patients and the lack of cultural understanding on the part of those who are providing care to the patients.

In a 2000 study of racism and the mental health of African Americans, Williams and Williams-Morris concluded that institutional racism can have an adverse effect. This is due to the level of crime and violence that African Americans are exposed to, the noise and overcrowding that exists in their neighborhoods, and the level of anxiety they live with as they experience various forms of discrimination in their daily encounter with white institutions. Moreover, since racism is an internalized assumption of superiority over another group, when blacks are treated in an institution, the providers may already assume that the treatment will not be effective since they have already a set of stereotypes against blacks. The authors noted that black clinicians have long argued that the popular misconceptions and inaccuracies of the psychology of African Americans could lead to the misdiagnosis of black patients. "The over-diagnosis of paranoid schizophrenia and the under-diagnosis of affective disorders are the most frequent types of misdiagnoses for Blacks" (Williams and Williams-Morris 2003: 256).

Many people may assume that black children have enjoyed equality in education since official segregation in education ended in 1954 with the Supreme Court's ruling that separate schools for blacks and whites were unequal and unconstitutional. Yet, institutional racism still persists in the education system. Institutional racism is manifested in how school districts are funded, the policies that authorities adopt to address education issues, and cultural and social stereotypes of blacks that are often found in books and the media. School districts are usually supported by property taxes. Citizens who live in affluent communities receive more money for their schools than do minorities who live in the inner cities or poor communities. Despite the rhetoric on quality of education for every child in the United States, most blacks attend mostly segregated schools in this society. Most of these schools do not have adequate funding to meet the needs of their students, and fewer of these children attend graduate schools. Of the minority children in the United States, 40 percent attend inner-city schools, and more than half of these children are poor and fail to achieve basic achievement levels. In 2000, about one-sixth of blacks attended schools in which 1 percent of their fellow students were white.

Residential segregation remains one of the most enigmatic problems that U.S. society faces today, because most communities are divided primarily between those who live in predominantly white neighborhoods and others who live in predominantly black or mixed neighborhoods. Institutional racism continues in the housing market when those who do not have significant savings or a history of credit are asked to come up with a large down-payment to obtain a mortgage. Blacks and other minorities are often unable to raise the money or find family members who can cosign a mortgage application for them because they do not have a history of credit or collateral to support the mortgage.

Mortgage lenders and insurance companies can also be involved in the politics of redlining. Redlining is a practice where banks and other financial institutions denied mortgage or home improvement loans to homeowners who live in certain geographic areas, regardless of the physical condition of the home or the credit worthiness of the potential buyer.

In a report published by the Federal Office of Thrift and Supervision, Feagin (1999) notes that "Black mortgage loan applicants have been rejected by savings and loan associations twice as often as White applicants." Other researchers noted that "White Americans made a series of deliberate decisions to deny blacks access to urban housing markets and to reinforce their spatial segregation" (Massey and Denton 1993: 19). More than 35 years after the adoption of the Fair Housing Act, institutional racism still exists in the housing sector, and it forces African Americans to live in ghettos that have substandard housing, few opportunities for employment, and inadequate health care and education.

On June 16, 2003, a Texas judge freed 12 African Americans in the town of Tulia after they had spent almost four years in jail on accusations brought by a lone white undercover narcotics agent. At the time of the arrests, the law-enforcement agent was hailed as a hero and decorated as the state's lawman of the year. Subsequently, it was discovered that the agent not only lied about the people he had arrested, but his methods of gathering the evidence were dubious. The most impressive aspect of this story is the rapidity of law-enforcement associations in the state of Texas in believing the charges that the agent brought against the defendants. The eagerness of whites to accept official police accusation of blacks has been the most pernicious effect of institutional racism in society today.

Institutional racism is manifested in the way that law enforcement, the courts, and the prison system disproportionately convict African Americans and other minorities for crimes. Blacks, who account for only 12 percent of the population, make up 45 percent of the people who are in prison. Law enforcement officials profile African Americans more than any other racial or ethnic group in America. For example, the Civil Rights Commission and the New York City Council reported recently that police officers in New York City tended to profile blacks at a higher rate than any other group in the city.

One of the most famous examples of institutional racism is New York State's Rockefeller Drug Laws. In 1973, Gov. Nelson Rockefeller pressed the state legislature to pass a series of stringent antidrug laws. These laws were the most severe in the country at the time. Their goal was to deter citizens from using or selling drugs and to punish and isolate from society those who had engaged in this enterprise. The laws required judges to impose a mandatory sentence of 15 years to life for "any one convicted of selling two ounces or possessing four ounces of narcotics drug." In 1973, the laws were amended by the legislature to include crack cocaine and to increase the amount of drugs needed to be convicted. As a result of these laws, the population of the state's prison system increased from 20,000 in 1980 to almost 62,000 in 1992. By the end of 2002, the prison population was expected to exceed 73,000 prisoners. Most of the prisoners are African American males, because crack cocaine is likely to be used by the poor and is found mostly in communities that are heavily populated by minorities. Of those convicted and incarcerated for drug offenses today in New York state, 94 percent are African Americans.

The fear of crime is not the exclusive purview of whites. Blacks are as much afraid of crime as whites and are more often the victims of crime. However, the deployment of police officers in black communities depends on the policies and priorities that are established by city officials. African Americans often find themselves underserved when it comes to having police officers patrol their community. Moreover, even when officers are deployed in their community, they are often ignorant of the needs of the community. As far back as 1968, the Kerner Commission, which investigated the causes of the riots of the summer 1967, reported that most police officers deployed in black neighborhoods had little knowledge of the community and therefore were unable to communicate effectively with residents. Police officers, who are often white because of past departmental hiring practices, have been seen to regard blacks no matter how good a citizen, in the role of the enemy.

Whether in private or public institutions, blacks often confront institutional racism in employment. This is expressed in the form of denial of promotion, paying them less than their white workers, or hiding information that could enhance their chances of being promoted. Although well-known African Americans, such as Colin Powell, Condoleezza Rice, Richard Parsons, and Kenneth Chenault, have occupied high-powered positions in government and the private sector, the reality is that there are fewer African Americans in the position of power in corporate or government

institutions than it appears. Corporate and government policies, such as the seniority system, exams, and tenure, often work against blacks and other minorities who are just entering these institutions.

Since the 1960s, there have been many efforts to end institutional racism in corporate and public institutions. Citizens have sued the police, fire, sanitation, parks, and private agencies over their testing policy, their recruitment practices, and their requirements, such as height, weight, or racial backgrounds, to force them to end institutional racism. There have been numerous victories since these lawsuits have been filed. However, there is still a long way to go before institutional racism is eliminated.

Francois Pierre-Louis

See also

Color-Blind Racism; Ideological Racism; Laissez-Faire Racism

Further Reading:

Carmichael, Stokely, and Charles Hamilton. *Black Power: The Politics of Liberation in America*. New York: Random House, 1967.

Davey, Monica. "Texas Frees 12 on Bond after Drug Sweep Inquiry." *New York Times*, June 17, 2003.

Feagin, Joe R. "Excluding Blacks and Others from Housing: The Foundation of White Racism." *Cityscape* 4, no. 3 (July 10, 1999).

Fletcher, Michael A. "Prophecy on Race Relations Came True." *Washington Post*, March 1, 1998: A06.

Hacker, Andrew. *Two Nations: Black and White: Separate, Hostile, Unequal*. New York: Scribners, 1992.

Lieu, Tracey, et al. "Racial/Ethnic Variation in Asthma Status and Management Practices among Children in Managed Medicaid." *Pediatrics* 109, no. 5 (May 2002).

Massey, Douglas S., and Nancy A. Denton. *American Apartheid*. Cambridge: Harvard UP, 1993.

Orfield, Gary, and Eaton Susan. "Back to Segregation." *Nation* 276, no. 8 (March 3, 2003).

Perle, Eugene D., and Kathryn Lynch, "Perspectives on Mortgage Lending and Redlining." *Journal of the American Planning Association* 60, no. 3 (Summer 1994): 344.

West, Cornel. *Race Matters*. New York: Vintage Books, 1993.

Williams, David R. "The Health of Men: Structured Inequalities and Opportunities." *American Journal of Public Health* 93, no. 5 (May 2003): 724.

Williams, David R., and Ruth Williams-Morris. "Racism and Mental Health: The African-American Experience." *Ethnicity and Health* 5, no. 3/4 (2000): 243–68.

Integration

The term *integration*, when used in a racial sense, describes a process of leveling barriers within the broader society or culture to jobs, housing, education, and free social interaction between members of different racial or ethnic groups or classes. It is therefore the opposite of segregation, the policy of maintaining separation between races in employment, schools, residential patterns, and general social engagement. Although this distinction is not universally accepted, integration is often seen as mainly a social process while desegregation is defined in largely legal terms. Both before and during the civil rights movement of the 1950s and 1960s, efforts to achieve integration, particularly in housing and schools, often led to racial violence.

Many riots in the United States were part of citizens' responses to changes in the racial make up of cities, workplaces, housing patterns, and public facilities. The influx of black migrants to urban centers in the early 20th century (*see* The Great Migration) is cited as one of the major causes of the rash of race riots that occurred during the Red Summer Race Riots of 1919. The attempt to bring blacks into the industrial labor force, often a move to break the collective bargaining powers of white workers, was the precipitating event in both the East St. Louis (Illinois) Riot of 1917 and a narrowly averted race riot at Ford's River Rouge Plant in Detroit, Michigan, in 1941. Housing has presented another challenge to peaceful black and white coexistence. In Detroit's Sojourner Truth Housing Project in 1942 and in Chicago's Trumbull Park Homes in 1953 and 1954, riots erupted when blacks attempted to move into public housing. Public spaces have also presented a challenge in the country's slow and as yet incomplete march toward integration, as blacks and whites meet one another outside the context of home and work. The Chicago (Illinois) Riot of 1919 started when a white man killed a young boy on the beach during a skirmish that erupted as blacks attempted to break the unwritten rules about segregated beaches. The attempt to desegregate schools, perhaps the most well-known chapter in American civil rights history, also brought race riots. Most notably, two years of violence marked the advent of busing in Boston in the 1970s (*see* Boston [Massachusetts] Riots of 1975 and 1976).

In 1919, 25 race riots occurred in the United States. The influx of black migrants was a source of anxiety for city residents across the country. In Chicago, for example, the black population had grown from 44,000 in 1910 to 110,000 in 1920, as blacks left rural farm labor in search of jobs in industry. Often violence followed any direct competition for jobs, or attempts by blacks to share housing and recreational facilities.

The early part of the 20th century was a period of widespread labor unrest. Some estimate that as many as 3,000 labor disputes broke out around the nation in 1919. In the East St. Louis Riot of 1917, white workers attacked blacks as part of a plan to stop black migrants from taking "their" jobs. Tensions reached a boiling point when management at the Aluminum Ore Company adopted a policy of hiring blacks in response to a successful strike the year before. The union attempted a strike in the spring of 1917, but the company won out. Even though most of the strikebreakers were white, union members blamed blacks for breaking the strike. The racialization of labor competition makes more sense within the larger context—the workers were residents of East St. Louis, a city that imagined itself in the middle of a black invasion because its African American population had grown to comprise 18 percent of its total population. The riot marks one of several events characterized by the failure of labor to overcome race prejudice and fully include blacks in labor organizing. The incident at Ford's River Rouge Plant is a rare instance of black-labor compromise. The Ford Motor Company began using blacks as strikebreakers and thugs during a 1941 white labor strike. Convinced that these actions would cause a race riot, local black leaders, convened by Louis Martin, came forward to condemn Ford's race-baiting tactics and announced their support of the UAW-CIO. Union leaders met with Walter White of the National Association for the Advancement of Colored People. As a result of this meeting, many black workers were persuaded to leave the plant, giving the union the power to bargain with management. The result was a contract that applied to all workers, regardless of race or national origin.

Although the River Rouge strike brought gains in black job security in Detroit, housing was another story. Blacks were excluded from all public housing, with the exception of the Brewster Housing Project. As a result, blacks paid relatively high rents—two and three times what similarly situated whites paid—to live in shacks without heat or hot water. In 1941, the Detroit Housing Commission approved the Sojourner Truth Housing Project for blacks. To the dismay of local leaders, the project was located in a white neighborhood, and whites mounted the inevitable protest. In 1942, the Federal Housing Commission backed down and declared that the Sojourner Truth housing would be for whites, but reversed this decision when no suitable location could be found for a black housing project. On February 28, a crowd of 1,200 whites met their would-be black neighbors, and violence ensued. Although no one was killed, officials postponed the move-in indefinitely. Finally, at the end of April, as police and state troopers kept the peace, African Americans were able to occupy their homes.

In 1953 and 1954, riots erupted during attempts to integrate Deering Park in Chicago. Since 1937, the Chicago Housing Authority (CHA) had an unwritten rule upholding white-only housing projects. However, in the 1950s, the housing authority accidentally integrated the projects by accepting the application for residence of fair-skinned Betty Howard and her husband Donald. Betty Howard's complexion was not the only thing that allowed her to bypass the authority's passive segregation tactics; to further complicate matters, she lived in a neighborhood with an unclear racial makeup, and the stark residential segregation that allowed the authority to deny black applicants by using their postal zone as a guide was of no service. When the couple moved in, crowds gathered and for weeks hurled insults and bricks at their apartment. The Howards required a police escort to leave the building. CHA Executive Secretary Elizabeth Wood proclaimed a policy of nonsegregation and threatened to evict tenants who participated in antiblack protests. The violence continued as CHA succeeded in moving 15 more black families into the projects by April 1954, often during the day when many Deering Park residents were at work. Although officials did not back down from the new policy of integration, white residents determined to make the neighborhood uninhabitable for blacks. The projects were the scene of sporadic outbursts of violence throughout the 1950s and the violence succeeded in stopping all but token integration of the project.

The Chicago Riot of 1919, although aggravated by issues such as black "infiltration," job competition, and housing, began when a skirmish broke out as blacks, attempting to violate the unwritten rule regarding segregation at the Twenty-Ninth Street Beach, were chased away. The black beachgoers returned with reinforcements, throwing rocks at the whites on the beach. The whites retreated only to return with their own reinforcements. During the fray, a white beachgoer stoned a black teenager, Eugene Williams, causing him to drown. A white police officer refused to arrest the murderer. The officer only made matters worse because as black witnesses protested his actions, he arrested a black man on the complaint of a white man. The events brought a long anticipated five-day race war to Chicago. Police and white mobs murdered 25 black men; the white death toll reached 16.

In 1974, Judge W. Arthur Garrity ordered the Boston School Committee to desegregate the city's schools. When the committee refused, arguing to uphold the conventional white neighborhood school policy, Garrity put the schools under federal receivership, and enacted a plan to desegregate the city's schools by busing students around the city. The plan impacted the poorest white neighborhoods in the city, including Southie, and left schools in suburban Boston largely untouched. Seventy-nine of the 80 schools received students without incident at the beginning of the school year, but rioting began as black students attempted to enter South Boston High. The protesters, who had gathered at the school carrying signs bearing racial slurs, began to hurl bottles and watermelon, among other things, at buses carrying black children. Violence marred the city's landscape, particularly around schools and in the affected neighborhoods, for the next two years, as protesters threw bricks at children on buses and white and black high school students fought one another around the city.

SHATEMA A. THREADCRAFT

See also

Boston (Massachusetts) Riots of 1975 and 1976; Desegregation

Further Reading:

Baulch, Vivian M., and Patricia Zacharias. "The 1943 Detroit Race Riots." *Detroit News Rearview Mirror* (2000).

Hallgren, Mauritz. "The Right to Strike." *The Nation* 137, no. 3566 (November 8, 1933): 530.

Hirsch, Arnold R. "Massive Resistance in the Urban North: Trumbull Park, Chicago, 1953–1966." *Journal of American History* 82, no. 2 (1995): 522–50.

Poinsett, Alex. "Walking with Presidents: Louis Martin and the Rise of Black Political Power." *The New Crisis* (February/March 1998).

Rudwick, Elliott M. *Race Riot at East St. Louis, July 2, 1917.* Carbondale: Southern Illinois University Press, 1963.

Tager, Jack. *Boston Riots: Three Centuries of Social Violence.* Boston: Northeastern University Press, 2001.

Tuttle, William M., Jr. *Race Riot: Chicago in the Red Summer of 1919.* New York: Athaeneum, 1970.

Intelligence Testing

Intelligence tests in the West emerged almost simultaneously in England, France, and Germany in the late 19th century. Researchers invigorated by Charles Darwin's *Origin of the Species* (1859) were eager to find a scientific way to measure mental ability, with many poised to initiate comparative studies that took a variety of indicators into consideration, particularly race and class. The implications of intelligence testing and the interpretation of test results were far reaching and fueled heated debates, particularly in the United States, a meritocracy whose democratic ideal had been persistently undermined by social inequality since the nation's inception.

The Western philosophical interest in intelligence emerged in Ancient Greece with Plato and Aristotle, who distinguished cognitive and emotive aspects of human behavior. Cicero later invented the term *intelligence*, but Plato suggested a correlation between intelligence and social class by arguing that human beings were made of different metals. Those made of gold were poised to be rulers; of silver, executives; and of iron and brass, to cultivate the soil or manufacture goods. Duties in the Republic that Plato imagined were to be assigned according to the innate abilities of those concerned, a pattern of stratification that was achieved in part in modern meritocracy.

By the 19th century, pseudoscientific theories claimed to offer valid proof that the races were innately arranged in a hierarchical relationship from greatest to least, with whites, particularly those of English, German, or French ancestry, occupying the first rung and those of African descent occupying the last. According to the pseudoscience of phrenology, the races were distinguished by phenotype and brain size. Such theories were often used to justify European expansion into Africa, Asia, and the Americas, and to offer explanations for slave societies and the colonial and postcolonial relationships emerging from them. Darwin's enduring theory of evolution presented in *Origin of the Species* catalyzed discussions that led researchers to test this theory and imagine its social and political implications. A scientific test to measure intelligence evinced this trend and emerged from a synthesis of scientific investigations in various fields, including statistics, physiology, and modern educational and social psychology, with its emphasis on understanding the cognitive and emotive aspects of human nature.

Philosopher Herbert Spencer, statistician Karl Pearson, and Sir Francis Galton, Darwin's cousin, argued that intelligence could be measured, and that such measurement was related to evolution and genetics. Physiologist John Hughlings Jackson and others conducted microscopic brain studies, which forwarded discussions by providing a scientific basis for understanding the relationship between brain activity and intelligence. Professor of psychology Charles Spearman argued that if a cognitive ability existed that allowed an individual to reason well, it should then be possible to test this ability through a series of different problems of varying complexity. Alfred Binet in France and Herman Ebbinghaus in German were creating such tests, but Spearman added that there was a positive correlation between cognitive tests of any kind when they were carried out. Spearman's tests

---

Lewis Terman (1877–1956)

Lewis Terman, a psychologist at Stanford University, was notorious for arguing in favor of hereditary differences in IQ scores among different racial groups. In 1916, Terman and his associates developed the Stanford-Binet scale of intelligence. Based on his research on intelligence tests, Terman claimed that a low level of intelligence is common among Spanish-Indian and Mexican families in the Southwest as well as among Negroes. He believed that many of the children from these families were uneducable beyond basic training and that education could improve their intelligence to the level that would allow them to be intelligent voters or capable citizens.

Terman is therefore one of the major scholars in the United States in the laying of the groundwork for biological racism, the view that racial minority groups have low levels of intelligence influenced by genetic differences.

PYONG GAP MIN

Charles Darwin was photographed by Julia Margaret Cameron shortly before the publication of his controversial book *The Descent of Man* (1871). (Library of Congress)

and early versions of the same measured verbal and quantitative skills, the format used in the United States throughout most of the 20th century.

Objective testing in the United States received its first great impetus with the civil service exam, established in 1883 by the Pendleton Civil Service Reform Act and administered first during World War I. A primary goal of the exam was to eliminate the spoils system that dominated access to certain federal positions and to enhance expertise by placing federal employees for certain posts on a merit system. The civil service exam in and of itself did not perturb blacks and other minorities, but the interpretation of test results and comparative analysis between black and white averages engendered enduring controversy and divided educators throughout the country.

The Pendleton Act applied only to positions with the federal government, but its implications were far reaching. As many blacks feared, test results were used increasingly to justify, structure, and reinforce inequality. Exams of similar structure were adopted at state and local levels, with the results impacting access to education and the quality thereof, employment, and general social mobility. In the Jim Crow South, many proponents of intelligence testing hoped to find definitive proof that whites were intellectually superior to blacks and other ethnic minorities and therefore innately meritorious of certain social and economic privileges.

Southern blacks, many of whose ancestors had barely transitioned from being property to owning property, were particularly suspicious of intelligence testing. Their collective historical experience with the random administering of tests affirmed that testing was designed to preclude their participation in the political process in the years immediately following Emancipation. Black Southerners who attempted to vote were sometimes required to recite the Constitution or to demonstrate reading proficiency before being permitted to vote. Literate black voters were prohibited from voting by the "grandfather clause," which stated that a person was ineligible to vote if his or her grandfather had been a slave.

But the controversy over comparative intelligence was not limited to the South. The intelligence question even affected whom one could marry in California before *Perez v. Sharp* (1948), when the California Supreme Court declared that antimiscegenation laws violated the Fourth Amendment. Prior to the new ruling, the state had prohibited interracial marriages on the grounds that the correlation between the social environment of poor black children and performance on IQ tests had not been resolved.

Researchers engaged in heated discussions about whether test performance reflected hereditarian or environmental influences. Others questioned the purported objectivity of intelligence tests, since cultural expectations regarding what a person should know by a certain age ultimately varied from one social group and context to the next, and since education, exposure to the testing conventions, and economic standing impacted the probability of test-takers' failure or success. Many were also concerned about the impact that the interpretation of test results would have on access to education, employment, and promotion. In a broad sense, they questioned the inherent conflict in a meritocracy in which the democratic ideal had been only partially achieved.

Historically black colleges and universities of the period responded to concerns about college entrance exams by maintaining open admissions policies, which welcomed students to earn college degrees regardless of their performance on standardized tests. Other universities developed admissions procedures that took a variety of factors into account, including but not limited to scores on standardized exams, which generally used white, urban, middle- and upper-class subjects as the standard.

The battle over intelligence testing and its ability to predict success continued throughout the Jim Crow era and beyond. Testing continues to impact access to education by the implementation of tracking and merit-based gifted and talented programs, which largely led to the near resegregation of American classrooms despite *Brown v. Board of Education* (1954), which acknowledged the negative psychological and social impact of Jim Crow.

Karen Kossie-Chernyshev

See also

Bell Curve: Intelligence and Class Structure in American Life; Biological Racism

Further Reading:

Aptheker, Herbert. "Literacy, The Negro and World War II." *Journal of Negro Education* 15, no. 4 (Autumn 1946): 595–602.

Eysenck, Hans Jurgen. *The Intelligence Controversy: H. J. Eysenck versus Leon Kamin*. New York: Wiley & Sons, 1981.

Gosset, T. F. *Race: A History of an Idea in America*. New York: Schocken Books, 1965.

Samuda, Ronald J. *Psychological Testing of American Minorities: Issues and Consequences*. New York: Dodd, Mead and Company, 1975.

Intergenerational Social Mobility

Intergenerational social mobility refers to the likelihood that an individual will attain a different level of socioeconomic status than the individual's family of origin. Usually, the term refers to upward mobility, individuals achieving a higher status than their parents; however, downward mobility is also possible. There are five forms of mobility: wage mobility, family income mobility, occupational mobility, educational mobility, and wealth mobility. Researchers in different fields tend to use different types of mobility to examine social mobility. For example, economists typically use family income mobility, while sociologists tend to use occupational mobility.

Social mobility, in all forms, is closely linked to inequality. There are a number of ways social mobility is related between wealth (land, properties, and other assets), and understanding the importance of wealth is vital to understanding racial and ethnic inequality in intergenerational social mobility. Proponents of meritocracy will often elevate the success of a few, exceptional people of color to illustrate the lack of barriers to success. Since his election in 2008, President Barack Obama, the first black president, has perhaps been the most common example.

A consistent stream of policy decisions at the federal and state level have systematically facilitated opportunities for intergenerational upward mobility for white citizens, while preventing nonwhite citizens from accessing the same opportunities. The GI Bill played a critical role in the creation of the suburban white middle class and maintaining the systematic exclusion of blacks from homeownership and other middle-class benefits. The GI bill, rather than facilitating upward mobility for black veterans, actually served to widen the already large racial gap in wealth. Increasing cultural pressure and unprecedented government incentives to suburbanize drove housing production up, prices down, and made home-ownership attainable for a much broader range of people than before in terms of income.

Section 235 of the 1968 Housing Act was created to shift funding for local housing authorities toward providing supply-side subsides to the private sector in order to stimulate home ownership for minorities and the poor, but it actually facilitated segregation in its implementation. As a result of Section 235, many whites were able to purchase new suburban housing, but black families with the means to purchase homes were mostly restricted to purchasing existing housing in the inner city. Homes in black neighborhoods appreciate at a much slower rate, and are more likely to depreciate.

Intergenerational social mobility, then, is facilitated or impeded on the basis of race through a variety of social mechanisms, including property ownership. Examining the effects of kin characteristics on account ownership and home ownership, Heflin and Pattillo (2002) found that having a poor sibling and living in a poor family during childhood are significantly and negatively correlated with home

Cultural Capital

Introduced to the sociological lexicon in 1979 by prolific philosopher and sociologist Pierre Bourdieu, *cultural capital* has been used widely by a number of scholars in a wide range of disciplines. Cultural capital is the knowledge of high culture that works to an individual's economic and social advantage. Some examples are exposure to what is considered to be high art, having a familiarity with wine, and the knowing the appropriate etiquette for a formal dinner party. The term is most frequently used in the field of education, as that was the area in which Bourdieu initially discussed it, but it has wide application in other aspects of the social world.

ownership, and that blacks are more likely to have poor siblings. This research speaks to the cumulative and intergenerational nature of wealth creation and disadvantage.

Poverty among Native Americans is an example of the ways in which race is intricately linked with wealth creation and maintenance. Poverty is among the highest among Native Americans compared to other racial groups in the United States. In 2000, the median household income for Native Americans was 25 percent lower than that of the entire U.S. population and Indians living on reservation have lower income levels and higher unemployment and poverty than those who do not. Historical mistreatment of native lands and resources have placed an obvious barrier to upward mobility for Native Americans, but government action and inaction in recent times has continued to hinder upward mobility for the group with the lowest amount of income in the United States. Mismanagement of Native land trusts, improper administration of benefits and other gross injustices on the part of the U.S. government have all contributed to a lack of intergenerational social mobility for Native Americans.

The most commonly recognized mechanisms for intergenerational social mobility are education and cultural capital. Racial differentials in educational access and achievement are generally well-known issues. But beyond impacting individual life chances in terms of college entrance or success in the workforce, lifetime earnings and wealth accumulation are also impacted. An alternative to education as a mechanism for mobility is Pierre Bourdieu's concept of cultural capital. Cultural capital is passed from parents to children in the family, and also through formal schooling. Cultural capital can be thought of as one of several resources, in concert with social, economic, and human capital, that can be converted into one another to maximize upward social mobility For example, a parent can use their economic capital to finance a private school education in which their child learns about high art and appropriate dress for upper-class social functions, thereby enabling the child to participate in upper-class social events where they make future professional contacts as an adult.

Renee S. Alston

See also

Downward Mobility; Educational Achievement Gap; Meritocracy

Further Reading:

Gotham, Kevin Fox. "Separate and Unequal: The Housing Act of 1968 and the Section 235 Program." *Sociological Forum* 15, no. 1 (2000): 13–37.

Heflin, Colleen M. and Mary Pattillo-McCoy. "Kin Effects on Black-White Account and Home Ownership." *Sociological Inquiry* 72 no. 2 (2002): 220–39.

Katznelson, Ira. *When Affirmative Action Was White: An Untold History of Racial Inequality in Twentieth-Century America.* New York: W. W. Norton, 2005.

Lareau, Annette, and Michèle Lamont. "Cultural Capital: Allusions, Gaps and Glissandos in Recent Theoretical Developments." *Sociological Theory* 6, no. 2 (1988): 153–68.

Reagan, Patricia B., and Robert J. Gitter. "Is Gaming the Optimal Strategy? The Impact of Gaming Facilities on the Income and Employment of American Indians." *Economics Letters* 95, no. 3 (2007): 428–32.

Internal Colonialism

Internal colonialism is a theory of interethnic relations based on the analogy of the relationship between the colonizers and the colonized. This theory gained significant currency in the 1960s and the 1970s when national liberation movements proliferated both within and without the U.S. border. Just as the Vietnamese and Algerians would fight for the independence of their nations, Native Americans, African Americans, Chicanos, and Puerto Ricans would demand their own autonomous nation-states.

The social situation of the colonized minorities in Africa differs from that of the immigrant minorities such as the Irish and the Germans of the Unites States in many aspects. The colonized minorities were indigenous and numerically a majority but forcefully subjugated to the domination of alien colonizers in their own homelands. Thus, they were minorities in terms of power. The colonial interethnic system usually allocated the most degrading jobs to the natives. Social mobility, if there was any, was extremely limited. Assimilation into the mainstream culture was impossible. The only hope lay in the overthrow of colonial domination and the establishment of an independent government of the indigenous people. The aspiration of the colonized for liberation took the form of nationalism. Political struggle for national liberation required solidarity as a nation based on the presumed common root of national history and identity and pride in the national language, religion, and culture.

Some tried to apply this colonial paradigm to the interethnic relations of the United States. Robert Blauner, author of *Racial Oppression in America* (1972), thought that the peoples of color in the United States shared essential conditions with the colonized peoples abroad: economic underdevelopment, a heritage of colonialism and neocolonialism, and a lack of real political autonomy and power. Indeed, as many argued, the historical experience of Mexican Americans could be better understood within the paradigm of internal colonialism than with that of assimilation. At first, Mexicans were colonized by the Spaniards and then by the Anglo Americans. The Anglo elite frequently intermarried or became *compadres* (god-relatives) with the landowning Mexican families. Many of traditional Mexican landowning elite lost their titles by the legal and illegal actions of the Anglo administration. The conquered people were kept at the bottom of the occupational structure as a cheap and controlled labor force, always filling the dead-end jobs. Unlike European immigrants, Mexican Americans confronted strong racial discrimination and found little opportunity for upward social mobility through the generations. In the 1960s, the protest movement of Mexican Americans developed into the Chicano nationalist movement fighting against Anglo imperialism. It called for the unity of the people of La Raza, who supposedly shared the cultural heritage from the Aztec, Inca, and Toltec, as well as the Spanish, civilizations. They sought community control in the hope that it would assure political and economic equity and preserve their cultural identity.

The theory of internal colonialism draws attention to the historical experience of African Americans, Mexicans, and Puerto Ricans, in contrast to that of European ethic immigrants. They were forcefully incorporated into U.S. society and remain the subordinated "others" instead of being assimilated into the mainstream American culture. Native Americans have suffered near extermination since the "discovery of America" in the 15th century and have survived with few resources, forced into reservations. Africans were forcefully brought to the United States only to be slaves at the discretion of the white masters, while the African continent became colonized by the European empires. Mexicans and Puerto Ricans became Americans through conquest.

DONG-HO CHO

Further Reading:

Acuna, Rodolfo. *Occupied America*, 2nd ed. New York: Harper & Row, 1981.

Blauner, Robert. *Racial Oppression in America*. New York: Harper & Row, 1972.

Montejano, David. *Anglos and Mexicans in the Making of Texas, 1836–1986*. Austin: University of Texas Press, 1987.

Moore, Joan W. *Mexican Americans*, 2nd ed. Englewood Cliffs, NJ: Prentice Hall, 1976.

Internalized Racism

Internalized racism is a product of the socialization process in the United States exhibited by many people of color at some point in their lives. People of color exhibit internalized racism when they collude with the racist ideas of the dominant white society. Internalized racism has both a conscious and an unconscious component. Conscious collaboration occurs when people of color knowingly (but not always voluntarily) accede to their own mistreatment to survive or maintain some status, livelihood, or other benefit, as when a person of color silently endures racist jokes told by a boss.

The more insidious form of internalized racism is unconscious. It occurs when people of color do not even know they are collaborating in their own dehumanization. Often, this occurs because they do not recognize that racism occurs at an institutional level; rather, they see prejudice and discrimination only at the individual level. An example of unconscious internalized racism is when a person of color who has been repeatedly passed over for promotions at work feels that the problem is his own—for example, that he needs to work harder—rather than recognizing his plight as a manifestation of his superiors' racist attitudes. Another form of internalized racism is denial of one's ethnic or cultural background, such as not wanting to speak one's native language or eat one's ethnic food. This denial of one's ethnic or racial background is also known as the "acting white" or "wanting to be white" stage of ethnic and racial identity development.

KHYATI JOSHI

See also

Clark Doll Study; Color-Blind Racism; Ideological Racism; Oppositional Culture

Further Reading:

Alexander, Michelle. *The New Jim Crow: Mass Incarceration in the Age of Colorblindness.* New York: The New Press, 2010.

Bonilla-Silva, Eduardo. *Racism Without Racists: Color-Blind Racism and the Persistence of Racial Inequality in the United States.* Lanham: Rowman and Littlefield Publishers, 2003.

Feagin, Joe. *Systemic Racism: A Theory of Oppression.* New York: Routledge, 2006.

Takaki, Ronald. *A Different Mirror: A History of Multicultural America.* Boston: Back Bay Books, 1993.

Internet Racism

Racism is a phenomenon of human social interaction that is not limited to personal contact, but can also exists in virtual worlds, such as television, radio, and even the Internet. Racism in computer-generated worlds is the distribution, through technology, of racial expression and ideals. Les Back (2002) defines Internet racism as the use and spreading of rhetoric of racial and/or national uniqueness and common destiny, ideas of racial supremacy, superiority and separation, a repertoire of conceptions of racial Otherness, and a utopian revolutionary world-view that aims to overthrow the existing order. Racist groups also us the Internet to organize, mobilize members, and raise money through the sale of merchandise.

There are various forms of racist activity on the Internet, which include Web sites, games, e-mails, chat rooms, discussion groups, and social networking sites. Each of these venues provides a technological tool for the dissemination of racism that allows a person to be exposed to very little backlash or criticism. Web sites represent static venues that advertise racist ideology and refer individuals to other racist resources. More interactive mediums, such as e-mail, chat rooms, and social networking forums, can create the "sense of community" that is essential to the formation of racist ideology. Games also allow individuals to "live out" their racist fantasies, such as violence against nonwhites.

Although Internet racism can take form in any of the multiple technological tools available, it appears in subtle and overt forms. Through the use of hidden agendas and multiple redirections of web traffic, individual anonymity is quite easy to accomplish. Jesse Daniels (2009) notes this through the idea of "cloaked websites," which "illustrate a central feature of propaganda and cyber-racism in the digital era: the use of difficult-to-detect authorship and hidden agendas intended to accomplish political goals, including white Supremacy" (661). According to Daniels, and others, this hidden agenda method has become more frequent throughout the Internet as a way to foster and promote racism.

Overt forms of racism are also likely to appear on the Internet, particularly in the realm of "fun" and "entertainment." Online computer games are one example of this phenomenon and are a form of racial vilification that is emerging largely because interaction with these technological tools does not require personal identification. One of the more sophisticated games is *Ethnic Cleansing*, which was principally advertised by on-line white power music distributors and released in 2002 on Martin Luther King Day. The goal of the game is to kill "sub-humans," namely ethnic and racial minorities, as is stated in its promotional materials:

> Run through the ghetto blasting away various blacks and spics in an attempt to gain entrance to the subway system … where the jews have hidden to avoid the carnage. Then if your lucky you can blow away jews as they scream "Oy Vey!," on your way to their command center. (Anti-Defamation League 2002)

The player can choose to have their character dressed in KKK robes, as a skinhead, or other racially supremacist

This screen capture shows the title page of the Internet video game *Border Patrol*. The online video game, in which the player shoots immigrants crossing the border, has sparked outrage over its racist content. (Getty Images)

attire, throughout the game. Various white power symbols can also be seen throughout the game, and it is played to a white power music soundtrack. These games are an example of racism and the nature of its operation in a virtual arena.

Another key feature of Internet racism is the blurring boundaries between front and backstage communication. Conversations about race, by whites, in particular, largely occur through hushed voices or private conversations (the backstage). While some may view overt expressions of racism a thing of the past, explicit racist comments are not gone, but occur in a *white-only spaces* (the backstage) (Picca and Feagin 2007). Social media and the Internet has changed this; as more white people spend time online, they often forget that the comments intended for the "backstage" (white-only spaces) are easily made public and shared in the "front stage" for everyone to view. As more of these expressions of racism come to light, it forces all of us to decide again and again what is socially acceptable.

Technology, of all forms, can be utilized in certain historical times and places to produce particular socially based effects. A particular technology has no inherent ideological or racially based orientation; rather, the relationship between the technologies and how people use them becomes the essential manner in which racism is expressed (Back 2002). The racism found on the Internet originates with individuals and the manner in which they communicate race-based ideas and values.

JAMES W. LOVE

See also

Digital Divide; Hate Groups in America

Further Reading:

Anti-Defamation League. "Racist Groups Using Computer Gaming to Promote Violence Against Blacks, Latinos and Jews." 2002. http://www.adl.org/videogames/default.asp (cited December 15, 2012).

Back, L. "Aryans Reading Adorno: Cyber-culture and Twenty-first Century Racism," *Ethnic and Racial Studies* 25 (2002): 628–51.

Daniels, Jesse. "Cloaked Websites: Propaganda, Cyber-Racism and Epistemology in the Digital Era." *New Media Society* 11 (2009): 659–83.

Daniels, Jesse. *Cyber Racism: White Supremacy Online and the New Attack on Civil Rights*. Lanham, MD: Rowman and Littlefield. 2009.

Picca, Leslie, and Joe Feagin. *Two-Faced Racism: Whites in the Backstage and Frontstage*. New York: Taylor & Francis, 2007.

Interracial Marriage

Intermarriage refers to a marriage between two partners of different groups. There are three forms of intermarriage: interethnic, interfaith, and interracial. *Interethnic marriage* is commonly used to refer to a marriage between partners of two different national origins or language groups, whereas *interracial marriage* indicates a marriage between persons who belong to two different racial groups. *Interfaith marriage* refers to a marriage between members of two different religious backgrounds. In the United States, interethnic marriages are more common than interfaith marriage, which are more common than interracial marriages. It suggests that physical differences are more difficult to overcome for friendship and intimate relations than are differences in national origin or religion, which indicates the tenacity of racism in the United States.

The most widely known and studied cases of interethnic marriages are those among descendants of European immigrants. More than 75 percent of third-generation and

Mr. and Mrs. Richard Perry Loving, an interracial couple, fought Virginia's law against interracial marriages in 1967. This landmark Supreme Court case established that state bans on interracial marriages are unconstitutional. (Bettmann/Corbis)

higher white Americans are involved in interethnic marriages across national origin. Before World War II, interethnic marriages among different white ethnic groups were at a considerably high level, but interfaith marriages were exceptionally few. This trend led to the triple-melting-pot hypothesis proposed in 1944, which claimed that intermarriage was occurring between various nationalities but only within the three major religious groupings (Protestants, Catholics, and Jews). But interfaith marriage rates have gradually increased since 1960, to the extent that the majority of Protestants, Catholics, and Jews now marry members of different religions.

Interethnic marriages among white Americans are now so common that most white Americans have difficulty tracing their ancestries. Intermarriage indicates the highest level of assimilation, so a high level of intermarriage among white ethnic groups means their high level of assimilation into American society. Interethnic marriages among different Asian, Latino, and/or black groups within each racial minority group have also increased since the 1980s as these minority populations have rapidly increased as a result of mass migration from Asian, Latin American, and Caribbean countries. But it remains to be seen whether third- and fourth-generation racial minority members will have high levels of intermarriage within each panethnic or racial group, comparable to multigeneration white Americans. It is anticipated that their high level of intermarriage will not lead to assimilation into American society because they belong to racial minority groups.

Interracial marriages are generally less common than the other two forms of intermarriages. African Americans in particular have had an exceptionally low intermarriage rate. During the periods of slavery, unions between whites and blacks were prohibited legally in almost all states, although many white slave owners raped black slaves and mixed-race children resulted. In the Jim Crow system, almost all Southern states established the antimiscegenation laws that banned interracial marriages between whites and members of other racial minority groups. Various antimiscegenation laws lasted until 1967, when the U.S. Supreme Court declared them unconstitutional. Such formal segregation and related discrimination certainly discouraged interracial marriage between whites and African Americans. Children of black-white interracial marriages were treated as black.

In fact, according to the one drop rule, one drop of African American blood identified a person as black.

Since the Supreme Court struck down antimiscegenation laws in 1967, black-white intermarriages have steadily increased. Nevertheless, a tiny proportion of African American marriages are interracial marriages. In the mid-1990s, only 1 percent of black women and 3 percent of black men were married to persons other than blacks, mostly to whites. Given the great social distance between African Americans and whites and a high level of residential segregation of African Americans, this extremely low rate of interracial marriage is not surprising. Of white-black interracial marriages, about 75 percent are marriages between black men and white women. Often, it is occupationally successful African American men who marry white women. This kind of interracial marriage is often interpreted as an exchange of black men's high occupational status with white women's superior racial status.

In 1990, about 40 percent of native-born Asian Americans had intermarried, most of them with white spouses. Their high intermarriage rate may be the result of a low level of social distance between Asian and white Americans and Asian Americans' high socioeconomic status. But it is also a result of their small population size. As its native-born adult population increases in the future, more and more Asian Americans may be able to marry members of their own ethnic group and other Asian Americans. Even though Hispanics are shown to have married interracially as often as (if not more than) Asian Americans, racial origins of their marriage partners are much more diverse, including both white and black. This is because of their diverse racial characteristics.

Native Americans have always shown a high rate of interracial marriage, which is due to their small population and a low level of segregation. Today, most Native Americans are children of interracial marriages between Native Americans and other racial groups. Children of interracial marriages between Native Americans and others have a wider option as far as their ethnic identification is concerned. In spite of this possibility, a high proportion of children of such interracial marriages tend to identify themselves as Native Americans.

SHIN KIM AND KWANG CHUNG KIM

See also

Anti-Miscegenation Laws; Hypodescent (One Drop Rule)

Further Reading:
Kennedy, R.J.R. "Single or Triple Melting Pot? Intermarriage Trends in New Haven, 1870–1940." *American Journal of Sociology* 49 (1984): 331–39.
Mathabane, Mark, and Gail Mathabane. *Love in Black and White: The Triumph of Love over Prejudice and Taboo.* New York: HarperCollins, 1992.
Qianm Zhenchao, Sampson Lee Blair, and Stacey Ruf. "Asian American Interracial and Interethnic Marriages: Differences by Education and Nativity." *International Migration Review* 35 (2001): 557–86.
Rosenblatt, Paul C., Terri A. Karis, and Richard Powell. *Multiracial Couples: Black and White Voices.* Thousand Oaks, CA: Sage Publications, 1995.

Intersectionality

Intersectionality, also known as "intersectional social analysis," refers to the study of intersections between various systems of oppression or discrimination. The concept of intersectionality originates primarily from the scholarly consideration among American women of everyday experiences of social inequality. Out of these lived experiences of inequality, intersectionality as a theory suggests that categories of identity such as race, class, gender, and sexual orientation can interact on multiple levels to contribute to a larger system of social inequality. Intersectional perspectives stem from the consideration of how women of different colors and classes experience their racial, gender, and class identities, leading to multiple forms of social oppression based on these identities (i.e., racism, sexism, and classism). The core scientific assumptions and theories of intersectionality research have been most fully articulated and developed by black and multiracial feminist American sociologists and U.S. social theorists.

At its core, intersectionality theory recognizes that a person lives simultaneously in multiple identity categories, including race, class, gender, and ethnicity, and therefore also lives under any and all social oppressions based on these identities. These various social oppressions can intersect to form a larger system of oppression for individuals and groups alike. The sociologists perhaps best known for their work on intersectionality theory are Irene Browne and Joya Misra. Browne and Misra have explained that intersectionality is one of the few theories that is actually capable of capturing the simultaneity or complexity of overlapping social variables like race, sex, class, and ethnicity, and their corresponding social oppressions, i.e. racisms, sexisms, classisms, and ethnicisms.

One fundamental premise of intersectionality holds that there are multiple forms of each type of social oppression. For example, intersectionality describes various racisms and sexisms rather than a single type of racism or sexism. According to intersectionality, black men and black women do not experience the same forms of racism, just as white and black women do not experience the same forms of sexism. Other theories have expanded on this concept, such as the theory of Black Feminist Thought. Often, social oppressions such as sexism and racism can overlap. For example, according to Black Feminist Thought scholar Patricia Hill Collins, sexisms for blacks are racialized, such that certain "controlling images" are applied to black women (e.g., the welfare queen, the Jezebel, the Hoochie, and the Church Lady) which cannot apply to black men (who experience male-sexist forms of racism such as the "black-dead-beat-dad"). This example illustrates that for blacks, there are at least two forms of sexism. Furthermore, these sexisms also result in distinct social experiences for women that are intricately tied to their race. Black women, for example, have among the lowest levels of privilege and advantage in U.S. society, and are the least likely of all to marry white men who have historically been at the opposite end of the spectrum with the highest levels of privilege and advantage. As a direct consequence of being the least likely to marry the most socially privileged white men, black women generally do not receive the racial privilege benefits that stem from being white wives and white daughters. Thus, the lived experience of black women in American society illustrates the core theory of intersectionality, which is that various forms of discrimination can intersect to create a much larger system of oppression for minority groups.

Intersectionality is very different from most previous understandings of social oppression and social identity. For example, nonintersectional approaches have tended to group black women along with black men, by race, when examining questions of social stratification and racial inequality. Likewise, these same nonintersectional approaches have tended to group black women with white women, by gender, when examining questions of sexism, gender inequality or sex stratification. Intersectional perspectives explain why analytically grouping black women with these two other populations of black men and white women should not be done in social analysis. Intersectionality holds that the system of oppression experienced by black women is very different than the one experienced by black men or white women.

Intersectional theories perhaps best explain the experience of black women, since this minority group experiences the dual oppressions of being both female and black. According to intersectionality, black women frequently occupy positions on the lowest rungs of society, preventing them from existing fully as Blacks, alongside black men, or as women, alongside nonblack women. Instead, intersectional theory proposes that it is within the confines of their own racial, gender, and class experience that black women experience gendered forms of racism not directed toward their black male peers. Furthermore, the racialized sexism directed towards a black woman is very different from the sexism facing her white female peers. Accordingly, this "racialized sexism" and "gendered racism" is also class differentiated in complex ways, cutting across racial and gender categories.

However, it has been difficult scientifically to assess the extent of these intersecting systems of oppression in U.S. society. It has not helped that early research programs tended to particularize and to separate from one another the three studies of race/racism, class/classism, and gender/sexism. For example, Marxism and Marxist forms of social analysis stress the primacy of class and classism, holding that gender and racial identities and oppressions all originate from forms of class and classism. Consequently, Marxists have tended to deemphasize the respective fights against sexism and racism in which women and racial minorities have engaged, claiming that struggles with racism and sexism will disappear once their underlying cause—classism—is eradicated. Theories such as Marxism that focus on one form of oppression over all others, instead of seeing oppressions as interrelated and overlapping, tend to minimize the experience of groups such as black women who experience discrimination on multiple social levels.

Such "either/or" approaches to social life—where things like racism and sexism are treated merely as forms of classism—have long been unattractive to groups like black women, who often experience both sexism and racism. These types of considerations where some social variables and oppressions, such as class and classism, come before others, such as race and racism, result in distorted forms of social analysis. Intersectionality holds that theories such as Marxism cannot address the sexual and racial divisions, identities, and social oppressions that differently impact people of different race-sex-class categories. Intersectionality offers a scientific approach that can transcend these limitations.

SALVATORE LABARO

See also
Discrimination

Further Reading:
Browne, Irene, and Joya Misra. "The Intersection of Gender and Race in the Labor Market." *Annual Review of Sociology* 29 (2003): 487–513.
Collins, Patricia Hill. "Moving Beyond Gender: Intersectionality and Scientific Knowledge." In *Revisioning Gender*, edited by Myra Marx Ferree, Judith Lorber, and Beth B. Hess, 261–84. Thousand Oaks, CA: Sage, 1999.
Collins, Patricia Hill. *Black Feminist Thought: Knowledge, Consciousness, and the Politics of Empowerment*. New York: Routledge, 2000.
Hurtado, Aida. "Relating to Privilege: Seduction and Rejection in the Subordination of White Women and Women of Color." *Signs* 14 (1989): 833–55.

Invisible Hand, The

Adam Smith, who lived during the 18th century, advanced the term the "invisible hand." This invisible hand guarantees the marketplace will provide for society's good. Whenever individuals follow their own pursuits, they are also helping the market—even though they might not know it. There is an invisible hand that guides the marketplace toward achieving the best for society.

As Smith writes in *Wealth of Nations*, "[An individual] neither intends to promote the public interest, not knows how much he is promoting. By preferring the support of domestic to that of foreign industry, he intends only his own security; and by directing that industry in such a manner as its produce may be the greatest value, he intends only his own gain, and he is in this, as in many other cases, led by an invisible hand to promote an end which was no part his intention" (2009). In other words, the marketplace can run and benefit society on its own. There is no need for governmental regulations to control the marketplace. According to this concept, regulations limit the power of the free market.

Equal opportunity advocates are often critical of the free-market ideology, because they believe the free market does not give equal opportunity to everyone. These advocates argue that legislation is needed to help ensure that everyone has the opportunity to get a job and not allow for any type of discrimination or racism. Such legislation includes affirmative action and antidiscriminatory laws. These laws are believed to expand the welfare of the nation and give it more prosperity. According to them, those who argue against such policy are putting aside the nation's problems.

Proponents of the free-market system say those who want to place restrictions on the market are imposing morality on the American population and are placing limitations on an individual's right to choose. Ideally, the marketplace will eliminate the effects of discrimination without any regulations. According to this logic, racist, white employers may hire a black employee over a white employee, because they can pay a black employee less due to the employer's racism. Then, those companies that hire white candidates and pay them more will go bankrupt, because they cannot compete with the companies who hire the black candidates for a much lower salary. They also say that companies that hire only white candidates have a smaller pool of candidates to use. This will cause the company to have a longer and much more extensive search. They will also have lost productivity due to the longer searches. Due to the scarce labor supply, they will have to pay higher wages. Thus, the marketplace is correcting itself.

The market may correct itself, but blacks are still discriminated against by receiving the low wages. The government needs to recognize the importance of minority labor and business to the work force and create an environment that encourages success.

ALAN VINCENT GRIGSBY

See also
Hiring Practices

Further Reading:
Bishop, John D. "Adam Smith's Invisible Hand Argument." *Journal of Business Ethics* 14, no. 3 (1995): 165–80.

Feiner, Susan F., and Bruce B. Roberts. "Hidden by the Invisible Hand: Neoclassical Economic Theory and the Textbook Treatment of Race and Gender." *Gender and Society* 4, no. 2 (1990): 159–81.

Harrison, P. "Adam Smith and the History of the Invisible Hand." *Journal of the History of Ideas* 72, no. 1 (2011): 29–49.

Joyce, H. "Adam Smith and the Invisible Hand." +plus magazine. March 1, 2001. plus.maths.org/content/adam-smith-and-invisible-hand. Accessed January 2, 2012.

Portillo, Javier, and Walter E. Block "Anti-Discrimination Laws: Undermining Our Rights." *Journal of Business Ethics* 109, no. 2 (2012): 209–17.

Rothschild, Emma. (1994). "Adam Smith and the Invisible Hand." *American Economic Review* 84, no. 2 (1994): 319–22.

Smith, A. *An Inquiry into the Nature and Causes of the Wealth of Nations.* Digireads.com Publishing, 2009 [1776].

Iran Hostage Crisis and Anti-Iranian Stereotypes

The Iran hostage crisis began on November 4, 1979, when a group of Iranian students seized the U.S. embassy in Tehran, taking its employees hostage. Ayatollah Khomeini, the charismatic leader of the Iranian Revolution (1978–1979), denounced the United States for its longtime support of the deposed leader Reza Shah Pahlavi. When the exiled shah entered the United States in October for medical care, many Iranians feared a repetition of the U.S.-assisted coup that had put him back on the throne in 1953. At Khomeini's encouragement, 52 Americans were taken hostage as a preventative measure. President Jimmy Carter immediately applied economic and diplomatic pressure on Iran; Iranian diplomats in the United States were expelled, oil imports from Iran were stopped, and around $8 billion of Iranian assets in the United States were frozen. At the same time, he began several diplomatic and military initiatives to free the hostages, all of which failed. Then, in exchange for the hostages, the United States agreed to unfreeze almost all the Iranian assets. Finally, on January 20, 1981—only a few hours after Carter left office—all hostages were released, after 444 days in captivity. Clearly, the hostages were used as pawns to deal a blow to Carter's incumbency. The hostage crisis occurred right after the revolution in Iran, which led to a massive influx of Iranian exiles into the United States.

Iran hostage crisis student demonstration in Washington, D.C., November 9, 1979. (Library of Congress)

Ironically, these exiles faced unfair targeting and scapegoating, despite their opposition to the new Iranian regime.

The hostage crisis prompted a presidential order referred to as the "Iranian Control Program." The program screened, on a case-by-case basis, almost 57,000 Iranian students—the single largest group of foreign students—to make sure that they were in the United States legally. After holding 7,177 deportation hearings, 3,088 students were ordered to leave the United States, and the departure of 445 was verified. The program was not aimed at students only, but in the words of the Immigration and Naturalization Service, the new policy "effectively prohibited the entry of most Iranians into this country." In light of the permanent closure of the American embassy in Iran, even a quarter of a century later Iranians seeking a U.S. visa must first travel to another country.

Iranian Americans become scapegoats every time conflict erupts between Iran and the United States. This started with the Iranian revolution, with its vehemently anti-American slogans, peaked during the hostage crisis, and flared up again in the post-9/11 era, when President George W. Bush included Iran in the "axis of evil" and the U.S. Department of Justice ordered the "special registration" of recent immigrant men, eventually leading to the detention of some in Los Angeles. There have also been widespread allegations that the Iranian government is acquiring the raw materials and technology to build an atomic bomb, although these have been toned down since June of 2004 because of the Iranian government's cooperation with the International Atomic Energy Agency's standards.

Iranian Americans are perceived as Islamic fundamentalists and, by analogy, terrorists. However, significant proportions of Iranians in the United States are not even Muslims; they overrepresent Iran's religious minorities—Christians (mostly Armenians and Assyrians), Bahais, Jews, and Zoroastrians. In general, Iranian Americans are one of the most educated and skilled immigrant groups and present few social problems. They have suffered disproportionately and inadvertently from widespread American stereotypes dating back to 1978–1979.

MEHDI BOZORGMEHR AND ANNY BAKALIAN

See also
Discrimination; Journalism and Racial Stereotypes; Prejudice; Racism

Further Reading:
Ehrlich, Howard J. *Hate Crimes and Ethnoviolence: The History, Current Affairs and Future of Discrimination in America.* Boulder, CO: Westview Press, 2009.
National Research Council. *Measuring Racial Discrimination.* Washington, D.C.: National Academies Press, 2004.
Omi, Michael and Howard Winant. *Racial Formation in the United States: From the 1960s to the 1990s.* London: Routledge, 1994.

Islamic Fundamentalism

Islamic Fundamentalism is known by other names, including "militant political Islam," "Islamic extremism," and the like. The vast majority of Muslims are keen on highlighting the fact that this type of Islamic practice is not generally representative of the aims of either Shi'ite or Sunni branches of Islamic faith. Even prior to September 11, 2001, Islamic fundamentalism as a term and concept was being increasingly linked to those Islamic groups that embraced jihadist (holy war) or other violent solutions to perceived problems, or practiced suicide bombing and other acts of "martyrdom" as an apt expression of fidelity to Allah. Algeria, Turkey, Egypt, Burma, India (Kashmir Region), and Afghanistan have all received significant political attention in the past 10 years because of their struggle with Islamic fundamentalist parties or groups that sought to alter the course of government in their respective countries. Both the Muslim Brotherhood (in Egypt) and Taliban forces (in Afghanistan) have been repeatedly associated with violent actions.

Muslim scholars seem to be in agreement that there are a number of factors that account for the growth in Islamic fundamentalism since the early 1990s. One of the most often cited reasons involves U.S. support for Israel and an apparent lack of proportionate support for Arabs. The legacy of a

Opposed Fundamentalisms?

Fundamentalism, despite the widespread usage of the term, has nonetheless been the object of some disagreement. Regardless of some disagreement about the definition of the term, fundamentalism has usually been associated with absolute moral commitment. As such, it is noteworthy that fundamentalism thrives in nations that may be perceived as politically opposed to one another. Islamic fundamentalism is stoutly identified with the control of women, a policy that rejects a plurality of views, and a movement that joins religion and politics in a way that many Americans consider in opposition to the separation of church and state. In this sense, Americans endorse a "secular" government. Despite the formal commitment to Thomas Jefferson's "wall of separation" between an established faith and governmental operations, this has not prevented Christian fundamentalism from influencing the American political process. Fundamentalism in the United States, in contrast, has been associated with staunch commitments to oppose gay marriage and abortion, while embracing prayer in school and a literalist view of the Bible. These views have affected the course of Republican politics, especially in the Southern regions of the United States. Despite some key differences, therefore, fundamentalism may thrive in countries that may otherwise not enjoy amicable relations.

perceived abuse of military power in Iraq during and after the Persian Gulf War has also served as fertile soil for the growth of oppositional groups. A number of grievances also emerged from perceived hypocritical relations with Islamic fundamentalist groups and Muslim monarchs or dictators during the latter half of 20th century. Bob Woodward's book, *Veil: The Secret Wars of the CIA 1981–87,* identifies intimate relations between the American spy agency and the Pakistani dictator Mohammed Zia ul-Haq, Sudan's Jaffar Numeiri, Egypt's Anwar Sadat, and a number of others. Also, a number of Muslims have found it appalling that the United States was willing to have close relations with Afghan Islamic fundamentalist groups between the end of World War II and the collapse of the Soviet Union, only to quickly abandon them

---

"Green Menace"

During the four decades of the Cold War, the Soviet Union—the "Red Menace"—was depicted as a sinister military and ideological threat to the American way of life. With the collapse of the Soviet Union and the rise of the United States as the dominant player in international politics, in recent years a "Green Menace" has emerged in the American popular and political imagination. The "Green Menace" represents the assumed danger posed by Islamic fundamentalism (Islam is represented by the color green). First given life in the 1970s through the Iranian Revolution and the Tehran embassy hostage crisis, the image of the Green Menace depicts Islamic revivalism as a virulent threat to American political dominance and the West's social and cultural order. Since the mid-1990s, terrorist activities against U.S. interests worldwide—culminating in the 2001 World Trade Center and Pentagon attacks—have cemented the picture of the United States under hostile attack from an ominous "green" power.

Like the "Red Menace" of previous years, the "Green Menace" is the product of political ideology, mass media, and popular culture. It is also the product of oversimplification. The creation of an identifiable menace may prove useful for political mobilization, because a clear enemy is presented against whom the United States can marshal military and financial resources. It may, however, have negative consequences as well, particularly for the rapidly growing Middle Eastern population of the United States. Television and media images that promote negative stereotyping of Arabs reinforce political messages of a sinister Islamic enemy. Islam is unfairly equated with fundamentalism, and fundamentalism with terrorist activity—this denies the immense diversity of Islam within both religious and political spheres. Also, propagation of the Green Menace imagery may encourage a monolithic, and wholly negative, view of Middle Easterners in America, who in fact have varied ethnic, national, and religious allegiances.

REBEKAH LEE

---

once the objectives of the United States were achieved. In this vein, there is an important historical development to appreciate. During the 1980s, Western policy makers and journalists called these same Afghan Islamic groups "freedom fighters," but then abandoned the moniker once collective Western perceptions of the Iranian arch-fundamentalist Ayatollah Khomeini took a turn for the worse. Khomeini was fond of calling the United States "the Great Satan," and apparently guided Iranian students to take control of the U.S. embassy in Tehran on November 4, 1979. It was these students that the media referred to as Islamic fundamentalists. Predictably, the term became a byword the world over, particularly in the United States and Europe.

Perhaps most important among the reasons for the growth of Islamic fundamentalism is the commitment to the unity of Muslims beyond any discrete or independent Muslim nation-states, which many Muslims consider to be alien to the faith of Islam at its roots. Hence, Osama bin Laden and his supporters, prior to the 9/11 attacks, had gained considerable support for the idea that a joint, international army of the ummah (Muslim faithful) was needed to counter

the alleged arrogance and hypocrisy of the United States and other Western nations.

Muhammad Ali-Siddiqi, however, argues for an important distinction between fanaticism and fundamentalism (Mustikhan 1999: 74). Central to this distinction is the claim that fundamentalism has always existed in one form or another in Muslim societies, just as Christian fundamentalism has likewise played a key role in the development of society in the United States. This is also valid for the fundamentalisms that have grown out of the Judaic, Hindu, and Buddhist faiths. Acknowledging this point is different, of course, from asserting that fundamentalism is always and necessarily tied to a "fanatic" that is willing to murder his or her enemies. By assuming that all Muslim fundamentalists are potential suicide bombers or terrorists, many have argued, the gap between Muslims and non-Muslims in the West has only widened, magnifying their disagreements and encouraging a deeper hold of prevailing stereotypes and prejudices between the camps. Put simply, the more extreme the assumptions made about Muslims in general, the more likely that the opposition will grow to be just that: extreme, both in its ideas about what actually amounts to fidelity to God in the present conflict and in its actions against others.

Finally, it is imperative, therefore, to take note of another point of contention in understanding the nature of Islamic fundamentalism. At issue here are not the standard practices of Islam: circumcising male children, girls and women wearing headscarves, praying five times daily, fasting during Ramadan, giving 2.5 percent of one's accumulated yearly wealth to the poor, or making the annual pilgrimage to the Kaaba in Mecca, Saudi Arabia (Mustikhan 1999: 74). With respect to fundamentalism, the notion of jihad (holy war) is crucial. Muslims are in disagreement as to whether the Quran prescribes jihad as aggressive self-defense or as offensive military subjugation in the name of expanding Islam. What is certain, indeed, is that the course of the violent strain of Islamic fundamentalism will depend on how Western nations handle their relationship with Muslim societies.

GABRIEL SANTOS

See also
Aryan Brotherhood; Patriot Act of 2001; Terrorism

Further Reading:

Barkun, Michael. "Religious Violence and the Myth of Fundamentalism." In *Religious Fundamentalism and Political Extremism*, edited by Leonard Weinberg and Ami Pedahzur, 55–71. London: Frank Cass Publishers, 2004.

Herriot, Peter. *Religious Fundamentalism: Global, Local, and Personal*. London: Routledge, 2009.

Mustikhan, Ahmar. "Different Faces of Islamic Fundamentalism." *World & I*, July 1999, 74.

Woodward, Bob. *Veil: The Secret Wars of the CIA 1981–87*. New York: Simon and Schuster, 2005.

Islamofascism

Islamofascism is a pejorative or derogatory term that gained considerable popularity during the presidency of George W. Bush, especially during the period following the extremist attacks of September 11, 2001. The term, more specifically, was employed to specify the character of terrorism that the United States was poised to confront by means of a multifaceted national security campaign in the homeland and abroad (measures generally referred to as the "War on Terror"). For instance, after British police thwarted a plot to detonate explosives in aircraft flying over the Atlantic Ocean, President Bush made the following statement in Green Bay, Wisconsin: "The recent arrests that our fellow citizens are now learning about are a stark reminder that this nation is at war with Islamic fascists." Remarkably, the term grew to such a degree of prominence that by October 2007, the well-known conservative policy advocate David Horowitz initiated an "Islamofascism Awareness Week," which was intended to run from October 22 to October 26, with the aim of rousing the biggest "conservative campus protest" ever (Marshall 2007: 17). Seventy campuses, including Georgetown University and George Washington University, participated in the events, which included screenings of *Obsession*, a documentary about Islamic radicalism and more formal talks about related foreign policy.

To be sure, the use of the term, as well as the term itself, has been highly contested. Many political and social critics have asserted it is highly misleading for several reasons. A number of these reasons are relevant to a consideration of the significant role of both religion and race with respect to Islamophobia and the ongoing "War on Terror." More importantly, the term has decisively shaped the views of American citizens and residents in the United States with respect to what constitutes loyal citizenship. Hence, it is fitting to summarize the more focal criticisms and praises directed at the term itself and then link these misgivings with critical racial issues surrounding Islam in the United States.

Islamofascism has caused quite a stir among scholars of fascism that find it difficult to identify the classic instances of fascism as a popular political movement during the 1920s and 1930s in Europe with the politics of Islamic nation-states or positions of other Islamic groups (whether Shi'ite or Sunni) in the late 20th and early 21st century. As Robert Paxton, author of *Anatomy of Fascism*, has argued, the use of the term *Islamofascism* is both a historical error and an inappropriate use of language to the extent that it misrepresents the actual characteristics of the groups to which it is supposed to refer. Indeed, the fascist regimes of the early to mid-20th century, primarily those of Benito Mussolini in Italy and Adolf Hitler in Germany, were nationalist revival movements that relied upon a populist dictatorship to strengthen their respective nations. Most interestingly, the nations that embraced fascism were relatively young democracies that failed or underwent momentous crises in response to which

> ## *World War IV: The Long Struggle Against Islamofascism*
>
> As the term *Islamofascism* garnered evermore attention in the national political scene, Norman Podhoretz's book, *World War IV: The Long Struggle Against Islamofascism*, pushed the debate to even greater levels of controversy. The book was published during the ongoing U.S. military engagement in Afghanistan and Iraq, defending these endeavors arising out of George W. Bush's "war" strategy that endorsed preemptive strikes, regime change, and the spreading of democracy in the Middle East. Notably, Podhoretz surmises that the struggle against Islamofascists has placed the United States in the midst of a global confrontation that he calls "World War IV," and that it may be more difficult to attain victory in this struggle than it was to do the same against the Nazis and the Soviet Union. The major threat, Podhoretz claims, is the possible possession of weapons of mass destruction among numerous well-financed violent Islamic fundamentalist groups that can possibly recruit even more militants in the next 10 years. Podhoretz endorses the view, considered outlandish by many, that up to 10 to 15 percent of Muslims are committed Islamofascists, which amounts to 200 million adherents. These claims and others, and their implications, catapulted this book to the center of the public discussion concerning Islamofascism.

dictatorship and the acceptance of limitations to certain freedoms was deemed necessary. None of these qualities seem to fit the groups to which the term *Islamofascism* seems to be directed. Most often Hezbollah and similar movements are understood as Islamic fundamentalist movements and hence have no appreciable relationship with failed democracy. In fact, Islamic movements that have been associated with violent attack (and which do not represent the vast majority of Islamic adherents) do not operate through an existing state—that is, by means of the centralized authority of a nation-state. As Paxton claims, the majority of "Islamic fundamentalists have contempt and hatred for existing Middle Eastern states like Saudi Arabia or Egypt or Jordan that are in the hands of conservatives" (Paxton in Neal 2006).

It is worth elaborating upon the condition of the nations that turned to fascism in the early 20th century: most of these nations were divided, economically weak, or politically unstable and hence sought some way to unify the citizenry, which often led them to embrace the need to expel any foreign, "contaminating" elements from the populace. This general policy of expulsion or exclusion leads directly to matters of race, racism, and racialized politics. It is for this very reason that the late social critic Christopher Hitchens argued that the term *Islamofascism* is valid: Islamic extremists tend to act as those exalting the "pure" and exclusive over against the "impure" and profane. In any event, to the extent that fascism points toward the demonization of a certain group that is labeled as biologically inferior or undeserving of a given nation, it is important to recognize how the extensive use of specific terms transforms the public language and prominent symbols that circulate throughout the political culture of a nation. Islamofascism has been adopted and promoted in a number of political contexts or situations as a supposedly helpful term that accurately characterizes certain oppositional, Islamic fundamentalist groups. This has been carried out during a post–September 11 period that has seen an increase in the popularity of highly racialized political perspectives that tightly associate, as if completely natural, the faith of Islam with cold-hearted and fanatical terrorists. Consequently, many followers of Islam are thereby deemed by many as worthy of exclusion from certain basic rights and freedoms and hence daily life is haunted by the constant threat of discrimination.

GABRIEL SANTOS

See also

Islamophobia; Patriot Act of 2001; September 11, 2001, Terrorism, Discriminatory Reactions to

Further Reading:

Conan, Neal. "What Is Islamofascism?" *Talk of The Nation*, August 31, 2006.

Hitchens, Christopher. "Defending Islamofascism." *Slate*, October 22, 2007. http://www.slate.com/articles/news_and_politics/fighting_words/2007/10/defending_islamofascism.html.

Marshall, Josh. "Islamofascism Fallacies." *The Hill*, October 26, 2007, Comment Section, Final Edition.

Podhoretz, Norman. *World War IV: The Long Struggle Against Islamofascism*. New York: Vintage, 2008.

Scruton, Roger. "Islamofascism." *Wall Street Journal*, August 17, 2006, A8.

Sugden, Joanna and Robert S. McCain. "Exposing Islamofascism." *Washington Times*, April 18, 2007, A02.

Islamophobia

Islamophobia, which as a term translates into "the fear of Islam," is a broad term that captures the prejudices, stereotypes, and discriminatory actions resulting from unjustified perceptions regarding Islam and Muslims. It is a widespread social condition that has grown in intensity since the attacks of September 11, 2001. Even prior to this event, however, Islamophobia had already created a social atmosphere in which Muslims were roundly denigrated and in many places treated as second-class citizens. This is evident in the initial response to the Murrah Federal Building bombing in Oklahoma City, after which two state legislators openly predicted that a Muslim must have been responsible for perpetrating the attack that killed adult federal employees, clients, and children located in the ground-floor daycare center. As we now know, a white American Gulf War veteran, Timothy McVeigh, took responsibility for the attack and was consequently charged, convicted, and executed. Prior to the discovery of McVeigh's involvement, it was not uncommon to hear reports of Muslim residents being threatened, openly insulted, or even physically attacked. During this same period, a local head of a Mosque in Oklahoma City daily urged the completely innocent adherents under his care that if any had been involved in the attack, they should confess to the crime quickly in order to prevent any escalation in local conflict.

Muslims and people of other faiths gather at the capitol in Hartford, Connecticut, to discuss what they call "Islamophobia" across the country and concerns for their safety during the holy month of Ramadan. (Associated Press)

Indeed, Islamophobia appears in a number of guises, and encourages stereotyping, prejudices, hostility, discriminatory treatment, and the denigration of the most sacred symbols of Islam. From a racial and historical perspective, there is a certain irony to the many factors that fuel this form of fear and opposition. Some commentators have drawn attention to the fact that certain Jewish residents of the United States and Israel, for whom racism in the form of anti-Semitism is well known, have endorsed Islamophobia and actively supported anti-Muslim organizations. Nina Rosenwald, the daughter of respected Jewish philanthropist, William Rosenwald, has purportedly supported a sizable number of anti-Muslim organizations, including the American Israel Public Affairs Committee (AIPAC). AIPAC has actively promoted a joint Israeli-American military attack on Iran for a number of years and routinely speaks against Sharia, ethical teachings that guide the daily life of Muslims. Remarkably, this case demonstrates how certain political commitments can override a common history of exclusion and degradation.

Some thinkers believe that the increasing number of Muslim citizens and asylum seekers in Western nations that wish to resist assimilation and preserve their own identity is also a contributing factor to the intensification of prejudice and discrimination regarding Islam and Muslims. A large number of Americans, themselves descendants of immigrants that entered the United States in the late 19th century and early 20th century, express bewilderment and even scorn toward Muslims that do not, as their forebears did, shed certain cultural practices or beliefs in order to assimilate into the American social order. The anti-Sharia campaigns that have grown since 2010 clearly demonstrate that Islamophobia persists as a practice of discrimination, not simply among residents and citizens of the United States, but even among their purported political and civic leaders.

One complicating factor in the challenge surrounding Islamophobia has emerged from evidently feminist criticisms about the unequal treatment of women, with special attention directed toward the apparent misogyny (women-hating) that characterizes the relationship between Muslim men and women. Is it possible, however, to raise valid ethical or moral questions about how Muslims understand and practice gender and sexuality without perpetuating Islamophobia—that is, without generating more reasons for undue fear, resentment, and opposition? Many feminists in the West have sternly criticized the treatment of women in a number of Muslim-majority nations, citing the mandatory wearing of the veil and overly submissive conduct toward men as directly opposed to the notion of gender equality and freedom of expression. In doing so, feminists imply that Western treatment of women is the model to be upheld in contrast to "oppressive Islam" (Hasan 2012: 57). This negative view of Islam, opponents argue, is unjustified and founded upon a lack of appreciation for Islamic faith from an insider's perspective. Without appreciating the many differences between and among Muslim-majority nations, which reflect a very wide range of women's experiences, the view that all Muslim women are "shackled" and oppressed has been employed to justify military campaigns against certain Middle Eastern nations.

GABRIEL SANTOS

See also

Cultural Racism; Culture; Racism; Xenophobia

Further Reading:

Bleich, Erik. "What Is Islamophobia and How Much Is There? Theorizing and Measuring an Emerging Comparative Concept." *American Behavioral Scientist* 55 (2011): 1581–1600.

Blumenthal, Max. "Islamophobia's Sugar Mama." *Nation*, July 2, 2012, 28–31.

Esposito, John, and Ibrahim Kalin. *Islamophobia: The Challenge of 21st Century Pluralism.* New York: Oxford University Press, 2011.

Hasan, Mahmudul Md. "Feminism as Islamophobia: A Review of Misogyny Charges Against Islam." *Intellectual Discourse* 20 (2012): 55–78.

J

Jackson, Jesse (b. 1941)

African American civil rights activist, minister, and politician Jesse Jackson was the first African American man to run for U.S. president, having a long career in social activism and involvement in the civil rights movement. Through the Rainbow PUSH Coalition (formerly the National Rainbow Coalition and People United to Save Humanity), Jackson has continually been involved in public debates over civil rights, racism, and the socioeconomic status of people of color, often mired in controversy.

Noah Robinson and Helen Burns's son, Jesse Louis Burns was born on October 8, 1941, in Greenville, South Carolina. However, Robinson was already married and thus Jackson was born out of wedlock. When Jackson was two years old, Helen Burns married Charles Jackson, who gave Jackson his surname. Jackson attended the segregated schools of Greenville. He also attended the Longbranch Baptist Church each Sunday for services. When Jackson was nine years old, he gave his first public speech at a Christmas pageant at church. Growing up in the Jim Crow South, Jackson experienced segregation and racial discrimination on a daily basis.

Throughout his years at the African American Sterling High School in Greenville, Jackson pursued class offices, having been elected president of the honor society and president of his class in the ninth grade. He was also an athlete, playing football, basketball, and baseball in high school. One of

Jackson's chief competitors was Dickie Dietz, the top quarterback at the all-white Greenville High School across town from Sterling High. In 1959, after graduating, both of them were approached by a scout for the New York Giants. However, Jackson discovered that while he was offered $6,000 a year to play for the Giants, Dietz had been offered $95,000 a year. Jackson refused the offer and decided to continue his education, accepting an athletic scholarship at the University of Illinois.

Jackson attended the University of Illinois from 1959 to 1960, but could not achieve his goal of being a quarterback on the college football team. African American players were expected to be halfbacks or ends. Jackson experienced the tacit segregation on the campus. At the end of his freshman year, Jackson transferred to North Carolina Agricultural and Technical College (now a state university). When Jackson arrived at A&T, he immediately joined the Congress of Racial Equality (CORE). He was soon in a leadership position, organizing marches and protests almost daily. He was also an honors student and president of the student body. In June 1963, Jackson was arrested, charged with inciting a riot in downtown Greensboro. His girlfriend and wife-to-be, Jacqueline Davis, stood by him during this time. Later, the two were married in a quiet ceremony at Jackson's parents' home in Greenville. In his senior year, 1964, he was elected president of the newly formed North Carolina Intercollegiate

Rainbow Coalition

The Rainbow Coalition is an organization founded in 1985 by Rev. Jesse Jackson with the goal of "uniting people of diverse ethnic, religious, economic, and political backgrounds" in a push for "social, racial, and economic justice" through political empowerment and changes in public policy. It sees itself as a child of the civil rights movement, using demonstrations and boycotts as well as litigation and lobbying to promote its interests. Since its founding, the Rainbow Coalition has been active in voter registration, getting people of color elected, lobbying for equal-opportunity employment in various industries, and bringing attention to U.S. foreign policy in South Africa and Haiti.

In 1996, the Rainbow Coalition merged with People United to Serve Humanity (PUSH), another organization that Jackson founded in 1971 to expand educational and employment opportunities for disadvantaged people of color. The united single organization is referred to as the Rainbow/PUSH Coalition. Rainbow/PUSH currently focuses on HIV/AIDS issues, advocating for minority and women-owned businesses, linkages between black churches, local civil rights issues, voter registration, prison ministry and services for prisoners, and health insurance for children.

MIKAILA MARIEL LEMONIK ARTHUR

Council on Human Rights, and became a field representative for CORE. His responsibilities included attending a number of workshops led by Dr. Martin Luther King, Jr. and his staff. After graduation, Jackson and his family, which now included daughter Santita, moved north to Chicago, where Jackson enrolled at the Chicago Theological Seminary (CTS). While at CTS, Jackson joined King's Southern Christian Leadership Conference (SCLC).

During the protest march in Selma, Alabama, in 1965, Jackson came to the attention of King and the SCLC. The SCLC leaders noticed that during a number of speeches held at Brown Chapel in Selma, Jackson also stood up and spoke, impressing the audience with his oratory skills. During 1966, the SCLC extended its economic program, Operation Breadbasket, northward. In January of that year, King flew to Chicago for a rally to promote the program, and Jackson was in the forefront, organizing the march. He gathered local ministers, urging their support, and marched through white neighborhoods. Jackson was so immersed in the civil rights activities in Chicago that he withdrew from CTS. In June 1968, he was ordained in the Baptist church, and in 1969 CTS granted him an honorary degree.

In the years following the SCLC march in Chicago, Jackson worked steadily to promote the SCLC's Operation Breadbasket, serving as its coordinator in Chicago for a year. Early in 1968, Jackson and other leaders of the SCLC began to plan the Poor People's Campaign that would include a march on Washington, D.C., to call attention to the thousands of poor and jobless in the country. Those attending built a tent city, Resurrection City, next to the Lincoln Memorial and named Jackson its city manager. King left the march to go to Memphis where sanitation workers were staging a strike, and Jackson followed. As a result, on April 4, 1968, Jackson was present at King's assassination. Jackson was on all the television news shows claiming he was the last man to speak to Dr. King. The story escalated to Jackson cradling the dying King in his arms. This situation displeased many members of the SCLC.

While Jackson was made the national director of Operation Breadbasket, he had lost much of the support of the SCLC. In 1971, Jackson staged a Black Expo in Chicago to aid African American business owners. There were rumors of Jackson refusing to share the proceeds from this event with the SCLC. Ralph Abernathy, the new head of the SCLC, went to Chicago to investigate. Although Abernathy found the charges were unfounded, he imposed a 60-day suspension from the SCLC on Jackson and ordered him to move to Atlanta where the SCLC could monitor him. As a result, Jackson quit the SCLC and started his own organization, Operation PUSH (People United to Save Humanity). Operation PUSH continued the same agenda in Chicago that Operation Breadbasket had begun. Jackson also promoted education through PUSH-Excel that worked to keep inner-city youth in school and to provide jobs for them.

After PUSH was organized in 1971, Jackson entered the political arena. He mounted a campaign against Chicago mayor Richard J. Daley, forming a third party, the Bread 'n Butter Party. However, he lacked support in the African

American community because he had alienated many of the local African American leaders by announcing his candidacy without consulting them. Jackson also faced the entrenched Daley Democratic political machine. Daley won by a wide margin. During the 1970s, Jackson continued to promote PUSH in Chicago, despite the fact that it had encountered a number of problems; paramount among them was the fact that the government, suspecting misappropriation of funds, was investigating its financial records. Jackson continued with his work and began earning an international reputation. In 1979, he traveled to South Africa to speak against apartheid, and to the Middle East to push for peace negotiations between the Palestinian Liberation Organization (PLO) and Israel. In contrast with South Africa, Jackson experienced outright hostility in Israel. He was criticized for allegedly endorsing the terrorist tactics of the PLO when he met with PLO leader Yasser Arafat.

On November 3, 1983, Jackson announced his intention to run for president at a rally held in Washington, D.C. The National Rainbow Coalition was established, with Jackson as its first and only candidate, as a coalition of various interests and ethnic groups. In 1984, he flew to Syria and successfully negotiated the release of Lt. Robert O. Goodman, a U.S. pilot who had been shot down and taken hostage. Jackson was praised by President Ronald Reagan for his efforts and gained credibility as a candidate. However, in February 1984, eight days before the New Hampshire primary, Milton Coleman, an African American reporter for the *Washington Post*, reported that Jackson had made a negative comment ("Hymietown") in reference to the large number of Jewish Americans in New York City. Although he publicly apologized, his campaign was tarnished. In the New Hampshire primary, Jackson finished fourth with only 5 percent of the vote. The charge of anti-Semitism would plague Jackson throughout his campaign and the rest of his political career. Despite this, at the 1984 Democratic National Convention, Jackson had won 384 delegates.

In 1988, Jackson ran for the presidency again. He had moved from Chicago to Washington, D.C., in an effort to establish political contacts. The Rainbow Coalition had more funds and far better organized. By the end of the various primaries, Jackson had won a number of them, including an unexpected victory in the state of Michigan. Although

his chances for a nomination for president at the National Democratic Convention were poor, Jackson was hoping to be asked to fill the vice presidential spot on Michael Dukakis's ticket. However, Dukakis chose Texas senator Lloyd Bentsen, without notifying Jackson beforehand. After an apology and discussion, Dukakis agreed to have Jackson introduce him at the convention; in return, Jackson would campaign on Dukakis's behalf.

Jackson did not run for the presidency in 1992 or 1996. In 1991, he ran and was elected "statehood senator" for the District of Columbia, a position established by the city to promote the statehood of Washington, D.C., in Congress. In February 1998, Jackson returned to Africa as the president's and secretary of state's special envoy for the promotion of democracy in Africa. During this trip, Jackson visited Kenya, the Democratic Republic of the Congo, and Liberia. In 1996, the National Rainbow Coalition was merged with PUSH as the Rainbow PUSH Coalition.

Jackson remained involved in politics while not actively running for office. He was critical of the George W. Bush administration on various occasions, particularly in regards to the Iraq War and the alleged irregularities in the 2000 and 2004 presidential elections. He generated significant controversy in 2001, when evidence was revealed of an extramarital affair with Karin Stanford, with whom he had a daughter. Moreover, it was alleged that he had given Rainbow PUSH Coalition funds to Stanford.

Jackson remains involved in politics through his leadership of the Rainbow PUSH Coalition and through his involvement in (often controversial) public debates over social justice in the national media.

JAMES HASKINS

See also

Civil Rights Movement; Sharpton, Al

Further Reading:

Haskins, James. *I Am Somebody!: A Biography of Jesse Jackson*. Hillside, NJ: Enslow Publishers, 1992.

LaBlanc, Michael L., ed. *Contemporary Black Biography: Profiles from the International Black Community*, Vol. 1. Detroit, MI: Gale Research, 1992.

"Special Envoy Jesse Jackson Travels Again to Africa." *Africa News Online*. Washington, DC: U.S. Department of State, 1998. http://www.africanews.org/usafrica/stories/19980206_feat3 .html. Accessed May 4, 1998.

James Byrd Jr. Murder

On June 7, 1998, James Byrd Jr., a 49-year-old black man, was murdered by three local white racists in Jasper, Texas. The exceptional brutality of the racially motivated crime drew national media attention and spurred a demand in Texas for the passage of special hate crimes legislation, which was opposed by then Texas governor George W. Bush.

While walking home along a country road near Jasper on June 7, Byrd was accosted by three white men in a pickup truck—John William King, 23; Shawn Berry, 23; and Lawrence Brewer Jr., 31. The men beat Byrd, attempted to slit his throat, and then chained him to the back of their truck, dragging his body for over three miles. An autopsy later suggested that Byrd was still alive for much of the dragging, and that he died only when he struck a culvert, which severed

Ricky Jason wears a photograph of James Byrd Jr. outside the Texas Department of Criminal Justice Huntsville Unit before the execution of Lawrence Russell Brewer in 2011. Brewer, one of two purported white supremacists condemned for the dragging death of James Byrd Jr., was executed on September 21, 2011. (AP Photo/David J. Phillip)

his head and right arm. Byrd's assailants were captured and tried for murder, with King and Brewer receiving death sentences and Berry sentenced to life in prison. These punishments led Gov. Bush to oppose a call for new state hate crimes legislation.

Since the three white men had apparently been members of white supremacy gangs during earlier periods of imprisonment in Texas, African American leaders, such as Jesse Jackson, denounced the Byrd murder as the most vicious form of racism. Basketball star Dennis Rodman offered to pay for Byrd's funeral and donated $25,000 to a fund created to support the Byrd family, which later created the James Byrd Foundation for Racial Healing to advocate for the passage of state and federal hate crimes laws. In 2001, Texas governor Rick Perry, who had succeeded to his office upon Bush's election as president in 2000, signed the James Byrd Jr. Hate Crimes Act, which amended existing state law on hate crimes to specifically cover and increase penalties for criminal acts undertaken on the basis of race, color, religion, national origin or ancestry, age, gender, disability, or sexual orientation.

In 2003, two films about the Byrd murder were released. *Jasper, Texas* was produced and shown on the Showtime Network. The documentary *Two Towns of Jasper*, a collaboration between black and white filmmakers, which used segregated crews to document black and white reaction in Jasper to the murder and the subsequent trial, was shown on the PBS *P.O.V.* series.

JOHN A. WAGNER

See also
American Literature and Racism

Further Reading:
Jasper, Texas. Directed by Jeffrey W. Bird. Written by Jonathan Estrin. Showtime Entertainment, 2003.

Texas NAACP, James Byrd Jr. Web site, http://www.texasnaacp.org.

Two Towns of Jasper. Produced and directed by Marco Williams and Whitney Dow, 2003.

Japanese American Citizens League (JACL)

The Japanese American Citizens League (JACL) is the nation's oldest and largest Asian American civil rights organization, with more than 30,000 members. The JACL was established in 1930, growing out of several local and regional organizations of the *nisei* (second-generation Japanese Americans). As a citizens league, the *issei* (immigrants) were excluded from joining the JACL. On the other hand, the *issei* community leaders did not approve the JACL's emphasis on Americanization. Japan's attack on the U.S. naval base at Pearl Harbor on December 7, 1941, changed the lives of both the *issei* and the *nisei*. Under Executive Order 9066, signed by President Franklin D. Roosevelt in 1942, all men, women, and children of Japanese descent in western coastal regions, including about two-thirds of the U.S.-born *nisei*, were rounded up and taken to guarded camps in the interior. The JACL wired President Roosevelt immediately after Pearl Harbor, demonstrating its loyalty to the United States, even if it meant agreeing to this mass evacuation and relocation.

After the war, however, the major political activities and legislative efforts of the JACL were directed at eradicating anti-Japanese discrimination. In 1946, the JACL embarked on a hard-fought campaign to repeal California's Alien Land Law, which prohibited all Japanese immigrants from purchasing and owning land in the state. In 1948, it supported the passage of the Evacuation Claims Act, the first of a series of efforts to rectify the losses and injustices of the World War II internment. In 1949, efforts by Japanese immigrants to become naturalized U.S. citizens, a right denied them for more than 50 years, were initiated. In 1978, the membership and board of the JACL decided to focus the organization's efforts on the recognition of, and reparations for, the internments during World War II. The Commission on Wartime Relocation and Internment of Civilians was formed, and in 1982 it found the government's actions unjustified and unconstitutional. The redress campaign culminated in the Civil Liberties Act of 1988, which provided monetary compensation of $20,000 to each victim if alive, or an heir if deceased, and a formal apology.

While the JACL's founding mission was to protect the civil rights of Americans of Japanese ancestry, since 1982 this organization has extended its services to protecting the rights of all segments of the Asian Pacific American community. This change came about when Vincent Chin, a young Chinese American, was murdered by two laid-off Detroit autoworkers who mistook him for being Japanese. Since 9/11, the JACL has also become a vocal defender of the civil rights of Arab and Muslim Americans who have become victims of the government's initiatives. The JACL has realized that the civil rights of one group can only be guaranteed by ensuring the rights of all Americans.

MEHDI BOZORGMEHR AND ANNY BAKALIAN

See also

Japanese Americans, Redress Movement for; Japanese Internment

Further Reading:

Hayashi, Brian Masaru. *Democratizing the Enemy: The Japanese American Internment.* Princeton, NJ: Princeton University Press, 2004.

Ng, Wendy. *Japanese American Internment During World War II: A History and Reference Guide.* Westport, CT: Greenwood Press, 2002.

Robinson, Greg. *By Order of the President: FDR and the Internment of Japanese Americans.* Cambridge, MA: Harvard University Press, 2001.

Japanese Americans, Redress Movement for

Japanese Americans won a major victory when the Civil Liberties Act of 1988 was passed by the Congress, authorizing a redress program for the internment of Japanese Americans during World War II. However, this victory did not transpire overnight; it was a product of decades of discussions, protests, and negotiations by individuals and groups across the nation.

Following the civil rights movements initiated by the members and supporters of the African American communities across the nation in the 1950 and 1960s, civil rights awareness began to intensify among other minority communities. This gradually fueled the movement to demand redress for Japanese American internment. The Japanese American Citizens League (JACL) approved a resolution in 1970 to seek both acknowledgement of and compensation for the injustice imposed through the World War II internment of Japanese Americans by the U.S. government. Although the framework for the redress movement was formed at this time, the JACL's resolution was initially received with apathy, skepticism, and disagreement within the Japanese American communities.

President Reagan signs the Reparations Bill, also known as the Civil Liberties Act, before a group of Japanese Americans on August 10, 1988. The Act granted $20,000 in compensation to each surviving World War II internee. (Ronald Reagan Library)

For instance, many community members thought that their communities would benefit more by forgetting the dark past and focusing on creating a bright future. They frequently cited the notable success among Japanese Americans in the postwar United States. For instance, in 1974, Japanese Americans Norman Mineta and George Ariyoshi had been elected a congressman of California and the governor of Hawaii, respectively. Others expressed their skepticism by stating that the American government would never apologize or compensate for its actions three decades before, and they feared that seeking redress was not the best use of their resources. Yet others thought that demanding monetary compensation would tarnish the legacy of their suffering in the internment camps, by reducing their collective experiences of injustice to a finite dollar amount.

Partly because of these ideological differences, it took the JACL several years to launch a major campaign to demand redress from the U.S. government. In 1978, the JACL unanimously voted to seek monetary compensation in two forms: a $25,000 payment to each individual who had been interned, or to his or her heirs; and a trust fund to help reestablish the Japanese American communities that were destroyed as a result of the internment programs. It initially sought to pursue these goals through a series of legal actions. However, recognizing the time-consuming nature of such processes, the JACL followed the advice of Japanese American senator Daniel Inoue of Hawaii and decided instead to recommend that a federal commission be established. As with most political movements, this decision prompted some members of the communities to branch out and establish their own organizations to tackle the redress issue differently. Such organizations included the National Council for Japanese American Redress and the National Coalition for Redress Reparations, both of which disapproved of having a governmental commission address their concerns.

In the midst of these disagreements, in 1980 President Jimmy Carter signed a bill to establish the Commission on Wartime Relocation and Internment of Civilians. This commission was designed to investigate whether the U.S. government had committed any human rights violations through their relocation programs involving Japanese Americans and to suggest any applicable remedies if such violations had indeed taken place. The commission conducted a series of public hearings across the nation, interviewed remaining survivors and their families, and reviewed documents. In 1983, the commission concluded, in its report entitled "Personal Justice Denied," that the internment programs were indeed reflective not of justifiable security considerations but of racism and wartime hysteria created by government officials.

The commission recommended that the surviving internees or their heirs, approximately 60,000, be granted compensatory payments of $20,000 each, that a statement of apology be issued by the U.S. government, and that a presidential pardon be granted for the Japanese Americans who were unjustifiably convicted of violating the curfew and internment orders. In 1988, the redress payments were finally approved by Congress; in 1990, the first redress payments were made, accompanied by letters of apology. Although these terms did not fully comply with its original resolution, the JACL nevertheless endorsed these recommendations, citing that this marked a major milestone in the lives of Japanese Americans, as it concluded one of the darkest episodes in the constitutional history of the United States.

DAISUKE AKIBA

See also

Japanese American Citizens League (JACL); Japanese Internment; World War II

Further Reading:

Daniels, Roger, Sandra C. Taylor, and Harry H. L. Kitano. *Japanese Americans from Relocation to Redress*. Seattle: University of Washington Press, 1991.

Hatamiya, Leslie T. *Righting a Wrong*. Stanford, CA: Stanford University Press, 1993.

Hohri, William Minoru. *Repairing America, Account of the Movement for Japanese American Redress*. Seattle: Washington State University, 1988.

Japanese Internment

On February 19, 1942, 74 days following the Japanese attack on Pearl Harbor, President Franklin D. Roosevelt signed Executive Order 9066, giving authority to the secretary of war or to military officers under his command "to prescribe military areas in such places and of such extent as he or the appropriate Military Commander may determine, from which any or all persons may be excluded, and with respect to which, the right of any persons to enter, remain in, or leave shall be subject to whatever restriction the Secretary of War or the appropriate Military Commander may impose in his discretion." This order set in motion a chain of events that culminated in the exclusion of Japanese Americans from the Western United States, the largest forced migration in American history, and the internment in concentration camps of over 120,000 innocent people, most of them until near the end of the war. However, the story of the internment of Japanese Americans during World War II does not begin with the bombing of Pearl Harbor. That travesty was the culmination of decades of discrimination and mistreatment.

The federal census of 1890 reported slightly over 2,000 Japanese immigrants in the United States, although several thousand more would fall under the jurisdiction of the United States with the annexation of Hawai'i in 1898. Those in the continental United States lived mostly in the Western states near the coast, primarily in rural and semirural areas. Most of the Japanese immigrants worked in agriculture or fishing. The anti-Chinese crusades in California that led to the passage of the federal Chinese Exclusion Act in 1882 had no immediate effect on Japanese Americans, but it galvanized racist views in the Western states, encouraging those who rejected Chinese immigrants to insist on a similar policy toward other East Asians. During the last decade of the 19th century and the first years of the 20th, tens of thousands of Japanese immigrated to Hawai'i and to the Western continental states. In 1905, the California legislature passed a resolution calling on Congress to restrict Japanese immigration. The following year, the school board in San Francisco voted to force Japanese children to attend the segregated schools that had been originally constructed for Chinese pupils. President Theodore Roosevelt was drawn into the controversy. He had developed ties with the leaders of the Japanese government with his participation in the diplomatic resolution of the Russo-Japanese War in 1905, and

Japan Bashing

As the U.S. economy suffered a decline in the 1980s and early 1990s, some politicians and media outlets blamed cheap imports, especially Japanese cars, for the failure of American industries. This fueled anew anti-Japanese sentiments among Americans and the scapegoating of Japanese Americans. Examples of Japan bashing include the brutal 1982 murder of Vincent Chin, a 27-year-old Chinese American in Detroit. The assailants, two autoworkers (one recently laid off), called him a "Jap" and blamed him for the loss of their jobs. In 1992, a Japanese businessman was stabbed to death in his home in Ventura, California. Two weeks earlier, two white young men, who blamed Japan for the economic crisis in the United States, had threatened him. There were also instances of graffiti on Asian American stores and crank phone calls to individuals or institutions with Asian names. A striking feature of Japan bashing is the inability of some Americans to differentiate among diverse ethnic/nationality groups of Asian Americans. This mistaken identity results in panethnic prejudice, discrimination, and racism every time one of these groups is involved.

In the past, the policies of the U.S. government were the chief source of anti-Japanese racism. At the turn of the 20th century, Japanese immigrants were severely restricted from entering the United States and from bringing their spouses and also barred from owning agricultural lands. Many observers believe that racist acts of Congress set the stage for the internment of 120,000 Japanese Americans in western states for a period of four years during World War II. Against all odds, though perhaps because of these occurrences, Japanese Americans mobilized and succeeded in American society. Along with the Jews, they are considered the most successful of American ethnic groups. They were elevated to "model-minority" status in the 1960s and 1970s. This phase came to an end when Japan emerged as an industrial giant and a serious competitor to the United States, once again triggering the malicious, if highly remote, association between Japan and Japanese Americans.

MEHDI BOZORGMEHR AND ANNY BAKALIAN

he was keenly aware of that government's objections to the discriminatory policies in California. Nevertheless, he was also sympathetic to the advocates of immigration restriction. In a series of diplomatic communications, Roosevelt negotiated the so-called Gentlemen's Agreements, whereby Roosevelt would oppose immigration restriction and the Japanese government would cease issuing visas to Japanese laborers wishing to immigrate to the United States.

Pressure to exclude Japanese did not cease with that fragile agreement. In 1913, the California legislature passed the Alien Land Law, also known as the Webb Law after its champion, California attorney general Ulysses S. Webb, which prohibited aliens ineligible for citizenship from acquiring, possessing, transmitting, or inheriting land. The courts had ruled that all East Asians were ineligible for citizenship, but the proponents of the legislation made no secret of the fact that the measure was intended to dispossess Japanese landowners. President Woodrow Wilson opposed the measure, but his efforts to stop it proved futile. Japanese farmers were able to lease land, but they no longer could expect to pass it on to their children, even if those children were native-born

American citizens. In some cases, they were able to hold the land in trust for their minor children, but efforts to modify the initial legislation made these arrangements more uncertain as the years passed. By 1920, Japanese farmers held less than 2 percent of the farmland in California through various forms of ownership, trusteeship, or long-term leases. Nevertheless, they still were responsible for 13 percent of the state's agricultural produce. That year, an initiative of the state ballot closed the loopholes that had allowed Japanese immigrants to maintain a tenuous hold on their property, forcing Japanese farmers into tenant farming and sharecropping. Japanese commercial fishermen encountered similar restrictions. Both Oregon and Washington prohibited aliens ineligible for citizenship from acquiring commercial fishing licenses. A similar measure was introduced in the California legislature in 1939, and was barely defeated.

The immigrant Japanese, or the *issei*, were objects of particular suspicion. In the Western coastal states, they tended to live in ethnically segregated communities and were less likely than either their children or other immigrants to assimilate into mainstream American society. Nativists overlooked the fact that the *issei* were proscribed from U.S. citizenship, and criticized them for disloyalty to their new home on the basis of their alien status. Nativist organizations such as the California Joint Immigration Committee and the Native Sons of the Golden West lobbied for stricter controls on Japanese immigration and further restrictions on the rights of those already in the United States. Newspaper editorials called for extending the ban on land ownership to the *nisei*, the American-born children of the *issei*, because they held dual American and Japanese citizenship under Japanese law.

In 1922, the U.S. Supreme Court in *Ozawa v. United States* confirmed the policy that refused citizenship to Japanese immigrants. Two years later, riding a wave of postwar nativism, Congress passed the Immigration Act of 1924, excluding most immigrants from Eastern and Southern Europe and effectively shutting off the last remnant of Japanese immigration. Section 13C of the law restricted from the United States all aliens ineligible for citizenship, a provision that applied in particular to Japanese after the decision in *Ozawa*. President Calvin Coolidge criticized the exclusion, but signed the legislation nevertheless.

After the immigration restrictions of 1924, the nativism that spawned them lost steam, although statutory and social discrimination against both *issei* and *nisei* continued on the West Coast. With the invasion of Manchuria by Japanese forces in 1931, the issue again arose. Although Franklin D. Roosevelt's New Deal did not explicitly discriminate against Japanese Americans, the actions of local and state officials in the Western states ensured that they would not benefit from relief programs. After Japan invaded northern China in 1937, the president's anger at the Japanese government spilled over into suspicion of Japanese Americans. Navy Secretary Frank Knox suggested that the administration consider the necessity of concentration camps should hostilities erupt between the United States and Japan.

When war came to the United States with the Japanese attack on Pearl Harbor, press accounts of Japanese duplicity and collaboration with enemy forces were rampant. Stories of Japanese agricultural workers in Hawai'i cutting huge arrows in fields pointing to Pearl Harbor were reported as fact on the mainland. Secretary Knox toured Hawai'i and reported to the president and to the press that Japanese on the islands contributed essential information to the attackers.

He suggested that the president order the removal of all Japanese from Hawai'i. Supreme Court justice Owen Roberts asserted that Japanese spies had aided the strike force.

With the fear of invasion, pressure mounted to arrest or to evacuate Japanese from Pacific coastal communities. The Justice Department drew up tentative plans to investigate and exclude *issei* living near sensitive and defense-related areas, but before any of those plans could be developed fully, the army was put in charge of the issue. Gen. John DeWitt of the West Coast Defense Command reported to his superiors in Washington that the West Coast Japanese were engaging in espionage and planning sabotage. He also claimed, without evidence, that every ship sailing from the mouth of the Columbia River into the Pacific was being tracked by Japanese ships with information provided by radio communication from the mainland. DeWitt issued a curfew for the West Coast, restricting Japanese aliens and Japanese Americans from traveling more than five miles from their homes or places of work, and that they remain in their homes between 8:00 PM and 6:00 AM. Although immediately after Pearl Harbor he had defended the *nisei* as American citizens, DeWitt quickly adopted the racist language of the Nativists. "A Jap's a Jap," he told a Senate committee. "It makes no difference whether he is an American citizen or not."

National news media reported these claims and other equally unsubstantiated rumors of sabotage and espionage. On December 22, 1941, *Life* magazine ran an article with two photographs to help readers to know "How to Tell Japs from the Chinese." Japanese American factory workers and professionals lost jobs as private employers and local governments dismissed them as security risks. In early February, DeWitt requested the authority to exclude Japanese aliens and American citizens from strategic areas of the West Coast. In response, President Roosevelt issued Executive Order 9066, giving DeWitt that authority. Executive Order 9201 the next month created the War Relocation Authority. Milton Eisenhower, the brother of Gen. Dwight Eisenhower, was appointed director, although he resigned after three months and was replaced by Dillon Myer, formerly employed by the Agriculture Department.

The *issei* were excluded from a large area of the coastal states, and a voluntary evacuation of both *issei* and *nisei* began by the end of the month. This effort soon was abandoned, as many *nisei* showed little willingness to comply, and because

Korematsu v. United States (1944)

Korematsu v. United States (323 U.S. 214 [1944]) was a U.S. Supreme Court case in which the Court upheld the internment of Japanese Americans during World War II. Just after the surprise attack on Pearl Harbor, Hawaii, by the Japanese on December 7, 1941, President Franklin D. Roosevelt issued Executive Order 9066. This order gave vast powers to restrict the movement of Japanese along the coast, due to fears of espionage. Acting under the president's authority, the military forcibly relocated more than 100,000 people of Japanese ancestry to internment camps—including U.S. citizens. By 1944, when the war hysteria had eased, the order was rescinded, and the camps were closed by 1945.

In *Korematsu*, the legality of the internment was challenged. A divided Supreme Court upheld the internment by a 6–3 vote, essentially stating that citizens of the United States have benefits as well as duties and that during wartime, each citizen is expected to do more. Additionally, the Court thought that, at the time they were hearing the case, the situation was calm compared with just after the Pearl Harbor attack. Therefore, they believed it was unfair to judge actions taken after the attack because those making the decisions did not know then that the actions they were taking were obviously unnecessary.

There was, however, a strong dissent. Dissenting Justice Frank Murphy argued that the internment violated the Constitution and was blatant racism. Eventually, in 1988, this strong dissent was vindicated as Congress, through the Civil Liberties Act, attempted to remedy the injustices endured by Japanese Americans. Congress apologized and gave $20,000 to each person still alive who had been interned. The issues in *Korematsu* continue to be debated today, especially with respect to terrorism and crime.

JOHN ETERNO

state officials in the Western states to which the Japanese Americans would move were openly hostile to the policy. In response, DeWitt on March 27, 1942, ordered the Japanese to end the voluntary evacuation and instead to report to assembly centers that were being constructed for the War Relocation Authority. From there they were sent to 10 relocation camps in Utah, Arizona, Colorado, Wyoming, California, Idaho, and Arkansas. Two-thirds of the internees were American citizens; one-third were children.

The War Relocation Authority was authorized to help evacuees from the West Coast dispose of or store property, but because of the haste with which the policy was executed and the indifference of many administrators to the plight of the Japanese Americans, most who left behind farms, homes, and cars never recovered them. Sympathetic neighbors, in many cases, stepped in to help Japanese families, but more often farms and homes were lost to unscrupulous bargain hunters.

The accommodations in the camps varied, but for the most part resembled makeshift military housing with poor ventilation and little consideration for comfort or privacy. Barracks were divided into rooms ranging in size from 20 × 16 to 20 × 25 feet. A family would be assigned a single room

and individuals who arrived alone or in smaller groups either would share a room or would be assigned to a room that already housed a small family. Meals were provided in crowded mess halls. Food shortages and spoilage was common, but conditions improved as internees began to grow and prepare their own food, insofar as conditions allowed. Military personnel guarded the barbed-wire-encircled camps, and searchlights kept internees awake at night. Internees were shot in what were reportedly escape attempts, at least one dying from his wounds. At Manzanar, two internees were killed and several others wounded when guards opened fire on a crowd. At Tule Lake, internees were beaten during a work strike.

At the beginning of the war, nearly 5,000 Japanese Americans were in the army. At first the War Department refused to permit any more *nisei* to join the armed forces, but with the wartime manpower needs, that policy was modified. The 100th Army Battalion, composed of members of the Hawai'ian National Guard, and the 442nd Infantry Regiment, recruited from the camps, served with distinction in Italy, France, and the Rhineland during the war. The two units were combined during their service in Italy, and the combined 442nd was the most decorated regiment in the wartime army. At war's end, 33,000 *nisei* were serving in the military.

Internees eligible for military service were released from the camps through the Loyalty Review Program, established in 1943. The program also made it possible, in theory, for internees to leave the camps and relocate east of the Rocky Mountains. The slow pace of the program, the difficulty of meeting requirements of sponsorship or employment, and confusion over the loyalty oaths rendered it ineffective. Few internees, except those who joined the military, were able to leave the camps under the program until near the end of the war.

The legality of the relocation and internment did not go unchallenged during the war years. Minoru Yasui was an Oregon-born attorney who was arrested in March 1942 for violating DeWitt's curfew order. The trial judge ruled that the curfew was unconstitutional when applied to American citizens, but then stripped Yasui of his citizenship because he had worked for the Japanese consulate in Chicago before the war. In *Yasui v. U.S.* (1943), the Supreme Court reinstated Yasui's citizenship, but reversed the trial judge's ruling that the curfew was unconstitutional. Another internee, Gordon Hirabayashi, also challenged the legality of the curfew order. He was arrested and convicted, and served 90 days on a roadside prison work crew, in addition to five months he spent in jail awaiting trial. In a unanimous decision, the Court held in *Hirabayashi v. U.S.* (1943) that the war powers of the executive allowed for the military curfew. The Court did not address the issue of the discriminatory nature of the order.

Fred Korematsu was arrested for disregarding the evacuation order. He had lost his job as a shipyard welder when the Boiler Makers Union expelled all Japanese American members after Pearl Harbor, and had been rejected for military service, when he decided not to report with his parents to the Tanforan Assembly Center. His efforts to elude authorities ended in May 1942, when he was arrested for refusing to evacuate. The Supreme Court agreed to hear his case and ruled in *Korematsu v. U.S.* (1944) that the evacuation orders were constitutional as a wartime necessity, even though martial law had not been declared.

The only favorable ruling for an internee was the case of Mitsuye Endo. Endo, born in California, had been an employee of the state Department of Motor Vehicles until that agency fired all of its Japanese American employees at the beginning of the war. She had never been to Japan and could not read or write Japanese. Her lawyers petitioned for a writ of habeas corpus and challenged her internment, asserting that the government had no authority to detain loyal citizens without charges. Without ruling on the broader issue of the constitutionality of the concentration camps, the Court held in *Ex parte Endo* (1944) that the government could no longer detain loyal citizens.

A 1949 study estimated that the Japanese Americans lost about $77 million in property due to the evacuation and internment. Those who filed for compensation recovered approximately 10 percent of their losses, and these payments often were delayed for years. In 1983, legislation was introduced in Congress to make payments to the surviving internees to redress their losses. Five years later, President Ronald Reagan signed the Civil Liberties Act of 1988, providing a payment of $20,000 to each of the approximately 60,000 survivors.

JAMES IVY

See also

Japanese American Citizens League (JACL); Japanese Americans, Redress Movement for; Nativism and the Anti-immigrant Movements; World War II

Further Reading:

Girdner, Audrie, and Anne Loftis. *The Great Betrayal: The Evacuation of the Japanese-Americans During World War II.* London: Macmillan, 1969.

Hayashi, Brian Masaru. *Democratizing the Enemy: The Japanese American Internment.* Princeton, NJ: Princeton University Press, 2004.

Irons, Peter. *Justice at War: The Story of the Japanese American Internment Cases.* New York: Oxford University Press, 1983.

Ng, Wendy. *Japanese American Internment During World War II: A History and Reference Guide.* Westport, CT: Greenwood Press, 2002.

Robinson, Greg. *By Order of the President: FDR and the Internment of Japanese Americans.* Cambridge, MA: Harvard University Press, 2001.

Jazz

Jazz is an American musical art form whose sociological features have been significantly shaped by Jim Crow segregation and ideology. Essentialist notions of race and culture have determined how people have defined and perceived jazz since the music's beginning. While historians agree that jazz emerged from a syncretism of numerous American music traditions, the belief persists that jazz is essentially "black music" and that African contributions are jazz's most defining traits. The story of how jazz became racialized is intertwined with the story of Jim Crow.

Historians generally agree that the musical style that eventually became known as "jazz" emerged in New Orleans in the first years of the 20th century. Too many historians reiterate without question the received wisdom that blacks invented jazz in the New Orleans ghettoes. However, the evidence for this origins narrative is scant. Contradictory evidence abounds, indicating that the early New Orleans musical scene that produced jazz was uncommonly diverse.

One challenge for investigators is to define exactly what "jazz" means. The early New Orleans jazz musicians called their music "ragtime." The word "jazz" first entered the American slang vocabulary on the central California coast in the early 1910s. It was used synonymously with pep, vigor, and energy. It was first published by sportswriters who used "jazz" to describe an enthusiastic approach to playing baseball. "Jazz" was eventually applied to a style of music being performed in California by a band of New Orleans expatriates who called themselves "The Original Creole Orchestra."

However, these pioneering jazz expatriates in California were not "black"; they were Creoles of color. They were the descendants of French and Spanish colonists in the New World who had formed unions with people of color. During Reconstruction, the close ties between the white Creoles and colored Creoles began to unravel. They supported opposing political parties, which created significant antagonism between the two formerly intimate populations. As Jim Crow segregation emerged across the nation in the late 19th century, racial lines hardened between New Orleans whites and the Creoles of color. When jazz emerged as a new style at the turn of the 20th century, the Creoles of color as a group were still culturally and socially distinct from freedmen and their descendants. They lived in their own neighborhoods, frequently owned their own homes, and worked at skilled jobs. They spoke French and went to Catholic churches. They were also racially distinct, possessing a lighter skin color on average than the freedmen population. They did

not consider themselves "black." Many took great offense at that racial label. Furthermore, the freedmen population of New Orleans harbored some degree of resentment and distrust towards the Creoles of color, seeing them as part of the old slave economy's power structure. This social division between freedmen and formerly free people of color was common throughout the South in the postbellum era.

The ideology of Jim Crow imagined a biracial society in which you were either black or white. Prior to Jim Crow, other variables determined social and racial status, such as education, degree of skin pigmentation, family history and accomplishments, and freedom versus slavery. But as early Jim Crow emerged in the late 19th century, these variables decreased in significance. Now, any visible amount of non-white ancestry was sufficient to classify a person as black. Many formerly free people of color resisted this binary race system. Some were able to maintain a distinct cultural identity by defending the social boundaries that distinguished them from freedmen. While whites under the thrall of Jim Crow rarely respected distinctions within the nonwhite population, the old antebellum social boundaries did foster the persistence of such subcultures well into the 20th century.

A significant proportion of the early pioneers of jazz were Creoles of color. Many of these musicians were born in the plantation region just west of New Orleans. The Creoles of color were not the only creators of jazz. Other jazz pioneers were of recent Caribbean or Mexican origin. Of course, there were a significant number of "black" and "white" American musicians in the mix as well. Furthermore, numerous early jazz musicians were of mixed ancestry.

Thus the black-white racial dichotomy used by so many jazz mythographers excludes any serious discussion of the uncommonly diverse origins of jazz's founding population. It fails to acknowledge that many of the jazz pioneers did not consider themselves black. The earliest jazz bands often included the word "Creole" as part of their ensemble's name, to distinguish themselves from the black population.

The historical evidence does not support the idea that jazz emerged solely out of black culture, as an expression of the freedmen's African roots. If that were the case, we should expect to see jazz developing in every region containing freed slaves. But the evidence shows that jazz developed in the unique cultural environs of New Orleans, with the city's freedmen descendants playing only a partial role in the project, along with musicians from many other backgrounds. New Orleans musicians then spread the music to other parts of the country during the first two decades of the 20th century.

Nor does the evidence support the idea that jazz is an expression of black culture alone. The evidence is overwhelming that there was significant cross-cultural influence between all of the various ethnic groups represented in the population of jazz musicians during the music's early years. Jazz could not have evolved the way it did without the contributions of artists from a host of different musical backgrounds and experiences.

Middle-class blacks were generally hostile to jazz and blues in the music's early decades, through the 1920s. They considered musicians to be part of a disreputable class, and jazz and blues to represent a dangerous secular tradition that was at odds with their Protestant religiosity. Many blacks were too poor to buy a radio, phonograph, or admission to a live performance. The black audience for jazz was found primarily in large cities, comprising a tiny cross-section of the black population. A broader black audience for jazz emerged during the swing craze of the 1930s, along with the rest of the country. Once jazz's brief moment as popular music began to wane, so did the black audience. During the 1950s, the black audience began to dwindle. Since the recording industry's inception, the economic fan base for jazz has been composed primarily of white listeners.

The "blacks invented jazz" narrative is attributable to Jim Crow in several ways. First, the ideology of Jim Crow was founded on an "essentialist" conception of race. American racial essentialism assumes that members of a race share an essence, a commonality that determines their shared skin color and racial appearance, and that also determines their shared culture. But the evidence is overwhelming that racial essentialism is false. There is no biological or cultural characteristic that is unique to members of one race. Culture is learned, and thus any cultural trait is potentially accessible to any human capable of learning it, regardless of racial category. In short, racial boundaries are imaginary constructs.

The ideology of Jim Crow reified racial essentialism, treating the white/black (or white/not white) binary as if it were real, and as if skin color itself set boundaries on human culture and behavior. Furthermore, reifying the white/black

binary denied the existence of groups with ambiguous status that did not easily fit into the black and white categories—groups such as the Gulf Coast Creoles of color. Not surprisingly, the jazz histories produced during the Jim Crow era reproduced this denial of interstitial status. Instead, jazz historiography reclassified the Creoles as "black." Their unique history and culture was conflated with that of freedmen and freedmen descendants. Meanwhile, Latin and Caribbean jazz pioneers were either ignored or trivialized—or recategorized as "black."

It is already dubious to insist on the artist's ethnicity as the most significant biographical element shaping his creation. But the simplistic illogic of Jim Crow racialism requires that musicians with mixed ancestries be reduced to either black or white. Furthermore, the Jim Crow racial binary also obscures ethnic distinctions among white Americans. During the first decades of jazz, Americans of Jewish or Italian descent suffered their own experiences of segregation and discrimination. Many of the early Jewish and Italian jazz musicians changed their names to sound more Anglo, in order to improve their chances in the music business. Jewish and Italian musical culture had a profound influence on the development of jazz and other American popular music styles. A number of prominent jazz musicians were of partial American Indian ancestry. But under the binary black-white racial ideology of Jim Crow, the only racial debate in jazz historiography has been over the significance of contributions made by essentially "white" musicians to what the first jazz critics mistakenly viewed as an essentially "black" folk art.

Much of early jazz criticism focused on the critics' perception of the music as an expression of primitivism. The primitivist aesthetic was popular in a number of art worlds in the early decades of the 20th century. Artists and critics became fascinated with the folk art of exotic, "uncivilized" cultures. The artist Pablo Picasso was inspired by African masks. The French composer Claude Debussy was inspired by Indonesian gamelan ensembles. The primitivist conception of jazz saw the music as the purely emotional expression of Noble Savage stereotypes, unfiltered by intellectual intent. For the primitivists, the jazz musician was an inarticulate, unreflective, and unsophisticated naïf who did not fully comprehend the artistic import of his creation. Since Jim Crow ideology stereotyped African Americans as emotional, instinctive, spontaneous, and unreflective, the primitivist myth of jazz became bound up with racial essentialism, and jazz was redefined as an essentially black music. An acknowledgment of the significance of "European" influences on jazz would have amounted to an admission that the primitivist thesis was flawed.

Not surprisingly, the primitivist myth was especially popular among critics who viewed jazz as an expression of African Americans' racial essence. In 1934, the French author Hugues Panassie published *Le Jazz Hot*, the first significant book of jazz criticism. Panassie held that "In music, primitive man generally has greater talent than civilized man. An excess of culture atrophies inspiration" (quoted in Jarrett 1999: 41). Winthrop Sargeant, an early American jazz critic, considered jazz to be a folk music, "the original primitive music of the American Negro."

For these early critics, "hot jazz" performed by black musicians was the only authentic expression. White musicians could only aspire to be imitators or exploiters of African Americans. Thus critics denied the possibility of Louis Armstrong's art deriving from an informed, reflective esthetic agency.

The primitivist perception of jazz reduced artistic creation into a spontaneous, instinctive, animalistic activity, devoid of cerebral, intellectual intent. The primitivists conceived jazz in terms that exactly match the Jim Crow stereotype of the African American as an intellectually limited slave to his emotions. But while primitivism is informed by the racist stereotypes of Jim Crow, it is not cognate with racism. Racism holds whites to be superior in every way. Primitivism reverses the equation, and instead valorizes the primitive's "natural, spontaneous" creations over hyperintellectual European art.

The primitivist myth reinforced the racial stereotypes of Jim Crow, but with a twist. Jim Crow denied the possibility of significant black accomplishments. The primitivists, on the other hand, celebrated black accomplishments, but denied the intellectual humanity driving black creation. The primitivists ignored the significance of New Orleans's French Opera in the city's cultural life at the dawn of jazz, even though a number of early jazz musicians performed in the opera or attended it often. The primitivists ignored the fact that a significant number of the early jazz greats were well-trained musicians, many of them college graduates. Those who did not have access to music lessons in their youth often sought out advanced training even after they were well established in the music business. The primitivists ignored the central place in jazz of musical instruments and traditions derived from European music, instead valorizing only those elements that they perceived to represent African primitivism. Primitivism ignores all of this, and instead falsely attributes jazz musicians' artistry to "the Negro's" racial essence—a conception of identity that the primitivists borrowed from the tenets of Jim Crow racial pseudoscience. Primitivism reinforces Jim Crow racial ideology, first by claiming jazz as an exclusively black creation, but also by denying that black musicians possess the intellectual powers of intense concentration and reflection, instead attributing their artistry to instinct and to racial characteristics inherited from Africa.

The racial essentialism of the primitivist myth was not unique to critics, but was also adopted by musicians themselves. Duke Ellington preferred to refer to his music as "Negro music" instead of "jazz." The composer Darius Milhaud held: "There is no doubt that the origin of jazz music is to be sought among the Negroes. Primitive African qualities have kept their place deep in the nature of the American Negro and it is here that we find the origin of the tremendous rhythmic force as well as the expressive melodies born of inspiration which oppressed races alone can produce" (Lemke 1998: 92).

The primitivist myth is hardly limited to jazz criticism. It has long been central to the economics of jazz. As early as the 1920s in Harlem, then New York City's black neighborhood, clubs opened to cater to white patrons in search of an exotic and transgressive experience. On one stretch of 133rd Street during the 1920s, 11 nightclubs operated for a whites-only audience, in the midst of a black ghetto. This area was known as "Jungle Alley," because many of these clubs adopted a jungle theme. They were decorated with palm trees and other exotic plants. Black employees dressed as stereotypical jungle savages. Chorus girls wore costumes representing loin cloths made of leopard skins. Duke Ellington's 1920s band was known for its "jungle sound," and cut records under the pseudonym "The Jungle Band." Even prominent black performers such as Louis Armstrong and Josephine Baker performed in costumes that symbolized "jungle" stereotypes. Thus financial motivations led entrepreneurs and performers alike to exploit the primitivist myth.

The racial binary of Jim Crow also structured the early recording industry. During the 1920s, recording sessions were segregated by race into "black" acts and "white" acts—at least for publicity purposes. Multiracial, multiethnic bands did record, but under pseudonyms that implied a monoracial identity for all of the band's members. For example, the Italian American guitarist Salvatore Massaro changed his name to "Eddie Lang," apparently assuming that his Italian name was a disadvantage in the music business. But on his records with the black guitarist Lonnie Johnson, he used the pseudonym "Blind Willie Dunn," thus impersonating a black bluesman. On other Lonnie Johnson recordings, the names of his white bandmates were simply left off the record. One of Massaro's records was released as "Blind Willie Dunn and his Gin Bottle Four." This band included King Oliver, a "black" trumpeter who worked in a "Creole" band, as well as the Italian American Massaro and the African American Johnson.

The primitivist myth manifested in the recording industry held that black musicians were superior performers of the more energetic, up-tempo "hot jazz" style, and that black audiences were more interested in this type of jazz. Meanwhile white musicians were stereotyped as better performers of the more commercial, pop-oriented "sweet jazz," and industry executives believed that white audiences preferred this style of jazz. The recording industry fostered these stereotypes by preferring to release "sweet jazz" records by white bands, while ignoring the white bands' actual live performance repertoire. Conversely, the recording industry took black bands whose repertoire contained a wide variety of waltzes and love ditties, and ensured that their recorded output consisted primarily of hot jazz numbers. Many musicians of the era—both black and white—have long complained that the skewed racial logic of the recording industry has prevented posterity from being able to appreciate the musicians' full accomplishments, instead focusing on only one aspect that may not be representative of their artistry.

The recording industry's primitivist "white-sweet/black-hot" stereotype functioned as a feedback loop. As the record-buying public consumed hot records from only black bands, and sweet records from only white bands, a racial stereotype with little basis in reality became a self-fulfilling prophecy, engrained into Jim Crow's musical culture.

Some opponents of Jim Crow ideology deployed the primitivist myth in an opportunistic manner that valorized racial essentialism. Jim Crow ideology denied the possibility of black talent. Consequently, Jim Crow's opponents sought out talented blacks as counterexamples, and among the shining lights of early jazz were many accomplished black musicians. This rhetorical strategy was popular with communist music critics in Europe, and later, the Communist Party and its sympathizers in the United States. For these critics and activists, to befriend and honor black artists was a symbolic blow against colonialism and Western hegemony. They used the obvious evidence of black genius to criticize the illogic of Jim Crow racism. But in doing so, they further engrained the primitivist myth that jazz was fundamentally a black creation. Thus in attacking Jim Crow, they also reproduced its core fallacy—the notion that racial essentialism is a valid construct.

One of the most convincing arguments in favor of the "jazz as essentially black music" narrative is the sheer number of black jazz stars. Certainly the prominence of black genius in jazz history is no myth. However, the predominant narrative obscures the role of white critics and gatekeepers in creating black stars, while they simultaneously deemphasized the significance of white jazz geniuses.

The popular narrative also obscures the social funneling effects of Jim Crow segregation in the American economy. Music was one of the few professions open to blacks during the Jim Crow era, and perhaps the only potentially lucrative profession available to blacks that did not require a college credential or privileged family background. Much of the creative energy and talent in the black community was funneled into the music business, because there were so few other arenas in which talented African Americans were permitted the opportunity to succeed. Thus, the predominance of black geniuses in jazz is explained by the alternative options available to white talent that were denied to black talent. White talent was drained from jazz and disseminated into more secure and lucrative careers in the symphonies, recording studios, or music industry boardrooms, or into the vast number of nonmusical professions to which whites had easier access.

The economic role of jazz during the Jim Crow era is analogous to the role of professional sports today—an arena in which a talented but disadvantaged striver has an opportunity to succeed in the broader society. There is no disputing that race is significant here, but black predominance in both jazz and basketball is an economic outcome of Jim Crow racism—and not attributable to essential racial characteristics. To attribute black predominance in jazz or basketball to black peoples' superior aptitude for these activities is to reproduce the core fallacy of Jim Crow ideology—racial essentialism—while simultaneously obscuring the central role that Jim Crow racism plays in producing black predominance in these arenas.

THOMAS BROWN

See also

Music Industry, Racism in; Rhythm and Blues; Rock and Roll

Further Reading:

Collier, James Lincoln. *Jazz: The American Theme Song*. New York: Oxford University Press, 1993.

Gioia, Ted. "Jazz and the Primitivist Myth." *Musical Quarterly* 73 (1989): 130–43.

Jarrett, Michael. *Drifting on a Read: Jazz as a Model for Writing*. Albany: State University of New York Press, 1999.

Lees, Gene. *Cats of Any Color: Jazz, Black and White*. New York: Oxford University Press, 1999.

Lemke, Sieglinde. *Primitivist Modernism: Black Culture and the Origins of Transatlantic Modernism*. New York: Oxford University Press, 1998.

Meltzer, David. *Reading Jazz*. New York: Oxford University Press, 1993.

O'Meally, Robert G. *The Jazz Cadence of American Culture*. New York: Columbia University Press, 1998.

Sudhalter, Richard. *Lost Chords: White Musicians and Their Contribution to Jazz, 1915–1945*. New York: Oxford University Press, 2001.

Jena Six

The Jena Six were six black teenagers, Robert Bailey, Mychal Bell, Carwin Jones, Bryant Purvis, Jesse Ray Beard, and Theo Shaw, convicted of beating a white student, Justin Barker, on December 4, 2006, at Jena High School in Jena, Louisiana. Jena is a town of about 3,000 people, 11 percent of which are black and 85 percent white. Various racial incidents that preceded the assault must be examined in order to understand why the case attracted thousands of protestors and why it is often cited as an example of racial injustice in the United States.

On August 30, 2006, during an assembly at Jena High School, a black student, Kenneth Purvis, asked the assistant principal whether black students were permitted to sit under the tree in the center of campus, a previously segregated gathering place, and the vice principal responded that they could sit wherever they want. The next day, nooses were found hanging from the tree in question, which prompted a silent protest of black athletes who sat under the tree where the nooses were hung. Several days later, District Attorney J. Walters Reed brought police officers with him to another assembly in which he threatened black students for protesting the incident stating that he had the power to ruin their lives. He also lectured them on how blacks are more likely to be victims of state violence than they are to be recipients of equal protection under the law.

Eventually, the three white students who hung the nooses were identified and punished with nine days at an alternative facility, two weeks of in-school suspension, Saturday detentions, and discipline court. The three students behind the noose incident claimed that they hung the nooses as a joke directed towards white students on the rodeo team, and the school committee agreed that there was no racial motivation behind the hanging of the nooses even though nooses have been specifically linked to the threat of violence against blacks throughout history.

Several months later on November 30, 2006, the main academic building of Jena High School was destroyed by arson. The next night, a black student was beaten up by a white student when he attempted to attend a white party, and the night after that, a white man pulled out a shotgun at a local convenience store after a confrontation with three black teenagers. The black youth were arrested and charged with disturbing the peace, theft of a firearm, second-degree robbery, and conspiracy to commit second-degree robbery while the white man was not arrested and no charges were filed against him.

Two days later at the high school, a white student, Justin Barker, was allegedly directing racial slurs, including the n-word, towards black students and was showing his support for the white students who hung the nooses and beat up the black student at the party. He was knocked down, punched, and kicked by six black students and taken to the hospital, treated, and released. Though he was well enough to attend a social event that evening, during the trial about his attack, Barker stated that he suffered temporary vision loss, headaches, and forgetfulness due to the incident.

A crowd marches through Jena, Louisiana, in support of six black teenagers initially charged with attempted murder in the beating of Justin Barker, a white classmate, 2007. (AP/Wide World Photos)

All six black teens involved in the beating were charged with second-degree attempted murder, though this charge was later determined to be unsubstantiated and reduced to aggravated second-degree battery and conspiracy to commit aggravated battery. This charge requires the use of a weapon, and it was determined by an all-white jury that the tennis shoes worn by Bell were in fact dangerous weapons. Bell was convicted in less than three hours and faced up to 22 years in prison; however, this verdict was later overturned because it was ruled that Bell should not have been tried as an adult. Bell eventually pled guilty to a reduced charge of battery and was sentenced to 18 months in a juvenile facility. The remaining five defendants pleaded no contest to the charge of simple battery for which they paid fines and received unsupervised probation.

The main source of controversy surrounding the Jena Six was the severity of the charges originally brought against the defendants and the unfair treatment of blacks within the American criminal justice system. Because of this, race scholars argue that the Jena case can be viewed not as an aberration, but rather as a status quo example of inequality on which the racist American legal system is founded.

All six men of the Jena Six have since moved out of Jena, and five of them went on to attend college. Robert Bailey played wide receiver on Grambling State University's football team. Mychal Bell also played football at Southern University at the position of cornerback. Bryant Purvis enrolled at Southeastern Louisiana University. Jesse Ray Beard played lacrosse at Hoftra University, and Theo Shaw attended the University of Louisiana at Monroe. Shaw now works as a community advocate for the Southern Poverty Law Center in New Orleans. Though all six men involved in the beating have left Jena, the victim, Justin Barker, remains, splitting his time between Jena and an oil rig in Texas where he works.

ADRIENNE N. MILNER

See also

Noose Incidents; Southern Poverty Law Center (SPLC)

Further Reading:

Bell, Jeannine. "The Hangman's Noose and the Lynch Mob: Hate Speech and the Jena Six." *Harvard Civil Rights-Civil Liberties Law Review* 44 (2009): 329–59.

Census Viewer. *Jena, Louisiana, Population: Census 2010 and 2000 Interactive Map, Demographics, Statistics, Quick Facts.* http://censusviewer.com/city/LA/Jena.

CNN. "5 Defendants Plead No Contest in 'Jena Six' Case." http://edition.cnn.com/2009/CRIME /06/26/louisiana.jena.6/.

"Jena Six, Louisiana Town Move On, Five Years Later." *Huffington Post.* http://www.huffingtonpost.com/2011/08/25/jena-six-louisiana-race_n_936076.html.

Southern Poverty Law Center. *'Jena Six' Teen Now an SLPC Community Advocate.* http://www.splcenter.org/get-informed/news/-jena-six-teen-now-an-splc-community-advocate.

Tibbs, Donald F., and Woods, Tyron P. "The Jena Six and Black Punishment: Law and Raw Life in the Domain of Non-Existence." *Seattle Journal for Social Justice* 7 (2003): 235–83.

Jensen, Arthur (1923–2012)

Arthur Jensen was born in 1923. An educational psychologist, Jensen received his PhD from Columbia University in 1956 and went on to teach at the University of California at Berkeley. A controversial figure, Jensen wrote that intelligence is primarily an inherited trait that is only slightly influenced by environmental factors. Based on tests that he performed in the 1960s on school children, Jensen divided cognitive ability into two groups, level 1, simple functioning, and level 2, higher-level thinking. Based on these tests, which he considered to be culturally unbiased, Jensen argued that level-1 abilities were distributed across racial groups but that level-2 abilities were not. According to Jensen's research, Asians as a group have the highest level-2 abilities, followed by whites. Blacks on average, according to Jensen, had the lowest level-2 scores.

Jensen argued that the differences he found reflect a fundamental biological difference only slightly affected by environmental factors. Critics, such as Stephen Jay Gould, argue that Jensen and other hereditarians make a fundamental mistake in equating observed differences with inborn, immutable differences. Critics of Jensen and other hereditarians note that even if it were accepted that the test scores are true reflections of intelligence—a leap that many, including Gould, are not willing to make—that does not mean that the scores reflect inborn ability that could not have been changed through environment. How much intelligence is mutable and how much it is inborn remains a controversial question.

ROBIN ROGER-DILLON

See also

Biological Racism; Hereditarians versus Environmentalists; Intelligence Testing

Further Reading:

Herrnstein, Richard J., and Charles Murray. *The Bell Curve: Intelligence and Class Structure in American Life.* New York: Free Press, 1994.

Jensen, Arthur R. "The Debunking of Scientific Fossils and Straw Persons." *Contemporary Education Review* 1, no. 2 (1982): 121–135.

Jensen, Arthur R. "How Can We Boost IQ and Scholastic Achievement?" *Harvard Educational Review* 39, no. 1 (1969): 1–123.

Jesse Washington Lynching

Jesse Washington, a 17-year-old illiterate black farm hand, was lynched in Waco, Texas, on May 15, 1916. Arrested on May 8, 1916, for murdering Robinson, Texas, resident Lucy Fryer, a 53-year-old white woman, Washington confessed to Fryer's rape and murder. Despite the public outrage among whites, Sheriff Samuel S. Fleming safely transferred Washington to Dallas County to await trial. The trial began in Waco, a town of 25,000 located seven miles south of Robinson, on May 15, 1916, at the 54th District Court, Judge Richard I. Munroe presiding. A sea of white faces pushed into the court until it filled to capacity, and hundreds more gathered outside, anxious to render their own justice. Twelve white men served as the jury. After hearing the evidence, they deliberated for less than five minutes and returned with a guilty verdict, which carried with it the death penalty. What happened next became known as the Waco Horror.

The verdict ignited an already incensed court. Shouts rang out for Jesse's immediate execution. Men rushed Jesse, pushing aside security and Jesse's lawyers (who did not resist the onslaught), grabbed the frightened boy, and ripped off his clothes. Some had clubs, others bricks, still others had shovels, guns, and knives. They dragged him outside where they wrapped a chain around his neck. Jesse's plea for mercy did not deter the crazed mob, now 15,000 strong. They swarmed Jesse, the chain tightening around his neck. As they dragged him to the City Square to be hanged, they beat him, stabbed him, and mutilated him. His fingers were cut off, his ears, his toes—body parts taken as souvenirs.

No matter the verdict, the townspeople had already judged Jesse guilty, evident in their reaction to the verdict and the debris for a bonfire they had built in the City Square outside the courthouse. The boxes and wood that they had piled under a tree were doused in coal oil, as was Jesse. Then the fire was lit, the chain around Jesse's neck was looped over a branch, and Jesse was hoisted up. The onlookers' gaze bespoke anger, pride, and victory as Jesse was lowered into the blaze. His screams fell on the deaf ears of women, children, and men. Indeed, Waco's finest, many donned in their Sunday best, did not flinch at the sight or smell of the burning youth.

In fact, Jesse Washington's lynching drew a crowd of everyday, law-abiding, church-attending, educated citizens—Waco's mayor and police officials included. The popularity of lynching between 1880 and 1930 was often captured in photos depicting satisfied mobs smiling and posing with their kill. Waco photographer Fred Gildersleeve took pictures of Jesse's lynching as it was in progress. He photographed scenes of the mob torturing Jesse. Gildersleeve had planned to use the photos as postcards to sell commemorating the event. Although some of the photos were made into postcards, Gildersleeve did not expect his photos to stir a nation to outrage or to shame and tarnish Waco's image as the Athens of Texas. Yet his photographs shone a spotlight on what was sometimes called the New Negro Crime and was instrumental in bringing national attention to the crime of lynching.

The violence against blacks dubbed New Negro Crime emerged primarily to quell the upward mobility blacks gained during Reconstruction and reflected the stereotype of white females as prey of black men. Hence, merely accusing a black man of raping a white woman was reason for a black man, any black man, to be hanged. Although the accusations were mostly false, mobs could only be satisfied when a snapped-neck black victim paid with his life. Jesse's guilt

was questionable, according to black journalist A. T. Smith. Smith alleged that George Fryer, Lucy Fryer's husband, murdered her, an allegation for which Smith was convicted of criminal libel and silenced.

Nevertheless, the New Negro Crime sealed Jesse's fate. His conviction, torture, mutilation, burning, decapitation; the bagging of his burnt body, dragging it back to Robinson, and hanging it in public as a warning to blacks occurred within an hour of his conviction. No one in the mob was charged.

REGINALD BRUSTER

See also
Lynching

Further Reading:
Bernstein, Patricia. *The Lynching of Jesse Washington and the Rise of the NAACP*. College Station: Texas A&M Press, 2005.
Carrigan, William D. *The Making of a Lynching Culture: Violence and Vigilantism in Central Texas, 1836–1916*. Urbana: University of Illinois Press, 2004.
Giddings, Paula. *When and Where I Enter: The Impact of Black Women on Race and Sex in America*. New York: Bantam Books, 1984.

Jewish-Black Conflicts

Jewish-black conflicts manifest the intricacy of race relations in the United States, because both Jews and blacks have long been the victims of racial discrimination and thus have a better chance of sympathy, if not of solidarity, in the struggle for racial justice. In fact, there have been efforts toward sympathy and solidarity between the two groups, particularly in the era of the civil rights movement. But several polls conducted in the 1990s found a noticeable increase of anti-Semitism in the black population to a greater extent than among any other ethic groups. It is surprising because since the 1960s, negative Jewish stereotypes have clearly declined among the general American public. On the other hand, most Jews were found to not support government spending for the benefits of blacks. Jews, more than other white ethnic groups, another poll found, disliked having blacks in their neighborhoods and black students in the same school with their children.

Black anti-Semitism may be traced back to the tradition of medieval Christian anti-Semitism that holds Jews as killers of Christ and shrewd money handlers. It was, however, socioeconomic disparity between two groups that reinforced the negative images of Jews. In spite of ethnic bigotry, most Jews as a group achieved an impressive upward mobility only with the span of two generations in the United States, while most blacks have remained at the bottom. Many saw the evidence of the inflated notion of Jewish control of the United States in the incredible success of Jewish Americans, combined with their disproportionate presence in media, film, and retail industries, and their influence in national politics. Blacks in large cities, particularly in New York City, often found themselves in financial deals with Jews because Jews owned a substantial number of small businesses and apartment buildings in black communities. Such transactions frequently turned Jews into the closest and most visible symbol of white oppression, and they became an easy target of black resentment.

Among other factors contributing to black anti-Semitism was the radicalization of the black freedom struggle toward Black Nationalism beginning in the mid-1960s. One extreme example was Louis Farrakhan, the leader of black Muslims, who, in his fiercely anti-Semitic rhetoric, bluntly condemned Jews for their supposed role in white domination. Black advocates of community control accused Jewish-owned small businesses in black neighborhoods of being parasitical. Militant black civil rights leaders did not want Jewish activists in their organizations, where they had once played active roles. In addition, the policies of the Israeli government toward Palestine also tended to strengthen the negative attitude against Jews among blacks, whose experience of racial oppression led them to identify with Palestinians.

Jews' racism toward blacks can be partially explained as a result of their successful assimilation into mainstream American culture. As they assimilated into U.S. society, some also adopted mainstream racism. The actual contact with poor blacks through their business activities could reinforce the negative stereotypes of blacks. Many Jewish intellectuals were wary of Black Nationalism, just as many black intellectuals were uncomfortable with Zionism. Jewish Americans also found that affirmative action worked against them, even though it was intended to compensate for the harms caused by past racial discrimination. Around 1920, many discriminatory quota systems had been introduced to curb the number of Jews in schools, occupations, and neighborhoods, and Jews had fought against those measures. Given the disproportionate concentration of Jews in higher education and high-ranking occupations, they argued, affirmative action acted in reality as reverse discrimination against Jewish Americans.

Dong-Ho Cho

See also

Anti-Semitism in the United States

Further Reading:

Anti-Defamation League. *Survey on Anti-Semitism and Prejudice in America.* New York, 1998.

Nathan, Glazer. *Affirmative Discrimination: Ethnic Identity and Public Policy.* New York: Basic Books, 1975.

Salzman, Jack, Colin Elman, and Mirium Fendius Elman, eds. *Bridges and Boundaries: African Americans and American Jews.* New York: George Braziller, 1992.

Smith, Tom W. *Jewish Attitude toward Blacks and Race Relations.* New York: American Jewish Committee, 1990.

Jim Crow Laws

The term *Jim Crow* originated from a song that Thomas "Daddy" Rice, a minstrel performer, overheard being sung by a black man. It is believed that the Jim Crow reference in the song alluded to a slave owner. Rice later popularized the term in the 1830s and 1840s in a blackface skit he called "Jump Jim Crow." For blacks, this skit was degrading. In 1841, the term *Jim Crow* was used by a railroad in Massachusetts to identify the rail cars restricted to blacks. Segregated rail cars had appeared as early as the 1830s. In the 1890s, the name Jim Crow was given to the various laws that mandated racial segregation in public facilities, such as schools, parks, restrooms, places of entertainment, businesses, and railway stations. These laws varied from state to state but were most prominent in the South. Violence was often used by whites to enforce Jim Crow laws and to punish the blacks who challenged them. The Jim Crow era, which spanned more than 70 years, was marked by violence.

Early attempts to protest racial segregation were not only unsuccessful but perilous. In the 1830s, free blacks were restricted from renting cabins on steamboats and were required to stay on deck even during storms. All blacks, regardless of their social or economic status, were excluded from white society in the South. Affluent blacks who lived in white neighborhoods in the North were rare. Blacks who paid for first-class train tickets were frequently forced to take second-class coaches, which were generally filthy, overcrowded, and inferior.

Mortified by this situation, blacks engaged in various forms of resistance on both individual and collective levels. Frederick Douglass regularly refused to give up his first-class seat, thereby forcing whites to physically remove him. On one occasion, Douglass and several white men struggled so much that his seat was torn from its foundation. In 1854, a white streetcar conductor in New York physically assaulted a black teacher who resisted the discriminatory laws. In 1889, black Baptists purchased first-class train tickets from Georgia to Indiana; in Indianapolis, Indiana, they were met by a white mob and beaten. In her youth, Mary Church Terrell managed to keep her first-class seat during her travel only by threatening the conductor that her father would sue the railroad for forcing her to ride in a Jim Crow car. Resistance from black politicians—and even the railroads (although for purely economic reasons)—was ineffective. In 1892, blacks tested the 1891 law that established segregated trains in Louisiana. In a gallant effort to protest segregation, Homer A. Plessy mounted a train but was arrested when he attempted to sit in the white-only section. His case went to the Supreme Court. In 1896, the U.S. Supreme Court ruled in favor of segregation. Justice Henry Brown justified the court's decision by stating that separate did not mean unequal. Opposition to a juggernaut of similar events proved futile, leading ultimately to the Jim Crow laws.

With federal backing from the *Plessy v. Ferguson* ruling and other similar Supreme Court decisions, Jim Crow laws took effect across America. But contrary to the *Plessy v. Ferguson* ruling, separate remained far from equal. Whites enjoyed better facilities, such as schools, textbooks, and hospitals. Even blacks with achievements equivalent to their white counterparts endured limited privileges, opportunities, and freedoms. Jim Crow laws effectively reinforced a miasma of volatile racial tension and hatred that let loose a deluge of violence against blacks. Prominent during the Jim Crow era was the lynching of black males of various ages and race riots. White mobs regularly assailed blacks for myriad reasons. Whites often accused black males of violating the rules of racial etiquette, especially when they pertained to white women. Thousands of black males were murdered for this reason alone. The lynching of Emmett Till was one of the most publicized cases. Till was lynched for speaking to a white woman on a dare. Incidents such as this were reminiscent of frontier justice, where law was enforced without due process. Oftentimes, white mobs did not cease with one lynching but spread their hostility into nearby black communities, attacking blacks who had nothing to do with the original incident. More often than not, the blacks had done nothing to provoke such atrocities against them. Lawlessness was rampant throughout the Jim Crow era.

Shortly after the inception of the Jim Crow laws in the 1890s, the United States experienced a wave of violence in its towns and cities that continued intermittently until the nascent civil rights protests of the 1950s and 1960s. Major race riots occurred in Phoenix, South Carolina (1898); Lake City, North Carolina (1898); Wilmington, North Carolina (1898); New Orleans, Louisiana (1900); New York City (1900); Springfield, Ohio (1904); Atlanta, Georgia (1906); Chattanooga, Tennessee (1906); Greensburg, Indiana (1906); Brownsville, Texas (1906); Springfield, Illinois (1908); and Palestine, Texas (1910). These riots were generally instigated by whites to maintain their supremacy and to enact revenge. For example, whites rioted in Phoenix, South Carolina, in response to blacks who took action to protest their disenfranchisement. A white mob attacked blacks after a black newspaper spoke out against white men who sexually violated black women. In Atlanta, Georgia, whites cruelly attacked blacks and their businesses over rumors of assaults against white women (*see* Rape as Provocation for Lynching).

Between 1917 and 1921, another wave of race riots hit the towns and cities to which blacks migrated for safety, better opportunities, and the promise of economic advancement. Riots occurred in East St. Louis, Illinois (1917); Houston, Texas (1917); Chester and Philadelphia, Pennsylvania (1918); Chicago, Illinois (1919); Elaine, Arkansas (1919); Washington, D.C. (1919); Omaha, Nebraska (1919); Charleston, South Carolina (1919); Knoxville, Tennessee (1919); and Tulsa, Oklahoma (1921). Over 20 riots occurred in 1919 alone. The riots in this period are known as the Red Summer

Race Riots of 1919. Racial tensions were particularly high as a result of a high influx of blacks into the cities during World War I. Competition for employment and housing, compounded by white racism, was the main catalyst for the violence of the Red Summer riots. White gangs played a significant role in these riots, as well as in the indiscriminate harassment of blacks in the cities. Jim Crow laws directly affected the 1919 outbreak in Chicago, which was triggered when a black youth unintentionally drifted into the section of a beach designated for whites. Whites pelted rocks at him and drowned him. The ensuing violence resulted in 38 deaths, 537 injuries, and nearly 1,000 individuals bereft of their homes.

Blacks who migrated to states such as Arkansas and Oklahoma after Reconstruction to escape the mass violence and subjugation experienced in the South were met with unexpected adversity. Blacks in Elaine, Arkansas, were forced to work as sharecroppers. Most sharecroppers received meager prices for their cotton, while white merchants and landowners hoarded much of the profit. In an effort to attain higher cotton prices, blacks formed a union. Trouble erupted when a deputy was shot and killed while trying to foil a union meeting. Whites murdered several blacks without repercussions, but 12 black men were sentenced to death, and 67 black men were given prison terms. The riot in Tulsa in 1921 broke out at a courthouse jail when blacks attempted to protect a black man accused of raping a white woman from a white mob. He was later found innocent. Whites customarily kidnapped blacks in or en route to jail and lynched them. Both whites and blacks suffered casualties. Whites then chased blacks into Greenwood, Oklahoma, which was one of several prosperous black towns. Whites decimated Greenwood. Rosewood, Florida, another black town, was destroyed in 1923 when a white woman falsely claimed that a black man beat her.

Rioting broke out again in World War II during the next wave of black migration. Riots occurred in Detroit, Michigan (1943); New York City (1943); Mobile, Alabama (1943); Columbia, Tennessee (1943); Beaumont, Texas (1943); and Cicero, Illinois (1951). Racial tensions and competition over employment and housing were at the root of most of these incidents. The Detroit riot was caused by racial tensions between black and white youths. Each group carried out aggressions on innocent bystanders. The full-blown riot

occurred when whites attacked a local black neighborhood. Whites at the Alabama Dry Dock and Shipbuilding Company went on a violent rampage when 12 blacks were hired as a result of federal regulations. Whites rioted in Beaumont when a black man was accused of raping a white woman.

Disturbances also occurred in other areas, particularly near or on military bases. Numerous racial conflicts broke out between Southern whites and black soldiers from the North who were not used to Jim Crow laws and etiquette. In many cases, blacks outright refused to play the docile role whites expected of them. Black soldiers instigated several intense confrontations, such as in Fayetteville, North Carolina (1941), for being forced to ride a Jim Crow bus; in El Paso, Texas (1943), following a rumor that a white man had raped a black woman; and at Camp Claibourne, Louisiana (1944), where a white mob murdered four blacks.

Black soldiers were not the only ones to defy Jim Crow laws. Black resistance to Jim Crow has a long history, although it is replete with violent backlash. Ida B. Wells-Barnett, a journalist who protested lynching in her writings in the early 20th century, was threatened on more than one occasion. Other outspoken newspaper editors, church leaders, and prominent figures, such as Henry McNeal Turner, Booker T. Washington, and W.E.B. Du Bois, remarkably survived the onslaught of terror inflicted upon blacks during their lifetimes. In 1909, the National Association for the Advancement of Colored People (NAACP) rose out of the violence of the riot in Springfield, Illinois. The NAACP was an organization composed of blacks and whites who waged battles in court against the discriminatory Jim Crow laws, disenfranchisement, and lynching. Their most significant and far-reaching win was the defeat of racial segregation in public schools in the 1954 *Brown v. Board of Education* case.

The 1950s and 1960s ushered in a massive new nonviolent movement to protest segregation. This movement, known as the civil rights movement, involved individuals, organizations such as the Southern Christian Leadership Conference (SCLC) and the Congress of Racial Equality (CORE), and student groups, such as the Student Nonviolent Coordinating Committee (SNCC). Participants in this movement engaged in bus boycotts, sit-ins, demonstrations, and marches. White mobs often challenged these peaceful demonstrations with violence. White mobs savagely attacked participants of the Freedom Rides. Police officers beat, gassed, and turned their dogs on protestors of all ages. Many men and women, including Dr. Martin Luther King, Jr., were murdered for their valiant struggle against discrimination.

Nevertheless, the civil rights movement was more effective than any other previous form of resistance. After considerable labor, the boycotts and court cases won by the NAACP resulted in the elimination of racial segregation on Montgomery buses. Further protests contributed to the enactment of the Civil Rights Act of 1957. Intensifying demonstrations, along with the exposure (thanks to television) of the violence inflicted upon peaceful activists, achieved a compelling victory when U.S. President Lyndon B. Johnson signed the Civil Rights Act of 1964, thereby eradicating all Jim Crow laws across the nation. What the act could not do was remedy the effects of prolonged racism and discrimination on the inhabitants of the Jim Crow-created ghettos, or prevent the imminent black rebellions.

GLADYS L. KNIGHT

See also

Civil Rights Movement; Great Migration; Lynching; Segregation

Further Reading:

Chafe, William H., ed. *Remembering Jim Crow: African Americans Tell about Life in the Segregated South*. New York: New Press, 2001.

Gilje, Paul A. *Rioting in America*. Indiana University Press, 1996, 151–61.

Hine, Darlene Clark, William C. Hine, and Stanley Harrold. *The African American Odyssey*. Englewood Cliffs, NJ: Prentice Hall, 2000, 146–47, 314–17.

Woodward, C. Vann. *The Strange Career of Jim Crow*, 3rd rev. ed. New York: Oxford University Press, 1974.

Jimmie Lee Jackson Murder

On February 18, 1965, Jimmie Lee Jackson was shot in the stomach by Alabama state trooper, James B. Fowler. It happened in Marion, Alabama, as Jackson tried to participate in a peaceful civil rights demonstration. His subsequent death from the gunshot wounds contributed to the decision for the Southern Christian Leadership Conference (SCLC) to hold the famous civil rights march from Selma to Montgomery on March 7, 1965. This demonstration was a pivotal event in the history of the civil rights movement. The images from that march have become symbolic in the struggle for black voting rights during that era. Because of the fatal assault on Jimmie Lee Jackson that preceded the Selma-to-Montgomery march, many citizens of Marion, Alabama, proclaim their city the cradle of the civil rights movement.

Jackson was born in Marion, Alabama, in December 1938. At the time of his death, he was 26 years old. Even at that age, he was the youngest deacon in his Baptist church. He was a Vietnam War veteran and was well respected in his community. In him there was clear potential for leadership not only in his community but in the civil rights movement. Yet he was not allowed to vote. He had attempted to vote at least five times. All efforts were unsuccessful.

In the 1960s, central Alabama, like a number of other places throughout the country, especially in the Deep South, was experiencing volatile racial conflicts. Through the civil rights movement, blacks and their supporters were pushing for change. One critical issue was for blacks to vote unencumbered, without unfair barriers such as poll taxes and literacy tests. In central Alabama there were formidable obstacles to overcome. There was Jim Clark, the sheriff who was an arch segregationist, who was determined to maintain the status quo. There was John Hare, the circuit court judge, who summarily issued court orders targeting civil rights workers by prohibiting marches, meetings, or even small gatherings. Then there were the citizens, many of whom resisted any changes in the way of life they had come to know.

In his position as sheriff, Jim Clark had several notorious encounters with nonviolent civil rights protesters. On one occasion, he punched Rev. C. T. Vivian, one of Martin Luther King, Jr.'s associates from the SCLC, as he gave a speech on the courthouse steps. Clark even had Vivian arrested for having the audacity to make a speech there.

In the midst of this environment, civil rights marches, protests, and sit-ins were growing. Students and other young people tried to desegregate a restaurant in Marion. They were arrested. They came in waves of different groups. All were arrested. A few days later, James Orange, a field secretary for the SCLC, was arrested too. His charge was contributing to the delinquency of a minor, alleging his responsibility for the students' actions in their desegregation effort. On February 18, 2006, local blacks and their supporters assembled at Zion United Methodist Church in Marion. They were planning to develop strategies to eliminate discriminatory practices, including the refusal to allow them to vote. Almost spontaneously, they decided to walk a few yards to the jail where Orange and some other civil rights protesters were being held. About 500 people left the church with plans to sing freedom songs outside the jail in a peaceful display of solidarity.

But before they reached the jail, they came face-to-face with a wall of city police officers, sheriff's deputies, and Alabama state troopers. The street lights went out. In addition to the large number of law enforcement officials, there suddenly appeared white men who looked as if they were regular citizens. Altogether they began to physically attack the people from the church—movement activists, journalists, civil rights supporters, and bystanders. During this attack, several of the people fled, taking refuge in a nearby business called Mack's Café. State troopers followed. When they entered the café, they wreaked havoc by knocking over tables where customers were eating. They bludgeoned patrons and protesters alike. During this rampage, state troopers beat 82-year-old Cager Lee down to the floor. Cager Lee was Jimmie Lee Jackson's grandfather. Viola Jackson, Jimmie Lee Jackson's mother, went to help her father. When Jimmie Lee Jackson went to assist his mother, a state trooper (Fowler) shot him in the stomach. Jimmie Lee Jackson was taken to Good Samaritan Hospital in Selma. Ten others were hospitalized. Many others were jailed.

On February 26, 1965, Jimmie Lee Jackson died of the gunshot wound. State Trooper Fowler gave an affidavit of a slightly different version of what happened that night. No action was taken against him. But by all reputable accounts, an innocent person was killed as a result of the events that occurred when he set out to participate in a peaceful march to show solidarity with a jailed civil rights worker.

When Jackson was shot, Martin Luther King, Jr. sent a prescient telegram to Nicolas Katzenbach, who was the U.S. attorney general. It read, "This situation can only encourage chaos and savagery in the minds of law enforcement unless dealt with immediately" (Fleming 2005). Jimmie Lee Jackson became a martyr for the civil rights movement, generally, and black voting rights, specifically. He epitomized nonviolence, the guiding philosophy of Martin Luther King, Jr. and the civil rights movement. He was murdered though he did not possess a gun or other weapon of destruction. His only crime was the desire to exercise his constitutional right to vote.

Every year there is a memorial held in Marion commemorating Jimmie Lee Jackson and his contribution to a movement that changed the nation. In the town near the spot where he was murdered, there is a marker that reads, "[He] gave his life in the struggle for the right to vote."

BETTY NYANGONI

See also
Bloody Sunday; Police Brutality

Further Reading:
Branch, Taylor. *Pillar of Fire: America in the King Years, 1963–65.* New York: Simon and Schuster, 1999.
Fleming, John. "The Death of Jimmie Lee Jackson. *Anniston Star*, March 6, 2005.
VoteJustice.org. "Sample Letter to the Editor and Opinion-Editorial: Re-authorize the Voting Rights Act of 1965."
Williams, Juan. *Eyes on the Prize.* New York: Penguin Group, 1988.

Johnson, Jack (1878–1946)

Jack Johnson was the first African American heavyweight boxing champion. As champion from 1908 to 1915, Johnson held the most important athletic title in all of American sports. Before him, white heavyweight champions refused to fight African American contenders. Battering whites in the ring, Johnson shattered the myth that white men were physically superior to African Americans. Outside the ring, he rebelled against white authority by defying the law and flaunting his relationships with white women. Johnson embodied a physical challenge to Jim Crow.

Arthur John "Jack" Johnson was born a year after the collapse of Reconstruction, in 1878, in Galveston, Texas. Johnson's father, Henry, labored as a school janitor, while his mother, Tina, worked as a laundress to support their six children. For five or six years, Johnson attended elementary school. His boxing education began when he started fighting in battle royals. In these humiliating contests, white men formed a circle around black youths, who were sometimes blindfolded, and forced them to fight each other until only one was left standing. The victor won a handful of pennies. By his late teens, Johnson traveled throughout the country boxing against minor professionals.

In 1901, Johnson fought Joe Choynski, an experienced fighter, in Galveston. After Choynski knocked out Johnson, both were locked behind bars for nearly a month for violating Texas laws that prohibited prizefighting. Freed from jail, Johnson continued to fight, defeating the best contenders Galveston had to offer. Later that year, he left for California to fight new opponents. At that time, Johnson had no chance at the heavyweight title. In 1892, champion John L. Sullivan drew the color line, refusing to enter the ring with African American challengers. Although African Americans fought white champions in other divisions, heavyweight title bouts remained segregated. For many Americans, the heavyweight champion represented the "king of men," and as long as a white man wore the crown, whites continued to believe in their own inherent racial superiority.

As a premier African American heavyweight, Johnson earned a shot at the Negro heavyweight championship against Denver Ed Martin in 1903. After defeating Martin, he defended his title against the best African American fighters, including Sam McVey, Sam Langford, and Joe Jeannette. Holding the Negro championship brought Johnson little fame and fortune. For the next three years, he fought the best black and white boxers in the country, but white champions ignored him.

By 1905, boxing seemed to decline in popularity. Five years earlier, reform-minded politicians banned the sport by law, claiming that prizefighting promoted corruption, gambling, and immoral behavior. With little interest in boxing, purses shrank, and the heavyweight champion Jim Jeffries retired undefeated. At the same time, Johnson fought against less-talented white fighters, often carrying his opponents round after round in order to dish out more punishment. He also hired a white manager who had the kind of connections that would help Johnson break the color barrier. Significantly, Johnson began traveling openly with white women, most of whom were prostitutes.

Johnson journeyed to Australia in 1907 to build up his international reputation. Later that year, he earned a match in Philadelphia against an aging former champion, Bob Fitzsimmons. Johnson dropped Fitzsimmons in two rounds and celebrated with a white prostitute named Hattie Mc-Clay, who became his travel companion over the next four years. The next year, Johnson chased heavyweight champion Tommy Burns to Australia hoping to arrange a title fight.

Boxer Jack Johnson in bowler hat and vested suit, 1909. (Library of Congress)

Burns rejected his overtures, but Johnson persisted. The champ eventually gave in, after Johnson agreed to let the white fighter keep $30,000 of the $35,000 purse.

From the opening seconds of the first round, it was clear Johnson would win. Toned and powerful, Johnson toyed with Burns. He laughed as Burns wailed away at his midsection, dispelling the myth that African American men lacked intestinal fortitude. Burns fought back with racial epithets. Johnson hammered him until the 14th round. For the first time in history an African American held the heavyweight championship.

Almost immediately, promoters searched for the "Great White Hope," a boxer who could restore the crown to the white side of the color line. As the search began, Johnson returned to America in 1909, more determined to live by his own rules. He bought flashy suits, fancy hats, and fast cars. The American public began to hear stories about his nightlife carousing with white women. In Chicago, he met a young prostitute named Belle Schreiber, who became one of his closest mistresses. Johnson lived recklessly, racing cars, ignoring speed limits, and racking up unpaid tickets. Jack Johnson insisted on being free.

After Johnson easily discarded every white challenger he faced, America finally found its White Hope, pressuring Jim Jeffries out of retirement. Now 35 years old and extremely overweight, Jeffries was far from prepared to save the white race. Nonetheless, the astronomical $101,000 purse and the fight's movie revenue provided plenty of motivation for him to lose more than 70 pounds before the match.

Originally scheduled for San Francisco, promoters moved the battle for racial supremacy to Reno, Nevada. The media depicted Johnson in Sambo cartoons, stereotypically portraying him as childlike and cowardly. More than 20,000 people traveled to Reno to witness the "fight of the century." Drunken gamblers placed bets right up until the opening bell. When the two men finally raised their gloves on July 10, 1910, it was clear that Johnson was the stronger boxer. He unleashed a series of counterpunches and uppercuts on Jeffries. By the 15th round, Jeffries's face had swollen as he struggled to stand upright. Finally, Johnson drilled him until he fell to the canvas. Jeffries's corner threw in the towel. The Great White Hope had fallen.

After Johnson's victory, white mobs attacked celebrating African Americans in numerous cities. To prevent further riots, authorities banned the showing of the fight film, while others called for an end to boxing altogether. The new champion struck fear in whites who viewed Johnson as a dangerous role model for African Americans. Johnson hoped his fame would translate into a successful vaudeville career, but theater promoters feared boycotts or riots would follow the champion on stage. Johnson added to his controversial reputation by marrying Etta Terry Duryea, a previously wed white woman. He angered his new wife by continuing his relationship with Belle Schreiber. Duryea could not share her husband, or stand his physical abuse, and eventually committed suicide.

Nearly two months after his wife's death, Johnson married another young white woman, Lucille Cameron. Cameron's mother charged Johnson with abduction and white slavery, a federal violation of the Mann Act, which forbade the transportation of women in interstate travel for immoral purposes. The case fell apart when Cameron admitted to practicing prostitution before she met Johnson. Although the federal government knew he was not guilty, they pursued conviction, persuading Schreiber to testify against him. In May 1913, Johnson was convicted of trumped-up Mann Act charges. The judge sentenced him to 366 days in prison and a $1,000 fine. Defiantly, Johnson fled to Montreal, Canada, and then set sail for France. Over the next year and a half, he staged shows, boxing exhibitions, and wrestling matches throughout Europe, but struggled to earn money with the onset of World War I.

After defending his title three times in Paris, Johnson arranged a fight with another White Hope in Cuba. On April 5, 1915, Johnson squared off against the six-foot-six "Pottawatomie Giant," Jess Willard. In the 26th round, Willard took advantage of the aging champion and landed a long right punch that knocked Johnson down. Many reporters believed that the fight was fixed. Johnson later maintained that he threw the match for a large sum of money and a lenient return to the United States. Historians doubt Johnson's claim. Nonetheless, Willard reinstated the color line, and not until 1937 did another African American, Joe Louis, win the heavyweight championship.

Jack Johnson's boxing career basically ended after the Willard fight. Over the next five years, he fought unspectacular boxers and took up bullfighting in Spain and Mexico. After seven years in exile, he turned himself in to U.S. marshals in July 1920 at the California border. Thereafter he served one year in prison in Leavenworth, Kansas. For the rest of his life he worked a variety of jobs, as a boxing promoter, museum lecturer, preacher, and nightclub owner. During World War II, he fought an exhibition at the age of 67 to raise money for the war effort. Johnson was no longer the fighter he once was, but he could still race cars. On June 10, 1946, his life ended when he crashed his speeding automobile in North Carolina.

JOHN MATTHEW SMITH

See also

Sports and Racism

Further Reading:

Roberts, Randy. *Papa Jack: Jack Johnson and the Era of White Hopes.* New York: Free Press, 1983.

Ward, Geoffrey C. *Unforgivable Blackness: The Rise and Fall of Jack Johnson.* New York: A. A. Knopf, 2004.

Johnson, John H. (1918–2005)

John H. Johnson built a publishing and cosmetics empire based on the promotion of healthy images for African Americans, in order to counter the prevalence of hurtful and damaging images of blacks in popular American media during the 20th century. Born in Arkansas City, Arkansas, in 1918 to Gertrude and Leroy Johnson, John H. Johnson's early life was stable and secure, though at times marked by tragedy. Leroy Johnson, a sawmill worker, died in an accident at the factory when his son was eight years old. Later that year, Johnson and his mother narrowly escaped the Great Flood of 1927, when the Mississippi River overran its banks in nearly every state between Louisiana and Minnesota. Johnson and his mother spent six weeks on a small island awaiting rescue. When they returned to Arkansas City, they found their house devastated. The family found a measure of stability in the years after the flood. Gertrude Johnson remarried, and John Johnson excelled in elementary and middle school.

After John Johnson completed eighth grade, the highest grade offered to black students in Arkansas City, Gertrude Johnson and her son moved to Chicago in 1933. Though Gertrude Johnson's education ended at the third grade, she found gainful employment as a domestic worker. The two moved in with Gertrude Johnson's daughter from an earlier marriage, Beulah. They were later joined by Gertrude's husband, James Williams. The family of four became permanent residents of Chicago, and it was in the city that he launched two of the most profitable and significant magazines in African American publishing, *Ebony* and *Jet*.

Chicago was a popular destination for Southern African Americans migrating northward after World War I. Seeking to escape the lynching, police brutality, segregation in housing, few employment prospects, and inferior education, blacks like John H. Johnson found that Chicago and other cities (such as New York and Kansas City) offered economic opportunity and middle-class respectability. By the mid-1930s, African Americans had established prosperous businesses across the city, including insurance companies, newspapers, beauty salons, and grocery stores.

Though the Great Depression hit the country hardest in the early 1930s, Gertrude Johnson's wages as a domestic worker kept the family afloat. Her son enrolled in Wendell Phillips High School in 1933. The initial years in Chicago ultimately proved beneficial to Johnson. His stepfather joined the family in 1933 in Chicago. Johnson left behind most of the ill effects of a segregated, limited education in Arkansas City. By his senior year in 1936, Johnson edited the school newspaper, was voted senior class president, and earned a partial scholarship to the University of Chicago. The family's fortunes took a turn for the worse in 1936, when the economic crisis that devastated the country eventually undid the prosperity enjoyed by much of black Chicago. The Johnson family found financial relief in New Deal projects, including the Works Progress Administration and the National Youth Administration. After graduation, Johnson worked at Supreme Liberty Life Insurance Company, one of the most profitable businesses in Chicago.

It was at Supreme Liberty that Johnson gained much of his education in business and entrepreneurship. Johnson became the personal assistant of Supreme Liberty's president, Harry H. Pace. Over the decade-long relationship with Pace, Johnson developed valuable business contacts and networked with Pace's personal friends, the wealthiest of Chicago's black elite. He even used his small office at Supreme Liberty as the mailing address for his first undertaking in journalism, the *Negro Digest*.

Johnson founded *Negro Digest* in November 1942, using his savings and a $500 loan from his mother as collateral to pay the printers. Though Chicago already had a number of popular black newspapers, most notably the *Chicago Defender*, the articles in the *Negro Digest* focused on positive images of achievement, hope, and success, rarely publishing articles about crime, delinquency, and violence. It also featured a regular column, "If I Were a Negro," in which famous white leaders answered questions about the "race problem," such as the morality of segregation and the scarcity of good education for black children. In less than a year, *Negro Digest* had nearly 100,000 subscriptions. Johnson used the profits from *Negro Digest* to fund his most successful magazine, *Ebony*.

Founded in November 1945, *Ebony* followed the same journalistic pattern set by *Negro Digest*—upbeat stories of accomplishment, advice for business success, births and wedding announcements, and celebrity interviews—and its complete focus on black life and culture. Johnson used his resources from the *Negro Digest* to completely finance *Ebony*, and after a year, *Ebony* outsold *Negro Digest*. In *Ebony*'s first year, Johnson opted against including advertisements, in order to maintain complete editorial control. As *Ebony* increased in popularity, it cost more money to produce. In 1947, Johnson partnered with Eugene McDonald, president of Zenith Radio, the most popular black-owned radio station in Chicago. The advertising revenue from Zenith underwrote the production of *Ebony* after the first 12 months, and later, its success. Johnson became a member of the board of directors of Zenith in 1971.

Johnson's financial acumen extended to two more ventures, *Jet* magazine in 1951 and Fashion Fair Cosmetics in 1974. By catering to an exclusively African American audience, the Johnson Publishing Company developed a loyal following for its periodicals and its products. For example, Fashion Fair Cosmetics spoke to the lack of cosmetics for African American women in the 1970s. Fashion Fair currently controls much of the nationwide market for African American women's beauty aids, and the products are advertised exclusively in *Ebony* and *Jet*. Similarly, *Jet* magazine featured news articles on black life and history in a digest format. All three enterprises, *Ebony*, *Jet*, and Fashion Fair, stayed true to Johnson's vision of achievement through loyalty, constructive images, positive role models, and hard work. However, by the late 1960s, Johnson's vision for African American success came under increased scrutiny. Influenced by the civil rights movement and the Vietnam War in the 1960s, black intellectuals and celebrities criticized Johnson, the magazines, and the Johnson Publishing Company for irrelevance or for falling out of touch with the needs of black communities. One intellectual, Harold Cruse, wrote that *Ebony* and *Jet* merely promoted black achievement, big and small, without critical engagement or measure. By the mid-1970s, Johnson's vision of upbeat, middle-class black Americans failed to address the crushing poverty and unemployment facing African Americans in urban areas. The Johnson Publishing Company had raised African American spirits during the era of Jim Crow, but it had not kept up with lingering economic and political impact of segregation.

Johnson responded that the needs of the black community were his chief concern. He partnered with corporations that pledged to support black education. Among several awards, he has been granted the Spingarn Medal of Freedom from the National Association for the Advancement of Colored People in 1966, the Presidential Medal of Freedom in 1996, and the "Greatest Minority Entrepreneur" by Baylor University in 2003. In his honor, Howard University rededicated its communication school to the John H. Johnson School of Communication. Though the *Negro Digest* (later renamed *Black World*) ended its run in 1970, *Ebony* and *Jet* remain tremendously successful, each earning over 100,000 subscriptions per year, the highest subscription rate of all-black periodicals in the world.

Johnson married Eunice Walker in 1941. They adopted two children. Their son, John Jr., died of sickle cell anemia at the age of 25. Their daughter, Linda Johnson Rice, graduated from the University of Southern California with a BA in journalism. She currently presides over the Johnson Publishing Company. Johnson died of heart failure in August 2005 at the age of 87. He is buried at Oak Woods Cemetery in Chicago.

Nikki Brown

See also
Cosmetics; Skin Lightening

Further Reading:

Cross, Theodore. "*Ebony* Magazine: Sometimes *The Bell Curve*'s Best Friend." *Journal of Blacks in Higher Education* 10 (Winter 1995–96): 75–76.

Johnson, John J. *Succeeding Against the Odds*. New York: Warner Books, 1989.

Johnson Publishing Company, http://www.johnsonpublishing.com (accessed June 2008).

Washburn, Patrick Scott. *The African American Newspaper: Voice of Freedom*. Evanston, IL: Northwestern University Press, 2006.

Johnson-Jeffries Fight of 1910, Riots Following

When the African American fighter Jack Johnson, the then heavyweight champion, defeated retired white champion James Jeffries in a much publicized fight in Reno, Nevada, on July 4, 1910, the result caused the outbreak of racial violence in numerous American cities, including Baltimore, St. Louis, and Pittsburgh.

As a youngster growing up in Galveston, Texas, during the post-Reconstruction era, Jack Johnson believed he was destined to be a great man. His parents, Henry and Tiny Johnson, were former slaves who managed to build their own home and see to it that Johnson and his four siblings learned to read and write. Unlike other Southern cities, Galveston was not distinctly racially divided, and Johnson never experienced the harsh apartheid of Jim Crow that beleaguered other Southern blacks living below the Mason-Dixon line. Racial lines were drawn in schools but neighborhoods were an ethnic mix as economic status was the dominant factor determining where people resided. Thus, as he played with white boys on Galveston's docks, Johnson matured with a mindset that he was inferior to no one and that no limits could be placed on his aspirations.

The young Johnson began to seriously pursue his boxing career in 1896. At 18, he was sparring with veteran fighters and traveling to cities looking for his own bouts. He was earning between $5 to $15 a night, more than manual laborers made in a week; however, his first big break would come six years later in Los Angeles when he faced Jack Jeffries, the younger brother of heavyweight champion Jim Jeffries. Although this was not a title fight, the media accentuated the racial implications calling the younger Jeffries a Greek god and referring to Johnson as a coon. Yet the contest was not the battle many expected, as Johnson won easily in five rounds and confidently whispered to the elder Jeffries: "I can lick you too" (Ward 2004: 46–48). The champion ignored Johnson as he had all other worthy black challengers who deserved a shot at the title. Prior to Johnson, five blacks had held crowns in lighter divisions, but the opportunity to contend for the heavyweight title had been denied them because legendary pugilists John L. Sullivan, Jim Corbett, and Bob Fitzsimmons drew the color line in the ring. Jeffries continued boxing's black code and vowed that the title would never go to a black fighter while he was champion.

Johnson went on to become the Negro heavyweight champion with a victory over Denver Ed Martin in 1903. By the end of that year, the *Police Gazette*, a prominent sporting publication, began to urge Jeffries to give Johnson an opportunity. Jeffries stubbornly refused, but the media continued to follow Johnson's rising star as he defeated the best black heavyweights, along with white contenders. By 1905, one of the top white fighters, Marvin Hart, agreed to a contest against Johnson. Hart won on a controversial call when he hit Johnson with a right hook that caused the Negro champion to stumble at the sound of the bell ending the 20th round. Johnson, who had prevented Hart from landing a solid punch throughout the fight, declared he had been robbed. Hart scornfully dismissed Johnson's allegations, saying, "That coon has enough yellow in him to paint city hall. Johnson is a fancy boxer, but when he gets stung he is strictly a 'tin canner and staller.' I'll never fight another nigger" (Ward 2004: 71).

Soon after Johnson's defeat by Hart, Jeffries retired at age 29, declaring that he had defeated all "logical challengers" (Ward 2004: 72). The former champion agreed that his title would go to the winner of the match between Hart and former light heavyweight champion Jack Root. Hart won the championship but lost it the following year to Canadian light heavyweight Tommy Burns. Burns claimed he would not draw the color line and that he would defend his title against any "black, Mexican, Indian, or any nationality," but the first opportunities would be granted to white fighters. This meant that Johnson, who was not a huge draw after his loss to Hart, would continue to be denied a chance to compete for the heavyweight title. Angered by this racial lockout, Johnson refused to be disregarded and he chased Burns around the world until an Australian promoter named Hugh D. McIntosh put up $30,000 to stage the fight in 1908. Johnson only got $5,000 out of the deal, but he finally had his chance at the title that had eluded him. The fight took place the day after Christmas in Sydney, and Burns was no match for the Negro champion. Both fighters taunted each other in the ring, but Johnson's verbal gibes, in addition to the physical punishment he laid on Burns, were extremely crude.

"Poor, poor Tommy," Johnson said as he mocked Burns after the Canadian landed a punch. "Who taught you to hit? Your mother? You a woman?" (Roberts 1983: 63). Very familiar with the racial stereotypes implying physical weakness of black boxers, Johnson urged Burns to hit him in the stomach. When Burns tried, Johnson derided him saying, "Is that all the better you can do, Tommy? Come on, Tommy, you can hit harder than that, can't you?" (Roberts 1983: 63). Johnson's defensive skills proved to be too much for Burns. The fight was stopped in the 14th round by McIntosh after Burns, bloody and bruised, quickly hit the canvas after two quick rights by Johnson.

With this decisive victory, Johnson upset the racial mores of the sporting world, and for the first time in boxing history, a black man held the heavyweight title. Johnson's triumph disturbed whites, but as historian Frederic C. Jaher points out, Burns was not an American, and the territorial imperatives of patriotism and race were absent since the fight took place in Australia. Naturally, whites were rooting for Burns, but he did not represent American nationalism. Nevertheless, novelist Jack London, who covered the fight for the *New York Herald*, urged Jeffries to come out of retirement and restore the heavyweight championship to white America. London placed the onus of race squarely on Jeffries' shoulders.

As heavyweight champion, Johnson was now a volatile symbol who greatly disturbed the white American male psyche. White men honored past boxing icons Sullivan, Corbett, and Fitzsimmons with messianic reverence. Each punch, uppercut, and knockout from these men during their heavyweight reigns had come to represent the strength and virility of white manhood. Johnson's victory over Burns challenged the doctrine of white supremacy, and thus the era of the Great White Hope was born.

During the nation's frantic search for this white savior, the media used the Sambo stereotype, the docile, buffoon, clownlike image, to characterize Johnson. He was featured in Sambo cartoons with an "ape-like head, large eyes, and red lips, nappy hair, and big feet" (Wiggins 1988: 253). Historian Joseph Boskin contends that whites, unable to restore the authoritative master–slave relationship, were determined to degrade blacks using exaggerated comic means. The dense Sambo was an effigy whites were comfortable with, but Johnson's demeanor did not personify this witless, lethargic stereotype. He was mainly perceived as an insolent "uppity n*gger" who had stepped out of his prescribed place in the American caste system.

Attempts to groom a White Hope for Johnson's defeat proved futile. Johnson defeated five White Hopes in 1909, including middleweight champion Stanley Ketchel. Jeffries came out of retirement to accept the call to defend the honor of his race a few months before Johnson and Ketchel fought on October 16, 1909. The much-awaited Johnson–Jeffries bout was nine months away and would eventually be scheduled for July 4, 1910, in San Francisco. Johnson agreed to prolong his fight with Ketchel to guarantee a nice film profit and ensure a large promotion as he prepared to meet Jeffries; however, Ketchel reneged on the arrangement in the 12th round and hit Johnson with a powerful right hand.

Shocked, Johnson punched the undersized challenger in the mouth, leaving him unconscious for several minutes. After this debacle, newspapers across the country showed Johnson standing over Ketchel's limp body. The stage was now set for the fight of the century as whites demanded Johnson's defeat at the hands of Jeffries.

Johnson was now viewed as the "bad nigger" who needed to be roughed up in the ring with Caucasian wrath, but some whites, especially Southerners, feared that race relations would be drastically altered if Johnson won. One Southern official remarked that black men would become so boastful with a Johnson victory that they would push white women off the sidewalks and cause unpardonable trouble in small towns.

However, Southern white men were not just concerned about white women being pushed aside on the streets. Their innermost fear was miscegenation. Johnson began to openly travel with a white woman named Hattie McClay after his victory over Burns and he later married a white woman named Etta Duryea. As his entourage grew, more white women were attracted to him, mostly prostitutes, and Southerners were terrified that young black men would emulate Johnson's sexual lifestyle.

In spite of the racial concerns from the South, the media continued to promote the contest as a race war. The *New York Daily Tribune* claimed that either the "son of a slave mammy of the Old South, Heavyweight Champion Johnson, or the son of a preacher, the undefeated Jeffries, will be declared the most perfect fighting machine in the history of the prize ring" (Banks 1993: 136). White intellectuals and boxers picked Jeffries mainly on race alone. Burns predicted that because Jeffries was deemed physically and mentally superior to Johnson, the Negro champion had no chance. Intellectuals overlooked Jeffries' deteriorated boxing skills and believed his education and breeding would be enough to dethrone Johnson. Although Johnson held the title, he was still thought to have no endurance or heart to fight a white man. His defensive skills, which caused his opponents to assist in beating themselves, were still dismissed as a lack of aggressiveness.

As the racial tension continued to heighten, there were also rumors spreading across the nation that the fight was fixed. Media reports claimed that Johnson knew that whites would never allow him to wrest the title from Jeffries, and even if he somehow managed to whip the former champion, the risk would be too great for his own life. Thus, Johnson had no choice but to "lay down for the money" (Ward 2004: 189). Ministers urged California's governor J. N. Gillette to stop the fight and even pleaded for President Taft to intercede. Gillette eventually decided to bar the fight just three months before it was scheduled to take place in San Francisco. Morality, as Geoffrey C. Ward asserts in *Unforgivable Blackness*, was not the reason; rather, Gillette wanted San Francisco to be considered for the 1915 Panama Exposition, which would bring in millions. The House Foreign Affairs Committee would not recommend a state that was home to a "prize-fighting city" (Ward 2004: 191).

With Gillette pulling California out, fight promoter Tex Rickard settled on Reno, Nevada. Reno's mayor assured him that a stadium could be built under the tight two-week deadline and Gov. Denver S. Dickerson guaranteed Rickard that no protest would influence him to cancel the fight. Scheduling the Johnson–Jeffries bout only added to Nevada's amoral reputation, but there would be no further obstacles hindering the July 4 racial showdown. Although Jeffries was heavily favored, he was not that confident within his camp. He was disturbed by the media coverage, especially by the *New York Times* report from John L. Sullivan's ghost writer that the fight "looked like a frame-up" (Roberts 1983: 101). Johnson, on the other hand, appeared extremely confident, which baffled reporters who thought he would be terrified of the White Hope chosen to overthrow him. When Sullivan asked Johnson if he was in shape, the Negro champion replied, "Cap'n John, if I felt any better, I would be afraid of myself" (Ward 2004: 197).

The black press highlighted the racial burden that Johnson carried, although Johnson never considered himself a trailblazer fighting against prejudice. Nevertheless, the *Chicago Defender* insisted that the welfare of the race rested in Johnson's fists and that whites across the nation would mourn because Jeffries would not be able to deliver the "pugilistic scepter" to them (Ward 2004: 201).

An estimated 18,000 to 20,000 traveled to Reno, mostly fans of Jeffries, to watch what they hoped would be the brutal pummeling of Johnson. They were sorely disappointed. Jeffries' size did not intimidate Johnson, and the ex-champion proved to be too slow and too old. Johnson taunted Jeffries just as he did Burns in Sydney. "Come on now, Mr. Jeff," Johnson said at the beginning of the third round. "Let me see what you got. Do something, man. This is for the championship" (Ward 2004: 208). Jeffries, however, could do nothing and endured a long, hot, and fierce beating. When the fight was stopped after Jeffries teetered along the ropes early in the 15th round, the former champion sadly confessed in his corner, "I couldn't come back, boys" (Ward 2004: 211).

The surprising Independence Day outcome evoked feelings of trepidation as well as anguish among whites. Unlike the Burns fight, where whites nonchalantly dismissed Johnson's loss as unofficial because Burns was "appointed" the title after his win over Hart, Johnson's win over Jeffries officially gave him the crown. More important, the Johnson–Jeffries title bout took place in America, which had nationalistic significance. Jeffries was a former American champion whose pugilist image upheld the white male emblem of masculinity, a factor that escalated the patriotic essence denoted in white America's racist outlook on the heavyweight title.

Now that a black man had indisputably triumphed over the most favored White Hope, the *New York Times* was quick to rescind its position on racial physical supremacy and claimed that brute force did not determine the prominence of a particular race.

After Johnson's victory in Reno, racial tensions rose around the country. Blacks were mercilessly beaten as whites vented their frustration. Violence broke out in New York; Washington, D.C.; Atlanta; New Orleans; and Chattanooga. Lower-class whites were often the instigators of the attacks as blacks celebrated Johnson's win.

It is estimated that disturbances occurred in 11 cities, mostly in the East and West, after the announcement of Johnson's defeat of Jeffries. The *Atlanta Constitution* reported that New York had more riots than the entire country as clashes broke out in seven sections of the city. One black man was dragged from a streetcar and brutally beaten before being rescued. Four blacks and eight whites were arrested in this incident. The most serious violence took place in what was called the black and tan belt, as a gang of disgruntled whites set fire to a Negro tenement on the middle West Side. The police were on the scene quickly enough to put out the fire before anyone was hurt. Another major outbreak in New York occurred on West 37th Street. The *New York Times* reported that every policeman in the precinct was on "fight duty" but it was impossible to prevent all the race confrontations. A gang of white men and boys had formed to attack any black man coming their way. Many of them carried clubs and beat their victims with lead pipes and other deadly objects. Cries of "Let's lynch the first nigger we see!" started a riot near 135th street as a middle-aged black man was pulled from a car and beaten. Police reserves hurried to the area and arrested the leaders of the riot.

In Washington, D.C., more than 250 arrests were made in the First and Sixth Precincts, and two hospitals were filled to capacity with blacks and whites who had been injured in street conflicts. The *Washington Post* stated that "Negroes were chased, captured, and beaten in many instances without apparent provocation. In a few cases, Negroes were attacked and maltreated because they had dared to hurrah for Johnson" ("Race Clashes in Many Cities," 1). Other jubilant blacks cheering Johnson's victory also met violent ends. In Atlanta, a black man was attacked instantly on a crowded downtown street by several white men after boasting about Johnson's triumph. Charles Williams, a black man shouting the outcome of the fight on a streetcar in Houston, had his throat slashed by an angry white passenger, and young onlookers in New Orleans attacked a black man announcing the Reno results on Camp Street.

The riots in the South included the cities of Uvaldia, Georgia; Clarksburg, West Virginia; Norfolk, Virginia; and Chattanooga, Tennessee. In Uvaldia, three blacks were killed and many others were wounded at a construction camp in a clash resulting from boasting that Johnson would kill Jeffries once the fighters entered the ring. Whites armed themselves to clean out the camp, and shots were exchanged, causing the blacks to flee into the woods. The fighting was so fierce that concerned citizens asked the governor to send troops to stop the unrest. State troops were also requested in Clarksburg when a posse of 1,000 white men gathered to stop blacks from celebrating the Reno outcome. The mob was preparing to lynch a man, leading him through the streets with a rope around his neck before the police stepped in.

Marines from the Navy Yard were called to aid police in stopping the riots in Norfolk. Enlisted whites from battleships had formed bands to attack blacks in the city. Many were injured, but no deaths were reported. Soldiers from Mississippi organized to attack black prisoners in a Chattanooga jail after a black man shoved a newspaper with the fight results under a Mississippi militiaman's nose. Stopped from entering the jail by police, the soldiers then raided a Negro settlement and the police were called again to subdue the outbreak.

In the West and Midwest, scores of uprisings occurred. Jeffries' home city of Los Angeles reported that eight men, three white and five black, were treated at a hospital as a result of violence started by blacks who had won some cash betting on Johnson. In the Ohio cities of Columbus, Dayton, and Cincinnati, riots broke out in downtown sections. Blacks celebrating the fight in Columbus organized a parade through the streets, and whites quickly formed mobs to break up the festivities. In Dayton, blacks assaulted a party of white men that resulted in police reserves being called out, and a mob of hundreds of whites in Cincinnati chased a black man on Vine Street, the city's leading thoroughfare ("Eleven Killed in Many Race Riots," 4; "Race Clashes in Many Cities," 11). Pueblo, Colorado, had the highest number of injuries as a crowd of 2,000 gathered at Bessemer City Park, located near the city's steel works suburb. Every police officer in Pueblo was sent to stop the outbreak.

The violent rioting by whites throughout the country exemplified their greatest fear: racial order being uprooted. With his undisputed victory over Jeffries, Johnson was now viewed as an independent Negro who no longer needed the white man's permission for anything, and Johnson was just that. The champion did exactly as he pleased. He lived lavishly, flaunting his money and his white women, and was not the least apologetic for it. Many whites hoped the race clashes would prevent blacks from aspiring to rise above their second-class citizenship, but the old, docile mentality of blacks, particularly those in the South, was beginning to wane. A folk song written after the fight expressed this newfound pride by exclaiming that no matter what the white man said, "The world champion's still a n*gger" (Roberts 1983: 110).

The Negro now had a hero and a champion whose accomplishments showed him that when given a fair chance, a black man could be the white man's equal. Leading black educators like William Pickens, president of Talladega College in Talladega, Alabama, maintained that Johnson's victory was very significant for the self-esteem of the race. "It was a good deal better for Johnson to win and a few Negroes be killed in body for it, than for Johnson to have lost and Negroes to have been killed in spirit by the preachments of inferiority from the combined white press," Pickens commented after the fight. "Many . . . editors had already composed and pigeonholed their editorials of mockery and spite—and we shall not conceal . . . our satisfaction at having these homilies and editorials all knocked into the wastebasket by the big fists of Jack Johnson" (Ward 2004: 217).

Johnson's fists indeed chipped away at the doctrine of white physical supremacy, and the race riots symbolized the altered status of white men. The uprisings primarily reflected the power struggle in the United States that would change, albeit slowly, as a result of Jeffries' loss. White men knew their social position was threatened with a black heavyweight champion. However, what disturbed them most was that Johnson played by their rules and won, and as he broke through the heavyweight division's color line, many blacks would follow Johnson's lead and no longer accept their subordinate position in American society.

As the racial violence subsided, whites, frustrated that they could not stop Johnson's exploits in the ring, decided to punish him outside it. In 1912, Johnson was brought under federal indictment for violating the Mann Act—a federal law declaring transporting of women across state borders for the intent of prostitution and debauchery illegal. While the Federal Bureau of Investigation was investigating him, Johnson married his second white wife, a young prostitute named Lucille Cameron, just weeks after his first wife, Etta Duryea, committed suicide. Since Johnson's marriages were regarded as sexually taboo, the government altered the true intent of the Mann Act (to convict white slavers) to castigate Johnson for his marriage to Cameron. Although Cameron and many of the other white women in Johnson's entourage were prostitutes, they were still considered ladies when it came to being involved with a black man. The government's chief witness against the champion was Belle Schreiber, a white prostitute Johnson had kept as a mistress. By 1913, their affair was over, but Schreiber gave the government

substantial testimony about their relationship that led to Johnson's conviction by an all-white jury. He and Cameron fled the country, and Johnson was in exile for seven years. He defended his championship abroad against lesser white opponents, but as he aged, he began to lose his defensive fighting form. He finally lost his title in 1915 to Jess Willard, a white boxer from Kansas, in Havana, Cuba. The media hailed Willard as the restorer of white superiority as he knocked out Johnson in the 26th round.

Johnson returned to the United States in 1920, served his prison term, and was released a year later. White Americans' obsession with him ceased after he returned home mainly because of the country's involvement in World War I. Cameron divorced him in 1924 and Johnson's marriage to his third white wife, Irene Marie Pineau, did not yield the public outrage of his previous unions.

Although Johnson's private life was no longer on extensive public display, it was very difficult for the ex-champion to make a living. Johnson was legally barred from the ring as boxing boards and licensing commissions were in place in the 1920s. Well past his prime, Johnson was no longer a serious contender for the title, but boxing authorities were determined to keep him completely locked out of the sport. Desperately in need of money, Johnson boxed in exhibitions against children in the 1930s. He became a hustler in the boxing world, refereeing, managing, and even involving himself in fixed fights. He tried to become a mentor to Joe Louis, but the younger black fighter was determined to keep his distance from the former Negro champion. Louis's managers diligently worked to make him a submissive public figure so that white Americans could be assured he was not the "bad nigger" Johnson had been. Louis's demeanor was always humble. He did not gloat when knocking out white opponents, and he did not violate America's sexual taboos by marrying a white woman. This meek disposition eventually made Louis the nation's first beloved black athlete.

Considered an outcast in Louis's camp, Johnson found himself further isolated from the black community. He involved himself in politics, endorsing Franklin D. Roosevelt, and he toured the lecture circuit promoting evangelical religion. Nevertheless, Johnson was never truly pardoned by whites for his intrepid lifestyle. When his life ended as the result of a car crash in 1946, there were few kind words, if any, expressed in obituaries. Although Johnson was remembered as one of America's most dominant prizefighters, the image that most whites retained was a pompous Negro who refused to be their subordinate. Johnson had all the characteristics that were admired in white boxers, and generally in most white men: courage, virility, strength, and wit. Yet, it was these same attributes that made him a threat to the American racial order.

JESSICA A. JOHNSON

See also

Race Riots in America; Sports and Racism. Documents: Report on the Memphis Riots of May 1866 (1866); Account of the Riots in East St. Louis, Illinois (1917); A Southern Black Woman's Letter Regarding the Recent Riots in Chicago and Washington (1919); The Cook County Coroner's Report Regarding the 1919 Chicago Race Riots (1920); The Final Report of the Grand Jury on the Tulsa Race Riot (June 25, 1921); Testimony from *Laney v. United States* (1923); The Governor's Commission Report on the Watts Riots (1965); Cyrus R. Vance's Report on the Riots in Detroit (1967); The Reports of the Oklahoma Commission to Study the Tulsa Race Riot of 1921 (2000–2001); Draft Report: 1898 Wilmington Race Riot Commission (2005)

Further Reading:

Banks, Michael. "Black Athletes in the Media." Ph.D. dissertation, City University of New York, 1993.

Boskin, Joseph. *Sambo: The Rise and Demise of an American Jester*. New York: Oxford University Press, 1986.

"Eight Killed in Fight Riots." *New York Times*, July 5, 1910, 1, 4.

"Eleven Killed in Many Race Riots." *Chicago Tribune*, July 5, 1910, 1, 4.

Jaher, Frederic. "White America Views Jack Johnson, Joe Louis, and Muhammad Ali." In *Sport in America: New Historical Perspectives*, edited by Donald Spivey, 145–92. Westport, CT: Greenwood Press, 1985.

"Race Clashes in Many Cities." *Washington Post*, July 5, 1910, 1, 11.

"Race Outbreaks at Chattanooga." *Atlanta Constitution*, July 5, 1910, 2.

"Racial Clashes Follow Victory of Jack Johnson." *Atlanta Constitution*, July 5, 1910, 1–2.

Roberts, Randy. *Papa Jack: Jack Johnson and the Era of White Hopes*. New York: Collier Macmillan Publishers, 1983.

Ward, Geoffrey C. *Unforgivable Blackness*. New York: Alfred A. Knopf, 2004.

Wiggins, William H. "Boxing's Sambo Twins: Racial Stereotypes in Jack Johnson and Joe Louis Newspaper Cartoons, 1908 to 1938." *Journal of Sport History* 15, no. 3 (1988): 242–54.

Journal of Negro History

In 1915, the Harvard University–educated, African American historian Carter G. Woodson founded the Association for the Study of Negro Life and History and the following year, 1916, launched the *Journal of Negro History*. The *Journal* (edited by Woodson until 1950) provided a strong and sustained response to white academic racism and challenged the racist bias in mainstream American historiography throughout the first half of the 20th century. Prior to the appearance of the association and its journal, black scholars struggled to contribute to the production of African American history, having been largely excluded from mainstream archives, libraries, history organizations, conferences, and periodicals. Containing original articles on various aspects of African and African American history, primary source documents, as well as critically informed book reviews, the *Journal of Negro History* offered valuable publishing opportunities for an emerging new generation of black scholars, as well as countering Jim Crow–era stereotypes of black intellectual inferiority and shattering the myth that black Americans had no history.

Perhaps nowhere was the antiblack sentiment of American historians more evident than in the field of slavery studies, where Ulrich B. Phillips's idea of benevolent planter paternalism was the dominant white academic interpretation until the appearance of Kenneth Stampp's *The Peculiar Institution* (1956). Phillips's *American Negro Slavery* (1918), for example, offered a white supremacist vision of plantation slavery, one that argued that the institution was a controlling, civilizing influence over an allegedly inferior race. Responding to this racist romance of American slavery, very much the ideological accomplice of the sugarcoated movie blockbuster *Gone With the Wind* (1939), black scholars in the *Journal of Negro History* were among the first to question the validity of Phillips's research. In his 1919 review in the *Journal*, Woodson pointed to numerous methodological defects in Phillips's account, not the least of which was his utter "failure to fathom the Negro mind." Building on Woodson's critique, Richard Hofstadter's 1944 article for the *Journal*, "U. B. Phillips and the Plantation Legend," called into doubt the reliability and relevance of Phillips's sources in attempting to render an accurate account of the Old South. Hofstadter highlighted how Phillips had tailored his evidence, sampling chiefly from the records of larger

Carter Woodson established a model for African American history through the Association for the Study of Negro Life and History, which helped to correct the prejudice with which historians and the general public viewed African American abilities. (AP/Wide World Photos)

slaveholders, so as to maintain a more favorable portrait of the chattel system.

Unlike Phillips, scholars writing for the *Journal of Negro History* did not neglect the African American perspective and were among the first to utilize slave narratives and interviews with former slaves in constructing their historical narratives. Other important subjects of African American history addressed by the journal, but on the whole neglected or distorted by white scholars, included slave revolts and resistance, the domestic slave trade, free black communities in the Northern and Southern United States, black culture and consciousness (especially spirituality and the formation of black churches), the black family (with important and influential work conducted by E. Franklin Frazier), antislavery activities, and Reconstruction. The interdisciplinary methods used by scholars in the journal (for example, calling upon anthropological, sociological, and psychological as well as historical approaches), together with their concern for so-called ordinary and everyday people, greatly anticipated the

spirit and the sentiment of the social history movement that gained momentum throughout academia in the 1970s.

Reflecting the political gains and heightened racial pride of the civil rights and Black Power era, in 1972 the Association for the Study of Negro Life and History became the Association for the Study of Afro-American (and later African-American) Life and History. However, perhaps due to its long history and established reputation, it took another 30 years before the *Journal of Negro History* became the *Journal of African-American History* in 2002.

STEPHEN C. KENNY

See also
Du Bois, W.E.B.

Further Reading:
Goggin, Jacqueline. "Countering White Racist Scholarship: Carter G. Woodson and *The Journal of Negro History*." *Journal of Negro History* 68, no. 4 (Autumn 1983): 355–75.

Journalism and Racial Stereotypes

The news industry has changed dramatically in the United States since the early 1990s. Stories cycle in and out at a much faster pace, which leaves little time to delve into details. Stories and the people involved are presented so quickly, but repetitively, that only caricature-like profiles are established. One result is the perpetuation of stereotypes, or unreliable, exaggerated generalizations, about all members of a group that do not take individual differences into account. Stereotypes tend to evolve from statements or facts that are somewhat truthful, until they are stretched beyond their initial scope and applied with a more liberal meaning than they were originally able to support. The repetitive nature of the news industry today means that inaccurate representations have a great number of opportunities to influence the beliefs and perceptions of the audience.

There are several ways in which journalism perpetuates stereotypical attitudes in the United States. First, bad outcomes are most often associated with minority communities. News stories convey the notion that crime happens in certain parts of town, primarily the parts where higher percentages of African Americans and Latinos reside. The full range of economic and social status experienced by racial minorities are not represented. Instead, minority communities are frequently depicted as economically disadvantaged. Local newscasts typically show photographs of whites with an attorney when they are accused of crimes, whereas they typically show African Americans when they are being arrested. Stories about drug abuse, drug-addicted babies, AIDS patients, and homeless people are usually accompanied by photographs of African Americans. The reality is that white Americans are the majority or at least a significant proportion of each of these groups.

For years, the Mexican American population was treated as nonexistent by mainstream media outlets. When the news industry finally offered coverage of the Mexican American community, simplistic and inaccurate images were presented. As media outlets were beginning to recognize the presence of Mexican Americans, farm-labor activist César Chávez and his United Farmworkers Union were highly visible, leading most Americans to identify Mexican Americans as farmworkers and rural dwellers. The reality is that most Mexican Americans and other Hispanics live in urban areas. Other stereotypical images of Mexican Americans that have been hard to dispel are those that represent them as illegal aliens, "wetbacks" who take public assistance without contributing tax dollars, drug dealers, and gang members.

Asian Americans are depicted as recent immigrants rather than citizens, regardless of how long they have been in the United States. A prime example of this is when, during the 1998 Olympics, U.S. news outlets reported that "the American beat Kwan," ignoring the fact that figure skater Michelle Kwan is also an American. The news industry also creates images of Asian Americans as disinterested participants in American society who prefer to remain segregated from mainstream society while benefiting from the resources that are available in the United States.

Muslims are portrayed not only as foreigners but also as undemocratic and unpatriotic. Arab Americans are depicted as threats to national security.

Attempts to offer humanized profiles of Native Americans typically involve concepts of spirituality and closeness to nature. These concepts at first glance seem complimentary, but on closer examination are really strategies for creating a perception of Native Americans as antiquated, behind the times, or out of touch with the modern world.

More often than not, images of Native Americans are not present at all.

Jewish Americans have been characterized as wealthy and materialistic. Jewish mothers are depicted as overbearing and asexual.

White Americans are frequently stereotyped as well, but the difference is that most of their stereotypes are positive, as they control the images that are released.

The stereotypes that are promoted by the news industry are dangerous, not only because they are inaccurate and often negative, but because the source is powerful. Despite the changes that have transpired in the last decade, journalism is still associated with a significant level of credibility. In the fast-paced 21st-century newsroom, the lack of time to commit to accuracy often translates into institutionalized stereotyping, which could be a precursor to institutionally sanctioned discrimination.

Romney S. Norwood

See also

Films and Racial Stereotypes; Stereotype; Television and Racial Stereotypes

Further Reading:

Enns, Aiden. "Questioning Our Images of Islam." March 2002. http://www.journalism. ubc.ca/thunderbird/2001–02/february/religion.html.

Jones, Jackie. "Stereotypes Don't Change Themselves: Survey on Whites' Misconceptions Shows Need for a New Generation of Minority Journalists." http://newsatch. sfsu.edu/columnists/nabj/080101jones.html.

Lester, Paul M., ed. *Images That Injure: Pictorial Stereotypes in the Media.* Westport, CT: Praeger Publishers, 1996.

Juneteenth Celebration

Juneteenth Celebrations honor an important date in African American history. On June 19, 1865 (two and a half years after the Emancipation Proclamation), slaves in Galveston, Texas, were informed about the conclusion of the Civil War and that all enslaved people were freed. This has become a widely known celebration of the end of slavery in many communities around the United States.

Maj. Gen. Gordon Granger made the following statement in Galveston, accompanied by Union Troops:

The people of Texas are informed that, in accordance with a proclamation from the Executive of the United States, all slaves are free. This involves an absolute equality of personal rights and rights of property between former masters and slaves, and the connection heretofore existing between them becomes that between employer and hired labor. The freedman are advised to remain quietly at their present homes and work for wages. They are informed that they will not be allowed to collect at military posts and that they will not be supported in idleness either there or elsewhere. (Lamont 1896: 929)

Although the Emancipation Proclamation had occurred over two years earlier, enforcement was slow to follow in states like Texas. Even after Gen. Gordon and the troops arrived in Galveston, some slaveholders were slow to free their slaves, though as Campbell points out, "most slaveholders became aware of it and freed their bondsmen during the summer of 1865" (1984: 140).

Eventually, the word of freedom spread to 250,000 slaves in Texas. The question of the exact date when slavery became illegal in Texas became controversial. This was "important to slaveholders because of its bearing on contracts involving slave property that had been signed during the Civil War. In spite of the Confederacy's waning fortunes as the conflict progressed, Texans continued to deal in slaves as personal chattels until the bitter end" (Campbell 1984: 140). After a number of court cases, the Texas Supreme Court eventually decided that June 19, 1865 would mark the end of slavery in Texas. Perhaps, as Justice Hamilton argued in 1868, the Emancipation Proclamation technically was effective from January 1, 1863, onward, but such reasoning would have ignored the de facto existence of slavery until the late spring of 1865. Moreover, a decision in favor of the earlier date would not in any case have had the effect that Hamilton appeared to want. He had insisted, as the report of his statement said, that neither party to "illegal" traffic in slaves after January 1, 1863, should "receive relief." A decision to enforce the Emancipation Proclamation as the legal death date, however, would have given relief to one party just as surely the use of June 19, 1865, gave relief to the other. Slaves as human chattels had been given all the protections that the laws of the United States typically extend to private property, and the legal implications of that situation could not be escaped immediately. Thus disputes over contracts constituted one of the ways, albeit a relatively minor one compared to racial and social questions, that the heritage of slavery maintained a hold on Texas after Juneteenth.

Regardless of the reason for the establishment of Juneteenth, it became an important date for African Americans in the United States. The first Juneteenth celebrations included political rallies and taught freed African Americans about their voting rights. Popularity declined for Juneteenth in the 1960s, but "in the 1970s African Americans' renewed interest in celebrating their cultural heritage led the revitalization of the holiday throughout the state" (Texas State Historical Association). It was made an official holiday in Texas in 1979. As African Americans migrated from Texas, the celebration of Juneteenth spread beyond Texas.

Juneteenth celebrations include family reunions, dramatic readings, parades, blues festivals, public entertainment, pageants, and barbecues. This is a celebration of thanksgiving where the hymn "Lift Every Voice" is often offered as an opening to the event.

KATHRIN A. PARKS

Further Reading:
Acosta, Teresa P. "Juneteenth." *Handbook of Texas Online.* http://www.tshaonline.org/handbook/online/articles/lkj01.
Campbell, Randolph B. "The End of Slavery in Texas: A Research Note." *Southwestern Historical Quarterly* 88 (1984): 71–80.
Lamont, D. S. *The War of the Rebellion: A Composition of the Official Records of the Union and Confederate Armies.* Washington, D.C., 1896. Series 1, vol. 48, part 2, p. 929.

K

Kansas Exodusters

The Kansas Exodusters were the thousands of rural, working-class African American men and women who tried to emigrate from the states of the Deep South to Kansas in 1879. "The Kansas Fever Exodus" pointed to African Americans' rejection of the new status quo in the Redeemer South following the collapse of Reconstruction. Rural blacks voted with their feet in opposition to rampant political and economic injustice: the violent intimidation of black voters and political leaders, persistent white terrorism, and ongoing economic exploitation and debt peonage at the hands of white plantation owners and shopkeepers. The mass departure to Kansas represented African Americans' hopes to build new a future where they could own land, cast their ballots, hold offices, and move about freely. The Kansas Exodusters hoped to be governed by the principles of the Thirteenth, Fourteenth, and Fifteenth Amendments, not the whims of Southern whites who wanted to destroy the legacies of Reconstruction and impose new systems of oppression that too closely resembled antebellum slavery.

The migrants came from Louisiana, Mississippi, and Texas. In these states, as well as the other Southern states, many years of white intimidation and terrorism shattered the constitutional and political promises made to African Americans during the years of Reconstruction. As blacks became free persons and citizens during the 1860s, whites in the South responded with violent hostility. For them, the idea that African Americans were equal under the law defied the most fundamental premise of white Southern culture: that white men could command and control the labor and status of African Americans. Initially in the spring of 1865, during the era of Presidential Reconstruction, whites in Southern state legislatures imposed "Black Codes" that were intended to constrict the newly freed's rights. Whites wanted to force blacks into strict labor contracts with Southern planters, curb their political activities, and preclude African Americans from testifying against whites in court. Whites wanted to build a new South that closely resembled the old. Radical Reconstruction, however, destroyed the Black Code regime. Angered by Southern whites' actions, the Republican Congress imposed military rule, gave blacks the vote and the right to hold office, and promised equality under the law. Southern whites continued to fiercely resist black empowerment, however. They deployed extralegal tactics such as nightriding and "bulldozing," and formed terrorist organizations such as the Ku Klux Klan and the White League, to intimidate and murder black Republican voters, candidates, and organizers. In election after election during the 1870s, Southern whites undermined the political process by stuffing ballot boxes, scaring away voters, forcing black candidates into exile, and murdering blacks who stood up to injustice. The terrible corruption and violence that overshadowed the

1st Stone Church

View of Washington Street in Nicodemus, Kansas, circa 1885. Nicodemus was an African American town settled by former slaves. (Library of Congress)

1878 elections in Louisiana convinced many blacks in the Gulf region that the South held no future for African Americans. In fact, some Louisiana parishes passed laws in 1878 that required blacks to carry passes when they traveled on public roads—distressing reminders of the days of slavery and the absence of democracy in the Redeemer South.

Unremitting poverty was the second major factor that gave rise to the exodus. In the years after the Civil War, poor blacks and landowning whites struggled to define the terms of labor and land use in the South. African Americans refused to submit to whites' demands that they become landless laborers, struggling to distance themselves from any labor system that resembled Old South slavery. Black men and women wanted to possess their own land and live independently. Rural whites, however, opposed black landownership, which would have signified equality among whites

and blacks. During the 1860s and 1870s, sharecropping and tenant farming emerged as the predominant labor and landholding arrangements that were available to blacks. As renters, African American families farmed a specified portion of a planter's land, perhaps between 15 and 20 acres, paying an annual rent with a portion of the cotton crop they produced. While tenancy allowed blacks to distance themselves from their former masters, the workings of tenant farming created a cycle of debt peonage. White planters, shopkeepers, and creditors forced black farmers into a state of permanent debt by setting high prices for the "ginning" of cotton bales, overpricing tools and supplies at local stores, and establishing high rents for land. Black families had to remain on the land as renters in order to work towards paying off their outstanding debts. They seldom made a profit, sinking deeper into debt every year. To make matters worse, contracts between landowners and tenants often stipulated that the landlord could seize a tenant's personal property—including farming tools, supplies, and mules—as payment. Whites never allowed African American farmers to climb out of poverty and tenancy to become landowners themselves, enforcing their will with the threat of violence. In 1879, after many years of struggle on Southern plantations, the Exodusters viewed emigration to Kansas as a way to finally achieve economic independence.

In the 1870s, Benjamin "Pap" Singleton, an aging former slave who once worked as a carpenter in Tennessee, popularized the notion of emigration to Kansas. Singleton viewed himself as a deliverer who would bring the oppressed of the South to the Promised Land. While Singleton called himself the "Father" of the migration, the Kansas Fever Exodus arose from the rural black working class itself. Between March and the end of the year, thousands of black men and women departed from Louisiana, Mississippi, and Texas. Despite their shortage of funds, the migrants determinedly made their way north and westward—doing so without the aid of a centralized leadership. Newspapers reported that 75 black men and women reached St. Louis in the early spring of 1879. The migration from the South rapidly expanded, much to the surprise of white observers. Between March and May, observers noted that the banks of the Mississippi River were crowded with Southern black families, all trying to secure passage to St. Louis and points beyond. The Kansas Exodusters reported to curious journalists that they were leaving the South for the land of John Brown. An estimated 4,000–5,000 migrants arrived in Kansas during 1879. Despite the groundswell that pushed the migration forward, the movement slowly began to fade. Many steamships refused passage to the migrants, and the poor black families who led this great migration quickly began to run out of money and could not complete the journey. Those who made it to Kansas found more opportunity than in the South, purchasing 20,000 acres of land, acquiring more than $40,000 in assets, and securing an average yearly income of $363. The migration would continue into the 1880s, but on a smaller scale.

The Kansas Fever Exodus was the high point of a broader pattern of grassroots emigrationism that unfolded in the post-Emancipation South. In response to the racial violence and injustice of the post–Civil War years, African Americans looked abroad to Africa and the Caribbean, as well as domestically to Kansas and Indiana, in the hopes of finding freedom and new opportunities to own land. For instance, hundreds of black Americans in Georgia, Tennessee, Virginia, and the Carolinas applied to the old American Colonization Society for transportation to the African nation of Liberia. Between 1865 and 1868, 2,232 African Americans relocated to Liberia from the South. The average number of those who emigrated to Africa in the 1860s (558 per year) was more than double the rate during the years between 1820 and 1861. During the 1870s, emigration sentiment intensified because of the efforts of a U.S. Army veteran, black civil rights advocate, and former slave named Henry Adams, who helped create the grassroots Colonization Council. Adams and the other members of the council tried to organize poor black farmers for emigration to Liberia, collecting the signatures of more than 69,000 rural black men and women. While a lack of funds prevented the organization from sending migrants overseas, the group popularized the idea of leaving the South and paved the way for the 1879 exodus to Kansas.

White reactions to the Kansas Exodusters varied. Early on, many white Southerners claimed the migrants had been duped into leaving by demagogues, while others expressed hopes that Southern labor might be more productive now that these quitters had left. However, as the migration intensified, whites in the South and North began to worry that the South would experience a labor shortage that would injure its fragile economy. African Americans generally endorsed the migration. However, some prominent blacks, including Frederick Douglass, criticized the migrants. Douglass believed the Exodusters had implicitly abandoned the struggle for citizenship in the South. While only a fraction completed the journey to Kansas, the fact that so many tried indicated that African Americans firmly opposed the political and economic practices that defined the post-Reconstruction South.

GREGORY WOOD

See also
Great Migration; Jim Crow Laws

Further Reading:
Foner, Eric. *Reconstruction: America's Unfinished Revolution, 1863–1877*. New York: Harper & Row, 1988.
Hahn, Steven. *A Nation Under Our Feet: Black Political Struggles in the Rural South from Slavery to the Great Migration.*

Cambridge, MA: Harvard University Press/Belknap Press, 2003.

Painter, Nell Irvin. *Exodusters: Black Migration to Kansas after Reconstruction*. New York: Alfred A. Knopf, 1977. Reprint, New York: W. W. Norton, 1992.

Kennedy, John F. (1917–1963)

John F. Kennedy, a Democrat, was president of the United States from January 1961 to November 1963. During his presidency, Kennedy contended with grave issues, such as the Cuban Missile Crisis, the Vietnam War, and the Cold War with the Soviet Union. On the home front, the nonviolent demonstrations of the civil rights movement and subsequent white retaliatory violence were generating an increasing amount of turmoil. The violence that was carried out by white mobs and police officers was covered on TV and in newspapers. This eventually caught the world's attention and forced Kennedy to take an aggressive stance in support of the movement.

Early in Kennedy's political career, his public support of blacks appeared questionable. He voted along with his party against the Civil Rights Act of 1957, but during the presidential election of 1960, he valorously advocated civil rights. Some have argued that the former move was calculated to help obtain his party's nomination for the presidency, while the latter was a strategy to win black votes. Whether or not this was a ploy, Kennedy did in fact personally support integration and civil rights for blacks. He demonstrated that he was earnest when, while campaigning in 1960, he saw to it that Martin Luther King, Jr. was released from an Alabama jail, where he was being held on trumped-up charges. Kennedy stirred hope in the hearts of many blacks, who saw in him a hero and a defender of their rights and causes.

After his narrow win over Richard Nixon, Kennedy's overt support of integration and civil rights disappeared. Despite the appearance of neglect, he charged his administration—particularly his brother, Robert Kennedy, whom he made attorney general—to foster civil rights and to work with the organizations within the civil rights movement. Speculation as to why Kennedy did this centered on his preoccupation with major crises with communist countries such as East Germany, Cuba, South Vietnam, and the Soviet Union.

It is argued that, by downplaying his role in the movement, Kennedy was trying to maintain the support of Congress and the American people. The United States, as a whole, was not interested in challenging discrimination or bettering conditions for blacks. Particularly in the South, whites were extremely hostile toward blacks and were strongly in favor of maintaining the status quo of social, economic, and political oppression. White mobs and organizations such as the Ku Klux Klan regularly enforced their racist sentiments with brute violence, as they had been doing since the Reconstruction era.

Nevertheless, Kennedy did effect some progress for blacks, although not without receiving his share of criticism. His achievements included the appointment of blacks to federal government positions, the enforcement of extant civil rights legislation through the use of the law courts, the integration of the Washington Redskins football team, and the creation of the Equal Employment Opportunity Commission. Kennedy believed that the realization of integration and the elimination of discrimination required patience, careful and quiet negotiations within the court system, and incremental steps to accommodate white opposition. He believed that it was the responsibility of the states, not the federal government, to manage their own affairs and denounced the tactics used by civil rights activists because he believed they were too radical and harmful to the reputation of the United States. On the other hand, as a direct result of their protests and passive resistance to white violence, activists generated a crisis that demanded the attention of the world and the president. Kennedy had no choice but to be drawn into the movement. Ultimately, he became one of its most formidable forces.

Although Kennedy wanted the activists to cease the Freedom Rides of 1961 so that the laws that disallowed segregation on public transportation and facilities could be tested, he permitted Attorney General Robert Kennedy to rescue the riders who had been abused and threatened by the Ku Klux Klan. He federalized the National Guard of Mississippi and Alabama in 1962 and 1963, respectively, to protect blacks who were integrating into previously white-only universities. In response to Kennedy's treatment of violence against blacks in Birmingham in 1963, King described how "a thoroughly aroused president told the nation that the federal government would not allow extremists to sabotage a fair and just pact. He ordered 3,000 federal troops into position near Birmingham and made preparations to federalize the Alabama National Guard" (King 1964: 107). That evening Kennedy gave a televised civil rights address, in which he proposed the forthcoming Civil Rights Act of 1964.

Tragically, Lee Harvey Oswald assassinated Kennedy on November 22, 1963, during an open-car motorcade in Dallas, Texas, prematurely ending the life of a man who, as King described him, was "undergoing a transformation from a hesitant leader with unsure goals to a strong figure with deeply appealing objectives" (King 1964: 144).

GLADYS L. KNIGHT

See also

Civil Rights Act of 1964; Civil Rights Movement; Kennedy, Robert F.

Further Reading:

Dallek, Robert. *An Unfinished Life*. New York: Little, Brown and Company, 2003.
King, Martin Luther, Jr. *Why We Can't Wait*. New York: Harper & Row, 1964.

Kennedy, Robert F. (1925–1968)

Robert Kennedy was a noted supporter of the civil rights movement throughout a political career that included serving as attorney general, congressman, and candidate for president. But his career was abruptly ended when, on June 6, 1968, he was assassinated during his campaign for the Democratic presidential nomination.

Robert Francis Kennedy, also known as RFK or simply Bobby, was born on November 20, 1925, the seventh of 12 children, into an illustrious family in Boston, Massachusetts. In 1960, RFK joined John F. Kennedy's presidential campaign. Among the issues on their platform was the promise to attack segregation. While on the campaign trail, the Kennedy brothers intervened to release Martin Luther King, Jr. from an Alabama jail in response to an urgent plea from King's wife, Coretta, who felt his life was in danger. This was

a bold act since the civil rights movement was not enthusiastically welcomed by Americans in general, or the South in particular. This happened again in 1963 when King was in a Birmingham jail.

John F. Kennedy won the 1960 presidential election and appointed RFK to be U.S. attorney general. Rather than take on segregation himself (and thus lose ground with the Southern Democrats), President Kennedy assigned this task to other members of his administration, most notably his brother. At first, the civil rights movement was not a pressing concern for either Robert or John. Although Robert was sympathetic to the victims of poverty and injustice, he was occupied with international concerns such as the Bay of Pigs and the Cold War with Russia. The raging violence against black protesters and its impact on the world altered his position and forced his involvement.

Kennedy was genuinely interested in integration and justice for all Americans. However, he did not agree with the tactics the civil rights activists used. To Kennedy, the protests, although nonviolent, inevitably provoked violent counterattacks—such as house, car, and church bombings; beatings; and killings—by whites. Kennedy also believed the civil rights activists were too impatient and uncontrollable. He urged protesters on several occasions to relent from their activities.

In 1961, the Freedom Rides tested the segregation laws on public transportation. When press coverage of racial violence exposed the reckless attacks against the protesters, RFK intervened. After the bombing of one of the buses, he called Alabama governor John Patterson to no avail, and then he contacted the Greyhound Company, which, not without considerable prodding, agreed to transport the activists. A Kennedy aide was enlisted to accompany the freedom riders. Nevertheless, white mobs assaulted the riders and the aide. RFK was unaware that Federal Bureau of Investigation agents stood by (only to take notes) and did nothing. Later, when King organized a rally for the riders at the First Baptist Church, Kennedy was impelled to "patch together a makeshift army" (Thomas 2000: 130). With 1,500 people and the remaining freedom riders inside, 3,000 whites besieged the church. King called Robert Kennedy. As they talked, the marshals arrived. Kennedy considered calling in federal troops, but Governor Patterson finally sent in the Alabama

National Guard. The next morning, the freedom riders were escorted to jail in Jackson, Mississippi, only to be replaced by more riders (Thomas 2000: 131).

In 1962, RFK provided protection for James Meredith, who was the first black man to integrate the University of Mississippi. At first, Kennedy attempted a series of long and complicated negotiations for Meredith's safe enrollment. He was averse to using head-on military force, as he had "vivid recollection of President Dwight Eisenhower's 1957 use of paratroopers, in combat gear with fixed bayonets, to integrate a high school in Little Rock, Arkansas" (Thomas 2000: 127). Nevertheless, Kennedy eventually agreed to the use of U.S. marshals, federal prison guards, and border patrolmen. A riot ensued between them and militant whites (Thomas 2000: 200–203), and Kennedy had no choice but to call in 23,000 federal troops to put an end to the chaos.

Violence spread across the nation in ensuing years. On November 22, 1963, Lee Harvey Oswald assassinated President Kennedy. In 1964, the administration of President Lyndon Johnson convinced activists to help garner suffrage in the Deep South. They felt that working toward voting rights (rather than protesting for civil rights) was a safer alternative. However, activists were met with more white violence. In the aftermath of the Mississippi Freedom Summer, many blacks replaced their nonviolent stance with militancy. In the same year, the first of numerous riots exploded in urban black ghettos. Unhappy with President Johnson's approach of facing violence with force, Kennedy came up with an ineffectual plan to help boost the economic growth of the ghettos.

In 1968, RFK began his campaign for the presidency. On April 4, Kennedy was prepared to speak at the ghetto in Indianapolis, Indiana, when he was told that King had been assassinated. Ignoring a warning not to go into the ghetto, he gave a moving impromptu speech, imploring all Americans, black and white, to abandon hatred, violence, and lawlessness. Indianapolis was one of the only cities to refrain from rioting in response to King's murder. Kennedy warmed the hearts of many, including some militant blacks. He openly supported programs to improve black ghettos. On June 6, 1968, Palestinian Sirhan B. Sirhan assassinated RFK because of his support for Israel. Both blacks and whites deeply mourned this terrible loss.

GLADYS L. KNIGHT

See also
Freedom Rides; Kennedy, John F.; Meredith, James

Further Reading:
Thomas, Evan. *Robert Kennedy: His Life.* New York: Simon & Schuster, 2000.

Kerner, Otto (1908–1976)

Otto Kerner Jr. was the governor of Illinois from 1961 to 1968. He was also a federal judge who had the misfortune of being the first sitting federal appeals court judge to be convicted of a felony.

Kerner was born on August 15, 1908, in the upscale Chicago suburb of River Forest. His parents were Otto Kerner, a lawyer and federal judge, and Rose Chmelik, of Czech roots. He graduated from the Chicago Latin School in 1926 and earned a bachelor's degree from Brown University in 1930. He then enrolled in Trinity College at Cambridge University in England during 1930–1931. He graduated with a law degree from Northwestern University in 1934. On October 20, 1934, Kerner married Helena Cermak. She was the daughter of Anton Cermak, the former Chicago mayor who died in Miami in 1933 when he was shot with a bullet intended for President Franklin D. Roosevelt. The couple had no children of their own but raised Helena's grandchildren after her daughter by her first marriage, Mary, was killed in a car accident.

Kerner was admitted to the bar in 1934 and worked for one year with the firm of Cooke, Sullivan, and Ricks. In 1935, he joined his father's firm, in which he remained a partner until 1947. His legal work was interrupted for five years during World War II.

Kerner became part of the Black Horse Troop of the Illinois National Guard in 1934 and was subsequently called to active duty in March 1941 as captain of the 33rd Infantry Division of the U.S. Army. After a year, he transferred to the Ninth Infantry Division as a major. During 1942–1943, he participated in the North African and Sicilian campaigns. He was then assigned to the 32nd Infantry Division as a lieutenant colonel and fought in the Philippines and Japan from July to December 1945. Kerner received an honorable discharge in March 1946, and his service was recognized with the Soldier's Medal and the Bronze Star. He continued his military association in the National Guard until 1951, retiring with the rank of major general.

Kerner was appointed attorney for the Northern District of Illinois in 1947. In 1954, the Democratic political machine led by Richard J. Daley supported his candidacy for Cook County judge. He won a second judicial term in 1958 but resigned to run for governor in 1960.

In 1960, Kerner was elected governor of Illinois. He was reelected in 1964. His administration increased revenue through an increase in sales tax and the corporate tax. Kerner supported legislation for nondiscriminatory employment, consumer credit, a new criminal code, and civil rights. He developed a reputation for integrity, which the political machine that supported him used to their advantage. Kerner, however, never seemed at ease with his association with the Daley machine; being educated and aristocratic, he felt himself somehow above such an organization.

During his second term, Kerner utilized the National Guard to battle racial riots in 1965, 1966, and 1967. His quick and decisive action during these crises, as well as his record for supporting civil rights, convinced President Lyndon B. Johnson to appoint Kerner as head of the president's National Advisory Committee on Civil Disorders. In 1968, the Kerner Report was completed. It stated that the nation "was moving toward two societies, one black and one white—separate and unequal." Civil rights groups applauded the document, but Johnson was dismayed by the report's demand for reforms in housing, law enforcement, employment, and welfare. He did not believe such programs could be funded, and subsequently, no important laws were passed due to the report's recommendations.

In 1968, Kerner resigned as governor of Illinois in order to assume his appointment to the U.S. Court of Appeals for the Seventh Circuit. Up to this point, his reputation had been impeccable, but in December 1971, a federal grand jury indicted him on 19 counts of conspiracy, tax evasion, mail fraud, bribery, and perjury. Kerner asserted his innocence but stepped out of his judicial responsibilities until the case was resolved. He was suspected of purchasing racing stocks at grossly discounted rates and then selling them at full price, making a hefty profit. Kerner's income tax records had been falsified with a purchase date of 1962 in order to report the stock profit as long-term capital gains and thus pay less

taxes. Then he apparently lied to the Internal Revenue Service about an entry on his 1967 tax return.

Kerner was convicted of 17 of the original counts on February 19, 1973. He remained composed and dignified in his assertion of innocence, stating that it was "more important than life itself, because it involves my reputation and honor, which are dearer than life itself." In April 1973, he was sentenced to three years in prison and a fine of $50,000, a relatively light sentence. Kerner appealed in October of that same year, but it was denied. On July 29, 1974, faced with impeachment, he resigned as judge. Kerner served his prison term at the low-security Federal Corrections Facility in Lexington, Kentucky. Interestingly, he continued to enjoy public support and was honored by the National Association for the Advancement of Colored People and the Illinois Academy of Criminology for his human service work.

The last years of Kerner's life were beset by a series of tragedies. His beloved wife died the same year he was convicted. In May 1974, he suffered a heart attack. Then, in early 1975, he was diagnosed with lung cancer, for which he underwent surgery on March 6, 1975. Following his recovery, Kerner made it his mission to speak on behalf of prison reform, especially in regards to the treatment of prisoners by administrators. In 1976, Kerner's health declined once more. During his hospitalization, both of Illinois's U.S. senators tried unsuccessfully to convince President Gerald Ford to pardon Kerner. Kerner died on May 9, 1976, and was buried in Arlington National Cemetery.

ABC-CLIO

Further Reading:
Boger, John Charles, and Judith Welch Wegner. *Race, Poverty, and American Cities*. Chapel Hill: University of North Carolina Press, 1996.

Messick, Hank. *The Politics of Prosecution : Jim Thompson, Marje Everett, Richard Nixon and the Trial of Otto Kerner*. Ottawa: Caroline House Books, 1978.

Kerner Commission Report (1968)

On July 28, 1967, after four summers of urban racial violence, U.S. president Lyndon Baines Johnson established a National Advisory Commission to investigate these civil disorders. In 1968, the commission issued a report named after its chairman, Illinois governor and later federal judge Otto Kerner. The 426-page Kerner Commission Report became a national best-seller, with over 2 million copies in print, largely because it was published a few weeks before the assassination of Dr. Martin Luther King, Jr., which sparked another wave of race riots around the country. In the national public culture, the Kerner Commission Report would be the new civil rights text on the American race problem, replacing the more politically placid *An American Dilemma* by Gunnar Myrdal, which would influence the moral tone of the *Brown* decision of 1954 but would be too tame for the 1960s, when the United States was engulfed in spasms of urban violence. The Kerner Advisory Commission was composed of a who's who in American politics and civic life.

President Johnson charged the commission with investigating what happened, why it happened, and what could be done to prevent it from happening again. For many years and for several generations, the Kerner Commission Report would be criticized left, right, and center for its silences, political biases, methodological flaws, and prophetic errors. Nevertheless, the report was an extraordinary feat for its day and has had an enduring impact on American public culture both directly and indirectly. Particularly powerful in its effect on American public culture was the Kerner Report's startling conclusion that white racism was the cause of the "urban civil disorders" and that the country was becoming "two societies, one black, one white" (Kerner Commission 1968). Over the years and generations, these findings would be criticized as being overly simplistic and exposing racism as attitudinal symptoms rather than as structurally rooted causes. However, considering the social background of the commissioners and the historical and political context of the times, this conclusion by members of a national black and white civic and political establishment about the source of the waves of urban violence was, to say the least, remarkable. Although President Johnson and others would privately question the findings of the report, it was the first public statement by a body charged by an American president to find that white racism was a systemic problem in the United States. That admission shook white America down to its foundational social roots with sustained aftershock waves in American public culture and life. Despite its ideological

and political restraints and its uneven methodological rigor, the Kerner Commission Report dispelled a number of myths embraced by President Johnson, Federal of Bureau of Investigation director J. Edgar Hoover, and other members of the American civic and political establishment. The main myth dismantled was that rather than being the handiwork of black extremists and radical white outsiders, the civil disorders were the sociological and psychological consequences of white discrimination in employment, housing, education, health, police relations, social services, media, and many other areas of inner-city life.

For most post–World War II whites, particularly in the urban North and West, where they had lived insular, segregated lives for generations with no significant daily contact with black people, this finding was viewed as shocking and unbelievable. But, no matter the dominant population perspective, the possibility that white racism had something to do with black inequalities would remain, over time, an issue of public debate involving different right, left, and center political persuasions.

Equally remarkable were the surprisingly progressive and empowering policy recommendations of the Kerner Commission Report, many of which have never been fully entertained publicly even for minute discussion. The recommendation about the development of police community relations expertise has probably had the greatest influence in shaping public policy. On the other hand, the recommendations to increase public investment in the education, employment, and social service sectors of predominantly black inner-city communities were initially ignored and then increasingly ridiculed in a national political culture that has moved progressively from left to right since the 1960s.

JOHN H. STANFIELD

See also

Kerner, Otto; Riots in America; Segregation

Further Reading:

Jones, Mack H. "The Kerner Commission: Errors and Omissions." In *The Kerner Report Revisited*, edited by Philip Meranto. Assembly on the Kerner Report Revisited, Institute on Government and Public Affairs, University of Illinois, Urbana, January 11–13, 1970.

Kerner Commission. *Report of the National Advisory Commission on Civil Disorders*. Washington, DC: U.S. Government Printing Office, 1968.

Lehrer, Jim. "A Nation Divided?" *News Hour with Jim Lehrer* transcript, with Elizabeth Farnsworth, Lynn Curtis, Hugh Price, Stephen Thernstrom, and Robert Woodson. March 2, 1998.

National Advisory Commission on Civil Disorders. *The Kerner Report.* New York: Bantam Books, 1968.

Thernstrom, Stephan, Fred Siegal, and Robert Woodson. "The Kerner Report and the Failed Legacy of Liberal Social Policy." Heritage Foundation Lecture No. 619. March 13, 1998.

King, Martin Luther, Jr. (1929–1968)

Martin Luther King, Jr. was an African American Baptist minister, a civil rights movement leader of the 1950s and 1960s, and a winner of the 1964 Nobel Prize for Peace. He was born in Atlanta, Georgia, into a family with a long tradition of Baptist preaching from both his parents' sides. This family environment exposed him to Christian ideas and black oratory since his childhood. In 1948, he earned a Bachelor of Arts in Sociology from Morehouse College in Atlanta, Georgia; in 1951 he received another Bachelor of Arts in Divinity from Crozer Theological Seminary in Chester, Pennsylvania; and in 1955 he obtained a PhD in Theology from Boston University. The same year, he became the leader of the Montgomery Bus Boycott, which was prompted by the arrest of Rosa Parks, a black woman who challenged southern Jim Crow laws by refusing to give her bus seat to a white man. From 1957, King headed the Southern Christian Leadership Conference, a predominantly Baptist organization that used the Gandhian strategies of nonviolence to achieve civil rights for African Americans. In 1965, in one of the dramatic events of the civil rights movement, King led a nonviolent protest march from Selma to Montgomery, Alabama, for voting rights. In his many speeches, King used the techniques of rhythmic and dramatic oratory, including call and response, and he consistently invoked biblical figures and ideas, African American history and literature, and world and American political and intellectual history to strengthen his arguments. For example, he drew quotations and concepts from the philosophies of Socrates, St. Augustine, T. S. Eliot, Martin Buber, and Gandhi. In the face of race violence, instead of advocating violence and the separation of the races like some of his contemporaries, he consistently

advocated racial harmony and reaffirmed his belief in the sound values contained in the Declaration of Independence. In his many writings and speeches, he envisioned an America united in the Christian values of love and brotherhood and in the principles that had founded the republic. "Letter from Birmingham City Jail," "I Have a Dream," and "I've Been to the Mountaintop," are three of his works that exemplify these ideas.

King wrote "Letter from Birmingham City Jail" on April 16, 1963, as a reply to an open letter from eight white Alabama clergymen who had called on his nonviolent resistance movement to let local and federal courts deal with the issues of integration to avoid inciting civil unrest. He argued that he was prompted by Christian values in his fight for social justice and that American democracy and morality were at stake. King's disappointment with his fellow clergymen and Southern Christians questioned their moral stand in the face of racism, segregation, and discrimination. The refusal of the city leadership to abolish segregation in its facilities and the triumph of violence against the black population had led King and his organization to boycott the goods and services of the city. He argued that his presence in Birmingham was justified by the fact that there was injustice there, and as the prophets of the Old Testament and the followers of Jesus Christ over centuries traveled to places outside their homelands, he had to go wherever there was injustice. King noted that the only reaction had been police brutality, blatant partiality in courts, and destruction of African American houses and churches, even though King and his followers had adopted the philosophy of nonviolence, which forbids the use of violence even in the face of violent attack. He further responded to the clergymen's idea that time would solve the problems by arguing that groups in power rarely gave up their privileges. About the accusation that he was breaking laws, his reply was that unjust laws were no laws at all, and he questioned the white moderates' obsession with civil order rather than justice and Christian values. In addition, he reminded his fellow clergymen that his struggle was rooted in Christian love, brotherhood, and nonviolent protest and that it was for freedom, an American ideal. He argued that action must be taken to awaken America to the injustice inflicted upon the black population even after the ratification of the Thirteenth, Fourteenth, and Fifteenth Amendments a century before. King concluded his letter with yet another

Martin Luther King, Jr., U.S. civil rights leader, at a press conference in Birmingham, Alabama, May 16, 1963. King was awarded the Nobel Peace Prize in 1964 for his work in the area of human rights. (Library of Congress)

reminder of the sacred values of Christianity and the Founding Fathers' ideals that created the nation, thus showing the moral bankruptcy that the oppression of African Americans has wrought upon the Republic.

King delivered his most famous speech, "I Have a Dream," on the steps of the Lincoln Memorial on August 28, 1963. With the expression "five score years ago," the speech fittingly opens with a reference to the opening of the Gettysburg Address, signaling the momentous significance of his own speech and at the same time invoking Abraham Lincoln, who signed the Emancipation Proclamation in 1863. In appealing to Lincoln's famous phrase "four score and seven years ago," King's play on words juxtaposes his reverence to American values and ideals but at the same time indicts America's failure to live up to them. He reminds America that "100 years later" the promise of the proclamation has not become a reality for African Americans, who are still victims of violence, segregation, discrimination, and disenfranchisement. He dramatizes America's betrayal of its black population through the metaphor of a check, the "promissory note" to all American citizens guaranteeing the enjoyment of rights contained in the Declaration of Independence and the Constitution, but America has refused to honor its "sacred obligation" to its black citizens.

The first part of King's speech is a true Jeremiad, lamenting the state of a nation that has betrayed its own covenant of "life, liberty, and the pursuit of happiness" for all its citizens. The use of biblical imagery permeates his speech to indicate the epic and moral nature of the civil rights movement. For example, invoking Psalm 23, he speaks of the "valley of the shadow of death" adapted as "the dark and desolate valley of segregation" in the speech. Likewise, "now is the time to lift our nation from the quicksand of racial injustice to the solid rock of brotherhood" is a reference to Jesus' parable of the wise man and the foolish man. Built upon the sand, the foolish man's house does not withstand the storm while the wise man's house, built upon the rock, remains unscathed. Both Psalm 23 (in which the psalmist also praises God for leading him through the dark valley) and the parable express indignation at the dark valley of racism and segregation and at the same time, in the tradition of the Jeremiad, demands drastic social change to forestall ruin. More biblical references are used to chastise America for its failure to deliver justice to African Americans. In the manner of prophets of the Old Testament, he threatens the continuation of revolt and lack of tranquility in America until African American freedom is achieved. He stresses, however, that his struggle is rooted not in "bitterness and hatred" and violence but in Christian love and nonviolence even in the face of police brutality and generalized social injustice.

King's catalogue of African American nightmares is further expressed in a series of appeals to the founding documents of the American republic (the Declaration of Independence and the Constitution) and to the many betrayed promises of the last century. Freedom has not become a reality for African Americans in spite of the Emancipation Proclamation; a few civil rights acts during Reconstruction; the Thirteenth, Fourteenth, and Fifteenth Amendments; and, more recently, the 1954 *Brown v. Board of Education* trial. In 1963, African Americans were still dealing with separate schools, churches, neighborhoods, public facilities for whites and blacks, as well as the denial of the right to vote and the generalized impunity of white-on-black crimes.

The "I Have a Dream" part issues a message of hope for an America where the "self-evident" truth of equality will be a reality; where brotherhood, justice, and Christian love will triumph; where "life, liberty, and the pursuit of happiness" will also be a reality for African Americans; and where people "will not be judged by the color of their skin but by the content of their character." He reiterates his belief in the founding values of the American republic ("a land of liberty"), where one day freedom will triumph and all God's children, black and white, and all religious creeds will one day be able to be rejoined in freedom regained.

King's last two allusions invoke two songs about two different kinds of freedom: "My Country 'Tis of Thee" and "Free at Last." The first is a hymn to freedom in America and the second is the expression of centuries-long aspirations for African Americans. The truth of "My Country 'Tis of Thee" has been repeatedly mocked by the lack of freedom and justice for a part of the country's citizens. King suggests that only when civil rights have been extended to all American citizens can the song have its full meaning. Only then can all citizens, black and white, sing it with conviction and loyalty. "Free at Last," on the other hand, is as much about freedom, but as a Negro spiritual, it is specific to African Americans. This old Negro spiritual song carries the hope for freedom that African Americans have expressed for a long time. King is suggesting that this clamor for freedom needs to become reality.

The power of King's celebrated speech depends, among other things, on the use of repetition and clusters of images and metaphors throughout the speech as well as in the delivery of the speech itself with its rhythmic building up to a climax, with interjections of call-and-response with the audience.

Martin Luther King Jr., delivered his last speech, "I've Been to the Mountaintop," at the Masonic Temple in Memphis, Tennessee, on April 3, 1968. He was there to support the city's sanitation workers. He first surveyed some of the great figures, moments, and civilizations in the history of humanity, culminating in Franklin D. Roosevelt's statement that we have "nothing to fear but fear itself" and concluding that the world was, in the 1960s, crying for freedom, particularly when it came to African Americans who had continued to suffer from neglect and poverty. Invoking the struggle and triumph against segregation and disenfranchisement in the past and the success of the nonviolent movement, King asked his audience to work together to defeat the modern pharaoh's attempt to keep African Americans enslaved, arguing that their collective power in the United States could be used to change hiring practices in the public and private sectors.

King ended his speech with an apocalyptic tone, comparing himself to Moses and asserting that his struggle for civil rights had taken him to the mountaintop and he had seen the glory of God and the Promised Land, a reference to an America where African Americans will fully enjoy the rights and privileges of citizenship. In a prophetic manner, he stated that, even though he was aware of threats on his life, he did not fear for his life. He was assassinated the next day.

King's choice to use nonviolence in his fight for African American rights at a time of great turbulence in the nation and when violence was advocated by other groups is a testimony to his attachment to Christian values of love, hope, inclusion, and brotherhood as well as to the ideals that founded the American Republic. His crusade for social justice and for a truly free and democratic America was, and continues to be, an inspiration to the nation and the world.

AIMABLE TWAGILIMANA

See also
Civil Rights Movement; Southern Christian Leadership Conference (SCLC)

Further Reading:
Hansen, Drew W. *Martin Luther King, Jr. and the Speech that Inspired a Nation*. New York: Ecco, 2003.

King, Martin Luther, Jr. "I Have a Dream." In *The Norton Anthology of African American Literature*, edited by Henry Louis Gates Jr. and Nellie Y. McKay, 107–9. New York: W. W. Norton, 2004.

King, Martin Luther, Jr. "I've Been to the Mountaintop." In *The Norton Anthology of African American Literature*, edited by Henry Louis Gates Jr. and Nellie Y. McKay, 110–16. New York: W. W. Norton, 2004.

King, Martin Luther, Jr. "Letter from Birmingham City Jail." In *The Norton Anthology of African American Literature*, edited by Henry Louis Gates Jr. and Nellie Y. McKay, 1896–908. New York: W. W. Norton, 2004.

King, Martin Luther, Jr. *The Measure of a Man*. Philadelphia: Fortress Press, 1988.

Miller, Keith D. *Voice of Deliverance: The Language of Martin Luther King, Jr. and Its Sources*. Athens: University Press of Georgia, 1998.

Knights of Labor

Originally the Noble and Holy Order of the Knights of Labor, the Knights of Labor was founded in secrecy by nine tailors in Philadelphia in 1869. The founder, Uriah Stephens, who originally planned to enter the ministry, took his personal goals for the United States and translated them into a platform for organizing labor. These ideas included the notion that prior labor organizations failed because of exclusive membership. Thus, Stephens and the Knights of Labor opened up their membership to include all workers, skilled and unskilled, and—eventually—African Americans and women.

New leadership emerged in the late 1870s, when Terence V. Powderly was elected grand master workman. Under Powderly's leadership, the secrecy dissipated, and this, coupled with falling wages in the early 1880s, triggered an increase in union membership. In addition, a successful strike against Jay Gould's Southwest Railroad in 1884 helped increase membership. By 1886, there were 15,000 local assemblies and somewhere between 700,000 and 1 million workers. This huge growth was highlighted by the merging of skilled and unskilled workers, and incorporating women, immigrants, and African Americans, groups that had previously been excluded from labor movements.

Prior to the Knights of Labor (and after) it was not uncommon for company owners to try to break organized labor by creating racial and ethnic strife within the workforce. The Knights of Labor sought to eliminate that paralyzing tactic and the violence that ensued.

Most African Americans joined all-black assemblies, but some locals had mixed memberships, even in the South. Knight membership included 60,000 African Americans. In some places like Virginia, black workers made up at least half of the local membership.

African Americans used the Knights of Labor to challenge racial discrimination, not only in the workplace, but in society in general. The national convention in Richmond, Virginia, in 1886 resulted in an attack on the Jim Crow structure of Richmond society resulting in the integrating, even if only temporarily, of Richmond's Academy of Music; this resulted in the largest racially integrated event in Richmond's history.

Powderly, while supporting African American pushes for equality, still attempted to placate Southern whites. He did not strive to shatter Southern racial conventions, and was willing to compromise black workers when it inhibited his ability to organize Southern whites. In the end, African American membership was often curtailed or limited in his attempt to attract more whites. And, despite its apparent openness, the union failed at crucial times to support black workers. In a strike among Louisiana sugarmen in 1887, 9,000 black workers went on strike. They refused to accept a higher wage without recognition of the Knights of Labor. In the end, shocked at the violence perpetrated by white society and government on the black workers, the Knights of Labor did not come to their aid and withdrew support, undermining the strike.

By 1890, it was apparent that most whites refused to join with blacks in pursuing solutions to economic problems, and they began to distance themselves from their black counterparts. By 1894, the Knights of Labor had abandoned African Americans and advocated returning them to Africa.

There was never total harmony among the groups that composed the Knights of Labor, but for a time the alliance was sufficiently stable to spark widespread fear among industrialists. In the end, the failure of some strikes, like the Missouri Pacific Strike of 1886 and the public's connecting the Knights of Labor to the violence of the Haymarket Square Riot, undercut their prestige and increased internal disputes among the skilled and unskilled workers, which shattered the all-inclusive nature of the union. The factional disputes, unsuccessful strikes, and the emergence of the American Federation of Labor led to a rapid drop in membership, so that by 1900, the Knights of Labor were practically nonexistent.

GARY GERSHMAN

See also

Labor Movement, Racism in; Labor Unions

Further Reading:

Dubofsky, Melvin. *Industrialism and the American Worker*. New York: Harlan Davidson, 1996.

Filippelli, Ronald L. *Labor in the U.S.A.: A History*. New York: McGraw-Hill, 1984.

Weir, Robert. *Beyond Labor's Veil: The Culture of the Knights of Labor*. University Park: Pennsylvania State University Press, 1996.

Knoxville (Tennessee) Riot of 1919

On August 30, 1919, an intruder shot and killed Bertie Lindsey, a 27-year-old white woman, in her Knoxville, Tennessee home. Her 21-year-old cousin, Ora Smyth, lay motionless in her bed. After the intruder grabbed a purse and ran away, Smyth fled next door to the house of a city policeman. A few hours later, Maurice Mays, a black man whom many people believed was the son of the Democratic white mayor of Knoxville, stood behind bars, charged with the slaying. By morning, roving bands of white men moved toward downtown, visibly upset with the news of the crime. Just before sundown, shooting began, as the mob stormed the county jail in search of Mays. Knoxville joined the numerous other American cities that experienced a riot during the Red Summer Race Riots of 1919.

Ostensibly, Knoxville was an unlikely candidate for racial violence. The city remained largely Republican more than 50 years after the Civil War's end. Only 12,000 blacks made up its 80,000 inhabitants. Many Knoxville blacks exercised their right to vote, held public office, sat on juries, and served on the police force. Also, the existence of Knoxville College, one of the first black schools established after the Civil War; the *East Tennessee News*, the area's biggest black newspaper; and a local chapter of the National Association for the Advancement of Colored People showed the growing role of African Americans in the community. However, severe animosities existed between the two races. For example, in June 1913, a gang of whites almost lynched a black man suspected of murdering a white policeman. Economic hardships and job competition aggravated the problem. Although World War I provided jobs, Knoxville's inability to accommodate new residents strained racial harmony. The postwar recession inflamed these hostilities as the city's industries closed. Some whites formed a local chapter of the Ku Klux Klan.

The situation remained tense in August 1919. The homicide of a white woman allegedly by a black man served as the catalyst that destroyed any remaining civility between the races. Only minutes after Ora Smyth sought help from her neighbors, several policemen rushed to the scene of the crime, where some 30 or 40 people had already congregated. One of the patrolmen, Andy White, immediately thought of Maurice Mays. More than once, others heard White castigate Mays for interacting with white women. Often at the center of controversy, the striking, eloquent, and married 31-year-old Mays attracted numerous women, both black and white. He owned a cafe and dance hall in Knoxville's red-light district frequented by both races. Mays also delivered the black vote to his father, John E. McMillan, who became mayor in 1915 and faced reelection soon. In fact, Mays handed out blank poll tax receipts for McMillan on August 29.

White and two other policemen were ordered to arrest Mays. They arrived at his house at 3:30 A.M., discovered him sleeping, and searched the premises for evidence. In his dresser they found a revolver, which the three lawmen claimed had recently been discharged. Both Mays's foster father and the black driver of the patrol wagon denied this claim, however. Moreover, although muddy tracks led away from the crime scene, Mays's clothes, shoes, and carpet were clean and dry. Nevertheless, White arrested Mays and took him to the crime scene for Ora Smyth to identify, which she promptly did after barely glancing at him. By 8:00 A.M., a sizable crowd congregated at the city jail, forcing the police chief to transfer Mays to the county jail. In the early afternoon, the Knoxville *Sentinel* circulated lurid front-page articles describing the crime and arrest. Rumors flowed. Again, the authorities decided that Mays would be safer elsewhere. They dressed him as a woman to conceal his identity and sent him to Chattanooga.

Concomitantly, large crowds gathered at various points around Knoxville. By 6:00 P.M., a mob of over 500 surrounded the county jail demanding Mays. In vain, officials allowed four different groups to tour the facility to see that Mays was not there. At Market Square, 5,000 whites worked themselves into a fury and marched toward the jail. By 8:00 P.M., a barrage of rocks and bullets battered the building, and the angry crowd soon broke down the doors. For the next few hours, hundreds—if not thousands—of people combed the jail looking for Mays. Although they could not find him, they discovered an impounded moonshine still and some liquor. Imbibing freely, the crowd ransacked the building, taking weapons and ammunition. The mob freed all the white prisoners, including convicted murderers, but neither liberated nor injured the African Americans.

Called in after the jailhouse assault, the Fourth Tennessee Infantry—scattered on weekend passes—slowly made its way to Knoxville. The first members arrived at the jail around 10:00 P.M. The 16 soldiers and their officer suffered

brutal beatings, along with the loss of their uniforms and firearms at the hands of the white mob. The adjutant general, accompanied by three companies, soon arrived and assured the crowd that Mays had been moved, but to no avail.

While the city's whites assaulted the jail, rumors of impending attacks circulated among Knoxville's blacks. Those who did not flee the city gathered weapons to prepare for an invasion. Well-armed men congregated at the corner of Vine and Central, the hub of the black district, waiting for the mob of whites to appear. Shortly after 11:30 P.M., the brawl between Knoxville's white and black citizens began. While several clusters of rioters from the jail headed for Chattanooga in search of Mays, the rest shifted their attention to shots coming from the black district. Members of the National Guard, strengthened but still badly outnumbered, received orders to march double-time to the scene of the new fight. The authorities could do very little, however, as the area became a battleground for the next few hours.

The reinforced National Guard finally sealed off the black district around 3:15 A.M., effectively preventing any whites from entering it or any blacks from leaving. The following day, accounts of lawlessness, mostly unfounded, continued to plague the authorities. As a result, some 200 white civilians became special deputies and patrolmen, and they dispersed throughout the city to maintain order. For the next two days, periodic bursts of violence erupted around Knoxville. But by midnight, August 31, most of the hostility had begun to diminish.

In the days after the riot, guardsmen searched blacks on the street. Things slowly began to return to normal, though, and most of the Guard left by September 2, the day after the black district reopened. Although newspapers recorded only two deaths, one black man and one white, and 14 wounded, the exact number of casualties remains unknown. Observers placed the number killed between 25 and several hundred. Authorities arrested 55 white men and women for their role in the riot, but many went free.

Under tight security, Maurice Mays returned to Knoxville on September 25, and his trial began a few days later. The all-white jury found him guilty of murder after only 18 minutes of deliberation. Two weeks later, the judge imposed the death penalty. However, the sentence was overturned on appeal because of judicial error. In a second trial, Mays received the same sentence. On March 15, 1922, as he continued to proclaim his innocence, Mays died in the state's electric chair.

ANN V. COLLINS

See also

Race Riots in America; Red Summer Riots of 1919. Documents: The Report on the Memphis Riots of May 1866 (July 25, 1866); Account of the Riots in East St. Louis, Illinois (July 1917); The Cook County Coroner's Report Regarding the 1919 Chicago Race Riots (1919); A Southern Black Woman's Letter Regarding the Recent Riots in Chicago and Washington (November 1919); The Final Report of the Grand Jury on the Tulsa Race Riot (June 25, 1921); Testimony from *Laney v. United States* Describing Events during the Washington, D.C., Riot of July 1919 (December 3, 1923); The Governor's Commission Report on the Watts Riots (December 1965); Cyrus R. Vance's Report on the Riots in Detroit (July-August 1967); The Reports of the Oklahoma Commission to Study the Tulsa Race Riot of 1921 (2000-2001); The Draft Report of the 1898 Wilmington Race Riot Commission (December 2005)

Further Reading:

Egerton, John. "A Case of Prejudice: Maurice Mays and the Knoxville Race Riot of 1919." *Southern Exposure* 11 (1983): 56–65.

Lakin, Matthew. "'A Dark Night': The Knoxville Race Riot of 1919." *Journal of East Tennessee History* 72 (2000): 1–29.

Ku Klux Klan (KKK)

The Ku Klux Klan (KKK), drawing on the Greek word *kuklos* meaning circle, and using the word "klan" as homage to the Scottish ancestry of its founders, was formed in Giles County, Tennessee, during the Reconstruction Era following the Civil War in the late 1860s. While the original motivations of the group were to engage in pranks to alleviate boredom, the KKK quickly morphed into a group whose primary aim was to reinforce white supremacy in the Southern United States through fear and violence. Today, the KKK is known as an extremist reactionary group that has historically expressed its views on white supremacy through terrorist acts. The KKK has experienced ups and downs in its membership and visibility since 1870, but as of 2012, it was still estimated to have between 5,000 and 8,000 members. Despite being classified as a hate group by several organizations including the Anti-Defamation League, the KKK has never been completely eradicated. The hateful attitude of the KKK has been directed at various groups over time, including African Americans, Republicans, Catholics, Jews, Mormons, and immigrant populations. The KKK spirit is one of fanaticism, contempt for the push towards equality, and a firm belief that in their right to accomplish by whatever means necessary the racist goal of preserving white Anglo-Saxon supremacy in the United States.

The KKK was founded in Pulaski County, Tennessee, in 1866 by James Crowe, Richard Reed, Calvin Jones, John Lester, Frank McCord, and John Kennedy—six former Confederate soldiers who had returned after fighting in the Civil War to a town where jobs and entertainment were rare. The early activities of the Klan were not malicious in nature nor aimed at any specific segment of society; instead, members attempted to break the monotony of their everyday lives by playing pranks around the town while dressed in white gowns and pointed hats. However, their activities quickly turned violent as KKK members adapted a more malicious goal. Primarily targeting free blacks, KKK members sought to reinstate the culture of the South prior to the Civil War where blacks were subservient to whites in all areas of life. Often using outright violence, the KKK terrorized and incited fear in Southern blacks.

Within a few months of the Klan's founding, Gen. Nathan Bedford Forrest became the head of the KKK and this new ideology of racial terrorism soon spread to adjacent counties and states. Many new chapters were formed, and groups sought to increase their visibility through announcements in local papers, meetings, and parades. Although it was billed as an organized group, local chapters of the KKK soon became uncontrollable and violence and other hate crimes against Southern blacks became rampant among group members. The Klan has been named responsible for at least 1,000 deaths during the first era of its existence alone. As a result of this widespread violence, in 1869 the Klan's leader Gen. Forrest issued General Order Number One, which called for the immediate disbandment of the KKK. While the Klan receded from visibility after the disbandment, they were by no means completely eradicated, and the years following World War I would see the largest increase in Klan membership in the nation's history.

The 1915 film *The Birth of a Nation* directed by D. W. Griffith offered an idyllic view of the KKK, glorifying

David Duke (1950–)

For more than 30 years, David Duke has been a local and national advocate of neo-Nazi, anti-Semitic, and white supremacist politics. He was perhaps the most widely known white supremacist in the United States in the 1990s.

As a student at Louisiana State University, Duke founded the neo-Nazi group White Youth Alliance. Duke attained national prominence as National Director (or "Grand Wizard") of the Knights of the Klu Klux Klan in the 1970s. During this time, he advocated the mainstreaming of the Klan, a tactic that boosted its national membership. After his association with the Klan, he founded the National Association for the Advancement of White People. He was elected in 1988 to the U.S. House of Representatives for Louisiana, where he authored anti-affirmative-action legislation. His election was widely understood as a testament to the tolerance for, and popularity of, overt racism in Louisiana politics. He ran unsuccessfully for the U.S. Senate in 1990, although he received over 43 percent of the Louisiana vote. He also ran for Louisiana's governorship in 1991 and the White House in 1992, winning neither.

Throughout the 1990s, he continued to promote himself as an advocate of "white civil rights" through his radio program and his autobiography and other publications. In December 2002, he pled guilty to tax and mail fraud, a case that involved the sale of his list of supporters to Louisiana governor Mike Foster, and he was sentenced to 15 months in prison. Currently, he is president of the European-American Unity and Rights Organization, which uses the Internet for the global advocacy of white supremacism and "white awareness" and for protesting affirmative action, U.S. immigration, hate-speech policies, and the Anti-Defamation League and other civil rights groups. He also sells products that appeal to racists and anti-Semites, including Confederate flags, videos like D. W. Griffith's *Birth of a Nation*, anti-Semitic books, and his own book, *Jewish Supremacism*.

VICTORIA PITTS

the original Klansmen. Films such as this, combined with the fear incited in white Americans due to the waves of immigrants arriving to the United States post-WWI, paved the way for the revival of the KKK.

This second era was led by Col. William J. Simmons, who was a Methodist minister in Alabama. Simmons was able to gain widespread support for the Klan by tapping into religious denominations across the United States who were concerned with the decline of morals, and by preying on widespread fears that white, Anglo-Saxon, middle-class values were being destroyed by immigrant populations. During this era, the Klan expanded beyond the Southern region to become a nationwide entity with membership growing to around 5 million by 1924—the highest in the history of the Klan. As with the first era, violence and intimidation against various minority groups was rampant among KKK members during this second phase. This second Klan embraced a now hallmark symbol of the KKK: the burning Latin cross. Clansmen embraced this symbol primarily as a means of intimidation, using it to incite fear in minority groups. Many opposing groups at this time fought to resist the KKK. The

National Association for the Advancement of Colored People created public education campaigns about Klan activities and lobbied in Congress against the KKK and its violent tendencies. By 1928, the popularity of the Klan was beginning to wane, and membership dropped substantially.

The third era of the Klan began in the 1950s when school segregation was struck down by the Supreme Court. This third phase of the KKK reached its pinnacle when the pressure for racial integration and the subsequent civil rights movement of the 1960s led to lunch counter sit-ins, freedom rides, and protests. In this climate, the KKK was reawakened as a violent reaction to the struggle for racial equality. While membership in this third era was nowhere near the millions the Klan attracted during the 1920s, they were still able to gain an estimated 20,000 followers. These KKK members began a violent attack against minorities that rivaled the violence of the Civil War–era Klan, including the use of intimidation in the form of cross burnings and Klan rallies that often ended in such violent acts as bombings and even murders. During this time period the vast majority of crimes committed by Klan members went unpunished and eventually, reactions to the Klan's overt violence and their seeming immunity to prosecution became an impetus to getting various pieces of civil rights legislation passed. After the passage of this legislation, the Klan experienced a decline in membership that lasted into the late 1980s.

Starting in the late 1970s the Klan entered their fourth era, which has been referred to as the public relations era of the Klan. Right-wing politician David Duke led this era of the KKK, working to raise the visibility of the Klan through his various appearances on talk shows and his political endeavors. Duke's main platform involved a belief that all races had the basic human right to preserve their own heritage. Duke specifically spoke out against Jews. Despite Duke's appeal to middle-class white America, this was an age of decline for the Klan as the civil rights acts they fought so hard to prevent had been passed and the courts were subsequently much more willing to prosecute and punish Klansmen.

The contemporary Klan is referred to as the fifth era. This current Klan is fragmented with over 40 different Klan groups totaling approximately 5,000 members. Nevertheless, this era of the KKK is still working to uphold white supremacy, and it has been identified by several civil rights coalitions as a hate group. Today's Klan has been characterized as both an underground paramilitary army of hardcore racists, and an aboveground political movement associated with the Christian coalition, whose goal is to elect extremist right-wing candidates. The Klan is now very heavily affiliated with other white supremacist groups such as the National Socialist Movement, Aryan Nations, and Christian Identity groups, among others. While the Klan today still directs its hateful acts towards minorities and immigrant populations as it always has, since 2006 they have also added homosexuals to the list.

Virginia R. Beard

See also

Christian Identity Hate Groups; Hammerskin Nation; Hate Groups in America

Further Reading:

Chalmers, David M. *Hooded Americanism: The History of the Ku Klux Klan*. Durham, NC: Duke University Press, 1987.

Randel, William P. *The Ku Klux Klan: A Century of Infamy*. Philadelphia: Chilton Books, 1965.

Ridgeway, James. *Blood in the Face: The Ku Klux Klan, Aryan Nations, Nazi Skinheads, and the Rise of a New White Culture*. New York: Thunder's Mouth Press, 1995.

Southern Poverty Law Center. "Ku Klux Klan." http://www .splcenter.org/get-informed/intelligence-files/ideology/ ku-klux-klan (accessed December 21, 2012).

Wade, Wyn C. *The Fiery Cross: The Ku Klux Klan in America*. New York: Oxford University Press, 1998.

L

La Raza Unida Party

La Raza Unida, "the People United," was a racially based third-party movement of Mexican Americans to challenge the political monopoly of the Democratic and Republican parties in the United States. It grew out of the militant Chicano movement that had proliferated throughout the Southwest and in some parts of the Midwest from 1966 to 1970. Many activists in the Chicano movement found neither of the two dominant political parties adequately responsive to the needs of most Mexican Americans, who were living in disproportionate poverty and experiencing racial discrimination. They also saw the traditional civil rights organizations of Mexican Americans, such as the League of United Latin-American Citizens, the GI Forum, and the Political Association of Spanish-Speaking Organizations, as being unwilling to work to bring about the social change demanded by the rising expectations of Chicanos.

The endeavor toward a Chicano political party emerged first in Texas and Colorado and expanded soon to California, New Mexico, Arizona, Utah, and the Midwest in the early 1970s. It could have flowered on the soil of Chicano grassroots social movements of an anticapitalist and nationalist bent, which provided the ideology, leadership, organization, constituency, and financial resources. La Raza Unida party in Texas came out of the Mexican American Youth Organization, founded in 1967 under the leadership of Jose Angel

Gutierrez. Colorado's La Raza Unida was organized by the Crusade for Justice, founded in 1966 by another prominent Chicano movement leader, Rodolfo "Corky" Gonzales. The explosive political atmosphere of the 1960s, both domestically and abroad, also emboldened Chicano activists. The party mainly appealed to radicalized students and poor Mexican Americans with anticapitalist and nationalist platforms, declaring that it was time for Chicanos' political self-determination to dismantle internal colonialism and systematic inequality.

La Raza Unida party's political success was, however, confined to several counties in Texas during the brief period from 1970 to 1975. Its achievement on state and national levels remained symbolic rather than real. In Texas, the party took over the local school boards and city councils of Cristal, Cotulla, Carrizo Springs, and other places where the Mexican American population predominated. It demonstrated how they could win political power and use it for La Raza. The newly elected Chicano officers had new schools built and old ones refurbished; implemented bilingual, bicultural education from kindergarten through 12th grade; promoted Chicano pride and multiculturalism; improved city services and infrastructure; and, though less successful, tried to advance Mexican American businesses. The success made Texas an inspiration for Chicano activists in other states. Even though La Raza Unida in Texas was an official political party on the

---

League of United Latin American Citizens (LULAC)

The League of United Latin American Citizens (LULAC) is the oldest and largest Hispanic civil rights organization that is still active. It was founded on February 17, 1929, by the merging of four Mexican American organizations: the Corpus Christi Council of the Sons of America, the Alice Council of the Sons of America, the Knights of America, and the Latin American Citizens League in the Rio Grande valley and Laredo. Although LULAC was created to address racial inequality, discrimination, and injustice Mexican Americans had suffered since the annexation of Mexico's territory after the Mexican War, the founders intended from the outset to include all Hispanics. The organizing efforts by a special task force called the "Flying Squad" frequently met intimidation by the Anglo authorities. By 1932, however, LULAC established local councils in Arizona, Colorado, New Mexico, and California. Today it represents all Hispanics in most of the United States, including Puerto Rico and Guam.

LULAC has always been a multi-issue organization. In 1945, a California LULAC Council successfully sued Orange County to desegregate its school system. In 1954, LULAC won another landmark victory in the Supreme Court case *Hernandez v. State of Texas*, successfully stopping the state's racist practice that had excluded Mexican Americans from jury duty. LULAC also started an early-childhood-education program, called "The Little School of the 400," which later became the model of the federal program Head Start. LULAC was also instrumental in creating Hispanic national organizations such as the American GI Forum, the Mexican American Legal Defense and Education Fund, and SER—Jobs for Progress. It also developed many low-income housing units.

LULAC has been a largely middle-class organization composed of skilled workers and small-business owners, as well as some professionals. Ideologically, it adheres to the mainstream American ideology: liberalism, individualism, free-market capitalism, anticommunism, and U.S. patriotism.

Dong-Ho Cho

---

ballot, it never won any statewide election. In the 1978 gubernatorial race, it lost its official party status. The party never regained its lost momentum after that and was defunct by 1981.

La Raza Unida's electoral record in other states did not match even that of Texas. But the political-party movement provided Chicano activists with a chance to put their radical demands on the state- and national-level political agenda, as well as an organizational impetus. No Chicano party movement survived the general turn toward political conservatism that has occurred since the 1970s, which saw the decline of antiwar, civil rights, and Chicano struggles. Restrictive election laws, lack of media access, insufficient financing, Democratic Party cooptation, and law-enforcement infiltration, which led to members being arrested on questionable drug charges, also contributed to the demise of the third-party movement. In addition to these external obstacles, internal strife, particularly the power struggle between two top leaders, Gutierrez and Gonzales, debilitated the movement. The internal conflict reflected the eclectic nature of La Raza Unida's ideology, a mixture of various types of nationalism and Marxism. Also inconsistent was its strategy. Whereas Gutierrez stood for a more pragmatic coalition approach, Gonzales opted for a direct ideological agitation of ultranationalism.

La Raza Unida, although it had little formal structure, never completely disappeared. Some activists have been working to revive El Partido Nacional de la Raza Unida. The increase of the Latino population, expanded financial resources, and Latino mass media, combined with the deteriorating economic and racial situations, may create suitable conditions for its revitalization in the 21st century.

Dong-Ho Cho

See also
Gonzales, Corky

Further Reading:
Garcia, Ignacio. *The Forging of a Militant Ethos among Mexican Americans*. Tucson: University of Arizona Press, 1997.
Muñoz, Carlos. *Youth, Identity, Power: The Chicano Movement*. New York: Verso, 1989.

Navarro, Armando. *La Raza Unida Party: A Chicano Challenge to the U.S. Two Party Dictatorship.* Philadelphia: Temple University Press, 2000.

Rosales, F. Arturo. *Chicano! The History of Mexican American Civil Rights Movement.* Houston: Arte Publico, 1996.

Labor Movement, Racism in

The year 1996 was a landmark year for the labor movement because for the first time in its history, most union members were not white and male. Indeed, the labor movement has come a long way from the days when blacks, if not completely excluded from unions, were forced to charter separate "colored" locals. Discrimination, however, does still exist in both the labor movement and employment at large in the United States.

Race has been a fundamental problem for the labor movement since the late 18th century, when the first unions were formed in Philadelphia and New York. The question of race in the labor movement has a complex history that can be broken down into three historical eras: from 1780 to the Civil War, from Reconstruction to the 1930s, and from the founding of the Congress of Industrial Organizations (CIO) in 1935 to the post–civil rights era of today. For most of its history, the labor movement was segregated if not outwardly racist. In California, for example, the Workingmen's Party was formed in large part as a means to deport Chinese immigrants. In the cases where blacks were allowed to join unions, they were forced to request separate charters from the American Federation of Labor (AFL) for "colored" locals. It was not until the formation of the CIO in 1935 that any unions pressed for integration as official policy. The United Mine Workers and the United Auto Workers were the most progressive of the CIO unions, and they pushed for interracial solidarity.

Because the labor movement emerged in the United States when slavery was the dominant mode of production in the South, "free labor" and civil rights for workers would come to be defined as being an issue exclusive to white workers. The construction of white identity and racism is intimately bound up with the rise of the labor movement: the concept of "whiteness" was developed during these years, and it would be a major obstacle for the labor movement after the Civil War, because it prevented interracial solidarity. Certain ethnic groups, such as the Irish and Italians, could "become white," but other groups could not. And, writing in 1935, W.E.B. Du Bois argued, "It must be remembered that the white group of laborers, while they received a low wage, were compensated in part by a sort of public and psychological wage." Before the Civil War, most white workers opposed ending slavery because they feared that free blacks would take their jobs. White workers suffered under harsh conditions in factories, working 12- to 14-hour days, six days a week for very low wages. But if they were exploited in the factories, white workers could still take pride in knowing that they were free and that another group of workers, namely African Americans, were not. This is what Du Bois referred to as a kind of compensation for their exploitation; white workers could promote themselves by denying job opportunities for blacks. As a result, white workers in the labor movement were more concerned with the supposed "threat" of free blacks than with challenging the power of capital and the erosion of independence created by the wage system and factory labor. The investment in whiteness proved more salient than interracial solidarity among workers.

There were a few exceptions to the predominance of racism among white workers. One union in particular, the Knights of Labor, which was founded in 1869, vowed not to discriminate against blacks on the principle that integration was necessary to build solidarity among workers and a powerful labor movement that could challenge the growing power of monopoly capital and the newly emerging corporations. Integration of workers and interracial organizing was an early goal of the AFL too, but as early as 1893, the AFL chose to allow racist locals to join the federation, and the AFL began the practice of allowing separate locals for black and white members. Nor did the AFL do anything to stop union members in California from attacking Chinese workers. The policy of tolerating racism among its rank and file is partly explained by the AFL's narrow focus on craft workers, or skilled workers, who were almost exclusively white and male. Blacks, Latinos, and Asians (especially the Chinese in California) were consistently shut out of high-paying, high-skilled jobs by both employers and unions. A. Philip Randolph, the president of the all-black Brotherhood of Sleeping Car Porters union, appealed to the AFL numerous times to abolish the practice of segregating locals in the AFL, to no avail. As a consequence, the labor movement continued to practice racial discrimination until the AFL was challenged by the CIO in the 1930s.

The CIO, an umbrella group of industrial unions, was founded by John L. Lewis of the United Mine Workers. The CIO was committed to organizing unskilled workers across craft lines and organized more than a million black workers between 1935 and the end of World War II. In many ways, the CIO was a precursor to the civil rights movement in the 1950s, in that many members of the CIO were also activists in the fight for equal rights for blacks. Many of the tactics first implemented by the organization drives of the CIO—including the sit-down strike and various other types of nonviolent civil disobedience—would later be used in the civil rights movements. Although the CIO made significant progress toward ending racial discrimination in the labor movement, many unions did not end the practice of segregation until they were forced to do so by the passage of the Civil Rights Act in 1964. Title II of the Civil Rights Act forced labor unions to integrate their locals. But even the CIO leadership did little to challenge Jim Crow in the South. In fact, the CIO suffered a spectacular failure to organize Southern workers when their campaign, Operation Dixie, collapsed under the weight of racism in the South. Still, black workers were able, in spite of the opposition, to form the National Negro Labor Council in 1951, an organization designed to pressure both employers and unions to end racial discrimination.

Today, blacks and other racial and ethnic minorities have risen into the ranks of leadership in many unions across the United States. One of the most progressive unions today is Janitors for Justice (JFJ), which grew out of the Service Employees International Union (SEIU). The JFJ is on the forefront of the fight to end discrimination in the workplace, and their union reflects the changing face of the labor movement. Today, the working class is the most diverse it has ever been, and the rank and file of the labor movement is no longer dominated by white men working in the blue-collar industries. Today, union members are more likely to be working in the service sector in hospitals, schools, and retail establishments and are more likely to be African American, Latino, and South Asian than white. There is still progress to be made, however. Minority communities suffer the most when companies downsize or shut down their operations altogether as more and more U.S. jobs are moved overseas in the process of globalization. The new challenge for the labor movement is to become truly international.

MICHAEL ROBERTS

See also

Affirmative Action; Day Laborers; Domestic Work; Garment Workers; Labor Unions; Migrant Workers; Sharecropping; United Farm Workers. Document: Glass Ceiling Commission: Summary of Recommendations (1995)

Further Reading:

Draper, Alan. *Conflict of Interest: Organized Labor and the Civil Rights Movement in the South, 1954–1968*. Champaign: University of Illinois Press, 1994.

Du Bois, W.E.B. *Black Reconstruction in the United States: 1860–1880*. New York: Atheneum, 1977.

Marshall, Ray. *The Negro and Organized Labor*. New York: John Wiley, 1965.

Roediger, David. *The Wages of Whiteness: Race and the Making of the American Working Class*. New York: Verso, 1996.

Saxton, Alexander. *Indispensable Enemy: Labor and the Anti-Chinese Movement in California*. Berkeley: University of California Press, 1995.

Labor Unions

Labor unions in the United States are affiliated organizations that function as the legal representatives for a multiplicity of workers in various industries. The history of labor unions during the era of Jim Crow is the history of struggle to overcome racism and discrimination within labor unions and the labor movement. It is also a history spotted with episodes of biracial activism. Because racial exclusionary policies are a very effective way to control the labor supply and, consequently, exercise bargaining power over the wages of workers, labor unions, particularly during the era of Jim Crow, have a long history of racial discrimination on their hands. Racial discrimination is fundamental to understanding labor unions during the era of Jim Crow, and, conversely, labor unions are fundamental to understanding racial discrimination in the Jim Crow era. Discrimination within unions during the Jim Crow era is unique given the fact that a majority of union leaders' rhetoric and theories were are always quick to include, or at least not explicitly exclude, African Americans by arguing that working-class consciousness would ultimately trump racism. However, in practice and organization techniques, they often fell short and were quick to embrace exclusionary policies that stemmed from Jim Crow policies.

The budding relationship between black workers and organized labor movements began to take form during the periods of the Civil War and post–Civil War Reconstruction. The Civil War not only freed 3.5 million people of African descent from a life of bondage and oppression by dismantling the institution of slavery but also transformed millions into free laborers, and resurrected union activity that had been static since the depression of 1837. However, it has been noted that it was not until the post–Civil War era that the United States completed abolition and had defined civil rights. The politically established principles of free labor had to confront the first nationwide labor organization by the late 1860s. Unions, arguably, were from the start not concerned with the plight and struggle of Africans Americans. That labor unions and early working-class people's opposition to slavery rarely rested on the claim that slavery was a moral injustice imposed upon bond(wo)men is testament to their peculiar strand of racism. Indeed, working-class people of the Midwest and the West became aware and raised concern over the proslavery 1854 Kansas-Nebraska Act—an act that would soon allow the expansion of slavery to proceed and expand into the open Midwestern and Western territories— and the Dred Scott decision—a court decision that declared that people of African descent, slaves and nonslaves alike, could never become citizens and declared that Congress had no authority to prohibit slavery in federal territories—not as an expression of the immorality of slavery or commiseration for those enslaved, but rather, expressed outrage over the fact that the expansion slavery might affect their working-class status. To be sure, working-class opposition to slavery was not so much against slavery per se, but against the expansion of slavery that would ultimately jeopardize their status as workers.

While the National Labor Union and the National Colored Labor Union fought unsuccessfully to preserve their respective unions during the devastating depression of 1873, the Noble Order of the Knights of Labor (KOL) successfully avoided the union-crushing depression and survived to see the early beginnings of Jim Crow. Uriah Stephens, a Philadelphia tailor and antislavery Republican, formed the KOL in 1869. Blacks were loyal to the Republican Party due to its abolitionist past. Originally, the KOL was formed as a secret union that embraced both trade and industrial unions. Moreover, the KOL's rhetoric of racial inclusiveness, Christian evangelicalism, and abolitionist heritage, backed by an unwavering appreciation for class unity, ultimately made the organization acceptable to black workers

Although the KOL at its birth practiced exclusionary policies vis-à-vis the black worker, it did lift its ban on black workers during the early shaping of Jim Crow in 1883. The fact that the KOL boasted an agenda of racial inclusiveness may have led to the dramatic increase in their union membership. By putting worker dissatisfaction, low wages, and class unity across racial lines at the front of their agenda, the KOL's membership increased dramatically throughout the 1880s. By the mid-1880s, the KOL had won several important strikes and saw its membership increase to approximately 750,000 official union members, of which 60,000 to 90,000 were black. The KOL's commitment to interracial activism trickled down to the workers and created cooperation across the color line. Due to the efforts of the KOL, throughout the Jim Crow South, episodes of interracial working-class unity were at work. Indeed, in the mid-1880s, the heyday of the KOL, the KOL and other unions saw a dramatic increase in the amount of interracial class unity experienced. While KOL District Assembly 194 sought negotiations with the nearby black Louisiana Sugar Planters Association in an effort to increase wages and better methods of pay, white and black miners of Alabama, under the auspices of the KOL, stood unified in strike against wage cuts for mine operators. In the end, prison laborers and Italian immigrants broke the miners' strike.

Although the Knights of Labor's rhetoric preached about racial inclusiveness, and while at times they even practiced racial inclusiveness, they too practiced a major policy that defined the Jim Crow South: separatism. While union leaders stood at the pulpit recommending black-white worker unity, they constantly and consistently advocated separate but unified black and white local organizations. Moreover, the Knights of Labor were ardent supporters of the anti-Chinese movement and refused to admit Chinese workers. In 1885, in

Truck with a billboard posted on side reading "Best of Luck A.F. of L. White Labor must smash the Color Line in its Own Interest" in front of building by the San Francisco Branch of the NAACP, ca. 1954–1960. (Library of Congress)

Spring Rock, Wyoming, the Knights of Labor led a riot that resulted in the deaths of 28 Chinese railroad workers. They also did not support European immigrants.

In retrospect, the KOL's racial inclusiveness may have been as much responsible for the union's increase in membership in the mid-1880s as much it was responsible for its decrease in the late 1880s. By 1890, 100,000 members remained in the KOL, few of whom were black. The violence of the Knights' strikes caused a decrease in support from blacks, who were once attracted to their peaceful revolutionary style. Despite the Knights' efforts, the period put blacks and the labor movement at further distance.

That the more racially restrictive American Federation of Labor (AFL) replaced the KOL and took control of the labor movement during the nadir of race relations—a racially complex time period starting in 1890 and enduring throughout the Jim Crow era until 1930, when blacks were forced back into noncitizenship and race relations, indeed, got worse—is evident in their workings as an organization. AFL delegates took their cue from the KOL's broad social vision of racial inclusiveness by focusing their efforts on securing higher wages, shorter working days, and improved working conditions for the unions and union members they represented across racial lines. Throughout the early 1890s, the KOL and AFL engaged in bitter disputes around the country as to what the goals of labor movement should be. The AFL rejected the KOL's favoritism of workers' cooperatives, and criticized their simply defined economic agendas. By the 1890s, the AFL became the dominant national labor organization.

While open to socialist and Marxist thought concerning the economic structure and the direction of the labor movement, AFL leaders, like the KOL leaders before them, remained perplexed about the race issue within the labor movement during the racial hostile period of Jim Crow. The AFL was an umbrella organization with which separate trade unions were affiliated. The AFL's constitution was quiet on race issues and implicitly included African Americans. AFL founder Samuel A. Gompers initially opposed the inclusion of racially exclusive organizations under the AFL's umbrella. However, due to the fact that the AFL focused on skilled labor, many African Americans, who were barred from such jobs and relegated to perform "unskilled" labor due to racial discrimination, received very little attention from the AFL. Like the KOL leaders before them, AFL leaders were quick to spout rhetoric in favor of racial egalitarian ideals. Gompers, who led the AFL from 1886 until his death in 1924, affirmed his commitment to racial egalitarianism at the 1891 annual convention. Although the AFL's commitment to racial egalitarianism remains suspect, there were episodes of biracial activism. In 1892, white and black longshoremen of New Orleans rallied behind the AFL banner and supported each other's strikes at substantial risk to themselves. Gompers would constantly herald the event as a landmark case of biracial union activism. More scattered episodes of interracial union activism carried on throughout the World War I era and into the 1920s. During the war, in Little Rock, Arkansas, the white-controlled labor council supported black women who worked in the city's steam laundries that served a nearby army base. Meanwhile, the black longshoremen labored on the docks of Philadelphia and became attracted to and strongly affiliated with the radical, Marxist, and, above all, racial egalitarian Industrial Workers of the World. African Americans and their white counterparts struggled, with varied success, to form unions that rose above the color line in places such as, Chicago, rural Louisiana, and Memphis. For example, AFL carpenter unions in rural 1919 Bogalusa, Louisiana, struggled together in an effort to preserve their biracial union. In the South Side of Chicago's packinghouses and stockyards, World War I–era interracial unity reached its peak. Fifty thousand men and women, both black and white, rallied behind the AFL's Amalgamated Meat Cutters (AMC), a very powerful AFL organization of skilled workers that did not ban blacks, side by side with the AFL's Chicago Federation of Labor (CFL) between 1916 and 1922 in a long-drawn-out struggle for equal rights and better working conditions in Chicago's meat packinghouses.

The president of the CFL, John Fitzpatrick, and a Railway Carmen Union organizer, William Z. Foster, both radical syndicalists who dedicated their efforts to turn the AFL on to socialism, led the Chicago labor activists and workers' struggle to effectively organize industrial unions and stockyards across the color line. Together they formed the Stockyard Labor Council (SLC) in an effort to unite all packinghouse workers regardless of color and gender. As a result of other, less-skilled unions segregating and banning blacks, the SLC and AFL became locals that blacks could join. The successful organization of meat industry workers was vital to the success of the labor movement as a whole. It presented the opportunity for the AFL to enlarge its influence by expanding from craft unions into one of the country's largest mass production industries. AMC affiliates, one of the AFL organizations that did not ban black workers, were ardent supporters of organizing across racial lines and continually, with mixed success, advocated the importance of nondiscrimination in the labor movement. The AMC, in an effort to show their commitment to black workers, created a black local. In fact, all the AMC locals representing workers in the South Side of Chicago included African Americans. The SLC shared the AMC's commitment to African American workers. The SLC pressed for dramatic changes, such as their call on the federal government to nationalize the meatpacking industry, the implementation of the eight-hour workday, and increased pay for unskilled workers, a category into which most African American workers fell. As the end of the Great War approached its demise, the SLC started pressing for a 100 percent union agreement with the packers, with blacks being the primary hurdle. Ninety percent of white workers and a meager 25 percent of African American workers were members. However, black gains in union membership and wages came at the cost of increased racial hostility between blacks and native-born and immigrant whites, which culminated in the vicious Chicago Race Riot of 1919.

The Chicago race riots might, indeed, be reflective of the collective consciousness of the American public at large during the racially daunting years of Jim Crow. Although a causal claim between the SLC's effort to organize black workers in Chicago cannot be verified, there is, no doubt, information that makes such a causal connection attractive. On the packinghouse floors, where native-born and immigrant whites toiled side by side with their African American coworkers and fellow union supporters, whites expressed their hostility and contempt for African Americans. European immigrant laborers who were "working toward whiteness" by reminding their native-born white coworkers that African Americans were, indeed, the "other" and the real problem, met African Americans with intense racial tension. In the summer of 1919, racial tension erupted onto the streets and an all-out riot ensued. The riot was sparked when a black boy was drowned for crossing into a white neighborhood on Lake Michigan beach. The event triggered racial violence that would last for weeks. Most of the mayhem was attributed to gangs of Irish immigrants. In the end, 23 blacks and 15 whites lay dead. The July race riots, arguably, ended the hope of the SLC to successfully organize black workers. Racist policies, although not explicitly written in the constitution, were a tradition for the AFL and its affiliated organizations from the beginning.

As Jim Crow policy tightened its grip on everyday life in the South, and newly arrived immigrants began competing with native-born whites and blacks for jobs, exclusionary policies vis-à-vis immigrants and African Americans increased. Immigrants were not welcome into the AFL or any affiliated organizations from the start. Gompers, a Jewish immigrant from Great Britain and once a supporter of racial egalitarianism, stated that the AFL's policy was to protect whites from the "evils" of the Chinese invasion. Chinese immigrants who toiled on the railroads were banned from unionization outright. While white workers led vicious, bloody massacres and anti-Chinese riots, writers and editors of union and labor newspapers were busy constructing the Chinese and other immigrant groups as "savage" and "uncivilized." As early as 1897, AFL leaders urged the adoption of a draconian literacy test in an effort to curtail immigrant labor. They argued that the plethora of early European immigrants who emigrated had not proved themselves assimilable or fit for union organization and ultimately posed a threat to the American worker whose wages they undercut.

The AFL's putative commitment to racial egalitarianism was a sham. They, like much of American society, had elements of both de jure and de facto segregation along with a history of violence against African American and Chinese laborers. The railroad unions proved to be the least accepting of African Americans and Asian immigrants. Blacks were often barred from unions or were forced to form separate unions. In fact, the early radical W. E. B. Du Bois, in a publication on union activity, revealed that of the 1 million AFL members, 40,000 were black. Moreover, 43 unions practiced Jim Crow policy to the point that they had no African Americans at all. The National Association of Machinists, an umbrella organization affiliated with the AFL, is a case in point to the AFL's ultimate commitment to party building, not to racial egalitarianism. The National Association of Machinists was founded in 1889 in Atlanta as an organization dedicated to organizing skilled railroad laborers. For five years, the AFL denied the admittance of the National Association of Machinists into the organization to do its constitution declaring white-only membership. However, in an effort to build union membership, AFL officials backed down from their commitment to racial egalitarianisms and biracial activism and admitted the National Association of Machinists in 1895. In the 1890s, firemen stood with the Brotherhood of Railway Trainmen in an effort to organize against the admittance of African Americans into their unions on a national scale. In 1899, the trainmen's union voted for the exclusion of African Americans from railroads worldwide.

Violent means were often used to ensure that railroad unions remained as segregated and off-limits to African Americans as possible. Violent outbreaks against African American railroad workers often sprung from strikes advocating white-only hiring policies. In an effort to maintain the color line, white workers in 1911 organized a strike against New Orleans, Cincinnati, and Texas Pacific railroads for employing African Americans. In the end, 10 African Americans were murdered. As a result, the strikers and the railroad companies decided that African Americans would not be employed north of Oakdale and Chattanooga, Tennessee. More still, the railroad companies concurred that the overall percentage of African American firemen would not rise on a national level. The AFL continued to ignore, or at least place secondary to increasing union numbers, African Americans and their complaints of racial discrimination into the 1920s. When union officials refused to make the Railroad Brotherhood of Railway Carmen strike the words "white only" from its constitution, and when they refused to grant international charter to the black Railway Coach Cleaners, blacks took the jobs of whites during the 1922 shopmen's strike. The results were tragic. Over 1,500 cases of attempted murder, kidnapping, dynamiting, and vandalism occurred in an effort to curtail blacks from acting as strikebreakers. African Americans' willingness to act as strikebreakers increased the AFL's hostility toward them. The AFL often blamed their lack of attention to African American workers on the African Americans themselves. As the Depression began to take a grip on the economy, and as racial tensions increased due to the lack of job opportunity, increased competition, and Jim Crow laws, African Americans made up only 50,000 of the nation's 2.25 million union members. However, as the Congress of Industrial Organization (CIO), arguably the most egalitarian significant union to emerge since the KOL, emerged as the primary labor organization in 1935, African Americans saw increased racial tolerance, and labor unions saw a dramatic increase in the number of African American affiliates.

The Congress of Industrial Organization

The Congress of Industrial Organization was, no doubt, the most racially egalitarian and radical labor organization to emerge since the KOL. While Jim Crow laws began to cripple the South, the CIO presented a viable opportunity to organize African Americans within a largely racist labor movement. CIO leaders took a divide-and-conquer, radical, Marxist approach to the racial question vis-à-vis the labor movement by contending that racial division was created by bourgeois employers who wished to disrupt working-class solidarity so as to keep wages low and create "super profits." Thus, the CIO's primary goal was to organize industrial sectors of the labor force, which, they realized, necessitated the inclusion of African American workers who by the 1930s made up a significant portion of the industrial labor. In the South, where labor union representation was comparatively weak to that of the North, unions desperately needed the support of African American workers if they wished to succeed in mining, steel, and a multiplicity of agriculture sectors of which African Americans dominated. As such, the CIO sought to reach out to African American workers and civil rights groups to create interracial, working-class solidarity. And reach out they did. The CIO, in a remarkable effort to preserve and create racial harmony, formed the Committee

to Abolish Racial Discrimination, and encouraged blacks to reject and speak out against the American Federation of Labor and other independent unions.

The congress took its cue from the United Mine Workers Association (UMWA), which had been promoting and practicing racial egalitarianism under the presidential leadership of John L. Lewis since the late 19th century. By the turn of the 20th century, African Americans made up one-quarter of UMWA's membership and enrolled at a much higher rate than their white comrades. The UMWA consisted of more than 20,000 black miners, approximately half of the AFL's black membership. In the depths of the Great Depression in 1934, the United Mine Workers boasted 90 new locals and 20,000 men, of whom 60 percent were African Americans. Even in the hostile time and space of Jim Crow Alabama in the 1890s, the United Mine Workers struggled to create interracial unity in the union locals of Alabama and other Southern states. Furthermore, Irish immigrants along with British immigrants made up a significant portion of union leadership. To be sure, the UMWA did, indeed, have its share of racial turmoil, but it was their effort to forge class unity across racial lines that caused the CIO to adopt the UMWA's organizing techniques. For example, UMWA organizers in Alabama made it clear that their commitment to African American workers did not embrace the idea of social equality, simply better wages and working conditions. At one point in 1920, white mine workers bombed the houses of a dozen black strikebreakers. Despite a few episodes of interracial hostility, the United Mine Workers Association proved its commitment to black workers.

Indeed, the CIO's efforts and commitment to African American workers did not go unnoticed. Unlike the AFL, which practiced Jim Crow policy if not in rhetoric or theory then in practice, the CIO transcended racial lines in its organizing process and made its way into the Piedmont region—southern Virginia to northern Alabama—and had organized 200,000 cotton textile workers. From the early stages of the Great Depression to the end stages of World War II, African American union membership increased radically from 60,000 to an impressive one million. African Americans became the CIO's main supporters. Other unions such as the KOL and AFL tried to organize across racial lines but ultimately fell pray to Jim Crow practices. The CIO represented the first massive effort to organize workers across racial and ethnic lines for a common movement This was indeed the case in Chicago's meatpacking industry, in which African Americans made up 20 to 30 percent of the labor force. Thanks to the efforts of CIO and other, mostly communist activists, the Packing House Workers Organization Committee brought together several unions to reach out to blacks by promising designated seats for blacks on the executive board, and by mandating a quota equivalent to the local population.

As World War II emerged, the labor movement more broadly, and labor unions in particular would again have serious consequences for African American workers. Blacks were direly needed in the industrial sector to produce goods for the war effort; however, their employers were very hesitant to hire them due to long-standing Jim Crow practices within the industrial sector. By the end of 1944, it is estimated that at least 1.25 million African American workers, a quarter of which were women, were performing industrial work, a 150 percent increase from 1940. During the time period of World War II, both the AFL and the CIO grew dramatically. The AFL had expanded its union affiliates from 4.2 million to just shy of 7 million. The CIO grew to 4 million members from 2 million members from 1940 to 1945. In all, union membership doubled from 1940 to 1945 to 15 million.

However, Jim Crow policies that pervaded the labor movement and unions would tighten their grip during the war effort, and blacks were forced to overcome racism and discrimination on a multiplicity of levels. Their struggle in the railroad unions and craft brotherhoods is a case in point. Railroad unions have a history of Jim Crow policy under the tutelage of the AFL, and they continued this tradition during the course of the war. While railroad employment increased to meet the demands of the war effort, so too did discrimination against black workers in labor unions. Black workers faced severe forms of discrimination, including contracts that limited the number and locations where blacks could work. The Brotherhood of Locomotive Firemen, for example, pushed to rapidly accelerate the removal of black workers. This culminated in the Brotherhood successfully winning Southeastern Carriers agreement, which limited the employment of "unpromotable" firemen to 50 percent and ended the increased hiring of blacks. While the Brotherhood of Locomotive Firemen practiced a strict form of Jim

Crow by virtue of job elimination, the International Boilermakers Brotherhood (IBB) did admit blacks, albeit in a Jim Crow fashion that separated black and white union members into separate locals. Black workers paid dues to the union but were denied membership. Additionally, the hierarchal structure of the union did not allow all black unions to exercise autonomy and set up "parent" all white unions to dictate their organization techniques and behavior. In short, the IBB openly practiced Jim Crow policies.

The postwar effort to organize across racial lines in the Jim Crow South proved fruitless. The Taft-Hartley Act—an amendment passed in 1947 to amend the National Labor Relations Act of 1935—provided little protection for black union members who were already in unions. The act permitted Jim Crow segregation in union locals and weakened the efforts of the AFL and the CIO to organize across racial lines. The act was effective. Black and white union members in the South remained largely segregated despite the fact that the AFL had 60 percent of its 7 million African American members located in the South. Soon after Jim Crow began to loosen grips on the policy and consciousness of the United States with the *Brown v. Board of Education* case in 1954, the AFL and CIO merged in 1955.

Both the AFL and CIO strongly and openly endorsed the black civil rights movement that emerged in the South in response to Jim Crow. The AFL-CIO led charges in favor of civil rights acts throughout the late 20th century, and played a significant role in bringing civil rights to the fore of national consciousness. Indeed, the Civil Rights Act of 1964—an act that outlawed public school and public workplace segregation, and guaranteed fair employment practices—and the Voting Rights Act of 1965, were all endorsed by the AFL-CIO, who now began to understand the civil rights and labor movements as organically linked phenomena, and acknowledged that biracial activism is the life's blood of the labor movement.

JACK A. TAYLOR III

See also

Communist Party; Knights of Labor. Document: Glass Ceiling Commission: Summary of Recommendations (1995)

Further Reading:

Bernstein, David. *Only One Place of Redress: African Americans, Labor Regulations, and the Courts from Reconstruction to the New Deal.* Durham, NC: Duke University Press, 2001.

Honey, Michael. *Southern Labor and Black Civil Rights: Organizing Memphis Workers.* Urbana: University of Illinois Press, 1993.

Moreno, Paul. *Black Americans and Organized Labor: A New History.* Baton Rouge: Louisiana State University Press, 2006.

Nelson, Bruce. *Divided We Stand: American Workers and the Struggle for Black Equality.* Princeton, NJ: Princeton University Press, 2001.

Obadele-Starks, Ernest. *Black Unionism in the Industrial South.* College Station: Texas A&M University Press, 2000.

Roediger, David. *Working Toward Whiteness: How America's Immigrants Became White: The Strange Journey from Ellis Island to the Suburbs.* New York: Basic Books, 2005.

Zieger, Robert H. *For Jobs and Freedom: Race and Labor in America Since 1865.* Lexington: University Press of Kentucky, 2007.

Laissez-Faire Racism

After the civil rights movement of the 1960s, racial attitudes, as reported in surveys, increasingly revealed whites had greater tolerance for African Americans as well as supported their integration and equal status. Whites reported they were more likely to support principles such as integrated housing and schooling, yet when questioned whether they would support *policies* to achieve these goals, they were not willing. The conflict between whites supporting principles of equality but not policies to achieve that equality is explained by the theory of laissez-faire racism. Laissez-faire racism argues that the overt, biological, and segregationist racism of Jim Crow has morphed into a more subtle and complex racism whereby whites explain and defend their white privilege through free market and egalitarian ideals.

Lawrence Bobo, James Kluegel, and Ryan Smith developed this theory of racism in their 1997 and 1998 papers on the transition from Jim Crow racism to laissez-faire racism. This new racial ideology formed because the overt racism of the Jim Crow era increasingly became viewed with disdain and became politically incorrect, yet whites needed some way to rationalize their continued privileged status and the lower status of blacks. Laissez-faire racism is discrimination that specifically developed out of the contemporary free labor economy to help defend white privilege and explain away blacks' lower social and economic statuses. This racism

emerges out of market inequality and informal racial bias, relies on negative stereotypes of blacks, and blames blacks for their low social positioning. Thus, rather than using biological or overtly racist ideological arguments to maintain the racial hierarchy, a logic of the free market and the cultural inferiority of blacks is used. For example, blacks don't do as well in school or at work because they don't have the skills and qualifications to get into that school/job; or blacks don't have the culture of hard work and dedication necessary for success. This new form of antiblack prejudice is a combination of two lessons taught early to whites: (1) lessons about traditional values such as individualism and the Protestant work ethic (those who work hard will be rewarded); and (2) lessons that foster negative feelings and beliefs about blacks. These attitudes solidify and evolve into resentment for blacks' demands for equality along with a simultaneous denial that blacks are currently experiencing discrimination.

The theory of laissez-faire racism is distinct from another popular theory of modern racism, symbolic racism, in two primary ways. First, laissez-faire racism, unlike symbolic racism, is not only a theory of attitudes and psychological beliefs but explains that these beliefs form the basis of a white response that gets "injected" into politics and becomes "in and of" politics (Bobo 2004). In this way, laissez-faire racism has real and serious consequences for the representation of blacks in the political system and the implementation of race related policies. Second, the theory of laissez-faire racism is historically rooted. This theory explains that a new racism emerged as a necessary response to the collapse of Jim Crow racism as overt racism would no longer work or succeed after the civil rights movement. Thus, rather than being primarily concerned with individual attitudes, it is more concerned with how general patterns of group relations and ideology change to maintain the system. However, laissez-faire has been criticized by Bonilla-Silva (2010) for not fully explaining how this new prejudice is connected to material relations and specifically why these new attitudes developed.

The theory of laissez-faire racism makes a significant contribution to understanding modern racism. It explains why whites support ideas of integration and inequality yet do not support the policies to achieve this end. The end of Jim Crow racism was the end of an overt racist ideology, but it did not end racial inequality; thus the new ideology of laissez-faire racism formed to explain and rationalize continued racial disparities. Race, group interests, ideology, and power combine to justify the continuing maintenance of white supremacy via the political system. Towards this end, laissez-faire racism also aids in understanding how beliefs and attitudes greatly affect the racial order as they become *political judgments* on the rights and status that blacks should have. Bobo (2004) suggests that laissez-faire racism can perhaps be counteracted by putting race back into the center of our conversations and by pushing for an explicit black political agenda.

HEPHZIBAH STRMIC-PAWL

See also

Color-Blind Racism; Cultural Racism; Ideological Racism; Racism; Symbolic Racism; Systemic Racism

Further Reading:

Bobo, Lawrence. "Inequalities That Endure? Racial Ideology, American Politics, and the Peculiar Role of the Social Sciences." In *The Changing Terrain of Race and Ethnicity*, edited by Maria Krysan and Amanda E. Lewis, 13–42. New York: Russell Sage Foundation, 2004.

Bobo, Lawrence, James Kluegel, and Ryan Smith. "Laissez Faire Racism: The Crystallization of a 'Kinder, Gentler' Anti-Black Ideology." In *Racial Attitudes in the 1990s: Continuity and Change*, edited by Steven Tuch and Jack Martin, 15–44. Westport, CT: Praeger, 1997.

Bobo, Lawrence, and Ryan Smith. "From Jim Crow Racism to Laissez-Faire Racism: The Transformation of Racial Attitudes." In *Beyond Pluralism: The Conception of Groups and Group Identities in America*, edited by Wendy Katkin, Ned Landsman, and Andrea Tyree, 182–220. Chicago: University of Illinois Press, 1998.

Bonilla-Silva, Eduardo. *Racism Without Racists: Color-Blind Racism & Racial Inequality in Contemporary America*, 3rd ed. New York: Rowman & Littlefield, 2010.

Jean-Baptiste de Monet, Chevalier de Lamarck, was a botanist and naturalist who proposed one of the first theories of evolution. Though Lamarck's evolutionary theory is now considered invalid, Charles Darwin, the father of modern evolutionary theory, credited Lamarck with laying the foundation for the new understanding of the evolution of the species. (Library of Congress)

Lamarckism Theory

Jean-Baptiste Lamarck (1744–1829), a French biologist, is known as the first contributor to evolutionary theory. Lamarck argued two important points about evolution. The first is *use or disuse*, which contends continuous use of an organ gradually strengthens and develops it whereas disuse of an organ weakens and deteriorates it. Moreover, if an organ is not used it will disappear or if it is used frequently it will change for the better. The second argument is *inheritance of acquired characteristics*. Lamarck believed an organism could acquire characteristics from the surrounding environment and could pass them to its offspring. In short, Lamarckism theory argues that variations developed by an organism can be inherited.

Lamarck's work on evolution preceded that of Charles Darwin; however, Darwin's theory of natural selection received much more attention in evolutionary science. The main difference between Lamarck and Darwin pertains to the causes of evolution. Darwin argued that favorable and frequently used organs become more common because of differential reproduction. That is, organisms who are more fit to the selective pressure(s) by their environment will leave more offspring than those less fit. This theory is known as *natural selection*. Furthermore, Darwin believed in systematic classifications and rejected Lamarck's arguments that evolution was fluid and indefinite.

Research during the 19th century generally failed to provide support for any Lamarckian processes in biological systems, and most evolution scientists dismissed much of Lamarckism theory. Modern synthesis, which has dominated evolutionary thinking much of the 20th century and was informed by Darwin, completely rejected the notion that hereditary variation could be affected by the developmental history of the individual. Rather, modern synthesis contends that evolution occurs through modifications from a common ancestor and is based on vertical descent.

Lamarckism theory was not as significant in shaping racial attitudes as natural selection. Whereas Lamarck did not emphasize racial differences or hierarchies, other evolutionists, such as Charles Darwin, were extremely influential in providing a scientific justification for biological beliefs in race. For instance, whites were considered the superior race because they were found to have larger brains. Larger brains were more valuable, and therefore whites were considered naturally fit to fill higher status roles. Eventually, much of these ideas were refuted and dismissed as pseudoscience, and race has become understood as a social construction—a socially invented category based only on scientific myths. However, arguments relating race to biology and genes have resurfaced given advances in medical technologies in the late 20th century and the Human Genome Project (HGP).

These medical technologies and the HGP have also redirected evolutionary thinking back to Lamarck. Outlined most succinctly in *Evolution in Four Dimensions*, scientists now accept that there are multiple processes that shape variations in DNA: genetic, epigenetic, behavioral, and symbolic. To sum, Jablonka and Lamb (2005) argue that living organisms depend on both genetic and epigenetic inheritance, animals transmit information behaviorally, and humans have the additional capacity to transfer information through symbolic communication. These arguments are largely influenced by Lamarckian ideas, insofar as variations can be developed and transmitted across generations, and often discussed under the term of *soft inheritance*. Sickle-cell disease provides an example of a scientific conclusion informed by Lamarck. That is, sickle-cell disease reveals how a small

Human Genome Project

The Human Genome Project (HGP) is known as one of the most important biological projects of the last two decades. The flagship endeavor of the HGP is human DNA sequencing, which can track genetic variations and in turn is argued to have significant medical implications, such as locating variations in risk of disease among individuals. Inherent in this endeavor is the belief that the environment contributes to gene variation and inheritance. Although the HGP has found that the human population has nearly 99.9 percent of its genes in common, race is still sometimes used as a proxy for group differences in biomedical research. For instance, one of the goals from the Human Genome Project was to explore how race, ethnicity, and socioeconomic status influence the understandings and interpretations of genetic information and genetic services (Collins et al. 1998).

DNA change can result in a large phenotypic change—severe anemia—for a group of people. Although sickle-cell disease is most prevalent in tropical regions, such as sub-Saharan Africa, India, and the Middle East, some Bedouin Arabs show only middle symptoms because they developed an allele for a different gene that counteracts the effects of the sickle-cell allele.

Lamarckian theory allows biology to be linked to sociology. Lamarckian theory, and inheritance of acquired characteristics in particular, argues that characteristics adapt to the surrounding environment. Social scientific research today accepts the social environment as one of the most significant factors in shaping health disparities, and as such it should continue to be engaged with the work of Lamarck.

Whitney Laster

See also
American Eugenics Movement; Genotype versus Phenotype; Social Darwinism

Further Reading:
Burkhardt Jr., Richard W. *The Spirit of System: Lamarck and Evolutionary Biology*. Cambridge, MA: Harvard University Press, 1997.
Collins, Francis S., Ari Patrinos, Elke Jordan, Aravinda Chakravarti, Raymond Gesteland, and LeRoy Walters. 1998.

"New Goals for the US Human Genome Project: 1998–2003." *Science* 282 (5389): 682–89.

Fisher, Ronald A. "Retrospect of the Criticisms of the Theory of Natural Selection." In *Evolution as a Process*, edited by J. S. Huxley, A. C. Hardy and E. B. Ford, 84–98. London: Allen and Unwin, 1954.

Hofstadter, Richard. *Social Darwinism in American Thought.* Boston, MA: Beacon Press, 1992.

Jablonka, Eva, and Marion J. Lamb. *Evolution in Four Dimensions: Genetic, Epigenetic, Behavioral, and Symbolic Variation in the History of Life.* Cambridge, MA: MIT Press, 2005.

Lamarck, Jean-Baptist. *Philosophie Zoologique.* Translated by H. Elliot as *Zoological Philosophy.* Chicago: University of Chicago Press, 1984[1809].

Lawson, James Morris, Jr. (b. 1928)

James Morris Lawson Jr. was a minister, teacher, and activist who performed an influential role during the civil rights movement. As an officer in the Student Nonviolent Coordinating Committee (SNCC), Lawson changed the tactics by which Americans fought for integration and racial equality. As a leading proponent and theorist of the resistance tactics of Indian leader Mahatma Gandhi, Lawson trained hundreds of young people to use nonviolence as a tool of mass protest. A close confidant of Martin Luther King, Jr. and other important leaders, Lawson led the lunch counter sit-ins in Nashville, Tennessee; participated in the 1961 Freedom Rides; and advised the Memphis sanitation workers' strike in 1968.

Born on September 22, 1928, in Uniontown, Pennsylvania, Lawson was the oldest son of a preacher who was heavily involved with the National Association for the Advancement of Colored People (NAACP). Lawson grew up in Massillon, Ohio, and attended schools with mostly white students. Just out of high school, Lawson got his first license to preach in 1947 and traveled a good deal for Methodist training and prayer meetings, soon coming to see race and poverty as the major divisive elements in American society. As a freshman at Baldwin-Wallace College in Berea, Ohio, Lawson joined the pacifist Fellowship of Reconciliation (FOR) in 1947. Lawson began to learn more about Gandhian resistance, or using nonviolent means to struggle against oppression, from the FOR's executive director A. J. Muste. Increasingly committed to pacifism, Lawson refused to comply with the military draft at the start of the Korean War and spent 13 months in federal prison beginning in 1950.

Following his parole, Lawson graduated from Baldwin-Wallace and became a professor at Hislop College in Nagpur, India, in April 1953. In India, Lawson studied Gandhian tactics and considered their usefulness for combating segregation, while reading eagerly of the Montgomery Bus Boycott (1955–1956) in Indian newspapers. Lawson returned to the United States to begin graduate work in theology at Oberlin College and met Martin Luther King, Jr. in February 1957. The two men connected instantly over discussions of nonviolent mass action, and King urged Lawson to move to the South. At Lawson's request, the FOR made him a field secretary in Nashville, Tennessee, where he also joined the Southern Christian Leadership Conference (SCLC). Upon his arrival in Nashville in January 1958, Lawson became the second African American student ever to enroll at Vanderbilt University's divinity school. Soon after Lawson's arrival, he met Dorothy Wood, whom he would marry in 1959.

If moderate by Tennessee standards, Nashville remained largely segregated in 1958, which included restaurants, the bus station, lunch counters, restrooms, hotels, cabs, neighborhoods, and schools. Lawson began holding workshops in nonviolent philosophy in November 1959 in the basement of Kelly Miller Smith's First Baptist Church. Sponsored by FOR, Lawson's workshops stressed the importance of complete pacifism in order to provoke a moral crisis in their opponents. Lawson trained students in actual protest tactics as well as the philosophy of peace. Students also began to test policies in different stores in late 1959 to choose targets for a sit-in protest. Among Lawson's mentees were Diane Nash, James Bevel, Bernard Lafayette, Marion Barry, and John Lewis, all of whom went on to work for civil rights through the 1960s with the SCLC, SNCC, and other organizations. The Nashville movement relied primarily on young people because they would be less vulnerable to pressure or stricture from white employers once they began protests against segregation.

When students in Greensboro, North Carolina, staged a sit-in on February 1, 1960, the Nashville students sprung into action. One hundred twenty-four students, all trained and prepared by Lawson, staged an initial sit-in at downtown

Nashville lunch counters on February 13, 1960. On February 27, Nashville police allowed mobs of angry whites to physically assault the activists and then arrested 81 demonstrators. However, the sit-ins had been organized such that replacements stood ready to fill empty seats at lunch counters. Lawson's strategy of "jail, no bail" meant that protestors remained in overcrowded jails for some time, financially burdening the city of Nashville and forcing the local government to become involved in the conflict. Segregationists on Vanderbilt's Board of Trustees, including *Nashville Banner* publisher James Stahlman, demonized Lawson in the press and in private meetings. Vanderbilt chancellor Harvey Branscombe subsequently expelled Lawson on March 3, 1960, and Nashville police arrested Lawson the next day for his involvement in the demonstrations.

Lawson and the Nashville leaders soon called for an Easter boycott of downtown stores that depended on African American business but refused access to restrooms and lunch counters, which heightened the pressure on Nashville mayor Ben West to intervene. On April 19, 1960, reactionaries bombed the home of Z. Alexander Looby, the attorney representing the arrested students. The Loobys were unharmed, but the furious Nashville students and ministers initiated a silent march towards the courthouse downtown. Confronted by Diane Nash on the courthouse steps, West publicly acquiesced that downtown lunch counters should be integrated, effectively ending the symbolic reign of Jim Crow in city restaurants. By May 10, 1960, six downtown stores had integrated, and more gradually followed. Over the next two years, the Nashville Movement built by Lawson integrated movie theatres and restaurants in Nashville as well.

A few days before the Looby bombing, on April 15 and 16, Lawson delivered the keynote address at a conference organized by SCLC member Ella Baker in Raleigh, North Carolina. Baker had called the meeting to build upon the work of students activists in Nashville and throughout the South. On the podium, Lawson criticized the NAACP for being too conservative and timid in its methods, and pointed to direct action as the only way to defeat Jim Crow. The Shaw University conference marked the birth of the SNCC, and also began a period wherein Lawson advised ever greater numbers of activists. In 1960, the SCLC made Lawson its director of nonviolent education. At the same time, Lawson finished

his master of divinity degree at Boston University (1960) and accepted an appointment to tiny Green Chapel Methodist Church in Shelbyville, Tennessee, just south of Nashville.

When the U.S. Supreme Court banned segregation in interstate travel facilities in *Boynton v. Virginia* (1960), the Congress of Racial Equality (CORE) organized Freedom Rides to test the integration of transportation facilities throughout the Deep South. Leaving Washington, D.C., on May 4, 1961 the Freedom Rides nearly dissolved in Anniston, Alabama, when the bus was firebombed. Activists from SNCC and CORE chapters reinforced the original riders in Birmingham and Montgomery after additional attacks. Lawson joined the riders in Montgomery, where he was made spokesperson for the initial bus sent to Jackson, Mississippi. Authorities in Jackson arrested Lawson and many others, and sent them to notoriously brutal Parchman State Penitentiary. Waves of Freedom Riders followed to attempt to integrate the Jackson bus station and nonviolently resist arrest. After repeated violence and national attention, Attorney General Robert F. Kennedy ordered the desegregation of bus terminals in November 1961.

In 1962, Lawson assumed the pastorship of Centenary Methodist church in Memphis, where segregation was more ingrained than Nashville. In June 1966, King asked Lawson to organize a replacement march after James Meredith was shot by a sniper on his solo walk against fear from Memphis to Jackson. During the march, Lawson became dismayed by increasing factionalism between the SNCC and the SCLC and wary of the separatist strain adopted by the SNCC under Stokely Carmichael's leadership. Lawson thought that greater militancy belied a turn away from nonviolence, a shift that Lawson could not support. Lawson also served as a counselor for King in Chicago, where he saw increasing weariness among nonviolent activists struggling to fight more complicated forms of Jim Crow that existed outside of the South.

Lawson also helped to fight racial injustice in Memphis as an advisor for the Memphis Sanitation Workers strike in 1968. Long underpaid, denied access to higher paying jobs, and without benefits, African American sanitation workers' frustration boiled over on February 1, 1968, when two workers were killed due to a short circuit in a garbage truck's crushing mechanism. Under Lawson's guidance the workers commenced a strike on February 12, making their slogan "I

AM A MAN" as visible as possible. Lawson reached for national exposure by inviting King to Memphis, suggesting the sanitation strike fit perfectly with King's burgeoning Poor People's Campaign against poverty. After a March 28 demonstration fell apart due to a number of disruptive elements, King agreed to return to lead another march. Fatefully, King was assassinated the day before he was to lead the second march. City officials and the sanitation workers settled the strike one week later.

Lawson moved with his wife and three sons to Los Angeles in 1974, and became pastor of Holman Methodist Church. Lawson continued to work for peace education and racial justice throughout the latter decades of the 20th century, and retired from the ministry in 1999. In the fall of 2006, Lawson returned to Vanderbilt University as a visiting professor.

BRIAN PIPER

See also
Student Nonviolent Coordinating Committee (SNCC)

Further Reading:

Ackerman, Peter, and Jack DuVall. "The American South: Campaign for Civil Rights." In *A Force More Powerful: A Century of Nonviolent Conflict*. New York: St. Martin's Press, 2000.

Halberstam, David. *The Children*. New York: Random House, 1996.

Inskeep, Steve, and James Lawson. "James Lawson: An Advocate of Peaceful Change." Radio interview, National Public Radio. http://www.npr.org/templates/story/story.php?storyId=6676164&sc=emaf (accessed July 2007).

Lovett, Bobby L. *The Civil Rights Movement in Tennessee: A Narrative History*. Knoxville: University of Tennessee Press, 2005.

League of United Latin American Citizens (LULAC)

Arguably the most important and historically most visible Mexican American organization in the United States, the League of United Latin American Citizens (LULAC) was founded in 1929 in Corpus Christi, Texas. From its inception, LULAC echoed the voices of middle-class Mexican Americans and embraced a reformist, rather than radical, approach to change. LULAC leaders have always stressed patriotism and the effective assimilation of Mexican Americans into mainstream American society. The organization's work to end discrimination against people of Mexican descent resulted in several significant victories during the 20th century and inspired change at the local and national levels. Although LULAC's fortunes have waxed and waned over the years, it remains a viable organization, headquartered in Washington, D.C., with chapters throughout the United States as well as in Puerto Rico, Guam, Mexico, and even on a U.S. military base in West Germany.

The violence of the Mexican Revolution of 1910, as well as the labor demands created in the United States as a result of World War I, encouraged many Mexicans to immigrate during the early decades of the 20th century. By the 1920s, and particularly with the onset of the Depression, peoples of Mexican descent became the target of discrimination. As the Great Depression took hold, Mexican immigrants, as well as some Mexican Americans living in the Southwest, became the targets of campaigns that forcibly repatriated them to Mexico. It was in this context that a group of middle-class Mexican Americans in south Texas (some of whom could trace their Texas roots back for generations) decided to form LULAC. Their immediate aim was to distinguish themselves from the new Mexican arrivals and to lessen the discrimination that threatened to undermine the gains that Mexican Americans had made.

LULAC's initial "Statement of Aims and Purposes" declared that the organization would "develop within the members of our race the best, purest, and most perfect type of a true and loyal citizen of the United States of America." The new organization stressed its patriotism (and sought to draw a distinction between Mexican Americans and newly arrived Mexican immigrants) in a variety of ways. Members pledged loyalty to the U.S. Constitution and U.S. laws, promising to push for change peacefully and legally. English was embraced as the official language of LULAC, and only U.S. citizens were accepted as members. The organization used legal and political pressure to combat discrimination while it sought to attain the goal of full citizenship for Mexican Americans primarily through voter registration drives and campaigns to make public schools (viewed as a key to assimilation) more accessible to Mexican Americans.

During the first two decades of its existence, LULAC won important legal victories, particularly in the area of school desegregation. It also successfully pressured the U.S. Census Bureau to reclassify as "white" those individuals of Mexican descent. By World War II, LULAC's membership had grown to around 2,000 and the organization had expanded from its base in south Texas to include groups in New Mexico, Colorado, and California.

The post–World War II period witnessed another wave of LULAC activism, encouraged by the determination of returning veterans to continue the struggle against discrimination. LULAC sponsored legal efforts to end segregation in public schools and other public facilities throughout the Southwest. LULAC attorneys also sought to end discrimination within the U.S. legal system, and they won a crucial victory in 1953 when the U.S. Supreme Court declared unconstitutional the exclusion of Mexican Americans from jury selection in a Texas murder trial. The patriotic line of LULAC persisted as well. Members continued to distinguish themselves from Mexican immigrants, and they supported citizenship and English classes in an ongoing effort to promote assimilation. In 1957 LULAC launched its "Little School of the 400" program, which taught Mexican children 400 basic English words before they entered the first grade. During the 1960s, this program was transformed into Project Head Start and received the endorsement of the federal government.

During the 1960s and with the emergence of the Chicano movement, LULAC's dominant position within the Mexican American community was challenged. From the beginning, elements within the Mexican American population had criticized LULAC for its insistence on assimilation and accused it of a kind of elitism. Chicano activists of the 1960s and 1970s likewise insisted on a more radical response to discrimination within American society and embraced a separate "Mexicano" identity. At the same time, LULAC's membership base was declining, and the organization was compelled to look for outside sources of support. Its name recognition and high profile helped LULAC secure funding from government and corporate sources, enabling the organization to continue with its own brand of activism. In 1965 a Houston LULAC chapter piloted a job placement program that eventually became the federally funded SER-Jobs for Progress program. Government support also helped establish the Mexican American Legal Defense and Educational Fund (MALDEF) in 1968.

The new reliance on corporate support was not without problems. In 1977 the LULAC Foundation (established as a tax-exempt body that could solicit corporate grants) began what would become a long-standing link with the Adolph Coors Brewing Company. The company was known for its antiunion policies and employed few minorities. It drew the ire of other Mexican American groups and heightened criticism of LULAC. Throughout the 1980s, LULAC leaders would work (with some success) to encourage the Coors Company to initiate more minority hiring.

Despite continuing difficulties with establishing a sizeable and active membership base, and despite financial and legal scandals involving the LULAC Foundation and LULAC leadership, LULAC remained a high-profile group during the last two decades of the 20th century. It continued its efforts on the legal and educational fronts, and its leaders issued public criticisms of the Official English movement and the anti–affirmative action sentiments that took hold among some politicians and voters during the 1980s and 1990s. As the 21st century began, LULAC remained an influential voice for Mexican Americans.

SUZANNE B. PASZTOR

See also
Mexican American Legal Defense and Education Fund (MALDEF)

Further Reading:
Márquez, Benjamin. *LULAC: The Evolution of a Mexican American Political Organization.* Austin: University of Texas Press, 1993.
San Miguel, Guadalupe. *"Let all of them take heed": Mexican Americans and the Campaign for Educational Equality in Texas, 1910–1981.* Austin: University of Texas Press, 1987.
Sandoval, Moisés. *Our Legacy: The First Fifty Years.* Washington, DC: LULAC, 1979.

Lee, Spike (b. 1957)

Often erroneously referred to as the black Woody Allen, Spike Lee has established himself as one of the leading African American filmmakers of the 20th and 21st centuries. His films have touched on subjects in the African American community that, in large part, have been ignored or treated with less complexity by others.

Shelton Jackson Lee was born on March 20, 1957, in Atlanta, Georgia. His father, Bill Lee, was a jazz musician, and his mother, Jacqueline Shelton Lee, was an art teacher. The eldest of five children, Lee had developed a tough demeanor, which earned him the nickname "Spike" from his mother. After living in the pre–civil rights era South when Lee was a small child, the family moved briefly to Chicago and then to Brooklyn's predominantly African American Fort Greene section. As an educator, Lee's mother made certain he was exposed to different facets of African American culture and history. Although his mother taught at a predominantly white private school, which afforded the family free tuition for their children, Lee instead opted to attend the predominantly black public schools in Brooklyn to ensure he would be amongst his peers.

After graduating from John Dewey High School, Lee decided to enroll at Morehouse College in Atlanta, his father and grandfather's alma mater, where he majored in mass communications. Unexpectedly, in 1977, his mother died of cancer. To take his mind off his troubles, Lee's friends would frequently take him to the movies, where he became enamored with the work of Akira Kurosawa, Martin Scorsese, and particularly Michael Cimino's *The Deer Hunter*. Lee soon decided to become a filmmaker, with the goal to bring a realistic African American experience to the big screen. When Lee graduated in 1979, he received an internship at Columbia Pictures. He returned to New York that fall to attend New York University's Tisch Institute of Film and Television, where he was able to study with Scorsese. His first-year project was a 10-minute film about a young black screenwriter assigned to remake D. W. Griffith's *The Birth of a Nation*. The faculty reaction was negative, a response Lee attributed to racism.

Lee received his master's degree in filmmaking in 1982. His final project was entitled *Joe's Bed-Stuy Barbershop: We Cut Heads*. The film was set in a barbershop in Brooklyn's Bedford-Stuyvesant neighborhood and had a score by Lee's father. For his work, Lee received the 1983 Student Academy Award for merit from the Academy of Motion Picture Arts and Sciences. The film was also selected by the Lincoln Center to be shown at its New Directors and New Films series.

Lee worked for a movie distribution house cleaning and shipping films while raising money for his first project. It was a semiautobiographical film entitled *The Messenger*, about a bicycle messenger coming of age. Lee ran into difficulties raising the money and getting a waiver to use non-union actors. By the end of the summer of 1984, Lee gave in to reality and canceled the project; he would later admit that the project had been beyond his means. He next determined to produce a small-budget film with commercial appeal.

With a budget of only $175,000, Lee released *She's Gotta Have It* in 1986. Lee wrote the script, directed, and filmed the movie in only 12 days; he edited the film in his apartment. The story was a comedy about a African American woman with three lovers, with Lee in the role of one of the men. Well received by critics, the film was shot in black and white and went on to win the Prix de la Jeunesse at the Cannes Film Festival for the best film by a newcomer. In the United States, Island Pictures distributed *She's Gotta Have It*, and the film eventually grossed $7 million. The success of *She's Gotta Have It* made it possible for Lee to continue making films with his vision. In 1988, he produced *School Daze*, an exposé of relations between blacks. Based upon his experiences at Morehouse College, *School Daze* showed how light-skinned African Americans discriminated against those with darker skin tone. The film's central theme stirred controversy within the African American community; while some community leaders applauded Lee's willingness to explore an ongoing, painful issue, many others were deeply offended. When Island Pictures pulled out of the picture, Lee arranged for backing by Columbia Pictures. *School Daze* grossed $15 million without much promotion by Columbia.

Lee's reputation as a screenwriter and director who was willing to undertake controversial subjects was enhanced by his next project. In 1989, he released *Do the Right Thing*. The movie captured the racial tensions between Italians and African Americans in the Bedford-Stuyvesant section of Brooklyn. In the film's climax, a predominantly white police force kills a black teenager, which leads to a race riot that destroys a local pizzeria. While Lee was criticized as promoting violence, he denied that was his intent. The following year, Lee released *Mo' Better Blues*, a story about a jazz musician's relationship with women, his family, and his music. *Mo' Better Blues* received only moderate praise. Lee's shallow characterization of women as well as the non–African American characters was especially criticized. Lee followed that film with *Jungle Fever* in 1991, which was inspired, in part, by the actual murder of an African American teenager by Italian American teenagers. Although the interracial romance between an African American man and an Italian American woman received mixed reviews, it was a commercial success.

Lee has often used public controversy over his movies to his advantage for commercial success and adheres to Malcolm X's theory that greater racial equality depends on greater financial equality. Besides his production company, Forty Acres and a Mule, Lee created Spike's Joint, a chain of apparel boutiques. He also owns his own advertising agency and a music company that produces soundtracks. He usually plays a supporting role in his movies. He has also directed music videos for such artists as Miles Davis and Branford Marsalis, as well as ads for Jesse Jackson's campaign for president in 1988. Lee has even directed commercials for such companies as Nike, The Gap, Ben & Jerry's, and Snapple. Not shunning the spotlight himself, he has also appeared in television and print advertising for Apple computers, National Fluid Milk Processors "Got Milk" commercials, and the famous Nike Air Jordan spots with Michael Jordan.

When it was announced that Norman Jewison was slated to direct a movie about Malcolm X's life, Lee publicly derided the idea that a white man could direct the film. As a result, Jewison stepped away from the project; Lee was hired in his place. Wanting the means with which to portray the civil rights leader accurately, he requested a budget of $40 million, but was countered with an offer of $20 million by Warner Brothers studios. Lee filled the budget gap by selling foreign rights and kicking in some of his salary from the film. Additionally, in an embarrassing move for the studio, he also sought funding from such prominent African American celebrities as Bill Cosby and Oprah Winfrey. The risks Lee took paid off and he was able to complete *Malcolm X*, which is now generally regarded as his masterpiece. The film, a critical and commercial success, led to a brief period of "Malcolm-mania" in pop culture; street vendors and even Lee himself, through Spike's Joint, manufactured baseball hats and other fashion items with large "X's" on them that were ubiquitous throughout the early 1990s.

The next three films made by Lee were box office disappointments. *Crooklyn* (1994), *Clockers* (1995), and *Girl 6* (1996) were panned by the critics and criticized for lack of character development. His less commercial films of the late 1990s were better received. In 1996, *Get on the Bus* told the story of a group of African American men who participated in the 1995 Million Man March on Washington organized by Louis Farrakhan. Lee followed that up with the documentary *4 Little Girls*, about the Sixteenth Street Baptist Church bombing in 1963, in which four young African American girls were killed. Channeling his love for basketball, in 1996, Lee produced the well-received documentary *Hoop Dreams*. In 1998, Lee combined his love of basketball with his passion for filmmaking in *He Got Game*. The movie tells the story of the corruption in the process of recruiting African American athletes for large sports programs.

Toward the end of the 20th century, Lee began to branch into directing and producing for television. He directed John Leguizamo's one-man show, *Freak* (1998), for HBO. In 1999, Lee explored the high-tension summer that gripped New York City the year that serial killer Son of Sam (David Berkowitz) went on a rampage in *Summer of Sam*. In 2000, Lee released the comedy tour movie *The Original Kings of Comedy* and *Bamboozled*, which took a scathing look at white perceptions of blacks in entertainment. He also wrote the teleplay *A Huey P. Newton Story* (2001), about Black Panther Huey Newton.

Following the World Trade Center and Pentagon attacks of 2001, Lee participated in the television special *The Concert for New York City* and, along with other New York City–based filmmakers who contributed spots about the metropolis, he directed a segment entitled "Come Rain or Come Shine." Lee then directed a film segment on jazz trumpet and a documentary on football player Jim Brown in 2002. That same year, he produced and directed *25th Hour*, starring Edward Norton, which centered on a convicted drug dealer's last day before he leaves for prison.

In 2003, Lee became embroiled in a legal battle over the use of the name "Spike" when a new cable channel was marketed with the same name. Ultimately, Lee and Viacom, the media company that owned the show, settled the matter in undisclosed terms. Lee took some time off before releasing his next film, *She Hate Me*, in 2004, which was variously received and did poorly at the box office. He continued with television projects like *Sucker Free City* and the miniseries *Miracle's Boys*.

In October 1993, Lee married lawyer Tonya Linette Lewis, and the couple has a daughter and a son. Lee is a trustee of

Morehouse College and, in 2004, sat on the advisory board of the inaugural National Geographic All Roads Film Festival. Lee's recent projects include working once again with *Malcolm X* star Denzel Washington on the film *Inside Man* (2006). In 2005, Lee entered the Toronto Film Festival with his film *All the Invisible Children* and made a short film for the United Nations Children's Fund about AIDS entitled *Jesus Children of America*, so named after a song title by Stevie Wonder. In 2006, Lee produced an acclaimed documentary on the aftermath of Hurricane Katrina in New Orleans titled *When the Levees Broke: A Requiem in Four Acts*. Lee directed the 2008 film *Miracle at St. Anna* that highlights the role of African American soldiers active in the Italian campaign during World War II.

Since Michael Jackson's death in 2009, Lee and his 40 Acres and a Mule Productions have annually held the Brooklyn Loves Michael Jackson commemoration of the singer's birthday each August. In August 2012, Lee released a documentary commemorating the 25th anniversary of *Bad*, using behind-the-scenes footage not previously seen.

TIM WATTS

See also

Films and Racial Stereotypes

Further Reading:

Abrams, Dennis. *Spike Lee: Director*. Broomhall, PA: Chelsea House Publishers, 2008.

Lee, Spike, with Kaleem Aftab. *That's My Story and I'm Sticking to It*. New York: W. W. Norton, 2005.

Patterson, Alex. *Spike Lee*. New York: Avon Books, 1992.

Lesbian, Gay, Bisexual, Transgender, Intersex, Queer, and Queer Questioning Community (LGBTQ)

LGBTQ is an acronym that stands for lesbian, gay, bisexual, transgender, and queer. The term has been in use since the 1990s, and is an adaptation of the earlier initialisms LGBT and LBG. These terms initially came into use in the late 1980s in order to replace the term *gay*, as many in that community felt the term did not accurately represent all of the people to whom it referred. The term LGBTQ is intended to reflect the diversity of gender and sexuality identities encompassed by this group, and is sometimes used to refer to anyone who is nonheterosexual. The letter Q was added around 1996, thereby including those who identify as queer or who are questioning their sexual identity. Initially, the term *queer* was commonly used as a derogatory term meaning "strange" or "abnormal," but this was disrupted by scholar Teresa de Lauretis in the early 1990s. Inspired by gay-affirmative activists in New York who used the word *queer* regularly, Lauretis sought to reclaim the term. Out of a history of being used as a slur, academics and activists turned the word *queer* into a theory that challenged assumptions of heterosexism and offered a new identity location. As queer theory continues to challenge heterosexism, the term *queer* has often been accused of not encompassing all experiences; therefore, LGBTQ has been offered as a way to describe the diversity of sexualities that exist.

The 1960s civil rights movements enabled discussions about oppression in its many forms, including not just racial oppression, but also the power and privilege of heterosexism. By the late 20th century, social issues such as gay rights and the Acquired Immune Deficiency Syndrome (AIDS) epidemic—which was commonly referred to as "Gay Cancer" before 1982—changed the visibility of the LGBTQ community and often invoked irrational fears about its members. There is a long history of prejudice and discrimination against the LGBTQ community in the United States. This is evident in the derogatory terms often used to refer to members of this group. The term "homosexual" carried negative connotations until about the 1960s, connotations which subsequently became attached to the word "gay." Throughout the twentieth century, gays and lesbians in the United States and beyond have attempted to reclaim their sexual identities as legitimate categories. Bisexual and transgender people have also joined in this struggle, which is reflected in the evolving nature of the term LGBTQ. In reclaiming terms such as *gay* and *queer* that initially held derogatory undertones, the LGBTQ community has used their title to serve as a positive symbol of inclusion.

However, the LGBTQ movement has not been without controversy. The term has been challenged, accused of reproducing Eurocentric perspectives since "LGBTQ" does not nominally include all individuals, including those in smaller communities like intersex or transsexual groups. In 1995, a group known as Queers of Color published a collective statement critiquing the Eurocentric nature of the queer liberation movement and the marginalization that occurred within the LGBTQ group. *Queers of color* is a term used to capture what queer theorist José Estaban Muñoz refers to as "identities of difference." The Queers of Color controversy illustrates the complexities of identity and oppression. According to this collective, the struggle against sexism is marked by an overlapping struggle against racism. Composed of lesbian black feminists, the Queers of Color collective calls for black women to struggle together with black men against racism, and within their communities to address sexism and patriarchy.

LGBTQ of color face many additional instances of prejudice and discrimination—struggles that their white LGBTQ counterparts rarely encounter. This is often evident in public spaces or when relationships are made visible, LGBTQ members of color in these situations frequently facing not just homophobia, but also racism and racial prejudice. Often, these include subtle forms of racism. People of color are often racialized in dating life; for example, Asians are assumed to be exotic while black men are assumed to be sexual predators. This racism can often underwrite the LGBTQ experience, and sometimes can result in blatant violence. Although the murder of Matthew Shepard in 1998 eventually led to the passage of the Matthew Shepard and James Byrd, Jr. Hate Crimes Prevention Act (2009) which made hate crimes illegal, LGBTQ of color continue to be particularly vulnerable to violence. For example, in 2004, a gay bar in the Castro district of San Francisco called the Badlands was picketed for discriminating against nonwhite customers. Minority customers were prevented from entering the bar because of stereotypes that having queers of color present would hinder business. In 2011, *Colorlines*—a magazine devoted to articles on race and culture—reported that 70 percent of anti-LGBTQ murder victims are people of color. It is clear that for nonwhite LGBTQ, the struggles for equality and legitimacy are doubly difficult, as they are fighting dual battles of heterosexism and racism, often experiencing invisibility even within their own LGBTQ communities.

Since 1996, gay marriage is the issue around which most discussions of the LGBTQ community have revolved. The

Lesbian feminist and activist Audrey Lorde (1934–1992), was a vanguard of the LGBTIQQ community, challenging Eurocentric and heterocentric feminist theory. Lorde's poetry was published throughout the 1960's and 1970's, and addressed issues pertaining to gay and civil rights. (Library of Congress)

debate over gay marriage has created a wide range of discussions, social movements, and reactions among the American public. In 1996, as Hawaii was contemplating legalizing gay marriage, the Clinton administration passed the Defense of Marriage Act (DOMA), a law that allowed states to refuse to recognize same-sex marriages. This was a major legal setback for LGBTQ rights, as it meant that same-sex couples were prevented from enjoying the same legal rights and benefits heterosexual couples receive through the institution of marriage. The battle over same-sex marriage has grown since the passage of DOMA, as individual states have increasingly legalized gay marriage. In 2004, Mayor Gavin Newsome of San Francisco legally married LGBTQ couples, and that same year Proposition 8 was put forth to ban same-sex marriage in California. Prop. 8 was passed in the November 2008

California state elections. Over the course of the battle for same-sex marriage, the racialization of the discussions have become clear. During the battle over Prop. 8, the majority of voters who were in favor of banning same-sex marriage were black and Latino.

There have been gains in recent years for LGBTQ equality. In 2010, a federal court ruled that Prop. 8 was unconstitutional, and DOMA was overturned in 2013. However, as of 2013, same-sex couples can only legally marry in 14 U.S. states: California, Connecticut, Delaware, Iowa, Maine, Maryland, Massachusetts, Minnesota, New Hampshire, New Jersey, New York, Rhode Island, Vermont, and Washington. Several states offer civil unions, which grant same-sex couples some of the benefits of marriage, but there are still 31 states with constitutional restrictions that limit marriage to a man and a woman. However, in 2012, President Barack Obama was the first president to speak vocally in favor of gay marriage, and Rep. Mark Takano of California became the first nonwhite openly gay member of Congress.

ANNIE ISABEL FUKUSHIMA

See also

Anti-Miscegenation Laws; Domestic Violence; Down Low; Illegitimacy Rates; Mixed Race Relationships and the Media; Tripping over the Color Line

Further Reading:

Abrajano, Marisa. "Are Blacks and Latinos Responsible for the Passage of Proposition 8? Analyzing Voter Attitudes on California's Proposal to Ban Same-Sex Marriage in 2008." *Political Research Quarterly* 63, no. 4 (December 2010): 922–32.

Combahee River Collective. "The Combahee River Collective Statement." In *Home Girls, A Black Feminist Anthology*, edited by Barbara Smith. New York: Kitchen Table: Women of Color Press, 1983.

Dettmer, Elizabeth. "Beyond the Gay Marriage; the Mainstreaming of the Gay Movement." http://www.prx.org/pieces/73983 -beyond-gay-marriage-the-mainstreaming-of-the-gay# description.

Halperin, David M. "The Normalization of Queer Theory." *Journal of Homosexuality* 45, no. 2–4 (2003): 339–43.

Han, Chongsuk. "They Don't Want to Cruise Your Type: Gay Men of Color and the Racial Politics of Exclusion." *Social Identities: Journal for the Study of Race, Nation and Culture* 13, no. 1 (2007): 51–67.

Steinbugler, Amy C. *Beyond Loving: Intimate Racework in Lesbian, Gay and Straight Interracial Relationships*. New York: Oxford University Press, 2012.

Levittowns

Created in 1947 by William Levitt, Levittowns were standardized, large-scale suburban developments. Levitt emphasized efficiency and mass-production methods, which put the cost of home ownership within reach of middle-class America. Designed to accommodate the housing needs of returning World War II veterans, Levittowns served as a symbol of the postwar American dream. However, Jim Crow practices and housing policies kept African Americans out of this utopian community. Levittowns are the exemplar of innumerable American developments that prohibited black suburbanization.

The first of many Levittowns was built on Long Island, New York. Thousands of modest houses in these subdivisions mirrored one another. Levitt's goal was to provide affordable, not designer, homes. Often known as "cookie cutter communities," similarities did not end with the architecture. Most of the Levittown residents were young, married with children, and held similar jobs. Possibly one of the most obvious and shared characteristics among Levittowners was race. The Levitt organization openly stated that Levittowns were solely Caucasian communities and made every effort to keep Levittowns segregated. Thirteen years after its inception, not one African American resided in a Levittown. Levitt and residents of Levittown worried that integrating the communities could cause the property values to plummet. Additionally, attitudes of white supremacy encouraged segregation to endure.

African Americans slowly began to break Levittown's race barrier in the mid-1960s, but it was not an easy feat. White realtors and financial institutions made it almost impossible for African Americans to move into all-white communities. Banks would refuse to lend money or offer only the most expensive rates to black families. White residents joined together to form homeowners' associations with the common goal to prevent integration. Many homeowners refused to sell or rent their home to African Americans. Moreover, desperate white segregationists resorted to threats, violence, and arson in hopes of scaring black families away. Even Jackie Robinson, one of the greatest baseball players of all time, had so much difficultly finding a home near New York that he and his wife eventually decided to reside in Connecticut.

These prejudicial practices became illegal in April 1968, when President Lyndon B. Johnson signed the Civil Rights Act of 1968, also known as the Fair Housing Act. This legislation prohibited "discrimination based on race, color, religion, sex, and national origin in the sale or rental of housing" and banned well-known discriminatory practices such as blockbusting, redlining, and real estate steering. Despite such legislation, according to the 2000 census, Long Island, New York, the first home to a Levittown, is the most racially segregated suburban area in the United States.

EMILY HESS

See also

Residential Segregation; Segregation, Suburban

Further Reading:

Civil Rights Act of 1968, Public Law 90–284, April 11, 1968, 82 Stat. (Title VIII, Fair Housing). *U.S. Statutes at Large, 90th Congress, 1968.*

Jackson, Kenneth T. *Crabgrass Frontier: The Suburbanization of the United States.* New York: Oxford University Press, 1985.

Leif, Beth J., and Susan Goering. "The Implementation of the Federal Mandate for Fair Housing." In *Divided Neighborhoods: Changing Patterns of Racial Segregation,* edited by Gary A. Tobin, 235, 261. Newbury Park, CA: Sage, 1987.

Wiese, Andrew. *Places of Their Own: African American Suburbanization in the Twentieth Century.* Chicago: University of Chicago Press, 2004.

Linnaeus, Carolus (1707–1778)

Carolus Linnaeus is the pen name of the great Swedish botanist Carol von Linne. Since his writings were in Latin, he is commonly known by his Latin name. He is best known for establishing binomial nomenclature, or the genus and species system of naming, as the standard means of organizing the biological world into a scientific taxonomy. Linnaeus's

This is an undated image of Swedish scientist Carl Linnaeus (1707–1778). Linnaeus, among other things, constructed a system of classifying all living organisms. (AP Photo/Scanpix)

major work *Systema Naturae* (1758) offered a simple method for ordering plants and animals into a nested hierarchy based on observable characteristics. In Linnaean taxonomy different species are recognized as being in relation to one another to a greater or lesser degree, based on shared features. This is the same basic principle used by modern biologists in classifying the living world, only today the focus is on genetics rather than observable physical characteristics. At the time of his death he was one of the most highly regarded scientists in the world.

Linnaeus is also known as the first person to offer a scientific explanation for the human races. In a move that shocked his contemporaries, Linnaeus placed humans in his taxonomy of the natural world, coining the name *Homo sapiens* for our genus and species. This was especially challenging to 18th-century Europeans because of the widely held belief that humans, having been made in God's image, were superior to everything in the natural world. Based on anatomical similarities, Linnaeus argued that humans ought to be classified with monkeys and apes in an order of mammals he called Primates. In Linnaeus's taxonomical description of *Homo sapiens* there were four races, which were defined by geography and skin color. These four races were: white European, red American, yellow Asian, and black African. Included with these physical descriptions were supposedly natural racial differences of temperament and intelligence. For example the white race was inventive and the black race was lazy, while the red race was stubborn and the yellow race was greedy.

Although Linnaeus departed from convention by placing humans within the natural world, he conformed in others. According to the dominant theological doctrine his day, all living things were created by God in their modern form. This "fixity of species," as it was known, precluded the possibility of change among populations over time. Therefore racial differences were seen as immutable because those differences were set down by God at the moment of creation. In anticipation of forthcoming theories of evolution, Linnaeus came to abandon the fixity of species later in life although he himself was not an evolutionist.

MATTHEW D. THOMPSON

See also

Blumenbach, Johann; Racial Taxonomy

Further Reading:

Benedict, Ruth, and Gene Weltfish. *The Races of Mankind*. New York: Public Affairs Committee, 1943.
Scheidt, Walter. "The Concept of Race in Anthropology and the Divisions into Human Races, from Linnaeus to Deniker." In *This Is Race*, edited by E. Count, 354–91. New York: Henry Schuman, 1950.

Little Rock Nine

The term "Little Rock Nine" refers to the group of nine students who in September 1957 became the first African Americans to attend Central High School in Little Rock, Arkansas. The nine students were Melba Pattillo, Minnijean Brown, Elizabeth Eckford, Ernest Green, Gloria Ray, Carlotta Walls, Thelma Mothershed, Terrence Roberts, and Jefferson Thomas. The Nine, who had been carefully selected for their role, submitted themselves to humiliation and physical danger in order to help desegregate the public schools of Little Rock.

On May 24, 1955, the Little Rock School Board unanimously approved a plan drafted by Virgil Blossum, the superintendant of schools, for the gradual integration of the city's schools, in compliance with the U.S. Supreme Court, which had ruled in the 1954 decision *Brown v. Board of Education* that segregated schools were unconstitutional, and that all schools were to be desegregated. The initial phase, when nine black students would begin attending classes at the previously all-white Central High School, would begin in September 1957. Local civil rights leaders and the Little Rock School Board understood that the first black students to attend the school would be under intense scrutiny, with any deficiency in academics or conduct used as an excuse to label the entire movement to integrate the schools a failure. The nine students were carefully selected by the local chapter of the National Association for the Advancement of Colored People for their high grades, solid attendance records, and lack of discipline problems in their previous school records. Daisy Lee Bates, a journalist and publisher who was active in the civil rights movement in Little Rock, provided continual advice and support to the Nine. The students were instructed to dress neatly, not to overreact to provocation, and in general to give segregationists no excuse to use them as an argument against integration.

White residents of the city formed "citizens' councils," which pledged themselves to uphold segregation, with force if necessary. Gov. Orval Faubus, a former liberal who had come to support segregation, promised white voters that he would keep Central High an all-white school. By inclination, President Dwight D. Eisenhower disliked heavy-handed government approaches, and preferred to remain aloof from the civil rights movement. However, he saw a crisis building in Little Rock, as segregationists rallied and planned during the 1956–1957 school year. Hoping to avoid a showdown between state and federal authorities, Eisenhower met with Governor Faubus to discuss the approaching integration. While Faubus remained noncommittal, Eisenhower apparently believed that although Faubus might speak against integration, he would ensure that federal laws were obeyed.

The initial attempts of the Nine to attend classes at the school on September 4, 1957, brought out large crowds of white adults, mostly parents of students attending the school, bent on maintaining segregation. The crowds had assembled around the school in the early morning to keep the black students out of the school. Governor Faubus mobilized part of the Arkansas National Guard with the mission to physically block the nine black students from entering the school. Faubus explained his actions as stemming from his concern for maintaining law and order, but the white mobs were the people violating the law, not the black students. Photographs of the day's events were published nationally, with the image of a row of white armed Guardsmen and the mobs of angry adult white adults blocking the small group of neatly dressed black students, all of whom were in their mid-teens, making a powerful impression throughout the nation. Eisenhower was furious at the actions of Faubus, seeing his stance as a direct challenge to federal authority. Eisenhower had the U.S. Department of Justice request an injunction against the use of the National Guard in U.S. District Court for the Eastern District of Arkansas. The injunction was granted, and Faubus was ordered to withdraw the National Guard or face contempt of court.

Faubus, having shown his commitment to his political base while holding himself and his city up to national ridicule, complied and withdrew the Guard on September 20, and city police took over the mission of ensuring the safety of the Nine. However, the situation at Central High was still tense, as a large crowd of whites, estimated in the hundreds, kept a vigil at the school in an attempt to ensure that the Nine did not enter the school. On September 23, the police were able to sneak the Nine into the school to begin attending classes. However, when the surrounding mob learned that the Nine were in the school, order began to break down. The police, seriously outnumbered, feared for the safety of the Nine, and escorted them away from the school.

Supporters of integration, as well as people who supported the rule of law and not the rule of mobs, realized that a stronger show of authority would be needed, or else the mobs around Central High would continue to keep the Nine away from school. Woodrow Mann, the Democratic mayor of Little Rock, formally requested that Eisenhower use federal soldiers to maintain order and ensure that the Nine were able to attend classes. On September 24, Eisenhower sent in the U.S. Army's 1,200-man 327th Battle Group of the 101st Airborne Division to Little Rock to take control of the campus. At the same time, he federally mobilized the entire Arkansas National Guard, about 10,000 Guardsmen, mainly to prevent Governor Faubus from attempting to use the Guard to oppose the federal soldiers. With this overwhelming show of disciplined soldiers, the threat from the mobs abated, although the shouting continued. The Nine were able to enter the school and begin attending classes on September 25.

The federal soldiers were deployed for the immediate crisis, but Eisenhower and the army wanted them returned to Fort Campbell, Kentucky, as soon as the situation allowed it. Originally, most of the National Guardsmen were ordered to remain at the armories. However, the army began organizing some of the federalized National Guardsmen into what became Task Force 153 on Camp Robinson, in North Little Rock, with the long-term mission of ensuring order at the school, while demobilizing most of the remainder of the Arkansas National Guard. By the end of November, the 101st soldiers were all withdrawn, and Task Force 153 assumed full control of the campus.

Although the Nine attended classes under tight security, they were still subjected to a host of threats, harassments, and even assaults, from white students throughout the year. Despite the hostile environment, the Nine remained at the school through the fall semester. Minnijean Brown was the only one of the Nine not to complete the school year. In December, a group of white male students began hassling her in the cafeteria. In the confrontation, she dropped her tray, in the process splashing some of her chili on one of the white students. For this, she was expelled from the school. Melba Pattillo suffered injury when acid was thrown in her face by a white student, but continued to attend Central and finished the school year.

However, the opponents of integration were not finished. With the support of the governor and the state legislature, the school board closed all public high schools in Little Rock after the end of the 1957–1958 school year. The public high schools remained closed only for one year, though. Under pressure from the Little Rock Chamber of Commerce, as well as the enormous negative publicity the city and state received nationally over the crisis, the school board reopened the high schools, as integrated schools, in the fall of 1958.

Of the eight black students who completed the first year, Earnest Green was the only senior, and at the end of the 1957–1958 school year, became the first African American to graduate from Central High. Elizabeth Eckford moved to St. Louis in 1958 and completed her college preparation there. Jefferson Thomas returned when Central reopened, and graduated from Central High in 1960. Terrence Roberts moved to Los Angeles after the end of the first year, and graduated from Los Angeles High School in 1959. Carlotta Walls, the youngest of the nine, also returned to Central High School when it reopened in 1959 and graduated in 1960. Thelma Mothershed completed most of her coursework by correspondence during the year the public schools were closed. She received her diploma from Central High by mail. Melba Pattillio moved to California after the first year and completed her high school program there. In 1999, each of the Little Rock Nine was honored with Congressional Gold Medals presented by President Bill Clinton, in recognition of their courage and their important role in knocking down segregation.

BARRY M. STENTIFORD

See also

Bolling v. Sharpe (1954); *Brown v. Board of Education* (1954); *Brown v. Board of Education* Legal Groundwork; *Cooper v. Aaron* (1958); *Cumming v. Richmond County Board of Education* (1899); Desegregation; Education; School Segregation; Segregation. Document: *Brown v. Board of Education* (May 1954)

Further Reading:

Fitzgerald, Stephanie. *Little Rock Nine: Struggle for Integration.* Mankato, MN: Compass Point Books, 2006.

Freyer, Tony. *The Little Rock Crisis: A Constitutional Interpretation.* Westport, CT: Greenwood Press, 1984.

Jacoway, Elizabeth, and C. Fred Williams, eds. *Understanding the Little Rock Crisis: An Exercise in Remembrance and Reconciliation.* Fayetteville: University of Arkansas Press, 1999.

Locke, Alain LeRoy (1886–1954)

Alain LeRoy Locke was an African American educator, writer, and philosopher, and is best remembered as a leader and one of the chief interpreters of the Harlem Renaissance.

Born in Philadelphia, Pennsylvania, on September 13, 1886, Locke graduated from Harvard University in 1907 with a degree in philosophy. He was the first black Rhodes Scholar, studying at Oxford from 1907 to 1910, and the University of Berlin from 1910 to 1911. He received his PhD in philosophy from Harvard in 1918. For almost 40 years, until retirement in 1953 as head of the department of philosophy, Locke taught at Howard University in Washington, D.C. During that time, he became a distinguished member in 1930 of the African American Greek organization Phi Beta Sigma Fraternity, the second member inducted into their Distinguished Service Chapter.

Locke stimulated and guided artistic activities and urged black painters, sculptors, and musicians to look to African sources for identity and to discover materials and techniques for their work. His many written works include *Four Negro Poets* (1927), *Frederick Douglass, A Biography of Anti-Slavery* (1935), *Negro Art—Past and Present* (1936), *The Negro and His Music* (1936), and his most notable work *The New Negro* (1925), an anthology of notable African American works.

The corpus of his work is seized upon for explaining and conceptually organizing the rising Harlem Renaissance movement that was indicative, for the first time (and across racial lines), of African American cultural aesthetic absorption by the mainstream white-dominated culture. In 1924, *Opportunity* magazine hosted a dinner at the Civic Club in New York City and made Locke master of ceremonies. This event is often considered the formal launching of the New Negro movement, which was named after Locke's cultural and literary endeavors.

Locke's engagement with race riots was most notable in regard to the Harlem (New York) Riot of 1935, which was caused by a rumor that a young African American boy stole a knife from a Kress Store on 125th Street in New York City. Further, it was rumored that the boy had been beaten and was either gravely injured or dead, though in reality he had fled. The rumors, coupled with charges of brutality and employment discrimination by Kress, triggered the rioting. At least 600 store windows were shattered and looting was rampant. The riot resulted in the deaths of three blacks and caused over $2 million in property damage. Police arrested 75 people, mostly black, and nearly 60 citizens were seriously injured. Resultantly, Locke wrote a short essay titled "Harlem: Dark Weather-Vane," which appeared in the August

Alain LeRoy Locke was a writer, philosopher, educator, and patron of the arts. He is best known for his writings on and about the Harlem Renaissance. (National Archives)

aesthetics. Locke termed his philosophy *cultural pluralism* and emphasized the necessity of determining values to guide human conduct and interrelationships. His philosophy was said to have been greatly influenced by his membership in the Bahá'í faith. Locke entered into the faith in 1918 and enjoyed a close relationship with Shoghi Effendi, the guardian of the Bahá'í faith and great-grandson of its founder, Bahá'u'lláh. Chief among Locke's values was respect for the uniqueness of individual personality, which he believed could develop fully and remain unique only within a democratic ethos. Locke died on June 9, 1954.

MATTHEW W. HUGHEY

See also
Harlem (New York) Riot of 1935

Further Reading:
Akam, Everett H. "Community and Cultural Crisis: The 'Transfiguring Imagination' of Alain Locke." *American Literary History* (Summer 1991): 255–76.

Burgett, Paul Joseph. "Vindication as a Thematic Principle in Alain Locke's Writings on the Music of Black Americans." In *The Harlem Renaissance: Revaluations*, edited by Amritjit Singh, William S. Shiver, and Stanley Brodwin, 139–57. New York: Garland, 1989.

Harris, Leonard. *The Philosophy of Alain Locke: Harlem Renaissance and Beyond*. Philadelphia: Temple University Press, 1989.

Locke, Alain Leroy. "Harlem: Dark Weather-Vane." *Survey Graphic* 25, no. 8 (August 1936).

Napier, Winston. "Affirming Critical Conceptualism: Harlem Renaissance Aesthetics and the Formation of Alain Locke's Social Philosophy." *Massachusetts Review* 39, no. 1 (Spring 1998): 93–112.

Washington, Johnny. *Alain Locke and Philosophy: A Quest for Cultural Pluralism*. New York: Greenwood Press, 1986.

1936 edition of *Survey Graphic* and expressed his view of the riot as variously diagnosed as a Depression spasm, a ghetto mutiny, a radical plot, and dress rehearsal of proletarian revolution. Whichever it was, like a revealing flash of lightning, it etched on the public mind another Harlem than the bright surface Harlem of the night clubs, cabaret tours, and arty magazines, a Harlem that the social worker knew all along but had not been able to dramatize—a Harlem, too, that the radical press and street-corner orator had been pointing out but in all too incredible exaggerations and none too convincing shouts. Locke was careful to debunk the fallacious story, but also provided keen insight into the multifarious causes of the riot related to the impoverished and terrorized social environment of Harlem in the Depression era.

Accordingly, Locke is often considered a humanist who was intensely concerned with social life and cultural

Long Hot Summer Riots (1965–1967)

The Long Hot Summer is the name given to the riots that occurred in the urban ghettos of the North between 1965 and 1967. Of the several hundred disturbances that occurred during each summer, the Watts or Los Angeles (California) Riot of 1965, Newark (New Jersey) Riot of 1967, and Detroit (Michigan) Riot of 1967 were the most intense. These riots signaled an unprecedented shift in the pattern of racial violence that had occurred previously in the United States. They also challenged the way Americans perceived and depicted black violence.

Prior to the 1960s, most race riots or incidents of racial violence were instigated by whites. The inciting event was often triggered by a perceived need to enforce economic, social, or political control, or by an alleged accusation of a crime or offense, no matter how minor. Once the white mobs or vigilante groups apprehended and executed the accused, they often went on long and violent rampages through the nearest black community. Murders were commonplace, and blacks were nearly always the victims. Local authorities rarely arrested the whites, who murdered numerous innocent blacks and obliterated their property and communities. This pattern persisted from Reconstruction to the end of World War II.

In the 1950s and 1960s, the focus of white violence shifted from the black communities to the nonviolent protests and demonstrations of the civil rights movement. Media scrutiny, intervention by local, state, and federal government institutions, and effective law enforcement deterred future attacks. The incidence of white rioting decreased dramatically. Meanwhile, activists continued to make strides toward ending racial segregation and, eventually, defeating Jim Crow laws altogether. Wealthier blacks moved out of the formerly black urban neighborhoods, leaving the destitute in their wake. The residents of the ghettos faced critical problems such as high crime and unemployment, broken families, poorly maintained housing, and feelings of powerlessness.

Local activists, city officials, and even the federal government made attempts to quell—if not permanently remedy—the tensions in the nation's ghettos. The Harlem Youth Opportunities Unlimited program was one of the first of its kind. The leaders of this program were Kenneth B. Clark, an esteemed black psychologist who made significant contributions toward desegregation, and members of the Harlem community.

President Lyndon B. Johnson also launched a gallant attack on poverty with his Great Society programs. These programs were unpopular to politicians and most white Americans. Politicians, "fearing that the federal government was subsidizing their opponents and undercutting their power, were especially threatened by programs that empowered the previously disfranchised and dispossessed" (Hine et al. 2000: 539). Others resented the idea that blacks were not pulling themselves out of poverty but rather depending on others to save them.

Under his Economic Opportunity Act of 1964, Johnson initiated programs such as Head Start, for the young children of impoverished families, and Upward Bound, to help direct underrepresented youth toward college. His New Careers program aimed to fill local positions, such as community coordinators, teaching assistants, and day care workers, from within the poor black communities themselves. These programs, reminiscent of the promises of Reconstruction, filled blacks with hope and gave them a reprieve from the despair of their circumstances. However, strong opposition, coupled with growing American entanglement in the Vietnam War, halted Johnson's plans. Ultimately, the riots in the ghettos were unaffected by Johnson's programs or by others like them.

In 1965, a new wave of race riots emerged out of the frustrations percolating within the ghettos, triggered by repeated incidents of police brutality and harassment. *The African American Odyssey* (2000) details other contributing factors as follows:

> As jobs moved increasingly to suburbs to which inner-city residents could neither travel nor relocate, inner-city neighborhoods sank deeper into poverty. School dropout rates reached epidemic proportions, crime and drug use increased, and fragile family structures weakened. It was these conditions that led militants like the Panthers to liken their neighborhoods to exploited colonies kept in poverty by repressive [and exclusive] white political and economic institutions.

Disturbances occurred primarily within black neighborhoods and were instigated by blacks who targeted their own property. Unlike the white riots of prior years, blacks did not aim to murder. In some cases, they attacked white bystanders, but they did not kill. Most deaths occurred as authorities attempted to restore order. Blacks looted and set fire to their own homes and businesses. In contrast to white riots, blacks were often arrested, charged, and convicted.

The first major riot occurred in Watts in the summer of 1965. Watts, a predominantly black neighborhood in Los Angeles, California, was troubled by the ills of high unemployment and crime, drug addition, and inadequate public facilities. Residents also were subjected to frequent police harassment and brutality. On August 11, 1965, a white police officer arrested a black man he had stopped on suspicion of drunk driving. A black crowd was present. After reinforcements arrived, blacks threw rocks, bottles, and other objects at the officers. A riot followed. Gov. Pat Brown neglected to call in the National Guard until the sixth day. By then, the rioters had destroyed their own community. In the aftermath, more than 900 individuals were injured, 34 were killed, and 4,000 were arrested.

The next major uprising occurred in the sweltering heat of July 1967 (a year that saw 59 riots) in Newark, New Jersey. Newark was "a majority black city, but one that operated on an inadequate tax base and under white political control" (Hine et al. 2000: 537). Black men in Newark had the highest unemployment rate in the nation. There was a prevailing feeling of animosity toward racist police officers and a judicial system that did not provide justice for blacks in the community, as well as a distrust of white-dominated institutions. Blacks living in the urban ghettos were beginning to embrace racially empowering ideologies, such as black pride, Black Power, and Black Nationalism.

In early July, a white police officer beat up a black cab driver. Outraged, blacks firebombed the police station where the driver was being detained. Police officers responded by clubbing the protestors. In retribution, blacks rioted for four days. The police and the National Guard killed 25 innocent bystanders. Two of the victims were children. One white police officer and one firefighter were also killed. The property damage was enormous.

The third major riot occurred in Detroit, Michigan, 11 days after the disturbance in Newark. Blacks in Detroit were also grappling with the effects of alienation, racism, and systematic social and economic oppression. Black Nationalism, Black Power, and the Nation of Islam movements were popular among blacks in Detroit. These ideologies infused blacks with a sense of purpose and value otherwise denied them in the society at large.

On July 23, more than 80 blacks gathered in an after-hours drinking establishment to celebrate the return of two Vietnam War veterans. White police officers raided the party and roughly handled blacks as they attempted to clear the club. Five days of rioting ensued. When the National Guard, 200 Michigan police officers, and 600 Detroit police officers failed to restore order, President Lyndon B. Johnson sent out 4,700 troops of the Army's elite 82nd and 101st airborne units.

Responses to this tumultuous period in inner-city history varied. Some blacks, such as Malcolm X of the Nation of Islam, sympathized with the rioters. The National Association for the Advancement of Colored People (NAACP) condemned the riots but acknowledged that genuine troubles had produced the desperate response. Both the Nation of Islam and the NAACP established programs to help the troubled communities.

Deeply concerned, President Johnson established the National Advisory Commission on Civil Disorders, which was headed by Otto Kerner and is thus known as the Kerner Commission. The objectives of the commission were to study the ghettos and determine the causes of the summer riots and develop solutions to help eliminate the harrowing conditions of poverty, discrimination, poor housing, inadequate health care, and other ills. In 1968, the commission published a report that showed racism as the primary cause of the riots (see Kerner Commission Report [1968]). The report recommended federal aid to develop better housing, to improve and integrate schools, and to fund new jobs. Unfortunately, the divisive Vietnam War was by this time attracting both the nation's attention and its resources.

In "Riots, Revolts, and Relevant Response," Charles V. Hamilton describes how whites were shocked and oblivious as to why blacks attacked their own communities, especially during a period when they assumed all blacks had achieved significant progress. He explained that too much emphasis was placed on the lawlessness of the acts and the defamation of blacks, thus causing many whites to seek greater restrictions and enforcement over blacks to maintain law and order. Hamilton opposed this solution, since extant tensions between blacks and law enforcement had caused the turmoil in the first place and more stringent action from the same source would only aggravate the situation. He also condemned those who wrongly characterized the blacks who participated in the rebellions as criminals and "hoodlums," while those who opposed the "unlawful acts" were "'right thinking.'" According to Hamilton, these perceptions were amiss and did not consider the underlying reasons for the rebellions.

Hamilton argued that the disturbances of the Long Hot Summer were revolts, not riots, and that blacks were exerting their power through violent protest against the brutalities and injustices they suffered at the hands of the police. The triggering event (for example, the officer who beat up the cab driver in Newark) was symbolic of the cumulative offenses blacks experienced. The violent reactions were not so different from how whites responded to perceived offenses during America's early years. Frontier justice was frequently enforced in the West. Whites often banded together to maintain law and order in the absence of formal enforcement. Vigilante organizations were instrumental in ensuring the safety and protection of their own lives, families, property, and livelihood. Hamilton explained that the police officers and the court systems had repeatedly wronged and abused blacks. Thus, the rebellions were not only protests but an execution of their own form of justice and a demonstration of their power. For over 100 years, belligerent Southern whites evaded punishment for, and criticism of, their violent activities, while blacks were imprisoned and even killed when they attempted to impose justice. Formally organized black vigilante groups were rarely successful.

The slave uprisings of the 1700s were similar to the ghetto rebellions of the 1960s in that they involved violent protest. The major difference was that the slaves often purposefully murdered whites, whereas blacks in the ghetto disturbances did not. Numerous accounts exist of slaves protesting their condition through violence. In New York City (1712), 27 Africans, seeking retribution for the abuses they suffered, set fire to a building, then killed nine whites and injured six. Six of the Africans killed themselves when whites apprehended them. Whites executed the other 21. Stringent law enforcement to control slave uprisings eventually thwarted future attempts.

In considering solutions to the rebellions in the ghettos, some—particularly those who characterized participants as criminals—proposed harsher law enforcement and control. Others proposed augmenting the increase of preventative programs within the ghettos. Although Hamilton agreed that programs were a viable solution, he recommended that blacks be allowed to control, lead, and hold significant positions within them. He believed white-controlled programs were problematic because blacks distrusted whites. The rebellions were evidence of that fact. Moreover, having blacks run the programs would be a significant step in empowering a people who had so long been dominated.

GLADYS L. KNIGHT

See also

Black Nationalism; Kerner Commission Report (1968); Race Riots in America; Harlem Youth Opportunities Unlimited (HARYOU). Documents: Report on the Memphis Riots of May 1866 (1866); Account of the Riots in East St. Louis, Illinois (1917); A Southern Black Woman's Letter Regarding the Recent Riots in Chicago and Washington (1919); The Cook County Coroner's Report Regarding the 1919 Chicago Race Riots (1920); The Final Report of the Grand Jury on the Tulsa Race Riot (June 25, 1921); Testimony from *Laney v. United States* (1923); The Governor's Commission Report on the Watts Riots (1965); Cyrus R. Vance's Report on the Riots in Detroit (1967); The Reports of the Oklahoma Commission to Study the Tulsa Race Riot of 1921 (2000–2001); Draft Report: 1898 Wilmington Race Riot Commission (2005)

Further Reading:

Gilje, Paul A. *Rioting in America*. Bloomington: Indiana University Press, 1996.

Hamilton, Charles V. "Riots, Revolts and Relevant Response." In *The Black Power Revolt*, edited by Floyd B. Barbour, 170–78. Boston: Extending Horizons Books, 1968.

Hine, Darlene Clark, William C. Hine, and Stanley Harrold, eds. *The African American Odyssey*. Englewood Cliffs, NJ: Prentice Hall, 2000.

Upton, James N. *Urban Riots in the 20th Century: A Social History*. Bristol, IN: Wyndham Hall Press, 1989.

Longoria, Félix (1917–1945)

Félix Longoria was a U.S. Army private who was killed in action in the Philippines in 1945. When a funeral parlor in Texas refused to accept his remains because he was Latino, the incident sparked a national outcry against racial discrimination.

Longoria was born into a Mexican American family in Three Rivers, Texas, in 1917. The city enforced strict segregation between the Latino and Anglo communities. In 1944, Longoria was drafted into the U.S. Army. He left his wife Beatriz and four-year-old daughter and went to the Philippines. On June 15, 1945, he volunteered to go on a patrol in the Cagayan Valley. While on patrol, he was shot by a Japanese sniper and killed instantly.

Longoria's remains were not repatriated to the United States until 1949. When the body arrived in Three Rivers, it was sent to the town's only funeral parlor. However, Tom Kennedy, the owner of the funeral parlor, refused to permit the body to lie in state in the chapel. He explained to Longoria's widow that local whites might complain. Outraged, Beatriz and her sister contacted Hector Perez Garcia, the head of the newly founded American GI Forum.

The AGIF was the nation's first Latino veterans' organization. It had been established to help combat the discrimination that many Latino veterans faced after returning home from the war. Garcia tried to convince Kennedy to change his mind. When he refused, Garcia organized a special meeting of the AGIF to publicize the incident. He also sent out telegrams to several Texas politicians alerting them to the case. Garcia's message called the funeral parlor's decision "a direct contradiction of those same principles for which this American soldier made the supreme sacrifice in giving his life for his country, and for the same people who deny him the last funeral rites deserving of any American hero regardless of his origin."

The AGIF's efforts to publicize the Longoria affair sparked national protests against racial discrimination. Leading radio and newspaper editors published editorials decrying the hypocrisy of a nation that would discriminate against its veterans. Several national radio commentators read Garcia's telegram on the air. Famed radio personality Walter Winchell, addressing the case on his program, observed that "the State of Texas, which looms so large on the map, looks so small tonight."

One of the first politicians to respond to Garcia's telegram was Texas senator Lyndon B. Johnson. Johnson expressed his outrage at the incident and made provisions to have Longoria's remains interred at Arlington National Cemetery in Virginia. He was buried there with full military honors on February 16, 1949. Despite the government's efforts to compensate for the discrimination suffered by Longoria's family, some family members were unhappy that their relative had to be buried so far from his home.

After the funeral, the Texas state legislature appointed a committee of inquiry to look into the Longoria case. It concluded that the family had not suffered from discrimination at the hands of the funeral parlor. However, several members of the legislature disputed the findings of the committee, and its report was never officially filed.

The Longoria incident brought the AGIF and the problem of discrimination against Latinos to national prominence. It is viewed as a watershed event in the history of the Latino civil rights movement. The incident also helped launch the career of Garcia, who went on to become one of the nation's most prominent civil rights activists. In 1968, President Johnson appointed Garcia to the United States Commission on Civil Rights. His efforts on behalf of civil rights have been recognized by several American presidents and by Pope John Paul II. Today, the Corpus Christi, Texas chapter of the AGIF is named in honor of Longoria.

ABC-CLIO

See also
American G.I. Forum (AGIF)

Further Reading:
Allsup, Carl. *The American G.I. Forum: Origins and Evolution.* Austin: University of Texas Center for Mexican American Studies, 1982.
Arlington National Cemetery. http://www.arlingtoncemetery.com.
García, Ignacio M. *Hector P. García: In Relentless Pursuit of Justice.* Houston: Arte Público Press, 2002.
Ramos, Henry A. J. *The American G. I. Forum: In Pursuit of the Dream, 1948–1983.* Houston: Arte Público Press, 1998.

Longview (Texas) Riot of 1919

In Longview, Texas, on the night of July 10, 1919, a white mob in pursuit of Samuel L. Jones gunned its way through the black part of town, shooting people and burning black homes and businesses, leaving four dead. Black residents defended their homes with organized resistance.

In 1919, there were just over 5,000 people living in the industrial town of Longview, the county seat of Gregg County, around 2,000 of whom were black. Longview was the home of the Kelly Iron Works and other manufacturers, and was considered a vibrant center of commerce. According to a Dallas newspaper at the time, Longview was "like a white pearl in the middle of a fine farming territory," and because its white and black citizens were able to work together in peace, both peoples had prospered ("The Great Battle" 1919). The article went on to say that the black population had good churches, schools, halls, and homes, as well as several stores and shops. The Dallas newspaper told only the optimistic side of the story, for all was not well in Longview.

The black community of Longview was cohesive, and a branch of the Negro Business League was active locally, with cooperative stores that offered competition with white merchants. Leaders in the community had been promoting the idea that black farmers should bypass the white cotton brokers in Longview and deal directly with buyers in Galveston. The national black news magazine, the *Chicago Defender*, was readily available, sold at the Quick Grocery, Benton's Market, McWilliams's Restaurant, and Leroy's Fountain, as well as sold on the street by newsboys.

Certain white citizens of Longview perceived the economic and cultural vitality of Longview's black community as a threat. By comparison, many whites in Longview were not enjoying a similar degree of prosperity. With racial tension at a high level, an article in the July 10 issue of the *Chicago Defender* began to circulate among local whites. The article described the death in mid-June of a young black man, Lemuel Walters, in Longview. It reported that a prominent white woman had declared that she loved Walters, and had she been in the North, would obtain a divorce and marry him. A white mob then went after Walters while he was jailed in police custody. The sheriff welcomed the mob into the jail and waved greetings to the mob as they seized the prisoner. Walters was taken to the outskirts of the town and shot, his nude body thrown to the side of the road. The *Chicago Defender* article also asserted that there had been an orchestrated cover-up of the incident by police and other local officials.

Angry that word of the lynching had gotten out, locals believed that Samuel L. Jones, a black activist who taught in the Longview school system and was a local correspondent for the *Chicago Defender*, was the source of the article. Despite his denial, two brothers of the woman attacked him. Jones escaped and sought medical treatment at the office of Dr. Calvin P. Davis. The article and the attack on Jones ratcheted up the tenor of the debate. Word got to Dr. Davis that Jones would be lynched if he did not leave town, and that Dr. Davis should leave too. Davis consulted with a group of black men who agreed to stand with Davis and Jones. They gathered at Jones's house to protect him. Around midnight the mob showed up, and four of its members came up onto the back porch, calling for Jones to come out. When there was no response, and they indicated they would force their way in, Davis fired the first shot. More than 100 shots were fired, and the mob retreated with its wounded.

At daybreak, the mob was reinforced with 1,000 white men armed with rifles, pistols, and ammunition stolen from the hardware store. The mob went to Jones's house, and finding it empty, set it on fire; they went across the street, shot the husband and wife who lived in that house and set it on fire; they then went to Davis's office and to his house, setting them on fire. The mob burned down Quick Hall, owned by Charlie Medlock, which had a store on the lower floor and dance hall above it. Jones left town and Davis escaped as well, disguised as a soldier. Marion Bush, Davis's 60-year-old father-in-law, was chased from his home and pursued until he was shot. The mob left his body in a cornfield three miles south of town.

During the commotion, local officials had requested assistance from the Texas Rangers and Texas National Guard. After Bush's death, Mayor G. A. Bodenheim requested more aid from the governor, who sent additional guardsmen to Longview and placed the entire county under martial law. The rangers arrested 17 white men on charges of attempted murder; each was released on $1,000 bond. Nine white men were arrested and charged with arson. Twenty-one black men were arrested and taken to Austin in protective custody. While Captain W. M. Hanson of the Texas Rangers asserted that any white man arrested in connection with the destruction of black homes would be charged with arson, none of the whites or blacks arrested was ever tried. The names of some of those arrested were Ernest White, Byron Oden, Elbert Keller, John Ethridge, Colton Moore, F. S. Wheeler, Brickbat Robertson, Will Rosson, Fred Nelson, Walter Beall, Lewis Bair, Lowell Smith, L. A. Mackey, Ed Nelson, M. F. Flanagan, Clifford Parr, and Robie Vick.

JAN VOOGD

See also

Race Riots in America; Red Summer Race Riots of 1919. Documents: The Report on the Memphis Riots of May 1866 (July 25, 1866); Account of the Riots in East St. Louis, Illinois (July 1917); The Cook County Coroner's Report Regarding the 1919 Chicago Race Riots (1919); A Southern Black Woman's Letter Regarding the Recent Riots in Chicago and Washington (November 1919); The Final Report of the Grand Jury on the Tulsa Race Riot (June 25, 1921); Testimony from *Laney v.*

United States Describing Events during the Washington, D.C., Riot of July 1919 (December 3, 1923); The Governor's Commission Report on the Watts Riots (December 1965); Cyrus R. Vance's Report on the Riots in Detroit (July-August 1967); The Reports of the Oklahoma Commission to Study the Tulsa Race Riot of 1921 (2000-2001); The Draft Report of the 1898 Wilmington Race Riot Commission (December 2005)

Further Reading:

Durham, Ken. "Longview Race Riot of 1919." *The Handbook of Texas Online* (2001). http://www.tsha.utexas.edu/handbook/online/articles/LL/jcl2.html.

"The Great Battle of Longview: The Other Name for the Race Riots Now Closing in Gregg County." *Dallas Express*, July 19, 1919.

Kitchens, John W., ed. *Tuskegee Institute News Clippings File Microfilm.* Sanford, NC: Microfilming Corporation of America, 1981. Reel 10, Frame 868.

Meier, Augus, ed. *Papers of the NAACP.* Frederick, MD: University Publications of America, 1981.

"Police Work to Keep Lynching a Secret." *Chicago Defender* 14, no. 27 (July 5, 1919): 2.

Tuttle, William M. "Violence in a 'Heathen' Land: The Longview Race Riot of 1919." *Phylon* 33, no. 4 (1972): 324–33.

Los Angeles (California) Riot of 1965

Also known as the Watts Riot or Watts Rebellion, the Los Angeles (California) Riot of 1965 was one of the major racially motivated urban insurrections of the 1960s. The riot lasted five days, 144 hours, from Wednesday, August 11, to Sunday, August 15, 1965. When it was over and the final curfew was lifted, 34 people were dead, thousands were injured, and nearly 4,000 were arrested. Besides the human devastation, millions of dollars of property was damaged and hundreds of buildings were burned to the ground.

The L.A. riot was not the first urban rebellion to occur during the 1960s. A year before the violent disturbance in California, there were riots in Harlem, New York (July 18, 1964), which lasted two days; Rochester, New York (July 24, 1965); and Jersey City (August 2, 1964) and Paterson, New Jersey (August 11, 1964). There were also riots in Philadelphia, Pennsylvania; Chicago, Illinois; St. Augustine, Florida; and Elizabeth, New Jersey. The 1960s was a turbulent decade marked by an insurgent civil rights movement that fought a

battle against segregation and other forms of racial discrimination on many fronts, and a burgeoning antiwar movement that protested American involvement in the Vietnam War.

Beginning in the early 1920s, Los Angeles was a deeply racially divided city. As the economy expanded, Mexicans and African Americans migrated to Los Angeles in hopes of earning a better standard of living, but they were never able to obtain the highest paying jobs. The Stock Market Crash (October 28, 1929) did not improve their circumstances. In fact, because of the economic crisis that ensued, thousands of Mexicans were deported back to Mexico. On December 7, 1941, when the Japanese attacked Pearl Harbor, 120,000 Americans of Japanese descent (40,000 of them from Los Angeles) were sent to internment camps.

World War II launched a period of immediate but temporary growth and prosperity. Because of the war industry, the population of Los Angeles County reached an astounding 4.7 million. And the African American community grew from approximately 75,000 in 1940 to almost 250,000 by 1950, and nearly 500,000 five years before the Los Angeles Riot of 1965. But even during this economic boom, racial tensions did not decrease. On June 3, there was a weeklong clash called the Zoot Suit Riot of 1943 between white off-duty sailors and Mexican American youths. During the course of the riot, American sailors beat and harassed Mexicans and Mexican Americans while the local authorities were reluctant to intervene. Although the African American population continued to increase, African Americans were restricted to living only in certain sections of the city. One of those areas was Watts.

Watts, originally called Mud Town, was an independent, working-class suburb of Los Angeles that was made up mostly of African Americans. It was named after C. H. Watts, a wealthy real estate broker from Pasadena. Watts was annexed by Los Angeles County in 1926, and it was, along with a few other areas of South Los Angeles, where working-class African Americans could rent, and in some cases, own property. Consequently, by the 1940s, the area that we now know as Watts became a predominantly African American community. At the time, adjacent neighborhoods like Florence were completely off limits to blacks. An African American caught walking or driving an automobile through Florence was subject to verbal and physical harassment. In an effort to deal with the influx of African Americans, primarily from the

June 1965: A suspect being searched by two armed police during the Watts race riots in Los Angeles, California. (Harry Benson/Getty Images)

South, the state of California constructed a series of housing projects including Nickerson Gardens, Jordan Downs, and Imperial Courts. Initially, these public housing units were integrated, but by the early 1960s they were almost entirely African American. Los Angeles became one of the most segregated cities in the United States, and once the boom from the war industry was over, the majority of lucrative employment went to European-Americans while non-Europeans, particularly African and Mexican Americans, became increasingly impoverished.

Around 7:00 P.M., on August 11, 1965, a white motorcycle officer, Lee Minikus, was on duty at 122nd Street. Responding to a tip, Officer Minikus pulled over a car driven by a young African American man on the corner of 116th Plaza and Avalon. The officer claimed the driver was going approximately 50 miles per hour in a 30-mile-per-hour zone. The driver of the car was 21-year-old Marquette Frye. His

brother, Ronald, was riding in the passenger seat. Ronald was one year older than his brother and had just been discharged from the Air Force. They were driving their mother's car on their way home after visiting friends. They had two blocks to go when they were pulled over by Officer Minikus. Since Frye admitted to drinking vodka and orange juice, Minikus asked him to step out of the car and proceeded to administer a sobriety test. In the meantime, Ronald ran the two blocks to his mother's house and let her know that Marquette was about to be arrested and her car was going to be impounded. By the time 49-year-old Rena Frye and her son Ronald arrived back on the scene, a crowd of 200 to 300 people had gathered, and Minikus had called for backup.

Initially, Mrs. Frye lashed out at her son for getting caught driving while intoxicated. Angered over his mother's public reprimands, Marquette directed his frustration toward the arresting officer. More and more people began to gather around the scene. Sensing danger, Minikus called for more backup. An altercation broke out between the Frye brothers, their mother, and the police officers. Marquette Frye was hit over the head by Officer Minikus's nightstick and received a gash over his eye. At this point, the police officer threw Frye face-down across the front seat of one of the patrol cars and handcuffed him. Ronald, in an attempt to prevent his brother's arrest, held onto Marquette's legs while Mrs. Frye jumped on the police officer's back. The other officers called to the scene by Officer Minikus now became involved in the struggle. Eventually, around 7:25 P.M., the officers arrested Mrs. Frye and her two sons. As the officers were leaving the scene, someone from the crowd spit at them. By the time the last patrol car drove away, the crowd, which had attracted more people, was on the brink of pandemonium. They began throwing rocks and bottles and anything else within reach at the retreating patrol cars.

After the arrest, the crowd that had gathered to watch the altercation did not disperse. Instead, they separated into small groups and wandered up and down the streets in the vicinity where Officer Minikus had initially stopped Marquette Frye. Around 8:00 P.M., there were reports of scattered outbreaks of violence. White motorists driving through the surrounding area were pulled from their cars and beaten. Others had rocks, bottles, and broken pieces of asphalt thrown at their vehicles. Black pedestrians, who had not witnessed the incident but had heard rumors that white police officers had beaten and brutalized an African American woman, began to attack patrol cars that drove through the community. By 11:00 P.M., three and a half hours after the initial incident, the disturbance had engulfed eight blocks. In response, the Los Angeles Police Department (LAPD) dispatched 100 officers to contain the unrest within the eight-block radius. The fact that the majority of the officers were white only served to infuriate the people of the neighborhood even more, and the disturbance escalated. The crowd went from throwing bricks and bottles and smashing windows to overturning automobiles and setting them on fire. Over 50 cars were burned or severely damaged, including two fire trucks.

At midnight, the police thought the civil disobedience had been brought under control, but by 1:00 A.M., the crowd had grown to over 1,500, which included men, women, and children, and there were intermittent reports of violence

and vandalism until dawn. By then, 34 residents had been arrested and 35 people, including 19 officers, were injured. At 4:00 A.M., on August 12, there were reports of a few random acts of violence but, for the most part, the crowd had dispersed. The news media descended on Watts, but other than the wreckage and wild speculation about what caused the insurrection, there was not much to report.

At 2:00 P.M., the Los Angeles County Human Relations Commission sponsored a meeting of community leaders in Athens Park in a desperate attempt to derail any further possibility of violence by giving residents an opportunity to discuss their troubles and then return to their homes. Because the media had already taken an interest, this was a well-publicized gathering. One of the most repeated headlines was the statement made by a 16-year-old African American who declared that the fire next time would cross the borders separating black and white neighborhoods. A proposal was made to withdraw white officers from the areas where the disturbance had occurred and replace them with plainclothes African American officers in unmarked cars. The proposal was rejected by Deputy Chief of Police Roger Murdock because the suggestion to use only African American officers in predominantly black communities ran counter to Police Department policy. By 6:00 P.M., on Thursday, an estimated 2,000 people had gathered at Athens Park, and the rioting began again.

As the disturbance spun out of control, Police Chief William Parker contacted Lt. Gen. Roderick Hill, the adjutant general of the California National Guard in Sacramento, alerting him that the National Guard might be needed to quell the violence. But the reactions of the LAPD did more to inflame the rioters. Chants of "Burn, baby, burn!" and "Get Whitey!" became the mantra that accompanied Thursday night's violence. And instead of rocks, bricks, and broken pieces of pavement, Molotov cocktails became the weapons of choice. The crude gasoline bombs were tossed at passing cars and used to incinerate buildings. When police and firefighters arrived to extinguish the flames, they were attacked. Under deteriorating conditions, the Emergency Control Center at Police Headquarters was opened at 7:30 P.M., Thursday night. After midnight, numerous angry, rebellious residents gathered in front of Police Headquarters. They were faced down by 500 police officers, deputy sheriffs, and highway patrolmen who used a variety of tactics to disperse the crowd.

By 4:00 A.M., the authorities felt that they had at least temporarily restored order.

At 9:00 A.M., on Friday, August 13, Police Chief Parker and Mayor Sam Yorty requested the intervention of the National Guard, asking for 1,000 troops. From early Friday morning to late Friday night, rioters jammed the streets, burning and looting stores and businesses. Anything that could be employed as a weapon was used, mostly to target white people. Along with other sections of the city, 103rd Street was systematically burned. The LAPD and the Sheriff's Department were no longer able to control the spreading violence.

By 5:00 P.M., Friday evening, 2,000 national guardsmen were on their way to Los Angeles. Two hours later, nearly 1,500 troops were on their way to strategic areas where the worst violence was taking place, but the troops were not actually deployed until 10:00 P.M. Evidently, more troops were needed because by midnight another 1,000 guardsmen were deployed. By midnight Saturday, nearly 14,000 troops were on the streets of Los Angeles.

Even with the arrival of the California National Guard, Friday night, August 13, 1965, was the worst night of violence. According to the McCone Commission Report (December 1965), the first death occurred between 6:00 and 7:00 P.M., when an unnamed African American bystander, trapped on the street between police and rioters, was shot and killed during an exchange of gunfire.

Also on Friday night, the burning and looting moved beyond Watts and spread over a wide area of Southeast Los Angeles. Despite the combined forces of the National Guard, the LAPD, and the Sheriff's Department, the riot had taken on a life of its own. Reports of major incidents of looting, burning, and shooting came at regular intervals. By 1:00 A.M., on Saturday, August 14, 100 engine companies were fighting fires in various areas of the city, but snipers hindered their progress. One fireman was crushed to death under a fallen wall, and a deputy sheriff was killed by friendly fire when another deputy's weapon was accidentally discharged.

When old strategies failed to produce the desired result, the authorities changed tactics. Police made sweeps on foot, moving along the streets in an effort to restore order; they marched shoulder-to-shoulder with the National Guard and members of the Sheriff's Department. However, in spite of these tactics, the disturbance continued throughout Friday night into Saturday morning. At this stage in the disturbance, Lt. Gov. Anderson appeared on television to impose a curfew. While the curfew was in effect, it was against the law for any unauthorized persons to be on the streets in the curfew area after 8:00 P.M.

On Saturday night, after the curfew was imposed, the streets of Watts, with the exception of a few sporadic outbreaks of violence, were quiet, even subdued. On Sunday, it was the same. The curfew was lifted on Tuesday, August 16, and for all intents and purposes the L.A. riot was over. According to the McCone Commission Report, the riot caused 34 deaths and 1,032 injuries. Among the injured were 773 civilians, 136 firemen, 90 police officers, 10 national guardsmen, and 23 individuals from other unspecified government agencies. The L.A. coroner ruled that 26 deaths were justifiable homicides, five were homicides, and one was accidental. In the case of the justifiable homicides, the coroner determined that 16 were caused by the LAPD and seven by the National Guard. Property damage was estimated at $40 million. More than 600 buildings were burned or looted, 200 of these destroyed completely by fire. A total of 3,438 individuals were arrested.

On August 24, California governor Edmund G. Brown appointed a blue ribbon commission headed by John A. McCone, former head of the Central Intelligence Agency, to investigate the riot. The commission's report was issued on December 2, 1965. The report warned that the Los Angeles Riot of 1965 was a curtain-raiser for future violence unless stronger efforts were made to deal with social problems. Some of the recommendations included a literacy program, a large-scale job training and placement program, improved means of processing complaints against the police, and increased mass transit.

During the four decades since the 1965 riot, much has changed and much has stayed the same in Watts. The changes include a new health center, post office, shopping center, savings and loan, and clothing store. However, unemployment hovers around 20 percent, almost three times the national average. More than one-third of the families in Watts live below the poverty line, and the community has the highest infant mortality rate, the lowest rate of immunization, the highest incidence of communicable disease, and the fewest doctors per capita in the country.

Beginning in August 2005, residents and representatives from organizations throughout the community came together to plan the Watts Renaissance, a year-long initiative that seeks to plan solutions to poverty. The people of Watts also host the Watts Summer Festival, which they claim is the oldest African American cultural festival in the United States. Growing out of the ruin and devastation of the 1965 riot, the festival was conceived during the summer of 1966 and incorporated in 1968 with the sole intent of redirecting the energies of the community into tangible, positive solutions and alternatives by developing pride, cultural awareness, and political conscious. It is also a memorial and tribute to the 34 residents who lost their lives in 1965. The Watts Summer Festival has drawn worldwide attention and support, and many African American artists have participated in it, including James Brown, Stevie Wonder, Isaac Hayes, Harmonica Fats, Richard Pryor, Nancy Wilson, Gil Scott-Heron, Barry White, the Watts Prophets, Charles Wright and the Watts 103rd Street Rhythm Band, and the Staple Singers.

The Watts Summer Festival has also received special proclamations and resolutions from the city, county, state, and federal officials. A few of its renowned grand marshals include Muhammad Ali, Coretta Scott King, Myrlie Evers, Dr. Betty Shabazz, Richard Pryor, and the Honorable Maxine Waters.

JOHN G. HALL

See also

Black Panther Party (BPP); Long Hot Summer Riots (1965–1967); Los Angeles (California) Riots of 1992; Malcolm X; Nation of Islam; Race Riots in America. Documents: The Report on the Memphis Riots of May 1866 (July 25, 1866); Account of the Riots in East St. Louis, Illinois (July 1917); The Cook County Coroner's Report Regarding the 1919 Chicago Race Riots (1919); A Southern Black Woman's Letter Regarding the Recent Riots in Chicago and Washington (November 1919); The Final Report of the Grand Jury on the Tulsa Race Riot (June 25, 1921); Testimony from *Laney v. United States* Describing Events during the Washington, D.C., Riot of July 1919 (December 3, 1923); The Governor's Commission Report on the Watts Riots (December 1965); Cyrus R. Vance's Report on the Riots in Detroit (July-August 1967); The Reports of the Oklahoma Commission to Study the Tulsa Race Riot of 1921 (2000-2001); The Draft Report of the 1898 Wilmington Race Riot Commission (December 2005)

Further Reading:

Bullock, Paul. *Watts: The Aftermath: An Inside View of the Ghetto.* New York: Grove Press, 1969.

Governor's Commission on the Los Angeles Riots (McCone Commission). *Violence in the City: An End or a Beginning?* Los Angeles, 1965.

McWilliams, Carey. "Watts: The Forgotten Slum." *The Nation*, August 30, 1965.

Peters, Jennifer. "The Watts Riot: Los Angeles, California 1965." *Race and Ethnic Relations*, November 30, 2004.

Reitman, Valerie, and Mitchell Landsberg. "Watts Riot, 40 Years Later." *Los Angeles Times*, August 11, 2005.

Watts Renaissance Planning Committee. *Watts 40th–Watts Renaissance.*

Los Angeles (California) Riots of 1992

The Los Angeles (California) Riots of 1992, also known as the 1992 L.A. race riots, the Rodney King riots, the Rodney King uprising, or the L.A. rebellion, were sparked on April 29, 1992, when a mostly white jury in suburban Simi Valley found four Los Angeles Police Department (LAPD) Officers (Sgt. Stacey Koon, Officer Theodore Briseno, Officer Timothy Wind, and Officer Laurence Powell) not guilty on various charges related to police brutality. All four officers were accused in the videotaped beating of African American motorist Rodney Glen King. Thousands of people in Los Angeles, mainly young African American and Latino men, joined in the riot, involving mass law-breaking, including looting, arson, and murder. In all, there were 50 to 60 deaths, over 10,000 arrests (that were 88 percent male and 80 percent between the ages of 18 and 34), more than 2,300 injuries, more than 1,000 buildings lost to fires, and an estimated $1 billion in damages. The riot secured a position in public memory as one of "the worst riots of the century" (Coffey 1992: 49).

In addition to the immediate acquittal verdict of the officers in the Rodney King trial that triggered the unrest, there were many other precipitating factors: the 1980s recession enabled high unemployment levels and cultural factors related to hopelessness and alienation among residents of South Central Los Angeles; the establishment of the Christopher Commission that found racial profiling and excessive use of force as a norm in the LAPD, which then led to the truce of the two largest L.A. street gangs, the Crips and the Bloods, wherein both groups worked together to make political demands of the police and the L.A. political establishment; specific anger over the light sentence given to a Korean shop owner for the shooting of Latasha Harlins, a young African American woman; the escalating racial tensions between the quadrilateral network of whites, blacks, Hispanics, and Asians in the South Central Los Angeles region; and the Rodney King beating and moving of the trial venue from Los Angeles to Simi Valley.

The recession of 1980s Reaganomics hit the lower-class areas of Los Angeles hard, especially the demographic of young black men. The area of South Central Los Angeles declined from traditional, highly unionized, high-wage manufacturing jobs and was full of openly negative attitudes toward black workers. The black male joblessness rate in some residential areas of South Central hovered around 50 percent. The rampant unemployment rates in South Central also coincided with 182,000 children under 18 years of age, 46 percent of those living with only one parent, and 10 percent with no parent. Additionally, the national housing budget was cut by more than 50 percent in the 1980s, health care became increasingly unaffordable, and the infant mortality rate in South Central Los Angeles had a poorer rating than many developing nations in Africa and Asia.

In addition, scholars point to the cultural effects of highways that were built through black neighborhoods, effectively demolishing previous cultural landmarks and separating and dividing communities' residents. Others point to the justified anger created from being told to endure and to trust in racist institutions (see Racism). Many sociologists report the preconditions of the L.A. riot as a cultural lag—the effect of one section of society lagging behind another section. The result of cultural lag was referenced in the Kerner Commission Report in 1968, which found that there were two hostile and unequal Americas: one black and one white. It went on to describe that racially segregated black communities' inhabitants are compelled to contend with the condition of alienation and normlessness whereby certain norms, tacts, taboos, and even epistemologies of certain groups are deemed inappropriate or lacking in relation to mainstream thinking. Both culturally and structurally–demographically, South Central Los Angeles was ripe for civil disobedience and disturbance. It contained a critical mass of young males who had no regular occupations, who felt

alienated without pragmatic recourse, and who had the time and physical capacity to engage in a riot and escape, evade, or outmaneuver police repression.

On April 1, 1991, amidst charges against the LAPD of racism and incompetence, L.A. mayor Tom Bradley announced that a commission headed by Warren Christopher, a former diplomat, would evaluate the performance of the LAPD. The commission released a report that found between January 1986 and December 1990, there were 8,274 total allegations from complaints by citizens made against LAPD officers and 24.7 percent of them were allegations of use of excessive force. Most of those complaints came from neighborhoods with concentrations of ethnic minorities, but investigations rarely took place because the decision to investigate was made by police officers themselves. As a result of many of the commission's findings, the two largest L.A. street gangs, the Crips and the Bloods, began meeting to formulate how to end police brutality. On April 26, 1992, just days before the King verdict was released, 60 Crips and Bloods representing gangs from Pomona to Inglewood signed a peace treaty at the Imperial Courts projects.

They later made several demands and offered proposals to the city of Los Angeles to increase educational programs and welfare benefits, and they requested that local drug lords take their monies and invest them in business and property in Los Angeles. This treaty was said by many to later organize portions of the riot into a rebellion, actually structuring and systematizing what was perceived as riot and chaos.

Acrimony between Koreans and African Americans reached a critical mass in a surveillance video that documented the March 16, 1991, incident in which a Korean woman, Soon Ja Du, fatally shot Latasha Harlins, a 15-year-old African American girl. The incident occurred approximately three weeks after the Rodney King beating (see Harlins, Latasha [1976–1991]). The African American community was outraged after Du was sentenced on November 15, 1991, to just five years' probation, community service, and fines as a result of a conviction of voluntary manslaughter.

The patterns of ethnic succession in differing parts of Los Angeles reveal a territorial competition and tension between the four racial groups of whites, blacks, Hispanics, and Asians. Commentators on the eruption of violence emphasize tensions rising from the changing demographics of South Central as building factors to the riots. Los Angeles received a sizable black population during and after World War II. That black population quintupled to about 993,000 by 1990. Yet, during the early 1990s, that growth slowed due to out-migration of blacks to Inglewood, Hawthorne, Downey, Paramount, and Long Beach. As blacks moved out, Hispanics moved in. The northeastern part of South Central Los Angeles was a Hispanic enclave, and the western area beside downtown (the Pico-Union district) became dominated by Salvadorian immigrants.

Additionally, the racial makeup of historically black neighborhoods changed as various aforementioned areas became Hispanic, and Koreans bought formerly black-owned liquor stores and small grocery stores. The Asian population of Los Angeles County more than doubled during the 1980s and, in the historically black areas affected by the riots, the Hispanic population increased 119 percent over the same decade. Economic competition between races in the labor force and in small enterprises provoked more racial animosity; in particular, the 1980s saw downtown Los Angeles's businesses fire most of their black-dominated janitorial staffs and replace them with Latino immigrants earning half the wages paid to their unionized black predecessors. The fracture between Korean-owned businesses and the black residents they served was especially pronounced, as the black community frequently complained of poor treatment by store owners and inflated prices.

On March 3, 1991, at 12:47 A.M., a California Highway Patrol (CHP) dispatch advised that their officers were in pursuit of a white 1988 Hyundai Excel that was refusing to stop. Minutes later, 25-year-old African American motorist Rodney King and two other African Americans (Freddie Helms and Bryant Allen) were stopped in the residential area of Lake View Terrace district by members of the CHP, LAPD, and the Los Angeles Unified School District Police. King, who had a record of drunk driving, was said to have been driving at speeds up to 115 miles per hour. When the police officers ordered him out of the car, he refused. Once he finally exited the car, King threw off four officers who were trying to wrestle him down, and it was then that Koon shot King with a 50,000-volt Taser. Such high voltage was considered to be enough to put a person down, and it was

because of the failure of the Taser that King was believed to be under the influence of PCP (phenylcyclohexylpiperidine), a pain-numbing drug (official test results were negative for PCP, although King's blood alcohol content was said to be twice the legal limit). King rose from the first Taser charge and was hit with a second Taser which brought him to the ground. King again rose and charged toward Officer Laurence Powell, at which point Powell struck him with his police baton. The other three police officers (Koon, Briseno, and Wind) then kicked King and struck him 56 times with nightsticks. In addition to those officers, 24 other law enforcement officers watched the beating. Some of them assisted in holding King down by placing their feet on his back while he was beaten.

The incident was captured on a videotape by a white plumbing company manager, George Holliday. The video, an 81-second surveillance of the event, was delivered to local television station KTLA the next day (March 4) and broadcast that evening locally to the greater Los Angeles viewing area. On March 5, the tape was obtained by CNN and played nationwide. The broadcast captured much of the U.S. public attention. It soon became an international media sensation and a touchpoint for minority activists in Los Angeles and the United States. It also caught the attention of the Federal Bureau of Investigation (FBI), which opened a civil rights inquiry into the King beating. LAPD Chief Daryl Gates wrote as follows in 1992:

> I stared at the screen in disbelief. I played the one-minute-fifty-second [sic] tape again. Then again and again, until I had viewed it twenty-five times. And still I could not believe what I was looking at. To see my officers engaged in what appeared to be excessive use of force, possibly criminally excessive, to see them beat a man with their batons fifty-six times, to see a sergeant on the scene who did nothing to seize control was something I never dreamed I would witness.

On March 7, LAPD Chief Gates announced that Koon, Briseno, Wind, and Powell would be prosecuted. The following day, March 8, District Attorney Ira Reiner announced that he would seek grand jury indictments against the officers. Also that day, it was announced that 15 law enforcement officers present at the scene of the King arrest had been suspended. Several days later, a *Los Angeles Times* poll reported that of those polled who had seen the Holliday videotape, 92 percent thought excessive force had been used against King.

On March 14, a grand jury returned indictments against Koon, Powell, Wind, and Briseno and two days later Judge Bernard Kamins set June 17, 1991, as the opening date for the trial. He denied a motion from the defense for a change of venue out of Los Angeles County, but the defense appealed the denial of their motion to the California Court of Appeals, which unanimously granted the change of venue motion. Judge Kamins was also removed due to an alleged improper ex parte message to prosecutors, and the case was reassigned to Judge Stanley Weisberg.

Supposedly, due to the enormous amount of media coverage and saturation of the story in Los Angeles, the trial was moved to a newly constructed East Ventura County courthouse in predominantly white and conservative Simi Valley in Ventura County, a place where "residents worship the police . . . and one that is politically, racially, and culturally as different from downtown Los Angeles as Manhattan is from the moon" (Pinkney 1993: 44). On February 3, 1992, the trial began with a jury of 10 whites, one Hispanic, and one Filipino-American. Among the jury members, the average age was 51; five were registered in the Republication Party and five in the Democratic Party.

Three were members of the (conservative) National Rifle Association, and three were relatives of police officers. Before the trial, of the 264 potential jurors, the six who were black were excluded from service by peremptory challenges (i.e., no reason had to be given for their exclusion). Contrary to popular belief, no Simi Valley residents served on the jury, which had been empanelled in Los Angeles County; however, the jury was drawn from the nearby San Fernando Valley. The four officers faced charges of official misconduct, excessive force, filing false police reports, and the felony charges of assault with a deadly weapon.

Of note during the trial was how the 81-second Holliday video was broken into scores of individual still pictures, each of which was then subject to endless reinterpretation. Then, since no single picture taken by itself could constitute excessive force, taken together, the videotape as a whole said something different—not incredibly clear evidence of racist police brutality, but instead ambiguous slices of

time in a tense moment that Rodney King had created for the police.

On April 29, 1992 at 3:15 P.M., the jury acquitted Koon, Wind, and Briseno of all charges. The charge of excessive force under the color of authority against Officer Laurence Powell was found inconclusive, resulting in a mistrial on that one count. Various explanations for the verdict were given: from the aforementioned frame-by-frame analysis of the video, to jury lawlessness, the change of venue, or the failure of the defense to properly humanize King to counter the defense's strategy of constantly objectifying him.

The riot, beginning in the evening after the verdict, peaked in intensity over the next two days, but would ultimately continue for several days. Continuous television coverage, especially by helicopter news crews, showed buildings being burned, stores openly looted, so-called innocent bystanders beaten, and rioters shooting at police. Hispanics, blacks, and some whites united against the police; the composition of the riot reflected the composition of the area. Of the first 5,000 arrests "52 percent were poor Latinos, 10 percent whites, and only 38 percent blacks" (Davis 1992). A curfew and deployment of California National Guard troops began to control the situation; eventually federal troops were sent to the city to quell disorder. Many fires broke out at unguarded businesses, as bricks, followed by Molotov cocktails, were thrown through windows. Cars were torched to block intersections, and some vehicles were stolen via carjacking. Allegedly, rescue personnel were fired upon with rifles and handguns. By darkness the first evening, fire officials refused to send firemen into the area for fear of their lives. Smaller, concomitant civil unrest occurred in other U.S. cities due to the King verdict, especially in Las Vegas, Atlanta, and San Francisco, but also including Oakland, New York, Seattle, Chicago, Phoenix, Madison, and even the Canadian city of Toronto.

Wednesday, April 29, at 3:43 P.M., just 28 minutes after the verdict was televised, the LAPD received a report that a young man had thrown a brick at a passing truck at the corner of West 67th Street and 11th Avenue in Hyde Park. Others began to join in the attacks of passing motorists, drawing a crowd that began to move toward shops and markets a few blocks away where looting began. A second disturbance was reported at 4:17 P.M. at Normandie and Florence, where passing vehicles were being pelted with stones, and where whites and light-skinned people were being dragged from their cars, beaten, and robbed.

Concurrently, there were two political protests at the Los Angeles County courthouse and at the Parker Center, the headquarters of the LAPD. By 6:00 P.M., several hundred demonstrators carrying signs gathered at Parker Center and demanded that LAPD chief Daryl Gates resign. However, Gates was not there to address the crowd and later drew sharp rebuke for attending a fundraiser that evening against Proposition F, a proposal for police reform that would put the police under more civic control. Long-established LAPD tactics and procedures held that the opening hours of a riot were critical, and that a full-force response was required. The LAPD did not respond quickly and decisively in the opening hours and suffered persistent criticism as a result. Many of the protestors at the Parker Center were white and carried signs identifying themselves with the Progressive Labor Party or the Revolutionary Communist Party. When the crowd began to break windows of the Parker Center, the police forced them back and they then turned down First Street, smashing automobiles and storefronts. By 10:00 P.M. that evening, rioting was occurring all over the city from the Santa Monica Freeway to Pico Boulevard. The CHP was closing exit ramps on the Harbor Freeway, trying to keep people out of the area on the surface streets. L.A. mayor Tom Bradley declared a local state of emergency and Gov. Pete Wilson ordered the National Guard to activate 2,000 reserve troops.

At 6:30 P.M., Reginald Denny, a white, male driver of an 18-wheel truck that was hauling 27 tons of sand, drove into the intersection of Florence and Normandie. He was unaware of the verdict and stopped at a traffic light, was dragged from his vehicle and severely beaten as news helicopters hovered above recording every blow, including a cinder block dropped on the head of the prostrate Denny. The police never appeared, having been ordered to withdraw for their own safety, although several assailants were later arrested and one was sent to prison. Denny was rescued by black neighbors who, seeing the assault live on television, rushed to the scene, put him in the cab of his truck and drove him to Freeman Memorial Hospital, where he would later recover after brain surgery. Due to the live coverage, Denny remains the best-known victim of the riots. However, Fidel Lopez, a contractor and Guatemalan immigrant, was beaten

on videotape near his home near the same intersection, and Choi Sai-Choi, an immigrant from Hong Kong, was dragged from his car, beaten, and robbed on videotape.

By the second day (Thursday, April 30) the violence appeared widespread and unchecked. Open gun battles were televised as Korean shopkeepers took to using firearms to protect their businesses from crowds of looters. Fire crews began reappearing with police escort. CHP reinforcements were airlifted into various parts of the city. Mayor Bradley declared a state of emergency and announced a dusk-to-dawn curfew. Then-president George H. W. Bush spoke out against the rioting, stating that anarchy would not be tolerated and that he had ordered the U.S. Department of Justice to investigate the possibility of filing federal civil rights charges against the LAPD officers. The *Los Angeles Times* reported that several of the King jurors had fled their homes and that Rodney King had been placed under psychiatric care. Carloads of rioters mobilized, traveling from South Central into Koreatown (between Pico and Santa Monica Boulevards). At night, Korean vigilantes organized to protect their businesses by erecting barricades and mounting armed guards. This had limited success, as by late into that evening, some minimalls in those areas were burned and/or looted.

Additionally, the *Los Angeles Times* reported a breakout of violence in Watts where a crowd of approximately 200 blacks and Latinos smashed through the gates of the Watts Labor Community Action Committee headquarters, an anti-poverty organization set up after the Watts riots (*see* Los Angeles [California] Riot of 1965). Sixteen cars that were used by the committee to shuttle residents to and from shopping centers and medical appointments were burned or vandalized, and a commercial center with a Laundromat, toy store, youth enterprise project, furniture and appliance shop, and food stamp office was also vandalized.

Early the next morning, Friday, May 1, at 1:00 A.M., Gov. Pete Wilson requested federal assistance, but it would not be ready until the following day. State guard units (now doubled from 2,000 to 4,000 troops) continued to move into the city. Additionally, a varied contingent of 1,700 federal law-enforcement officers from different agencies began to arrive to protect federal facilities and assist local police. The most notable event of that day was punctuated by live footage of a shaken Rodney King asking, "People, I just want to say ... can we all get along? Can we get along? ... We'll get our justice. They've won the battle, but they haven't won the war. ... We all can get along. We've just got to, just got to. We're all stuck here for awhile. Let's try to work it out" (Baker 1993: 45). In the evening, as darkness fell, the main riot area was further hit by a large power outage. President George H. W. Bush denounced lawlessness and outlined the federal assistance he was making available to local authorities.

From Saturday, May 2 through Monday, May 4, 4,000 soldiers from the U.S. Army and Marines were deployed from Fort Ord to suppress the crowds and restore order. Calm began to reappear as the federal presence spread. With most of the violence under control, Korean people conducted a march demanding that Koreatown be rebuilt. Whether in response to the riots, or simply the verdict, on May 2, the Department of Justice announced that it would begin a federal investigation of the Rodney King beating.

Overall quiet set in on May 3, and Mayor Bradley assured the public that the crisis was "pretty much under control" (Mydans 1993: 11). However, in an isolated incident, a motorist was shot in an evening encounter with national guardsmen.

Although Mayor Bradley lifted the curfew on May 4, signaling the official end of the rioting, sporadic violence and crime continued for a few days afterward. Schools, banks, and businesses reopened. Federal troops, reluctant to leave residents unprotected, would not stand down until May 9; the state guard remained until May 14; and some soldiers remained as late as May 27.

After the riots, pressure mounted for a retrial of the officers. The acquittals survived appeals in the state courts, but federal charges of civil rights violations were brought against the officers. Near the first anniversary of the acquittal, the city tensely awaited the decision of the federal jury; seven days of deliberations raised speculative fear of an incendiary outcome in the event of a not-guilty verdict. Mindful of accusations of sensationalist reporting following the first jury decision, media outlets opted for more sober coverage, which included calmer on-the-street interviews. Police were fully mobilized with officers on 12-hour shifts, convoy patrols, scout helicopters, street barricades, tactical command centers, and support from the National Guard and Marines.

The federal jury's decision was read at an atypical time of 7:00 A.M. at a Saturday court session on April 17, 1993. The retrial convicted Sgt. Stacey Koon and Officer Laurence Powell for violating Rodney King's civil rights. The jury acquitted Timothy Wind and Theodore Briseno. Federal District Court Judge John Davis sentenced Sergeant Koon and Officer Powell to 30 months in prison, at the Federal Prison Camp at Dublin, California, often used to house so-called white-collar criminals.

Some scholars consider the events of Los Angeles from April 29 to May 4, 1992, more than a riot, regarding it as a rebellion or a revolutionary activity. "These events constituted a 'rebellion,' the explosion of a powder keg of economic, social, and political injustices that had oppressed their communities for years" (Hunt 1997: 2). At times it is referred to as an uprising as an attempt to find a neutral middle ground between rebellion and riot. Some feel that the events, and not the name, should be the focus, "the 'riot,' 'insurrection,' 'rebellion,' 'anarchic criminal chaos'—call it what you will" (Baker 1993: 45). Still, most think the nominal framing of the event has an explicit connection with the meaning-making of the incident.

The techniques utilized to convince the Simi Valley jury of the reasonableness of the use of force on Rodney King are linked to the struggle, in a quite different legal arena, over whether to permit race-conscious, affirmative-action programs; both those arenas are, in turn, related to the conflict over whether to see the events in South Central Los Angeles as an "insurrection," as Rep. Maxine Waters characterized it, or as a "riot" of the "mob," the official version presented in dominant media and by the president of the United States.

Additionally, Los Angeles was a hybrid social revolt with three major dimensions. It was a revolutionary democratic protest characteristic of African American history when demands for equal rights had been thwarted by the major institutions. It was also a major postmodern bread riot—an uprising of not just poor people, but particularly of those strata of poor in Southern California who had been most savagely affected by the recession. Third, it was an interethnic conflict.

All in all, various scholars read the events of 1992 in different ways. Some have argued that the riots drew attention to the continuing importance of race. Others stated that not-guilty verdicts were a reality check for the African

American community in regard to their continued status as second-class citizens, and still others contend the events are often discussed by politicians in reductionist, overly simplified terms with the purpose of winning over the white vote. Despite the difference in how the events are named, interpreted, or represented, most scholars agree that the riots were a wake-up call for continued critique and problem solving in the troubled intersection of race, crime, and justice in the United States.

MATTHEW W. HUGHEY

See also

Los Angeles (California) Riot of 1965; Police Brutality; Race Riots in America; Rodney King Beating (1991). Documents: Report on the Memphis Riots of May 1866 (1866); Account of the Riots in East St. Louis, Illinois (1917); A Southern Black Woman's Letter Regarding the Recent Riots in Chicago and Washington (1919); The Cook County Coroner's Report Regarding the 1919 Chicago Race Riots (1920); The Final Report of the Grand Jury on the Tulsa Race Riot (June 25, 1921); Testimony from *Laney v. United States* (1923); The Governor's Commission Report on the Watts Riots (1965); Cyrus R. Vance's Report on the Riots in Detroit (1967); The Reports of the Oklahoma Commission to Study the Tulsa Race Riot of 1921 (2000–2001); Draft Report: 1898 Wilmington Race Riot Commission (2005)

Further Reading:

Baker, Houston A. "Scene . . . Not Heard." In *Reading Rodney King, Reading Urban Uprising*, edited by Robert Gooding-Williams. New York: Routledge, 1993.

Baldassare, Mark, ed. *The Los Angeles Riots: Lessons for the Urban Future.* Boulder, CO: Westview Press, 2004.

Cannon, Lou. *Official Negligence: How Rodney King and the Riots Changed Los Angeles and the LAPD.* New York: Times Books, 1997.

Coffey, Shelby, III, ed. *Understanding the Riots: Los Angeles Before and After the Rodney King Case.* Los Angeles: *Los Angeles Times*, 1992.

Crenshaw, Kimberle, and Gary Peller. "Reel Time/Real Justice." In *Reading Rodney King, Reading Urban Uprising*, edited by Robert Gooding-Williams. New York: Routledge, 1993.

Davis, Mike. "In L.A., Burning All Illusions." *The Nation* (June 1, 1992).

Gates, Daryl F. *Chief: My Life in the LAPD.* New York: Bantam, 1992.

Hunt, Darnell M. *Screening the Los Angeles "Riots": Race, Seeing, and Resistance.* New York: Cambridge University Press, 1997.

Los Angeles Times Staff. *Understanding the Riots.* Los Angeles: *Los Angeles Times*, 1992.

Matheson, Victor A., and Robert A. Baade. "Race and Riots: A Note on the Economic Impact of the Rodney King Riots." *Urban Studies* 41, no. 13 (December 2004): 2691–96.

Mydans, Seth. "Verdict in Los Angeles; Fear Subsides with Verdict, But Residents Remain Wary." *New York Times*, April 19, 1993, Section B, Column 1, 11.

Oliver, Melvin L., and James H. Johnson Jr. "Inter-Ethnic Conflict in an Urban Ghetto: The Case of Blacks and Latinos in Los Angeles." *Research in Social Movements, Conflict and Change* 6 (1984): 57–94.

Pinkney, Alphonso. "Rodney King and Dred Scott." In *Why L.A. Happened: Implications of the '92 Los Angeles Rebellion*, edited by Haki R. Madhubuki. Chicago: Third World Press, 1993.

Pollard, Gail. "Latinos Bring Racial Mix to Boil." *Guardian* (London) (May 1, 1992): 7.

Rosenberg, Howard. "Los Angeles TV Shows Restraint." *Chicago Sun-Times*, April 19, 1993, Section 2, 22.

Staten, Clark. "L.A. Police Acquitted, Rioting Strikes S.E. Los Angeles." In Emergencynet NEWS Service (ENN). *Three Days of Hell in Los Angeles.* Chicago: Emergency Response & Research Institute, April 29, 1992.

Tisdall, Simon, and Christopher Reed. "All Quiet on the Western Front after King Verdicts." *Guardian* (London) (April 19, 1993): 20.

Los Angeles Chinatown Massacre of 1871

The Los Angeles race riot of October 24, 1871, also known as the Chinese Massacre, was an act of mob violence by white citizens of Los Angeles against Chinese immigrants. Xenophobia over the arrival of Chinese immigrants in California had been previously concentrated in San Francisco and other areas of northern California, which was home to a far greater number of Chinese. It was the violence in Los Angeles, however, that brought nationwide attention to the anti-Chinese movement in California, which led to passage of the Chinese Exclusion Act in 1882.

The Chinese population in Los Angeles at the time of the riot was relatively small (barely 200) but had grown considerably during the 1860s. The unstable economic conditions in the region, along with the willingness of the Chinese to work at low-paying jobs for long hours, produced tension between many Californians and the Chinese immigrants.

Still, Los Angeles had experienced less of this tension than San Francisco, and the city sent no representatives to an anti-Chinese convention held in San Francisco in August 1870.

In Los Angeles, many Chinese lived on a street known as Calle de los Negros, or "Nigger Alley." Helping the Chinese adapt to American life, there were immigrant associations known as tongs. The tongs created social connections and helped with job procurement, but some were involved with organized crime. Los Angeles at the time was known for its lawlessness, its police force ineffective against a rapidly growing population. Lending to the atmosphere of intolerance was a law passed by the California legislature during the height of the Civil War in 1863. The law stated that a Chinese victim of a crime (as well as other groups from the Asian continent) could not testify in favor or against a white perpetrator in a civil or criminal case. This had the effect of placing the Chinese outside the court system and gave sway to any white person wanting to commit a crime against these immigrants.

The race riot began as a dispute between two tongs over a woman. A mounted policeman who attempted to restore order was caught in the crossfire and shot and killed by one of the Chinese men. That action produced a frenzy among white men. A participant later wrote of his shock that "Chinese had dared to fire on whites, and kill with recklessness outside their own color set." In the five hours after the shooting, a mob estimated at 500 whites gathered and murdered roughly 20 Chinese men and boys, many by lynching.

Sheriff James F. Burns and other prominent residents unsuccessfully tried to calm the angry crowd. Of the 11 white men who tried to help protect the Chinese and stop the rioting, one was shot. Throughout the city, many whites hid Chinese in their homes in the event the riot expanded outside of what would later become Los Angeles's Chinatown. The entire incident focused national attention on Los Angeles and forced a grand jury inquiry. While anti-Chinese sentiment in the northern parts of the state certainly contributed to the riot, the grand jury also found that ineffective law enforcement and the Wild West atmosphere in 19th-century Los Angeles were also factors.

Nonetheless, the riot brought nationwide attention to Chinese immigration to the United States. By 1876, the anti-Chinese movement in Los Angeles had begun in earnest, as the local economy deteriorated and Chinese immigration to the area increased with the construction of a railroad between San Francisco and Los Angeles. In 1882, the Chinese Exclusion Act became law, suspending immigration from China.

ABC-CLIO

See also

Baraka, Amiri; Race Riots in America. Documents: Report on the Memphis Riots of May 1866 (1866); Account of the Riots in East St. Louis, Illinois (1917); A Southern Black Woman's Letter Regarding the Recent Riots in Chicago and Washington (1919); The Cook County Coroner's Report Regarding the 1919 Chicago Race Riots (1920); The Final Report of the Grand Jury on the Tulsa Race Riot (June 25, 1921); Testimony from Laney v. United States (1923); The Governor's Commission Report on the Watts Riots (1965); Cyrus R. Vance's Report on the Riots in Detroit (1967); The Reports of the Oklahoma Commission to Study the Tulsa Race Riot of 1921 (2000–2001); Draft Report: 1898 Wilmington Race Riot Commission (2005)

Further Reading:

Dorland, C. P. "Chinese Massacre at Los Angeles in 1871." *Historical Society of Southern California*, vol. 3, 1894.

Lowery, Joseph (b. 1928)

A confidant of Martin Luther King, Jr. and prominent pastor in the Southern Christian Leadership Conference (SCLC), Joseph Echols Lowery played a key role in the peak years of the civil rights movement in Alabama. He was born in Huntsville, Alabama, in 1928, and spent part of his youth in Chicago. He attended Knoxville College and Alabama A&M College from 1939 to 1942. Lowery was an avid student of divinity and Christianity, studying theology at Paine Theological Seminary in Augusta, Georgia, and the Chicago Ecumenical Institute. In 1952, he was ordained as a pastor in the United Methodist Church, a denomination that partnered with thriving African American congregations since the 19th century. As pastor of the Warren Street Methodist Church of Mobile, Lowery used his position to advance a program of social justice and civil rights for African Americans in the South.

Alabama stood as one of the most racially divided states in the South, as nearly every aspect of life, including public

Southern Christian Leadership Conference president Joseph E. Lowery during an interview in his Atlanta office, July 19, 1985. (AP Photo/Ric Feld)

accommodations, cemeteries, political parties, and education, were strictly segregated. After the *Brown v. Board of Education* decision, political leaders in Alabama had pledged to resist desegregation for as long as they could. Despite the ruling, throughout Alabama, blacks were routinely threatened with violence or were victimized by police action for challenging Jim Crow.

In 1957, Lowery was asked to join Martin Luther King, Jr. and Ralph Abernathy in the founding of the SCLC. Based in Alabama, Lowery served as the vice president of the organization, and his leadership was vital to its early success. Lowery and Abernathy knew the political landscape better than most black preachers, as they had been born, raised, educated, and lived in the state for much of their lives. Lowery

helped the SCLC navigate the most contentious aspects of Jim Crow in Alabama, understanding that some cities and constituencies were more open to nonviolent civil action than others. Lowery's public role as the vice president of the SCLC led to the consolidation of political power in black congregations, direct challenges to diffident white ministers, petitions to the city governments of Montgomery and Birmingham, and the long-term organization of the nonviolent protests of black residents of the state.

Lowery's leadership in the SCLC also put him at considerable risk of retaliation from the white institutions he challenged. Most notably, Lowery and three other preachers, Abernathy, Fred Shuttlesworth, and S. S. Seay, were the defendants in a lawsuit initiated by the attorney general of the state of Alabama in 1962. At issue was an advertisement appearing in the *New York Times* urging readers to donate to the Martin Luther King Legal Defense Fund in April 1962. The city government of Montgomery claimed that the four preachers, whose names appeared in the margins of the ad, had libeled the city for targeting King with racist intentions. In a landmark case, *Sullivan v. New York Times* (1964), Lowery and the other ministers were vindicated by the U.S. Supreme Court, which had overturned an earlier ruling for the plaintiff, Police Commissioner L. B. Sullivan. Though the original judgment was upheld by the Alabama State Court, the Supreme Court found that the ruling violated the free speech rights of the four ministers and the First Amendment rights of the *New York Times*. The state of Alabama returned to Lowery all of his personal assets and property, which totaled nearly $100,000.

His position in the SCLC provided critical moral and logistic support to the Birmingham campaign in 1963 and the Selma marches in 1965. In order to expose the injustice of segregation in Birmingham, Lowery was joined by Shuttlesworth, E. D. Nixon, King, and other prominent ministers in the SCLC, who made the crucial decision to launch Project C, the Children's Crusade, in the spring of 1963. Project C organized African American youth for nonviolent marches challenging the segregation in Birmingham. With segregation viciously enforced by Sheriff "Bull" Connor, the nationally broadcast images of police dogs and water cannons turned on teenagers were critical to public condemnation and Birmingham's eventual capitulation to the desegregation efforts.

In 1965, Lowery moved to Birmingham, where he served as the pastor for the St. Paul's Methodist Church and an organizer in the Alabama Christian Movement for Human Rights. He then moved to Atlanta in 1968, and for the next 18 years, he was the head pastor at the Central Methodist Church, a predominantly black congregation whose donations raised enough funds to establish its own housing complex for low-income residents. After a divisive battle over the aims and future development of the SCLC, in 1977, Lowery became the president of the organization. With Lowery as its leader, the SCLC confronted ongoing problems left in the wake of Jim Crow, such as lackluster interest in voting, economic disempowerment, and apartheid.

Lowery has maintained his steady commitment to civil rights and social justice issues. He founded the Lowery Center for Justice and Human Rights at Clark Atlanta University. He maintains a rigorous schedule as a lecturer and activist in Atlanta.

NIKKI BROWN

See also
Southern Christian Leadership Conference (SCLC)

Further Reading:

Branch, Taylor. *Parting the Waters: America in the King Years, 1954–1963*. New York: Simon and Schuster, 1988.

Fairclough, Adam. *To Redeem the Soul of America: The Southern Christian Leadership Conference and Martin Luther King, Jr.* Athens: University of Georgia Press, 1987.

Lowery Institute for Justice and Human Rights. http://www .loweryinstitute.org (accessed May 24, 2008).

Russell, Thaddeus. "Joseph Lowery." In *Encyclopedia of African-American Culture and History*, 1344–45. Detroit, MI: Thomson Gale, 2006.

Lowndes County Freedom Organization (LCFO)

On March 1, 1965, 39 black residents of Lowndes County, Alabama, gathered at the county courthouse and attempted to register to vote. Predictably, the county's racist voting registrars turned them away. At the time, not a single black resident of the county was registered to vote. Indeed, in this poverty-plagued rural hamlet located in the heart of the Alabama Black Belt, the exclusion of African Americans from the political process was absolute. To coordinate future voter registration tries, 28 local people met secretly on March 19 and formed the Lowndes County Christian Movement for Human Rights (LCCMHR). Days later, LCCMHR members partnered with a cadre of Student Nonviolent Coordinating Committee (SNCC) field secretaries headed by veteran Mississippi organizer Stokely Carmichael. Carmichael had used the Selma to Montgomery March, which passed through Lowndes for the better part of three days beginning on March 22, to make known SNCC's interest in helping the county's black residents organize.

Throughout the summer of 1965, Carmichael and his team of organizers assisted a group of dedicated local activists, led by LCCMHR chairman John Hulett, a 37-year-old black landowner, in coordinating a grassroots voter registration

717 Lucy, Autherine (b. 1929)

campaign. By the end of July, they had succeeded in getting more than 1,000 African Americans, or over 20 percent of the county's eligible black voters, to file voter registration applications. White intransigence, however, remained high, prompting the county's registrars to reject almost every application received. Fortunately, on August 14, federal registrars sent by the U.S. Department of Justice in compliance with the Voting Rights Act arrived, enabling more than 40 percent of the county's eligible black voters to register by October 1965.

The reenfranchisement of African Americans prompted activists working in Lowndes to discuss the most effective use of black votes. Carmichael, who had not forgiven the Democratic Party for refusing to support the Mississippi Freedom Democratic Party's attempt to replace Mississippi's prosegregation delegates at the 1964 Democratic National Convention, suggested to Lowndes residents that they make use of an obscure Alabama law to form their own countywide political party. In December 1965, after attending a series of workshops at the SNCC's Atlanta headquarters designed to teach local activists about the mechanics of county government and Alabama election law, John Hulett announced plans to form the politically independent Lowndes County Freedom Organization (LCFO). He explained that the LCFO would field a full slate of black candidates for local office in the November 1966 general election. For a ballot symbol, Lowndes activists chose a snarling black panther because, as they put it, cats chase roosters, and a rooster was the symbol of Alabama Democrats. Incidentally, in October 1966, two community college students in Oakland, California, Huey P. Newton and Bobby Seale, adopted the LCFO ballot symbol as their own, naming their newly formed civil rights group the Black Panther Party for Self-Defense.

In May 1966, nearly 1,000 LCFO supporters nominated seven working-class men and women as candidates for sheriff, tax collector, tax assessor, coroner, and school board. Significantly, the success of the nomination convention catapulted Stokely Carmichael to the chairmanship of SNCC. It also convinced SNCC members to make the formation of grassroots political parties the basis of their new organizing program, which Carmichael introduced to the nation as Black Power during James Meredith's March Against Fear in June 1966.

Despite six months of intense organizing, the LCFO's candidates lost in November. Voter fraud and intimidation contributed significantly to their defeat. White landowners, for instance, used the threat of eviction to compel hundreds of black sharecroppers to vote for white candidates. Nevertheless, the LCFO polled 40 percent of the total vote, a remarkable feat for an upstart third party.

In 1970, the LCFO, which had been renamed the Lowndes County Freedom Party after its strong showing in the 1966 general election, merged with the LCFO-inspired National Democratic Party of Alabama, an independent, statewide party supported mainly by Black Belt African Americans and left-leaning whites. That same year, Lowndes County's black residents elected three of their own to county government, including John Hulett to the sheriff's office. Black residents successfully placed an increasing number of independent candidates in the county courthouse throughout the early and mid-1970s, and black Democrats starting in the late 1970s. By 1980, African Americans occupied a majority of the offices in the county courthouse, a tribute to the experiment in independent politics launched 15 years earlier.

HASAN K. JEFFRIES

See also
Racial Gerrymandering; Voter ID Requirements

Further Reading:
Carmichael, Stokely, with Ekwueme Michael Thelwell. *Ready for Revolution: The Life and Struggles of Stokely Carmichael (Kwame Ture)*. New York: Scribner, 2003.

Carson, Clayborne. *In Struggle: SNCC and the Black Awakening of the 1960s*. Cambridge, MA: Harvard University Press, 1981.

Lucy, Autherine (b. 1929)

Autherine Lucy was the first African American to attend the University of Alabama. Born in October 1929 and raised in Shiloh, Alabama, Autherine Juanita Lucy was the youngest of 10 children born to Minnie Maud Hosea and Milton Cornelius Lucy. The Lucy family resided on a 110-acre farm in Shiloh, and escaped much of the desperation of the Great Depression by raising cotton, watermelons, and sweet potatoes. Lucy attended public school in the Shiloh area, and graduated from high school shortly after World War II. She continued her education at two historically black institutions, Selma University and Miles College. She graduated from Miles College in 1952 with a BA in English. Lucy's tremendous feat of desegregating university education in Alabama began when she decided to pursue another BA in 1952, in library science.

She applied in 1952, with her friend from Miles College, Pollie Myers, a student and civil rights activist. The University of Alabama initially accepted the two women for admission, apparently without realizing they were African American. The University of Alabama, however, maintained a policy of rejecting the applications of African Americans solely on the basis of race. When the university realized its mistake, under pressure from the Alabama White Citizens Council, it withdrew its offer of admission. Lucy and Myers approached the National Association for the Advancement of Colored People (NAACP) with their case, and they were assigned its top attorneys, Thurgood Marshall, Constance Baker Motley, and Arthur Shores. The NAACP team sued the university, and three years later, Judge Harlan Hobart Grooms of the federal District Court ruled on *Myers and Lucy v. Adams* (1955) in favor of the plaintiffs. It was just two months after the U.S. Supreme Court desegregated public schools in the *Brown v. Board of Education* decision. The University of Alabama reinstated its acceptance to Lucy, but denied admission to Myers. Lucy enrolled in February 1956.

However, Lucy's matriculation at the University of Alabama was not the end of her journey. Indeed, the most troubling part of her experience lay ahead when she began attending classes. The University of Alabama gave her little help in securing room, board, and books. White students resented her presence in the classroom, while hate groups and white supremacists phoned in bomb threats and burned crosses on the university campus and on her attorney's lawn. In some of her classes, the other students were also of little help. Some declined to sit next to her, and angry mobs of students followed her to her class. In other classes, such as children's literature, she was politely, and sometimes warmly, greeted by fellow students. Eager to chronicle the story, reporters and photographers also trailed Lucy, adding to the chaotic atmosphere. Lucy's first day had ended without serious incident, but trouble mounted, as parents,

students, and groups not associated with the university grew increasingly hostile.

On February 6, Lucy's third day as a student, she required a full-time police escort to walk her to and from classes. After each class, a violent and angry mob awaited her, throwing rotten eggs and gravel at her. One mob chanted, "Let's kill her!" Another mob vowed to lynch her to "Keep 'Bama white!" Fueled by the Ku Klux Klan and other hate groups, crowds swelled across the campus, threatening Lucy's education at the school and, eventually, her life.

The University of Alabama suspended Lucy on the evening of February 6, for her protection and for the protection of the other students. On February 29, the NAACP filed a lawsuit against the University of Alabama, arguing that the university had not shielded Lucy from danger. In effect, the lawsuit claimed that the university acted in collusion with the mobs to drive Lucy out of the school. The NAACP was unable to prove its case and later withdrew the lawsuit. In retaliation, the university expelled Lucy for slander. Though the NAACP could have contested the decision, the entire episode exhausted Lucy, and she declined to pursue it. In March 1956, her attorney, Thurgood Marshall, invited Lucy to stay with his family in New York to recover from the ordeal.

Lucy married Hugh Foster in April 1956, and moved with him to Texas. In the first year of their marriage, she remained active in the civil rights movement; she traveled the country and frequently lectured about her time as a student at the University of Alabama. She was unable, however, to find a teaching position for many years. Her family settled first in Texas, but they later moved to Louisiana and then Mississippi. In 1974, Lucy Foster, her husband, and her five children relocated to Birmingham, Alabama, where she worked as a substitute teacher.

Her fortunes took a surprising turn in early 1988. Invited to speak at the University of Alabama about her experience 35 years earlier, Lucy was asked afterward whether she would ever pursue her education again at the university. She answered that she would consider it, but the expulsion on her record had virtually nullified the possibility. An emergency petition to the university, then the Board of Trustees, resulted in the overturning of her expulsion in spring 1988. She entered the University of Alabama in fall 1989 as a graduate student in elementary education. In May 1992, Lucy graduated with an MA in elementary education; she was joined in the commencement ceremonies by her daughter, Grazia Foster, who earned a BA in corporate finance.

The University of Alabama named an endowed professorship in honor of Lucy, and a portrait is on display at the Ferguson Center, the student union of the university. The 40 years between Lucy's initial enrollment and her eventual graduation signify two important themes in Jim Crow: the tremendous courage of ordinary citizens who challenged institutionalized racism, and the time it takes to rectify the damages caused by decades of Jim Crow.

NIKKI BROWN

See also

College Admissions, Discrimination in; School Segregation

Further Reading:

Carter, Dan T. *The Politics of Rage: George Wallace, the Origins of the New Conservatism, and the Transformation of American Politics.* Baton Rouge: Louisiana State University Press, 2000.

Clark, E. Culpepper. *The Schoolhouse Door, Segregation's Last Stand at the University of Alabama.* New York: Oxford University Press, 1995.

Lynching

One of the most shameful chapters in the great epic that is American history is the lynching of African Americans. Although used against every race, ethnicity, and both genders, by the late 19th century it had become a code word for the random and wanton murdering of blacks, especially black men. As such, generations of blacks grew up knowing that their lives could be snuffed out for the most trivial of reasons or no reason at all.

The National Association for the Advancement of Colored People (NAACP), the first national organization to catalog and study lynching, defined it as the illegal killing of a person by three or more people claiming to be serving the cause of justice or upholding tradition. The venerable *Chicago Tribune* began tracking lynchings in the late 19th century. It reported that there were 4,951 lynchings in the United States from the years 1882 through 1930; they had been reported in every state of the union except Connecticut, Maine, Massachusetts, Nebraska, Nevada, Rhode Island, Vermont, Washington, and Wisconsin. Of the victims,

3,513 were black and 1,438 were white; 92 were women and 76 of those women were black. Eighty-two percent of the recorded lynchings occurred in the 11 states of the former Confederacy. Yet mob violence in America was not new to the post-Reconstruction era.

The use of mob violence in America can be traced back to colonial times. The mob acted as finders of fact and assessors of guilt. Mob violence was especially popular during the Revolutionary period; because of the excesses of British authority, many colonists had lost respect for regular law and order. After the Revolution, this kind of mob violence gradually fell out of favor in more settled regions of the country.

Within the dynamics of the mob, there is a sense of anonymity that permits members of the mob to lose themselves within it. Because of this, there is often confusion about what exactly has taken place; it is easy for members of the mob to draw erroneous conclusions. Moreover, while there is often a supposed leader within the mob, the leader, too, often loses perspective of the situation and is easily swept up in activities in which that particular person might not participate under normal circumstances.

Lynching as a means of punishment was also very common during the antebellum years. Thieves, gamblers, and others who were considered deviants in the West and South were often hanged for their crimes. Deviant behavior was not the only reason lynchings flourished during this time period: the system of justice in the southern and western portions of the United States was often pitifully slow; therefore, mob violence was often employed.

Those people who were lynched during the antebellum years, however, were much more likely to be whites or free blacks. Slaves were seldom killed; they represented a considerable monetary investment to their masters. It was probably abolitionists who were the first group to see lynching as extralegal violence that was directly connected with the racism that caused slavery and the intimidation and coercion that was so much a part of the institution. Abolitionists also pointed out that the Southern code of honor and the protection and preservation of white feminine virtue combined to make Southern men quick to respond to real or perceived violations of either.

Ironically, the increasing effectiveness of the abolitionist movement and Nat Turner's rebellion were important elements in the revival of lynch law in settled areas. Southern

---

Leo Frank (d. 1915)

The April 26, 1913, murder of Mary Phagan, a 12-year-old girl employed in an Atlanta factory, initiated a sensational chain of events culminating in the lynching of Leo Frank, the man convicted of this crime but who was probably innocent. This bloody incident has been the subject of books, articles, films, exhibits, and a musical. It is of historical significance because bound up in these two murders and the reactions to them are the central tensions, changes, and conflicts that the American South experienced in the early 20th century: industrialization and class conflict, anti-Semitism, new racial stereotypes and etiquette, discomfort with newcomers from the North, and changing gender roles and work roles for females.

The murder of a young girl who had to work in a factory outraged the public. Leo Frank, a Jew from New York, was superintendent of the factory in which Mary Phagan worked and was killed. He and six Georgians were arrested, and with little evidence the prosecutor put Frank on trial. During and after the trial, anti-Semitic rhetoric flowed, led by Tom Watson, who was well known for his hatred of blacks and Jews. Frank was convicted and sentenced to death. While appealing the verdict, threats on his life made it necessary to transfer him from Atlanta to a prison in Milledgeville, Georgia. After hearing evidence that cast doubt on the verdict, Gov. John Slaton commuted Frank's sentence to life in prison. This enraged those who believed Frank guilty and wanted him to die. On August 17, 1915, a group calling themselves the Knights of Mary Phagan abducted Frank from prison, brought him to Marietta, and lynched him. This case soon led to organizing along very different directions: the Anti-Defamation League of B'nai B'rith gained support in its fight against anti-Semitism, while the Ku Klux Klan was revived to defend white Protestant Americans against perceived threats. Much later, in 1986, Georgia posthumously pardoned Frank.

CHARLES JARET

---

whites lived in terror that slave insurrections, some of which were encouraged by abolitionists, could occur at any time. These fears presaged the institution of more severe penalties for slaves who disobeyed their masters' orders or attempted to escape, and the whites, free blacks, or mulattos who helped them.

Extensive use of mob violence as an extralegal instrument of justice again flourished during the later portion of the 19th century as frontier America was being settled. In areas where tools of justice such as the constable, courts, and jails had yet to be established, it was natural that extralegal methods to ensure that justice would be realized would be employed. This extralegal violence was often directed at Indians, and widespread prejudice against Native Americans ensured that public reaction was such that whites were seldom punished for this activity. Organized, semipermanent bodies of citizens often came together to suppress crime and enforce community standards and the law. As the West developed, legal means of social control did also, and mob violence was less likely to be employed. Lynchings in this area of the country gradually tapered off during the last third of the 19th century.

However, just the opposite happened during this period in the South. The number of lynchings of blacks by whites actually increased during this period, and the manner in which they were carried out became more barbarous as the 19th century drew to a close. Race prejudice was clearly a factor in the number of blacks lynched in the United States. The institution of slavery was based on the idea that blacks were inferior to whites in every way; blacks could not have been enslaved if this were not true. The South's loss of the Civil War was particularly galling to white Southerners, and their views on the inferiority of blacks were heightened because of that loss.

Reconstruction was the first time the federal government moved to protect the rights of African Americans; in the decade after the Civil War, a flurry of federal legislation was passed. In 1865, the Bureau of Freedmen, Refugees, and Abandoned Lands helped slaves resettle, find jobs, and gain an education, and the Thirteenth Amendment to the Constitution, which outlawed slavery, was passed. A strengthened Freedmen's Bureau Bill and the Civil Rights Act of 1866 granted blacks citizenship and entitled them to the protection of the federal government. The Fourteenth Amendment to the Constitution, passed in 1868, strengthened the Civil Rights Act of 1866. Especially galling to white Southerners was the passage of the First Reconstruction Act in March 1867. Passed over President Andrew Johnson's veto, it divided the South into five military districts, each under the command of a general. These military personnel protected the lives and property of blacks until new civilian governments could be passed. Two laws were passed in 1870. The Fifteenth Amendment prohibited discrimination in voting based on race, color, or previous condition of servitude; the Enforcement Act of that year prohibited the wearing of masks or disguises, and protected the civil rights of citizens. The Ku Klux Klan (KKK) or Enforcement Act of 1871—Southerners called it the Force Act—made it a federal crime to interfere with an individual's right to vote, serve on a jury, hold public office, or enjoy the equal protection of the law.

Clearly, for a short time after the Civil War, the federal government, under the leadership of radical Republicans, worked actively to promote and ensure black rights. But the giants of radical Republicanism who had done so much to extend and protect African Americans' rights were passing from the scene. By 1870, Thaddeus Stevens had died, Benjamin Wade had been defeated in his bid for reelection, and Charles Sumner had been stripped of much of his congressional power. The Civil Rights Act of 1875, which prohibited racial discrimination in public accommodations, transportation, places of amusement, and public schools, was the last piece of legislation designed to help African Americans until well into the 20th century.

In the midterm elections of 1874, the Democrats won control of the House of Representatives for the first time since 1861. The Democratic Party, with its solid Southern base, moved quickly to solidify the results of the midterm election. Competition for jobs between poor whites and black men gave the Democratic party an opportunity to appeal to the economic fears of poor whites. The party also used psychological and economic intimidation against those blacks who tried to vote. Its best weapon, though, was a resurgent Ku Klux Klan. The Klan often operated with the tacit approval and assistance of officials in the Democratic Party.

It was the presidential election of 1876, though, that rang the death knell for Reconstruction and resurrected the crime of lynching. Republicans nominated Ohio Gov. Rutherford B. Hayes; the Democrats ran Samuel Tilden, famed

African American Chandler Colding hangs from a branch of a tree near Ocala, Florida, on January 26, 1926. A mob of 250 men had stormed the sheriff's office and seized Colding, who was accused of raping a 77-year-old white woman. Lynching, the putting to death (usually by hanging) of an individual by a mob under the pretense of administering justice, occurred throughout the United States in the 19th and 20th centuries, although it was especially common in the South. From the 1880s until the practice ended in the 1960s, the vast majority of lynching victims were African American. (UPI-Bettmann/Corbis)

prosecutor of the corrupt Boss Tweed ring in New York City. Tilden won a majority of the popular votes, but the electoral vote was close because both candidates claimed victory in Florida, Louisiana, and South Carolina. Congress established an electoral commission of 15 members, five each from the House, Senate, and U.S. Supreme Court. Voting 8–7 along party lines, the commission awarded the disputed electoral votes to Hayes. Democrats threatened a filibuster, and an informal agreement, the so-called Compromise of 1877, was reached. Hayes's supporters agreed to withdraw troops from the South and not to block the formation of all-white governments; southern Democrats agreed to deal fairly with black Americans.

Although Republicans kept their part of the agreement, Democrats did not. Upon the withdrawal of Northern troops from Louisiana and South Carolina, their Republican governments collapsed, and white Democrats took over. By the close of the 19th century, virtually all of the Reconstruction-era laws designed to give equal opportunity to blacks and wipe out racial discrimination were repudiated by states' rights supporters and conservative judges. By 1880, black Southerners had been stripped of their legal and civil rights and abandoned by the U.S. government. Emboldened by this lack of government oversight, the governments of the 11 states of the Confederacy set about returning to lives that were as close to pre-Civil War conditions as possible, and lynching quickly became the preferred way of dealing with blacks who dared resist.

Mob violence differed in various regions of the country. In the South, those who participated in lynchings and mob violence were likely to be a cross-section of their communities: public officials, members of the Ku Klux Klan, the poor, and the working class. Moreover, in the South it was not uncommon for entire black communities to be destroyed during mob violence, especially if members of the communities fought back. In the Northern and Midwestern portions of the country, whites who participated in lynchings and mob violence were less likely to be from the middle and upper classes, nor did law enforcement and officials of the criminal justice system participate as often and on the same scale as in the South. Although Klan membership in some Northern and Midwestern states was high, there does not appear to be a strong link between that membership and participation in lynching and mob violence.

Whites used many excuses for the lynching of blacks. Among the most common was the need to protect white women from sexually depraved black men. However, if this were true, a few lynchings would have been enough to make the point. Other excuses included real or perceived transgressions against the social order, the inability of the criminal justice system to function properly, and a callousness toward black life that allowed killing blacks as a sport. Irrefutable empirical evidence, however, shows that lynching was aimed primarily at blacks who possessed the characteristics of the New Negro: they failed to pay sufficient deference to whites,

excelled economically and socially, and dared to assert their rights under the laws and the Constitution. Each year, the number of lynchings and the extreme cruelty with which they were carried out increased. It was not enough merely to kill the victims; they were often tortured before death and their bodies mutilated afterward. Victims were beaten, set afire, had their extremities cut off; one pregnant woman was lynched hanging by her feet, burned afterward, and had the baby she was carrying cut from her womb, after which its head was crushed by the mob. There can only be one explanation for this kind of behavior: race hatred.

By the last decade of the 19th century, lynchings were so common as to have their various elements ritualized. The accusation of wrongdoing, the rush to judgment by whites, the gathering of the crowd, the hunting down of the victim, and the discussion of how the victim would be killed all had a purpose. Eventually, killing would not be enough; a spectacle to which the public would be invited was needed, even a special vocabulary was developed: *Negro barbeque* and *necktie party* were among the most common phrases used to describe lynchings.

By the close of the 19th century, lynching had morphed from merely a way to punish criminals and those who transgressed the social order to the savage and depraved way that whites used to maintain their racial caste system.

White Southerners gave myriad reasons for why they lynched blacks with such impunity: they were upholding the Southern code of honor, protecting the chastity of white women, enforcing communal values. Even Progressive reformers such as Jane Addams did not decry lynching so much as express contempt for the lawlessness it represented. Many whites simply accepted lynching as an occasional happening and the price Southern society paid for the social engineering of Reconstruction and black depravity; they only spoke critically of it when it was carried out in an exceptionally brutal manner.

Lynching began to be seriously studied in the early 20th century, partly in response to the tremendous increase in its numbers from 1880 through 1900. These early researchers were psychologists who were especially concerned with the concept of social pathology; that is, society, made up as it is of individuals, was sick and acted out its illnesses by engaging in deviant behavior. Those explanations faltered, however, since in many lynchings, the leaders of the community and law enforcement played active roles; society's leaders are not generally looked upon as deviant or depraved.

Psychologists also theorized that individual psychopathologies could explain lynching. By the 1890s, the frenzy with which the mob carried out lynchings—its use of lynchings as entertainment spectacles, the mutilation of the victims, and the focus on black sexuality as the primary explanation of lynching—were all a means of allowing the mob to vent its frustration, anger, and resentment over a rapidly changing economic and social system. Because poor whites could not challenge the white elites of Southern society, their frustration could only be relieved by targeting the one group of people that was considered beneath contempt.

African American leaders vociferously disagreed with various white theorists about why lynching occurred and vehemently protested against lynching. It was they who conducted the first empirical studies of the crime, challenging the myths whites had spun. One of the most famous black critics of lynchings was Ida B. Wells-Barnett.

Born a slave in Holly Springs, Mississippi, in 1862, Wells-Barnett grew up during Reconstruction. As a child, she witnessed her father casting his first vote. Orphaned at 16 and left with the responsibility of raising her siblings, Wells-Barnett had to give up her dream of finishing Rust College and took a teaching job. She later moved to Memphis, Tennessee, and, politicized by the appalling conditions of the Jim Crow society she found there, began speaking out on the horrors of racism. She sued a Memphis railway company after they tried to force her to ride in a car designated for blacks.

Although she won $500, her judgment was later reversed on appeal. In 1892, one of her closest friends, Thomas Moss, was lynched in Memphis because he operated a grocery store that was more successful than that of his white competition. Galled by this act, she began speaking out against racism and especially the crime of lynching, traveling alone throughout the South investigating lynchings—often in disguise because a bounty had been issued for her.

Wells-Barnett's careful empirical studies exploded the sexual myth that whites had used to justify lynching. She pointed out that fewer than one-third of the black men who were lynched were accused, much less found guilty, of raping white women. She became an early and ardent supporter of federal anti-lynching legislation. Uncompromising in her

Clarence Triggs (1942–1966)

Clarence Triggs was slain by nightriders in Bogalusa, Louisiana, on July 30, 1966.

Born in 1942, Triggs had just moved to Bogalusa from Jackson, Mississippi, with his wife, Emma. He had served in the armed forces and was working as a bricklayer. Triggs had never been active in the civil rights movement, but when he came to Bogalusa and saw that it was still a Jim Crow town, he joined civil rights marches and attended meetings organized by the Congress of Racial Equality (CORE). It was believed that Bogalusa had more Ku Klux Klan (KKK) members per capita than any other region in the South during the mid-1960s. Triggs was one of the many blacks in the area who supported the movement for equality, yet he was never considered a leader in the movement; in fact, few people knew who he was in Bogalusa. Less than a month after marching at a civil rights demonstration, Triggs was found dead on the side of the road with a bullet wound in his head.

Believing that the police were covering up Triggs's murder—especially since his wife was not allowed to identify her husband's body at the scene—civil rights leaders organized nightly marches until someone was arrested. Two days later, the police arrested two white men, Homer Richard Seale and John W. Copling Jr., and charged them with murder. Seale was never tried for this crime and a jury deliberated for less than an hour before finding Copling innocent. The motive for the deadly attack was never released, and the death of Clarence Triggs remains a mystery.

PAULINA X. RUF

support for an end to lynching, Wells-Barnett's implacability drew her into a number of public disagreements with some of the leading figures of her day, including Booker T. Washington; Frances Willard, the founder of the Women's Christian Temperance Union; and the great Progressive social worker, Jane Addams, all of whom worked to end various social ills of the day but who were not supportive enough in the campaign to end lynching. But as critical as Wells-Barnett was of white individuals and organizations that equivocated in their support for anti-lynching remedies, she joined the Association of Southern Women for the Prevention of Lynching and worked tirelessly to ensure that the crime was punished and eventually eradicated.

Other than Wells-Barnett, no other African American studied the crime of lynching more thoroughly than Walter White. Born in Atlanta, Georgia, in 1893, White, who had white skin, blue eyes, and blond hair, could easily have passed for white. At the age of 13, however, he had an experience that burned his racial identity forever in his mind and ensured that the eradication of lynching and racism would be his life's work.

White's father—who was as light as his son—was a letter carrier, a good job for a black man in a Southern city in 1906. He also owned a large house in the black section of Atlanta; it was virtually the only house that was kept up, and for this he drew the ire of whites who were jealous of him. During the bitter political campaign of 1906, Thomas E. Watson, a candidate for governor of Georgia, broke from his long-standing support of agrarian radicalism and interracial cooperation and joined in the race baiting so popular among candidates in the South. The campaign, along with a newspaper circulation war between the *Atlanta Journal* and the *Atlanta News*, ensured that only the most negative and inflammatory information would be printed about the black population in Atlanta. This included many untrue stories about black men raping white women, and soon the town was a seething cauldron of racial tension that culminated in a full-scale race riot. A number of innocent blacks were killed, and White's father was targeted by his white neighbors who resented his industry and all it had earned for him.

Like Wells-Barnett, White relied on empirical studies and his own eyewitness accounts; his color and features enabled him to talk freely with participants of mob violence, law enforcement officials, and neighborhood residents. His book *Rope and Faggot*, published in 1929, was an effort to isolate and examine what he said were the ingredients of lynching: economic forces, race prejudice, religion, sex, politics, yellow journalism, and theories of racial superiority and inferiority based on pseudoscience. White concluded that whites in America had taught their children that lynching was an acceptable way to correct all social ills, especially if they involved black Americans.

According to White, there were several factors that created and perpetuated the psychology of the lyncher. First,

government officials were derelict in their duty to uphold the laws faithfully and fairly. Second, humans love excitement, and will often do in a crowd what they would never do alone. Third, whites were unwilling to admit that they did not know or understand blacks. In fact, they had merely decided that there were only three types of blacks: the happy-go-lucky uncle or auntie, the habitual criminal or brute, and the humble, shuffling black of the antebellum years. Because of these prejudices, whites were unable to accept blacks in any other role.

Like Wells-Barnett, White concluded that it was the white man's inability to accept black economic and social advancement that caused most lynchings; it was black progress, not black crime, that frightened whites. This fear, and the pathological need to defend white supremacy, drove many whites to membership in the Ku Klux Klan.

White also looked at the connection between religion and lynching; he asserted that lynching could only happen in a *Christian* nation. It was the Christian church, after all, that had acquiesced in the evil of the slave trade. Furthermore, the Christian church helped slave owners use color as a justification for slavery and all the barbarities that went with it. Finally, White blamed religious leaders, particularly evangelical Protestants and holiness denominations for unleashing the torrid emotions of their congregations in their vocal condemnation of sex, especially sexual relations between white women and black men. White thought that Southerners were obsessed with sex, and that obsession promoted widespread antiblack feeling.

By the beginning of the 1920s, the number of lynchings began to drop sharply. White credited the drop with a nationwide campaign to combat lynchings led by the NAACP, and the introduction of the Dyer Anti-Lynching Bill, which was introduced in Congress by Leonidas C. Dyer, a Republican congressman from Missouri. The bill sought to make lynching a federal crime and to give the government the authority to investigate, fine, and punish those who took part in lynchings and members of the law enforcement community who did nothing to stop them. Although the bill passed the House in 1922, it was killed by a Senate filibuster that same year. It again passed the House in 1937 and 1940; it failed in the Senate in each of those years due to real or threatened filibusters by Southern Democrats and conservative Northern Republicans.

White Capping

The term *white capping* refers to the violent intimidation of blacks to rob them of their property. The individuals responsible for this violence were known as White Caps, nightriders named for the distinctive headgear they used to disguise themselves. The term seems to have originated in Indiana in 1887. The stated aim of the White Caps was to regulate the morality of the community, and their most common form of intimidation was whipping.

Between 1900 and 1929, the white capping epidemic reached its peak, chiefly in Southern rural areas. In addition to whipping, the White Caps terrorized, beat, and lynched blacks to unlawfully take their land. The phenomenon often occurred during periods when the competition for land was high. At other times, the purpose was to crush prosperous landowning blacks or to simply confiscate desirable property. Between 1887 and 1900, 239 incidences of white capping were reported. Despite the fact that White Caps violated black rights under the Fourteenth Amendment, the federal government did little, if anything, to protect blacks or their property.

Exacerbating the phenomenon of white capping was the fact that for blacks to acquire land in the first place was a Sisyphean task. Although rumors abounded of blacks being awarded "40 acres and a mule" after the Civil War, the majority of blacks received no land. In their everyday lives, blacks were forced to surmount gargantuan obstacles—poverty, racism, and discrimination—making it nearly impossible for them to eke out the most meager of existences. Nevertheless, blacks did manage to purchase land as a result of their own efforts.

In 1999, steps were taken by organizations such as the Race Relations Institute of Fisk University to address land theft and to locate its victims. The ultimate goal was to submit these cases to the court system in the hope that reparations might be forthcoming.

GLADYS L. KNIGHT

While the Dyer bill was never passed, it can still be credited with the sharp drop in the lynchings of black men during this period. The increased scrutiny connected with lynchings and the bad publicity they drew clearly alarmed Southern elites. They wanted no repeat of Reconstruction when the federal government was such an omnipotent presence in the region. Moreover, black migration north and the return of black soldiers from World War I were interfering with the South's efforts to attract the black manual laborers it so desperately needed. It, therefore, made concerted efforts to decrease the practice of lynching. There were 83 blacks lynched in 1919; by the time the Dyer bill was introduced in 1922, that number had dropped to 61. By 1927, the number of lynchings had dropped to 21.

As executive secretary of the NAACP, White ensured that it was the premier American organization in the forefront of defining the crime of lynching, recording its numbers, and eradicating its existence. The NAACP was founded in 1909 by a group of black and white intellectuals who were alarmed at the increasing segregation of American society and the subservient way in which the leading black spokesman of the day,

Booker T. Washington, chose to fight it. By 1918, the NAACP was the leader in seeking federal intervention by its support of the Dyer bill and campaigned tirelessly for its passage.

Unlike other organizations or individuals that equivocated on lynching and sometimes excused the practitioners of it, the NAACP took a very straightforward position. Eschewing common legend that lynchings occurred because of defective justice systems, community rabble-rousers, and lecherous black men who would strip defenseless white maidens of their sexual purity, it described lynching as a means that whites used to maintain economic and psychological hegemony over blacks. For whites, what was at stake was their theory of color caste: they were extremely concerned with racial purity and the prevention of amalgamation and were determined to do anything to ensure that race mixing did not happen. To the NAACP, lynching was a crime with its roots in race hatred and an elaborate myth of white superiority and black inferiority. Whites needed no particular reason to lynch blacks.

In campaigning against lynching, the NAACP was assisted by faculty at Tuskegee Institute who developed a classification of the causes of lynching into seven types: (1) homicide, (2) felonious assault, (3) rape, (4) attempted rape, (5) robbery and theft, (6) insult to white persons, and (7) all other causes. The Tuskegee scholars had difficulty classifying each lynching, in part because of the inability to obtain accurate information. However, some generalities can be made. Murder was the most frequently cited reason for lynching, followed by rape. In fact, the data showed that of the 1,399 lynchings from 1889 through 1930 recorded by the Tuskegee faculty, only 214 were tied to homicide and 622 to rape.

Like Wells-Barnett and White, the NAACP found that the reasons why African Americans were lynched ranged from the trivial to the serious and were as numerous as the people found in a lynch mob. Some of the more common reasons included incest, rape, murder, being disrespectful of white people (especially women), drunkenness, failing to pay debts, possessing a bad character, gambling, and theft. In many cases, the Tuskegee scholars found no offense had been committed or alleged; the lynching victim was merely in the wrong place at the wrong time.

The study of lynching in the latter part of the 20th century has, for the most part, been carried out by psychologists and sociologists. These social scientists looked at issues such as individual and social pathology much as did those in the 19th century. It was not until Jacquelyn Dowd Hall published *Revolt Against Chivalry* in 1979 that the study of lynching wriggled free from the grip of psychologists and sociologists. Like Ida B. Wells-Barnett and Walter White, Hall connected the violence of lynching with the Southern need to preserve the hierarchical relationship between blacks and whites. Hall also discussed the culture of violence in the American South, the economic and social dislocation wrought by modernism in the region, and the sexual tension between whites and blacks. Her research opened the door for a profusion of articles and books on the subject.

Indeed, the scholarship on lynching has never been more dynamic. Scores of historians, sociologists, and psychologists are breaking new ground in the study of lynching. Their theories range from economic distress to tension over race and sex, to individual psychopathologies. Little-known issues connected with lynching, such as the lynching of black people by black mobs, and lynchings in Northern states, are also being studied; the latter promises to be fertile ground as it has rarely been studied. In October 2002, scholars from all over the United States and several other countries gathered at Emory University in Atlanta for the first ever International Conference on Lynching and Racial Violence. Scholars and students from a number of disciplines presented a wealth of new research on lynching, its history, and its impact on American arts and letters, politics, and the criminal justice system. Held in conjunction with the conference was the first Southern exhibition of lynching artifacts, including postcards and photos, collected and owned by James Allen.

Lynching has all but disappeared. There are undoubtedly a number of reasons for this: modernization, industrialization, the civil rights movement of the 1950s and 1960s and the sweeping changes it brought to American society. Interracial dating and marriage, once illegal in the South and barely tolerated in the rest of the country, are much more common, and the pathological fear whites had of sexual activity between white women and black men has diminished. Yet the African American community still bears its scars. A majority of African Americans continue to believe that America operates a dual criminal justice system—often referred to as *legal lynching*—one for whites and another for blacks, and that it is impossible for blacks to be treated fairly or receive any semblance of justice. The explosion in the number of black men and women in prison and continued police brutality in large urban areas serve as proof of this belief.

Lynchings still occur in the United States, albeit rarely, and whites and blacks still react to them in starkly different ways. The 1998 dragging death in Jasper, Texas, of James Byrd Jr. by three white men shocked much of white America with its callousness and depravity. Many blacks, however, immediately made the historical connection to the lynching of black men in the South: the three white men overpowering the lone black one; the dark, lonely road; the fact that Byrd was tortured before his death and mutilated afterward did not seem to surprise most of black America. It must be pointed out that just as lynching was ritualized in the 19th and 20th centuries, so is the nation's reaction to it in the 21st century. There is the often vociferous condemnation of the violence by a large portion of the white community; the soul-searching questions about how and why human beings are so cruel to one another and why in 2005 race is still a flashpoint in America. These days, most law enforcement officials seek to help, not hinder, the investigations of lynching, and the justice system generally comes forth with the appropriate punishment.

Recently there has been increased awareness of, and attention to, so-called legal lynching, or the application of the death penalty in the United States. African American males are still more likely to be tried, convicted, and executed than white men for the same crimes. The state of Illinois issued a moratorium on the death penalty in 2000 after 13 death row inmates were exonerated. Several states are studying similar action. Although the occasional lynching still occurs, it is clear that lynching as the main way of maintaining the racial caste system is, for the most part, no longer accepted or tolerated in the United States.

MARILYN K. HOWARD

See also
Anti-Lynching League; Anti-Lynching Legislation; Black Women and Lynching; Costigan-Wagner Anti-Lynching Bill; Hate Crimes; Jim Crow Laws; Noose Incidents; Rape as a Provocation for Lynching; "Strange Fruit"; White Supremacy

Further Reading:
Brundage, W. Fitzhugh, ed. *Under Sentence of Death: Lynching in the South.* Chapel Hill: University of North Carolina Press, 1997.

"Civil Rights Memorial." http://www.tolerance.org/memorial/memorial.swf.

Dray, Philip. *At The Hands of Persons Unknown: The Lynching of Black America.* New York: Random House, 2002.

Holmes, William F. "Whitecapping: Agrarian Violence in Mississippi, 1902–1906." *Journal of Southern History* 35 (1969): 165–85.

Litwack, Leon. "Hellhounds." In *Without Sanctuary: Lynching Photography in America,* edited by James Allen and Hilton Als, 1–34. Santa Fe, NM: Twin Palms Publishers, 2000.

Wells-Barnett, Ida B. *On Lynchings.* Salem, NH: Ayer Company Publishers, 1991.

White, Walter Francis. *Rope and Faggot: A Biography of Judge Lynch.* New York: Arno Press, 1969.

M

Mack Charles Parker Lynching

Mack Charles Parker was a young African American man who was lynched in Mississippi in February 1959 for allegedly raping a white woman. Parker, whose life and death are recounted in Howard Smead's *Blood Justice: The Lynching of Mack Charles Parker*, in many ways served as the impetus for the civil rights legislation of the 1960s and helped bring an end to an era of open and publicly sanctioned acts of violence against African Americans.

Parker was a 23-year-old truck driver who lived in Lumberton, Mississippi. Although he married following his service in the Army, he later divorced and became the sole supporter for his mother, younger sister and her child, and four-year-old brother. Although recognized by his neighbors for taking on the responsibility of this mother and siblings at such a young age, Parker also liked to go out and have a good time with his friends. One such night was Monday, February 23, 1959, when Parker and four friends (Tommy Lee Grant, Curt Underwood, Norman "Rainbow" Malachy, and David Alfred), after receiving their paychecks, went out for the night.

During that same night, June Walters was traveling with her husband, Jimmy, and four-year-old daughter along a road between Poplarville and Lumberton in Pearl River County, Mississippi. At about 11:30 P.M. that night, the Walters' family car stalled and June's husband decided to travel to the nearest town, Lumberton, for assistance. June, who was two months' pregnant, and her daughter remained behind, locked in the car. While Jimmy was walking along the desolate road toward Lumberton, Parker and his friends drove by and noticed the car. This is where the events of the night of February 23 and the truth diverge.

What is known is that June Walters and her daughter were attacked. June was taken to an isolated field, beaten, and raped. Her daughter was accosted. After Parker dropped his friends at their homes, he returned to his own home briefly and then went out again. A truck driver found June stumbling along the road, in shock, with her daughter. She claimed that she was attacked by a black man. Parker, who had no previous arrest record, was accused of the crime and jailed. The intersection of race, class, politics, ambition, and hate colored the intervening facts of the case and, inevitably, determined the outcome and Parker's death.

Although no direct evidence connected Parker to the rape of June Walters, this fact did not stop the police from targeting Parker as their primary suspect early in the case. One of the friends with him that night, Curt Underwood, claimed that when they drove past the Walters' car, Parker told him he intended to go back. The father of another of Parker's friends, David Alfred, stated that Parker was the person the police were looking for. In addition, Parker's car was seen that night by a Poplarville police officer. When Parker was

Mack Charles Parker's relatives and friends at his funeral, May 1959. (Time & Life Pictures/Getty Images)

Local sentiment was fueled when Parker's mother hired two African American attorneys to defend her son. There was concern that the attorneys would be allowed to cross-examine a white woman—June Walters—if the case ever went to court. In addition, there was talk that Parker might be cleared of the charges or, if convicted, might win on appeal. The belief that a conviction might be overturned on appeal was a real concern. There were no African Americans on the grand jury that indicted Parker, and there were no African Americans eligible to serve as jurors.

The case transcended the need to convict the person who raped and assaulted June Walters. It was transformed into an occasion to uphold a way of life local residents believed was being challenged and derided. African Americans across the country were demanding legal recognition of their civil rights, demanding the right to vote without encumbrance, the right to equal opportunity in the workplace, and equal educational opportunities. Change was on the horizon, and small isolated hamlets and towns like Poplarville felt that they were being ignored by the federal government and the rest of the country, and they were ready to fight back. The incident involving Mack Charles Parker provided them with an opportunity to take a stand and to make a statement.

By the time Parker was transferred to a jail in Poplarville, which served as the county seat for Pearl River, plans were well underway to lynch him. Other prisoners were warned that something might happen and were directed to point Parker out if it did. On the night of April 24, several cars pulled up to the Pearl River County jail and courthouse, and from among that group, three men entered the jail and forcibly took Parker. They were later identified as J. P. Walker, a former deputy sheriff; James Floren Lee, an itinerant preacher; and Jewel Alford, an officer at the jail.

Although it may not have been a surprise that a lynch mob would come after Parker, it appears that no one who observed the events of that night was prepared for what they saw. Parker, young and strong, despite the beatings given to him by police some months earlier, struggled valiantly for his life. The three men bludgeoned and kicked Parker until he was on the brink of unconsciousness and then dragged him down the jailhouse steps, leaving a trail of blood, and placed him into one of the waiting cars. The mob, minus Jewel Alford, traveled from Mississippi to Louisiana and then back again, stopping at the Pearl River. Parker was bound, beaten

brought to the Lumberton jail, after sustaining a bloody beating by police, Walters was unable to identify him in a lineup. Yet, when Parker and the other men in the lineup were asked to repeat the words allegedly spoken by the rapist, Walters identified Parker as the person who attacked her.

From his initial questioning by police until his death, Parker proclaimed his innocence and denied that he had raped June Walters. It wasn't long after Parker was arrested and charged with kidnapping and criminal assault that some of the white residents of Pearl River County began to talk about carrying out their own form of justice. The facts that the victim was unable to identify Parker physically, that there was no evidence linking him to the crime, and that the two lie detector tests he took were inconclusive were not enough to deter locals from wanting to go after Parker. These threats were not taken lightly by Parker, his family, or the local African American community.

Those involved in the conspiracy were from every segment of the Poplarville area community—business owners, laborers, law enforcement officers, farmers, and a preacher.

and kicked, and then shot in the heart. His body was then weighed down with chains and tossed into the river.

Lynch mobs in the past had little to fear in terms of retaliation or of being arrested. Yet, it was apparent almost immediately that this lynching would be different. The first evidence of this was Gov. Coleman's decision to contact the Federal Bureau of Investigation (FBI). Only hours after Parker's kidnapping, torture, and death, the FBI, the U.S. Department of Justice, and the White House had been informed of the lynching. In addition, the national press descended on the residents of the county with questions and cameras.

The FBI quickly moved into Poplarville and started their formal investigation. Although some of the residents in Pearl River and the surrounding counties, including Jimmy and June Walters, thought Parker should have been able to stand trial, they also resented what they perceived as the federal government's intrusion. It became clear that not everyone agreed with the actions of the mob, but they would, without hesitation, defend their neighbors, county, and state. More than 60 FBI agents, along with the state police, began an investigation into Parker's disappearance and attempted to locate him.

Ten days after Parker was murdered, on May 4, his body, bloated and decomposed, surfaced. While he was being laid to rest, the FBI accelerated its investigation and attempted to gather evidence that the mob had carried Parker across state lines, from Mississippi to Louisiana, in order to make the charges a federal offense. At every turn, the FBI was met with silence out of fear of retaliation and resentment over their presence. Two potential witnesses who did participate in the investigation later attempted suicide.

Although no confessions were forthcoming from any of the participants in the lynching, the FBI believed that it had enough evidence, including Alford's admission that he helped the mob to gain entry to the jail, to bring indictments and convictions. Despite the testimony of key government witnesses, of the two grand juries (in 1959 and 1960) convened to examine the evidence, neither brought an indictment against any of the members of the mob or their accomplices. None of the individuals who participated in Parker's kidnapping and murder were ever jailed or arrested.

Nonetheless, many Pearl River County residents did not view the inaction of the grand juries as a victory. Tired of the press, government intrusion, and embarrassed that the state's judicial process was not allowed to resolve the case, local citizens were disappointed that Mississippi was not able to show the rest of the country, and the world, they were capable of handling their own problems in a fair and legal manner. This shift in thinking later opened the door for social change in Poplarville, Pearl River County, and the state of Mississippi.

No member of Parker's family remained in Pearl River County after the case was closed. Mack Charles Parker was interred in a simple grave that displayed no vestiges of his horrific death.

ROBIN DASHER-ALSTON

See also

Hate Crimes in America; Lynching

Further Reading:

FBI Summary Report. *Civil Rights Investigation into the Abduction of Mack Charles Parker from the Pearl River County Jail in Poplarville, Mississippi.* April 1959. http://foia.fbi.gov/foiaindex/parker.htm.

Smead, Howard. *Blood Justice: The Lynching of Mack Charles Parker.* New York: Oxford University Press, 1986.

Madrigal v. Quilligan (1978)

Madrigal v. Quilligan (1978) was a class-action suit that raised public awareness of coerced sterilization of Mexican American women in California. In 1909, California passed a sterilization law that permitted health care supervisors at prisons and mental institutions to sterilize a patient or prisoner to improve their condition. In the 1910s, the law was expanded to allow doctors to sterilize patients who had a mental illness that may be passed on to their children. By the 1960s, sterilization was viewed as a means to protect the collective public health and some called for the procedure to be used to address concerns of overpopulation. Immigrants, women of color, and low-income women were targeted for sterilization because of eugenic stereotypes that they procreated at a higher rate, would bear illegitimate children, and would be a burden on public services.

In 1973, Dr. Bernard Rosenfeld reported widespread sterilization abuses that he had witnessed as a resident physician at the Los Angeles County-University of Southern California

Medical Center and presented information to the Los Angeles Center for Law and Justice (LACLJ). In 1975, LACLJ attorney Antonia Hernández filed *Madrigal v. Quilligan* on behalf of 10 plaintiffs against the hospital and state and federal officials. All of the plaintiffs were working-class, Spanish-speaking, Mexican immigrants who had been surgically sterilized within hours of giving birth through cesarean section at the hospital between 1971 and 1974. During the physical stress of labor, the patients were asked by doctors to undergo tubal ligation surgery. Some of the plaintiffs had not agreed to the procedure, while others gave their consent because hospital staff withheld treatment, wrongly informed them it was necessary for their health, told them the procedure was reversible, and falsely claimed that their husbands had agreed to the procedure. The procedures had been funded through federal family planning initiatives from the War on Poverty (1964). Claiming that their civil and constitutional rights to procreate had been violated, the plaintiffs sought financial compensation and requirements for federally funded hospitals to provide counseling and consent forms in Spanish before performing sterilization procedures.

When the trial began in 1978, the court heard testimony from the plaintiffs. Additionally, Dr. Karen Benke, a medical student at the hospital, testified that she had observed coercive tactics used by doctors and that the head of Obstetrics and Gynecology believed poor minority women should be sterilized because they had too many children and put a strain on society. At the conclusion of the trial, the judge sided with the defendants, stating that the doctors had acted in good faith and did not intend to harm the women. Instead, he attributed the cases to a breakdown in communication between the doctors and their patients.

Though the plaintiffs lost the trial, the case drew widespread attention due to the efforts of Comisión Femenil Mexicana Nacional, which rallied public support and lobbied for laws to protect the reproductive rights of Latinas. In 1974, the U.S. Department of Health, Education and Welfare implemented federal guidelines that mandated a 72-hour waiting period between consent and operation; an explanation of the risks, benefits, family planning alternatives, and continued access to welfare even if they refused the procedure; a signed statement of consent; and restrictions on sterilizing patients under the age of 21. In 1979, California repealed its sterilization law.

Madrigal v. Quilligan also served as a rallying point in the Latina feminist movement, which continued to advocate health issues and reproductive rights for Mexican American women.

ABC-CLIO

See also
Sterilization of Native American Women

Further Reading:
Espino, Virginia. "Woman Sterilized As Gives Birth: Forced Sterilization and Chicana Resistance in the 1970s." In *Las Obreras: Chicana Politics of Work and Family*, edited by Vicki L. Ruiz. Los Angeles: UCLA Chicano Studies Research Center Publications, 2000.
Hernández, Antonia. "Chicanas and the Issue of Involuntary Sterilization: Reforms Needed to Protect Informed Consent." *Chicano Law Review* 3 (1976): 3–37.
Stern, Alexandra. *Eugenic Nation: Faults and Frontiers of Better Breeding in Modern America*. Berkeley: University of California Press, 2005.
Vélez-Ibañez, Carlos G. "The Nonconsenting Sterilization of Mexican Women in Los Angeles. Issues of Psychocultural Rupture and Legal Redress in Paternalistic Behavioral Environments." In *Twice a Minority: Mexican American Women*, edited by Margarita Melville. St. Louis: C. V. Mosby, 1980.

Magical Negro Films

Magical Negro films are understood as cinema featuring a lower-class, uneducated, black stock character that possess supernatural or magical powers that are used to help or save disheveled or broken white characters and transform them to able and content persons. Most of the white characters helped by the Magical Negro are male. Some examples of these movies are *The Green Mile* (1999), *The Legend of Bagger Vance* (2000), the *Blade* trilogy (1998, 2002, 2004), the *Matrix* trilogy (1999, 2003, 2003), *Bruce Almighty* (2003) and *Evan Almighty* (2007).

The Magical Negro character was developed from the Noble Savage, a character in 17th-century European literature from the "New World" colonies that possessed qualities of harmony, generosity, simplicity, and a strong moral character that would always do what was right under any circumstance. During the early 20th century, the racial "others," including Latinos, African Americans, and Native Americans, were framed as criminals and at the same time, possessive of a spiritual or moral power and insight. For example, African Americans were thought to have greater sexual potency and spiritual insights than most Europeans. As this trope entered the 1950s and 1960s, it emerged in American films as the "ebony saint"; a friendly yet wise black man, who would befriend and assist down-on-their luck white counterparts. By 2007, even then-presidential candidate Barack Obama was referred to as a "Magical Negro" in mainstream and conservative media outlets.

Magical Negro films contain certain common elements. The black character often appears (1) in a situation of economic extremity, such as abject poverty or as a prisoner; (2) is culturally or socially deficient and thought the host of various social pathologies; 3) possesses an unexplainable folk wisdom; 4) disappears for no reason at the end of the film; and 5) possesses a kind of primordial magic. Conversely, the white character being aided by the Magic Negro often (1) has socioeconomic upward mobility; (2) learns a moral lesson; (3) is involved in a white romance; (4) has little connection to spirituality; and (5) often pursues an idyllic and ideal white self, often called "hegemonic whiteness." While the representations of a black person possessive of magical powers have been praised as progressive, and while the characters' on-screen interracial cooperation and friendship is a departure from asymmetrical relations of the past, these films continue to endorse a subtle message of white supremacy. The Magical Negro character is represented as less than human, and as an object whose entire purpose is to fix and help white people rather than pursue their own interests or raise their social condition. While these apparently viewer-friendly and post-racial films promote strong black characters and cooperative racial relationships, and while many lump praise on these viewer-friendly depictions of race relations, they contain an implicit message of white superiority and contain antiblack stereotypes of contented servitude.

BIANCA GONZALEZ SOBRINO AND MATTHEW W. HUGHEY

Further Reading:

Baldwin, Gayle R. "What a Difference a Gay Makes: Queering the Magic Negro," *Journal of Religion and Popular Culture* 5 (2003).

Cozine, Joshua. "Mina: The Magical Female." *Film International* 5, no. 2 (2007): 43–47.

Ehrenstein, David. "Obama the 'Magic Negro.'" *Los Angeles Times.* http://www.latimes.com/news/opinion/commentary/la-oe-ehrenstein19mar19,0,3391015.story, 2007.

Hughey, Matthew W. "Cinethetic Racism: White Redemption and Black Stereotypes in 'Magical Negro' Films," *Social Problems* 56, no 3 (2009): 543–77.

Hughey, Matthew W. "Racializing Redemption, Reproducing Racism: The Odyssey of Magical Negroes and White Saviors," *Sociology Compass* 6, no. 9 (2012): 751–67.

Vera, Hernán, and Andrew M. Gordon. *Screen Saviors: Hollywood Fictions of Whiteness.* Lanham, MD: Rowman & Littlefield, 2003.

Magnet and Charter Schools

After the *Brown v. Board* decision of 1954, where segregated schools were deemed inherently unequal, freedom of choice plans were implemented in much of the South. However, while freedom of choice plans gave parents the opportunity to choose what school their child attended, these plans did not always dismantle school racial segregation. However, advocates of school choice believe that it will pave the way for competition among schools, because they would compete against each other to offer the best curriculum and teachers to their students. Since the notion of school choice emerged, a number of different schools have been created to meet students' needs, and magnet and charter schools are two popular avenues.

Magnet schools, the largest sector of choice in the United States, are public schools that have specialized themes and instructional methods. During the 1970s, as racial desegregation plans were being implemented in school districts throughout the country, magnet schools became a popular choice as they provided an alternative to school busing or mandatory reassignment, while encouraging racial balance within schools. Since magnet schools are part of the public school system, they receive funding from the state; however, they receive more money per pupil for supplies, teachers, and other materials. Most magnet schools are located in urban areas and their main goals include: promoting racial diversity, providing a specialized curriculum, and improving academic outcomes. Although magnet schools can cater to any grade level, most magnet schools serve students in

Ray Budde (1923–2005)

Born in St. Louis, Missouri, in 1923, Ray Budde is recognized as the first person to propose the concept of charter schools. Interested in education reform, Budde taught seventh grade English and also served as an assistant principal. He earned his master's degree in business administration from the University of Illinois, and then proceeded to Michigan State University for his doctorate, which he earned in 1959. He began teaching educational administration at the University of Massachusetts, Amherst, and retired in 1973. At first, Budde's ideas were ignored; however, in the 1980s after the *Nation at Risk Report*, Budde became adamant about the idea of educational freedom. His initial ideas, which concerned working within existing schools where teachers would receive charters from the school board, have been expanded on throughout the years. Albert Shanker, a former American Federation of Teachers president, is one proponent that has expanded Budde's original ideas. Ray Budde died in 2005, at the age of 82.

elementary school. Since their implementation, the number of magnet schools has increased dramatically, with their current enrollment just over 2 million students in 31 states. Magnet schools are a popular choice among parents, and with the high demand that exists in many districts that offer magnet schools, different admission processes are used for entry. While some schools rely on a lottery format, others schools utilize a first-come, first-served approach.

Although some research has shown that students in magnet schools have higher achievement levels than their traditional public student counterparts, critics argue how magnet schools perpetuate existing racial and class inequality, as middle-class parents are more knowledgeable about school options. Thus, although magnet schools were created during the 1970s as a means of desegregation, many scholars have cited that they still segregate by race and class.

In the late 1980s, due to decisions of the Supreme Court, schools started to dismantle their desegregation plans. When this occurred, public attention for magnet schools diminished while charter schools became the focus of school choice proponents. Similar to magnet schools, charter schools are public schools that have innovative methods; however, they are not subject to the same rules and regulations inherent in public schools. Instead, accountability plans are created and if the school is successful, the school's charter can be renewed for three to five years. Almost anyone can apply to start a charter school. Each school, however, needs a board of directors and certified teachers. Comparable to magnet schools, most charter schools are located in urban communities and serve elementary students. Since their inception, student enrollment in charter schools has increased exponentially. Between 1999–2000 and 2009–2010, student enrollment in charter schools grew from 0.3 million to 1.6 million students. There are currently over 4,500 charter schools throughout the United States.

Research has cited a number of reasons for the popularity of charter schools. First, charter schools have the freedom to use innovative teaching techniques since they operate outside of the regular school system. Second, the curriculum at charter schools is geared towards students' needs. And last, charter schools demonstrate an alternative means of improving the academic scores of students.

Thus, while proponents argue that charter schools improve educational outcomes through innovative strategies while offering traditional public school students a way out of failing schools, opponents have cited how charter schools create racial, economic, and linguistic isolation. For example, while some studies have shown that racial minorities are often more segregated in charter schools than they would be in public schools, other research has cited how charter schools are admitting a disproportionate amount of affluent and white students. Without policies designed towards racial integration, black, Hispanic, and white isolation often emerges. Further, although the goal is to increase academic outcomes, studies are mixed concerning whether or not charter schools produce higher academic outcomes compared to traditional public schools.

While the data remains mixed on the success magnet and charter schools have on improving academic outcomes, the school choice movement is still very popular among parents, students, educators, and elected officials. Alternative means of education will remain at the forefront of public policy, even if the creation of charter and magnet schools siphons money away from traditional public schools. Until educational gaps begin to narrow among different racial, ethnic, and social class groups, the popularity of school choice, specifically charter schools, will not dissipate.

BOBETTE OTTO

See also

Educational Achievement Gap; Vocational Education

Further Reading:

Civil Rights Project. "Renewing the Civil Rights Movement by Bridging the Worlds of Ideas and Action." http://civilrightsproject.ucla.edu/.

Frankenberg, Erica, Genevieve Siegel-Hawley, and Jia Wang. "Choice without Equity: Charter School Segregation." *Educational Policy Analysis Archives* 19 (2011): 1–96.

Frankenberg, Erica, and Genevieve Siegel-Hawley. "The Forgotten Choice? Rethinking Magnet Schools in a Changing Landscape: A Report on Magnet Schools in America." *Civil Rights Project* 2008: 1–64. http://civilrightsproject.ucla.edu/research/k-12-education/integration-and-diversity/the-forgotten-choice-rethinking-magnet-schools-in-a-changing-landscape/frankenberg-forgotten-choice-rethinking-magnet.pdf.

Nathan, Joe. *Charter Schools: Creating Hope and Opportunity of American Education*. San Francisco: Jossey-Bass, 1997.

National Center for Education Statistics. "Fast Facts." http://nces.ed.gov/fastfacts/display.asp?id=30.

Smrekar, Claire, and Ellen Goldring. *School Choice in Urban America: Magnet Schools and the Pursuit of Equity*. New York: Teachers College Press, 1999.

Wells, Amy Stuart. *Time to Choose: America at the Crossroads of School Choice Policy*. New York: Hill and Wang, 1993.

Williams, Kenton, Rose Duhon-Sells, and Harriet A. Pitcher. *Charter Schools: Answering the Call; Saving our Children*. Edited by Ashraf Esmail and Alice Duhon-Ross McCallum. Lanham, MD: University Press of America, 2012.

Malcolm X (1925–1965)

Malcolm X, or El-Hajj Malik El-Shabazz, was a charismatic religious leader, a relentless activist for black liberation, a brutally honest public speaker, a social scientist, an international revolutionary, and an unequivocal cultural icon during the mid-20th century of the United States. He ascended to prominence through his public speaking appointment with the Nation of Islam (NOI, or "The Nation"), the heterodox religious Black Nationalist/separatist North American organization, during the mid-1950s and early 1960s. He traveled the nation, and the globe, speaking on behalf of the NOI, and its spiritual leader, Elijah Muhammad (d. 1973), while critiquing the remnants of white supremacy, questioning "civil rights," and advocating black self-defense. Along with speaking to ethnically mixed audiences in public forums, Malcolm participated in countless interviews and debates, which appeared on numerous popular television programs and in print media such as newspapers and magazines. His oratory abilities affected his notoriety, though his eloquence and terse way of speaking did not translate into prolific writing. Indeed, Malcolm was not known as an author, but he was very involved in the publication of the once-popular NOI newspaper, *Muhammad Speaks*.

He was born Malcolm Little on May 19, 1925, in Omaha, Nebraska, to a Baptist minister, the Rev. Earl Little, and his wife, Louise Little, who were members of the Universal Negro Improvement Association and African Communities League (UNIA). The organization was founded in the early 20th century by the provocateur of rights for all people of African descent in the United States, Marcus Garvey. The seventh child of 10, Malcolm spend his early life growing up in foster homes, and with family members, after the murder of his father at the hands of the local Ku Klux Klan. Subsequently, Louise was institutionalized years later on the diagnosis of insanity.

Once older, he worked menial jobs amidst traveling between Lansing, Michigan; Boston, Massachusetts; and New York City during the early 1940s, but was eventually lured by the desire for bigger profits through criminal means in the street life of the big city. Influenced by lack of opportunity sanctioned by a Northern version of Jim Crow, and the survivalist mentality born from an environment of criminality, Malcolm experimented with peddling dope, larceny, running numbers (gambling), and pimping. Consequently, he was arrested in 1946, and served a brief period of imprisonment as a young adult. While serving an eight-year prison term for larceny and burglary, Malcolm was introduced by his brother Reginald to the teachings of Elijah Muhammad.

The NOI, or the "Black Muslims" as the press called them, was an organization founded in Chicago during the Great Depression of the 1930s by Elijah Poole. He was taught "Islam" and the "legacy" of blacks by a mysterious man, Wallace D. Fard, who appeared in the Chicago slums. Fard was a silk peddler who claimed to be a messenger of

Black Muslim leader Malcolm X holds up a paper for the crowd to see during a Black Muslim rally in New York City on August 6, 1963. (AP/Wide World Photos)

God from the East, and would "convert" would-be followers to Islam for a nominal fee. However, when law enforcement officers began to question neighborhood inhabitants for information on Fard, he fled. Poole, who was a staunch believer in Fard's rhetoric, recognized an opportunity, and developed a palatable theology for the growing numbers of uneducated former Christian-turned-Muslim followers. Now as Elijah Muhammad, he began to spread the message to blacks that Fard was God incarnate, and that he was to be considered God's (Fard's) prophet. Thus, the then "Lost-Found Nation of Islam in the American Wilderness" was founded, which was essentially an amalgamation of three other preceding movements: Marcus Garvey's Pan-Africanism, Noble Drew Ali's Moorish Science Temple, and, to a

lesser extent, the Ahmadiyyah Movement. The confluence of these three movements was important, because they served as "pillars" for the NOI's religious-based Black Nationalism. For example, the Moorish Science Temple was more religious than political in its ideologies, while Garvey's program through UNIA was strictly political. A considerable number of followers from both organizations were among those who joined the NOI at its inception during the 1930s. Both organizations, and their leaders in particular, prioritized agendas for "escape" from the "implications of being black in a white-dominated society."

Noble Drew Ali founded the Moorish Science Temple of America, which was a sect of Islam influenced by Buddhism, Christianity, and the Freemasons. The Moors, as they were often called, maintained the reactionary ideology that whites were naturally demonic, and expressed the only way for minority salvation was through conversion to Islam. Drew Ali decided to change the mental condition of blacks by introducing a new nomenclature of Arabic names and new cultural symbols such as "Nationality and Identification" cards for his followers—i.e., Black Moors—while Garvey believed in secession in, or complete emigration from, predominately white America.

The Ahmadiyyah Movement came to the United States during the late 19th century from the Punjabi region of British-ruled India, and was led by spiritual leader and Indian Muslim Mirza Ghulam Ahmad. As a studious young man, Ahmad was convinced he was a prophet and a messiah sent to earth to receive and disseminate what he believed to be revelations from God. This claim drew tremendous criticism from orthodox Punjabi Muslims, who believed that the descent of revelation was completed when the final verses of the Holy Qur'an came down from Heaven to the Arab prophet, Muhammad ibn Abdullah, during the later years of his life in seventh-century Arabia. Thus, Ghulam Ahmad and his followers, who would later spread their teachings to America's shores, were violently persecuted for their heretical beliefs.

The introduction to the NOI was pivotal in young Malcolm's life, considering the context of the United States at the time. Affronted with a system that infringed on their inclusion in cultural and political participation within America, historically blacks had found solace in the Christian church. The black church was a refuge from the misery of white racism, a cornerstone of any black community, and a crucial, relatively safe haven for public discussion. And as Malcolm would often point out through his later speeches, what was surprising to him was that Christianity was a religion given to blacks by their enslavers, and yet they clung to it tightly.

The dilemma was that in the church, some black Americans discovered an equivalent difficulty to challenge oppression in American Christianity, because it remained dominated by a similar white supremacy to that of the secular society. Thus, in a race-conscious society in which blacks were disproportionately imprisoned, openly discriminated against by Jim Crow laws in the Southern as well as Northern states, unprotected by a biased legal system, collectively held the least amount of property, and terrorized by the Ku Klux Klan with the constant threat of death, American Christianity's appeal as the path to liberation was contested.

Growing weary of the treatment they received from their Christian brethren, some black Christians debated whether Christianity was a source of liberation or oppression for their peoples. Few black Americans decided to challenge the white supremacy in Christianity from within, while others "took a leap of faith" and left Christianity completely. As other black Americans before him sought an alternative path to cultural and political equity, the teachings offered by the NOI ignited something in Malcolm, and served as a catalyst for his program of self-education on subjects, such as world and U.S. histories, literature, and philosophy.

Once released from prison on early parole in 1953, Malcolm began to attend NOI temples and, shortly after, was given responsibility as a minister under the guidance, and personal attention, of Elijah Muhammad. After spending time in NOI temples in New York City, Philadelphia, and Chicago, Malcolm later ascended to the position of national representative for the NOI from the late 1950s until 1963, which allowed him to further the organization's black separatist rhetoric. Through the heterodox interpretation of the religion of Islam, blacks sought out an alternative cultural and religious experience to become not honorary Arabs or whites, but truer, more authentic black men and women. The author of the seminal book *Black Muslims in America*, C. Eric Lincoln, had the opportunity to conduct firsthand research on the Nation during the height of its popularity, and conducted personal interviews with Elijah Muhammad and Malcolm. Lincoln wrote that the NOI espoused ideas such as self-reliance, economic empowerment, and high morality, and was an exemplar of black social protest for social change. Malcolm, with the teachings of Elijah Muhammad, and the NOI as his base, exemplified these characteristics.

Further, the NOI promoted ideas such as: "getting equality now instead of salvation in heaven later"; prohibition of consuming harmful food products, e.g., pork, alcohol, cigarettes, and other narcotics; refraining from gambling; chastity, responsibility, and honesty and practicing. Additionally, the NOI offered a discourse of black superiority to challenge white supremacy, and they firmly believed that Islam was the natural religion of black people.

Organization of Afro-American Unity (OAAU)

The Organization of Afro-American Unity (OAAU) was founded in 1964 by Malcolm X, after his break with the Nation of Islam. It was formed to coordinate political action and self-organization among blacks toward the goal of racial equality. Its secular character and more inclusivist ideology distanced the OAAU somewhat from the black militancy espoused by the Nation of Islam. However, the OAAU's mission to restore African identity and an ethos of self-determination to black people in America remains relevant to this day, despite Malcolm X's assassination in 1965.

At its core, the OAAU saw slavery as having robbed blacks of their connection to an African sense of culture and history, and their links to each other. The OAAU resolved to foster unity among blacks through a platform that embraced pan-Africanism, education, and political militancy. The OAAU advocated a "Basic Unity Program," which included the restoration of cultural links to and knowledge of Africa; reorientation to include a larger pan-African consciousness and agenda; education designed to free blacks from "mental bondage," programs to promote economic security; and self-defense against white domination.

The OAAU's political agenda can be seen as an outgrowth of Malcolm X's own evolving politics. Although calling for black self-organization and militant black action, the OAAU did not advocate black separatism as an end in itself but as the only means necessary to achieve full racial equality. However, the OAAU's acceptance of a multiethnic "future" needs to be seen alongside its fervent commitment to an African-centered cultural, political, and spiritual restoration project.

REBEKAH LEE

Along with the rather docile empowerment concepts, there were two theories that distinguished Malcolm and the NOI. One of the most disturbing theories asserted by Malcolm was the race-tinged generalization of white Americans based on the world history that all white peoples were "devils," as taught to Elijah Muhammad by his teacher, W. D. Fard. The second was their call for a separate area in North America for blacks, because they rejected the idea of integration as a ploy to resubjugate blacks. This was a departure from the ideas of Garvey's Back to Africa Movement, and was an obvious break from orthodox Islam's historical tradition of leaving a home to establish a society that would abide by justice, or egalitarian principles not available. Due to the persecution they experienced in their home city of Makkah (Mecca), Allah (God) commanded His believers through the Prophet of Islam, Muhammad, to establish a truly Muslim community in Madinah in 622 CE.

In a move to emulate tradition, the NOI prioritized connecting Black Muslims in the West to the broader Muslim world community. Their slant was that they emphasized the "brownness" of the larger community, who had been, in most cases, oppressed like blacks on the North American continent. In a constructed prophesy, Elijah Muhammad "foretold" of America's destruction for its treatment of the darker humankind. Likewise, he tried to make the case for black non-Muslims to see their condition in America as a microcosmic representation of what was happening globally wherever the "white man" went. Earlier, Muhammad even admonished his followers to not fight against Japanese military forces in World War II, because they were victims of white racism also.

Continuing this rationale, the analysis of the political infrastructure of the U.S. government by the NOI, and Malcolm in particular, was a lucid interrogation of U.S. history, U.S. domestic policies, and the claim of democracy in the United States for its citizens. Malcolm, in his eloquent manner of oration, took the government to task, delivering now infamous speeches, such as "The Message to the Grassroots," "A Declaration of Independence," "The Ballot or the Bullet," and "The Black Revolution." Through his words, whether speaking to audiences in Detroit, Harlem, Cleveland, or London, Malcolm also questioned the intellectual coherence of blacks who desired to be in the political establishment, and spoke suspiciously of the loyalty of white liberals.

In terms of political philosophy, he considered Democrats to be identical to Republicans in that they supported the white supremacist infrastructure. It made no difference whether the discussion was on the Northern or the Southern states, because where the North provided more economic opportunities, there was unemployment and disparate housing. Alternatively, in the South, blacks faced those conditions in addition to threats of being terrorized by the Ku Klux Klan, or even lynched or murdered, for no serious reasons. Being a critic of the altruistic tactics of protesting nonviolently, Malcolm advocated the constitutional right to bear arms for all blacks in the United States as a means to protect their bodies, families, and communities where the government had failed to do so.

For these reasons, Malcolm argued that Democrats, or as he called them, "Dixiecrats," were most often "Southern" in political orientation, and not really friends of blacks. In numerous speeches, he directly referenced the absence of voting rights for Southern blacks as an abomination to democracy, being that the Civil Rights Act had been signed in 1957. Malcolm continuously emphasized being aware of the words by white liberals (Dixiecrats) in Washington, D.C., and the actions of the Republicans and their constituents in the Southern states, because white liberals kept blacks disenfranchised with no hope of casting votes in the best interest of themselves. As the March on Washington took place in 1963 where Martin Luther King, Jr. gave the famous "I Have a Dream" speech, Malcolm only witnessed a ploy to appease the frustrated blacks around the country with no real gains.

In early 1964, he left the NOI after being silenced for making unauthorized comments about the assassination of President John F. Kennedy, and over confirmed reports that the person who saved his life, his father-like figure, Elijah Muhammad, had fathered several children with young secretaries within the NOI. He formed a new organization, Muslim Mosque, Inc., in Harlem, New York City, to support the smaller Muslim community outside of the Nation of Islam. In the spring of 1964, through the financial generosity of his sister Ella, he traveled to Makkah, Saudi Arabia, to perform the hajj (the required pilgrimage of all orthodox Muslims). Also on this extended trip, he was able to make contacts in foreign countries such as Egypt, Morocco, Algeria, Nigeria, Ghana, and Lebanon.

While on hajj, Malcolm was struck by the sense of "brotherhood" he experienced, as he witnessed no racial divisions among men and women, but saw only a unity of being for the worship of Allah (God). By observing and sharing quarters with white European Muslims, Malcolm, now identifying himself as Malik El-Shabazz, concluded that the race problems of the United States could be, potentially, solved by Christian, white America's conversion to Islam. Additionally, the experience of hajj solidified his decision to increase the call for Black Nationalism in black communities in the United States, and to replace efforts for civil rights with a more internationalized consciousness towards human rights for blacks.

Through the contacts he made on his extended trip abroad, Malcolm felt certain that with a Pan-Africanist perspective, his people in the United States could receive more support from partners within United Nations if the focus was on obtaining human rights instead of civil rights. Upon his return to the United States, he formed a new secular group, Organization of Afro-American Unity, to complement Muslim Mosque and address social, political, and economical issues facing the broader, disenfranchised, non-Muslim black community in the United States.

Malcolm would never see his plan materialize, as an unexplained chain of events began to happen in his life. He was attacked by assailants, was to be evicted from his family home by the NOI, and his house was under constant surveillance by the FBI. In early February 1965, Malcolm's family home was firebombed with Molotov cocktails thrown by assailants in the early morning hours as he, his wife Betty Shabazz, and their four daughters slept. This was an obvious attempt on his life by assassins, though who was responsible for sending them was left to speculation. However, while giving a speech before an audience of supporters in the Audubon Ballroom in Harlem, New York City, assassins infiltrated the crowd, and fatally shot Malcolm several times. El-Hajj Malik El-Shabazz, posthumously called the "Black Prince" and "our manhood" by film actor, playwright, poet, activist, and friend Ossie Davis at his funeral, died from those wounds on February 25, 1965.

MIKA'IL A. PETIN

See also
Nation of Islam

Further Reading:
Breitman, George. *Malcolm X Speaks*. New York: Grove Weidenfeld, 1990.
Chapman, Mark. *Christianity on Trial: African-American Religious Thought Before and After Black Power*. New York: Orbis Books, 1996.

Haley, Alex, and Malcolm X. *The Autobiography of Malcolm X: As Told to Alex Haley.* New York: Ballantine Books, 1964.

Jackson, Sherman. *Islam and the Black American: Looking toward the Third Resurrection.* New York: Oxford University Press, 2005.

Lincoln, C. Eric. *Black Muslims in America.* Boston: Beacon Press, 1961.

Strum, Philippa, and Taratolo, Danielle, eds. *Muslims in the United States.* Washington, DC: Woodrow Wilson International Center for Scholars, 2003.

Turner, Richard Brent. *Islam in the African American Experience.* Bloomington: Indiana University Press 1997.

Manifest Destiny

Manifest destiny was an ideology prominent in the United States from the mid-19th until the early 20th century. It was fundamentally an expansionist ideology that attempted to justify American attempts to increase its territorial claims. Manifest destiny was used to muster political and popular support for events ranging from the annexation of Texas, American entry into war with Mexico and Spain, and the acquisition of territories that make up present-day California, New Mexico, Puerto Rico, Guam, and the Philippines.

The term *manifest destiny* was first coined by John L. O'Sullivan, a journalist. Writing in the July–August 1845 edition of the *United States Magazine and Democratic Review*, O'Sullivan argued for the annexation of Texas. As justification, he asserted that it was America's right and duty to expand its borders westward to the Pacific, to spread its doctrine of liberty and freedom throughout the continent. Though the term was first penned by O'Sullivan, scholars suggest that the ideological origins of manifest destiny can also be traced to 17th-century Puritan notions of predestination and divine right. Of particular importance was the idea that Puritan settlers were graced by God with a divine mission to create a new "city upon a hill." This sense of a preordained design to settlement in an alien and hostile land was to permeate later American expansionist efforts.

Manifest destiny rapidly became a driving ideological force in the latter half of the 19th century, adopted not only by expansionist politicians but also by a broad cross-section of the American population, including settlers, slaveholders, and businessmen. Its power derived from its ability to serve a variety of economic and political agendas. Strategically, the doctrine of manifest destiny was seen as helpful in bolstering a fledgling country's position against possible encroachments by the British, which in the mid-19th century still had a foothold on the West Coast and Mexico to the south, which was newly independent from Spain in 1821. Commercially, the ability to access valued ports on the Pacific to engage with the lucrative East Asian trade was seen as a highly desirable goal. Expansion was seen as politically expedient for Southern states who sought more leverage in Washington, D.C., by working to increase the number of slave states added to the Union. Also, expansion provided a practical and profitable outlet for the burgeoning slave populations in the South. Technological change, such as the development of the telegraph in 1844 and the increasing use of steamboats, made communication and travel to remote places far more possible. Also significant was the view of expansion as a natural solution to excessive urbanization and the unhealthy concentration of political and economic power. Implicit in the concept of manifest destiny was this notion that, ultimately, expansion would increase opportunity and allow for the growth of personal freedom and prosperity.

However, manifest destiny was decidedly a racialized ideology as well. From its inception, the beneficiaries of expansionism were meant to be white settlers and landowners. Manifest destiny can be read as an attempt to justify white settler acquisition of land from nonwhite peoples. Land was characterized as essentially "unoccupied" and "cheap," though Native Americans, Mexicans, and other indigenous peoples had to be forcibly removed to make room for American settlement. Manifest destiny can be likened to the "civilizing mission," which was used to legitimize European colonialism in Africa and Asia. Because America had the duty to spread the civilizing influence of freedom and democratic culture to "other" people, it could engage in territorial imperialism.

Manifest destiny was tested almost immediately, with America's engagement in the Mexican-American War from 1846 to 1848. This war was the result of Mexican objection to the annexation of Texas and repeated border disputes along the U.S.-Mexican border. American victory in 1848 meant that California and New Mexico were ceded to the United States. Combined with the acquisition of the Oregon territory through the Oregon Boundary Treaty of 1846 with Great Britain and the Gadsden Purchase in 1854, the borders of what would later be the lower 48 states were set. America had attained its goals of expanding westward to the Pacific and south to the Rio Grande. Because of growing sectionalism that culminated in the Civil War, manifest destiny retreated to the back of the American political landscape. However, the turn of the century saw a renewed interest in American expansionism, this time beyond the contiguous borders of the United States. As a result of the defeat of Spain in the Spanish-American War (1898), the United States acquired Guam and Puerto Rico and purchased the Philippines for $20 million. In line with American desires to extend its reach into the Pacific, Hawaii was placed under American control in 1898. Hawaii eventually became America's 50th state in 1959.

REBEKAH LEE

See also

Mexican American War; Race

Further Reading:

Anders, Stephen. *Manifest Destiny: American Expansionism and the Empire of Right.* New York: Hill and Wang, 1996.

Graebner, Norman, ed. *Manifest Destiny.* Indianapolis: Bobbs Merrill, 1968.

Merk, Frederick. *Manifest Destiny and Mission in American History: A Reinterpretation.* New York: Vintage Books, 1966.

Mara Salvatrucha (MS) 13

Mara Salvatrucha 13, more commonly known as MS 13, originated in Los Angeles in the late 1980s. El Salvadoran youth formed the gang to protect themselves from the already established Calle 18 street gang, the largest non-Mexican Latino gang in the area at that time. Although LA County hosts many Latino gangs, most of their members are of Mexican descent. Young refugees from the Civil War in El Salvador were living in California among the mix of immigrants from other Latin American countries. The young immigrants could join Calle 18 or they could start their own gang since the other Latino gangs were exclusively Mexican. They began a competing group and chose the name Mara Salvatrucha. Their name uses "mara" meaning gang and the combination of Spanish words for shrewd and Salvadoran; 13 is the placement for M in the alphabet. Mara Salvatrucha created an alliance with the Mexican Mafia, the large prison gang with members in and out of prison. Out of deference to the gang, the gang added the 13 to the initials MS.

During the 20 years since its inception MS 13 has become one of the most violent, criminal groups in the gang community with estimates of 30,000 to 50,000 members worldwide. The prominence of MS 13 stems from two overlapping causes. California crime drew Latin Americans to the area where they learned street gang culture and criminality. Secondly, the immigration policy of 1996 deported felons in droves. Any noncitizen felon serving a year or more would be sent back to his country of origin. El Salvador's large portion of deportees came from those who fled their country during the civil war. The country was ill-prepared for their return and the violence and crime accompanying them. Gangs were already a problem in Latin America and known for their capacity for violence.

The gang maintains a large presence in both El Salvador and the Unites States, and each country actively works to stop their criminal activities. The FBI designated MS 13 a transnational criminal organization, or TCO, and this designation gives law enforcement rights to seize any assets used in a criminal enterprise. The approach is a rigorous crime control strategy used to cripple the gang financially. The El Salvadoran government has used negotiation tactics with gang members to reduce their crimes in exchange for improving social conditions for the poor, a chief concern for MS 13 members. MS 13 agreed to stop recruiting young members and reduce the rate of kidnapping in El Salvador while the government creates employment opportunities. Not all public officials work against the gang; some corrupt members of the political and judicial systems in El Salvador work with MS 13 members to win elections and stay in power.

MS 13 accomplishes their criminal activities by using established routes to traffic in the human and drug trades. They can return to the United States after deportation along these routes and maintain their crime syndicate in two countries.

Their geographic location situates them between the cocaine producers in Colombia and the cocaine users in the United States, making them a transnational criminal organization. These two factors mean large revenues for the gang, but also catch the attention of several criminal justice systems. Their crimes include kidnapping, extortion, prostitution, and murder for hire. Their motto is "Mata, roba, viola, controla," which translates to "Kill, steal, rape, control." Like other street gangs, membership in MS 13 brings protection, criminal opportunity, identity, and violence. Gang tattoos use the full name or its shortened version with their hand sign, the thumb holding down the two middle fingers while the pointer finger and pinky stand up.

Although their membership is spread through different cities and countries, MS 13 leaders manage criminal activities for multiple locations. The loose alliance of MS 13 cliques throughout the United States makes them a more efficient criminal syndicate as activities are coordinated through different geographic areas, a key piece of their evolution into a TCO. The National Gang Unit of ICE's Homeland Security Investigations arrested 4,000 known gang members between 2006 and 2012, and they continue to pursue criminal investigations into MS 13 gang activity.

M. KELLY JAMES

Further Reading:

Arana, Ana. "How Street Gangs took Central America." *Foreign Affairs* 84, no. 3 (May–June 2005): 98–110.

Farah, Douglas. "Central American Gangs: Changing Nature and New Partners." *Journal of International Affairs* 661 (Fall–Winter 2012): 53–62.

Federal Bureau of Investigation. *National Gang Threat Assessment: 2009*. Washington, DC: U.S. Department of Justice, Federal Bureau of Investigation, 2009.

Honda, Mike, and Ami Carpenter. "In Fighting Gangs, U.S. Should Look to El Salvador." *Christian Science Monitor*, December 28, 2012.

Howell, James, and John Moore. "History of Street Gangs in the U.S." *National Gang Center Bulletin* 4 (May 2010): 1–25.

Klein, Malcolm, and Cheryl Maxson. *Street Gang Patterns and Policies*. New York: Oxford University Press, 2006.

Manwaring, M. G. *A Contemporary Challenge to State Sovereignty: Gangs and Other Illicit Transnational Criminal Organizations in Central America, El Salvador, Mexico, Jamaica, and Brazil.* Carlisle, PA: Strategic Studies Institute, U.S. Army College, 2007. www.StrategicStudiesInstitute.army.mil.

Seper, Jerry. "U.S. to Go After MS-13 Street Gang's Financial Assets." *Washington Times*, 2012, 6.

March on Washington Movement

The origins of the March on Washington movement can be traced to a September 27, 1940, meeting between A. Philip Randolph, the president of the Brotherhood of Sleeping Car Porters; Walter White, head of the National Association for the Advancement of Colored People (NAACP); T. Arnold Hill of the Urban League; and President Franklin D. Roosevelt. Randolph urged Roosevelt to promote equal employment opportunities and to desegregate the armed services. When the meeting did not produce a positive response from Roosevelt, Randolph decided that he would bring the case directly to the American people by staging a march on Washington, D.C.

African Americans had benefited less than other groups from New Deal programs during the Great Depression, and continuing racial discrimination was excluding them from the job opportunities in the defense industries that were expanding as the world plunged into World War II. At a September 1940 union convention held at Madison Square Garden, Randolph discussed the problem of discrimination in the defense industry. Government training programs excluded blacks; defense contractors announced that they would not hire blacks or would only hire them for menial positions, and that despite the shortage of construction workers, contractors would not hire experienced blacks. During this time, the armed forces were segregated: in an army of half a million men, there were only 4,700 blacks. There were no blacks in the Marine Corps or the Army Air Corps, and even the Red Cross blood supply was segregated. In the audience the evening of Randolph's speech was First Lady Eleanor Roosevelt, who was going to speak to the convention the following evening. She learned from Randolph that the president's staff had refused to set up a meeting between Roosevelt and Randolph. Through her efforts, the September 27 meeting took place.

At the meeting, Randolph pointed out the discrimination in the defense industry, the refusal of skilled labor unions to admit blacks, and the discrimination in the armed forces. Roosevelt responded that progress was being made, although his secretary of the navy, Frank Knox (who also attended the meeting), asserted that it would be impossible to desegregate the navy. Roosevelt told the black leaders that he would consult his cabinet and military leadership and respond to their concerns. The response they received was

Six leaders of the nation's largest black civil rights organizations meet in New York's Hotel Roosevelt on July 2, 1963, to plan a civil rights march on Washington. From left, are: John Lewis, chairman, Student Nonviolence Coordinating Committee; Whitney Young, national director, Urban League; A. Philip Randolph, president, Negro American Labor Council; Dr. Martin Luther King, Jr., president, Southern Christian Leadership Conference; James Farmer, director, Congress of Racial Equality; and Roy Wilkins, executive secretary, National Association for the Advancement of Colored People. (AP Photo/Harry Harris)

not from the president, but was instead a statement by Roosevelt's press secretary, Stephen Early, who announced that the military would not be desegregated, and implied that the black leaders Roosevelt had met with agreed with the decision. Randolph and the others publicly announced that this was not the case, and the requested another meeting with the president, which was not forthcoming.

This led to a change in tactics. Randolph had sought change through letter writings and meetings with government officials. He now believed direct action was essential, and started making public statements to this effect.

Randolph, along with Bayard Rustin, the youth director of the Fellowship of Reconciliation, and A. J. Muste, the executive director of the Fellowship of Reconciliation, proposed a march on Washington to protest discrimination in government and the defense industry as well as segregation in the armed services. They established a March on Washington Committee (MOWC) to organize the march. Their slogan was: "We loyal Negro Americans demand the right to work and fight for our country." By late 1940, Randolph had established a National March on Washington Committee with chapters in 18 cities.

Randolph made his formal proposal in January 1941, and spent months gathering support for his plan and preparing for the march, which was scheduled for July 1, 1941. His union, the NAACP, the Urban League, and the black press played major roles in generating interest in the march. In "The Call to March," which appeared in the May 1941 issue of *The Black Worker*, he wrote that "[o]nly power can effect the enforcement and adoption of a given policy. Power is the active principle of only the organized masses, the masses united for a definite purpose."

Roosevelt, who had continued to refuse to meet with Randolph, became concerned about the political impact of the march, which had originally promised to bring more than 10,000 marchers to the nation's capital and had grown to where more than 100,000 marchers were expected. Randolph had indicated that all the marchers would be black, and Roosevelt feared that there might be violence, and that such a march would then become a precedent for other groups. Also, given the Roosevelt administration's opposition to the fascist regimes in Europe, a march by blacks against discrimination would be embarrassing to the country, which presented itself as a model of democracy. Also, Roosevelt was concerned about the reaction of Southern Democrats to such a march.

At the president's request, Eleanor Roosevelt wrote to Randolph asking him to call off the march. Randolph refused. Randolph then met with the first lady, who concluded that the only way to stop the march would be for the president to meet with Randolph. President Roosevelt met with Randolph and White on June 18, 1941, to urge him to call off the march. Roosevelt told them that the armed forces would remain segregated, but that he would consider an investigation of discrimination if the march was called off. Randolph's response to the president was that the march would be called off only if Roosevelt issued an executive order. Roosevelt agreed, and Randolph worked with Roosevelt's staff to draft the order.

On June 25, 1941, Roosevelt issued Executive Order 8802, which made discrimination based on race, creed, color, or national origin illegal in the defense industry, and establishing the Fair Employment Practices Committee (FEPC) to investigate charges of racial discrimination. This was the first executive order concerning the rights of African Americans since President Abraham Lincoln issued the Emancipation Proclamation during the Civil War. In response, Randolph announced in a radio address from Madison Square Garden on June 28, 1941, that he had agreed to suspend the march. In his speech, Randolph said that he had not cancelled the march, but had only suspended it. By leaving open the possibility of a march, Randolph asserted that this was the movement's "ace in the hole" to ensure that the government would not backtrack on its commitment.

The decision to suspend the march led Rustin, who believed that Randolph had "sold out" by not holding out for desegregation of the armed forces, to break (temporarily) with Randolph. In 1942, Rustin would help found the Congress of Racial Equality.

While suspending the march, the effort continued. By December 1941, the MOWC had become a dues-paying organization in order "to help create faith by Negroes in Negroes." During 1942, the MOWC mounted rallies in New York, Chicago, and St. Louis. The goal of the organization was to mobilize African Americans into an effective pressure group. Nearly 2 million African Americans worked in the defense industries by the end of 1944. However, the FEPC did not effectively tackle discriminatory practices in the South, and following Roosevelt's death, the FEPC was abolished as Congress refused to fund the agency. It ceased operation in 1946. Randolph and Rustin would initiate the effort that would culminate in the March on Washington of 1963.

JEFFREY KRAUS

See also

War and Racial Inequality; World War II

Further Reading:

Garfinkel, Herbert. *When Negroes March: The March on Washington Movement in the Organizational Politics for FEPC.* Glencoe, IL: Free Press, 1959.

Goodwin, Doris Kearns. *No Ordinary Time.* New York: Simon and Schuster, 1994.

Pfeffer, Paula F. *A. Philip Randolph, Pioneer of the Civil Rights Movement.* Baton Rouge: Louisiana State University Press, 1990.

March on Washington of 1963

The emotional high point of the first half of the Civil Rights Movement, the 1963 March on Washington for Jobs and Freedom brought together nearly 250,000 Americans to the nation's capital, all pledging their support of a transformation in race relations. It was a triumph in rhetoric, compassion, and civil rights, heralding the approaching demise of Jim Crow. The March on Washington also marked the end of the first, nonviolent stage of the modern civil rights movement; the second half of the civil rights movement, ranging from 1963 to 1970, took a decidedly more militant turn. The gathering of nearly 250,000 Americans also signaled to the administration of President John F. Kennedy that the time had come for the federal government to make its allegiance to the civil rights movement plain.

The 1963 March on Washington was influenced by an earlier attempt to gather African Americans for protest in the nation's capital. Led by A. Philip Randolph, the 1941 March on Washington Movement was intended as a peaceful demonstration against the widespread problem of racial discrimination in defense work during World War II. Randolph, a well-respected labor leader and president of the Brotherhood of Sleeping Car Porters, had spoken directly with President Franklin D. Roosevelt about the problem of African American exclusion from lucrative employment in the defense industry, which provided aircraft and munitions for the war in Europe. When Roosevelt balked, saying that he could do nothing to prevent private contractors from employing whomever they chose, Randolph called on 10,000 blacks to stage a "March on Washington" and to use the slogan, "We Loyal Negro-American citizens demand the right to work and fight for our country." Roosevelt eventually gave in to some of Randolph's demands, and in June 1941, he created the Fair Employment Practices Committee to police the desegregation of the defense industry in a presidential decree, Executive Order 8802.

In the years between the end of World War II and the 1963 March on Washington, several civil rights organizations had gained a considerable membership supporting their challenge of Jim Crow using nonviolent tactics. The National Association for the Advancement of Colored People (NAACP) and its Legal Defense Fund won several key U.S. Supreme Court decisions, including *Brown v. Board of Education*, that gravely wounded the institution of segregation. The Southern Christian Leadership Conference (SCLC) and the Student Nonviolent Coordinating Committee (SNCC) staged successful sit-ins and boycotts of cities, transportation systems, and department stores. The Congress of Racial Equality (CORE),

formed by peace activist James Farmer, led a series of Freedom Rides in the summer of 1961 that tested the application and enforcement of desegregation laws. The National Urban League's plan for economic growth and independence provided an avenue of support for African American businesses. Together, these five organizations coordinated a one-day mass movement that spoke to Randolph's vision of African American empowerment by way of peaceful, yet urgent protest.

The events of the spring and summer of 1963 also revealed the national urgency for an awareness of the vicious backlash to the civil rights movement. In early 1963, Martin Luther King, Jr. and the SCLC went to Birmingham, leading boycotts of stores in downtown Birmingham and protest marches through the streets of the city. Though the demonstrations were peaceful, the televised images of African American children and adults attacked by police dogs and fire hoses, ordered by police chief "Bull" Connor, horrified the nation. In April, King and his confidant, Ralph Abernathy, were arrested and placed in solitary confinement in Birmingham; King used the time to write his moving polemic, "Letter from a Birmingham Jail." In May, the A. G. Gaston Motel, the headquarters of the SCLC in Birmingham, and the home of King's brother, Alfred Daniel King, were bombed by the Ku Klux Klan. In June, Medgar Evers, executive secretary of the Mississippi NAACP, was shot and killed by Klan sympathizer Byron de la Beckwith. Just one day earlier, President Kennedy had proposed a strong civil rights bill that would have made such hate crimes federal offenses. Yet, the legislation was having difficulty garnering support in Congress, as the Southern bloc of the Democratic Party strongly resisted any usurpation of states' rights in favor of a federal mandate.

By the summer of 1963, the five main civil rights groups—the Urban League, SCLC, NAACP, SNCC, and CORE—had decided to pool their efforts and organized a March on Washington. A. Philip Randolph, in a nod to the march called off in 1941, inaugurated the march as the March on Washington for Jobs and Freedom. Randolph was joined by Bayard Rustin as chief organizers of the march. Rustin, a Quaker and a Freedom Rider for CORE, drew upon his wide network in peace activism to raise funds and awareness of the event. With a budget of $120,000, Rustin, the chief coordinator, collected donations from African American celebrities, churches, and business, as well as through selling buttons and posters for as little as 25 cents.

On the morning of August 28, 1963, hundreds of chartered buses from across the country arrived in front of the Lincoln Memorial. Marchers also traveled over thousands of miles by chartered train and cars. One group of CORE volunteers walked over 200 miles from New York to Washington, D.C., to show their solidarity. Eventually, nearly 250,000 people crowded the national mall for the march, the largest political assembly in American history.

With 17 components of the program, the 1963 March on Washington unfolded over eight hours. Marian Anderson, who had once been denied the opportunity to sing at Constitution Hall, sang the national anthem. Randolph gave the opening remarks, and the program included a tribute to the struggles of African American civil rights workers Daisy Lee Bates, Diane Nash Bevel, Rosa Parks, Merlie Evers, and others. As president of the SNCC, John Lewis denounced the passivity of the Kennedy administration in securing a civil rights bill. Gospel singer Mahalia Jackson sang "I've Been 'Buked and I've Been Scorned"; folk singers Bob Dylan and Joan Baez later joined Jackson on stage. Other speakers included Whitney Young, president of the National Urban League; Roy Wilkins, executive secretary of the national NAACP; Joachim Prinz, president of the American Jewish Congress; and James Farmer, national director of CORE.

The March on Washington is best remembered for King's "I Have a Dream" speech. King had delivered the speech as a sermon on several occasions in the early 1960s, but it was his experience in solitary confinement during the Birmingham campaign that honed the finer rhetorical points. In his earlier version of "I Have a Dream," King stressed a number of social justice issues of the period—a federal promise to supersede states' rights, prosecution of police brutality, the elimination of Jim Crow, and the passage of Kennedy's proposed civil rights legislation. These previous drafts were intended to nudge the national conscience into recognizing the debilitating effects of violent repression on the peaceful movement.

At midpoint in the speech, however, King abandoned the policy initiatives that had weighed down the language of the speech in favor of the passionate sermon that he delivered in churches and rallies across the South. Calling for freedom and equality, King's most famous words still resonate: "I have a dream that one day even the state of Mississippi, a desert state sweltering with the heat of injustice and oppression, will be transformed into an oasis of freedom and justice. I have a dream that my four little children will one day live in a nation where they will not be judged by the color of their skin but by the content of their character." By granting a vision and mission to the civil rights movement beyond boycotts and sit-ins, King's language of hope and change ushered in a phase of clear-focused determination on the greater goals of social justice. The peaceful end to the march helped Kennedy win victory for a number of his social programs. The astounding success of the 1963 March on Washington, coupled with his steadfast support of nonviolence in the civil rights movement, led to the conferral to King of the Nobel Peace Prize in 1964.

However, the success of the 1963 March on Washington did not spell an end to the violence. In September 1963, a bomb left at the Birmingham Baptist Church killed four African American girls, Addie Mae Collins, Denise McNair, Carole Robertson, and Cynthia Wesley. In November 1963, President Kennedy was shot and killed in Dallas while on a campaign stop. Assassinated before he could see his Civil Rights Bill reach fruition, Kennedy was succeeded by Lyndon B. Johnson, who made the passage of the Civil Rights Act of 1964 a priority.

The 1963 March on Washington, ultimately, heralded the urgent need for a second Reconstruction for African Americans. It also served as a harbinger of hopefulness in the 1960s, before assassinations of political and spiritual leaders, the war in Vietnam, and the free speech movement lent the patina of turbulence. In front of a national audience, Americans across generations and racial lines pledged their support for the moral objectives of the civil rights movement. As much a success for the entire nation as it was for the civil rights movement, the 1963 March on Washington spelled the death of Jim Crow through peaceful, orderly, and steadfast affirmation.

NIKKI BROWN

See also
Civil Rights Movement; King, Martin Luther, Jr.

Further Reading:
Branch, Taylor. *Parting the Waters: America during the King Years, 1954–1963*. New York: Simon and Schuster, 1988.

Branch, Taylor. *Pillar of Fire: America during the King Years, 1963–1965*. New York: Simon and Schuster, 1998.

Carson, Clayborne, et al., eds. *The Eyes on the Prize: Civil Rights Reader: Documents, Speeches, and Firsthand Accounts from the Black Freedom Struggle*. New York: Penguin, 1991.

Lewis, John. *Walking with the Wind: A Memoir of the Movement*. New York: Harvest Books, 1999.

Marked

In her notable book, *Marked: Race, Crime, and Finding Work in an Era of Mass Incarceration*, Devah Pager shows how ex-offenders who are white still have a better chance at obtaining a job than blacks and ex-offenders who are black. She used audit studies to document this discrepancy.

As a part of her research, Pager matched up pairs of young, male individuals, and she sent each pair to apply to real job openings in Milwaukee, Wisconsin. These testers were matched according to age, race, physical appearance, and how each individual presented himself. Before sending them out, she randomly assigned one individual from each group with a criminal record. Then, for every other job application, the duo rotated who had the criminal offense. Aside from the criminal offense, everything else about the job application was identical. The goal of this experiment was to see who would likely get hired in an entry-level job. After each individual submitted his application, he also filled out a six-page form which included additional details that could not be obtained from just receiving a call back. This included the behavior of the employer and comments the employer said which may have included some bias.

Results from this experiment showed that 17 percent of white ex-offenders and 34 percent of whites with no records were called back for the next stage in the job process. However, only 5 percent of black ex-offenders and 14 percent of blacks with no criminal record were called back. These results show that blacks who have a clean background have a tough time getting hired, and black ex-offenders have an even more difficult time. As Pager writes, "[A]s vast racial disparities have become emblematic of our criminal justice system, the findings of this study suggest that black ex-offenders may be doubly disadvantaged: not only are blacks more likely to be incarcerated than whites; according to the

Wage Discrimination

Besides discrimination in hiring in the workplace, there is also wage discrimination. Cancio, Evans, and Maume Jr. looked at the effects of the government backing away from antidiscrimination policies in the 1980s. These sociologists say this trend in the government resulted in a backlash against blacks, which produced organizational discrimination against blacks. It also added to disparity in the wages earned by blacks compared to whites.

During the 1970s, blacks saw a boost in wages, especially when the federal government passed the Civil Rights Act of 1964. Due to this boost, many whites believe that racial discrimination has been solved. For this reason, antidiscrimination laws have weakened. In addition, Reagan had weakened the Equal Opportunity Commission that enforced laws under Title VII of the 1964 Civil Rights Act. The EOC helps file lawsuits against large corporations. Once the enforcement was weakened, the number of lawsuits decreased, meaning more corporations could get away with discrimination. In addition, Reagan also weakened the policies used to enforce affirmative action. Through their research, Cancio et al. found that the ratio in wages between blacks and whites increased, meaning the wages for blacks gradually became lower.

findings presented here, they may also be more strongly affected by the stigma of a criminal record" (2007: 71).

After the publishing of her book, Pager, Bart Bonikowski, and Bruce Western went even a step further. They also tested how a marked record would affect Latinos in New York City's low-wage job market. They followed the same audit method Pager had used, and they matched white, black, and Latino job applicants based on their demographic characteristics and interpersonal skills. Like blacks who have a marked record, Latinos who also have a marked record are less likely to be hired for a job than whites who also have a criminal offense conviction. Yet, Latinos were more likely to be hired than blacks. Whites received callbacks in 34 percent of the cases, Latinos received callbacks in 15 percent of the cases, and blacks received callbacks in 15 percent of the cases. Seeing how employers hired blacks at a much lower rate in each of the two experiments shows that discrimination plays a major role in the hiring process.

Beyond her discoveries, what is unique about Pager's research is her use of an audit experiment. Not many people use an audit design in their research. However, according to Pager and Bruce Western, the audit design combines experimental methods with the real-life context. Such a methodology makes it easier for researchers to determine the causal factors rather than relying on observations or correlational data. Also, such audits can offer both qualitative and quantitative data, like the forms each individual completes.

Although a criminal offense is a barrier when it comes to employment, steady work is considered a way to decrease the incentives that lead to crime. Policies geared to help ex-offenders gain work center around two ideas—"promoting reentry" or "reducing risk." Policies that promote reentry focus on antidiscrimination legislation and removing legal barriers. On the other hand, policies that promote the reduction of risk center upon protecting employers from the risks of hiring an ex-offender. For example, an ex-offender may be dangerous or may have some unusual forms of behavior. Risk-reducing policies protect the employer from such threats. Pager believes working on such policies, in an independent manner, is not the correct method. Pager writes, "For reentry policy to be successful, the concerns of ex-offenders, employers, and the public must be simultaneously taken into account" (2007: 506).

Kurlychek, Bushway, and Brame (2012) studied the trajectories of ex-offenders after they had been arrested. By comparing their trajectory to a cohort of men who had not offended, they discovered that recidivism declines six to seven years after the arrest. Thus, employers who are concerned about the risks of hiring an ex-offender may have more confidence in hiring an ex-offender after the critical six or seven years have passed. Pager also suggests more use of intermediaries who would function as a liaison between the employer and the ex-offender. Liaisons can ease the transition for ex-offenders. Above all, Pager says race must not disappear when discussing public policy. To ensure equal opportunity for all, there must be more active protections in place.

ALAN VINCENT GRIGSBY AND RASHA ALY

Further Reading:

Cancio, A. Silva, T. David Evans, and David J. Maume. "Reconsidering the Declining Significance of Race: Racial Differences in Early Career Wages." *American Sociological Review* 61 (1996): 541–56.

Kurlychek, Megan, Shawn D. Bushway, and Robert Brame. "Long-term crime desistance and recidivism patterns: evidence from the Essex County convicted felon study." *Criminology*, 50 (2012): 71–103.

Pager, D. *Marked: Race, Crime, and Finding Work in an Era of Mass Incarceration.* Chicago: University of Chicago Press, 2007.

Pager, Devah. "Identifying Discrimination at Work: The Use of Field Experiments." *Journal of Social Issues* 68, no. 2 (2012): 221–37.

Pager, D., B. Bonikowski, and B. Western. "Discrimination in a Low-Wage Labor Market: A Field Experiment." *American Sociological Review* 74, no. 5 (2009): 777–99.

Marrow of Tradition, The

Charles Chesnutt's 1901 novel, *The Marrow of Tradition*, based on the Wilmington (North Carolina) Riot of 1898, represents everyday manifestations of racism of the era, explores Southern white anxiety about the ascendance of African Americans to political power, and portrays the 1898 riot as a ploy engineered by politicians and journalists to disenfranchise black voters. Set in the town of Wellington, the narrative illustrates the social and political backdrop of the riot through the intertwined histories of the Carteret and Miller families, and a large cast of supporting characters. Maj. Philip Carteret, editor of Wellington's *Morning Chronicle* newspaper, is an avowed white supremacist determined to end "Negro domination" of the South, in league with Capt. George McBane (based on labor leader and Redshirt Mike Dowling), a former prison labor contractor, and General Belmont (based on politician and journalist Alfred Moore Waddell), known collectively as the *Big Three.* McBane, Belmont, and Carteret foment latent white racism into a riot, which serves as a pretext to drive out Wellington's black and white Republicans and Populists (who had run together as "Fusionists"), and install white Democrats in local government.

Wellington's racial climate emerges through the experiences of the novel's various African American characters. There are servants still awaiting the material benefits of emancipation, such as Sandy Campbell, who mimics the old-fashioned manners of his employer; Jerry Letlow, who scrounges for tips but is scorned for his craven loyalty to Major Carteret; and Aunt Jane Letlow, who raises Carteret's son and dies in the street at the hands of a white mob. Dr. William Miller, an African American doctor educated in the Northeast and Europe, runs a black hospital in Wellington. As a black professional, Dr. Miller is continually faced with the disparity between his social status as a gentleman and the indignities imposed by racist legal and social institutions, such as being forced to switch, mid-conversation with a colleague, to a segregated railroad car during a trip back to North Carolina from Philadelphia, and having an invitation to assist in an operation on Major Carteret's son rescinded. In sharp contrast to Dr. Miller's accommodationist stance and aspirations to bourgeois respectability is the radical attitude of Josh Green whose father was killed by McBane. During the riot, Green installs a group of black resistors in Miller's hospital for a last stand and takes vengeance on McBane before being killed himself.

Instances of racial ambiguity, doubling, and crossing abound in the novel. The Carteret and Miller families are joined across the color line by Mrs. Carteret and Mrs. Miller, who are half-sisters. The unjust divestiture of Mrs. Miller from her inheritance (Mrs. Carteret's aunt hides their shared father's will and proof of his second marriage) represents one case of the broad disenfranchisement of Southern black citizens of their property rights. In another case, profligate white scion Tom Delamere dresses up as his black servant Sandy, in whose guise Tom wins a cakewalk contest and later commits murder, for which Sandy is almost lynched, hinting at the barely submerged violence that surfaces in the riot.

Of *The Marrow of Tradition*, William Dean Howells wrote, "The book is, in fact, bitter, bitter" (1996). But the astringent view of white anxiety, voter disenfranchisement, and post-Reconstruction race relations represented in the novel suggest hope that publicizing the political machinations behind the riot will lead to reform. As Chesnutt wrote in the *Cleveland World*, "The book is not a study in pessimism, for it is the writer's belief that the forces of progress will in the end prevail, and that in time a remedy may be found for every social ill" (1901).

ALEX FEERST

See also
American Literature and Racism; Wilmington (North Carolina) Riot of 1898

Further Reading:
Chesnutt, Charles W. "Charles W. Chesnutt's Own View of His New Story *The Marrow of Tradition*." *Cleveland World*, October 20, 1901, Magazine Section, 5.
Duncan, Charles. *Absent Man: Narrative Craft of Charles W. Chesnutt*. Columbus: Ohio University Press, 1999.
Howells, William Dean. "A Psychological Counter-Current in Recent Fiction." Project Gutenberg Release #726 (November 1996). http://onlinebooks.library.upenn.edu/webbin/gutbook/lookup?num=726.
McWilliams, Dean. *Charles W. Chesnutt and the Fictions of Race*. Athens: University of Georgia Press, 2002.
Wilson, Matthew. *Whiteness in the Novels of Charles W. Chesnutt*. Jackson: University of Mississippi Press, 2004.

Marshall, Thurgood (1908–1992)

The lead attorney for the National Association for the Advancement of Colored People (NAACP) in the 1954 *Brown v. Board of Education* case and the first African American to sit on the U.S. Supreme Court, Thurgood Marshall was born in Baltimore, Maryland, on July 2, 1908. Named for his great-grandfather, Thoroughgood, who had escaped slavery, Marshall grew up comfortably in middle-class, but segregated, black Baltimore (Marshall shortened the name himself to Thurgood as a child because he found his name too long to write out). His father, William, was a Pullman porter and a waiter at a white club, while his mother, Norma, was a schoolteacher.

In 1925, Marshall followed his older brother, Aubrey, to Lincoln University in Pennsylvania, one of the nation's most prestigious black universities. At Lincoln, Marshall was not an exceptionally serious student and was suspended from school for his involvement in hazing freshmen. When he returned to school, his racial consciousness was stoked by a fellow Lincoln student, the poet Langston Hughes, who was leading the charge to have Lincoln's all-white faculty integrated. Marshall, like most Lincoln students, initially opposed integrating the faculty, but he eventually became a supporter of the idea, and took over the campaign when Hughes graduated. As a senior, Marshall pushed a student

Lawyers for the National Association for the Advancement of Colored People celebrate outside the Supreme Court after successfully challenging school segregation in *Brown v. Board of Education* (1954). From left to right are: George E. Hayes, Thurgood Marshall, and James Nabrit. (Library of Congress)

referendum to force the administration to integrate the faculty, and the school's first black faculty member was hired the following year.

Marshall married Philadelphia native Vivian "Buster" Bury, a University of Pennsylvania student, in 1929. He graduated from Lincoln the following year but was relegated to working as a waiter at Maryland's all-white Gibson Island Club, with his father, as the onset of the Great Depression had left jobs scarce. Marshall, who had been an excellent debater in college, then decided that he wanted to go to law school. He and Buster lived with his parents in Baltimore, so he applied to the all-white University of Maryland Law School, but was rejected because of his race, bringing him face to face with the Jim Crowism that he had mostly avoided growing up in black Baltimore and at Lincoln University. Angered at the rejection, his only other option seemed to be to apply

to the historically black Howard University Law School in Washington, D.C. Howard's reputation at this time was poor, as the law school was not accredited by the American Bar Association or the Association of American Law Schools.

Marshall was admitted to Howard Law in the fall of 1930, at a fortuitous time in the school's history. Harvard-educated Charles Hamilton Houston, who had joined Howard's faculty in 1924, had recently been promoted to dean of the law school, and, along with Howard University's first African American president, Mordecai Johnson, was determined to increase Howard's academic standards and become a fully accredited law school. Despite some opposition to his rigorous policies, Houston succeeded in toughening admission requirements to the school, and by 1931, it was accredited by both the American Bar Association and the Association of American Law Schools. Most importantly, Houston was committed to using Howard Law School to develop a cadre of black lawyers to fight racial injustice. It was into this vigorous academic environment that Marshall entered in 1930.

At Howard, Marshall quickly became a disciple of Houston and fellow Howard faculty member William Hastie. Along with fellow student and future NAACP attorney Oliver Hill, Marshall developed as Houston's protégée, accompanying him to court and sitting in on strategy sessions for NAACP cases. Through Houston's tutelage, Marshall became aware of the power that lawyers could wield in bringing about change, and he wanted to be a part of it. Following his graduation from Howard in 1933, first in his class, Marshall traveled South with Houston to examine the state of black elementary schools throughout the region. The trip was part of Houston's research in developing a legal strategy for the NAACP to challenge segregated education; it was the basis of what would eventually culminate in the *Brown* decision.

Marshall was offered a scholarship to pursue an advanced degree at Harvard Law School in 1933, but instead decided it was time for him to begin his own practice and earn some money for his family, so he opened his own firm in Baltimore. However, the clientele available for a black attorney in Depression-era Baltimore was slim, and Marshall had a very difficult time making ends meet. The clients he did have often had a tough time paying his fees, but he developed a reputation of not turning anyone in need away. His reputation also brought him to the notice of the Baltimore branch of the NAACP, which retained him as its counsel, and in December 1933, Marshall began preparing his first civil rights case, what became *Murray v. Maryland*.

As Marshall knew all too well, the University of Maryland's law school refused to admit black students on account of their race. Marshall and the local NAACP wanted to challenge the legality of this segregationist policy, but they were hampered by the Supreme Court's 1896 *Plessy v. Ferguson* "separate but equal" decision, which ruled that segregation was constitutional. This decision was the great hurdle for black lawyers like Marshall and Houston to overcome, as once the Supreme Court has ruled on a decision, it rarely overturned itself, a practice known as *starre decisis* (Let the decision stand).

Houston, however, had been working on a different approach to challenge school discrimination, and when Marshall informed him that he planned to sue for the right of Donald Murray to attend the University of Maryland Law School, Houston sought to put his strategy to the test and join his former pupil on the case. He and Marshall would not challenge the *Plessy* decision, they would embrace it. Houston and Marshall argued not that Maryland had to admit Murray to its law school because segregation was unconstitutional (overturning *Plessy*), but instead that Murray had to be admitted under the "separate but equal" statute, because there was no public law school open to African Americans in the state of Maryland. Houston's strategy was relatively simple: in the *Murray* case, he did not have to prove the inequality between black and white law schools (the way he would have to with black and white elementary schools, for instance), because there was no black law school in the state; it was a question of exclusion, not equality, and therefore not allowed by *Plessy*.

Houston and Marshall prevailed in the *Murray* case when the Maryland Court of Appeals upheld the lower court's decision to admit Murray to the law school and the state decided not to appeal the case to the U.S. Supreme Court. It was Marshall's first civil rights victory, and it began a strategy that he and Houston would pursue in attacking school segregation for another 15 years, in cases such as *Missouri ex rel. Gaines v. Canada* (1938), *Sipuel v. Board of Regents of the University of Oklahoma* (1948), and *Sweatt v. Painter* (1950). In all of these cases, Marshall and/or Houston focused on

graduate educational facilities and did not challenge the legality of separate but equal, but instead on the lack of education programs provided for black citizens. With each victory, the NAACP lawyers chipped away at the legitimacy of school segregation and laid the groundwork for the eventual assault on *Plessy*.

While Marshall is most famous for his work on school desegregation during this era, he was involved in a host of other cases for the NAACP as well. In 1936, he closed his unprofitable one-man firm in Baltimore and became a full-time employee of the NAACP, focusing on cases in Maryland and Virginia. Many of the cases he pursued successfully were pay equalization cases for African American public school teachers and employees. In 1938, he took over as head of the NAACP's legal division, replacing Houston, who was in ailing health. Two years later the NAACP Legal Defense Fund, Inc., was founded as a organization separate from the NAACP to focus on civil rights litigation, and headed by Marshall from its inception until 1961, when he became a federal court of appeals judge.

With Marshall at the head of the NAACP's legal wing, the organization flourished. In addition to continued work on school integration and pay equalization, he instituted successful litigation that eliminated the white primary (*Smith v. Allwright*, 1944) and restrictive housing covenants (*Shelley v. Kraemer*, 1948). Marshall even traveled to Japan and Korea in 1951 to investigate discrimination by the U.S. Army against black soldiers, who were being court-martialed at much higher rates than whites, mostly on vague charges of "cowardice" and "incompetence." Between August and October 1950, 32 black servicemen in Korea were convicted under the 75th Article of War—"misbehavior in front of the enemy"—in comparison to only two white soldiers; blacks also got harsher penalties for being convicted for the same crimes as whites. Marshall's investigation revealed a pattern of discrimination in the court-martial process, going back to World War I. Marshall blamed the army high command, specifically Gen. Douglas MacArthur, for continued discrimination against African American soldiers, as the army leadership continued to resist integration two years after President Harry S. Truman's Executive Order 9981 mandating the end of discrimination in the armed forces.

In 1950, Marshall also believed that the time had finally come for a frontal attack on *Plessy*, and the NAACP announced that it was looking for plaintiffs who would be willing to challenge school segregation. For almost 15 years, the NAACP had pursued the legal strategy developed by Houston of using *Plessy* to gain equal educational facilities for African Americans (with the hope that the cost of making schools truly equal would force school integration). Now, Marshall decided that the Supreme Court was ready to hear a challenge to the constitutionality of school segregation itself. His team compiled five cases—from Kansas, Virginia, South Carolina, the District of Columbia, and Delaware—which became known as *Brown v. Board of Education*.

The cases came before the Supreme Court in 1952. Marshall's strategy in arguing *Brown* was controversial, in that he based much of his argument on evidence provided by psychologists Kenneth and Mamie Clark and their famous doll experiment. The Clarks' study of three- to seven-year-old children revealed that white superiority was so ingrained in society that young black children preferred white dolls (which they identified as "pretty" or "nice") instead of black dolls (which they described as "ugly" or bad"). While derided as sociological garbage by opposing counsel, Marshall's use of the "doll test" proved to be powerful evidence that school segregation caused a sense of inferiority in black children that was a violation of their Fourteenth Amendment right of equal protection of the laws. The justices agreed with Marshall's arguments, and in 1954, the Supreme Court overturned *Plessy*, ruling that "separate is inherently unequal in the area of education."

While the *Brown* decision was a dramatic victory for Marshall and the NAACP, the culmination of almost two decades of legal attacks on segregation in education, it did not bring about the immediate desegregation of the nation's schools. At the conclusion of *Brown*, the Court asked lawyers from both the NAACP and the states to return the next year to present their plans for a timetable on how *Brown* should be implemented. In his brief for the high court, Marshall recommended that integration plans go into effect in 1955, with complete school integration by the fall of 1956. Lawyers for the states asked instead that the court set no timetable for integration, but to leave the decision on how and when to integrate to local school boards. In what became known as *Brown* II, Chief Justice Earl Warren sided with the gradualist approach of the states in 1955 by refusing to set a timetable for integration, ruling instead that integration should

proceed "with all deliberate speed." This infamous order set the stage for massive resistance against school integration, as many school districts throughout the South simply refused to integrate until finally forced to by the federal government following the passage of the Civil Rights Act of 1964.

The same year as his professional setback with *Brown* II, Marshall suffered a personal loss when Buster, his wife of 25 years, died of cancer. His personal fame, however, in 1955, was at an all-time high. Known even before *Brown* in the African American community as "Mr. Civil Rights," he became well known throughout the nation as a result of the *Brown* decision, even appearing on the cover of *Time* magazine. As black protests regarding Emmett Till's murder in Mississippi and the Montgomery Bus Boycott in Alabama developed, Marshall also emerged as a lightning rod in the civil rights movement. He believed that the best way for African Americans to enact change was through the courts, not the streets; he was not always totally supportive of the protest movement, and was highly critical of black separatist organizations.

Despite some of his reservations over public protests, Marshall and the NAACP did provide legal assistance to the protesters. Marshall was directly involved in the Montgomery Bus Boycott case, working with local NAACP attorney Fred Gray as the case was eventually settled in their favor by the U.S. Supreme Court in 1956. He also continued to work for school integration, including representing Autherine Lucy in her fight to integrate the University of Alabama. Marshall, who remarried in 1955 to Cecilia ("Cissy") Suyat, an NAACP secretary, enjoyed a personal joy when his first child, Thurgood Jr., was born in 1956. The couple later had a second son, John.

In 1961, Marshall left the NAACP after a quarter-century of service when President John F. Kennedy appointed him as a federal appeals judge. As counsel for the NAACP, Marshall had argued 32 cases before the U.S. Supreme Court, winning 29 of them. Four years after his appointment as a federal judge, President Lyndon B. Johnson appointed Marshall as U.S. Solicitor General. As the nation's top litigator, Marshall won numerous other decisions before the Supreme Court on behalf of the United States. After less than two years in that post, Johnson appointed Marshall to the U.S. Supreme Court, becoming the first African American to serve on the nation's highest court in 1967.

During Marshall's 24-year term on the Supreme Court, he consistently supported civil rights, voting with the court's liberal majority in the 1970s on landmark cases regarding affirmative action, abortion, defendant rights, and school desegregation. As the court took a conservative turn in the 1980s, Marshall increasingly found himself arguing with the minority, and many of his written opinions became angry and bitter, especially in regard to cases in which he believed that the court was trying to turn back the clock on civil rights. Frustrated by the conservative nature of the court and in failing health, Marshall retired in 1991. The decision to appoint Clarence Thomas, a conservative African American with little experience as a litigator or a judge, hurt Marshall, but he accepted it with dignity, meeting with the new justice for more than two hours when Thomas joined the Court. Thurgood Marshall died the following year, at age 84.

THOMAS J. WARD, JR.

See also

Brown v. Board of Education, Legal Groundwork for

Further Reading:

Davis, Michael D., and Hunter R. Clark. *Thurgood Marshall: Warrior at the Bar, Rebel on the Bench*. New York: Carol Publishing Group, 1992.

Tushnet, Mark V. *Making Civil Rights Law: Thurgood Marshall and the Supreme Court, 1936–1961*. New York: Oxford University Press, 1996.

Williams, Juan. *Thurgood Marshall: American Revolutionary*. New York: Times Books, 1998.

Martin Luther King, Jr. Assassination

Rev. Dr. Martin Luther King, Jr., leader of the American civil rights movement, was assassinated on April 4, 1968, at 6:01 P.M. on the balcony of the Lorraine Motel in Memphis, Tennessee. King was in Memphis because he had been preparing to lead a local march in support of the predominantly black nonunion sanitation workers there, who had gone on strike as a response to a January 31, 1968, incident in which 22 black sanitation workers had been sent home without pay during bad weather while all the white workers remained on the job. Because the City of Memphis would not negotiate with the 1,300 striking workers, King and other civil rights leaders had been asked to visit Memphis to offer support.

On Monday, March 18, 1968, King spoke to over 15,000 people at Mason Temple, calling for a general work stoppage in Memphis. Promoting nonviolence, he agreed to return to lead a march in support of the striking sanitation workers. Ten days later, he returned to Memphis to do so. As King led the crowd on March 28, a few protestors began inciting violence, smashing the windows of a storefront and looting. The violence spread, and police moved in to disperse the crowd. Some of the marchers threw stones at the police, and the police responded with tear gas and nightsticks. According to a *New York Times* report, a black teenager was killed, 62 persons were injured, and 200 were arrested. Distressed by the violence that had erupted in his own march and his inability to control the activists, yet determined not to let violence prevail, King consented to lead a second Memphis march and scheduled it for April 5. He returned to Memphis on April 3, a little later than planned because there had been a bomb threat on his flight before the plane took off. That evening he delivered his "I've Been to the Mountaintop" speech to a few thousand who had braved the bad weather to hear him. After the speech, King went back to the Lorraine Motel to rest.

On the evening of the next day, April 4, King and his friends were preparing to have dinner with Memphis minister Rev. Billy Kyles. After getting dressed, King emerged from his room, and he and Kyles stepped out from the motel room onto the balcony, a walkway that connected the motel's second-floor rooms. Kyles began descending the stairs, while Rev. Ralph Abernathy remained in the motel room. A shot rang out. Some of the men who were waiting below—James Bevel, Chauncey Eskridge, Jesse Jackson, Hosea Williams, Andrew Young, and the driver of their car, Solomon Jones Jr.—initially thought a car had backfired, but others concluded that the sound was a rifle shot. King fell to the concrete floor of the balcony with a large, gaping wound covering his right jaw.

Kyles went into the motel room to call an ambulance, while Marrell McCoullough, an undercover Memphis police officer, tried to stop the flow of blood with a towel. Within 15 minutes of the shot, King, unresponsive and barely alive, was rushed to St. Joseph's Hospital, one and a half miles away, with an oxygen mask over his face. He had been hit by a 30.06-caliber rifle bullet that had entered his right jaw, then traveled through his neck, severing his spinal cord, stopping in his shoulder blade. The physicians attempted emergency surgery, but their efforts to revive him failed. King, 39 years of age, was pronounced dead at 7:05 P.M.

Shortly after King was pronounced dead on the evening of April 4, 1968, his body was taken from St. Joseph's Hospital to John Gaston Hospital, where an autopsy was performed by Dr. Jerry T. Francisco, the medical examiner of Shelby County, Tennessee. His body then lay in state at the R. S. Lewis & Sons Funeral Home in Memphis. The next day, April 5, King's body was flown to Atlanta on a plane chartered by Sen. Robert F. Kennedy. The body was accompanied by King's widow (Coretta Scott King), Abernathy, and other Southern Christian Leadership Conference (SCLC) staff members.

The news of King's assassination evoked expressions of dismay, shock, anger, and grief throughout the nation. It also precipitated one of the worst cases of racial riots and violence in the United States. Having received word of King's death, all three television networks interrupted programming with the news. The immediacy of this coverage prompted riots in over 60 American cities including Chicago, Denver, and Baltimore. These riots continued for more than five days, affecting at least 125 cities in 28 states and the District of Columbia. Racial disturbances swept the nation April 4–11, 1968, in the wake of King's assassination. King's murder also provoked demonstrations and disorders among students at various high schools and colleges across the country.

Looting and vandalism erupted in Washington, D.C., late on April 4 after Stokely Carmichael, ex-chairman of the Student Nonviolent Coordinating Committee (SNCC), led about 50 youths down 14th Street to urge stores to close as a sign of respect for King. The group swelled to more than 400 persons about a mile north of the White House. The District of Columbia government reported on May 1, 1968, that the April rioting had resulted in 9 deaths, 1,202 injuries, and 6,306 arrests.

In Chicago, federal troops and national guardsmen were called to the city to quell the disorders, in which more than 500 persons sustained injuries and approximately 3,000 persons were arrested. At least 162 buildings were reported entirely destroyed by fire, and total property damage was estimated at $9 million.

In Baltimore, the National Guard and federal troops were called to curb the violence. More than 700 persons were reported injured April 6–9, more than 5,000 arrests were made, and more than 1,000 fires were reported. Gov. Spiro T. Agnew declared a state of emergency and crisis on April 6, calling in 6,000 national guardsmen and the state police to aid the city's 1,100-man police force.

Some scholars have concluded that the riots following King's assassination represented a shift from an emphasis on local issues to a national focus, as the disruptions were so widespread. Regardless, events within the civil rights movement went forward. On April 5, Abernathy was named to succeed King as president of the SCLC, and the first activity was to carry out the march in support of the striking sanitation workers in Memphis that King had planned to lead. The march King had planned was held April 8 with Coretta Scott King taking her husband's place in the front ranks, ahead of an estimated 42,000 silent marchers, including thousands of whites. The march ended with a rally in front of Memphis City Hall, where Mrs. King urged the crowd to carry on because that was what her husband would have wanted. The strike eventually was settled on April 16, exactly 65 days after it had started.

Four days after King's death, President Lyndon Johnson declared a national day of mourning for the lost civil rights leader. The various institutions and activities that closed or were halted as a result included many public school systems, public libraries and museums, many businesses, the stock exchange, and seaports from Maine to Texas as longshoremen and seamen stopped work. The United Nations flag was flown at half-mast; the opening of the baseball season, scheduled for April 8, was postponed; the Stanley Cup hockey playoffs and the playoffs in the American Basketball Association and National Basketball Association were postponed; Hollywood's Oscar awards presentation ceremony was postponed, and the presidential nomination campaign was temporarily suspended.

TV and radio networks and stations canceled entertainment programs and commercial announcements to carry live coverage of King's funeral service on April 9 at the Ebenezer Baptist Church. To honor Mrs. King's request, the service included a tape-recording of her husband's last sermon, preached at the Ebenezer church on February 4, 1968. After the service, King's casket was placed on a faded green sharecropper's wagon and drawn by two Georgia mules for four miles to the Morehouse College Campus. Rev. Ralph Abernathy conducted the graveside service, and King was buried in a white marble crypt bearing the epitaph: "Free at last, free at last, thank God Almighty, I'm free at last." A crowd of 300,000, including national leaders, attended his funeral and burial.

The search for King's assassin was immediate. Aided by fingerprints found on an abandoned rifle left near the rooming house in Memphis and various other clues, local law enforcement agents and the Federal Bureau of Investigation (FBI) initiated a manhunt for King's assassin. On April 19, the FBI announced that Eric Starvo Galt was an alias of James Earl Ray, 40, of Illinois, who had escaped from the Missouri State Penitentiary on April 23, 1967, after serving seven months of a 20-year sentence for armed robbery and auto theft. The FBI released photos of Ray and placed him on its 10 Most Wanted List on April 20, 1968.

Two months after King's assassination, James Earl Ray, a career criminal and open racist, was captured and arrested by Scotland Yard detectives and captured on Saturday, June 10, at London's Heathrow Airport. He had attempted to board a plane for Brussels using a false Canadian passport in the name of Ramon George Sneyd. Ray was extradited by a London court on July 2, 1968, and returned to Tennessee on July 19. At his arraignment on July 22, he was charged with murder and carrying a dangerous weapon. He entered a plea of not guilty.

The facts of the assassination were presented. Allegedly, Ray, who had rented a room at a flophouse across the street from where King was staying, rested his rifle with a sniper scope on the window sill of the bathroom, and fired a single shot at King. No witness saw Ray shoot, although one man, Charles Stephens, claimed that he saw a man leaving the bathroom around the time of the act. A bag containing a rifle was found in front of a store near the rooming house. The rifle bore two of James Earl Ray's fingerprints. Records showed that Ray had purchased a pair of binoculars and the rifle six days before the shooting.

On March 10, 1969, Ray confessed to the assassination, pleading guilty in Memphis to King's murder, although three days later he recanted this confession. As a result, a trial was waived and Ray was subsequently sentenced to a 99-year prison term in the state penitentiary. Judge W. Preston Battle ordered Ray sent to the Tennessee State Penitentiary in Nashville after brief court proceedings during which Ray indicated that he disagreed with the prosecution's theory that there had

been no conspiracy. The case was settled in Shelby County Courthouse, during a short hearing at which prosecutor Phil M. Canale presented evidence against Ray to a 12-man jury. The 99-year sentence allowed parole after completion of half the sentence. If Ray had pleaded not guilty and had been convicted of first-degree murder, he could have received either a life sentence (and have been eligible for parole in 13 years), or he could have been sentenced to death.

Within three days of his arrival, Ray had written to the court requesting that his guilty plea be set aside and that he be given a trial. Despite many appeals, none of Ray's many attorneys ever produced evidence to convince a court of law to open the case. On the advice of his attorney, Percy Foreman, Ray pled guilty to avoid a trial conviction and thus the possibility of receiving the death penalty; some argue that it would have been highly unlikely that he would have been executed even if he had been sentenced to death, since the U.S. Supreme Court's 1972 decision in the case of *Furman v. Georgia* invalidated all state death penalty laws then in force.

Without much delay, Ray fired Foreman as his attorney, calling him "Percy Fourflusher." Ray proceeded to claim he had been framed by a shady character with the alias "Raoul" whom he had met in Montreal, Canada, while engaging in smuggling operations. Ray argued that Raoul was involved in the assassination, as was his brother Johnny. Ray went on to assert that although he didn't "personally shoot Dr. King," he may have been "partially responsible without knowing it," hinting at a conspiracy.

A federal investigation in 1977–1978 by the Select Committee on Assassinations of the U.S. House of Representatives, 95th Congress, was conducted. Hearings were conducted on August 14, 15, and 16, 1978. In January 1979, this committee published its final report, *Investigation of the Assassination of Martin Luther King, Jr.*, finding no complicity on the part of any government agency, including the CIA and FBI. Ray, the report concluded, was a lone gunman.

Shortly after Ray testified to the House Committee that he did not shoot King, Ray and six other convicts on June 10, 1977, escaped from Brush Mountain State Penitentiary. They were recaptured on June 13 and returned to prison. More years were then added to Ray's sentence for this attempted escape.

In spite of the 1979 government report, conspiracy theories continued to emerge. Ray, in fact, spent the remainder of his life attempting (unsuccessfully) to withdraw his guilty plea and secure a trial he never had. No Raoul ever materialized, until conspiracy investigators rounded up, in 1994, a retired auto worker from upstate New York, whom Ray said he recognized from a photo. The man was easily cleared of any involvement.

William F. Pepper, Ray's last attorney, promoted the conspiracy notion, claiming that Ray had been set up by the U.S. government. In his 1995 book *Orders to Kill: The Truth Behind the Murder of Martin Luther King*, Pepper alleged that the CIA, the Memphis police, the FBI, and Army intelligence were involved in the assassination plot. The key elements of Pepper's story were disproved, although Coretta Scott King (King's wife and a civil rights leader herself) and several of the King children announced their belief in Ray's innocence and the existence of a government plot. In 1997, Martin Luther King's son, Dexter, met with Ray in prison and publicly supported Ray's efforts to obtain a trial. Ray died in prison on April 23, 1998.

In 1998, however, attention was paid to Ray's case, particularly by Judge Joe Brown's court in Memphis. King's family publicly stated their belief that Ray did not kill King. Coretta Scott King asked President Bill Clinton and Attorney General Janet Reno to form a truth commission patterned after the one in South Africa to encourage those with evidence to come forward without fear of prosecution. In August 1998, Reno reopened a limited investigation into the assassination.

In 1998, Donald Wilson, a retired FBI employee, said he found scraps of paper in Ray's car after the 1968 shooting that had the name *Raul* written on them. Wilson allegedly took this evidence home and stored it in his refrigerator for the next 30 years. The FBI claimed that Wilson was not part of the search team and that his evidence was fabricated.

In December 1999, a Memphis jury awarded Coretta Scott King and her family a symbolic $100 in a wrongful death civil trial against Lloyd Jowers and other unknown co-conspirators. Jowers claimed to have received $100,000 to arrange King's assassination. The jury of six whites and six blacks found Jowers guilty and indicated their belief that governmental agencies were parties to the assassination plot. Few journalists, scholars, or law enforcement officials familiar with the case have given credence to the court's findings, and King biographers David Garrow and Gerald Posner disagreed with Pepper's claims that the government killed King.

The assassination of Dr. Martin Luther King, Jr. is a significant moment in the history of the civil rights movement and American race riots, as well as in the history of the United States. In death, as in life, Dr. King influenced millions of Americans, and this legacy continues even as the controversy surrounding the circumstances and details of his assassination remain unsettling and unsettled for some.

CAROL E. DIETRICH

See also

Civil Rights Movement; King, Martin Luther, Jr.; Southern Christian Leadership Conference (SCLC)

Further Reading:

Branch, Taylor. *At Canaan's Edge: America in the King Years 1965–68*. New York: Simon & Schuster, 2006.

Garrow, David J. *Bearing the Cross: Martin Luther King, Jr., and the Southern Christian Leadership Conference*. New York: William Morrow, 1986.

"James Earl Ray." *QuickSeek Encyclopedia*. 2005. http://jamesearlray.quickseek.com/.

Knight, Janet M., ed. *Three Assassinations: The Deaths of John & Robert Kennedy and Martin Luther King, Jr.* New York: Facts on File, 1971.

Pepper, William F. *Orders to Kill: The Truth Behind the Murder of Martin Luther King*. New York: Carroll and Graf Publishers, 1995.

Pepper, William F. *An Act of State: The Execution of Martin Luther King*. London and New York: Verso, 2003.

Posner, Gerald. *Killing the Dream: James Earl Ray and the Assassination of Martin Luther King, Jr.* New York: Random House, 1998.

Rugaber, Walter. "A Negro Is Killed in Memphis." *New York Times*, March 29, 1968.

Mary Turner Lynching

Mary Turner was herself a victim of lynching after protesting the lynching of her husband, Hayes Turner, two days earlier. Turner's death is a popular point of reference for black human rights, and is mentioned in dozens of books and articles, discussed in academic conferences on the black American experience, and is often used to emphasize American racism against and violence toward blacks.

In 1918 in Valdosta, Georgia, Hampton Smith and his wife were murdered by Sidney Johnson, a black field hand who worked on Smith's plantation to pay off a fine for gambling. After working a significant number of hours beyond what was required, Johnson demanded payment; however, Smith refused. Johnson withheld his services from Smith, who then pursued and physically accosted Johnson. After lying in wait a few days, Johnson shot Smith through his window. Mrs. Smith was injured but survived, and Hampton Smith was mortally wounded. After the shootings, a crowd of whites gathered, and giving no concern for who was killed in Johnson's absence, a white mob of men kidnapped and lynched two innocent black men, Will Head and Will Thompson. The next day, Hayes Turner was kidnapped and imprisoned. While allegedly being taken to a safe place away from the white mob, Turner, while handcuffed behind his back, was also lynched by the mob. In protest, Turner's wife, Mary, who was eight months' pregnant at the time, publicly vowed to report the identities of the murderers to authorities. Members of the white mob kidnapped her, taking her to a densely forested area, where they bound her by the feet, hung her face-down, doused her with motor oil and gasoline, and burned her alive. Miraculously, the burning did not kill her, and while still alive, her clothing was sheared off and her unborn child was barbarically extricated from her womb, only to have its head crushed under the foot of one white person at the base of the tree from which Turner was hung. Finally, Turner was riddled with over 150 bullets. In addition to the lynchings of Head, Thompson, and the Turners during the racial fray, Eugene Rice, Chime Riley, Simon Schuman, and Sidney Johnson were also lynched.

The lynching and disembowelment of Mary Turner and the crushing of her child's head are a case of American racial violence that has reached beyond the original contextual borders, affecting other aspects of black culture and life, including politics, nationalism, and literature. Turner's death lent credibility to the increasing need for black self-defense by emphasizing the extreme violence against blacks in the South and the lack of legal redress afforded them, despite the Fourteenth Amendment. The details of the Turner lynching have made the Black Nationalist case for self-defense and unification of all Africans in the diaspora. However, it is within black literature that Mary Turner has had considerable impact, particularly during the Harlem Renaissance.

Angela Grimké's story "Goldie" (the 1920 revised edition of "Blackness") treats the Turner incident, although Margaret Sanger was suspected of publishing the work in *Birth Control Review* to discourage black reproduction. Jean Toomer's *Cane* (Kabnis) also re-creates the death of Turner, changing the circumstances of the death, but not the motive.

National Association for the Advancement of Colored People (NAACP) investigator Walter White wrote about the lynching of Turner after his probe into the lynching of blacks in general, and Turner's murder in particular, which was published in *The Crisis* in 1918.

The cruelty and barbarity of the killings of Mary Turner and her unborn child continue to be a reference point in arguments for human rights across the nation. Deleso Alford Washington, co-chair of the Legal Strategies Commission for the National Coalition of Blacks for Reparations in America, used Turner's murder to make his argument for H.R. 40, the Commission to Study Reparations Proposals for African Americans Act, before Congress in 2005, attesting to the political similarities between her murder and the 1998 lynching of James Byrd Jr. in Jasper, Texas. In his address to the 2005 audience at the NAACP's convention, Julian Bond discussed the lynching of Turner to bring to the foreground the American government's consistent refusal to pass anti-lynching laws, or to apologize for the treatment of blacks.

ELLESIA ANN BLAQUE

See also
Black Women and Lynching; Lynching

Further Reading:

Als, Hilton, and James Allen. *Without Sanctuary: Lynching Photography in America.* Santa Fe, CA: Twin Palms Publishers, 2000.

Brown, Mary. *Eradicating This Evil: Women in the American Anti-Lynching Movement, 1892–1940.* New York: Garland, 2000.

Dray, Phillip. *At the Hands of Persons Unknown: The Lynching of Black America.* New York: Random House, 2002.

Ginzburg, Ralph. *100 Years of Lynchings.* Baltimore: Black Classic Press, 1997.

Masculinity, Black and White

A concept traditionally associated with the appearance and behavior of men, masculinity serves as a defining characteristic of maleness in many cultures. Masculinity refers to the meaning that a culture attaches to being male rather than the physical or biological category itself. Although recent scholarship reveals ways in which biological sex is also subject to societal definitions, masculinity is culturally constructed and can be interpreted differently by disparate groups. Cultural definitions of masculinity have changed and continue to change over time and between regions and cultures, and it is impossible to classify all black or white men under a particular definition of masculinity.

The gender concept of masculinity is often tied to economic, familial, and spatial issues. Men are often considered to be the primary economic forces in society. Masculinity can be defined through space. Since men can control access to certain types of work and leisure places, they therefore can control what type of work women can perform. Masculinity is typically differentiated from that of femininity. Throughout the history of the United States, different economic classes, ethnic groups, and religious and political organizations have defined family and gender roles for men and women in various ways. A "traditional" family was frequently defined as a man who made important decisions and provided financial resources and physical protection for his family, a feminine woman who cared for the home and children but was not necessarily responsible for the family's economic well-being, and children who were subordinate to the demands of both father and mother. Although societal reality did not always conform to a true gendered division of labor in the home and workplace, this concept is pervasive in American culture. Masculinity and manhood were intimately tied to male domination over the family structure, as well as in economic and political affairs.

Men have also frequently defined masculinity or manhood in relation to what men are not, or what society says men should not be. The opposite of masculine is not only feminine, but also childish, brutal, or animal-like. In the United States, homosexual, unmarried, unemployed, or pacifist men may be considered less masculine than other men. Although a cultural definition of masculinity includes particular types of men, it excludes many others. Control over women or other men was never complete, nor did all men support the same ideals.

In the earliest years of North American colonial settlement, issues of race and gender intertwined. White patriarchs controlled labor systems, property rights, and sexual access to both black and white women. Since white men had the power to define the rights of all people, they used discourses of race and gender to solidify their own economic and political authority. The importation of African slaves as laborers was a recent development, and slavery was not yet defined as the status of only black workers. Since they did not want black men to have access to white women, white patriarchs discredited the masculinity and intellectual abilities of black men. Conversely, elite white men guaranteed their own sexual access to black women by classifying them as morally weak. White women needed the moral protection of white men, but black women did not merit physical protection.

Colonists created their households based on the English assumptions of patriarchy and female domesticity. White men chose to maintain social control by placing women, children, and all people of color in subordinate roles. White women were spatially restricted to the home and domestic labor, while black women were forced to work as slaves. Since communal standards dictated that white men had to control their own households and white women had to adhere to their assigned gender role, aggressive women and weak husbands were publicly humiliated through customs such as charivari. Elite white men solidified control over working-class white men and black workers by feminizing dissent and severing ties between laborers who might otherwise join in solidarity. By emphasizing race as an important division, elite white men enlisted the support of poorer white men against black slaves. Free white men defined masculinity as the opposite of both female and slave. Since all white men could be potential patriarchs over their homes, whiteness and masculinity were closely tied to the colonial endeavor in North America.

As racialized slavery became more pervasive in the colonial era and solidified during the early years of the United States, black men found it more difficult to attain traditional masculine roles. Enslaved men had to endure the knowledge that white slaveholders held power over themselves and their families. Not only did white owners dictate the types of labor slaves must perform, but also had control over housing, food, travel, religious gatherings, and other freedoms. The threat of sale away from one's family was ever present. Enslaved families were not always able to live together as a unit. At times, the father was located on another plantation, or was sold away entirely. Children could be sold at the discretion of the master. In a society in which protecting one's family was a sign of masculinity, black men were unable to protect their wives or daughters from the sexual advances of white men. This vulnerability undermined the patriarchy and masculine roles of enslaved black men.

Free black men in the antebellum period were subject to discrimination in jobs and housing. Those men who managed to save wages and purchase their own freedom often worked to free the rest of their family, but they faced tremendous difficulties in doing so. In the years leading to the Civil War, many states passed manumission laws that prevented white slaveholders from freeing their slaves, or required that freed slaves had to leave the state immediately. Whether free or enslaved, black men confronted challenges to their masculinity.

Race played an important part in the antebellum discourse of masculinity. Elite white men in the colonial era had established patriarchy through the control of the household and property ownership. They maintained this masculine dominance through paternalism. Slaveholders believed that they were benevolent and were "civilizing" their enslaved workers. They believed that their actions were honorable and benefited society, and used the rhetoric of honor to glorify the system of enslavement. Both Southern slaveholders and abolitionists often adopted fatherly attitudes toward black Americans, which allowed them to believe that they were acting in the best interests of enslaved people.

Although far from wealthy, Southern yeomen farmers also had a vested interest in maintaining a system of slavery. These farmers could not prove their paternalism by dominating a large number of slaves, and they were often ashamed that their wives had to work alongside them in the fields rather than serve in a purely domestic role. Yeomen, however, conceded political power to the planter class in order to maintain patriarchal authority over their families. White yeomen farmers not only claimed equality with planters because they were all white, but also because they exerted authority over women and black men. In exchange for a measure of public influence, Southern yeomen supported the system of slavery as an extension of their own white, masculine authority.

In urban areas of the early 19th century, few white men could afford to own property and control their own livelihood. As wage labor became more common, white workers feared that they were being reduced to "wage slaves," or men enslaved to the capitalist system. These workers invoked the language of slavery to argue for the masculine ideal of free labor. They considered themselves men as long as they owned their own labor. In order to justify their jobs and find pride in their circumstances, white workers intentionally distanced themselves from black slaves. Once again, a system of racial slavery was solidified by the lack of solidarity between workers.

The Civil War provided the opportunity for both black and white men to prove their masculinity. Most men were greatly motivated by issues of home, family, and protection. Union soldiers emphasized the Victorian ideals of manly restraint, virtue, self-discipline, and loyalty, while Confederate soldiers abided by Southern codes of honor and protecting one's home. Both sides of the conflict placed great importance in displays of courage and valor. Soldiers feared that they would be branded as effeminate or cowards if they ran away from battle. At the same time, other soldiers feared that killing would make them brutal and inhuman. Soldiers were angry at pacifists or civilians who refused to fight. Many young men, away from home for the first time, experienced vice and a sense of adventure, but feared that their families would disapprove.

Black soldiers, especially former slaves, were anxious to fight for their own freedom and that of other enslaved people. They equated manhood with the ability to direct one's own destiny, which slavery had denied them. White politicians and soldiers on both sides of the conflict argued that black soldiers were unfit for warfare and would run at the first sign of danger. With the ongoing threat of slave rebellions in mind, Southern slaveholders viewed regiments of armed black men as their greatest fear. White Union officers often assumed that black soldiers were docile and childlike, traits bred into them through years of slavery and oppression. Black soldiers directly challenged these assumptions as they exhibited courage in battle. In time, many white officers grew to respect their black regiments, finding them strong, well disciplined, and fearless under fire. Members of the United States Colored Troops had to endure unequal pay, fatigue duty, dangerous assignments, and the threat of death or enslavement at the hands of Confederate troops. The courageous performance of black men in battle had a profound impact on the Union's fight for emancipation and racial equality.

Following the Civil War, black men throughout the country experienced a renewed sense of hope and manhood. With the passage of the Thirteenth, Fourteenth, and Fifteenth Amendments to the Constitution, African American men secured the right to vote and access to full citizenship in ways they had previously been denied. Black politicians sought to secure land, educational support, and equal legal protection for former slaves. Many men left their former employers and chose their own occupations for the first time. Once free to protect and control their families, some black men implemented patriarchal power in their homes. Black men and women legalized their marriages, although some women were subject to coercion or abuse as a result. Many men adopted middle-class notions of domesticity and family roles and urged their wives to stay at home. Not only did they want to be the primary breadwinner for their family, but they also hoped to protect their wives and children from abuse by white employers. Under the system of slavery, white men had free sexual access to black women, and black men wanted to end this practice.

The hopes of Reconstruction were short-lived. White men throughout the country feared the potential backlash of free black men. White laborers continued to use the rhetoric of race and wage slavery to distance themselves from black workers. With so many black workers no longer under the economic control of white men, former white planters feared physical and economic repercussions. Black people were not able to purchase large amounts of land, and white landowners still needed black labor to run their farms. A system of sharecropping and tenant farming was the solution. Although black laborers technically worked for themselves, they were still economically dependent on white people. Black workers throughout the country experienced job discrimination and low wages. African American freedom was undermined by racial injustice.

In order to reclaim masculine control in the South, white men formed organizations such as the Ku Klux Klan to intimidate black men politically, economically, and physically. Although black women had always been susceptible to white men's sexual access and violence, white men did not want black men to have sexual access to white women. White men exerted control through the invented myth of the "black beast rapist," a hypermasculine black man with animalistic and brutal sexual impulses who preyed on innocent white women. Implementing a process of torture and murder called lynching, white men used the reality and threat of violence to control black behavior. Black men were frequently physically emasculated, and their cultural and political activities were limited.

As years since the Civil War passed and veterans aged, regional hostilities became less important in light of economic and cultural similarities among white people. Northern industries had economically invested in the New South, and veterans of both armies wanted to celebrate their wartime heroism and courage rather than their differences. Across the country, veterans emphasized their manliness and valor while undermining challenges from independent black men and suffrage-seeking women. Northern cities, fearing the effects of so many black residents, looked to the South for a solution to the "Negro problem."

The South's answer to controlling black people continued to lie in violence, disfranchisement, economic marginalization, and segregation. White Southern politicians appealed to the ideal of white supremacy and white fears of black brutes to undermine any attempts for interracial political organization. Democratic political victories at the end of the 19th century resulted in the loss of black men's right to vote. Since manhood and citizenship had been linked throughout American history, black men were excluded from male privilege, and thus citizenship, by their inability to participate in the political system. In order to avoid violence, black men often had to adopt a servile demeanor rather than a public masculinity.

As black men's masculinity and patriarchal control was undermined in the Gilded Age and Jim Crow era, white men articulated a new type of masculinity. Fearing that the Victorian ideals of self-discipline and restraint were having a feminizing impact, white men placed great emphasis on a vigorous, aggressive masculinity. White men claimed to share the virile, primitive, "masculine" qualities of black men while maintaining a superior moral, civilized "manliness." Many white men believed that experiences with nature and violence would regenerate their moral character. Since white men controlled many of the economic and intellectual resources of society, they could spread this particular idea of masculinity to many people and advocate for a "strenuous life." Progressive Era reformers condemned aggressive sports such as prizefighting and football, arguing that such activities taught children to be brutal. Even as black soldiers once again proved their manly courage in the Spanish-American War, white men continued to argue that black men could never claim the civilized manliness of white men.

With the onset of World War I, many black people migrated to Northern cities. They not only hoped to escape the financial difficulties of sharecropping, but also desired to leave behind disfranchisement and lynching violence in the South. Expanded economic opportunities allowed them to provide for their families, and they were not subject to such extensive abuse at the hands of white men. Many black men believed that they could attain true citizenship in the North, where they would be allowed to vote, and through their military service. Black soldiers once again proved their courage and equality in battle, but encountered racism and competition for jobs and housing when they returned to the United States.

Men in the black middle class urged newly arrived workers to prove their equality through good behavior. Reformers tried to educate migrants in the dominant cultural ideals of thrift, sobriety, cleanliness, efficiency, and respectability. The middle class advised black men to be the sole breadwinners for the family and indicated that women should stay at home rather than enter the workforce. However, it was financially impossible for many black families to meet this ideal. The black middle class was also critical of how black workers spent their free time and money. The reformers recommended that working-class African Americans refrain from disreputable or excessive forms of leisure. Middle-class leaders did not want the whole race to be judged poorly by the behavior of some.

Black migrants were often limited to particular types of jobs in Northern cities. Although black men did not want to be viewed as either brutal or servile, they were often forced into roles, such as Pullman porters, that re-created the master/servant system of slavery. Better-paid industrial workers faced threats from white unions and returning veterans. In the Red Summer of 1919, tensions between black and white people erupted in brutal race riots. Many people, mostly black, died in the violence. Unlike racial violence under slavery or white supremacy, black people were willing and able to fight back. Organizations such as the National Association for the Advancement of Colored People and many black publications like the *Chicago Defender* advocated that the "New Negro" assert his rights and race pride. Although white men tried to maintain cultural and economic dominance, there were continual challenges.

Segregation and racial violence continued throughout much of the 20th century. Black men fought for their rights to provide for their families and be treated as societal equals, and white men asserted their dominance at every opportunity. All men experienced threats to their masculinity during the Great Depression as they found it more and more difficult to act as breadwinners. Although black men could gain employment through some New Deal programs, discrimination continued to impact their economic situation.

Black men were forced to serve in segregated units during World War II, but once again hoped that their military service would translate into equal citizenship. Through the Double V Campaign, black people demonstrated their patriotism and their demands for civil rights. This initiative called for military victory abroad and civil rights victory at home. Although the campaign was a step toward the future civil rights movement, black veterans continued to experience discrimination when they returned to the United States. Black soldiers did not receive equal treatment under the G.I. Bill, which hampered their access to housing and education benefits. Segregation and discriminatory practices at times thwarted notions of black masculinity.

As the civil rights movement gained strength through the 1950s and into the 1960s, both white segregationists and black civil rights leaders articulated their arguments in terms of masculinity. The defense team of the white men accused of killing Emmett Till in Mississippi in 1955 argued that the men had the right to protect their families, especially white women. They tried to invoke the image of the black beast to divert attention from the fact that Till was a 14-year-old boy. Although some white Southerners rallied to the defense, most white people throughout the country were sickened by the murder. Discomfort with racial mixing still existed, as evidenced by the turmoil following the *Brown v. Board of Education* decision, but changes were on the horizon.

As consumption became more important in the 20th century, white industrialists and landowners tried to maintain economic dominance. Housing segregationists claimed that they were protecting their economic investments rather than acting as racists. Both black and white men felt some threat from the rise of second-wave feminism and women's greater role in the workplace and civic culture. Black men viewed the Moynihan Report of 1965 as yet another challenge to their manhood and their ability to provide for their families. At times, black women were able to make political statements in ways that men were not, which some thought was a challenge to black masculinity. The Black Power movement advocated a shift from nonviolent protest to a more aggressive type of masculinity. Manhood was articulated in a variety ways among both black and white men.

Concepts of black and white masculinity continue to be relevant in the late 20th and early 21st centuries. Events such as the Million Man March highlight a particular type of black manhood, while gangsta rap conveys another. Issues of race and masculinity are prevalent in social and religious organizations like the Promise Keepers, and continue to be addressed in political forums on job discrimination, military action, welfare, and inner-city violence. Just as ideas of family, honor, and economics were expressed early in the history of the United States, they are still relevant to masculinity today.

SHANNON SMITH BENNETT

See also

Hypodescent (One Drop Rule)

Further Reading:

Bederman, Gail. *Manliness and Civilization: A Cultural History of Gender and Race in the United States, 1880–1917.* Chicago: University of Chicago Press, 1995.

Brown, Kathleen M. *Good Wives, Nasty Wenches, and Anxious Patriarchs: Gender, Race, and Power in Colonial Virginia.* Chapel Hill: University of North Carolina Press, 1996.

Clinton, Catherine, and Nina Silber, eds. *Divided Houses: Gender and the Civil War.* New York: Oxford University Press, 1992.

Estes, Steve. *I Am a Man!: Race, Manhood, and the Civil Rights Movement.* Chapel Hill: University of North Carolina Press, 2004.

Gilmore, Glenda Elizabeth. *Gender and Jim Crow: Women and the Politics of White Supremacy in North Carolina, 1896–1920.* Chapel Hill: University of North Carolina Press, 1996.

Glatthaar, Joseph T. *Forged in Battle: The Civil War Alliance of Black Soldiers and White Officers.* New York: Meridian Free Press, 1990.

Kantrowitz, Stephen. *Ben Tillman and the Reconstruction of White Supremacy.* Chapel Hill: University of North Carolina Press, 2000.

Roediger, David R. *The Wages of Whiteness: Race and the Making of the American Working Class.* New York: Verso, 1991.

Summers, Martin. *Manliness and Its Discontents: The Black Middle Class and the Transformation of Masculinity, 1900–1930.* Chapel Hill: University of North Carolina Press, 2004.

Wood, Amy Louise. "Lynching Photography and the 'Black Beast Rapist' in the Southern White Masculine Imagination." In *Masculinity: Bodies, Movies, Culture*, edited by Peter Lehman. New York: Routledge, 2001.

Matched-Pair Housing Audits

In order to investigate the practice of housing discrimination based on race, matched-pair housing audits have been utilized. These are also known as fair housing audits and were developed by fair housing organizations. Prior to fair housing legislation, it was common practice for real estate professionals to discriminate against potential buyers based on race. Often racial minorities were subject to racial steering, which are "actions by a real estate agent, or other housing provider, that result in minority and nonminority home seekers who have the same housing needs and qualification being shown different housing options" (Butters 1993: 153). This often plays out so that people of color are shown properties in areas that have a high proportion of minorities and whites are shown properties in mostly white areas. In order to determine that discrimination has occurred, it is important to make it clear that the variable that caused the differential treatment was race. Matched-pair housing audits are a way to prove that racial discrimination is at play. Notably, housing discrimination can occur in a variety of ways: renters being quoted different prices, differential credit or background check requirements, deceit about the availability of rental units, and so forth. Matched-pair housing audits are important because they can detect any number of these acts of discrimination and they offer direct measurement of discrimination. As Yinger (1986) points out, prior research estimated discrimination by looking at the prices of housing in minority areas compared to white areas or by looking at overall patterns of residential discrimination. Matched-pair housing audits provided a new type of data on housing discrimination.

"In a fair housing audit, an individual from the white majority and an individual from a minority group, who have been matched according to their family and economic characteristics, successively visit a landlord or real estate broker in search of housing. By comparing the treatment minority and majority auditors receive, a researcher can isolate discrimination, which is defined as systematically less favorable treatment for the minority auditors" (Yinger 1986: 881). Importantly, auditors must be matched on several characteristics, which often include age, family characteristics, and income. This is important so that race can be isolated as the cause of differential treatment. In Yinger's (1986) investigation of housing discrimination in Boston, he also accounted for whether the auditor of color or the white auditor visited the agency first, as well as the status of the housing market in the area. He created a statistical model in order to eliminate as much possible bias as he could in order to determine if race was the primary factor in differential treatment of auditors. He found that whites were more likely to be invited to inspect housing units compared to African Americans. "Overall, blacks must search much harder than whites to find equivalent housing; a black renter would have to visit 8 housing agents to receive as many invitations to inspect as a white receives from 5 agents" (Yinger 1986: 885).

Additionally, Yinger found that white preferences in housing tend to be what drives discriminatory behavior:

In the Boston audits, racial discrimination in housing generally does not vary with the characteristics of the black auditor or the characteristics of the housing agent, although in actually showing houses for sale, it is stronger against lower-income blacks and black families with children. On the other hand, discrimination does vary by location, with high discrimination in white areas and no discrimination in some areas undergoing racial transition. These results indicate that the primary cause of racial discrimination in housing is that housing agents illegally promote their economic interests by catering to the racial prejudice of their current or potential white customers. (Yinger 1986: 892)

A 2005 study in Boston shows that housing discrimination has not been alleviated. Using matched-pair audits, researchers found:

a pattern of differences in treatment that disadvantaged homebuyers of color in 17 of the 36 matched paired tests. In other words, African American and Latino homebuyers experience disadvantageous treatment in just under half of their attempts to purchase homes in Greater Boston's suburbs. The pattern of differences can be broadly divided into four categories: access to agents, access to properties and listings, mortgage requirements, and encouragement versus screening. (Fair Housing of Greater Boston 2005: 11)

These practices contribute to the continuation of residential segregation and the various social problems related to that issue. Ondrich, Ross, and Yinger (2001) examined data from the Housing Discrimination Study in four metropolitan areas (Atlanta, Chicago, Los Angeles, and New York) and found that "real estate agents sometimes withhold houses near their offices from black customers, presumably in attempt to protect their business with prejudiced white customers" (Ondrich, Ross, and Yinger 2001: 235). They claim that this practice makes housing discrimination difficult to detect, thus making it even more important to monitor.

KATHRIN A. PARKS

See also

Fair Housing Audit; Hypersegregation; Reverse Redlining; Segregation; Urban Renewal

Further Reading:

Butters, Robert D. "The Real Estate Industry's View of Audit Results: Comments." In *Clear and Convincing Evidence: Measurement of Discrimination in America*, edited by M. Fix and R. J. Struyk, 153–63. Washington, DC: Urban Institute Press, 1993.

Fair Housing of Greater Boston. "You Don't Know What You're Missing . . . A Report on Discrimination in the Greater Boston Home Sales Market." 2005. http://portal.hud.gov/hudportal/documents/huddoc?id=DOC_7412.pdf

Ondrich, Jan, Stephen Ross, and John Yinger. 2001. "Geography of Housing Discrimination." *Journal of Housing Research* 12 (2001): 217–37.

Yinger, John. "Measuring Racial Discrimination with Fair Housing Audits: Caught in the Act." *American Economic Review* 76 (1986): 881–93.

Mays, Willie (b. 1931)

Willie Mays was one of the greatest stars in the history of baseball. The ultimate "five-tool player," Mays could run, hit, hit with power, field, and throw, and he played the game with energy, style, and charisma. In his extraordinary career, the "Say Hey Kid" was named to the National League All-Star team 24 times, more than any other player in history. Younger than Jackie Robinson and Satchel Paige, Willie Mays was, nevertheless, a product of Negro League Baseball. But he played into the 1970s, tracing an arc from Jim Crow segregation to acceptance as an icon of major league baseball.

Mays was born in Westfield, Alabama, outside Birmingham, where his father and grandfather had played for black baseball teams in the Tennessee Coal and Iron League. His mother had been a high school track star. At age 16, in 1948, Mays joined the renowned Birmingham Black Barons of the Negro National League. Two years later, after he had graduated from high school, he was signed by the New York Giants in the wake of Jackie Robinson's initial success with the Brooklyn Dodgers. Mays became known for his spectacular ability as a center fielder before he established himself as a hitter. By the 1954 season, though, he was topping the league with a .345 batting average, hitting 41 home runs, and leading the Giants to the world championship. From that time, through the late 1960s, he was one of the brightest stars in baseball and, for a time, the game's highest paid player. Over the course of his career, Mays hit 660 home runs and batted .302. Most of his contemporaries commented that the most impressive thing about Mays was not his raw power or ability. What impressed them was his reckless and breathtaking style of play.

His success was unlikely. In a family with 11 children in rural Alabama, Mays grew up with poverty and segregation. He attended a vocational high school and trained to work in a laundry. He was a phenomenal athlete in high school, though, starring in football and basketball, and he played semipro baseball. With the Birmingham Black Barons, he played against Negro League legends Satchel Paige, Josh Gibson, and Buck Leonard. Following the success of Jackie Robinson, major league ball clubs were looking to develop young black talent, and within a couple of years, Mays was batting .330 and slugging .547 for Birmingham. Giants scout Eddie Montague wrote manager Leo Durocher, "This was the

Willie Mays is considered to be one of the greatest baseball players in history. He is among the all-time leaders in many offensive categories and was noted for his spectacular defensive plays. Mays also appeared in a record 24 All-Star Games. (Hulton Archive/Getty Images)

greatest young player I had ever seen in my life or my scouting career."

After signing him in 1950, the Giants wanted to send Mays to its minor league affiliate in Sioux City, Iowa, but the city would not accept a black player, so he was assigned to Trenton of the Interstate League. "I was the first black in that particular league," he would write. "And we played in a town called Hagerstown, Maryland. I'll never forget this day, on a Friday. And they call you all kinds of names there, 'nigger' this, and 'nigger' that. I said to myself, 'Hey, whatever they call you, they can't touch you. Don't talk back.'"

His first year in major league baseball, at the age of 20, Mays led the Giants to the World Series. He was voted National League Rookie of the Year, and his manager, the legendary Leo Durocher, claimed that "just to have him on the club, you had thirty percent of the best of it before the ball game started. In each generation, there are one or two players like that, men who are winning players because of their own ability and their own . . . magnetism." Nevertheless, when Mays returned to the Jim Crow South after the season was over, he tried to patronize a Woolworth's lunch counter and was refused service.

Mays served in the U.S. Army during the Korean conflict, although he spent most of his time playing with a stateside army baseball team. When he returned to the Giants in 1954, he began a dozen years of unbroken excellence. He won the batting title in his first year back, and he hit 51 home runs the following year. He led the National League in stolen bases four years in a row. And he won 12 consecutive Gold Gloves, awarded to the top fielder at each position. His talent and drive prompted historian Jules Tygiel to comment, "Mays, with his indisputable excellence, convinced all but the most stalwart resisters to integration of the need to recruit African-Americans."

When the Giants moved from New York to San Francisco before the 1958 season, Mays was not warmly welcomed, in part, because he was black. Soon after he moved into his new home, a brick crashed through his living room window. By 1963, though, Mays was the highest paid player in baseball, making $105,000, and his personal stature provided the impetus for integration. When the Houston Astros were formed in 1965, for instance, team ownership wanted to make certain that the city would not force the great Willie Mays to sleep in a Jim Crow hotel.

Mays was a pragmatic thinker and urged moderation in race relations. During the 1964 season, when manager Alvin Dark publicly expressed the view that Spanish-speaking and black players were not as mentally alert as white players, many of the Giants' Latino players threatened to boycott their games unless Dark was immediately fired.

Mays argued that such a move would be disastrous for their season and told a team meeting that Dark had always given everyone a fair chance to play, no matter his racial views. "I'm telling you he helped me," Mays told his fellow players. "And he's helped everybody here. I'm not playing Tom to him when I say that. He helps us because he wants to win, and he wants the money that goes with winning. Ain't nothing wrong with that." Mays urged the Latino players, "Don't let the rednecks make a hero out of him." At the same time, Mays himself continued to play, but he did not speak to Dark for the rest of the season, after which Dark was fired.

Mays was voted the National League's Most Valuable Player in 1954, and again 11 years later, in 1965, a testament to his consistency and drive. Although his skills had diminished by the end of the 1960s, Mays was voted Player of the Decade by the *Sporting News*. He was traded to the New York Mets in 1972, then retired the following year, his skills eroding fast, in the city where he began his major league career.

By the time he finished playing, Mays was acclaimed by everyone in the world of baseball, black and white. Home run legend Hank Aaron said Mays was the better player. Ted Williams commented at his own Hall of Fame induction that the All-Star game was made for Willie Mays. And Joe DiMaggio claimed that Willie Mays came as close to perfection as any ballplayer he had ever seen.

Elected to the Hall of Fame in his first year of eligibility, Mays again demonstrated moderation in the racial views he shared during his induction ceremony. In spite of his Jim Crow upbringing, at his induction ceremony, Mays was gracious. "This country is made up of a great many things. You can grow up to be what you want. I chose baseball, and I loved every minute of it. I give you one word. Love."

LOUIS MAZZARI

See also
Robinson, Jackie; Sports and Racism

Further Reading:
Durocher, Leo. *Nice Guys Finish Last.* New York: Pocket Books, 1975.
Einstein, Charles. *Willie's Time: A Memoir.* New York: J. P. Lippincott, 1979.
Linge, Mary Kay. *Willie Mays: A Biography.* Westport, CT: Greenwood Press, 2005.
Mays, Willie. *Willie Mays: My Life in and out of Baseball.* New York: E. P. Dutton, 1966.
Mays, Willie, and Lou Sahadi. *Say Hey: The Autobiography of Willie Mays.* New York: Simon & Schuster, 1988.
Negro League Baseball Players Association, "Willie Mays," http://www.nlbpa.com/mays_willie.html (accessed July 2007).

Saccoman, John. "Willie Mays." The Baseball Biography Project, http://bioproj.sabr.org/bioproj.cfm?a=v&v=l&bid=388&pid=9039 (accessed July 2007).

Tygiel, Jules. "The Negro Leagues." *Organization of American Historians Magazine of History* 7 (Summer 1992).

McCleskey v. Kemp (1987)

McCleskey v. Kemp (1987) was a 5–4 U.S. Supreme Court decision that upheld a death sentence for Warren McCleskey, rejecting the claim that statistical evidence of racial bias in sentencing could prove an individual's death sentence unconstitutional. McCleskey was an African American man sentenced to death in Georgia for killing a white police officer, Frank Schlatt, during an armed robbery. McCleskey, represented by the NAACP Legal Defense and Education Fund (LDF), challenged his death sentence, arguing that Georgia's death penalty was racially biased and thus violated the Eighth Amendment's ban on cruel and unusual punishment and the Fourteenth Amendment's guarantee of equal protection of the law. The Court accepted the sophisticated statistical evidence of a racially biased administration of justice in Georgia, but found that McCleskey could not demonstrate conscious, deliberate bias in his individual case and that racial disparities in sentencing were "an inevitable part of our criminal justice system." This latter finding has led legal scholars and advocates to condemn the decision, comparing it to *Dred Scott v. Sanford* (1857), which denied persons of African descent the protections of the U.S. Constitution. Below we discuss the decision and its racial consequences for American legal jurisprudence and equality.

From its inception, the American death penalty has been plagued by racial disparities in sentencing and executions. While the landmark Supreme Court *Furman v. Georgia* (1972) decision sought to eliminate the capricious and arbitrary nature of states' administration of their death penalty statutes, scholars continued to show that race plays a pivotal role in determining sentencing outcomes. One of the most sophisticated statistical studies of racial disparities in capital sentencing, the Baldus study, was introduced by the LDF during *McCleskey* as evidence of racial bias in Georgia's death sentencing. The study, conducted by University of Iowa professors David Baldus, Charles Pulaski, and George Woodworth, examined the details of roughly 2,500 murder cases in Georgia. Accounting for race and 35 additional nonracial variables, the study's findings were unequivocal: defendants convicted of killing whites were significantly more likely to be sentenced to death (4.3 times more likely than those involved in killing black victims) and this relationship was particularly pronounced for black defendants charged with killing whites, demonstrating that race was clearly a driving factor in Georgia's death sentencing schema.

The LDF argued that this evidence posed an "impermissible risk" that racial bias was a factor in McCleskey's death sentence, and thus, was a violation of the Constitution. The Baldus study did indeed demonstrate that prosecutorial discretion was a factor in the racial sentencing disparities in Georgia. Of cases involving black defendants and white victims (similar to *McCleskey*), prosecutors sought the death penalty 70 percent of the time, compared to 19 percent of cases involving white defendants and black victims.

By a one-vote margin, the majority Court found that the statistical findings of the Baldus study were valid but because McCleskey could not demonstrate "exceptionally clear proof" of an individual actor's deliberate and conscious intent to discriminate in his case, aggregate-level evidence of racial bias in sentencing did not prove unequal treatment under the law and could not suffice as a means to overturn a death sentence.

Striking a further blow to abolitionists and legal advocates was the Court's majority admission that racial disparities were "an inevitable part of our criminal justice system" and that accepting racial bias as a means to overturn a sentence could call into "serious question the principles that underlie our entire criminal justice system." Recognizing such an unjust practice had the potential to force a reexamination of the nature and entire structure of the American criminal justice system, a point Justice William Brennan ridiculed in his dissent as "a fear of too much justice." Warren McCleskey was executed on September 25th, 1991.

In 1994, retired Justice Lewis F. Powell Jr., who wrote the majority opinion for *McCleskey*, shared with his biographer that it was the only case he wished he could have decidedly differently. The legacy of *McCleskey* reaches far beyond the capital punishment system. *McCleskey* erected a "crippling" burden of proof in requiring evidence of an individual actor's

Racial Justice Acts

In *McCleskey*, the defendant was unable to sufficiently prove racial bias as a factor within the court's decision in his individual sentencing, not only upholding his death sentence but establishing that statistical racial discrimination was not a valid defense in further cases at the federal level. To challenge this decision, legislators have pushed, mostly unsuccessfully, for racial justice acts that would legitimize racial discrimination as an unconstitutional factor that plagues capital decision sentencing. The first, introduced by Rep. William "Don" Edwards in 1994, sought to make use of statistical evidence alongside evidence of race as an extralegal factor in sentencing. Like similar federal bills presented years prior and years since, it has failed to pass. While no current federal provision exists to address racial discrimination in capital sentencing, some states have made efforts to acknowledge statistical evidence of bias. For example, Kentucky's Racial Discrimination Act of 1998 focuses only on capital sentencing discrimination within prosecutorial discretion, limits who can bring about claims of bias, and ignores race-based statistical evidence as relevant to individuals' cases. North Carolina's 2009 Racial Justice Act allows for the examination of discriminatory measures in multiple stages of the capital system and allows for the use of statistical evidence to demonstrate bias. Unlike Kentucky's Act, the North Carolina Racial Justice Act is retroactive for death row inmates. In 2012, Marcus Robinson became the first person to have his death sentence repealed under North Carolina's Racial Justice Act, paving the way for others to challenge their death sentences as racially discriminatory based on statistical evidence and instead receive a sentence of life without parole.

discriminatory intent, a type of evidence nearly impossible to find or demonstrate in an era of post–civil rights color-blindness where racial bias is rarely admitted. *McCleskey* effectively ended the ability to file challenges to racial disparities in the criminal justice system, of which there are clearly many if one is to examine the racial dynamics of police practices, sentencing, or mass incarceration where citizens of color are grossly overrepresented throughout the criminal justice system. Twenty-five years after *McCleskey*, two states have passed Racial Justice Acts to allow evidence of racial discrimination in the administration of justice to serve as a means for appealing a death sentence.

JAZMINE BRAND AND DANIELLE DIRKS

See also

Racial Disparities in Capital Punishment. Document: *Furman v. Georgia* (1972)

Further Reading:

Baldus, David C., George Woodworth, and Charles A. Pulaski Jr. "Reflections on the 'Inevitability' of Racial Discrimination in Capital Sentencing and the 'Impossibility' of Its Prevention, Detection, and Correction." *Washington & Lee Law Review* 51 (1994): 359–430.

Chemerinsky, Erwin. "Eliminating Discrimination in Administering the Death Penalty: The Need for the Racial Justice Act." *Santa Clara Law Review* 35 (1995): 519–34.

Gross, Samuel R. "David Baldus and the Legacy of *McCleskey v. Kemp*." *Iowa Law Review* 97 (2012). http://www.uiowa.edu/~ilr/issues/ILR_97–6_Gross.pdf.

Johnson, Sheri Lynn. "Unconscious Racism and the Criminal Law." *Cornell Law Review* 73 (1995): 1016–37.

Kennedy, Randall L. "*McCleskey v. Kemp*: Race, Capital Punishment, and the Supreme Court." *Harvard Law Review* 101, no. 7 (1998): 1388–443.

"*McCleskey v. Kemp*." Oyez: The U.S. Supreme Court Media. 2005. <http://www.oyez.org/cases/1980–1989/1986/1986_84_6811>

Means, Russell (1939–2012)

Arguably one of the most well-known modern advocates of American Indian rights, Russell Means exhibited a spirited outspokenness that helped open a dialogue that changed the course of American Indian history in the late 20th century.

An Oglala Lakota, Means was born on November 10, 1939, on the Pine Ridge Reservation in southwestern South Dakota. Wishing to escape the limitations of reservation life, his mother, Theodora Louise Feather Means, moved the family to Vallejo, California, where his father, Walter "Hank" Means, found work as a welder at the navy shipyard on Mare Island. Hank's alcoholism contributed to an unstable family life for Russell, whose teenage years were marked by school truancy, drug and alcohol abuse, and petty criminal activity.

In 1964, the 26-year-old Means, recently fired from his job as a night watchman at the Cow Palace in San Francisco, accepted an invitation to accompany his father and a small assemblage of Indians living in the San Francisco Bay area on a symbolic takeover of the recently abandoned federal prison on Alcatraz Island. Russell later confided that his father's willingness to stand up for Indian treaty rights "made me proud to be his son, and to be a Lakota."

Five years later, as a new cadre of urban Indians readied once again to occupy Alcatraz, Means was in Cleveland, Ohio, where he joined two Anishinabe Indians from Minnesota, Clyde Bellecourt and Dennis Banks, in their effort to develop the American Indian Movement (AIM)—arguably the principal agency for American Indian empowerment during the late 1960s and early 1970s. Means later acknowledged "here was a way to be a *real* Indian, and AIM had shown it to me. No longer would I be content to 'work within the system.' . . . Instead, like Clyde and Dennis and the others in AIM, I would get in the white man's face until he gave me and my people our just due. With that decision, my whole existence suddenly came into focus. For the first time, I knew the purpose of my life and the path I must follow to fulfill it. At the age of 30 I became a full-time Indian."

On Thanksgiving Day 1970, Means, Banks, and other AIM leaders joined local Wampanoag activists in Plymouth, Massachusetts, to observe a national day of Indian mourning at the 350th anniversary celebration of the arrival of the Pilgrims. Speaking at the base of a larger-than-life statue of Chief Massasoit overlooking Plymouth Harbor, Means delivered an impassioned speech praising the ancestral Wampanoags who welcomed the Pilgrims and denouncing the white man's culture. Within 24 hours, Indian activists seized the *Mayflower II* (a full-scale replica of the original *Mayflower*), painted Plymouth Rock red, and brought national attention to the American Indian Movement.

Following its success at Plymouth, AIM elected Means the first national coordinator of the movement. He participated in the AIM-sponsored protest at Mount Rushmore in June 1971 and in the Trail of Broken Treaties, which led to the seizure of the Bureau of Indian Affairs building in November 1972. On the evening of February 27, 1973, Means, along with Dennis Banks, organized the occupation of Wounded Knee, South Dakota, the most renowned episode in the history of American Indian Movement. The takeover of the community, the proclamation of an Independent Oglala Nation, and the subsequent 71-day siege by the federal government led to the national attention—albeit short-lived—that Means and AIM desired.

In 1974, Means, beset with legal fees and court cases in the aftermath of the Wounded Knee occupation, nevertheless began his career in politics when he ran unsuccessfully for the Oglala Sioux tribal chair against the incumbent, Dick Wilson, in a contested election marked by voter fraud. In 1976, Means was tried for and acquitted of the murder of Martin Montileaux in the Longhorn Saloon in Scenic, South Dakota. Two years later he entered the South Dakota State Penitentiary, ultimately serving only 12 months of his four-year conviction for participating in a riot in a Sioux Falls courthouse in 1974. He joined Larry Flynt in 1983 in the pornographer's unsuccessful bid for the Republican presidential ticket in 1984. Hoping to force the Republican party to aid him in his struggles against the religious right in exchange for his withdrawal from the race, Flynt waged an outrageous campaign punctuated with publicity stunts. Disenchanted with the publisher's sincerity in championing First Amendment rights, Means ultimately removed his name from the ticket.

A supporter of indigenous rights worldwide, Means traveled to Nicaragua in 1986 to aid the Miskito Indians in their struggle against the Sandinistas. The move cost him the support of some of his more liberal supporters in AIM and elsewhere who saw his actions as condoning the pro-Contra dealings of the Reagan administration. Likewise, his 1986 speaking tour, sponsored by Reverend Sun Myung Moon's controversial Unification Church, further isolated Means from the Left. While the so-called Moonies used his lectures on Nicaragua as a venue to distribute literature about their church, Means saw the association as a vehicle to inform the public about the plight of the Nicaraguan Indians.

In 1987, Means accepted an invitation to enter the primary race for the Libertarian party's presidential candidate in 1988. The party's principles appealed to Means, and he mounted an extensive national campaign, only to lose in the end to former Republican Congressman Ron Paul at the

Libertarian party convention in Seattle. With residences in both South Dakota and New Mexico, Means tried in 2001 to enter the gubernatorial race in New Mexico as a candidate from the Independent Coalition party, only to drop out after a controversy over the filing deadline. Choosing instead to run, once again, for the presidency of the Oglala Sioux tribe, Means won the primary in 2002, but lost in the general election to incumbent John Yellow Bird Steele.

In addition to his activism and political aspirations, Russell Means developed a parallel career in the arts. In 1992, Means starred as Chingachgook in *Last of the Mohicans* and provided the voice of Chief Powhatan in Disney's *Pocahontas* in 1995. Most recently he worked with *The Last Horseman*, released in 2010. He also has had roles in more than 10 other films to date as well as numerous guest appearances on television dramas and talk shows. His autobiography, *Where White Men Fear to Tread*, was published in 1995. He also has produced two music CDs and several works of art.

Means remained active in issues of Indian self-determination and injustice in North America and abroad. Most recently, he focused his efforts on a campaign to abolish Columbus Day. No stranger to controversy, Means's exploits reaped both supporters and critics. There is no doubt, however, that his unremitting presence on the national stage in the late 20th century helped draw attention to issues of import to American Indian peoples.

Means spent his last years on his ranch in San Jose, New Mexico; on the Pine Ridge Indian reservation, Porcupine, South Dakota; and part of his time at his office in Santa Monica, California. Although he claimed to have played a role in the development of the Porcupine Health Clinic (the only nongovernment-funded clinic in Indian Country) and KILI radio, the first American Indian–owned radio station, current affiliates of AIM (with whom Means has been disassociated since 1988) believe he may have misappropriated funds.

Means was diagnosed with esophageal cancer in 2011. When he was told that his cancer was inoperable, Means favored herbal and other Native American remedies over mainstream medical treatments; however, the cancer continued to spread to his tongue, lymph nodes, and lungs. Means died on October 22, 2012, at his ranch in Porcupine on the Pine Ridge Reservation. He was 72 years old.

BARRY M. PRITZKER

See also
American Indian Movement (AIM); Bellecourt, Clyde; Peltier, Leonard

Further Reading:
American Indian Movement: http://www.aimovement.org.
Means, Russell. *Where White Men Fear to Tread*. New York: St. Martin's Griffin, 1995.
Smith, Paul Chaat, and Robert Allen Warrior. *Like a Hurricane: The Indian Movement from Alcatraz to Wounded Knee*. New York: New Press, 1996.

Medgar Evers Assassination

On June 12, 1963, civil rights leader Medgar Evers was shot and killed by white supremacist Byron de la Beckwith. The first well-known civil rights leader to be assassinated, Evers became the first martyr to the cause. Born in Decatur, Mississippi, on July 2, 1925, Medgar Evers grew up amid the violence and racial discrimination that permeated the South during the Jim Crow era. As a young boy, Evers was frequently harassed by gangs of whites who took pleasure in hurling insults and objects at African Americans. When Evers was just 11 or 12 years old, he witnessed the lynching of a family friend, William Tingle, who was beaten, dragged, and then hung from a tree for talking back to a white woman. Incensed by the absence of justice for Tingle and scores of others who were tortured and murdered at the hands of whites, Evers chose to fight back. He enlisted in the Army at the age of 17, and fought overseas during World War II. The liberal treatment Evers received from white Europeans strengthened his conviction to fight for racial equality back home and gave Evers an even greater appreciation for the democratic system of government.

Upon his return to American soil in 1946, Evers decided to exercise his own democratic rights and registered to vote in the next election. Together with his brother, Charles, and three friends, Evers made his way to the county courthouse on Election Day, only to be driven away by an angry white mob. Although he did not vote that day, Evers would not be dissuaded in his efforts.

Following his graduation from Alcorn A&M College in Mississippi in 1952, Evers began selling life insurance for Magnolia Mutual, one of the few African American–owned businesses in Mississippi at the time. It was at Magnolia Mutual that he met Aaron Henry, a long-time member of the National Association for the Advancement of Colored People (NAACP). Although the NAACP had made serious inroads in the fight for civil rights throughout the United States, the organization had been unsuccessful to date in effecting change in the state of Mississippi. Medgar Evers hoped to change that. In 1954, Evers left his job at the insurance company and accepted a position as field secretary of the NAACP in Jackson, Mississippi. Evers spent the next eight and a half years fighting for the enfranchisement of African Americans in the South. In addition to recruiting new members to the organization, Evers was also responsible for investigating and publicizing racial atrocities for the NAACP. Organizing demonstrations, boycotts, and sit-ins throughout Mississippi, Evers quickly became one of the most outspoken and recognizable civil rights activists in the state. In the fall of 1957, Evers was quoted in the *New York Times* as saying that Mississippi would be completely racially integrated within five years. Evers's prediction did not, however, sit well with segregationists. It was not long before he began to receive threatening phone calls, which quickly escalated into physical violence. In 1958, Evers was assaulted while trying to integrate a bus in Meridian, Mississippi. Two years later, he was harassed by a white mob when he tried to free a fellow NAACP member from prison. The following year, Evers was the victim of police brutality while attending the trial of some fellow civil rights demonstrators. Then, in the spring of 1963, Evers' home was firebombed following a civil rights demonstration in Jackson.

Despite the constant threat of violence, Evers continued to wage war on Mississippi's segregationists. On May 20, 1963, just three weeks prior to his assassination, Evers appeared on a local television station criticizing the segregationist sentiments of Jackson's mayor, Allan Thompson. Never before in the state of Mississippi had an African American been afforded this kind of public forum to express his views on segregation. Unfortunately for Evers, his public denunciation of the segregationist stance would cost him his life. Just after midnight on June 12, 1963, Medgar Evers was gunned down in front of his house after returning home late from a civil rights rally. The assassin, Byron de la Beckwith, shot Evers in the back with a high-powered rifle. Evers' wife,

Myrlie, and their three children, who had stayed up late to watch President John F. Kennedy's civil rights address to the nation, ran outside to find Evers lying face down in the driveway. Scattered about the dying man were a handful of sweatshirts inscribed with the words "Jim Crow Must Go."

Three days later, thousands of mourners, including Martin Luther King, Jr. and the head of the NAACP, Roy Wilkins, gathered to pay their respects to the fallen civil rights leader. Following the funeral and silent march, several hundred African American youths began demonstrating in the streets. Filled with rage over the senseless slaying of Evers, the youths demanded that his killer be brought to justice. As the crowd moved toward the white business district, a battalion of armed riot police were dispatched to the area. The angry youths began pelting the police with bricks, rocks, and glass bottles, yelling, "Freedom! Freedom! Freedom!" Then, just as the police were about to be unleashed on the crowd, the unthinkable happened. A U.S. Department of Justice official named John Doar stepped between the demonstrators and the riot police. A momentary hush fell over the crowd as they listened to the interloper plead with them to disperse. Unmoved by Doar's pleas, the mob advanced toward the unarmed man. In a final, desperate move, Doar appealed to the crowd's reverence for their fallen leader, stating, "Medgar Evers wouldn't want it this way" (Vollers 1995). Doar's words had the desired effect, and the crowd dispersed. One week later, Beckwith was arrested and charged with Evers's murder.

It would take another thirty years, however, for justice to be served. On February 7, 1964, an all-white jury was unable to reach a verdict in the case against Beckwith, and a mistrial was declared. Fearing a repeat of the violence that occurred on the day of Evers's funeral, the mayor of Jackson dispatched 300 police officers to the Jackson State College campus. Five students were injured when police fired upon a group of nonviolent demonstrators. Beckwith was freed from jail a few months later when a second mistrial was declared. Twenty-five years later, the grand jury in Jackson reopened the case, and Beckwith stood trial for a third time. On February 5, 1994, a multiracial jury found Byron de la Beckwith guilty of the murder of Medgar Evers, and sentenced him to life in prison.

Carol Goodman

See also
Civil Rights Movement; Hate Crimes in America

Further Reading:
Ghosts of Mississippi. Directed by Rob Reiner. Castle Rock
    Entertainment, 1996.
Linder, Douglas O. "Bending Toward Justice: John Doar and the
    Mississippi Burning Trial." *Mississippi Law Journal* 72, no. 2
    (Winter 2002): 731–79.
Nossiter, Adam. *Of Long Memory: Mississippi and the Murder of
    Medgar Evers*. Cambridge, MA: Da Capo Press, 1994.
Vollers, Maryanne. *Ghosts of Mississippi: The Murder of Medgar
    Evers, the Trials of Byron de la Beckwith, and the Haunting of
    the New South*. Boston: Little, Brown, 1995.

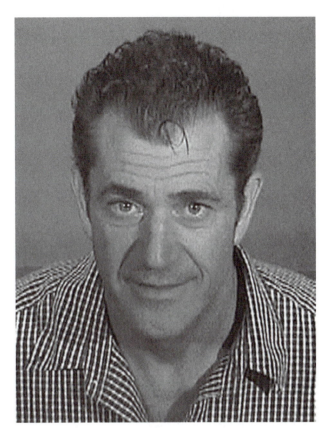

In this July 28, 2006, file photo originally released by the Los Angeles County Sheriff's Department, actor-director Mel Gibson is seen in a booking photo taken after his arrest on drunken driving charges. During the arrest, the Oscar-winning actor made anti-Semitic slurs to Deputy James Mee, who is Jewish. Attorneys for Mee say the case was settled pending approval of a $50,000 payment by the county. (AP Photo/Los Angeles County Sheriff's Department)

Mel Gibson Incidents

Mel Gibson is an American actor perhaps best known for being crowned *People* magazine's "Sexiest Man Alive" in 1985 and for winning a Best Director Oscar in 1996 for *Braveheart*. However, in 2006, Gibson was arrested for driving under the influence, and once he was in custody, he made several anti-Semitic comments that put him in the national spotlight.

At the time of his arrest, Gibson had recently enjoyed tremendous financial and popular success with his film *Passion of the Christ*, but on that night, he suddenly found himself in considerable trouble. It was not just the charge of drunken driving, but what happened after Gibson was in custody that got the attention of the world's media. Gibson was belligerent, loud, and uncooperative with the police, initially refusing to get into the patrol car. Once inside, Gibson made a series of anti-Semitic remarks to the officer. At the police station, Gibson continued to be confrontational, referring to a female officer using sexist language.

Unbeknownst to Gibson, the entire conversation in the police car had been audiotaped, and within hours of his arrest, Gibson's rant and mug shot were all over the news. The following day, Gibson issued an apology, which many observers—especially those in the Jewish community—felt was insincere. Gibson later issued a second apology for his remarks. At a hearing in mid-August 2006, Gibson pleaded no contest to driving under the influence. He was sentenced to three years' probation, ordered to attend regular Alcoholics Anonymous meetings, and paid $1,300 in court costs.

In 2010, Gibson's racist side once again came to light after his estranged girlfriend, Russian-born musician Oksana Grigorieva, released secret telephone recordings of the actor's rants, which included racial slurs directed at African Americans. By all accounts, it had been a tumultuous relationship, resulting in the couple's separation in 2010.

Such statements, along with others that are now immortalized on YouTube, did not help Gibson's tarnished reputation. Leon Jenkins, president of the Los Angeles chapter of the NAACP, referred to Gibson as an "out-of-date and out-of-control racist." However, many Hollywood celebrities came to Gibson's defense, including comedian Whoopi Goldberg, who stated publicly that she did not believe Mel Gibson to be a racist. Goldberg and others attributed Gibson's remarks to alcoholism rather than to an underlying attitude of racism.

In March 2011, Gibson entered a no contest plea to a charge of domestic violence after Grigorieva accused him of punching her in the face. He was sentenced to three years' probation, one year of domestic violence counseling, and 16 hours of community service. In September 2011, Gibson agreed to a $750,000 settlement with Grigorieva along with providing additional funds for housing and child support.

Colleagues in the film business with Gibson in Hollywood have pointed to two distinct sides of Mel Gibson. According to reports that emerged from his colleagues, Gibson could be supportive and kind one day, but dark and difficult the next. Yet, according to the author and journalist Christopher Hitchens, what Gibson represents is more than just overt racism. Hitchens has identified Gibson as a symbol of the violence, cruelty, bigotry, and sexual hypocrisy that underwrites the values and mindsets of many white American men. According to Hitchens, Gibson's objectionable rhetoric and behavior can be viewed as a consequence of his religious beliefs more than anything else. Gibson had long been noted as possessing a bizarre religious ideology, one that had been percolating a long time and was allegedly embedded under the tutelage of his father, Hutton Gibson, who has been identified as having a sideline in Holocaust denial. Journalist Philip Adams has referred to Hutton Gibson as a compelling and charismatic promoter of "rancid racism." Mel Gibson is very defensive of his father, refusing to discuss him or his peculiar ideas in interviews with the press.

In 2011, actor Robert Downey Jr. urged Hollywood to forgive and forget his friend's transgressions. At an awards show for the American Cinematheque in Los Angeles, Downey asked a crowd to forgive Gibson and "let him work." In the years following, it appears the film industry is still deciding whether to do so. Gibson continues to be dogged by controversy. In April 2012, respected Hollywood screenwriter Joe Eszterhas, who had been working closely on a project with Gibson, sent the director a letter alleging, "You hate Jews," and voicing his objections to Gibson's persistent racial slurs.

DANIEL M. HARRISON

See also
Michael Richards Incident

Further Reading:
ABC News. "Mel Gibson's Statement on His DUI Arrest." http://abcnews.go.com/Entertainment/story?id=2251961#.UOSCueSxySo (accessed February 4, 2013).
Adams, Philip. "Mel's Affliction Seems Hereditary." *The Australian*, August 8, 2006.
Anti-Defamation League. "Mel Gibson's Apology to the Jewish Community." http://www.adl.org/main_Anti_Semitism_Domestic/gibson_apology_20060801.htm (accessed February 4, 2013).
Day, Elizabeth. "Am I Forgiven." *The Australian*, July 30, 2011.
Hammond, Pete. "Robert Downey Jr. Asks Hollywood to 'Forgive' Mel Gibson." *Deadline*. October 15, 2011. http://www.deadline.com/2011/10/robert-downey-jr-accepts-american-cinematheque-award-asks-hollywood-to-forgive-mel-gibson/ (accessed February 4, 2013).
Hitchens, Christopher. "Mel Gibson Isn't Just an Angry Narcissist." *Slate*. July 19, 2010. http://www.slate.com/articles/news_and_politics/fighting_words/2010/07/mel_gibson_isnt_just_an_angry_narcissist.html (accessed February 4, 2013).
Leonard, Tom. 2012. "Gibson's New 'Tirade.' *Daily Mail*, April 13.
Los Angeles Times. "Transcript: Mel Gibson Arrest," http://www.latimes.com/news/local/la-gibson1aug01-transripit,0,3469141.story (accessed February 4, 2013).
Weekend Australian. "Mad Mel in Strife Again for Racist Tirade." July 3, 2010.
YouTube. "Mel Gibson Racist Rant." http://www.youtube.com/watch?v=xwWAeufYTlM (accessed February 4, 2013).
YouTube. "Whoopi Goldberg Defends Mel Gibson's Racist Rant." http://www.youtube.com/watch?v=8ccAPIEfAIU (accessed February 4, 2013).

Melting Pot Theory

The tem *melting pot* has its origins in the 19th century when it was believed that the many nationalities that made up America would melt into a single "American" culture. The term was also used to describe one of the interrelated models that the sociologist Milton Gordon (1964; 1972) used to explain the future of ethnic relations in the United States under the broader term of *assimilation*. The other two models were *Anglo-conformity* and *cultural pluralism*.

The Anglo-conformist model sees immigrants to the United States adapt themselves to the traditions and culture of the dominant, English-speaking culture. This is what people commonly think of when they think of the term *assimilation*. In contrast, with cultural pluralism, the traditions and cultures of both the preexisting and immigrant populations are seen as equally valid and valuable and are allowed to co-exist. In the third option of the melting pot, however, the traditions and cultures of both groups are blended to form a new cultural pattern taking on aspects of both groups and changing as new immigrants arrive. The culture is therefore dynamic and continually evolving. Gordon used the term *assimilation* to cover all three of these possible models, noting they all had their part in describing the development of American ethnic relations.

Some researchers such as historian Frederick Jackson Turner have argued that the melting pot is the best description of American cultural development in the 19th century. Turner noted the unifying effect that settling the expanding American frontier had on immigrants as they shared the same hardships and work as settlers and farmers. This is undoubtedly true when looking at the predominantly Protestant immigration from Western and Northern Europe that took place throughout most of the 1800s. But the late 19th and early 20th centuries brought both the closure of the frontier and increased immigration from Southern and Eastern Europe and from Asia. These immigrants did not have the unifying frontier experiences. Instead they moved to ethnic enclaves in the rapidly industrializing cities. Here they tended to live, work, and socialize in neighborhoods that were culturally homogenous. The people that they interacted with tended to be very similar to themselves. This limited social interaction left them without the means to melt or blend as had been done on the frontier. However, they did have the interaction of religion.

The Yale sociologist Ruby Jo Reeves Kennedy noted that in New Haven, Connecticut, intermarriage was taking place across ethnic and national boundaries, just as would be expected in a melting pot situation. At the same time, marriage was staying strictly within three general religious groups: Protestant, Catholic, and Jewish. This created what she referred to as the "triple melting pot." Italian, Irish, and Polish Catholics were more likely to marry each other since they shared a common religious tradition and often

Food as Metaphor

In many cultures, aspects of social and cultural life are talked about and experienced in terms of food. This is because of the universality of food itself. Rightly or wrongly, people use food both to symbolize a culture (e.g., linking chocolate and the Swiss) and to explain things within their own culture (e.g., using hamburger vs. filet mignon to describe social class). Interestingly, these metaphors may not always have meaning outside of the culture that creates them. Would the term "melting pot" be as effective in a culture that had no culinary tradition of foods that melt like cheese or chocolate?

a common priest. Similarly, a German Jewish immigrant was more likely to marry a Russian Jewish immigrant than a German Protestant who shared all other aspects of their culture. This concept was based on a study done in New Haven, but it was later expanded into use for explaining ethnic relations for the entire country by the religious scholar Will Herberg.

Throughout the late 20th and early 21st centuries, Americans liked to think of the melting pot concept as how the assimilation of immigrants should work. It is even taught to school children as part of our national mythology. However, the melting pot is only an accurate model when applied to some historical aspects of cultural development in the United States. As the triple melting pot thesis suggests, there is a need to look at a more culturally pluralistic view of American society, since there has never really been one "American" culture. Because of this, the "Salad Bowl" approach of thinking about assimilation has become more common than the Melting Pot. The Salad Bowl approach is more pluralistic, noting that the many different cultures that make up the United States do not melt into one another as much as combine like a salad. Each of the various ethnic groups retain some aspects of their distinctiveness while still acting as a unified whole. How "American" an individual is considered is based on their actions as a citizen, not their willingness to abandon their ethnic culture.

Donald P. Woolley

See also

Assimilation; Pluralism; Segmented Assimilation

Further Reading:
Gordon, Milton. *Assimilation in American Life: The Role of Race, Religion and National Origins.* New York: Oxford University Press, 1964.
Gordon, Milton. *Human Nature, Class, and Ethnicity.* New York: Oxford University Press, 1978.
Herberg, Will. *Protestant-Catholic-Jew.* Garden City, NY: Doubleday, 1955.
Kennedy, Ruby Jo Reeves. "Single or Triple Melting-Pot? Intermarriage Trends in New Haven, 1870–1940." *American Journal of Sociology* 49 (1944): 331–39.
Park, Robert E. *Race and Culture.* Ann Arbor: Free Press, 1950.

Mendez v. Westminster (1947)

Mendez v. Westminster (1947) was a federal court case that challenged racial segregation in schools in Orange County, California. In its ruling on the case, the U.S. Court of Appeals for the Ninth Circuit ruled that the segregation of Mexican American students into separate schools was unconstitutional. Despite this victory, de facto segregation continued. However, the *Mendez* case did set a precedent for the important *Brown v. Board of Education* victory in 1954, in which the U.S. Supreme Court held that separate facilities were inherently unequal.

Impelled by the revived movement for civil rights at the end of World War II, Mexican American parents in Orange County filed suit in 1945 against four elementary school districts, including Westminster. They asserted that the districts placed their children in separate classes solely because of their ethnic background. Their attorneys, provided by the League of United Latin American Citizens, pointed out that this segregation violated constitutional guarantees embodied in the Fifth Amendment and Fourteenth Amendment to the Constitution.

In February 1946, federal court judge Paul McCormick, agreeing with the complainants, ruled that such segregation violated not only the U.S. Constitution but also California statute law. Besides, he added, segregation was socially unhealthy; it fostered antagonisms and denied students the benefits of interaction with other cultures in the classroom. He ruled that separate schools, even with like technical facilities, did not provide "equal protection of the laws" and ordered the school districts to end the separation.

Unwilling to accept the court's decision and desegregate, the school districts appealed the decision, arguing that the facilities were completely equal and that the federal court had no jurisdiction. A year later, the Ninth Circuit Court in San Francisco, California, upheld Judge McCormick's ruling, agreeing that the school districts were in violation of both California law and the Fourteenth Amendment to the U.S. Constitution.

MATT MEIER AND MARGO GUTIERREZ

See also

Brown v. Board of Education (1954). Document: *Brown v. Board of Education* (May 1954)

Further Reading:
Flores, Rubén. "Social Science in the Southwestern Courtroom: A New Understanding of the NAACP's Legal Strategies in the School Desegregation Cases." B.A. Thesis, Princeton University, 1994.
McWilliams, Carey. "Is Your Name Gonzales?" *Nation* 164 (March 15, 1947): 302.
Ruiz, Vicki L. "'We Always Tell Our Children They Are Americans': *Mendez v. Westminster* and the California Road to *Brown*." *College Board Review* 200 (Fall 2003): 20–27.
Ruiz, Vicki L. "Tapestries of Resistance: Episodes of School Segregation and Desegregation in the U.S. West." In *From Grassroots to the Supreme Court: Exploration of Brown. v. Board of Education and American Democracy*, edited by Peter Lau. Durham, NC: Duke University Press, 2004.
Wollenberg, Charles. *All Deliberate Speed: Segregation and Exclusion in California Schools, 1855–1875.* Berkeley: University of California Press, 1976.

Meredith, James (b. 1933)

James Howard Meredith was a reluctant civil rights pioneer known for his integration of the University of Mississippi, but he always eschewed such honorific labels as well as the public spotlight.

Meredith was born on June 25, 1933, in Kosciusko, Mississippi. After graduating from high school, Meredith enlisted in the U.S. Air Force, in which he served from 1951 to 1960. During his service, he spent time overseas. Additionally, Meredith began to take college courses offered through military outreach programs. Upon his honorable discharge from the air force, he returned to Mississippi and attended historically black Jackson State College, completing two years of study. On January 31, 1961, Meredith applied to the University of Mississippi. From the outset, university officials stalled the admission process by using, what Meredith would describe in his letter to the U.S. Justice Department in which he appealed for assistance, "delaying tactics."

Anticipating the struggle he faced in his attempt to be admitted to the University of Mississippi, Meredith also wrote to Thurgood Marshall, seeking representation from the National Association for the Advancement of Colored People (NAACP) Legal Defense and Education Fund. Near the end of May 1961, the NAACP proceeded with litigation to have Meredith admitted, and the case eventually ended up in the U.S. Supreme Court. On September 10, 1961, the Supreme Court decided that Meredith should be allowed to attend the university.

What followed was a showdown between the state of Mississippi and the federal government over states' rights and opportunities for equal education. Segregationist governor Ross Barnett took active steps to prevent Meredith from registering for classes by physically blocking Meredith's entrance into the appropriate university office. Tensions grew in the area and boiled over with riots that encompassed the entire campus. In response to Barnett's defiance of the Supreme Court, President John F. Kennedy ordered the mobilization of federal marshals and federal troops to Mississippi to enforce the order admitting Meredith. This step only further riled the segregationists in the area, and there were several violent clashes between the protesters of Meredith's admittance and the federal authorities. The conflicts were bloody, with two deaths and scores of serious injuries. Finally, the violence abated after pleas from all sides, and Meredith attended his first class on October 1, 1962. He went on to graduate from the University of Mississippi, pursue further studies in Nigeria, and receive an LLB from Columbia University.

Meredith took a leadership role in the March Against Fear in 1966. He was shot by Aubrey James Norvell while participating in the march from Memphis, Tennessee, to Jackson, Mississippi. He recovered from the wound and was able to complete the journey. Meredith then retreated from the limelight and became a businessperson who seemed to want to put his contributions behind him. After this period, he relocated to Washington and worked on the staff of Senator Jesse Helms on matters of domestic policy. He made several unsuccessful runs for Congress as a Republican and wrote a number of books and articles.

As the 40th anniversary of Meredith's entry into the University of Mississippi approached, his attendance at the ceremony remained in doubt. In the end, Meredith reluctantly attended the ceremony, but he again expressed his desire to be viewed only as a humble U.S. citizen who sought the protections and opportunities offered by the government and not as a civil rights hero. Nonetheless, many still view Meredith as a significant contributor to the civil rights movement and, at the same time, respect his wishes to be thought of as just another American standing up for himself and others through action.

AARON COOLEY

See also
College Admissions, Discrimination in; School Segregation

Further Reading:
Klarman, Michael. *From Jim Crow to Civil Rights: The Supreme Court and the Struggle for Racial Equality*. New York: Oxford University Press, 2004.
Meredith, James. *Three Years in Mississippi*. Bloomington: Indiana University Press, 1966.

Meriam Report

In 1926, the Secretary of the Interior, Hubert Work, commissioned a team of 10 social scientists, led by Lewis M. Meriam, to study the conditions of Indian reservations. Meriam was the principal investigator at the Institute for Government Research at Johns Hopkins University. The survey team conducted fieldwork by visiting 95 different jurisdictions, including reservations, agencies, hospitals, schools, and many communities to which Indians had migrated. Officially entitled *The Problem of Indian Administration*, the Meriam Report was published in 1928.

The voluminous 872-page report contained a general policy evaluation and recommendations on various aspects of the Indian community, such as health, education, economic conditions, and the legal aspects of the Indian problem. Even though results varied from reservation to reservation, the major findings were that an overwhelming majority of the

Hubert Work was a noted physician who served as secretary of the interior and postmaster general in the administration of President Warren G. Harding. The Meriam Report exposed the horrible treatment of American Indians at the hands of the federal government. (Library of Congress)

Indians were not adjusted to the economic and social system of the dominant white society. For example, the study found that Indians had a higher infant mortality rate than any other minority group. Diseases such as measles, pneumonia, tuberculosis, and trachoma (an infectious eye disease) were rampant on the reservations, and material conditions related to diet, housing, health care, and the like were deplorable. These appalling conditions were closely associated with widespread food shortages, poor health, inadequate housing, and a lack of education.

According to the report, the Indians' poverty was caused mainly by the fact that the economic basis of their culture had been largely destroyed by the encroachment of white civilization. The report also pointed out that the U.S. government's effort to assimilate the Native Americans had been a total failure. The report singled out the U.S. government's allotment policy as the greatest contributor to Indian peoples' impoverishment. The allotment policy forced Indians to give up their traditional ways of life and adopt Western ways of living by making them farm the plot of land that was allotted to them. In the conclusion, the report called for a complete reexamination of the Bureau of Indian Affairs and of national Native American policy, and suggested what remained to be done in terms of improving the socioeconomic condition of Native American communities. The report recommended that the allotment program be stopped and that more funds be available for health and educational programs for Native Americans. It also recommended that the Bureau of Indian Affairs, which was created in 1824, should oversee the operation of the reservations and that the bureau hire Native Americans as employees.

Thus, the Meriam Report led government leaders to substantially reconstruct the nation's policy toward Native Americans. The Indian Reorganization Act (IRA), passed in 1934 during the Roosevelt administration, was the government's direct response to the call to reform its policy toward Native Americans. Under the impact of the IRA, Native Americans finally gained an opportunity to rebuild their cultural heritage and self-reliance.

SOOKHEE OH

See also

Bureau of Indian Affairs (BIA); Indian Reorganization Act (1934); Indian Reservations

Further Reading:

Brookings Institution (Institute for Government Research). *The Problem of Indian Administration.* Baltimore: Johns Hopkins University Press, 1928.

Johansen, Bruce Elliott. *The Encyclopedia of Native American Legal Tradition.* Westport, CT: Greenwood Press, 1998.

Meritocracy

Meritocracy is a system in which advancement in social position, resources, and other social goods are distributed based on individual talent, ability, and ingenuity. Meritocracy is the dominant ideology in the United States, as stratification in every social institution is generally attributed to individual merit, rather than social barriers like discrimination. It is widely accepted by Americans to be an accurate description of the way that social resources are distributed, as well as the most just way to distribute these resources. The concept of the American Dream is very closely related to the idea of meritocracy, as the individual successes attained in the American Dream are gained as a result of hard work, responsibility, and individual talent. Social stratification by race, class, and other factors challenge the notion of meritocracy; however, most Americans hold fast to the belief that if an individual works hard enough, that individual can become successful, regardless of where the individual started out.

Differences in income are commonly associated with differences in skill and effort, which is considered to be acceptable because social mobility is assumed to be high (Sawhill 2012). That is, most Americans believe that inequality is acceptable because it is possible to advance one's position with work and skill. Sociologist Kathleen Newman (1999) sees meritocracy as having some advantage even in the case of downward mobility, because the individualism associated with meritocracy includes a belief that personal striving can improve one's status. Evidence of discrimination is contrary to the idea of the United States as a meritocracy. As a result, racism and discrimination are often minimized or reframed in order to conform to a meritocratic frame.

The fact that people of color have consistently lagged on socioeconomic indicators of success continues to be discussed in ways that further the notion of meritocracy. Lack of human capital, low levels of parental involvement in school, a lack of work ethic, and other individual-level factors are often given to explain racial disparities. Attempts to ameliorate the effects of historical and contemporary discrimination are often met with great resistance. Affirmative action initiatives are an example of such attempts and the backlash to them. Labeling these measures as reverse discrimination, opponents of affirmative action have argued that rather than compensating disadvantaged groups for discrimination, affirmative action gives preferential treatment to protected classes.

Merit-based factors such as intelligence are often used to explain inequities. For example, *The Bell Curve* by Herrnstein and Murray (1994) was a wildly popular and controversial book arguing, among other things, that intelligence

---

Affirmative Action

Affirmative action is a set of laws and government policies developed to remedy historical discrimination against disadvantaged groups including women and racial minorities. The purpose was to ensure access to opportunities and resources such as jobs, higher education, and business contracts, as well as remedy the underrepresentation of women and minorities in workplaces, business ownership, and educational institutions. Membership in a protected identity group, one recognized as underrepresented, is treated as a positive factor in decisions affecting access to these resources. The federal government established the Office of Federal Contract Compliance Programs and the Equal Employment Opportunity Commission to ensure compliance with affirmative action policies. Affirmative action policies are extremely controversial, as proponents view the policies as a means of correcting historical injustices, opponents view the policies as "reverse discrimination," arguing that they give preferential treatment to protected groups rather than relying on merit.

---

is a better predictor of personal outcomes including income, criminality, and job performance than are socioeconomic status or education level, and that genes as well as environmental differences are related to racial outcomes. Merit has also been associated with particular attitudes or values such as work ethic, diligence, perseverance, and willingness to defer gratification. Researchers like McNamee and Miller (2009) argue that nonmerit factors like access to educational opportunities, good health care, and cash infusions from family members contribute greatly to socioeconomic well-being and success, and that nonmeritocratic social forces can suppress, neutralize, or negate the effects of merit in an individual's ultimate success.

Meritocracy has been an especially contentious issue in the institution of higher education. College admissions processes are often complicated and vary by institution, but have historically restricted admittance to white, middle-class applicants. Once legal discrimination in admissions based on race was no longer permissible, college admissions processes continued to favor the privileged group of applicants using seemingly meritocratic criteria like test scores and grade point averages. Affirmative action policies adopted by many institutions have been consistently challenged on the grounds of necessity and fairness, as well as the argument that affirmative action allows applicants who would have otherwise not been qualified for admittance to college. Central to the issue is the definition of merit. While standard measurements of academic merit have been shown to be related to the probability of college success, they are not the only ways to measure merit or potential for success. Standard measures of merit tend to privilege whites, middle-class applicants, those from suburban settings, and other already-privileged groups. Standardized tests have been shown to strongly favor privileged groups, despite advocates' determination of their innate fairness. In addition to the advantages white applicants enjoy through meritocratic measures, legacy admissions have been a sustained advantage for white applicants, operating as an opportunity-hoarding mechanism, perpetuating the advantage many white applicants have over applicants of color.

While most Americans believe in America as a meritocracy, belief in meritocracy varies by both race and class, and changes over time. For example, poor blacks, who tend to be concentrated in inner cities and often have access to few resources, have maintained the same level of belief in the American dream as they had in the 1960s. However, middle-class blacks, who have gained more access to education, employment opportunities, and other resources since the 1960s, believe in the American dream less than in the 1960s.

RENEE S. ALSTON

See also

Bell Curve; Downward Mobility; Intergenerational Social Mobility; Opportunity Hoarding

Further Reading:

Espenshade, Thomas J., and Alexandria Walton Radford. *No Longer Separate, Not Yet Equal: Race and Class in Elite College Admission and Campus Life*. Princeton, NJ: Princeton University Press, 2009.

Herrnstein, Richard J., and Charles A. Murray. *The Bell Curve: Intelligence and Class Structure in American Life*. New York: Free Press, 1994.

McNamee, Stephen J., and Robert K. Miller. *The Meritocracy Myth*. Lanham, MD: Rowman & Littlefield, 2009.

Newman, Katherine S. *Falling from Grace: Downward Mobility in the Age of Affluence*. Berkeley: University of California Press, 1999.

Sawhill, Isabell. *Are We Headed Toward A Permanently Divided Society?* Center of Children and Families at Brookings—CCF Brief #48. March 2012. Washington, DC: Brookings.

Mexican American Legal Defense and Education Fund (MALDEF)

The Mexican American Legal Defense and Education Fund (MALDEF) was founded in 1968 in San Antonio, Texas, to protect the civil rights of Latinos and promote their empowerment and full participation in society. As a leading national nonprofit organization, MALDEF conducts litigation, advocacy, and educational outreach work through multiple regional sites located across the United States, including Atlanta, Los Angeles, Sacramento, San Antonio, Chicago, Phoenix, Albuquerque, Houston, and Washington, D.C. MALDEF works to advance public policies, laws, and programs that protect Latino civil rights in employment, education, immigration, political access, and the equitable distribution of public resources.

Modeled after the National Association for the Advancement of Colored People's Legal Defense Fund and started with an initial $2 million Ford Foundation grant, MALDEF's extensive works in civil rights litigation have set precedents in electoral processes (to ensure that Latinos have a fair opportunity to elect representatives of their choice and/or run for elective office), in educational and employment practices, and immigrant rights, including language rights. A recent landmark MALDEF victory was the final settlement of the *Gregorio T. v. Wilson* (1995) case, which essentially struck down California's Proposition 187, the intent of which was to deny public services, including education, health care, and social services, to the state's undocumented population. MALDEF's work in such key areas as census enumeration and political redistricting, equity in public-resource allocation, and community education seeks to fully engage Latinos in advocating for policy changes that protect and advance civil rights and social justice.

TARRY HUM

See also

Asian American Legal and Defense Fund; League of United Latin American Citizens (LULAC)

Further Reading:

Gómez Quiñones, Juan. *Mexican Students for La Raza: The Chicano Student Movement in California, 1967–1977.* Santa Barbara, CA: Editorial La Causa, 1978.

Rosales, F. Arturo. *Chicano!: The History of the Mexican American Civil Rights Movement.* Houston: Arte Público Press, 1996.

Rosales, F. Arturo. *Testimonio: A Documentary History of the Mexican-American Struggle for Civil Rights.* Houston: Arte Público Press, 2000.

Mexican-American War

In May 1846, the United States invaded the Mexican territories of California, New Mexico, and central Mexico. Mexico surrendered and signed the Treaty of Guadalupe Hidalgo on February 2, 1848, under which the United States took California, New Mexico, Nevada, Utah, Colorado, and most of Arizona, in addition to Texas, which had already been annexed before the war. The war completed the westward movement of the Anglo-Saxons in the New World and appeared to bring to fruition the white men's vision of a transcontinental republic spanning from the Pacific to the Atlantic. Mexicans who had lived in those conquered territories entered the U.S. society as a conquered people. The first generation of Mexican Americans found themselves subjugated, discriminated against, and oppressed under the racist domination of the Anglo society, even though they were offered U.S. citizenship. The war is also called the Mexican War, the U.S.-Mexican War, and the U.S. Invasion of Mexico, revealing controversy over the historical understanding of the war. Most contemporary historians agree that the war can be best understood in the context of the U.S. expansionism of the 1840s.

Territorial expansion had been a contested political agenda in American history before the United States invaded Mexico. The Whig party vehemently warned against the undermining of the Jeffersonian democracy that expansion would inevitably entail. Abolitionists opposed it because the southwestward expansion would add more slave states. Even within the largely expansionist Democratic Party, some argued for a gradual process, while others insisted on a bold move.

In the late 1830s, there was a sudden surge of the expansionist passion. Technological, demographic, economic, and political factors converged to fuel the desire. Even if some may have dreamed of a transcontinental republic since the beginning of the United States, the expansionist vision did not become a viable goal until the 1840s, when innovations in transportation and communications technology conquered enormous physical distances that hitherto looked insurmountable. Steamships connected commercial centers through waterways. Railroad systems integrated eastern markets with cities and towns on the western slope of the Appalachians. In 1844, the telegraph opened up a new world of modern long-distance communication. Urbanization and the ever-increasing immigrants from Germany and Ireland also pressed the need for territorial expansion, although there still remained vast unoccupied lands. Leaders of the Southern slave states were particularly anxious to add new slave states because they would strengthen their political power and also serve as an outlet for the growing slave population. The U.S. control of the Pacific coast would provide American corporations with a greater competitive edge over the formidable rival Great Britain for the Asian trade. The economic crisis of 1837 made U.S. farmers desperate for new foreign markets. Policymakers coveted San Francisco and other coastal ports for their strategic and commercial advantages. All of these aspirations and calculations, combined with the fear of "being hemmed in" by Great Britain, inflamed the expansionist frenzy. In the early 1840s, countless books about California were published, all marveling at its richness, mild climate, and ports.

The U.S. expansionism of the 1840s was marked by an extreme version of Anglo-Saxon racism. In the early 1830s, the use of the phrase Anglo-Saxon in a racial sense was rather rare in political discourse. By the mid-1840s, the idea of the Anglo-Saxon race as the noblest stock chosen to dominate the New World had emerged. God had reserved America for a special people of Saxon blood. By the time of the Mexican-American War, the Mexicans who stood in the way of southwestward expansion were depicted as a mongrel race, adulterated by extensive intermarriage with an inferior Indian race. They were idle, thriftless, and, thus, it was believed, unable to govern such a beautiful land as California.

Texas Rebellion

The Texas Rebellion began in 1835 when the residents of Gonzales, East San Antonio, Texas, expelled Mexican forces in rebellion, and eventually led in 1836 to Texas's independence from Mexico. In the 1820s, the Mexican government allowed U.S. citizens to immigrate into Texas under the conditions that they be loyal to the Mexican government, learn Spanish, and become Roman Catholics. But the remoteness of the area made the government's control ineffectual. By the early 1830s, new settlers outnumbered the Tejanos and found themselves at odds with the Mexican government, which tried to regain its control over the territory. Many settlers were slave owners who engaged in cotton production, and Mexico's abolition of slavery in 1831 would have undermined their existence, if consistently enforced. Slave owners turned to the United States, which tolerated slavery.

To secure its power over Texas, the Mexican government stopped immigration and imposed heavy duty on imports. In 1833, General Antonio López de Santa Anna launched his effort to strengthen national unity. Disgruntled settlers rebelled against the Mexican forces with the help of the United States. Santa Anna's army prevailed at first and killed hundreds of settlers at Alamo and Goliad. But Santa Anna was captured in the Battle of San Jacinto and released only upon concessions of Texan independence and movement of the border southward, at the Rio Grande. In 1836, Samuel Houston, newly inaugurated president of the Republic of Texas, sent a representative to Washington and repealed the prohibition on slavery. Texas was not annexed until the Treaty of Guadalupe Hidalgo (1848).

Dong-Ho Cho

"In the hand of an enterprising people," lamented California missionary and author Richard Dana, "what a country this might be!" Like Indians and Negroes, the Mexicans must have faded away or been subordinated with the destined progress of the Anglo-Saxon race. To John L. O'Sullivan, editor of the *United States Magazine and Democratic Review*, any interference with the U.S. expansion amounted to a futile attempt to reverse a natural process. In the summer of 1845 he boldly criticized other nations that stood in the way of the United States "for the avowed object of thwarting our policy and hampering our power, limiting our greatness and checking the fulfillment of our manifest destiny to overspread the continent allotted by Providence for the free development of our yearly multiplying millions." He also suggested that the United States should claim its right to Oregon, based on the notion of Manifest Destiny. Since Representative Robert C. Winthrop of Massachusetts used the phrase in Congress in 1845, Manifest Destiny became the focal point of political debate on territorial expansion.

Following its conquest in 1521 by Conquistador Hernán Cortés, Mexico remained a colony of the Spanish Empire for 300 years. But the offspring of Spaniards in New Spain aspired to independence, spurred on by the independence of the United States in 1776 and the French Revolution in 1789.

On September 16, 1810, Miguel Hidalgo Costilla, a priest from the village of Dolores, Guanajuato, incited a rebellion against Spanish rule, and his compatriots, after 11 years of fighting, gained independence at last in 1821.

The northern regions of Mexico posed a particularly vexing problem to the Mexican government. They were not only far from the center of power, they also bordered with the expansionist America. Also they were sparsely populated, mostly by Native Americans and a smaller number of Mexicans. In an effort to stem the westward movement of Anglo Americans, in 1820 the Spanish crown took a desperate measure and granted foreigners—mostly Anglo Americans—the right to settle in Texas. Moses Austin received the first colonization contract, and in 1821 his son Stephen began to settle in eastern Texas. In subsequent years other families followed. By 1830, about 20,000 Anglos were living in Texas, constituting a numeric majority. Already in the late 1820s the Anglo settlers became troublesome elements to the Mexican government. Despite their promise to abide by Mexico's laws, they engaged in illegal homesteading, land speculation, smuggling, and support of slavery. They preferred the U.S. federalism and regarded the Mexican government as despotic and the Mexican culture as retarding economic development. They became increasingly rebellious.

During the 1820s, many Anglos also poured into California and New Mexico. It was against the law, but the Mexicans accepted them warmly. The earlier immigrants tried hard to assimilate themselves to the Mexican culture, learning Spanish, converting to Catholicism, and marrying native women. Intermarriage brought them citizenship and legal access to real estate and to political position. Both the Mexican elite and the lower class saw intermarriage with Anglo entrepreneurs as an opportunity to upgrade their social status by "whitening" their families and to improve economically. The later Anglo intruders, however, had no respect for Mexicans, whom they thought descended from a mongrel race and were prone to indolence, immorality, cowardice, filthiness, debauchery, cruelty, and frivolity.

The 1824 Mexican constitution, the first democratic constitution, granted autonomy to states and provinces. But the federalist principle did not apply to the northern frontier regions. New Mexico and California were under direct control of the national congress. Texas was incorporated into the state of Coahuila. The coup of 1835 by Antonio López de Santa Anna ended federalism throughout Mexico, restricting provincial autonomy. The central government began sending military rulers to the northern regions, which triggered the Texas Rebellion. On March 2, 1836, the Texans declared their independence from the Republic of Mexico and gained it on April 21, 1836, by defeating Santa Anna's troops at San Jacinto, although Mexico did not recognize it yet. In the same year, groups of Californians declared their independence, although by 1837 they had compromised with the Mexican government. New Mexico saw a rebellion among the lower classes in 1837, but it was suppressed by the ruling class.

Democrat James K. Polk was elected U.S. president on an expansionist platform in 1844 when the sense of urgency for the U.S. expansion prevailed. Polk quickly moved to invite Texas to be the 28th state of the United States. The Polk administration held Mexicans in contempt and assumed that firmness would force them to yield to American wishes—the annexation of Texas and the purchase of California—without resorting to physical force. The U.S. minister in Mexico, Wilson Shannon, said in October 1844, "I see it predicted in some of the papers in the U.S. that Mexico will declare war against the U.S.; there is as much probability that the Emperor of China will do so." To Mexico, however, the annexation of Texas was inadmissible because it violated the sovereignty of Mexico over its territory and would create a dangerous precedent threatening Mexico's territorial integrity. Yet Mexico did not want a war with the United States. The Jóse Joaquin de Herrera administration attempted in vain a double-edged diplomacy to avoid both the Texas annexation and a war with the United States. Mexico would even have recognized the independence of Texas if the Texans refused annexation. On July 4, 1845, however, Texas agreed to the annexation. Since its separation from Mexico, Texas had claimed the Rio Grande as the border instead of the traditionally recognized Nueces River, about 150 miles to the north of the Rio Grande.

The Herrera administration had no choice but to deploy federal troops to protect the disputed area between the Nueces River and the Rio Grande. President Polk promised the Texans that if they accepted annexation he would uphold their claim to the Rio Grande. Yet the Mexican government still wanted a negotiation with the United States. Any attempt at a diplomatic solution failed partly because of the lack of internal consensus in Mexican society. But it also failed because the United States sent John Slidell as the U.S. plenipotentiary secretary to demand what Mexico could hardly accept: recognizing the annexation of Texas and ceding the territories of New Mexico and California. Upon the abortion of the Slidell mission, President Polk ordered General Zachary Taylor to move his troops to the Rio Grande. It was obviously provocation of an armed confrontation. To the Mexican government, the deployment of the U.S. troops in the disputed area was an outright attack on Mexico's territorial integrity and a clear demonstration of the U.S. intention not to respect the 1828 border treaty. Mexico's new centralist president, Mariano Paredes, declared a war on April 4, 1846. Battles broke out. The report of a Mexican attack helped persuade Congress to vote for war with an overwhelming majority, 174 to 14 in the House of Representatives and 40 to 2 in the Senate. A handful of antislavery congressmen opposed the war on the grounds that the Mexican war would add to the number of slave states. Joshua Giddings of Ohio called the war measure "an aggressive, unholy, and unjust war." Pacifist Henry David Thoreau refused to pay tax, denouncing the Mexican war, and was put in jail. Based on this experience, he gave a lecture entitled "Resistance to Civil Government" two years later and published it in the famous essay, "Civil Disobedience."

The United States declared war against Mexico on May 11, 1846. In the declaration, President Polk stated: "Mexico had crossed over the U.S. border, had invaded our territory and had caused the shedding of U.S. blood in U.S. territory." This declaration suggested that the purpose of the war was the defense of U.S. territory, which the United States had unilaterally defined. Contradicting the spirit of the declaration, Polk ordered the occupation of the territory south of the Rio Grande, the territories of New Mexico and California. General Stephen Watts Kearny entered Santa Fe on August 18, 1946, meeting no resistance. He headed for California and finally established a provisional government in 1847 after a series of military victories gained with the help of other leaders. Meanwhile, General Winfield Scott entered Mexico City on September 12, 1847. Internal division disabled Mexico to launch a unified and effective military operation. Seven different Mexican presidents led the country during the two years of war.

The war ended with the signing of the Treaty of Guadalupe Hidalgo in February 1848. Mexico ceded California and New Mexico and recognized U.S. sovereignty over Texas north of the Rio Grande. From 1845 to 1848, the United States added 1.2 million square miles to its territory, a gain of more than 60 percent. In return, the United States paid $15 million to Mexico.

There were about 75,000 Mexicans living in the conquered territories at the time of the war's conclusion. They were given the choice of either moving to Mexico or staying in the United States. If they decided to stay, they could choose either Mexican or U.S. citizenship. If they did not declare their choice in a year, they would become U.S. citizens automatically. But soon they found themselves foreigners in their native land. The war may have expanded freedom and democracy to some, but it also expanded subordination and racial domination.

The war had been justified by the racist idea of Manifest Destiny: that the Anglo-Saxon race was destined to dominate the whole United States. Now the victorious war proved that was indeed the case. The heightened sense of racial superiority on the part of Anglo Americans reinforced Mexican Americans' ethnic awareness as La Laza. After 1848, the word *barrio* (meaning neighborhood in Spanish) came to denote a discernable section of a town populated by Mexican Americans.

Some Mexican Americans with property and business acumen, of course, found an economic niche in the new situation. But most farmers were dispossessed of their ancestral lands. Once owners failed to pay taxes or debts, county courts under the control of Anglo-Americans sold lands at public auction. Some Anglos used friendships with influential political figures to usurp the land titles from natives. Mexican American farmers, who were not familiar with the U.S. system, were easily victimized by Anglo-Americans' administrative and legal manipulation. Massive land loss made it harder for the lower classes to find jobs as common workers on ranches and farms. Displaced from agriculture and craft occupations, most Mexican Americans found themselves at the bottom of the occupational ladder in the new society. They sought a livelihood as day laborers, cooks, and servants. Racial oppression and discrimination often led to revolt and resistance in the conquered zones.

Many more Mexicans have immigrated to Texas, California, New Mexico, and other parts of the former Mexican territory since the United States took control of those areas in 1848. Thus, only a tiny proportion of Mexican Americans are the descendants of the indigenous Mexican population conquered by Anglo Americans. However, the legacy of the Anglo conquest of Mexico is the blatant anti-Mexican prejudice that has continuously affected Mexican Americans. Mexican Americans currently living in barrios face many of the problems of poverty and disadvantage that residents of inner-city black neighborhoods do.

DONG-HO CHO

See also

Guadalupe Hidalgo, Treaty of

Further Reading:

Castillo, Richard Griswold del, and Arnold De León. *North to Aztlán: A History of Mexican Americans in the United States.* New York: Twayne Publishers, 1996.

Fraizier, Donald S., ed. *The United States and Mexico at War: Nineteenth Century Expansionism and Conflict.* New York: Macmillan Reference USA, 1998.

Horsman, Reginald. *Race and Manifest Destiny: The Origins of American Racial Anglo-Saxonism.* Cambridge, MA: Harvard University Press, 1981.

Singletary, Otis. *The Mexican War*. New York: Oxford University Press, 1960.

Zinn, Howard. *A People's History of the United States: 1492–Present*. New York: HarperCollins, 2001.

Mexican Repatriation

Repatriation was a program run by various federal, state, local, religious, and social service agencies to facilitate the return of Mexicans to their homeland during the Great Depression. At its most benign, repatriation helped destitute families return home, but at its most inhuman and racist, it served to indiscriminately round up Mexicans and Mexican American U.S. citizens and force them onto trains to be dumped across the border.

When the economy was failing and did not have a chance of recovery, Congress passed the 1929 Immigration Act, which served as a partial victory for Texas congressman John C. Box and other nativists, who had pressed for a specific Mexican immigration ban throughout the 1920s. Although it was not aimed specifically at Mexico, the Immigration Act became the most restrictive legislation affecting Mexicans up to that point. Its provisions called for imprisonment of one year for those caught without documents a second time and a $1,000 fine. When William Doak was named secretary of labor in 1930 by President Herbert Hoover, he decided to use this new law against Mexicans. Throughout the country, Department of Labor agents zealously pursued undocumented Mexican immigrants, working hand in hand with local law enforcement officials.

The Great Depression of the 1930s, which dislocated millions of Americans, presented the greatest challenge to Mexican immigrants as the collapsed economy left hundreds of thousands homeless or without jobs. During the worst of the crisis, industrial cities like Detroit were plagued with 75 percent unemployment. Mexicans, so desirable as workers in the previous decade, were now discharged from their jobs by the thousands and then pressured to leave by community authorities. Between 1929 and 1936, at least 600,000 Mexican nationals and their children, many of whom were born in the United States, returned to Mexico—this represented about one-third of the U.S. Mexican population.

Out of work and unable to acquire adequate shelter and food, most Mexican immigrants wanted to return home. But they resented Americans' attitude—that Mexicans had no right to be in the United States. In the past, opposition to Mexicans living in the United States—from nativists and white workers—had not been transformed into successful campaigns to expel them. This was mainly because of powerful employers who were anxious to protect the Mexican immigration influx, but now nativists could do their worst.

The most zealous repatriation campaigns took place in Los Angeles. Even before the passage of the 1929 act, Los Angeles law enforcement officers conducted vagrancy sweeps to clear Los Angeles streets of unemployed workers, of which a disproportionate number were Mexicans. Charles P. Visel, Los Angeles County coordinator for unemployment relief, worked hand in hand with federal agents sent to Los Angeles by Secretary of Labor Doak and local Los Angeles police to arrest as many undocumented Mexicans as possible. A strategy was devised to intimidate "aliens" into leaving on their own by publicizing raids where hundreds of Mexicans were rounded up, regardless of whether or not they carried documents. It turned out that only a small percentage of the Mexicans harassed in this manner were undocumented.

In 1931, President Hoover implemented the President's Emergency Committee for Employment (PECE), his solution to unemployment. It was no more than a public relations ploy to make people feel good about providing a marginal number of jobs through the private sector. But the PECE in Los Angeles, of which Visel was a member, worked closely with county officials to coordinate the voluntary repatriation of Southern California Mexicans—in other words, those not deportable under the 1929 act. In 1931, Visel traveled to Mexico, hoping to arrange a program to settle the thousands of Mexicans whom county officials and Visel hoped to repatriate.

The Mexican government did cooperate with various groups in the United States, including Visel's program in Los Angeles County that raised funds to send Mexicans to the border by promising to take responsibility for the repatriates once they crossed the border. Unfortunately, the engine of repatriation on the American side was more efficient than the one south of the border, resulting in bottlenecks that left thousands of the discarded Mexicans marooned in border towns with little to eat and nowhere to sleep.

The repatriation movement effectively depopulated Mexican and Mexican American communities. That, coupled with the economic downturn, meant a curtailment of the cultural life offered by Hispanic theaters, newspapers, and publishing houses. The majority of Spanish-language newspapers and publishing houses in the Southwest ceased publication; theater houses either shut their doors or converted to movie houses and laid off their actors, technicians, playwrights, orchestras, and other personnel.

F. ARTURO ROSALES

See also
Immigration and Customs Enforcement (ICE); Japanese Internment

Further Reading:
Balderrama, Francisco E., and Raymund Rodríguez. *Decade of Betrayal: Mexican Repatriation in the 1930s.* Albuquerque: University of New Mexico Press, 2006.

Miami (Florida) Riot of 1982

The Miami (Florida) Riot of 1982 was a black-incited disturbance that arose after Luis Alvarez, a Hispanic police officer, shot and killed a young black man named Nevell Johnson. Two years earlier, Miami had experienced its largest black-incited riot, which had erupted in response to the acquittal of white police officers who beat to death Arthur McDuffie, a 33-year-old black man. The 1982 riot was much smaller. Nevertheless, the fact that the riot occurred illustrates the failure of the state, local, and federal governments to address the issues that caused black rioting two years earlier.

Black rioting was not a new concept, having emerged in many American cities during the 1960s (*see* Long Hot Summer Riots [1965–1967]). Many whites did not understand what provoked black youths to loot, vandalize, and set fire to buildings within their own community. Journalists and television reporters who covered the riots imprinted images of blacks ravaging stores, homes, and buildings and sometimes beating and killing unfortunate and innocent white

victims. The rioters were labeled as criminals, and conservative whites demanded law and order, while liberals, both black and white, advocated social reform and community programs. Blacks who subscribed to militancy and radical Black Power encouraged the riots, referring to them as revolutions and revolts. Other blacks, such as those associated with the civil rights movement, disapproved of the riots but sympathized with the young rioters who had been too long the victims of police brutality and systematic oppression and neglect. Scholars such as Darryl Harris have presented arguments to illustrate that black riots were often a form of protest that had roots in the black slave rebellions of the 18th and 19th centuries.

Miami blacks did not participate in the riots of the 1960s. In fact, the riots of that period were largely restricted to Northern black communities, where the civil rights protests and demonstrations were less active. The civil rights movement generally took place in the South and was led by middle-class blacks. The movement effectively squashed the discriminatory Jim Crow ordinances forced on blacks, but nothing was done to remedy the alarming state of black life, particularly in the North, which was characterized by dire economic, educational, and social disadvantages. In comparison to whites and other minority groups, blacks, overall, were the hardest hit.

Although many blacks in the South benefited from the civil rights movement, Miami blacks did not. Miami blacks competed with Cuban immigrants for resources and opportunities. As a result, their lives were more similar to those of Northern blacks than to blacks who lived elsewhere in the South. Blacks who lived in the sections of Miami known as Overtown, Liberty City, and Coconut Grove faced poverty, poor housing, and inferior schools just like blacks who lived in the ghettos of the North. Their predicament was an accumulation of the effects of slavery, racism, discrimination, oppression, and, as Harris (1999) states, white domination.

Antiblack violence was another problem historically confronting blacks in Miami and across the nation. Following the emancipation of black slaves in 1863, white mobs and racist organizations regularly assaulted and murdered blacks, often with little or no repercussions in Florida and across the nation. Through the mid-20th century, blacks, especially in the North and in Miami, were subjected to police misconduct, harassment, beatings, and killings. Generally, the justice system ignored the complaints or let the offending police officers go with little or no punishment.

Having repeatedly been denied justice, black Miamians turned from nonviolent demonstration to violent protest. Thirteen small riots, which occurred during the 1970s, preceded the larger and more infamous 1980 Miami riot. Local, state, and federal government responded immediately by pouring aid into the community. Numerous social programs were established. A commission was established to investigate the disturbance in Miami. It found that "the black community experienced isolation and subjugation in the full range of affairs—political, economic, education, housing, and criminal justice" and made a number of recommendations that were not fully implemented (Harris 1999: 113–14).

President Jimmy Carter's plan to help rebuild the sections of the city that had been badly damaged was unsuccessful. The U.S. Department of Labor provided financial assistance to support minority-owned businesses and to set up summer jobs and Job Corps programs for young adults. Several local black and white businesses "endeavored to improve blacks' socioeconomic status in Miami" (Harris 1999: 36). Overall, these programs and others like them failed, mostly because the assistance did not directly benefit blacks but was instead filtered mostly to whites and to other minority groups. Also, these programs were essentially quick fixes. Harris addresses another issue that intensified tensions in Miami—the 1981 election of Republican president Ronald Reagan, who did not support social change for the poor, the defenseless, and the marginalized.

In December 1982, Officer Luis Alvarez entered an arcade "as part of a training exercise of a rookie officer assigned to him" and after approaching Nevell Johnson, a young black man playing a video game, Alvarez shot and killed him (Harris 1999: 93). Alvarez claimed that "he thought that Johnson was reaching for a gun in his waistband" (Harris 1999: 93). Blacks insisted that this was another case of black injustice, and they rioted. The riot was less extensive than that of 1980; only "several hundreds took part in the 1982 uprising, causing just one death and eight injuries and resulting in twenty-nine arrests" (Harris 1999: 85). Howard Gary, the black city manager of Miami, was responsible for the quick restoration of order through the use of a crisis response team and

measures such as the closing down of all bars, liquor stores, and gasoline stations and the setting up of guards throughout the town (Harris 1999: 96). Because this disturbance was less publicized and considerably smaller than the riot of 1980, there were fewer programs established in its wake. Seven years later, another riot erupted in Miami. This was also a small riot, and once again brought about little, if any, change.

GLADYS L. KNIGHT

See also

Police Brutality; Race Riots in America. Documents: The Report on the Memphis Riots of May 1866 (July 25, 1866); Account of the Riots in East St. Louis, Illinois (July 1917); The Cook County Coroner's Report Regarding the 1919 Chicago Race Riots (1919); A Southern Black Woman's Letter Regarding the Recent Riots in Chicago and Washington (November 1919); The Final Report of the Grand Jury on the Tulsa Race Riot (June 25, 1921); Testimony from *Laney v. United States* Describing Events during the Washington, D.C., Riot of July 1919 (December 3, 1923); The Governor's Commission Report on the Watts Riots (December 1965); Cyrus R. Vance's Report on the Riots in Detroit (July-August 1967); The Reports of the Oklahoma Commission to Study the Tulsa Race Riot of 1921 (2000-2001); The Draft Report of the 1898 Wilmington Race Riot Commission (December 2005)

Further Reading:

Harris, Darryl B. *The Logic of Black Urban Rebellions: Challenging the Dynamics of White Domination in Miami.* Westport, CT: Praeger, 1999.

Michael Richards Incident

Before a certain stand-up performance at a California comedy club in 2006, Michael Richards was best known for his portrayal of Cosmo Kramer, the lanky, lovable, and at times rather creepy neighbor on the long-running hit NBC comedy show, *Seinfeld.* Michael Richards won three Emmy Awards for Outstanding Supporting Actor during the show's six-year run.

Although many people associated with *Seinfeld* went on to experience further professional and financial success, Richards was not one of them. Failing to attract solid work, he went back to performing in nightclubs, where he had gotten his start in the 1970s. On November 17, 2006, the 57-year-old

Richards was performing at the Laugh Factory in West Hollywood, when he became offended by the behavior of some noisy patrons in the balcony. This is what happened next:

> *Richards*: Shut up! 50 years ago we'd have you upside down with a fu****g fork up your ass. You can talk, you can talk, you can talk! You're brave now, motherf***er! Throw his ass out, he's a n****r. He's a n****r! He's a n****r, a n****r! Look, there's a n****r!
>
> *Patron*: That was uncalled for. ("Michael Richards")

The following Monday, November 20, it so happened that Jerry Seinfeld himself—a man who remains one of Richards's staunchest defenders—was a guest on the *Late Show with David Letterman*. Seinfeld had arranged to have Richards appear via satellite from California. He told Letterman, "I was extremely upset about it, and he is extremely upset about it . . . It was one of those awful, awful things" ("Kramer's Apology"). Seinfeld said he wanted to give Richards an opportunity to apologize and explain himself.

The whole segment was rather awkward. The three comedians were trying to talk about a serious subject of racial hatred, and the audience didn't know how to react. In response to the incident, Richards said: "I lost my temper on stage . . . I got heckled and took it badly, and went into a rage, and said some pretty nasty things to some Afro-Americans . . . I'm really busted up over this and I am very, very sorry" ("Kramer's Apology"). He claimed he was not racist and that the bile that came spurting out of his mouth came from some unknown place deep inside him. Richards said he would seek out help and counseling.

Sociologically, the event exposed a racist vein in U.S. society normally hidden from public view and—at least for a few news cycles—drew considerable media attention to the persistent use of the "N-word" in popular culture. Some black celebrities were so appalled by the display that they said they would never use the word again. In a few minutes, Richards' career had imploded, and the actor largely disappeared from public view. Yet thanks again to his friend Jerry Seinfeld, he did make an appearance on the latter's Internet comedy show "Comedians in Cars Getting Coffee" in 2012. Seinfeld picked up Richards at his home in a 1962 VW bus/utility truck, and the two went to a Los Angeles café to get coffee and reminisce. Most of their interaction was fairly jokey, but it took a serious turn when they began discussing the difference between working "selflessly" instead of "selfishly" ("Comedians in Cars").

Richards went on to thank Seinfeld for sticking with him over the years. Seinfeld suggested that Richards had been weighed down from the incident for too long, and it was up to him to let it go: "That's up to you to say, 'You know what, I've been carrying this bag around enough, I'm going to put it down'" ("Comedians in Cars"). The episode closes with the two friends hanging out and taking pictures with fans in the parking lot.

DANIEL M. HARRISON

See also

Mel Gibson Incidents

Further Reading:

"Comedians in Cars Getting Coffee." http://www.youtube.com/watch?feature=player_embedded&v=Wriy3ICfF9U (cited February 4, 2013).

Farhi, Paul. "'Seinfeld' Comic Richards Apologizes for Racial Rant." *Washington Post*. November 21, 2006. http://www.washingtonpost.com/wp-dyn/content/article/2006/11/21/AR2006112100242.html (cited February 4, 2013).

Fish, Stanley. "The Moving Finger Writes." *New York Times*. December 10, 2006. http://opinionator.blogs.nytimes.com/2006/12/10/the-moving-finger-writes/ (cited February 4, 2013).

Harker, Joseph. "Nothing to Laugh at in Kramer's n-Word Routine." *Guardian*, November 2, 2006.

"Kramer's Apology," http://www.youtube.com/watch?v=EC26RI-Ria8 (cited February 4, 2013).

"Michael Richards Spews Racial Hate," http://www.youtube.com/watch?v=BoLPLsQbdt0 (cited February 4, 2013).

Middleman Minorities

The term *middleman* refers to the stratum a group occupies between the elite and the masses in traditional societies. Middleman minorities may also play a role between producers and consumers in modern economies when there is a status gap or noticeable division. Ironically, middleman status is itself a by-product of being discriminated against economically in the first place. Unable to get decent jobs in the mainstream economy, some ethnic/religious groups specialize in specific occupational niches, such as trade, commerce, crafts, or the independent professions. Geographic mobility is an important characteristic of these occupations because middleman minorities' structural position makes them vulnerable to economic and political crises in the host society. Jews, Armenians, and the Chinese are classic examples of middleman minorities, often spread out around the globe as a diaspora.

Middleman minorities are particularly prevalent in agricultural societies as intermediaries between the aristocracy and the peasantry. They sometimes continue to exist in postcolonial societies after the elites have been removed. (Some examples are the Chinese in southeast Asia, Asian Indians in Africa, and Parsees in India. In advanced industrial societies, they are called immigrant or ethnic entrepreneurs.) Under favorable historical circumstances, middleman minorities acquire special resources such as entrepreneurial values, beliefs, institutions, and social networks that enhance their financial success. These resources are often passed on to their descendants, who in turn continue the "family" tradition. In essence, their biggest asset is their cultural heritage of entrepreneurship. Bolstered by their international ties, middleman minorities tend to thrive in business even after they migrate repeatedly.

Historically, middleman minorities managed to form semiautonomous communities in host societies. They maintained their ancestral language and culture while adapting fairly successfully to their host society. A separate and distinctive group identity and a sojourner ideology made them turn inward for trust, mutual help, friendships, and marriage partners. They developed an elaborate infrastructure for serving their community needs, whether for schools, presses, houses of worship, or social and recreational associations. These activities made them highly visible and were the cause of accusations of being clannish and foreign.

The very factors that bestow economic success on middleman minorities (e.g., cohesion, outsider status, and business visibility) can provoke host hostility during turbulent periods. Middleman minorities are often hated by the majority population and envied by other minority groups in the host society. Because middleman minorities are numerically small, their livelihood depends on elite protection. When the elite are removed, as in times of political crisis, middleman minorities are likely to suffer reprisals by the masses, who begrudge them their economic success. The elite may also use them as a peon for their own gains, accusing them of disloyalty and of pilfering the country's resources. Hostile reactions to middleman minorities can run the gamut from boycotts to riots to expulsions and may even culminate in genocide. Extreme examples include the estimated 1.5 million Armenians who perished at the hands of the Ottoman and Young Turk regimes between 1915 and 1923 in Asia Minor; the Holocaust that killed more than 6 million Jews during Nazi Germany; and the expulsions of Indians from Uganda by Idi Amin in 1974. It is important to point out that the structural position of middleman minorities, and not their cultural traits as it is popularly believed, accounts for their vulnerability.

Sociologists have argued that minorities frequently perform a middleman role because their "stranger" (outsider) status enables them to be objective and impersonal in business dealings. These very same advantages can, however, be a source of friction between the middleman minorities and the customers they serve, often resulting in all-out conflict and violence. But host hostility can actually reinforce the middleman minorities' ethnicity and group solidarity, locking them into their precarious position. Thus, what may have begun as a voluntary segregation can become a forced one. Relinquishing plans of eventual return to an ancestral homeland, as well as economic and social integration over several generations, remove the boundaries that make this group distinct. Inevitably, both cultural and structural forces contribute to the development, continuity, and eventual demise or assimilation of middleman minorities.

MEHDI BOZORGMEHR AND ANNY BAKALIAN

See also

Segmented Assimilation; Split-Labor Market Theory

Further Reading:

Blalock, Hubert. *Toward a Theory of Minority-Group Relations.* New York: John Wiley, 1967.

Bonacich, Edna. "A Theory of Middleman Minorities." *American Sociological Review* 38 (1973): 583–94.

Zenner, Walter. *Minorities in the Middle: A Cross-Cultural Analysis.* Albany: State University of New York Press, 1991.

Migrant Workers

Migrant workers move from place to place engaging in short-term (usually seasonal) work. Migrant workers may cross national borders or be internal migrants moving within a nation. American labor history includes two notable examples that helped foster a shared, negative perception of migrant workers: the Dust Bowl Okies and Latino migrant agricultural workers. Migrant workers and their families are often perceived as being a burden on local resources. They are also often treated as outsiders due to their mobile existence. Today, migrant workers remain most prevalent in agriculture and face a high risk of job-related illness and injury.

At the heart of migrant worker life is a sense of mobility, moving from job to job as need and demand dictates. For example, agriculture workers move as the seasons change and as specific crops are planted or harvested in other locations. Migrant workers are often found in agriculture jobs, such as tending, planting, and harvesting. However, they occasionally also appear in skilled professions (e.g., electricians and plumbers), and in low-skill jobs requiring significant physical labor (construction). For example, many Latinos relocated to New Orleans following Hurricane Katrina to fill a demand for construction workers.

El enganche

El enganche translates as *the hook* and is a term used to describe recruiting processes utilized to bring early Mexican migrant laborers to the United States. As the supply of Chinese and Japanese laborers shrank (due to both the Chinese Exclusion Act of 1882 and the 1907 Gentleman's Agreement), U.S. demand for physical labor led private labor contractors (called *enganchadores*) to heavily recruit labor from rural parts of southern Mexico. Recruiters misleadingly touted high wages and easy work to attract potential employees. Recruiters often seemingly sweetened the deal by loaning recruits money to make the trip, with the understanding that the loan would be deducted from wages. However, the loans often had high interest rates and took extended periods of time to pay back. Hence, many workers felt themselves *hooked* into the job for an extended period of time simply to pay back the loan.

During the Great Depression, many migrant workers moved from the Midwest to California looking for work. Increased farming demands, a lack of soil conservation practices, and a seven-year drought created the Dust Bowl. During the Dust Bowl, valuable topsoil literally blew off farmland, leaving many farmers and their families without a livelihood. Collectively, these migrants were called *Okies*, and they relocated to California with hopes of working the many crop cycles in California's warmer climate. Many Dust Bowl migrants arrived in California to find the state government overwhelmed with new temporary residents while still other migrants were turned away at the border. The preponderance of farmers weakened the demand in the labor pool, leading to depressed wages for migrants as well as California residents. Large, unsanitary camps of unemployed migrant workers created additional public health concerns. The prevalence of Okies continued until the start of World War II, which saw both Okies and Californians leaving the state for jobs in the military or relocating to booming manufacturing plants and shipping ports along the West Coast. This new labor shortage, in part, helped create a need to recruit migrant laborers from Mexico.

Latino (particularly Mexican) agriculture workers have been employed in U.S. farms for over a century. Private recruiters heavily recruited Mexican laborers as the supply of Asian labor dwindled in the late 19th and early 20th centuries. This period also coincided with the mechanization of agriculture in Mexico, leaving many rural residents without work or land. This made work in the United States additionally appealing. The start of World War I further increased demand for workers, a need that persisted until 1922 when many Mexicans were temporarily repatriated. Demand soon increased, but Mexican laborers were again deported from 1929 to 1941. The start of World War II led to the Bracero Program, designed to recruit Mexican farmworkers to fill jobs in U.S. agriculture. This program continued until 1964, as concerns over exploitation and civil rights formally ended the program and led to a long period of unauthorized migration into the United States due to a lack of legitimate access to U.S. employment. At its height, the Bracero Program employed 400,000 agriculture workers per year. Today, the H-2A visa similarly provides agriculture workers from Mexico, but at a much lower level of utilization, ranging from as few as 30,000 in 1999 and growing to 86,000 in 2009.

A Mexican woman stoops while picking melons in the Imperial Valley, California, 1937. Due to the poor tools they were given, many workers had back problems for the rest of their lives. (Library of Congress)

for bacterial urinary tract infections. This, in turn, creates a weakened immune system in close quarters with other weakened immune systems and provides the opportunity for infectious disease (such as tuberculosis) to spread rapidly. Workers also must worry about lacerations from farming equipment. Hence, migrant workers often pay a high cost for their employment.

JAMES MAPLES

See also
Bracero Program; Day Laborers; H-2A Visa

Further Reading:

Fussell, Elizabeth. "Hurricane Chasers in New Orleans: Latino Immigrants as a Source of a Rapid Response Labor Force." *Hispanic Journal of Behavioral Sciences* 31, no. 3 (2009): 375–94.

Gregory, James N. *American Exodus: The Dust Bowl Migration and Okie Culture in California*. New York: Oxford University Press, 1991.

Massey, Douglas S., Jorge Durand, and Nolan J. Malone. *Beyond Smoke and Mirrors: Mexican Immigration in an Era of Economic Integration*. New York: Russell Sage Foundation, 2002.

Thompson, Gabriel. *There's No Jose Here: Following the Hidden Lives of Mexican Immigrants*. New York: Nation Books, 2006.

Migrant workers are often perceived as being a burden on local resources. Migrants are perceived as taking jobs from local residents, utilizing resident resources (such as schools) without contributing financially, and increasing crime. Migrants also receive a negative reaction based on their status as outsiders to the community and the mysterious quality of their hidden existence as migrants and often unauthorized migrants.

Latino workers continue to be an important source of migrant labor, albeit exploited labor. For example, Latino farm workers experience a high risk for harm on the job site. Employers expose workers to pesticides in high doses in the workplace, often without proper safety precautions. Pesticides then follow workers home as tainted clothes come into contact with food via washing in the family sink. The presence of pesticides through active use and residue from previous applications has led to numerous birth defects, miscarriages, and reproductive health issues. Workers face high instances of sun-related illnesses such as heat stroke and skin cancers. A lack of bathroom facilities and an emphasis on holding one's urine creates the opportunity

Minstrelsy

Minstrel shows were the first form of musical theater that was uniquely American, based on American history and featuring uniquely American social relations. Minstrelsy began in the 1820s and went on to become America's most popular form of entertainment for nearly 100 years (although blackface depictions date back to the 1750s, before the American Revolution). The very phrase "Jim Crow" came into existence by Thomas D. Rice's depiction of a black man who "Jumped Jim Crow" and later became *the* image of African Americans in the United States. For these shows, whites used burnt cork to darken their skin and lipstick to enlarge their mouths to depict a stereotype of Africans and African Americans in a wide variety of American settings

Minstrel shows used stereotypes for white profit by simultaneously constructing black and white identities in the national imagination. Minstrel shows represent the most provocative and, perhaps, revealing form of entertainment in the late 19th and early 20th centuries. Their enticing use of black bodies and representations created, enforced, and disseminated ideas about whiteness and white privilege, and, conversely, black inherent inferiority and subservience. By both portraying blacks a certain way, generally in line with racial stereotypes of the time, as well as articulating statements that voiced political, social, and economic concerns, minstrel shows became both a principal site of struggle in and over the perceived culture of blacks.

The image of blacks that appeared in minstrel shows, Jim Crow, was based on a caricature of a black homeless man, dressed in ragged clothes, singing and dancing on stage. Though a gross misrepresentation of blacks, these depictions were perceived as reality and taken as truth when depicted by working-class whites in blackface. During minstrel shows, white audiences witnessed blacks in a wide variety of settings, ranging from slave ships to plantations to the urban North. Nearly all included (mis)representations of "authentic" black dancing styles. To attract large audiences, minstrel shows featured popular American music, most notably "Dixie," a nostalgic song dreaming of the "good old days" of white aristocracy rooted in blacks' plantation life. Contributing to these shows were many famous American songwriters, including Stephen Foster, who wrote lyrics to accompany blackfaced actors performances.

The content and subjects of minstrelsy changed with each historical epoch in America. The largest shifts appeared after slavery and emancipation and then again during the early part of the 20th century, which coincided with both the Great Migration of blacks northward and out of the South and mass migration of Southern and Eastern Europeans into America. This inexpensive entertainment for the masses provided many urban dwellers who spent their evenings watching minstrel shows with sufficient information about blacks to develop racial (and racist) attitudes about many of the men and women with whom they often lived in close proximity and/or competed with for jobs. However, traveling minstrel shows, which were extremely popular, brought these forms and ideas to countless Americans in the Midwest who never had any contact with blacks, thereby allowing them to participate in both American cultures and ideologies.

After the Civil War, minstrel shows featured nostalgically longing depictions of the "good old days" of slavery, when slaves were happy and content on the plantations. The new content of minstrel show also resulted in the introduction of new characters into the shows. Prominent characters included Zip Coon, Sambo, the mammy, and the brute. Characters were depicted as whites' conceptions of good blacks (Sambo and Mammy), the "brute nigger" who delighted in carrying knives and starting fights, and the dandy, who attempted to imitate upper-class white styles of dress and speech. The inhumanity and cartoon-like nature of these characters distanced real blacks from being perceived as equal to whites. Finally, black children, often referred to as "pickaninnies," were ignorant youths often prone to thievery and other forms of deviance with little potential aptitude for the new public education system in America that few wanted to extend to blacks.

Particularly fearful to whites was the black brute intent on raping white women. These depictions of these rapacious black men fueled a century of lynchings that took countless lives of innocent black men and women oftentimes only on the whispered rumor of a rape, or even a sideways glance, deemed inappropriate, at white women. Deeply embossed in American culture, the nation's first feature-length film, *The Birth of a Nation* (based on Thomas Dixon's book, *The Clansman*), featured the black brute, a white man in blackface depicted as chasing after a white woman who would rather jump from a cliff to her death than lose her chastity and virginity to a black man.

Throughout their long history, minstrel acts reflected an admiration and longing for values and characteristics of blackness in line with racial ideologies of the time period. Childish, emotional, and musical and rhythmic characteristics of blacks conveyed to white audiences that blacks were intellectually inferior to whites and lacked the intelligence and other mental resources to succeed in any profession beyond servile positions. In this way, caricatures of blacks in minstrel shows also embodied the past for which whites longed, thus voicing a conscious wish for black social and economic inequality implicit in slavery.

Minstrelsy is a useful example of how race was learned and perpetuated through popular culture, entertainment, and media forms. Minstrel shows, like lynchings, focused on a black otherness that unified whites and led to the creation of a unique American identity. These images of blacks supported, dispelled, and reinforced ideologies of white superiority ranging, depending on the time period, from environmental causes for degradation, inherent inferiority, romantic racialism, paternalism, social Darwinism, and progressivism. These images then provided whites, many of whom in the North likely knew few blacks, with the knowledge necessary to shape their own identity to the contrary of this perceived black inferiority.

As black culture developed, whites appropriated parts and pieces of it to use for their own economic advantage and political purposes, thereby shaping their own culture in turn. When blackness was vague and uncertain whites took what they saw and assumed that it was authentic, combined these visions with previous stereotypes, prejudices, and images about savages in Africa and created a blackness they could use to their advantage. In this way, blackness became integral to both the American identity and culture, even though most whites rarely maintain any kind of sustained relationship with their black counterparts.

As the first true and realized white entertainment in the nation, and in the world, minstrel shows emphasized the white identity of its audience and actors, and their difference from those whom they were imitating. In line with the racial ideologies of the time, particularly Romantic racialism, minstrel shows usually portrayed blacks as emotional characters who, although they had qualities whites often lacked, had a number of others that made success in America impossible—they were shiftless and lazy, brutish and sex-crazed, dirty and incompetent. In other words, they were everything whites were not, and thus something against which whites could use to measure themselves. Minstrel shows thereby educated Northern whites and new immigrants who may have rarely encountered blacks in their daily lives, as to these characteristics, thereby disseminating a highly damaging and long-lasting racial ideology of white supremacy.

Unskilled immigrants from Europe, particularly Ireland, during the second half of the 19th century were flooding America's shores and competing with blacks for the lowest paying jobs in the North. Mocking blacks through minstrel shows in the late 19th and early 20th centuries ensured that blacks would be considered neither citizens nor workers on the same plane as whites. Instead, minstrelsy further identified the presumed differences between blacks and whites, even among those working in similar positions in the North.

The license with which blackface provided whites allowed them to make statements about their own social circumstances that reflected the longing, fears, hopes, and prejudices enmeshed with being among the white working class in the 19th century. Minstrel shows inhibited cross-racial coalitions by ideologically suppressing black workers and obscuring any similarities between the two groups.

In addition to existing on the historical stage, minstrel figures continue to exist in many popular forms. For example, the vast majority of television programs and movies lack depictions of blacks in middle-class and professional roles and instead often appear as sidekicks, clowns, or criminals. Advertising, historically, drew on America's longing for the ideal and "simple" days of the plantation era. For generations, stereotyped caricatures of blacks have appeared on a wide variety of popular brands (such as the Gold Dust Twins and Nigger Brand oysters, tobacco, and toothpaste) and household products (ashtrays, piggybanks, kitchen accessories, etc.). A trip to a modern supermarket will find the legacies of these products and images in Aunt Jemima and Mrs. Butterworth's (classic examples of the Mammy figure) and Uncle Ben (an Uncle Tom figure) remain on store shelves.

Minstrel figures have also appeared in popular cartoons, particularly Bugs Bunny cartoons by Warner Brothers and a variety of cartoons by Walt Disney (including *Brer Rabbit and the Tar Baby*), through the 1980s. These cartoons often featured happy, smiling, banjo-playing, watermelon-eating, big-lipped, barefoot blacks in the South in a plantation setting or in Africa, as comic savages, roasting the hero in a pot, alluding to cannibalism. Therefore, while these images appeared from stage shows prior to World War II their lasting legacy continues to influence new generations of youth, including the current one.

MELISSA F. WEINER

See also
Amos 'n' Andy; Blackface

Further Reading:

Dates, Janette L., and William Barlow. *Split Image: African Americans in the Mass Media*, 2nd ed. Washington, DC: Howard University Press, 1993.

Fredrickson, George M. *The Black Image in the White Mind: The Debate on Afro-American Character and Destiny, 1817–1914*. New York: Harper & Row, 1971.

Hale, Grace Elizabeth. *Making Whiteness: The Culture of Segregation in the South, 1890–1940*. New York: Vintage, 1999.

Lott, Evan. *Love and Theft: Blackface Minstrelsy and the American Working Class*. New York: Oxford University Press, 1993.

Roediger, David R. *The Wages of Whiteness: Race and the Making of the American Working Class*. Rev. ed. New York: Verso Books, 1999.

Minuteman Project, The

The Minuteman Project is an activist organization of civilian volunteers founded for the purpose of monitoring the flow of illegal immigration across the U.S.-Mexican border. Its main focus is the Arizona and California borders, and it has spread only weakly to Texas and New Mexico. The group also engages in harassment of workers (such as day laborers) in interior areas of the country. Minuteman Project volunteers often carry arms and wear military or pseudo-military clothing, and they operate by spotting putatively undocumented migrants and reporting them to the Border Patrol and other law enforcement agencies. It has been alleged that volunteers have seized undocumented migrants and held them coercively, either by threat of force or by exploitation of the migrants' fear, until released or turned over to government authorities. The Department of Homeland Security has voiced disapproval of the Minuteman Project's volunteer law enforcement activities, but it is unclear whether and how collaboration actually occurs between this group and government officers in the field. The mass media greatly exaggerated the scale of the Minutemen, and by 2006, the organization's members had fallen into fighting among themselves over organizational names and assets, policies, and personalities, including serious charges of malfeasance directed at two key leaders, Chris Simcox and Jim Gilchrist.

Gilchrist founded the Minuteman Project in 2004 as a result of his dissatisfaction with the federal government's handling of immigration laws. The organization's name is derived from the Minutemen, members of the American colonial militia during the Revolutionary War. The group forms part of a network of anti-immigrant or immigration restrictionist organizations, some small and others with significant budgets and presences in Washington. Individuals associated with the Minuteman Project have reputedly participated in white supremacy and direct military action movements, and there is some overlap between racist ideologies and Minuteman Project rhetoric, although the connections are not always present, and not all members of the group are white.

The Minuteman Project has garnered support from such politicians as California governor Arnold Schwarzenegger, who has praised the organization's efforts along the border, and Texas governor Rick Perry, whom the group endorsed in his 2010 reelection campaign. Members of the mass media, including conservative commentators Michael Savage and Sean Hannity and former CNN television host Lou Dobbs, have also expressed support for the group's activities. However, the Minuteman Project has also generated controversy and criticism. The Southern Poverty Law Center has classified the group as a "nativist extremist" organization, charging that Minuteman members target individual immigrants instead of immigration policies. In addition, President George W. Bush in 2005 voiced his opposition to the project, characterizing its members as "vigilantes."

The Minuteman Project and its focus on Mexicans and the border can be seen in the context of ideological tendencies in some sectors of U.S. society. From the most general to the most specific, these include anxiety about a changing and disorderly world (e.g., September 11 terrorism, economic globalization), for which Latin American immigrants can be seen as scapegoats. The border, then, is a clear line that maintains "here" versus "there," safety versus danger, and symbolically holds back the influx of disorder.

JOSIAH HEYMAN

See also

Immigration and Customs Enforcement (ICE)

Further Reading:

ACLU of Arizona, New Mexico, and Texas. *Creating the Minutemen: A Misinformation Campaign Fueled by a Small Group of Extremists*. November 3, 2006.

Beirich, Heidi, and Potok, Mark. "Broken Record: Lou Dobbs' Daily 'Broken Borders' CNN Segment Has Focused on Immigration for Years. But There's One Issue Dobbs Just Won't Take On." Southern Poverty Law Center Intelligence Report, no. 120 (Winter 2005).

Southern Poverty Law Center. "Anti-Immigration Groups," Intelligence Report no. 101 (Spring 2001). http://www.splcenter.org/get-informed/intelligence-report/browse-all-issues/2001/spring/blood-on-the-border/anti-immigration-.

Miscegenation

"Miscegenation" refers to the mixing, interbreeding, sexual union, marriage, or cohabitation of people of different races or ethnic groups, especially whites and nonwhites. Given the pejorative and racist implications of its historical application, the term is considered offensive and has largely dropped from contemporary usage. From Thomas Dixon to Gunnar Myrdal, two poles in the evolution of mainstream American racial thought, it was expressed as common knowledge that the primary reason for segregation during Jim Crow was the fear of the ultimate taboo of miscegenation. Ostensibly, the issue of miscegenation can be considered the linchpin of racial antipathy during the Jim Crow era.

The term first appeared during the war election of 1864 as the title of an anonymous pamphlet, *Miscegenation: The Theory of the Blending of the Races, Applied to the American White Man and Negro.* While the term "amalgamation" had been used previously, the anonymous author explained his need to invent a new term from the classical Latin *misc*, "to mix," and *genus*, "race," in order to be more specific. The pamphlet, which sold on newsstands for 25 cents in the summer of 1863, turned out to be a hoax concocted by copperhead journalists David Goodman Croly and George Wakeman in order to sabotage President Abraham Lincoln's reelection campaign and Republican control of Congress. The treatise, pretending to represent the radical Republican goal of "social equality," argued in favor of race mixing, stating not only that all races originated from one type and are therefore equal, but, even more controversially, that racial mixing would actually strengthen the human race and should be adopted as national policy. In actuality, these views represented the polar opposite of what appeared regularly in scientific and popular literature from the mid-19th century through the first few decades of the 20th century.

Unlike in the West Indies and Latin America, the attitude toward miscegenation as one of reprobation appeared in written legislation during the early colonial period in the late 17th and early 18th centuries. One of the earliest surviving colonial records from Virginia shows that in 1662, the Virginia colony established a law that imposed additional punishment for fornication between whites and blacks. Other legislation of the period already referred to the "mulatto"

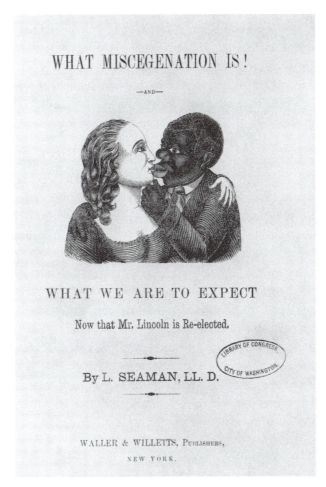

Title page of book against the mixing of races, published in 1864. (Corbis)

offspring of interracial sexual relations as "mongrel" and "spurious" and attempted to formally bastardize such progeny. Through such legislation, the mulatto came to be legally characterized as black and thus faced the same slave codes as blacks of predominantly African heritage.

The difference in the history of white treatment of mulattoes among the European colonies in the New World largely depended upon the ratio of white men to black and Indian women in the population. To a lesser degree, but a significant one, the status of white women and attitudes toward the family played a role in white attitudes toward miscegenation, or more properly, how to classify mixed progeny. In the United States, where there came to be a high ideal placed on the white family and likewise the purity of the white race and its dominance, it became more important to distance mulattoes from the master class.

Through antimiscegenation law and the legal classification of mixed-race offspring as black, illegitimate, and, if enslaved, property, the white male ruling class was able to have it all: increased slave labor supply, indulgence of sexual fantasies and desires, maintenance of white purity, and maintenance of white power. The classification of mulattoes as black also allowed white men to deny that miscegenation ever occurred and thereby allowed them to relieve, to some degree, their guilt over their inability to control their sexual desire. However, despite legal classification, mulattoes remained an ostensible reminder of their actions, and whites attempted to cover their tracks with particular rhetorical stringency against the practice.

Before the Revolutionary War, only two states, Virginia and North Carolina, bothered to write the taboo of miscegenation into law, although for all states (except Louisiana), common attitudes and regulation prevailed. After the Revolutionary War when the free black population increased, however, slave states began coming up with their own laws. These laws often defined the percentage of black "blood" present in one's heritage to determine one's race. Over time, these laws would become more stringent and morph into the so-called one-drop rule.

In the antebellum lower South, where demographics more closely resembled those of the Caribbean and Latin America, free mulatto classes did develop, particularly in the cities, but also in rural areas. Louisiana, and the city of New Orleans in particular, with its more recent history of Spanish and French colonialism, exhibited a more overt likeness to the southern part of the hemisphere with its general acceptance of interracial relationships and its intermediary mulatto class. While concubinage was prevalent throughout the Cotton Belt, it was practically institutionalized in Louisiana through the practice of *plaçage* and the related "quadroon balls." Likewise, before the Civil War, attempts to legalize blood quantum usually failed in Louisiana. South Carolina, especially Charleston, was a close runner-up in terms of the prevalence of a free and accepted mulatto class, although all of the lower South exhibited this phenomenon to some extent. Savannah, Georgia, and Mobile, Alabama, are two other major examples of cities with a history of thriving free mulatto communities.

The mulatto communities of the lower South maintained only a fraction of the population, yet they comprised a large percentage of the free black population. They were often property owning and sometimes even well off. Nonetheless, they were consistently distinguished from whites, despite the groups' cultural similarities. This situation created an atmosphere of color discrimination within the black population whereby lighter-skinned mulattoes would employ racialist justifications for their superiority over darker-skinned blacks.

Whites in the lower South achieved a degree of loyalty from the free mulatto class that they saw as a level of security, a buffer, between the planter class and the slaves—a view much like that held by white planters in the Caribbean and Latin America. However, the free mulatto class represented just a fraction of mulattoes in the United States during slavery. Most mulattoes were enslaved.

Approaching the Civil War, attitudes toward the free mulatto class began to change. The discourse of racial purity and the unnaturalness of interracial sex began to permeate the (lower) South from the North, particularly as the idea of race gained currency apart from the condition of servitude, and as the United States witnessed increased attention toward the biological and social scientific disciplines as authorities for explaining folk impressions about racial differences.

Within 50 years after emancipation, the "one-drop rule" emerged alongside increasingly popular scientific classifications and explanations of race. Whereas during slavery, there was a relatively unsophisticated correlation between skin color and status of enslaved or free, after emancipation, various scientific endeavors sought biological evidence of racial differences. In 1758, Swedish botanist, zoologist, and physician Carl Linnaeus developed a simple classificatory system of races—Caucasian, Ethiopian, Mongolian, and American—based largely on external, visible factors. A short while later in 1775, German anatomist and naturalist Johann Friedrich Blumenbach recovered this system and added a fifth category—Malayan—to complete the schema, which inaugurated the modern notion of race.

Anthropology in the 19th century drew upon this classificatory system in the attempt to link race to intelligence and behavior. The practice of phrenology, which consisted of taking cranial measurements, weighing brains, and charting head shapes and sizes, served as the precursor to evolutionary psychology and social evolution introduced by

Racial Purity

Racial purity refers to the idea that "races" should be kept biologically separate from one another. This idea is based on the false assumption that racial groups are fundamentally different and that it is unnatural or harmful for racial groups to blend. Proponents of racial purity often view racial groups as being similar to different species of animals, a notion that is rejected by contemporary science. Antimiscegenation laws, which outlawed interracial marriage primarily to prohibit mixed-race children, were common in the United States until they were found unconstitutional in 1967. Defining who belonged to a particular race was a particular challenge for those that promoted the idea of racial purity. Areas in the American South maintained the infamous "one-drop rule" for many years. Under this rule, any black ancestor—one drop of "black blood"—meant a person was not white. In contrast, a person could have one Native American ancestor and still be classified as white. Other countries have also attempted to maintain racial purity. Most notoriously, Nazi Germany committed genocide in the name of racial purification. It is still common for countries, including Japan, to have intricate laws determining who is truly Japanese. Therefore, while American antimiscegenation laws were struck down by the Supreme Court long ago and the term racial purity is now used primarily by fringe groups, the underlying concept that racial and ethnic groups are biologically different and should not mix still remains powerful. Nonetheless, it has no scientific basis.

ROBIN ROGER-DILLON

Herbert Spencer, and later, the eugenics movement of the Progressive Era.

The Civil War marked a turning point in popular conceptions of racial scientific theories. The Provost Marshall-General's Bureau and the U.S. Sanitary Commission both engaged anthropometric studies that used soldiers as subjects to gather cranial measurements and other racial data. These studies added "scientific evidence" to folk claims of racial difference. As well, this "war anthropometry" marked the beginning of the popular scientific notion that so-called mixed-bloods are weak and inferior to pure "breeds." Miscegenation was thought to be a serious social error, not simply for its effects in creating a physically and morally weak hybrid species, but mainly for its role in degenerating the white race.

The language of blood, breed, and racial species that gained such powerful ideological currency from the Civil War years through the Jim Crow era begins with the debate over the monogenetic or polygenetic origins of the various races. *Monogenesis* refers to the idea that all races have the same human origin, while *polygenesis* implies that all of the races evolved independently. This latter notion was considered by many to be heretical in that it goes against a literal reading of Biblical creationism, which links all humans to the Adamite family. Still, this view eventually prevailed in the scientific community and in the public consciousness since it correlated with prevailing folk understandings of race. As emerging scientific disciplines attempted to prove polygenetic theories in the middle to late 19th century, religion in general had to make room for the dominance of science as the master narrative of the social. Thus, while folk theories about race pervaded in the era of piety in the United States, race as it is known today, and as it came to be enforced in the Jim Crow era, was inextricably linked to the scientific age.

By the late 19th century, polygenist notions inherent in the Great Chain of Being were replaced by more contemporary strains of thought, namely Jean-Baptiste Lamarck's environmentalism, and Charles Darwin's hereditarian determinism. Nevertheless, the core of polygenist thought permeated both schools and shaped racial theory between Reconstruction and World War I—and beyond.

It was the polygenist notion of separate "species" that effected conversations on "amalgamation," or what came to be termed "miscegenation." The interbreeding of species was considered unnatural and counterproductive to the advancement of human civilization and the preservation of the so-called superior race. The tripartite logic of the polygenist view rested on the notions of mulatto infertility and sterility, the unnaturalness of race mixing, and the importance of racial purity. Despite advances in the biological and social sciences into the 20th century, the impressionistic and anecdotal bases of polygenist racial theory continued to shape academic and popular theories about race and race mixture.

Darwin's theory of evolution became very influential on scientific thought in the late 19th century, even though it is based on the idea of monogenesis. Nevertheless, it was easily adapted to popular notions. Lamarckianism—the doctrine of the inheritance of (environmentally) acquired characteristics within a racial group over time—on the other hand, did not contradict the polygenist view. Lamarckianism and Neo-Lamarckianism (post-Darwinian recuperations of evolutionary psychology) conflated culture and biology and suggested that the social was reified in the biological. Additionally, Lamarckianism put forth the notion that race prejudice had biosocial origins developed for the preservation of the species. In other words, while race mixing did occur, the subconscious instinctual aversion to other groups would eventually predominate to maintain a healthy species. This view justified race prejudice as natural and desirable. Though at odds with Darwinian hereditary variation, Lamarckianism succeeded in its ability to incorporate Darwinian evolutionism and polygenist ideas. In any case, the three strains of thought together dominated the discussion of racial difference far into the 20th century.

Franz Boas's anthropological work between 1890 and 1910 eventually developed the notion of culture as distinct from race. Boas's work in this regard helped to shape a more progressive and contemporary view of race which competed against the polygenist view and its legacy. Boas stressed the importance of accident and environment over the biological in cultural development, and eventually paved the way for the notion of human equality (of cognitive capacity). *The Mind of Primitive Man* (1911) noted a turning point in anthropological thought, ushering in the notion of cultural relativism and the ethnological method. By 1910, due in large part to Boas's advances in racial theory, Lamarckianism was largely dead and the notion of culture as separate from biological race was adopted. However, the predominance of intelligence testing in the social sciences and eugenics in the biological sciences continued with success to try to put scientific fact with racialist impression.

The American eugenics movement gained popular attention in 1912 after the first of three International Congresses on Eugenics; the second two were in 1921 and 1932. However, the interest in the scientific movement traveled over the Atlantic from the teachings of Sir Francis Galton as early as the late 19th century, about three decades after the publication of Darwin's *Origin of Species*. In the first three decades of the 20th century, the founding of several U.S.-based journals including, *Eugenics and Social Welfare Bulletin* (1906), *Eugenical News* (1916), and *Eugenics: A Journal of Race Betterment* (1928), in addition to the American Breeders Association (ABA) in 1905, J. H. Kellogg's Race Betterment Foundation in 1906 and the Eugenics Record Office in 1910 officially established eugenics as a reputable field of study. Once in the United States, the American eugenics movement metamorphosed into a unique and elaborate state project.

The state and the science collided in their shared concept of rights—the right to *eugenes*, "good genes," or the right to be "well born" was the mantra of the movement, which could be heard just as frequently from scientists, statesmen, and welfare officers. With genes, or "gene plasm" (the common term), as an organizing concept, eugenics policies of immigration restriction, sterilization and race segregation were juridically enacted at a time when the United States had to decide the shape and character of American identity. By the second decade of the 20th century, the eugenics movement and a concern with genes had taken root in the scientific community. One of its primary concerns was to address the ongoing "problem" of miscegenation. Eugenics specifically sought political and cultural ends to its academic products, particularly in the form of changing law and public sentiment.

Eugenicists were convinced—or convinced themselves—that the "mongrel" was the living embodiment of why the mixing of races should never occur. Reports in eugenics journals attempted to pile up the ways in which the racial hybrid was considered a "bodily maladjustment" based on the quasi-Mendelian idea that "racial" traits are linked traits and that to unlink these traits is to undo years of evolution and to unleash unnatural and harmful genetic combinations into the general population. In other words, the condition of miscegenation was a type of congenital disease. It is interesting to observe that eugenicists relied on Mendelian genetics to support their claims about the disharmony of miscegenation, yet actively ignored Mendel's discovery of "hybrid vigor," or the claim that the mixing of alleles from parents of different "breeds" can produce more vigorous offspring.

Instead, they saw the mongrel as a particular abomination who should be kept from the general population.

Those involved in propagandizing the notion of racial inferiority relied upon the testimony of the academic community to justify their claims to a public. In the mid-19th century, popular writers and scientists were often hard to distinguish, since either title had more to do with reputation among the scientific community than about training in a given field. However, even when, at the turn of the century, the scientific community became more discriminating, folk knowledge of race and race theory changed little. The professionalization of the academic disciplines and the establishment of academic journals in midcentury began to isolate the intellectual community from the public so that popular writers became the primary interlocutors between racial theory and popular consciousness. Ironically, these writers relied on claims to scientific fact in order to convince a public increasingly shaped by science's dominant authority. Since actual scientific advancements were often involved in disproving older folk claims, popular writers would cite any scientific source—old or new, accepted or not—to justify their claims.

Also at this time, religious arguments proclaimed the blasphemy of miscegenation. Despite popular interest in the authority of science, the United States remained a highly religious nation that paid particular attention to its consecrated leaders. Extreme clerical contributors to popular race theory attempted to use the Bible to prove miscegenation as inherently evil. Some, such as William H. Campbell, writing toward the end of the 19th century, argued that the great catastrophes of the Bible were all God's punishment for human attempts to mix pre-Adamic species of the genus homo with *Homo sapiens*, the direct line of Adam and Eve. Much of the propaganda coming from the religious community paradoxically incorporated insights from the scientific community that contradicted a literal interpretation of the Bible, the polygenist thesis being a prime example.

Popular themes of the mulatto in the late 19th century reflected those of the scientific literature, but were often elaborated in the context of racialist propagandizing. Miscegenation was considered an "abnormal perversion" of the "instincts of reproduction" which threatened white civilization culturally, morally, and genetically. Products of miscegenation were described as physically and genetically weak, fragile and incapable of hardships, prone to consumption and venereal disease, unlikely to live into old age, sterile like the hybrid mule (from which the term *mulatto* originates), and in this way anomalous, monstrous, or diseased in condition. Mulattoes were also described as immoral, cruel, vicious, lazy, malignant, treacherous, criminal, sensual, brutal, innately depraved, the epitome of moral degradation, and the embodiment of the sin that begat him or her. Mulatta women were seen as especially lewd and hypersexual, seductive threats to white men's moral willpower, and men as especially mischievous, carnal, and indecent.

Despite the belief that products of miscegenation would inherit the worst traits of both parent races, it was assumed that mulattoes inherited an enhanced mental faculty from their white parents. This cognitive advantage, however, was seen as a dangerous threat. Racialist logic reasoned that the bestial nature of the Negro and the audacity and intellect approaching the white man present in the mulatto made for the most dangerous form of criminality. Mulatto mental superiority to the so-called pure Negro, it was believed, made him a likely instigator of revolution. With all this, the mulatto was considered a burden to the integrity of the Negro race, but far more importantly to this logic, a threat to the white race and the American nation. Many foresaw that increased miscegenation within the United States would render the nation vulnerable to the superior, pure white civilizations of Europe. In other words, American sovereignty depended on its racial purity.

The escalation of fear and paranoia over the threat of miscegenation stemmed in part from the popular concern in the South at this time about "Negro retrogression," the notion that blacks were retrogressing to a more savage state. Popular race theorists justified this notion by citing statistics demonstrating a spike in crime, particularly the rape of white women and girls. Panic over this issue was deeply linked with a sense that miscegenation was burgeoning out of control. The idea that black men were on a quest for "social equality," a term euphemistically understood as a rape-quest to miscegenate America, reached the level of popular hysteria and can explain the culture of the Jim Crow South

In the decades surrounding the turn of the century, the South witnessed a hysterical, frenzied radicalization of racial attitudes defined by these popular notions that resulted in many an effort to combat the so-called yellow peril. Solutions to the problem of miscegenation circulated within the public sphere often came down to a tripartite answer: send the Negroes back to Africa, re-enslave them, or exterminate them. A combination of legal apartheid and disenfranchisement, an economic system of indentured servitude that closely resembled slavery, and campaigns of white pride coupled with racial terror organized largely by the leadership of the Ku Klux Klan became the immediate solution under Jim Crow.

Lynching appeared as a regular practice of extralegal justice in the United States as early as the Revolutionary War. However, lynching developed a distinctly racial and regional character by the 20th century. The majority of lynchings occurred in the South, perpetrated by whites on black victims. The first major spike in the 1890s coincided with the rise of the Ku Klux Klan, and by the Klan's second incarnation in the late 1910s and early 1920s, lynchings became public affairs organized by mobs and drew crowds of up to 10,000 spectators. Daytime lynchings were attended by men, women, and children in plain clothes who came, at times, with picnic lunch in hand to enjoy the brutal spectacle. Victims were tortured in ritualistic fashion, often sexually mutilated for symbolic import, and body parts were cut off and passed around as souvenirs. Nearly 5,000 people, most of whom were black, were executed in this brutal fashion during the Jim Crow era in the United States.

The ritual of lynching was propelled by many possible anxieties regarding interracial sex embedded in white patriarchal culture. These include that black men stood in for the repressed desires of white men, which they had to kill off in ritual sacrifice; that only white men had privileged access to interracial sex; that the keepers of racial purity, white women, needed actual and symbolic protection; and that white women should be frightened into a position of docility, vulnerability, and subservience to maintain white men's proprietary relationship to them. With all these possible psychological motives driving the peculiar nature of the ritual, the primary impetus for lynching black men, as discussed previously, was the purported tendency of black men to rape white women and the dire consequences of a miscegenated America. This pernicious myth was indelibly captured on screen in D. W. Griffith's landmark film *The Birth of a Nation*, which in its blockbuster success single-handedly rekindled

a spike in racial violence in the South and in Ku Klux Klan membership nationally. The film, based on Thomas Dixon's novel *The Clansman*, celebrates the rise of the Ku Klux Klan as a response to advances in "social equality" during Reconstruction and an antidote to a war-torn nation. Vividly bringing to the popular imagination the major notions of race theory, the film features three villains, a black rapist, a hypersexed mulatta temptress, and the mulatto conspirator of the black takeover of the South.

While popular representations of the anxieties surrounding miscegenation appeared in films such as Griffith's in the first few decades of the 20th century, those same anxieties eventually prompted censorship under the miscegenation clause of the Motion Picture Production Code of 1930 (the Hays Code). The trend in the representational ban on interracial relationships was unofficially lifted with the release of Stanley Kramer's acclaimed film *Guess Who's Coming to Dinner* in 1967, the same year as the *Loving v. Virginia* case that would undo an epoch of antimiscegenation legislation.

While extralegal "lynch law" cropped up as a method of enforcing racial barriers in the Jim Crow South, the institution of statutory law worked to regulate intermarriage and the racial status of individuals of mixed heritage in nearly all states. Under the so-called miscegenation laws, all interracial marriages and the offspring of those marriages were considered illegitimate, and rights commonly extended to blood relations were denied.

The criminalization of miscegenation, namely interracial marriage and sexual relationships, had begun in the colonial period. Maryland passed the first miscegenation statute in 1661, which criminalized marriage between white women and black men. During slavery, all Southern states and many Northern ones had antimiscegenation statutes on the books. Although they were enforced almost universally in the case of white women and black men, they were ignored nearly universally in the case of interracial sex between white men and black women. The children of interracial relationships between white men and black women under slavery were bastardized, denied the usual rights of relation, and became the property of the slave master who was also oftentimes the father. Slave statues that declared that the mulatto children of slaves were also slaves both helped to create clear demarcations between slave and free, black and white, and also granted white masters and overseers the dual benefit of unrestricted sex and an increased slave labor supply.

Legislators and judges paid increasing attention to miscegenation from the mid-19th century through the Reconstruction period. The Civil War amendments (1865–1870) and the Civil Rights Acts of 1866 and 1875 threatened to legitimize interracial sex and marriage, and as a result, state courts and legislators acted more aggressively to police interracial relations. After Reconstruction, however, the federal government became equally interested in the enforcement of antimiscegenation legislation.

In *Pace v. Alabama*, the major precursor to the landmark *Plessy v. Ferguson* decision, the U.S. Supreme Court decided that the state of Alabama's antimiscegenation statute was constitutional. In 1881, Tony Pace, a black man, and Mary Cox, a white woman, were both charged and convicted to two years in prison for "adultery and fornication" under Section 4189 of the Code of Alabama. The couple appealed their sentences with the Alabama Supreme Court, which upheld their convictions. Upon bringing their case to the U.S. Supreme Court, the plaintiff's charge that the statute violated the equal protection clause of the Fourteenth Amendment to the U.S. Constitution was denied. The opinion of Justice Stephen J. Field argued similarly to the Alabama Supreme Court case that since both the white and black parties involved in the crime of miscegenation are punished equally, equal protection under the law is upheld. While the federal court more or less reiterated the state decision, Justice Field did not comment on the State's argument that Section 4189 did not aim to discriminate against the person involved in the crime, but rather against the offense itself, whose "evil tendency" threatens to bring forth a "mongrel population and a degraded civilization."

By the second decade of the 20th century, in most of the states, the penalty for participating in one of these prohibited marriages involved a fine of up to $2,000 and up to 10 years in jail. Particularly into the 20th century, it became clear that the "evil" behind antimiscegenation legislation was not so much the act of fornication, which has its own legislative history, as it was the tendency of the offense to lead to a mongrel population that threatened white purity and white dominance in the United States.

Antimiscegenation laws and the prohibition on interracial relationships were originally targeted at African American and white marriages. However, the discourse on miscegenation in the United States applied to other races as well, albeit with great variation. In the case of the American Indian, antimiscegenation law was enforced but with notable leniency. For example, while "quadroons" and "octoroons" were generally treated under the law as "black," persons one-quarter or less American Indian were considered white, depending on the state and the year in history. Evidence of a more lax attitude toward Indian-white mixing is exemplified in the Pocahontas exception of the Virginia Antimiscegenation Act of 1924, which states that those white persons who could trace their ancestry back to the union of John Rolfe and Pocahontas were considered by law to be fully white. Long before the rising fear of miscegenation reached its pinnacle in the early 20th century, claiming lineage to the legendary Powhatan princess was a privilege withheld for Virginia's aristocratic families. Racial visibility played a crucial role in identification as well, and American Indian lineage, as well as the lineage of the other nonwhite races, was considered harder to detect than "Negro blood."

In 1850, the federal census first began taking note of "mulattoes," but in 1890, the census became more specific, designating mulattoes, quadroons, and octoroons. The accuracy of these records, of course, is dubious, considering the inability of the record taker to determine blood quantum by appearance. At different points in history, it was possible to possess a black lineage so "diluted" by white "blood" as to be legally insignificant. However, by the 20th century, the one-drop rule deemed that any evidence whatsoever of Negro ancestry determined black identity. Despite the laws that dealt with percentages, there are no cases that show attempts to prove white identity through them. In reality, identification was made through visual appearance. In *Hudgins v. Wright* (Va. 1806), the court made the decision that three generations of women with straight black hair were Indian, not black, and therefore free. This decision legally established that racial appearance, even more than calculated percentages, determined a person's race.

The particular obsession with racial appearance and the one-drop rule, which distinguished race relations in the United States (and Canada) from those in Latin America and the Caribbean, brought on the common practice among light-complexioned persons of color of "passing," or identifying as white. During slavery, racial passing was often employed as a strategy for escape. In the years after emancipation, some chose to pass in order to experience the benefits of being part of the racial majority. Passing was often considered a risky endeavor in that the discovery of one's true racial identity could result in dire, sometimes violently fatal, consequences. Such has been the theme of many works of literature from the Jim Crow era. Some notable examples include Frances Ellen Watkins Harper's *Iola Leroy*, Mark Twain's *Pudd'nhead Wilson*, Nella Larsen's *Passing*, James Weldon Johnson's *The Autobiography of an Ex-Colored Man*, George Schuyler's *Black No More*, Jessie Faucet's *Plum Bun*, and William Faulkner's *Light in August*.

It was not until 1967 that the opinion in *Pace v. Alabama* was overturned in the case of *Loving v. Virginia*, in which Chief Justice Warren observed that "the fact that Virginia prohibits only interracial marriages involving white persons demonstrates that the racial classifications must stand on their own justification, as measures designed to maintain White Supremacy." The opinion thus states that "there can be no doubt that restricting the freedom to marry solely because of racial classifications violates the central meaning of the Equal Protection Clause." However, the California State Supreme Court *Case Perez v. Sharp* actually made a similar decision in 1948, nearly 20 years earlier.

DANIELLE C. HEARD

See also

Anti-Miscegenation Laws; Interracial Marriage; Mixed Race Relationships and the Media

Further Reading:

Courtney, Susan. *Hollywood Fantasies of Miscegenation: Spectacular Narratives of Gender and Race, 1903–1967*. Princeton, NJ: Princeton University Press, 2005.

Croly, David Goodman, and George Wakeman. *Miscegenation: The Theory of the Blending of the Races*. New York: H. Dexter, Hamilton, 1864.

Dailey, Jane, Glenda Elizabeth Gilmore, and Bryant Simon, eds. *Jumpin' Jim Crow: Southern Politics from Civil War to Civil Rights*. Princeton, NJ: Princeton University Press, 2000.

Johnson, Kevin R., ed. *Mixed Race America and the Law: A Reader*. New York: NYU Press, 2003.

Lemire, Elise. *"Miscegenation": Making Race in America*. Philadelphia: University of Pennsylvania Press, 2002.

Mencke, John G. *Mulattoes and Race Mixture: American Attitudes and Images, 1865–1918*. UMI Research Press, 1979.

Zack, Naomi, ed. *American Mixed Race: The Culture of Microdiversity*. Lanham, MD: Rowman & Littlefield, 1995.

"Missing White Woman" Syndrome

Twenty-first century technologies expose consumers to the media's penchant for seizing on, sensationalizing, and scrutinizing particular stories. In the relentless 24/7 news cycle, some stories never appear while other stories that conform to dominant news paradigms, like celebrity scandal, dominate the airwaves for weeks and months.

This excessive attention to particular stories is glaringly evident in the saturated coverage of missing white women, like Laci Peterson, Chandra Levy, Natalee Holloway, Stacy Peterson, and other white women who have tragically disappeared. So common is this disproportionate coverage that it has garnered a label: "Missing White Woman Syndrome" (MWWS), which is defined as the inordinate media attention paid to missing white women who are attractive, petite, young, and generally affluent and the concomitant lack of media attention of missing persons of color.

Also referenced as "Damsels in Distress" and "Missing White Girl Syndrome," MWWS percolated to public consciousness during the intense media coverage of Natalee Holloway, an attractive 18-year-old woman from Alabama who disappeared in Aruba in 2005. Mainstream media ceaselessly reported on her disappearance, scrutinizing every police action and scouring over every detail; for instance, there were 1,880 print and broadcast stories regarding her disappearance from May 30, the date of Holloway's disappearance, to Labor Day of the same year. Conspicuously absent during the blanket coverage of Holloway was any mention of similarly missing women of color, like Latoyia Figueroa, a 24-year-old woman of African American and Latina descent from Philadelphia who was pregnant with her second child when she vanished in July of 2005. The juxtaposition of these two women demonstrated such a stark contrast in coverage that even the media engaged in a self-critique of its reporting, a critique that became a national story itself. Indeed, Figueroa's disappearance garnered media attention only after a groundswell of criticism initiated by Philadelphia-based citizen journalists made the story impossible to ignore, confirming what Tom Rosentiel, director of Project for Excellence in Journalism, candidly commented, "To be blunt, blond white chicks who go missing get covered and poor, black, Hispanic or other people of color who go missing do not get covered" (quoted in Curry 2005).

Journalists and academics offer several plausible explanations for the existence of MWWS. For instance, some journalists speculate that MWWS exists because of the racial demographics of consumers of media, mainly consisting of white, relatively affluent people: a pretty missing white woman garners higher ratings, then, because it's a story with which a largely white audience can more closely identify. Additionally, the phenomenon may exist because of the underemployment of people of color in newsrooms. In their 2012 diversity census that surveyed nearly a thousand daily newspapers, the American Society of Newspaper Editor's reported that persons of color comprised only 12.32 percent of the workforce in newsrooms, confirming the insight of Eric Van Dijk and Henk Wilke: "News is largely produced by White journalists who have grown up with a set of dominant White group norms and values, which tend to define an overall White perspective on news events" (1997: 245). Because of these white group norms and values, white journalists exercise what Don Heider (2000) calls "incognizant racism" in that the norms in which they have been socialized make them utterly oblivious to the perspectives and experiences of people of color. As a result, a news media composed mainly of white journalists might often unconsciously frame their reporting to accentuate particular details, like the race, wealth, and beauty of missing white women, that more closely resonate with the white norms and values of predominantly white viewers.

Because the disproportionate coverage of missing white women can significantly affect how consumers of media perceive reality, it may produce several negative consequences. For instance, MWWS perpetuates the narrative that only affluent, attractive white women matter. Such coverage, then, may also reinforce inequitable racial hierarchies. Moreover, MWWS pressures authorities to focus solely on missing white women, creating the possibility that the concentration of coverage may influence the investment of scarce resources by authorities.

Although MWWS persists in spite of its conspicuousness, some organizations and media have collaborated to counteract its effects and publicize the disappearances of people of color. For example, in 2012, TV One, an African American cable network, and the Black and Missing Foundation produced *Find Our Missing*, a weekly TV program that dramatically tells the stories of people of color who have disappeared. The goal of such programming is not to dismiss the tragedies of missing white women; rather, it is to provide more fair and balanced coverage so that all of those who are missing may be found.

Nicholas N. Behm

See also

White Privilege; Whiteness Studies

Further Reading:

American Society of Newspaper Editors. *2012 Census: Total and Minority Newsroom Employment Declines in 2011 But Loss Continues to Stabilize.* April 4, 2012. http://asne.org/content.asp?pl=121&sl=122&contentid=122.

Curry, George E. "White Damsels in Distress." *New Pittsburgh Courier*, July 13, 2005. http://www.georgecurry.com/columns/white-damsels-in-distress.

Heider, Don. *White News: Why Local News Programs Don't Cover People of Color.* Mahwah, NJ: Lawrence Erlbaum Associates, 2000.

Liebler, Carol M. "Me(di)a Culpa?: The 'Missing White Woman Syndrome' and Media Self-Critique." *Communication, Culture & Critique* 3 (2010): 549–65.

Moody, Mia, Bruce Dorries, and Harriett Blackman. "Invisible Damsels: Black and Mainstream Media's Framing of Missing Black and White Women in the Mid-2000s." *Media Report to Women* 37, no. 4 (2009): n. p. http://miamoody.blogspot.com/2011/09/invisible-damsels-black-and-mainstream.html.

Osunsami, Steve. "Getting More People to Care about Missing Black Women." *ABCNews.com,* January 18, 2012. http://abcnews.go.com/blogs/headlines/2012/01/getting-more-to-care-about-missing-black-women/.

Pokorak, Jeffrey J. "Rape as a Badge of Slavery: The Legal History of, and Remedies for, Prosecutorial Race-of-Victim Charging Disparities." *Nevada Law Journal* 7 (2006): 101–58.

Robinson, Eugene. "(White) Women We Love." *Washington Post*, June 10, 2005. http://www.washingtonpost.com/wp-dyn/content/article/2005/06/09/AR2005060901729.html.

Stillman, Sarah. "'The Missing White Girl Syndrome': Disappeared Women and Media Activism." *Gender and Development* 15, no. 3 (2007): 491–502. doi:10.1 080/1355 2070701630665.

Van Dijk, Eric, and Henk Wilke. "Is This Mine or Is It Ours? Framing Property Rights and Decision Making in Social Dilemmas." *Organizational Behavior and Human Decision Process* 71 (1997): 195–209.

Mississippi Plan (1890)

The Mississippi Plan was a pioneering strategy for African American disenfranchisement that endured well into the

20th century. The Mississippi Plan helped build the "Solid South" with its monopoly of white political power situated largely within the Democratic Party.

The Mississippi Plan of the Jim Crow era was less violent than proscriptive when compared to its 1875 forerunner. Previously, angry Southern whites (Redeemers) had taken to the streets with paramilitary forces to terrorize Republicans of both races and wrest control of state and local governments. The new approach relied upon statutory manipulation interlaced with the tacit threat of physical coercion. In 1890, white Mississippians convened a constitutional convention that subverted the intent of the Fifteenth Amendment to guarantee that race, color, and previous condition of servitude not determine voter eligibility. Poll taxes, literacy tests, and residency requirements were established that facilitated the targeting of blacks without overt employment of racial language or standards. A predominantly poor, uneducated, and transient population would soon feel the full force of these arbitrary requirements.

Other Southern states did not immediately follow suit due to the soul-searching engendered by the rise of the Populist reform movement in the early 1890s. With a platform celebrating the aspirations of the common man, Populists faced an uphill struggle in an age in which corporate elites and political machines openly cooperated to protect narrow interests. Challenging this oligarchy required mobilizing new constituencies and utilizing the discourse and tactics of inclusion. Some Populists genuinely hoped to forge an enduring biracial alliance, while others at least judged pragmatically that black support was instrumental for a third party's survival. Perceiving the Populists as a legitimate threat, some Democrats reluctantly courted the black vote as a form of inoculation against this political insurgency. The possibility of reformers galvanizing Northern public opinion against the injustice of the Mississippi Plan further encouraged Southern caution. The next state to employ the measure, South Carolina, would not do so until 1895.

Once the Populists were defeated in the 1896 presidential election, the Southern political landscape better favored blatant disenfranchisement. Democrats had nominated the Populist favorite, William Jennings Bryan, as their own standard-bearer and co-opted enough of the Populist platform to dilute the movement's appeal and splinter its organization. Consequently, the "reform" impulse in regional politics manifested itself strictly in efforts to widen the franchise for whites under the aegis of the Democratic Party. Figures such as embittered Populist Tom Watson argued that only by denying blacks the vote could the integrity of the electoral process be ensured. This argument signified a crass attempt to manipulate legitimate outrage over a nationwide epidemic of electoral fraud and coercion into tolerating a racially motivated vendetta. The U.S. Supreme Court decision *Williams v. Mississippi* (1898) validated the Mississippi Plan and highlighted the sort of reactionary thinking in political and social affairs that dominated the Gilded Age. Between 1898 and 1910, the rest of the former Confederacy (as well as Oklahoma) had enacted some facsimile of the Mississippi Plan.

Successful implementation of this measure in its early years owed as much to the lethargy of its opponents as to the audacity of its backers. Segregationists counted on the prevailing Northern view that racial questions were just too divisive anymore following the carnage of the Civil War. Sectional healing was paramount while the black population served as a convenient whipping-boy around which to cement a new alliance; a pathetic example of a "blame the victim" mentality. Developments in U.S. foreign policy only reinforced this trend. Angling to join the colonial powers of Europe, authorities engineered a conflict with Spain in 1898 whose rationale rested largely upon a hierarchy of race with embedded notions of dominance and paternalism. The heady expansionism of the times was often expressed in terms of spreading Anglo-Saxon civilization to "mongrel" and benighted peoples of color. The rise of eugenics and social Darwinism provided superficial rationalizations for exploitation as though a versatile, "scientific" template could be superimposed over any scenario. Soon, the denizens of Cuba, the Philippines, Guam, Puerto Rico, Samoa, and Hawai'i fell under the paradoxical influence of a republic that behaved like an empire. With the anti-imperialist movement at the turn of the century failing to elicit a fundamental reassessment of foreign policy assumptions and objectives, the liberation of the permanent underclass at home remained unlikely. Even white Republicans could not unify against the Mississippi Plan, since many saw it enabling the GOP to compete for the white vote without the need to cater to blacks or contend with race baiting.

The movement behind the Mississippi Plan reflected not only the desire to retain the antebellum status quo in race relations, but also a struggle over precisely which whites would dominate regional politics. Those whites residing in the Black Belt counties tended to be the strongest advocates for disenfranchisement against others from predominantly white communities. The latter group was often placated by favorable redistricting (gerrymandering) in the state legislatures. A perversion of the U.S. Constitution was thus sanctioned through the most banal form of political horse trading.

Poorer whites rightfully feared that the Mississippi Plan would be employed as an instrument of class warfare, despite assurances to the contrary by political leaders. Most states did not allow property ownership as a substitute for literacy in determining voter registration. As yeoman farmers expressed their anxieties in the 1890s, safeguards were enacted to protect their status. Mississippians fashioned an "understanding clause" whereby anyone who demonstrated a command of the state constitution could forego the literacy test. This highly subjective examination would be administered by white officials free to let their prejudices dictate their assessments. Louisianans adopted a "grandfather clause" stipulating that anyone whose father or grandfather could vote as of January 1, 1867 (before the Fourteenth Amendment went into effect guaranteeing equal protection under the law—i.e., whites only), could avoid both the literacy and property tests. Although various forms of special dispensation proliferated among the Southern states, the poll tax remained in effect. Yet, without a receipt or payment well in advance of an election, one could still be disqualified.

The response of the African American community did little to threaten the Mississippi Plan. In keeping with what he deemed a realistic philosophy, Booker T. Washington merely contended that any restrictions upon voting should be applied equally to all races. His 1895 Atlanta Compromise called for black disengagement from political affairs in favor of concentrating upon economic self-improvement. In what seemed to be an acceptance of white stereotypes on some level, he argued that blacks must use their occupational performance to demonstrate their worthiness for full citizenship. Although sometimes mischaracterized as a toady to the white power structure, Washington unwittingly facilitated a silencing of African Americans that would last for generations. Although a much younger man not yet at the height of his influence, W.E.B. Du Bois argued conversely to fellow blacks that the dignity and self-respect desired by Washington could never be achieved through submission, regardless of how it was justified. A New England native, Du Bois commented more bluntly on the reality of Southern society as a caste system with its nearly immutable class boundaries. His call for an appreciation of the higher aspirations in life that transcended materialism was underappreciated amidst crushing poverty. A combination of apathy and oppression ensured the absence of a large-scale, grassroots campaign among Southern blacks to defeat the Mississippi Plan.

In a final act of disrespect for democratic principles, all but one state convention that composed a version of the Mississippi Plan avoided using a popular vote for ratification. Meanwhile, the white primary replaced the old convention system as a vehicle to allow party officials at the state and local levels to marginalize and exclude any undesired voters who had navigated the obstacles inherent to the new registration process. In conjunction with tenant farming, sharecropping, Jim Crow laws, and lynching, the Mississippi Plan demonstrated that the promise of Reconstruction had gone unrealized.

These repressive techniques helped mire the South in a state of moral and cultural stagnation that the modern Civil Rights Movement would confront at its peril. The Voting Rights Act of 1965, promoted by President Lyndon B. Johnson, sounded the death knell of the Mississippi Plan, though subsequent legislation over the following two decades was necessary to augment this initiative.

JEFFREY D. BASS

See also

Atlanta Compromise; Tillman, Ben; Watson, Thomas E.

Further Reading:

Kousser, J. Morgan. *The Shaping of Southern Politics: Suffrage Restriction and the Establishment of the One-Party South, 1880–1910.* New Haven, CT: Yale University Press, 1974.

McMillen, Neil. *Dark Journey: Black Mississippians in the Age of Jim Crow.* Urbana: University of Illinois Press, 1989.

Williamson, Joel. *A Rage for Order: Black-White Relations in the American South since Emancipation.* New York: Oxford University Press, 1986.

Woodward, C. Vann. *Origins of the New South, 1877–1913.* Baton Rouge: Louisiana State University Press, 1971.

Mixed Race Relationships and the Media

In spite of a long history of racism that led to laws that banned interracial marriage, the media shifted public perception as early as the 1940s. Between the 1940s and 1950s popular media portrayals in popular magazines such as *Ebony* and *Jet* featured celebrities who married across racial lines, in particular black and white. These celebrities included singers and actresses, composers, musicians, and civil rights activists. Walter White, executive secretary of the National Association for the Advancement of Colored People, was a biracial African American who walked both sides of the color line, able to speak with people of color as an African American and also being able to "pass" in white American communities. His first wife, Jane White, was an African American actress. In 1949 White divorced his wife of 20 years and married Poppy Cannon, a white woman. Mixed-race intimate relationships occur across a diversity of racial lines. According to mixed-race studies scholar Dan Lichter, the shifts in attitudes towards interracial relationships are viewed as an example of a postracial or colorblind society, but not emblematic of a multiracial society.

The visibility of interracial relationships in the media and in community leadership is a sign for the changing attitudes towards people of color. In 1967 *Time* magazine featured Peggy Rusk and Guy Smith, "Mr. & Mrs. Guy Smith / An Interracial Wedding." A year later in 1968 *Time* magazine noted that interracial dating on college campuses was open. The social shifts were reflected in the changing laws during the civil rights movement that led to desegregation and enabled interracial marriage. In a 1965 Gallup Poll 72 percent of Southern whites and 42 percent of non-Southern whites said they approved of laws prohibiting interracial marriage. By 1970, the numbers declined: 56 percent of Southern whites and 30 percent of non-Southern whites favored laws that prohibited interracial marriages. In 2011, the tides of attitudes have dramatically shifted with 96 percent of African Americans and 84 percent whites accepting interracial relationships.

The trend of interracial relationships is one of a slow increase since antimiscegenation laws were ruled unconstitutional in 1967. In 1960, 20,000 couples in the South identified as mixed race with 60 percent being a white man with a black women. Between 1980 and 2010, interracial marriages have doubled; Pew Research Center found that 15 percent of all new marriages in the United States were between spouses of different race or ethnicity, an 8 percent increase in interracial marriages. In 2010, 21 percent of same sex couples (133,447 couples) were mixed. The regional difference of interracial marriages was evidenced in the 2010 U.S. census in which the states with the highest interracial marriage included: Hawaii (37.2 percent), Oklahoma (17.2 percent), Alaska (17.1 percent), Nevada (13.3 percent), California (12.8 percent), and Washington (10.9 percent), with all other states falling under 10 percent.

Interracial marriages differ across racial divides. White men have higher rates of marrying Asian women. And Hispanic men are two-thirds more likely than married black men to have a white spouse. And Hispanic women who are married are four times more likely than black women to have a white husband. However, of all ethnic minorities, Asian Americans are more likely than any other major racial or ethnic group to enter into interracial marriages. In 2012, 29 percent of Asian newlyweds married outside their ethnic group compared with the 26 percent of Hispanics, 70 percent of blacks, and 9 percent of whites that married someone of a different race. Asian women are twice as likely to marry out. Among whites and Hispanics there are no differences in gender. As interracial marriages increase in small increments, interracial dating continues to be one in which it is clear that most racial groups prefer to date within their own communities. This is most apparent with trends in online dating.

The challenges that couples face when dating and marrying across racial difference leads to their intimacy as being both hypervisible and invisible. Interracial couples deal with a host of social, cultural, and historic meanings that are applied to their relationships. These meanings are embedded in racist stereotypes of African Americans, Asian Americans, Latinas/os, Native people/indigenous people, and white Americans that are also gendered. In spite of the increasing acceptance of interracial coupling, the experience for interracial couples continues to include negative responses. The invisibility interracial couples experience may occur in public spaces (i.e., waiting in line together to be seated in a restaurant, only to have one member of the couple ignored) or one of hypervisibility—from stares to racist reactions. Race also impacts intimate partner relationships, in spite of contemporary love myths and assumptions about assimilation.

ANNIE ISABEL FUKUSHIMA

See also

Anti-Miscegenation Laws; Domestic Violence; Down Low; Illegitimacy Rates; Lesbian, Gay, Bisexual, Transgender, Intersex, Queer, and Queer Questioning Community (LGBTQ); Tripping over the Color Line

Further Reading:

Jayson, Sharon. "Census Shows Big Jump in Interracial Couples." *USA Today.* http://usatoday30.usatoday.com/news/nation/story/2012-04-24/census-interracial-couples/54531706/1.

Kellogg, Alex. "The Changing Face of Seeing Race." *NPR.* http://www.npr.org/2011/10/14/141235709/the-changing-face-of-seeing-race.

Rochman, Bonnie. "Love Isn't Color-Blind: White Online Daters Spurn Blacks." *Time.* http://healthland.time.com/2011/02/22/love-isnt-color-blind-white-online-daters-spurn-blacks/.

Romano, Renee C. *Race Mixing: Black-White Marriage in Postwar America.* Cambridge, MA: Harvard University Press, 2003.

Steinbugler, Amy C. *Beyond Loving: Intimate Racework in Lesbian, Gay and Straight Interracial Relationships.* New York: Oxford University Press, 2012.

Wang, Wendy. "The Rise of Intermarriage: Rates, Characteristics Vary by Race and Gender." *Pew Social & Demographic Trends: PEW Research Center.* February 16, 2012.

Model Minority Thesis

In the United States, model minority usually refers to Asian Americans and is often understood or interpreted as referring to a socioeconomically successful minority, since model and success are often used as synonyms in this context. The model minority thesis was invented by Caucasian scholars and reporters in the mid-1960s, at the height of the civil rights movement, urban riots, and social unrest, to exemplify the socioeconomic success of Asian Americans, and their educational achievements, occupational mobility, rising income, and low rates of mental illness and crime. The term *model minority* was first coined to portray Japanese Americans and Chinese Americans, and starting in the 1980s, it was extended to Asian Americans as a whole.

Beginning in the late 1970s, scholars started to criticize the model minority thesis. One of the major criticisms is that the model minority is a "myth" rather than a reality. In other words, it has no factual basis. Another major criticism is that the model minority concept is anti-Asian, or detrimental to Asian Americans. Despite these criticisms, the model minority thesis has persisted until today.

Is the model minority a myth or reality? Empirical evidence suggests that the model minority image is not totally a myth, nor is it completely a reality. In other words, the model minority image is not without any factual basis, but it inflates the success story of Asian Americans. Statistics show that Asian Americans generally fare better than blacks, Hispanics, and Native Americans in terms of all major socioeconomic indicators and even better than whites in education, occupational status, and family income. However, they lag behind whites in per capita earnings and wealth. They have not "outwhited whites."

Is the model minority image beneficial or detrimental to Asian Americans? A thorough and impartial assessment of the model minority thesis is in order. This seemingly positive image definitely has many negative effects on Asian Americans. First, the model minority image conceals the diversity among Asian American groups and excludes the truly needy Asians, especially recent Asian immigrants and refugees, from receiving governmental assistance. Second, it downplays racial discrimination against Asian Americans. The message of the model minority thesis is that Asian Americans have made it and have overcome discrimination through hard work. Hence, discrimination against Asian Americans is not insurmountable. Third, it may contribute to blaming other, less successful minority groups for their problems. The message of the model minority thesis is that hard work and strong cultural values enable Asian Americans to succeed. Other minorities do not fare well because their cultures have problems or they do not try hard enough. If Asian Americans can make it without the government's assistance, why cannot blacks, Latinos, and Indians make it too? By emphasizing the importance of culture, the model minority thesis contributes to the tendency to blame the victim for victimization. Fourth, it divides minority groups and pits one group against another. The concept implies that some minorities are model, or good, while other minorities are non-model, or bad. In part, it serves an ideological purpose and is a way to control minorities. Fifth, the exaggeration of the success story of Asian Americans could partly spur anti-Asian resentment, especially on college campuses. Sixth, it serves to exclude Asian Americans from some social programs designed to help minorities, such as affirmative action, in some institutions. Finally, it puts undue pressures on Asian American students to do well in school.

Does the model minority concept have any positive effects on Asian Americans? Scholars are usually silent about this. In reality, this image is not without its usefulness. Historically, it helped turn around the negative stereotypes of Asian Americans—for example, that they are unassimilable aliens and enhance the positive image of Asian Americans. It shows that Asians are not unassimilable but in fact have assimilated well into American society. In contemporary times, the model minority image helps people recognize the remarkable achievements of Asian Americans, it helps people appreciate Asian cultures and traditions, and it may increase the acceptance of Asian Americans in school, employment, and residential neighborhoods.

In summary, the model minority is a new, positive stereotype of Asian Americans in contrast to old, negative ones. Although this concept has a statistical basis, it is an oversimplification and an exaggeration of the Asian American experience. It ignores the diversity among Asian groups: there is no single model minority. While its historical contribution to countering the negative stereotypes against Asian Americans and its contemporary utilities should not go unnoticed, its many problems or potential problems overshadow its positive lights.

Philip Yang

See also

Segmented Assimilation; Stereotype

Further Reading:

Cheng, Lucie, and Philip Yang. "Asians: The 'Model Minority' Deconstructed." In *Ethnic Los Angeles*, edited by Roger Waldinger and Mehdi Bozorgmehr. New York: Russell Sage Foundation, 1996.

Kim, Kwang Chung, and Won Moo Hurh. "Korean Americans and the 'Success' Image: A Critique." *Amerasia Journal* 10 (1983): 3–21.

Suzuki, Bob. "Education and the Socialization of Asian Americans: A Revisionist Analysis of the 'Model Minority' Thesis." *Amerasia Journal* 4 (1977): 23–51.

Takaki, Ronald. *Strangers from a Different Shore*. New York: Penguin Books, 1989.

Modern Racism

Modern racism refers to subtle, conscious or unconscious prejudicial attitudes and behaviors that allow for the discrimination of people of color. Modern racism's development coincided with the demise of the Jim Crow South and the sharp decline in popularity of that era's supporting belief system, sometimes described as "old-fashioned racism," which incorporated a biologically based theory of African racial inferiority and support for racial segregation and formal racial discrimination. Modern racism may be defined as "the expression in terms of abstract ideological symbols and symbolic behaviors of the feeling that people of color are violating cherished values and making illegitimate demands for changes in the racial status quo." Modern racism is not often malicious by intent but is pernicious by effect.

In modern racism, prejudiced behavior is characterized by a subtlety that can make it much more difficult to identify—and to define as expressly and exclusively racial discrimination—than the older forms of racism. Modern racism perpetuates the idea that people of color are inferior to whites, although that idea is not extended into legal policies. It is thus a type of racism that cannot be undone by laws like the 1964 Civil Rights Act, but it allows for the perpetuation of individual acts of racism that have harmful effects. Indeed, while more difficult to detect, modern racism can have effects just as severe as overt racism.

Modern racism can take the following forms:

• Avoidance of Contact. Modern racism may be manifested in decisions, conscious or unconscious, not to have social or professional contact with people of color; in not making an effort to learn about communities of color; and in living in all-white communities, exercising the option not to be involved in the lives of people of color, the option that whites often have by virtue of economic privilege. Whites thereby maintain a lack of familiarity with members of other races that is self-perpetuating. A by-product is the likelihood of unconsciously discriminating against people of color, such as by seeing a person of color in one's neighborhood as being out of place.

- Blaming the Victim. In this modern form of racism, racist ideas are expressed by attributing the results of systemic oppression to the target group; ignoring the real impact of racism on the lives of people of color today; blaming people of color for troubled economic times; and subjecting successful target-group members to scrutiny or criticism that a similarly situated white would not have to confront.

- Dysfunctional Rescuing. This term, popularized by Valerie Batts, describes the "helping" of people of color when it is based on an assumption that they cannot help themselves. The "helped" person may be set up to fail by the situation the helper creates or may be treated by the helper in a patronizing or condescending manner. In this situation, the "helping" helps maintain the status quo with respect to the stratification of society. This "help that does not help" may be motivated out of guilt or shame but is carried out in a way that limits recipients' ability to help themselves.

- Cultural and Religious Marginalization. In this manifestation, modern racism involves the minimizing of obvious physical or behavioral differences between people and discounting the influence of culture or the experiences of people of color. Characterized by the phrase "color-blind," it ultimately has a pernicious effect on both the agent and the target. It masks the agent's discomfort with difference while undercutting the legitimacy of the target's lived experience.

KHYATI JOSHI

See also

Color-Blind Racism; Laissez-Faire Racism; *New Jim Crow, The*; Race Relations in the Post-Civil Rights Era; Racism

Further Reading:

Batts, Valerie. *Modern Racism: New Melody for the Same Old Tunes*. Rocky Mount, NC: Visions Publication, 1989.

McConahay, J. B. "Modern Racism, Ambivalence, and the Modern Racism Scale." In *Prejudice, Discrimination, and Racism*, edited by J. F. Dovidio and S. L. Gaertner, 91–126. New York: Academic Press, 1986.

Montgomery Bus Boycott

Starting in December 1955, the African American community of Montgomery, Alabama, boycotted the city bus system for over a year. Demanding equal and fair treatment, blacks refused to ride until their requests were met. Organized by the Women's Political Council (WPC) and Montgomery's National Association for the Advancement of Colored People (NAACP) branch, this boycott is often referred to as the beginning of the modern Civil Rights Movement.

In the 1950s in Montgomery, the city bus system was segregated. African Americans were not hired as drivers, rode in the back of the bus, and were expected to surrender their seat at a white passenger's request. Black passengers entered the front of the bus to pay the fee, exited the bus, and re-entered at the back entrance. At times, bus drivers would leave black passengers standing at the sidewalk after paying the bus fee. Although 75 percent of passengers were African American, they were constant victims of public degradation and humiliation.

For several years, the WPC, led by Jo Ann Robinson, and Montgomery's NAACP branch, formerly led by E. D. Nixon, had discussed the inequalities of the city bus system and possible resolutions. In 1954, Robinson sent a letter to Montgomery mayor W. A. Gayle requesting the buses' Jim Crow practices be put to an end and warned of a potential boycott if the demands were not met. Gayle paid no attention to Robinson's warning.

Even though the WPC had been organizing a possible boycott, the challenge of rallying the entire black community remained. A successful boycott required full participation. Due to fear of losing jobs, harassment, and racial violence, few African Americans publicly acknowledged their discontent of second-class citizenship. These organizations waited for the right person who would stand up against the ways of the South. That day came on Thursday, December 1, 1955, when Rosa Parks stepped on one of the city buses. It had been a long day of work, the bus was almost completely full, and Parks sat in the first row of the black section. At the next stop several white passengers entered the bus. A white male wanted Parks's seat. Parks refused. The bus driver ordered her to move or he would call the authorities. Parks did not move. Parks was arrested, and the inspirational story Nixon and Robinson had waited for arrived. The soft-spoken,

Rosa Parks, whose refusal to give up her bus seat to a white passenger sparked the Montgomery Bus Boycott and fueled the civil rights movement, sits in the front of a bus on December 21, 1956. After the court ruling, the Interstate Commerce Commission banned segregation in public transit. (Library of Congress)

respectable Parks served as the perfect symbol to mobilize African Americans for the bus boycott.

Days following the arrest, over 200 volunteers passed out 30,000 flyers calling for a one-day boycott of the Montgomery bus system on Monday, December 5, 1955. The one-day boycott was successful, and that evening the black community gathered in Holt Street Baptist Church to decide if the boycott should continue. Thousands attended the meeting. The church overflowed to the outside stairs and sidewalks.

The Montgomery Improvement Association (MIA) was developed to coordinate, support and organization the

demonstration. Martin Luther King, Jr., the new preacher in town, was elected MIA's president and chosen to give a speech at the first mass meeting at Holt Street Baptist Church. With less than an hour to prepare, King delivered a speech that inspired the crowd to vote unanimously to continue the boycott. This speech also marked the beginning of King's role as leader in the civil rights movement.

Through the efforts and sacrifices of the black community, the Montgomery bus boycott lasted 381 days. Boycotters walked to work, established a large carpool system, and ran extensive fund raisers to finance the car pool system.

Even on the coldest of days, some walked as far as 12 miles a day. Only a month after the boycott began, James H. Bagley, the superintendent of the Montgomery City Bus Lines, expressed frustration with the lack of patronage. The bus system was losing close to $400 daily, as expenses greatly outweighed income. Forced to reduce expenses, Bagley cut schedules, fired drivers, and increased the cost of bus fares. However, the movement needed federal legislation to change Jim Crow practices.

On February 1, 1956, NAACP lawyers Fred Gray and Charles Langford filed a lawsuit in the U.S. Circuit Court against Alabama and Montgomery's unconstitutional segregation laws. Gray and Langford filed this suit on behalf of five African American women: Aurelia S. Browder, Susie McDonald, Jeanetta Reese, Claudette Colvin, and Mary Louise Smith. Throughout the year, boycott leaders and participants faced much racial violence. Both King's and Nixon's houses were bombed, crosses were burnt on front lawns, and several were arrested for participating in "illegal" boycotts. Through Alabama's state courts, white Montgomery officials successfully made carpooling illegal. Interestingly enough, this state legislation passed the same day the federal court found Alabama's segregation laws unconstitutional.

On December 21, 1956, African Americans boarded the Montgomery city buses and sat where they pleased. This achievement sparked the modern civil rights movement and heightened racial tensions across the South as more and more blacks demanded freedom.

EMILY HESS

See also

Parks, Rosa; *Plessy v. Ferguson* (1896). Document: *Plessy v. Ferguson* (1896)

Further Reading:

Burns, Stewart, ed. *Daybreak of Freedom: Montgomery Bus Boycott*. Chapel Hill: University of North Carolina Press, 1997.

Robinson, Jo Ann, with David Garrow. *The Montgomery Bus Boycott and the Women Who Started It: The Memoir of Jo Ann Gibson Robinson*. Knoxville: University of Tennessee Press, 1987.

Williams, Donnie, and Wayne Greenhow. *The Thunder of Angels: The Montgomery Bus Boycott and the People Who Broke the Back of Jim Crow*. Chicago: Lawrence Hill Books, 2006.

Moore v. Dempsey (1923)

An important legal victory for the National Association for the Advancement of Colored People (NAACP), the U.S. Supreme Court decision in *Moore v. Dempsey* (261 U.S. 86 [1923]) declared that criminal convictions secured in trials dominated by the threat of mob violence deprived the defendants of their rights to due process as guaranteed by the Fourteenth Amendment. Rising out of the trials of African Americans arrested during the Elaine (Arkansas) Riot of 1919, *Moore v. Dempsey* was the first Supreme Court case of the 20th century that concerned the quality of justice provided to blacks in the American South.

During the course of the disorders that convulsed Phillips County, Arkansas, in 1919, bands of armed whites and federal troops dispatched by the governor killed over 200 blacks and detained some 700 others. In the aftermath of the riots, an all-white grand jury set about determining which of the detainees would be tried and which released. Those blacks who agreed, often after beatings or electric shock torture, to testify against others, or to work under whatever terms their white landlords imposed, were set free, while any prisoner suspected of being a ringleader or otherwise troublesome was indicted. On November 2, 1919, authorities in Phillips County put 12 black defendants on trial for the murder of five white men. After a series of perfunctory trials, during which the defense attorneys, who did not meet their clients until the proceedings began, called no witnesses, offered no evidence, and put no defendant on the stand, all 12 were convicted and condemned to death. No trial lasted over an hour, and jury deliberation averaged less than 10 minutes. Additionally, during the trials, armed white mobs surrounded the courthouse shouting that any defendant found not guilty would be lynched (*see* Lynching).

Dispatched to Arkansas in October 1919, NAACP investigator Walter White, who could pass for white, interviewed the governor and investigated the proceedings. Forced to leave when his identity was discovered, White published his findings in the *Chicago Defender*, *The Nation*, and the NAACP's own journal, *The Crisis*. Although the governor asked the U.S. Postal Service to prevent the mailing and distribution of these publications, White's report generated much hostility and controversy. The NAACP raised more than $50,000 to hire lawyers of both races, such as Scipio Africanus Jones, an African American attorney from Little Rock, and George W. Murphy, a Confederate veteran and former Arkansas attorney general, to appeal the convictions.

Acting on a technicality, the Arkansas Supreme Court reversed the verdicts in six cases, but allowed the other six to stand, finding that the threat of mob violence and the use of coerced testimony did not deny the defendants due process. After winning a stay of execution from the state chancery court, the NAACP attorneys were eventually able to take the case to the U.S. Supreme Court, where, in a 6–2 decision, the justices held that the mob-dominated proceedings violated the due process provisions of the Fourteenth Amendment. Written by Justice Oliver Wendell Holmes Jr., the majority opinion declared as follows:

> But if the case is that the whole proceeding is a mask—that counsel, jury, and judge were swept to the fatal end by an irresistible wave of public passion, and that the State Courts failed to correct the wrong, neither perfection in the machinery for correction nor the possibility that the trial court and counsel saw no other way of avoiding an immediate outbreak of the mob can prevent this Court from securing to the petitioners their constitutional rights.

The Court sent the case back to the lower courts to determine if the claims of mob violence and forced testimony were true. As a result of these proceedings, the state of Arkansas eventually freed all 12 defendants as well as all those convicted of lesser charges who were still imprisoned. *Moore v. Dempsey* set precedents for stricter Supreme Court scrutiny of state trials and for the broader use of federal habeas corpus actions to oversee state trials that may have been conducted in violation of federal constitutional rights.

JOHN A. WAGNER

See also

Lynching; National Association for the Advancement of Colored People (NAACP); Sharecropping; White Mobs

Further Reading:

Cortner, Richard. *A Mob Intent on Death: The NAACP and the Arkansas Riot Cases*. Middletown, CT: Wesleyan University Press, 1988.

Mosque at Ground Zero

"The Mosque at Ground Zero" is the nickname given to Park51, the 13-story Islamic community center planned for construction in Lower Manhattan two blocks from the World Trade Center site. Although Park51 contains plans for a Muslim prayer center inside the building, it is not a mosque, and it is not technically located at Ground Zero, the name for the site where the World Trade Center Towers once stood. Nevertheless, critics have nicknamed the project the "Ground Zero mosque" in an attempt to build public resistance to the project.

The plans for Park51—originally named Cordoba House—began in the summer of 2010 and were quickly met with public outcry, triggering a season of serious conflict in New York. The proposed site for construction of Park51 became the object of extremely passionate grievances from many Americans. The core issue for critics of the project was clear: namely, is it ethically justifiable to build an Islamic center so near to the site of the September 11, 2001, attacks? The September 11 attacks are generally agreed to have been launched by the Islamic terrorist group al-Qaeda, and for critics of the Park51 project, it seemed incomprehensible to celebrate Islam at the site of such attacks. Opponents nicknamed the project the "Ground Zero mosque," arguing that the building would serve as a celebration of the religion from which the September 11 attackers came. However, supporters of Park51 have pointed out that these arguments against the building are based on the false notion that Islam itself, rather than Islamic radicals, were responsible for the September 11 attacks. Most supporters of Park51 argued that those who will likely utilize the Islamic community center should not be associated with the extremists who carried out the attacks—that is, al-Qaeda agents are not representative of ordinary Muslims. Furthermore, Park51 is planned to be open to the general public and is designed to promote interfaith dialogue, hopefully working to prevent the type of radicalism responsible for the September 11 attacks.

The "Ground Zero mosque" controversy grew quickly to include a host of national and international thinkers and politicians. For these public figures, issues of governmental intervention became integral, along with arguments about cultural sensitivity. The mayor of New York City at the time of the attack, Rudolph Giuliani, went public with his adamant support for an alternative proposal that would move the community center to a location farther from Ground Zero. However, the mayor of New York City at the time the plans were publicly released, Michael Bloomberg, opposed this alternative and proclaimed that the very principle of religious liberty was at stake. Plans for Park51 have moved forward steadily since developer Sharif El-Gamal announced them in 2010. In September 2011, El-Gamal opened a smaller Islamic center at the Park51 location in the hopes of building public support for the larger project.

However, after the 2010 assault of a New York City cab driver named Ahmed Sharif, during which the accused assailant made numerous anti-Muslim remarks, the controversy surrounding the proposed Islamic center reached a new high. After this incident, the debate around Park51 began to address racial and religious prejudice much more explicitly than it had before. The cover of the August 30, 2010 issue of *Time* magazine released immediately following the cab driver attack read, "Does America Have a Muslim Problem?" The main article in the magazine claimed that anti-Muslim bias and discrimination had become acceptable among Americans in the nine years since the September 11 attacks, accounting for the level of public outrage surrounding the Park51 project. In the same magazine, conservative writers attempted to counter such arguments, responding that the FBI had reported a sizable drop in hate crimes against Muslims between 2001 (554 incidents) and 2008 (105 incidents). The same pundits also noted that Jews were still the most common hate crime victims, linked to 1,013 attacks in 2008. They claimed that the "real" problem, therefore, was not Anti-Muslim sentiment but an enduring Anti-Semitism that remains pronounced. Others were quick to note in reply that the FBI only records offenses for which they receive reports from state and local law enforcement agencies, thus leaving a potentially large number of offenses unaccounted for in official statistics. Many forms of discrimination, in fact, do not occur as direct, physical violence, but may take on the indirect forms of collective withdrawal of support, premature cessation of employment, and avoidance. Indeed, these forms of discrimination seem to characterize the outcry against the Park51 project and the attempts by its detractors to reduce public support and funding for the project.

Democracy Is Messy: Should the Government Intervene?

The controversy that attended the prospect of building a mosque near the Ground Zero site prompted many Americans to think again about what exactly democracy looks like in action. Joseph Bottum, a writer for the popular religion and civics journal, *First Things*, opined that unless the investors that proposed to build the mosque were doing something illegal, then a "messy" democratic process involving protest, arguing, negotiating, and the like should be the only means for resolving the problem. In other words, government officials, regardless of rank, should not be regulating any of public responses to the mosque initiative. Bottum argued that we need to steer clear of the notion that the government must resolve all the problems of the citizenry. In contrast, *New York Times* columnist Maureen Dowd called for former president George W. Bush to enter the chorus of voices, which already included current President Obama, current New York City mayor Michael Bloomberg, and many others. These figures, it is argued, should give citizens a reason to calm down and think clearly about the legality of the issue and simply standing up for the constitutionality of the proposed mosque construction. Where do you stand?

Even so, a number of public critics of the plan maintained that simply because they opposed the initiative to build the Islamic community center near Ground Zero did not mean they were bigots. Indeed, many New Yorkers and families of victims of the September 11 attacks expressed concerns about the scale of the project, not necessarily the fact that Muslims might worship there. In response, supporters of the project noted that prayer meetings were being held at the proposed building site with no complaint until the scope of the community center project was revealed. With the backing of a well-known figure in interfaith dialogue, Imam Abdul Rauf, many supporters of the project upheld it as a necessary symbol of tolerance. The opposition countered that such pleas for tolerance placed the need to avoid ill thoughts toward Muslims as more important than the need to establish a place of remembrance about the attack on New York, even though the two are not mutually exclusive. In fact, current plans for Park51 have proposed a memorial to the victims of the September 11 attacks as part of the community center. The debate surrounding Park51 continues, with critics still referring to it as the "Mosque at Ground Zero." In many ways, as political journalist Mehdi Hasan has pointed out, the "Ground Zero mosque" debate exemplifies the seemingly irreconcilable clash of civilizations that the perpetrators of September 11 wanted to initiate.

GABRIEL SANTOS

See also

Islamic Fundamentalism; Islamofascism; Islamophobia; Muslims, Terrorist Image of; Racial Threat Theory; September 11, 2001, Terrorism, Discriminatory Reactions to

Further Reading:

Azhar, Hamdan. "Ground Zero Mosque: Islamophobic Extremists are Fueling the Controversy." *Christian Science Monitor.* August 4, 2010, 1.

Bottum, Joseph. "Holy War Over Ground Zero." *First Things: A Monthly Journal of Religion and Public Life.* October 2010, 3–4.

Federal Bureau of Investigation. *Uniform Crime Reports.* http://www.fbi.gov/about-us/cjis/ucr/ucr (accessed December 27, 2012).

Greenfield, Heather Emory. "International Law, Religious Limitations, and Cultural Sensitivity: The Park51 Mosque at Ground Zero." *International Law Review* 25 (2011): 1317–69.

Hasan, Mehdi. "Fear and Loathing in Manhattan." *New Statesman.* November 1, 2010, 22–25.

Liyakat, Takim. "The Ground Zero Controversy: Implications for American Islam." *Religions* 2 (2011): 132.

Tobin, Jonathan S. "The Mosque and the Mythical Backlash." *Commentary.* October 2010, 24–29.

Motley, Constance Baker (1921–1985)

Constance Baker Motley was a lawyer, civil rights activist, politician, and judge. In addition to being a major activist in the movement, she personally broke down many racial and gender barriers during her life.

Motley was born in New Haven, Connecticut, on September 14, 1921. She was the ninth of 12 children. Her parents had immigrated to the United States from Nevis in the Caribbean. Motley explained that her parents had settled in New Haven because New Englanders traded with the Caribbean during the 18th and 19th centuries. Her father, Willoughby Alva Baker, was a chef on the Yale University campus, and her mother, Rachel Baker, was a founder of the New Haven Chapter of the National Association for the Advancement of Colored People (NAACP).

Early in her life, she had been exposed to segregation. As a 15-year-old, she was turned away from a beach in Milford, Connecticut, because she was black. She was also denied admission to a roller skating rink. These incidents caused her to become interested in civil rights, and she became the president of the local NAACP Youth Council. She also decided that she wanted to become a lawyer. After graduating from high school in 1939, she worked for a short time as a maid. She then took a job with the New Haven office of the National Youth Administration, a New Deal–era government agency that provided part-time jobs to young people between the ages of 16 and 25. Her family's modest means seemed to preclude her from attending college.

A turning point in her life occurred when she was speaking at the Dixwell Community House, an African American social organization. Her speech, in which she talked about the need for African Americans to be more involved in the organization's operations, was heard by Clarence Blakeslee, the white philanthropist and grandson of abolitionists who had built the Community House. He was so impressed by her speech that he offered to pay for her college education, including her law school tuition. Of Blakeslee, Motley quoted him in her autobiography telling her, "I guess if I can send [my grandson] to Harvard, I can send you to Columbia."

Baker entered Fisk University, a black college located in Nashville, Tennessee, in 1941. However, in June 1942 she decided to transfer to New York University's Washington Square College, from which she graduated with a bachelor's degree in economics in 1943. In 1944, she was the first African American woman admitted to the Columbia University Law School, and she graduated with an LLB degree in 1946. She married Joel W. Motley, a real estate broker, in 1946. They had a son, Joel Motley III. She was called to the bar of the State of New York in 1948.

In 1945, while still a law student at Columbia, she met Thurgood Marshall, who offered her a job with the NAACP Legal Defense and Education Fund (LDEF) as a law clerk.

Following her graduation from Columbia, she was the LDEF's first female attorney and became an assistant general counsel and later associate general counsel. Many of the early cases she worked on concerned the treatment of African American military personnel during World War II, working on appeals of courts-martial. Many of these appeals were based on the premise that African American soldiers were often given more severe sanctions than white soldiers who had been convicted of the same offense. She became the LDEF's chief trial counsel and was also a legal strategist, helping to desegregate Southern schools, buses, and coffee shops.

In 1950, she wrote the original complaint in the case of *Brown v. Board of Education*, the landmark 1954 U.S. Supreme Court case that ended de jure segregation of public schools. During the 1950s, she traveled throughout the South representing plaintiffs in school desegregation cases, including the black children denied entry to Central High School in Little Rock, Arkansas. She became the first African American woman to argue a case before the U.S. Supreme Court when, in *Meredith v. Fair* (1962), she successfully argued that James Meredith should be allowed to attend the University of Mississippi, which had refused to admit African Americans, a court decision that had to be enforced by the use of federal troops. Altogether, she won nine of the 10 cases she argued before the Supreme Court.

She also represented many of the freedom riders jailed during the 1961 effort to force the Kennedy administration to enforce Supreme Court rulings prohibiting the segregation of passengers in interstate transportation. She also successfully argued for the reinstatement of more than 1,000 Birmingham, Alabama, school children who had been expelled for demonstrating.

Baker became interested in politics in the mid-1950s. In 1958, she was appointed to the New York State Advisory Council on Employment and Unemployment Insurance, a post she held until 1964. In February 1964, she won a special election to the New York state senate, serving out the unexpired term of James Watson. Motley, a Democrat, became the first African American woman elected to the New York state senate. She was elected that November. In her brief time in the state senate, she introduced legislation to establish low- and middle-income housing in urban areas. In February 1965, she was chosen by the New York City Council

Constance Baker Motley rose from humble beginnings to become a trailblazing American woman. She was the first African American female federal judge in U.S. history. (Library of Congress)

to fill a vacancy as Manhattan borough president, the first woman and the first African American in that position. She was elected to a four-year term in November 1965 with the support of the Democratic, Republican, and Liberal parties. As borough president, she worked to decrease racial segregation in Manhattan public schools and for the revitalization of Harlem and East Harlem. In March 1965, she represented New York City on the historic civil rights march from Selma to Montgomery, Alabama.

In late 1965, President Lyndon B. Johnson nominated Motley for a seat on the U.S. Court of Appeals for the Second Circuit. However, opposition to her nomination was so intense that on January 26, 1966, Johnson withdrew her nomination and instead nominated her as a federal district court judge for the Southern District of New York; the first African American woman named to the federal bench. She was confirmed by the U.S. Senate on August 30, 1966, despite continuing opposition from Southern senators. She would remain on the bench until her death. In 1982, she became the first African American women to become a chief judge. In 1986, Baker assumed senior status. Among the cases she handled was a 1978 case in which she ruled that the New York Yankees would have to admit a female reporter to the locker rooms at Yankee Stadium and another case that upheld the right of gay protestors to march in front of St. Patrick's Cathedral.

In 1993, she was inducted into the National Women's Hall of Fame, located in Seneca Falls, New York, the site of the first women's rights convention. In 2001, she received the Presidential Citizens Medal, which recognizes American citizens who have performed exemplary deeds of service for the nation, from President Bill Clinton. The NAACP awarded her the organization's highest honor, the Spingarn Medal, in 2003.

Motley died on September 28, 2005 in New York City.

JEFFREY KRAUS

See also
Civil Rights Movement

Further Reading:
Motley, Constance Baker. *Equal Justice under Law: An Autobiography.* New York: Farrar, Straus and Giroux, 1998.

Movimiento Estudiantil Chicano de Aztlán (MEChA)

Movimiento Estudiantil Chicano de Aztlán (Chicano Student Movement of Aztlán, or MEChA) is the most widespread and largest Chicano student organization. Promoting higher education, cultura, and historia, MEChA was founded on the principles of self-determination for the liberation of *la raza*. The founders believed that political involvement and education were the avenue for change in society. There are literally hundreds of MEChA chapters in universities scattered across the United States. The official national symbol of MEChA is an eagle holding a machete-like weapon and a stick of dynamite.

In March 1969, in Denver, Colorado, the Crusade for Justice organized the first National Chicano Youth Liberation Conference that drafted the basic premises for the Chicano movement in El Plan de Aztlán. The following month, in April 1969, more than 100 California Chicano students met at the University of California, Santa Barbara, in a conference that became one of the most crucial events in the Chicano movement. It was sponsored by the Coordinating Council on Higher Education, a network of students and professors who earlier had attended the Chicano Youth Conference in Denver and had returned full of enthusiasm and energy. By now, the Chicano student community was ready to implement a higher education plan that would go beyond previous pronouncements. A major objective was the creation of college curriculum that was relevant and useful to the community. Higher education, the students judged, was a publicly funded infrastructure that nevertheless enhanced the business community and other white bastions of power even as very little was expended on the needs of the tax-paying Chicano community.

The students at the Santa Barbara meeting wrote *El Plan de Santa Barbara* (*The Plan of Santa Barbara*), a cultural and political message articulating the ideology that would be used by future Chicano studies programs and students. A major tenet of the document emphasized a mildly separatist nationalism that members of MEChA had to embrace. This meant a rejection of assimilation into American culture. In fact, adamant rejection of the label "Mexican American" meant rejection of the assimilation and accommodationist melting pot ideology that had guided earlier generations of activists. Chicanismo involves a crucial distinction in a political consciousness between a Mexican American and a Chicano mentality. Mechistas (members) still strove to better the Chicano community through education through collective efforts, not just individual success that came from rejecting the roots of Chicanos. As such, the group decided to bring all California Chicano student groups under one standard, called *El Movimiento Estudiantil Chicano de Aztlán*. Before the creation of this symbolic nomenclature, most student groups employed the term "Mexican American" when naming their organizations. For example, in southern California, a number of United Mexican American Students (UMAS) chapters existed on university campuses. Bay area campuses were home to various chapters of the Mexican American Student Confederation (MASC), and many other such groups existed in Arizona, New Mexico, and Texas. By the late 1970s, most of these organizations had been replaced by MEChAs or had changed their names to MEChA.

Chicano student organizations, both before and after appropriating the name MEChA, succeeded in bringing about numerous and significant changes in institutions of higher education. Since the 1960s, most Chicano and Mexican American studies programs were initiated after pressure was brought to bear by these groups. Cultural awareness projects and events, the promotion of multiculturalism on and off campuses, and remaining vigilant to see that these gains were maintained, often fell under the purview of Mechistas. Official MEChA activities often included poetry readings and *teatro chicano* (Chicano theater) performances. Many of the MEChA chapters supported their own theater groups.

Today, although MEChAs still exist in many colleges and even high schools, and they hold national conferences, their influence has waned. Hundreds of Mexican American student groups still celebrate cultural pride but just as zealously promote the political and economic success of Hispanics through education and integration into mainstream society. Indeed, the ideological stance taken by early organizations has been diminished somewhat; often MEChA chapters are very similar to their more tame counterparts. Perhaps one of the most significant accomplishments of the earlier militant groups is that they served as a training ground for a generation of politicians who, after the zeal of the Chicano movement began to wane, succeeded in entering mainstream electoral politics. Notably, long term mayor of Los Angeles, Antonio Villaraigosa, was a MEChA leader at the University of California, Los Angeles.

More recently, MEChA has lent its support to other on-campus organizations working with marginalized populations. At Notre Dame, MEChA has pledged its support to the gay, lesbian, bisexual, transgender and questioning population, explaining "the struggle these friends are facing now is not unlike the struggle many of us have faced in the past." In addition, MEChA has become involved in non-political activity on some college campuses, including breaking ground on "Jardín Tonatiuh," a community garden outside the Chicano Studies House at California State University, Northridge (CSUN), intended to promote healthy living and sustainability among students and the community. Nonetheless, MEChA continues with activity it has traditionally made its focus; in February 2010, MEChA at CSUN held a walk-out and teach-in to protest faculty furloughs in the Chicano Studies department and tuition increases. MEChA has also used its influence to draw attention to the issue of Fair Food Trade, both nationally and internationally.

F. Arturo Rosales

See also

Chicano Movement

Further Reading:

Rosales, F. Arturo. *Chicano! History of the Mexican American Civil Rights Movement.* Houston: Arte Público Press, 1996.

Moynihan, Daniel Patrick (1927–2003)

Daniel Patrick "Pat" Moynihan was an American sociologist, U.S. senator, ambassador, professor, and author of social policy. He is best known as the author of the *Moynihan Report*, a controversial and groundbreaking 1965 analysis of the African American family.

Moynihan was born in Tulsa, Oklahoma, on March 16, 1927. When he was six, his family moved to New York City, where he attended various public, private, and parochial schools before graduating from Harlem High School. Moynihan participated in four successive presidential administrations, beginning in 1961 with the John F. Kennedy administration and continuing through 1977 with the Lyndon Baines Johnson, Richard M. Nixon, and Gerald R. Ford administrations. During the Kennedy and Johnson administrations, Moynihan was assistant secretary of labor for policy planning. His responsibilities included formulation of national social policy for what would later become known as President Johnson's War on Poverty Program. During his tenure as undersecretary of labor, Moynihan wrote two controversial documents: *Beyond the Melting Pot: The Negroes, Puerto Ricans, Jews, Italians, and Irish of New York City* (1963), which he coauthored with Nathan Glazer, and *The Negro Family: The Case for National Action*, better known as the *Moynihan Report* (1965).

Completed in March 1965, the *Moynihan Report* was initially distributed only to certain members of the Johnson administration; however, in June, when President Johnson delivered the commencement address at Howard University in Washington, D.C., he included in his speech a passage about the black family from Moynihan's report. The report was not released to the White House press corps until August, during the Los Angeles (California) Riot of 1965, in what was a half-disguised attempt to provide an explanation for the violence.

Whether or not the *Moynihan Report* satisfactorily explained the causes of the Los Angeles riot and the other urban insurrections that occurred in the mid-1960s (*see* Long Hot Summer Riots, 1965–1967), it did accomplish several things, not all of which were to the advantage of Moynihan and the Johnson administration. First, the press coverage the report received propelled Moynihan from civil servant to celebrity status. He was portrayed in the press as an expert on race relations. However, by October 1965, the report had begun to draw criticism both from other social scientists and from the African American community. Sociologist William Ryan used the phrase "blaming the victim" (1971) to describe the findings in Moynihan's report.

The *Moynihan Report* inspired great animosity because of the methodologies its author used to arrive at his conclusions and the disparaging assumptions that he interpreted as facts regarding the African American family. Moynihan wrote that at the heart of the deterioration of African American society was the disintegration of the African American family; Moynihan saw the family as the primary cause of weakness in the African American community. To conclude his study, Moynihan referred to the condition of the African American family as "the tangle of pathology" (1965).

In 1965, Moynihan left the Johnson administration to become director of the Joint Center for Urban Studies at Harvard University and the Massachusetts Institute of Technology. In 1968, he joined the Nixon White House staff as an urban affairs advisor. From 1973 to 1975, he served as ambassador to India. Moynihan was elected to the U.S. Senate from New York in 1976, and reelected in 1982, 1988, and 1994. He chose not to run for a fifth term in 2000 and was succeeded by former first lady Hillary Rodham Clinton in 2001. Moynihan died on March 26, 2003.

JOHN G. HALL

See also
American Dilemma, An

Further Reading:
Billingsley, Andrew. *Climbing Jacob's Ladder: The Enduring Legacy of African American Families.* New York: Simon & Schuster, 1992.
Cherry, Robert. *The Culture-of-Poverty Thesis and African Americans: The Work of Gunnar Myrdal and Other Institutionalists.* New York: Journal of Economic Issues, 1995.
Glazer, Nathan, and Daniel P. Moynihan. *Beyond the Melting Pot: The Negroes, Puerto Ricans, Jews, Italians, and Irish of New York City.* Cambridge, MA: M.I.T. Press, 1963.
Moynihan, Daniel Patrick. *The Negro Family: The Case for National Action.* Washington, D.C.: Office of Policy Planning and Research United States Department of Labor, 1965. http://www.dol.gov.
Ryan, William. *Blaming the Victim.* New York: Vintage Books, 1971.

Muhammad, Elijah (1897–1975)

Born Elijah Poole on October 7, 1897, in Sandersville, Georgia, the Most Honorable Elijah Muhammad was the leader of the Nation of Islam from 1934 until his death on February 25, 1975. Muhammad died four days following the 10th anniversary of the death of Malcolm X (1925–1965), one of his most devoted and controversial ministers. Elijah Muhammad was considered by his followers to be the messenger of Allah to the black man and woman in the United States.

The story of Elijah Poole's life is significant because it chronicles the plight of African Americans of his generation, the first generation of free blacks born after slavery. His parents, Wali, a Baptist minister, and Marie Poole, were born in slavery and later became sharecroppers. Elijah, the sixth of the Pooles' 13 children, quit school when he was 14 years old to help support his family. Two years later, Elijah left home and supported himself by doing odd jobs. During his travels he met Clara Evans, whom he married on May 2, 1917. In 1923, the couple moved to Detroit, becoming

Elijah Muhammad, as spiritual leader of the Nation of Islam in the United States, established a religious organization that gave poor urban African Americans a sense of racial pride and economic and political self-sufficiency. (Library of Congress)

part of the Great Migration of blacks from the South to the North during the first decades of the 20th century. The causes of black migration are varied, but the violence and brutality African Americans faced was a significant factor. The violence came in the form of racial segregation or Jim Crow laws, which forced blacks to live in a world controlled by whites.

Groups like the Ku Klux Klan terrorized entire neighborhoods with burnings, lynchings, rapes, and murders. Violence in the form of racial rioting also became an effective weapon, with the summer of 1919 becoming known as the Red Summer because so many race riots occurred during those months. Hundreds of blacks were killed or wounded. In 1923, Elijah Poole rescued his family from this tragic cycle of violence and death. Later, remembering scenes from his life in the South, he stated that he "saw enough of the white man's brutality to last me 26,000 years" (Clegg 1997).

In Detroit, Elijah worked for the American Can Factory and the Chevrolet Motor Company. But the stock market crash on October 29, 1929, left Poole and millions of others out of work. It was during this period that Elijah met W. D. Fard (1877–?), the founder of the Nation of Islam. Elijah had also been a member of the Moorish Science Temple of America, founded by Noble Drew Ali (1866–1929). Ali, an adherent of Islam, who possibly introduced Elijah to the faith, was arrested in 1929 and died in jail while awaiting his trial.

Fard founded the Lost and Found Nation of Islam in the Wilderness of North America. According to his teachings, human culture began in Africa, and white people were inferior. He also preached the philosophy of Black Nationalism and separatism, which celebrated the beauty of people of African descent, and indicated that black people should establish a separate nation within the United States. He advised his followers to renounce their Christian or "slave" surname and replace it with "X" to symbolize their independence and rejection of Western culture. Elijah Poole became one of Fard's most committed converts. He changed his name to Karriem and, in 1934, when Fard mysteriously disappeared, Karriem (soon to be known as Elijah Muhammad) became leader of the Nation of Islam, stating that Fard had anointed him Messenger of Allah.

Muhammad's leadership did not go unchallenged. Fard's sudden disappearance and Muhammad's rise to power were too coincidental for some people, and a power struggle ensued. Muhammad moved to Chicago, where he established another temple. But even in Chicago, he was not free from the infighting. He then moved to Washington, D.C., where he remained until 1941.

After criticizing the government's internment of Japanese citizens after Pearl Harbor, Muhammad was sentenced to five years in federal prison in Milan, Michigan, for being a draft evader. Released in 1946, he returned to Chicago to assume leadership of the temple he had started 10 years before. This time, his authority was not challenged. He became the undisputed leader of the Nation of Islam and proclaimed himself Allah's last prophet. His mission was to deliver black people out of white slavery. He urged blacks to renounce Christianity and the vices of white society and build a separate black Nation of Islam; separation, not integration, was Muhammad's ultimate goal.

During the 1950s, Malcolm X, with his charismatic leadership, gave the Nation of Islam national visibility. By the early 1960s, he had become chief spokesperson and heir apparent to Elijah Muhammad. However, his meteoric rise to power was abruptly derailed in 1963 when he made inflammatory remarks about the assassination of President John F. Kennedy. Muhammad reprimanded Malcolm X and forbade him to make any public statements in the name of the Nation of Islam. This rupture between Malcolm X and Elijah Muhammad was never healed. Malcolm X was assassinated on February 21, 1965, by men thought to be loyal to Elijah Muhammad, but Muhammad denied any complicity.

The Nation of Islam never fully recovered from the murder of Malcolm X. In the years following Malcolm's death, Muhammad led a quieter, more solitary life. During his last years, he suffered from numerous physical ailments. He died of congestive heart failure in 1975. More than 20,000 of his followers attended his funeral to bid farewell to one of the most powerful African American leaders of his generation.

JOHN G. HALL

See also

Garvey, Marcus; Malcolm X; Nation of Islam

Further Reading:

Clegg, Claude Andrews, III. *An Original Man: The Life and Times of Elijah Muhammad.* New York: St. Martin's Press, 1997.

Lincoln, C. Eric. *The Black Muslims in America.* Boston: Beacon Press, 1961.

Magida, Arthur J. *Prophet of Rage: A Life of Louis Farrakhan and His Nation.* New York: Basic Books, 1996.

Malcolm X, with Alex Haley. *The Autobiography of Malcolm X.* New York: Grove Press, 1965.

Muhammad, Elijah. *The Fall of America.* Chicago: Muhammad's Temple No. 2, 1973.

Muhammad, Elijah. *Message to the Blackman in America.* Chicago: Muhammad Mosque of Islam No. 2, 1965.

Murphy, Larry G., J. Gordon Melton, and Gary L. Ward, eds. *Encyclopedia of African American Religions.* New York: Garland Publishing, 1993.

Multiculturalism

The term *multiculturalism* is commonly used to refer to an ideology that emphasizes the importance of maintaining cultural diversity in the United States or the social movement organized to achieve such a culturally diverse society. Multiculturalism is also used to indicate the government policy aimed at facilitating the preservation of cultural diversity in the United States. As an ideology, multiculturalism demands that the unique cultures of African Americans, Asian Americans, Latinos/as, Native

Americans, European Americans, and multiracial people be recognized and given a place in the curricula of schools and universities and in the societal contexts of the workplace. The multiculturalist ideology and the multicultural movement among minority members and women have led to changes in government policies, written and unwritten, on matters related to racial, gender, and sexual-identity diversity in the public sector.

The ideological seeds of multiculturalism are found in the United States' formation myths of individual rights, human dignity, and social justice. Multiculturalism's response to the "melting pot" is the metaphor of the "salad bowl" or "mosaic." According to the multicultural ideology, immigrants and other minorities do not have to give up their values and traditions by assimilating or melting together. Rather, they can keep their unique cultural norms, traditions, and behaviors while still sharing common national values, goals, and institutions. The ideology of cultural pluralism can be traced to the writings of the Jewish philosopher Horace Kallen. Beginning in 1915, Kallen argued in favor of an ideology of cultural pluralism based on the belief that the members of every ethnic group in America should be free to participate in all of the society's major institutions, including education, employment, and governance, while they retain their own ethnic heritage.

Multiculturalism as a movement is an attempt to establish this ideology in the reality of contemporary America. It has since developed beyond the mere validation of diversity to encompass an agenda of reducing and ultimately eliminating racial oppression and inequalities that exist in contemporary American society. Multiculturalism's political coming of age can be traced to the 1960s, when a number of minority movements—the civil rights movement, the Black Nationalist movement, the Third World movement, the gay rights movement, and the women's movement—challenged the Euro-male–centric educational system and social fabric.

Black Nationalism that started in the late 1960s was the earliest expression of the multicultural ideology. Other social movements by people of color, such as Latinos' La Raza (the race) movement and the American Indian movement, also incorporated multiculturalist thought with a leftist political agenda. Simultaneously, the United States saw the growth of gender-related activism—including the successful advocacy of the Equal Pay Act of 1963 and the movement to pass the women's Equal Rights Amendment to the United States Constitution. Likewise, the Stonewall Riots of 1969 marked the beginning of the modern gay rights movement, which also incorporated elements of multiculturalist thought. The environmental movement, long present on the American stage, was revived at the same time, often around issues such as environmental justice for indigenous people, communities of color, and people in the developing world, who most often bear the brunt of toxic pollution.

Multiculturalism's rise was abetted by the evolution of the mass media, which made it possible for what were seen as local problems, like the early civil rights movement, to become national issues for debate. The sudden visibility of Jim Crow racism to political moderates and liberals in the North galvanized broad-based and national opposition to Southern segregationist policies and brought the issue of African Americans' rights—and their sociocultural uniqueness—to the forefront. The post–World War II changes in American demography and geography, and in particular the movement of American whites to the suburbs, caused issues such as redlining and white flight to become topics of broad discussion.

The educational arena is the multiculturalist movement's central forum. While decisions like *Brown v. Board of Education* and *Lau v. Nichols* affirmed a person's legal right to "equal educational opportunities" regardless of race or national origin, the process of enforcing such decisions against recalcitrant school districts has lasted decades. More important, the legal requirements of federal legislation and court opinions do not meet the standard that multiculturalism sets for schools: to be genuinely inclusive, to provide not only "opportunities" but also validation and visibility to ethnic, racial, religious, and social groups and pedagogy that addresses the marginalization and oppression of minority groups.

Contemporary multiculturalism in education is characterized by two modes of thought. The first and more widely known involves merely the appreciation and celebration of cultural diversity. Integrating the history and culture of dominated groups into public-school curricula and textbooks is an end unto itself, rather than a starting point toward empowering oppressed people and thereby achieving social change. The second mode of thought, which is becoming the subject of greater attention and support, incorporates the first but also looks to address prejudice and discrimination at the individual and institutional levels. This multiculturalism says that while celebration of diversity is essential, it alone is inadequate; schools should change their policy and pedagogy to examine and address injustice at all levels. Advocates of this multiculturalism criticize the earlier school as offering only "heroes and holidays"—the obligatory study of noted minorities in history and cursory celebration of non-Christian holidays—without addressing the societal and cultural patterns that perpetuate the very need to offer up such heroes and holidays every year. This mode of fostering multiculturalism calls for critical and multifaceted analysis of contemporary societal problems, and responses to those problems that unabashedly address white Christian dominance.

Colleges and universities have been battlefields in the war between multicultural education and Eurocentric education. The multicultural movement on college campuses can also be traced to the 1970s when the Third World Liberation Front, a student organization made up of African American, Asian American, Latino/a, and Native American students at San Francisco State University and the University of California at Berkeley, called a strike demanding a Third World, Ethnic Studies College. After months of protests, teach-ins, and strikes—during which authorities deployed as many as 10,000 armed men each day for nearly two months in an attempt to quell the uprising—San Francisco State University became the first university to establish a black studies department and a college of ethnic studies. Ethnic studies programs, along with women's studies and, later, queer studies programs, thereafter came to be established on other university campuses. Along with multicultural representation in academics, student organizations that focus on ethnicity, religion, gender, and sexual orientation were established on campuses; these organizations have engaged students, faculty, and school administrations in public events and debates on a plethora of issues related to multiculturalism. Opponents of the multiculturalist ideology argue that the addition of non-European materials to the academic canon "waters down" curricula by spreading intellectual resources too thinly and by mandating less intellectually worthy pursuits. They also argue that it could "Balkanize" society by focusing individuals and communities on their respective dissimilarities and uniqueness, creating artificial interethnic competition, and damaging the cohesive effect of common "American culture."

Alongside the deep cultural changes already noted, multiculturalism seeks changes in the contemporary racial and cultural lexicon. Specifically, it advances the notion that any given group should be called by a name—a "label"—of its own choosing. Perhaps the best example of the effects of a group's deliberate attempt to name or "rename" itself is the evolution of the popular term for people of African heritage: from Negro in the middle of the 20th century to black, Afro-American, and African American over the course of recent decades. Another example is the switch from Oriental to Asian American or East Asian to describe people of Japanese, Chinese, and Korean descent. The decision to name one's group is political as well as linguistic, and it responds to the need for group self-determination and autonomy.

Driven by the social movements of the modern age, government policy has changed from one of Anglo conformity to multiculturalism since the early 1970s. Fueled by the general social ferment of the civil rights movement and the war in Vietnam, the federal government enacted social and educational reform legislation in many areas related to multiculturalism. For example, the Voting Rights Act of 1963 eliminated race-based bars to suffrage, and the Equal Pay Act passed the same year required that men and women occupying the same position be paid equally. The Civil Rights Act was passed in 1964 to address discrimination in housing, employment, and education.

Again, the shift in government policy toward multiculturalism is particularly evident in the educational policy sector. Many civil rights–era legislative initiatives were aimed at past discrimination in the educational arena. Titles IV and VI of the Civil Rights Act aimed to end school segregation and provide authority for implementing the U.S. Supreme Court's decision in *Brown v. Board of Education*. The Bilingual Education Act of 1968 obligated schools to provide programs for children whose first language was not English. Title IX of the Education Amendments of 1972 prohibited gender-based discrimination against students and employees of educational institutions, and the Education of All Handicapped Children Act of 1975 required schools to assume the responsibility for education of all children in the least restrictive environment possible. In 1967, the U.S. Commission on Civil Rights was established to investigate complaints alleging violations of the Voting Rights and Civil Rights Acts. The Indian Education Act of 1972 provided financial assistance to local schools to develop programs to meet the "special" educational needs of Native American students, a response to a 1969 report condemning past discrimination against Native Americans. Bilingual education, one of the most hotly debated topics related to multiculturalism, was officially born in 1974 when the U.S. Supreme Court issued its decision in *Lau v. Nichols*. In Lau, the high court ruled that the San Francisco public school system violated the Civil Rights Act of 1964 by denying non-English-speaking students of Chinese ancestry a meaningful opportunity to participate in the public educational program. The decision stated that "merely by providing students with the same facilities, textbooks, teachers, and curriculum," the school district was not meeting its obligation to ensure that they received an equal educational opportunity. The *Lau* decision was important because it extended civil rights protections to linguistic minorities, that is, to students who did not speak English, by applying the Civil Rights Act's prohibition on discrimination based on "national origin." Bilingual education continues to be a hotly debated topic as the number of immigrant students increases every year in public-school systems across the country.

Policies and practices related to multiculturalism are present at the local and state government levels in noneducational arenas as well. More recently, some states have directed resources to support "gay/straight alliances," organizations aimed at combating homophobia and ensuring equal educational access for gay, lesbian, bisexual, and transgendered students. State and local governments also have provided grants to programs that support the maintenance of different ethnic heritages. Government-supported social-service organizations have implemented translation programs to make sure all people get the services they need and that language is not a barrier. Vermont has enacted legislation giving gay couples rights substantially similar to those enjoyed by heterosexual married people, and Massachusetts has effectively been ordered to do the same by its state supreme court.

Of course, legal sanction does not equal social sanction. The legislation and court decisions described above did not guarantee social and educational equal opportunity to all. Historical disparities remain and are perpetuated by individual and institutional discrimination. American culture remains dominated by Anglo norms, and these lingering divisions still make structural pluralism a rarity in the early years of the 21st century. Multiculturalism—as an educational ideology and a social movement—will therefore remain a factor in contemporary education and public policy for years to come.

KHYATI JOSHI

Further Reading:

Banks, James, and Cherry McGee Banks, eds. *Handbooks on Research on Multicultural Education*, 2nd ed. San Francisco: Jossey-Bass, 2004.

McLemore, S. Dale, and Harriett D. Romo. *Racial and Ethnic Relations in America*, 5th ed. Boston: Allyn & Bacon, 1998.

Nieto, Sonia. *Affirming Diversity: The Sociopolitical Context for Multicultural Education*, 4th ed. White Plains, NY: Longman Publishers, 2003.

Spring, Joel. *Deculturalization and the Struggle for Equality: A Brief History of the Education of Dominated Cultures in the United States*, 4th ed. Boston: McGraw Hill, 2003.

Multiracial Identity

Multiracial identity refers to the identities of individuals who are from two or more racial heritages. Other commonly used terms include biracial, interracial, and mixed-race. Although most scholars recognize that racial mixture is by no means a new phenomenon and is centuries old, some suggest that the current idea of multiracial identity has rapidly accelerated as a matter of public and academic interest since the mid-to-late 1980s. Others reference the 1967 *Loving v. Virginia* Supreme Court decision, which dismantled antimiscegenation laws in the United States, as launching a new wave of multiracial individuals and thus amplifying discussion about multiracial identity. Notwithstanding the origins of the debate, individuals identifying as multiracial have increasingly inserted their experiences into racial discourse and are speaking openly about their multiracial identity and racially different ancestors. For some scholars in the field, the fact that there is an increasing demand for recognition of one's racial mixture as a unique category and point of identity signals a crossroad in the discourse of race, racism, and racial identity.

Mestizo

Mestizo is a term most frequently used in Latin America to designate a person of mixed European ancestry, especially Spanish and indigenous. In the complex hierarchy of color mixture in Latin America, mestizos held greater power and higher social status than Indians or black slaves, but were lower socially than white Spaniards and *criollos* (the Spaniards' descendants born in the colonies). In the 18th and 19th centuries, mestizos were often defined more by their social status and spatial location than by their racial and ethnic mixture and physical appearance. In Mexico, for example, rural mestizos were called peasants and studied by social scientists with the analytical categories of social class, while more economically and spatially marginal mestizos were called Indians and studied by social scientists with the analytical categories of ethnicity. In Andean countries the differences between mestizos and Indians often hinged on rural or urban location, command of the Spanish language, or dress. Throughout Latin America *mestizaje* denotes the generalized process of white/Indian mixture initiated by the Spanish conquest and colonialism, and in Mexico of the early 20th century, *mestizaje* came to be seen as the quintessential process of the country's national identity.

Carmenza Gallo

Attention to multiracial identity is also in part connected with the development of the multiracial movement. The multiracial movement refers to the mainstream presence of mixed race experiences in books, novels, blogs, Web sites, daytime television talk shows, among celebrities, as well as hair products, toys, and other items all designed by and for multiracial individuals and other members of interracial families to address what is seen as a unique experience of being multiracial. This attention supported the movement's mandate to create spaces in which multiracial individuals could engage with other multiracial people and be seen as legitimate. Most early works on multiracial identity were organized mainly under the scholarly and analytical umbrella of Maria Root's work *Racially Mixed People in America* (1992) and *The Multiracial Experience: Racial Borders as the New Frontier* (1996). Issues of multiracial identity further accelerated in the 1990s partly due to the popularity of golfer Tiger Woods, who publicly claimed that he was not black but "Cablinasian," a cross between Caucasian, Asian, and black.

The issues concerning multiracial identity that are most commonly addressed (in public and academic debates) have included personal accounts of family relationships, stories by parents about their relationships with their multiracial children, the challenges and rewards of growing up multiracial, and the pressures to define oneself according to public perceptions of racial identity, including informal applications of hypodescent and the challenges many face when choosing an identity outside of accepted binary racial identification categories. Public and private advocacy for multiracial identities has also sought to challenge the image of the tragic mulatto as the dominant experience of those who are mixed, and attempts to draw awareness to alternative experiences, including whether racially complex bodies are capable of transcending racial categories.

Perhaps the most notable impact of the movement and growing multiracial identity claims has been the attention placed on self-naming and the interrelationship between identity, recognition, and state structures, including efforts to legitimize multiracial identity as a category on the 2000 U.S. Census. Multiracial organizations such as Project RACE (Reclassify All Children Equally) and the Association for MultiEthnic Americans were highly involved with the movement to change the Census 2000 form to allow people to identify as belonging to more than one racial group. The U.S. 2000 Census debate (which began in the late 1980s and early 1990s) reflected claims that within the U.S. system and racial framework, multiracial individuals were unrecognized and therefore excluded. This effort further contributed to the development and support of a multiracial group consciousness and led multiracial supporters to emphasize specific terms such as *multiracial* rather than *mulatto*, as a method of moving away from derogatory terminology and history. The driving force behind the Census debate and calls for either the inclusion of a multiracial category or the option to select multiple groups, was the claim that mixed race people share a different experience, that they have different health concerns related to psychological well-being, that they deserve (have the "right") to be fairly counted and represented just like everyone else, and that such changes in racial categories (and formal structures) could address the unique oppression that multiracial people may experience.

Tension and scholarly criticism around multiracial identity abounds. Critical race scholars suggest that claims for a shared identity and common multiracial community are problematic because such organizing and identity claims risk reinforcing the notion of fixed races. Although some multiracial advocates claim that a multiracial identity can challenge rigid racial categories by making them more complex, others warn that such claims ultimately assert racial privilege through a desire to avoid being black or other racial locations, reinforce ideas of racial purity and false beliefs about biological race, all of which endorse racial hierarchies rather than challenge them. Some worry that increases in multiracial identity may fragment communities of color, which counters advances from the civil rights movement. Further criticisms caution against a multiracial identity that may advocate a form of postrace dismissal, detract from antiracist endeavors among other racialized groups, and make no challenge to white privilege or the purity of whiteness.

Despite these ongoing tensions, debates about multiracial identity do not appear to be slowing. Regardless of where one stands on its significance, what is clear is that the feelings of belonging among, treatment of, and attention to multiracial individuals in popular, political, and personal arenas points to larger processes of racial stratification. Multiracial identity raises questions about the relationship between phenotype and racial identity, and points to the ways in which society continues to categorize according to phenotype and physical features despite one's racial identification.

LEANNE TAYLOR

See also

American Eugenics Movement; Hypodescent (One Drop Rule)

Further Reading:

Aspinall, P.J. "The Conceptualization and Categorization of Mixed-Race/Ethnicity in Britain and North America: Identity Options and the Role of the State." *International Journal of Intercultural Studies* 27 (2003): 269–96.

Daniel, Reginald. *More Than Black: Multiracial Identity and the New Racial Order*. Philadelphia: Temple University Press, 2002.
Elam, Michele. *The Souls of Mixed Folk: Race, Politics and Aesthetics in the New Millennium*. Stanford, CA: Stanford University Press, 2011.
Glazer, Nathan. "American Diversity and the 2000 Census." *Public Interest*. 144 (2001): 3–18.
Ibrahim, H. *Troubling the Family: The Promise of Personhood and the Rise of Multiracialism*. Minneapolis: University of Minnesota Press, 2012.
Root, M. P. P. *Racially Mixed People in America*. London: Sage Publications, 1992.
Root, M. P. P. *The Multiracial Experience: Racial Borders as the New Frontier*. Philadelphia: Temple University Press, 1996.
Sexton, J. *Amalgamation Schemes: Antiblackness and the Critique of Multiracialism*. Minneapolis: University of Minnesota Press, 2008.
Spencer, Rainier. "Assessing Multiracial Identity Theory and Politics: The Challenge of Hypodescent." *Ethnicities* 4, no. 3 (2004): 357–79.

Music Industry, Racism in

Racism in the music industry cuts across the entire business spectrum: from exploitation of musicians to discrimination in the management of record labels to segregation within the musicians' union, the American Federation of Musicians. Racism in the music industry in the United States goes all the way back to the mid-19th century minstrel shows in which white musicians and performing artists dressed in "blackface" and ridiculed African American culture. Racial discrimination in the music industry continued all the way through the 20th century as black musicians created many popular music forms—including jazz, blues, rhythm and blues, and rock 'n' roll—but have never been compensated adequately for their work or creativity. White-owned record labels have been the beneficiaries of black creativity, and some have referred to the American music recording industry as a system of "black roots and white fruits."

Exploitation of black musicians by record labels happens in two ways. First, in the early years of the recording industry, black musicians were often denied "authorship" or copyrights to songs they composed and recorded. Under U.S. copyright law, when a musician writes a tune, he or she is entitled to the income derived from that song, which includes mechanical royalties—income based on record sales—and performance royalties—income based on the radio air play of the song or record. It was typical in the early days of the music recording industry for black musicians to compose and record a song for a record label, get paid a small fee for the work in the studio, and then lose the rights to the song because they were deceived by unscrupulous record-label owners and producers. Many African American recording artists were not aware of U.S. copyright law, and as a result most could be fooled into turning over their rights to the record label that recorded their songs. As a result, many black recording artists never received any royalties that they were entitled to under U.S. copyright law. Instead, record-label owners claimed that they were the "authors" of the songs, and they reaped all the royalty income. One notorious example was that of Fred Parris, who wrote the song "In the Still of the Night." Conservative estimates show that "In the Still of the Night" sold between 10 and 15 million copies. Based on those numbers, Parris should have received at least $100,000 in royalty payments, but because someone else was given credit for writing the song, Parris earned only $783 from the hit tune that he wrote. Another example of egregious racial discrimination in the music recording industry comes from an interview with Ahmet Ertegun, the founder of Atlantic Records. Ertegun recalls a conversation he had with an executive at Columbia Records in the 1950s, who boasted to Ertegun that his label did not pay African American recording artists on his roster any royalties.

Another example of exploitation that became common in the 1950s was the practice of "covering" records or songs. White artists—such as Pat Boone, who started his own cover label called Dot Records—would cover or record a song originally written by a black artist, such as Little Richard. When Pat Boone covered "Tutti-Fruiti" by Little Richard, Boone was able to take advantage of the distribution system of the major record labels, whereas Little Richard's independent record label had a much smaller network of distribution and retail outlets. Radio listeners often did not know that records they were buying by white artists were records originally written and recorded by black artists. As a result, Pat Boone made many times more money than Little Richard off of sales of the single "Tutti-Fruiti" even though Little Richard wrote, recorded, and performed the song.

Racial discrimination also takes place in both the management operations of record labels and in the union that represents musicians in the United States, the American Federation of Musicians. In the 1980s, the National Association for the Advancement of Colored People (NAACP) conducted a study of the recording industry and found that African Americans were seriously underrepresented among management and professional positions in the industry. Most African Americans employed by record labels work in the A&R (artist and repertoire) departments, the lowest level of management. The NAACP found that the typical mid-sized record label has about 35 management positions and fills only four of those positions with African Americans. On the labor side, discrimination was widespread until 1964, when the American Federation of Musicians (AFM) was forced by the federal government to integrate its locals. Under the Civil Rights Act of 1964, labor unions were forced to end racial segregation. Before 1964, apart from a few exceptions like New York City, the majority of musicians' locals in the AFM chartered separate white and black locals. In most cases, the white locals monopolized the good jobs, excluding black musicians from the better-paying engagements in the cities or towns where they had jurisdiction. During the civil rights movement, black members of the AFM successfully challenged and defeated racial discrimination in the union by appealing to the 1964 Civil Rights Act.

Recent research on the music recording industry shows that racial discrimination continues to exist. According to Kelley (2002), rap and hip-hop music—a predominantly black musical form—is now the second largest musical genre in the United States, accounting for 13 percent of all record sales, but black musicians still earn a miniscule portion of the income from the music they produce. Worth more than $1.8 billion in annual sales, hip-hop and rap music is still controlled by white-owned establishments. Compare that with the figure for the entirety of revenues generated by black-owned entertainment companies: $189 million dollars in the year 2000. There are a few profitable black-owned record labels in the industry such as Def Jam records, owned by Russell Simmons, and Bad Boy records, owned by Sean Combs. But even these labels are still dependent on white-owned and -controlled record companies for distribution. There are no fully independent, black-owned major record labels anymore since the 1993 sale of Motown records, which is now a subsidiary of the giant multinational corporate conglomerate Universal/Vivendi. Black musicians have made important gains in the recording industry, but discrimination remains a problem for future generations as they continue the struggle for equality in an industry that earns billions from their creativity.

MICHAEL ROBERTS

See also

Blues; Hip-Hop; Jazz; Rap Music; Rock and Roll

Further Reading:

Garofalo, Reebee, and Steve Chapple. *Rock 'n' Roll Is Here to Pay*. New York: Nelson-Hall, 1977.

George, Nelson. *The Death of Rhythm and Blues*. New York: Plume, 1988.

Kelley, Norman. *Rhythm and Business: The Political Economy of Black Music*. New York: Akashic Books, 2002.

Kofsky, Frank. *Black Music, White Business: Illuminating the History and Political Economy of Jazz*. New York: Pathfinder, 1998.

Muslim Brotherhood

The Muslim Brotherhood is an Islamic organization that was founded in Egypt by Hassan al-Banna in 1928 as a political response to the Westernization of Islamic culture and people. The Brotherhood is the largest and most organized Egyptian entity other than the Egyptian government and military. They have spent most of their existence as an outlawed organization that has a history of violence and has been viewed by some scholars as the theoretical roots of Islamic terrorism.

The founder of the Muslim Brotherhood, Hassan al-Banna was disturbed by the changes he was witnessing among citizens of his country whom he believed were too entranced by American culture. In 1928 he founded the Muslim Brotherhood with the goal of encouraging Egyptian citizens, especially the youth, to follow the way of the prophet Mohammed. He believed that the solution to the widespread problems he was witnessing in Egypt was a return to a society and government that was run based on a strict adherence to the basic principles of Islam. After its founding, the ideas of the Brotherhood drew immense support and recognition and by 1949 it was reported that the Brotherhood had over 1 million members. Despite an immense following the ideas of the brotherhood were in conflict with the increasingly secular government who had the goal of creating a modernized Egypt. The friction between the Egyptian government and the Muslim Brotherhood often erupted in violence with the Brotherhood engaging in multiple bombings, murders of those who disagreed with them, and assassinations of political figures. During the 1950s the Brotherhood attempted to assassinate President Abdul Nasser who was a strong proponent of modernization and secularization in Egypt. In retaliation, Nasser killed and jailed members of the Brotherhood and declared their organization illegal. The Brotherhood remained illegal but active in Egypt and neighboring Muslim countries until 1967 when they once again became a dominant force within Egypt whose citizens were experiencing apathy with the idea of modernization. This new era of the Brotherhood still proclaimed that "Islam is the answer" but rather than adopting the overt violent means of enforcing their ideologies of the past they stressed a program of reform that included and still includes political activism within the current system.

Today, the Muslim Brotherhood is the dominant political organization in the Muslim world with estimates of several millions of members. They have branches in over 70 countries throughout the Arab and Islamic worlds as well as in Europe and North America. While they have publicly denounced the Jihadist attacks against American targets, they are actively opposed to American influence and occupation of Iraq and the Israeli Occupation of the West Bank and Gaza, and have encouraged resistance to this occupation. The Brotherhood has been accused of fostering rebellion and supporting al-Qaeda. Within their branches in the United States and Europe their stated goal is to help Muslims gain political and economic power. Despite their

Hundreds of protestors from the Egyptian Muslim Brotherhood and opposition movement Kefaya demonstrate in Cairo as they protest against the government and Egyptian president Hosni Mubarak on September 1, 2005. (Mona Sharaf/Reuters/Corbis)

current moderate stance, many are concerned that this is simply a front that is being used to help members gain power, at which point they will revert to their previous violent methodologies as their current testament is "Allah is our objective, the messenger is our leader, Quran is our law, and Jihad is our way. Dying in the way of Allah is our highest hope."

VIRGINIA R. BEARD

See also

Black Separatism; Hate Groups in America; Sharia Law

Further Reading:

Fradkin, Hillel, and Lewis Libby. "Egypt's Islamists: A Cautionary Tale." In *The Reference Shelf: The Arab Spring*, edited by Paul McCaffrey, 70–76. Ipswitch, MA: H. W. Wilson, 2012.

Hendawi, Hamza. "With Eye on Political Power, Egypt's Muslim Brotherhood Treads Carefully After Election Win." In *The Reference Shelf: The Arab Spring*, edited by Paul McCaffrey, 82–86. Ipswitch, MA: H. W. Wilson, 2012.

Palmer, Monte, and Princess Palmer. *At the Heart of Terror: Islam, Jihadists, and America's War on Terrorism.* New York: Rowman & Littlefield, 2004.

Smith, Jane I. *Islam in America.* New York: Columbia University Press, 1999.

Muslims, Terrorist Image of

The image of Muslims as terrorists is not unfamiliar in the iconography of Western culture. European painters depicting the Crusades often used the same typology to portray the infidel Saracens, Moors, and Mohammedans as they did to portray Satan. Indeed, both the devil and the Muslims were believed to have a common objective—the downfall of Western civilization.

The fight to establish the state of Israel in 1948 saw the rebirth of the Muslim terrorist stereotype when Jewish "freedom fighters" battled displaced, stateless Palestinian "terrorists." Palestinians were all considered incorrectly to be Muslims in the public eye. These terrorist images were further enforced and ingrained into popular culture by highly visible terrorist attacks at the Munich Olympics in 1972; the bombing of the Marine Corps barracks in Lebanon in 1983; the bombing of the World Trade Center in 1993; the bombing of American embassies in Nairobi, Kenya, and Dar Es Salaam, Tanzania, in 1998; and finally, the attacks on Washington, D.C., and New York City on September 11, 2001.

These events, along with numerous less sensational ones, have caused the happier but still stereotypical image of Muslims as rich, mysterious, turbaned sheikhs, as seen in Rudolph Valentino's 1921 silent movie *The Sheik*, to be replaced almost completely by the Muslim terrorist stereotype image. Replays of terrorist attacks appeared constantly on television, sometimes accompanied by jingoistic commentary and using the terms "Muslim terrorists" and "Arab terrorists" interchangeably. Characters in television dramas began fighting terrorists and even superheroes had to fight terrorists in comic books. These television and comic book terrorists always seemed to look Middle Eastern.

The human drama and experience of terrorism became excellent grist for the Hollywood mill. True to its tradition, Hollywood could make a lot of money out of stories in which good always triumphed over evil and stereotypical "bad guys" got their comeuppances. In World War II films, the bad guys were warmongering Germans and sneaky Japanese, only to be replaced during the Cold War by godless Russians. Now the bad guys became "Middle Eastern–looking" terrorists.

Actor Sean Connery discovered a terrorist plot to sell a Middle Eastern country a nuclear bomb in the 1981 film *Wrong Is Right*. *Wanted Dead or Alive* was updated in 1986 from a western to a tale about the deadly struggle between an ex-CIA man and an international terrorist. In the 1987 film *Death Before Dishonor*, Fred Dryer took on an entire group of terrorists who had stormed an American embassy in the Middle East and taken hostages. Arnold Schwarzenegger and Jamie Lee Curtis found themselves in the midst of an international terrorist crisis in the otherwise rather humorous *True Lies*, which came out in 1994. Two years later, Kurt Russell and Halle Berry saved the day in *Executive Decision*, after Islamic terrorists took control of an airplane filled with hundreds of people and bombs filled with nerve gas. Denzel Washington, Bruce Willis, and Annette Bening have rough going in *The Siege* (1998) when New York City is targeted for attacks by terrorists after U.S. military forces abduct a Muslim leader. In the 2000 film *Rules of Engagement*, Samuel L. Jackson saved the U.S. ambassador to Yemen and killed the terrorists and demonstrators who had invaded the embassy. When these films left theaters, they then went into American homes.

Organizations such as the Muslim Public Affairs Council, the American-Arab Anti-Discrimination Committee, and the Council on American Islamic Relations (CAIR) protested long before the 9/11 events that the constant bombardment of negative Arab and Muslim stereotypes was feeding the fire of prejudice against Arabs and Muslims in the United States. The civil rights of these groups were eroding in the face of it. Furthermore, the unceasing use of the terrorist stereotype throughout the media had falsely connected terrorism to the religion of Islam in the minds of many Americans. Because American media products are spread all around the world, the images of Arabs and Muslims were being damaged globally.

The problem had reached global proportions after 9/11, so the Arab League met in Cairo, gathering over 70 Islamic scholars from 20 countries to figure out how to present to the world a truer understanding of Islam. They were especially concerned about the well-being of Arabs and Muslims living in the West. There was general agreement that the chasm between Muslims and Christians, between East and West, which existed since the prophet Mohammed's time on earth, needed to be closed somehow. Muslim scholars and clerics had to spread the word of true Islam to non-Muslims in the West. Islam itself needed to be interpreted in one way, not many. It needed to be rejuvenated.

While the 9/11 tragedy provided spokespersons from Muslim and Islamic organizations in the United States with airtime on radio and television networks that were looking for experts, their efforts to separate a few militants from the mainstream of Islam may have fallen on deaf ears. The persistence of the terrorist stereotype and the anxiety of the moment inhibited any desire to see another side. And the stereotype will persist until Muslims and Arabs are integrated into the American fabric and not viewed as voices from the outside.

Benjamin F. Shearer

See also

Arab American Institute; Arab/Muslim American Advocacy Organizations; Islamic Fundamentalism; Islamofascism; Islamophobia; September 11, 2001, Terrorism, Discriminatory Reactions to; Sharia Law

---

Myrdal, Gunnar (1898–1987)

A distinguished Swedish economist in his own right on many subjects, Gunnar Myrdal's lasting legacy and enduring contribution to American race relations is his book *An American Dilemma: The Negro Problem and Modern Democracy* (1944). Myrdal began the long journey of researching this subject when asked by Frederick Keppel, president of the Carnegie Corporation, to travel to the United States in order to study the problem firsthand, especially in the South, where approximately 75 percent of African Americans were living at the time. Keppel and other Carnegie trustees understood that the enormous importance and complexity of the problem required someone akin to Alexis de Tocqueville, the great 19th-century French observer of American democracy—someone with proper distance and objectivity, and yet (unlike Tocqueville) someone from a country not tainted with an imperialist past that could cause African Americans to question the validity of the study and its outcomes.

In his capacity as an economics professor at the University of Stockholm, Myrdal had already visited the United States as a Rockefeller Fellow in 1929–1930 and was preparing for a second visit to deliver the Godkin Lectures at Harvard when the invitation was extended to travel through the Jim Crow South. The evil he witnessed shocked and rattled him to the core as he began to grapple with the political implications of the problem. Firsthand observation of discriminatory segregation and injustice was a beginning, but by no means an end. Far from a travelogue of a gifted writer's observations, Myrdal assembled a diverse team of scholars to examine the problem from several angles using different methodological perspectives.

The methodological approaches to the research and the diversity within his own research team, combined with his evolving theories of equilibrium and change in economic dynamics to form a multicausal explanation, linking discrimination, education, housing, political empowerment, jobs, health care, belief, and other factors into a complex whole. These interlocking dynamic factors could pull segments of the population downward in what he called a "vicious circle" or, alternatively, be reversed through a "virtuous circle." No single explanation or solution was adequate.

However rigorously Myrdal explored these individual factors and their interrelationships, he believed that a moral dilemma lay beneath them all. Using the (now antiquated) language of his day, he wrote in his introduction to *An American Dilemma*:

> The American Negro problem is a problem in the heart of the American. It is there that the interracial tension has it focus. It is there that the decisive struggle goes on. This is the central viewpoint of this treatise. Though our study includes economic, social, and political race relations, at bottom our problem is the moral dilemma of the American—the conflict between his moral valuations on various levels of consciousness and generality. The "American Dilemma" ... is the ever-raging conflict between, on the one hand, the valuations preserved on the general plane which we shall call the "American Creed," where the American thinks, talks, and acts under the influence of high national and Christian precepts, and, on the other hand, the valuations on specific planes of individual and group living, where personal and local interests; economic, social, and sexual jealousies; considerations of community prestige and conformity; group prejudice and particular persons or types of people; and all sorts of miscellaneous wants, impulses, and habits dominate his outlook.

In other words, the high ideals embedded in the white majority American beliefs and values did not square with their actions and attitudes towards African Americans, contradicting their own "creed" and ideas about justice and democracy.

Overall, *An American Dilemma* was received favorably by academics, though criticized heavily by those with Marxist leanings. But in the political realm, little happened until 10 years later, when it influenced Chief Justice Earl Warren, who cited it in the *Brown v. Board of Education* decision, documenting the detrimental effect of segregated education upon children. The contradiction between American ideals and practice was a theme that civil rights leader Martin Luther King, Jr. picked up on, as is evident in his famous 1963 "I Have a Dream" speech. Myrdal's careful research and recommended reforms received more attention and exerted greater influence on public policy years after the publication of *An American Dilemma* than in his own day.

DOUGLAS MILFORD

See also
American Dilemma, An

Further Reading:
Clayton, Obie, Jr., ed. *An American Dilemma Revisited: Race Relations in a Changing World*. New York: Russell Sage Foundation, 1996.
Jackson, Walter A. *Gunnar Myrdal and America's Conscience: Social Engineering and Racial Liberalism, 1938–1987*. Chapel Hill: University of North Carolina Press, 1990.